SYSTEMATIC THEOLOGY

Volume One

PROLEGOMENA

THEOLOGY

ANTHROPOLOGY

CHRISTOLOGY

Morton H. Smith
Professor of Systematic Theology
Greenville Presbyterian Theological Seminary

WIPF & STOCK · Eugene, Oregon

Wipf and Stock Publishers
199 W 8th Ave, Suite 3
Eugene, OR 97401

Systematic Theology, Volume One
Prolegomena Theology Anthropology Christology
By Smith, Morton H.
Copyright©1994 Greenville Presbyterian Theological Seminary
ISBN 13: 978-1-5326-9845-3
Publication date 8/7/2019
Previously published by Greenville Seminary Press, 1994

To my wife, Lois

To the glory of God

in memory of

Professor John Murray

PREFACE

This work had its beginnings as lectures given at Reformed Theological Seminary, Jackson, Mississippi. It has been revised and enlarged in connection with lectures by the author, while teaching at Greenville Presbyterian Theological Seminary of Greenville, South Carolina.

Remembering from his own student days, his hand sometimes cramped from seeking to set down the full text of the lectures presented in Systematic Theology, the author hoping to relieve his students of this same trial, has prepared the material appearing in this work as the basic substance of his own theological lectures. This work does not pretend to be an original theological work, but rather a "boiling down" of the thought of many theologians who have gone before. An effort has been made to present some of the best statements made by the various theologians on the subject being considered..

The writer wishes to acknowledge his deep debt to the late Professor John Murray, who held the chair of Systematic Theology at Westminster Theological Seminary in Philadelphia. It was Professor Murray who set the example of systematic theology done exegetically, and not philosophically. This is the exemplar the present author has striven to follow, with varying degrees of success. Following this model, the interest is more in what the Bible says than in what different theologians have said, even when they have been cited. In particular, not much space is given to the refuting of various unorthodox opinions. This is a work designed to prepare men to understand and to preach the Gospel of Christ, not to carry on theological debate.

When the author first began his study of theology, he received from an elderly kinsman a very much used copy of Robert L. Dabney's *Lectures in Systematic Theology*. It was obvious that this book had been the constant companion of its previous owner, who was not an ordained minister. It is the hope of the author that this work may become a handbook to theology for the Christian family, as well as for the theological student, and the minister of the Word.

In order to make the text more readable, use of foreign languages has been kept to a minimum. A simplified, non-technical transliteration of Hebrew and Greek words is used in the text, with the original appearing in the footnotes, which are kept on the bottom of the page for ready reference. Hopefully this will make the work more popular than the standard systematic theology textbook.

Due to the contemporary theological climate, there are some sections that have received more attention than is generally given in most systematic theologies. For example, the *locus* on Ecclesiology is more extensive than usual, including a chapter on the cessation of the revelatory gifts.

It is the author's hope that this work may be used of the Lord to preserve the orthodoxy of the Church, and to advance the propagation of the full counsel of God.

Morton Howison Smith
Brevard, North Carolina
December, 1993.

PUBLICATION SPONSORS

A special word of thanks goes to the following, who made generous gifts toward the publication of this work:

Mr. and Mrs. Robert S. Hart

William H. Huffman

Donald J. Ottomeyer

Carl G. Russell

Samuel Warfield Smith

APPRECIATION

The author wishes to express his appreciation to the following who have assisted in proofreading and in the preparation of the text for publication. Mr. Ben Shaw, Mrs. Joy Ptacek, Mrs. Linda Small and Mr. Billy Stevens. Of course, the responsibility for any remaining errors rests upon the author alone.

CONTENTS OF VOLUME I

DIVISION I PROLEGOMENA

Chapter I Introduction 11

Chapter II The Idea, Task and Methodology of
Systematic Theology 19

Chapter III The Source or Principle of Theology 33

Chapter IV Revelation (Principium Cognoscendi Externum) 39

Chapter V The Scripture (Principium Cognoscendi Externum)
(continued) 69

Chapter VI The Principium Cognoscendi Internum 89

DIVISION II THEOLOGY

Chapter VII The Knowability and Incomprehensibility of God 97

Chapter VIII The Revelation of God in His Names 107

Chapter IX The Being and Attributes of God 121

Chapter X The Doctrine of the Trinity 147

Chapter XI The Decrees of God 155

Chapter XII Predestination 163

DIVISION III ANTHROPOLOGY

Chapter XIII Creation 179

Chapter XIV Angels: Their Creation, Nature and Functions 197

Chapter XV God's Work of Providence 207

Chapter XVI The Creation of Man 225

Chapter XVII The Image of God 233

Chapter XVIII Man: His Nature - Biblical Psychology 243

Chapter XIX Man in the Covenant of Works 275

Chapter XX Sin: Its Origin and Nature 291

Chapter XXI The Effects of Sin 301

Chapter XXII Original Sin 311

DIVISION IV OBJECTIVE SOTERIOLOGY - CHRISTOLOGY

Chapter XXIII The Plan of Salvation 323

Chapter XXIV The Counsel of Peace 329

Chapter XXV The Covenant of Grace 333

Chapter XXVI The Person of Christ 341

Chapter XXVII The Work of Christ 365

Chapter XXVIII The States of Christ 405

CONTENTS OF VOLUME II

DIVISION V SUBJECTIVE SOTERIOLOGY

Chapter XXIX The Ordo Salutis 425

Chapter XXX Calling and Regeneration 431

Chapter XXXI Conversion: Repentance and Faith 441

Chapter XXXII Justification 455

Chapter XXXIII Adoption 465

Chapter XXXIV Sanctification 471

Chapter XXXV Union with Christ 491

Chapter XXXVI Perseverance 499

Chapter XXXVII Assurance of Faith 507

DIVISION VI ECCLESIOLOGY

    Chapter XXXVIII The Biblical Idea of the Church 515

    Chapter XXXIX Christ and the Church 535

    Chapter XL The Holy Spirit and the Church 549

    Chapter XLI The Holy Spirit and the Cessation
        of the Revelatory Gifts 575

    Chapter XLII The Doctrine of the Church Formulated 595

    Chapter XLIII The Means of Grace 603

    Chapter XLIV The Word as a Means of Grace - A- 607

    Chapter XLV The Word as a Means of Grace - B -
        The Law of God 617

    Chapter XLVI The Sacraments 655

    Chapter XLVII Baptism 659

    Chapter XLVIII The Lord's Supper 673

    Chapter XLIX Prayer 697

    Chapter L Prayer and the Persons of the Godhead 707

DIVISION VII ESCHATOLOGY

    Chapter LI The Old Testament Eschatology 721

    Chapter LII The New Testament Eschatology 727

    Chapter LIII The Meaning of the Present Age 737

    Chapter LIV The Kingdom of God 745

    Chapter LV The Holy Spirit and Eschatology 751

    Chapter LVI Physical Death and the Intermediate State 757

    Chapter LVII The Coming of Christ 765

    Chapter LVIII Signs of the Coming of Christ 791

Chapter LIX The Coming of Christ and the Millennial Views 795

Chapter LX The Judgment and the Final State 803

COMPREHENSIVE OUTLINE 817

BIBLIOGRAPHY 835

INDICES

Selected Scripture Index 839

Selected Subjects and Authors 845

DIVISION I PROLEGOMENA

Chapter I - Introduction

I. The Name - Systematic Theology

Throughout the history of the church, there have been various names used for works that might properly be described as systems of theology. The earliest writer to give us a system was Origen, who entitled his work *Peri Archon*[1] (Concerning Principles). We have only fragments of the original Greek text, but we have, from the fourth century, a translation of Origen by Rufinus in the Latin under the title *De Principiis*. Origen divided his work into four books:
(1) God (God, Trinity and angels).
(2) The world (creation and the incarnation, the judgment and the resurrection).
(3) Freedom (free will, salvation and eschatology).
(4) Scripture (inspiration, authority and interpretation), and a recapitulation of the doctrine of the Trinity.
We see here the beginning of a systematic structure of Scriptural doctrines, though not well worked out. Augustine, writing in the fifth century, entitled his work *Enchiridion* (meaning Handbook), and added the following: "*sive de fide, spe et cartate*" (or faith, hope and love).

John of Damascus wrote a systematic treatise entitled *Ekdosis akribes tes orthodoxou pisteos*[2] (An Accurate Description of the Orthodox Faith). This work of John's approaches most closely the modern treatment of systematic theology. It is divided into four books:
(1) God and the Trinity.
(2) Creation and the Nature of Man.
(3) Christ and His Incarnation, Death, and Descent into Hades.
(4) The Resurrection and Reign of Christ.
All of these works from the early church failed to be real systematic theologies in that they treated the various disputed doctrines of their day too broadly, and failed to consider many other doctrines that should be handled in a systematic theology.

We are indebted to Isidorus Hispalensis for the name *Sententiae* (Thoughts or Maxims). The most important of these scholastic works under this title was *De Libores Sententiarum* by Peter of Lombard. This book was largely a gathering together of material from the earlier church fathers together with Peter's own original thought. It remained the handbook for the study of theology for the next three centuries. Thomas Aquinas used the term *Summa Theologica* (The Chief or Summary of Theological Matters) for his work in theology.

With the coming of the Reformation, Melancthon introduced the new name *Loci Communes Rerum Theologicarium* (Leading Conceptions in Theol-

---

1. Περὶ Ἀρχών
2. Ἔκδοσις ἀκριβὴς τῆς ὀρθοδόξου πίστεως

ogy). This work was based on the commentary on the Epistle to the Romans. The title *Loci Communes* became generally used by Lutheran and Reformed theologians. Zwingli wrote a work called *Commentarius de Vera et Falsa Religione* (Commentary on the True and False Religion). This has sometimes been called the first systematic exposition of the Reformed Faith. Calvin entitled his great work *Christianae Religionis Institutio* (Institutes of the Christian Religion). The name "institutes" has been used by a number of theologians since Calvin.

The century following the Reformation, the word *Theologia* became commonly used by Lutheran and Reformed theologians, but with the broadening of the subjects under this title, it became necessary to limit it with an adjective when treating systematic theology. Reinhart (1659) was the first to have used the term "dogmatics" in his work *Synopsis Theologiae Dogmaticae*. An interesting development then took place; namely, the dropping of the word theology and the preservation of just the word dogmatics, which technically defines the Christian Faith as held by the Church.

Schleiermacher introduced the title *Christlicher Glaube nach den Grundsaetzen der evangelischen Kirche*. From this has come the simple title *Doctrine of Faith* or *Christian Faith*. Among the titles used in the last two centuries, the following are examples: *The Christian Faith* used by both Haering and Curtis; *Christian Theology* used by Knapp, Pope, and Valentine; *Dogmatik, Gereforemeerde Dogmatiek, Christliche Dogmatik* used by Cafton, Bavinck, and Hoenig, respectively; Shedd and Hall writing in English used the title *Dogmatic Theology*; Raymond, Hodge, Miley and Strong used the title *Systematic Theology*.

Theologians of Germany and the Netherlands tend to use the title *Dogmatics*, whereas American theologians more commonly use *Systematic Theology*. It has been argued that the term *Systematic Theology* is somewhat redundant. All theology, whether historical, exegetical, or dogmatic, is systematic. This view fails to take into consideration the real idea of systematic theology, namely, that it is a discipline in which the material is presented in the form of a system.[3] It might be noted that American Presbyterians have generally used the term *Systematic Theology*, and this is the best term for us to use in our present historical situation.

II. Definitions

A. Theology

Theology is derived from the Greek *theos*[4] meaning God and *logos*[5] meaning word, or discourse or rational thought. Theology, then, is that division of rational thought dealing with God. As such, it has sometimes been called the science of God. Under this concept is included the study of God and of his relations to the universe. Such is the definition as set forth by Thornwell and A. H. Strong of the last century, and by Buswell and Van Til of the present century.

---

3. See Warfield "The Idea of Systematic Theology" in *Studies in Theology* (New York: Oxford University Press, 1932), p. 49f.
4. θεός
5. λόγος

B. Religion

One derivation of the word "religion" is from the Latin *religare*, meaning "to bind fast" or "to bind back." The thought is that it denotes man as bound back or brought to relation to God. Another possible derivation is to see it coming from the Latin *relegere*, meaning "to go over again," "to ponder carefully." The thought here is that the word has come to mean reverence or reverent observance to God.

The basic idea of religion, then, is that of life with God-- a life lived in recognition of God, in communion with him, under the control of his Spirit. If this concept of the term *religion* is kept in mind, and if there is but one true God, then there is only one religion, namely, the Christian religion. *Religion* thus deals with the life under God, and it cannot be described simply as consisting of matters of the intellect, affection, or will. In other words, the term *religion* is broader than theology, which treats more the intellectual aspect of religion. It is broader than ethics, which treats more the aspect of the will, and it is broader than experimental religion, which treats essentially the aspect of experience and affections.

It may be argued, however, that due to the modern usage of the term *religion* to encompass not only Christianity but other so-called religions, then the definition of theology as the study of religion is confusing. There have been those who have contrasted Christianity and religion. They reserve the term *religion* for all non-Christian faiths and Christianity for the only true faith. Buswell makes a point of the fact that the English Bible supports this modern and somewhat confused usage of the term *religion*. For example, in Galatians 1:13, 14, the phrase "the Jews' religion" translates *ioudaismos*.[6] The word *religion* is used to translate *threskeia*,[7] or the adjective *religious* translates *threskos*.[8] This root has to do primarily with ritual acts of worship. It is used in James 1:26 of that which is false and in James 1:27 of that which is true religion. One other word is translated by the English adjective *religious*, namely, *sebomenos*.[9] This root carries with it the idea of devout attitude of heart or religious devotion. As Buswell concludes in his study of these usages, the English Bible seems to support the broad usage of the term *religion* that we find in our modern language as well. It is probably best, when using the term, to speak either of the Christian religion or of non-Christian or pagan religions. Due to this confusion, we agree with Van Til in declining to define theology as the science of religion. He says, "Fundamental to everything orthodox is the presupposition of the antecedent self-existence of God and of his infallible revelation of himself to man in the Bible. Systematic theology seeks to offer an ordered presentation of what the Bible teaches about God."[10]

---

6. Ἰουδαϊσμός
7. θρησκεία
8. θρῆσκος
9. σεβόμενος
10. Cornelius Van Til, *An Introduction to Systematic Theology*, (unpublished syllabus, 1949), p. 1.

C. Systematic

The term *systematic* is used in our title. It is derived from *sunistano*.[11] This is a Greek verb meaning to put together as a whole, or to organize. This, of course, is exactly what is implied in the title *Systematic Theology*. It is the attempt to put together the whole system of thought found in the Bible, or to organize the thoughts of the Bible into a unified system. We shall have more to say about the goal of systematic theology and the methodology of attaining this goal later.

III. The Theological Encyclopedia

A. General

The term *encyclopedia* comes from the Greek *egkuklopaideia*,[12] which denotes the whole circle of general education. Theological encyclopedia, thus, is that area of thought designed to orient the student to the entire circle of theological study.

Since all truth comes from God, and since every fact is, therefore, revelational, it necessarily follows that the whole circle of human learning is theological. It all comes from God. As man learns the truth in each particular field, he is learning something about God. One might thus divide the total area of encyclopedia into two major divisions: the first being those subjects which deal with God directly, that is, theology proper; and secondly, those which deal with God more indirectly. Under the latter are included the general areas studied in the university, while the former are the subjects studied in the theological seminary or the divinity school.

B. Directly Theological

The distinctly theological area with which we are dealing has been divided into four major sections. They are: exegetical, historical, systematic, and practical.

1. Exegetical Theology

Exegetical theology is that branch of theology devoted to the interpretation of the Bible itself. It may be further divided into the following four subdivisions:

a. General Introduction

Under general introduction, the first subject covered is that of the Canon of Scripture. This division is sometimes designated by the term *higher criticism*.

---

11. συνιστάνω
12. ἐγκυκλοπαίδεια

The next subject covered under general introduction is that of the text, including a study of the method of textual criticism.

Third, the study of the Biblical languages or Biblical philology is included here.

Fourth, Biblical archaeology falls under general introduction.

Fifth, hermeneutics, which is the study of rules and principles of Biblical interpretation, falls in this division.

Sixth, the history of interpretation also should be studied here.

b. Special Introduction

Special introduction treats each particular book in the Bible by itself with a study of its authorship, occasion, design, etc.

c. Exegesis Proper

This is the application of the principles learned under the General and Special Introduction division to the actual text in which passages are studied and interpreted according to all the proper rules of grammar, etc.

d. Biblical Theology

This is a study of the gradual development of the revelation of God through the Bible. It is historical in its nature and yet also exegetical. The attempt is made to understand what each particular historical period in the Bible would have understood about various different aspects of the revelation of God made to them down to that point.

2. Historical Theology

Historical theology may be divided into two basic divisions, namely, Biblical and ecclesiastical history.

Biblical history is easily divided into the periods of the Old and New Testaments.

Ecclesiastical history may be divided into the various periods: ancient, medieval and modern. Special historical studies may be made on such themes as the history of literature, Christian archaeology or the history of Christian thought. The history of doctrine together with the history of symbolics, that is, the history of creeds, may be placed either here or in the field of systematic theology.

3. Systematic Theology

Various different methods of distribution of the material of Systematic Theology have been used in the history of Christian thought. The principle governing this distribution has been derived from the subject matter of the theology, from the source materials, from the manner in which it is treated or from the historical development of doctrine. As one considers the question of such a principle, it seems obvious that the subject matter should govern the division and not the sources, the manner of treatment, or the historical development. The following methods have been used by Protestants since the Reformation.

a. The Trinitarian Method

The Apostles' Creed follows the arrangement of statements about each of the persons of the Trinity. Calvin and Zwingli followed this same distribution as they wrote about theology. It has been adopted by some of the seventeenth century Dutch theologians as well as by Hagle and by Martensen of the Lutheran Church. The weakness of this position lies in the fact that there is an excessive emphasis on the separate persons of the Godhead. There can be no really logical treatment of the doctrine of the Trinity itself except as an introductory chapter and there is a tendency not to see the unity of the Godhead. Further, the other areas, such as anthropology and soteriology do not receive the full emphasis that belongs to them. In other words, this view is a rather unbalanced treatment of the total materials of systematic theology, and it has not been adopted by a great many theologians.

b. The Analytical Method

Calixtus (1614-1656) began with the final cause or end of theology, namely, blessedness. From this, he proceeded to treatment of the subjects of God, man and sin; and finally, he considered the means by which the end would be secured, namely, predestination, the Incarnation, Christology, justification, the Word and sacraments. This sort of an arrangement, of course, tends to place God on a par with angels and men. All are coordinated together to be the recipients of the final blessedness. There tends to be less emphasis upon the subject of soteriology.

c. The Covenantal Method

Coccejus was the first to divide theology on the basis of the covenants. His division was, first of all, two-fold, the covenant of works and the covenant of grace. Under the covenant of grace, he had three subdivisions: before the law, under the law, and after the law. He was followed in The Netherlands by Witsius and Vitringa. These men, of course, wrote in Latin, and their works were known to the early American theologians at Princeton, Union and Columbia Seminaries. Thornwell tended to follow this same division. He states his principle in terms of moral government. He spoke first of moral government alone, then moral government modified by the covenant of works, and then moral government modified by the covenant of grace. The principle of distribution of this system is the historical development of the doctrine rather than the subject matter itself. It would fit better with what we today call Biblical theology than with systematic theology.

d. The Christological Method

Based on the view that all genuine Christian theology should be Christocentric, a number of theologians have made the principle of distribution of theology to be based upon Christ or his saving operations. Among those who have done this are Hase, Thomaius, Schultz, T. B. Strong, A. Fuller, H. B. Smith, and D. Gerhart. To a certain extent, Karl Barth also falls into this school of thought. The general outline followed by the Christological method is to treat God, man, and sin as antecedents of redemption. Redemption itself and its consequences become the main body of the theology. As Berkhof says, Christ is indeed the center of God's revelation but for that very reason, cannot be the starting point. In Gerhart, a danger of this method is seen in that he identifies Christ and not the Scripture as the external source of theology. This is again being repeated today in neo-orthodox theology which identifies Christ as the Word and not Scripture. There is, generally speaking, a lack of real balance of the full teaching of Scripture in the various *loci* of theology under this method.

e. Method Based on the Kingdom Idea

Ritschl taught the Kingdom of God is central in theology. Though he himself and some of the leading Ritschlian theologians do not make this the principle of distribution, we do see the attempt made by the Dutch theologian, Van Oosterzee. Actually, he uses the classic synthetic divisions but applies the name *Kingdom* to them. He discusses God the Supreme King, man the subject of the kingdom, Christ the founder of the kingdom, redemption or soteriology as the constitution of the kingdom, the church as the training school, and eschatology as the completion of the kingdom. It is highly questionable whether the idea of the kingdom of God gives us the basic principle under which various aspects of theology can properly be discussed.

f. The Synthetic Method

The classic way of dividing theology has been that of the synthetic method. This is found in a number of the Reformed Confessions and Catechisms, in particular, in the Westminster Standards. After treating the revelation of God in the Bible, this method takes its starting point with God, and then moves in a logical order step by step from God to his decrees, to the execution of those decrees, the creation of man, the fall into sin, the doctrine of Christ, the plan of salvation, the Church, and finally, the last things. This system may be summarized under seven basic *loci*:

    I. Prolegomena - Encyclopedia, Revelation, Scripture
    II. Theology - The Being and Nature of Gód, the Doctrine of the Trinity, the Decrees of God
    III. Anthropology - Man and his Fall
    IV. Christology - the Person and Work of Christ
    V. Soteriology - Salvation, the Doctrine of Salvation Applied
    VI. Ecclesiology - the Doctrine of the Church, the Means of Grace
    VII. Eschatology - the Last Things

The synthetic method gives the best over-all balance to the entire structure of systematic theology. For this reason, we shall follow this method of distributing the materials.

In addition to these seven *loci*, which constitute the basic structure of the system of theology, there are also other areas generally covered under the department of systematic theology. They are: the history of doctrine, the study of the development of the creeds, apologetics and ethics.

Though it is true that these various fields of study may properly belong with systematic theology, we shall limit our consideration to the seven *loci* that specifically constitute the system.

4. Practical Theology

Practical theology has been defined as "the science and art of the various functions of the Christian ministry for the preservation and propagation of the Christian religion at home and abroad."[13] Schaff goes on to say "it is the crowning consummation of sacred learning to which all other departments look and by which they become useful for the upbuilding of the kingdom of God in the world."[14] He goes on to divide the various branches of practical theology as follows:

    I. Theory of the Christian Ministry
    II. Ecclesiology - Church Polity
    III. Liturgics - Worship
    IV. Homiletics - Preaching
    V. Catechetics - Teaching
    VI. Poimenics - Pastoral Work
    VII. Evangelistic - Evangelism and Missions

---

13. Philip S. Schaff, *Theological Propaedeutic* (New York: Charles Scribners Sons, 1909), p. 448.
14. *Ibid.*

Chapter II - The Idea, Task and Methodology of Systematic Theology

I. The Idea of Systematic Theology

We have already indicated that theology is properly defined as the science of God and of his relations with all of his created universe. We have also seen that to add the word *systematic* carries with it the idea of the full organization of the materials of theology into a system. It is more than just a systematic organization, however. It is a presentation of the material in the form of a *system*. Such a view of systematic theology implies the idea that it is essentially a science. When we say this, we are saying that it is an area of human knowledge in which we seek to discover what is true. In other words, the design of systematic theology is to discover and declare absolute truth. It aims at the organization of this truth into a complete self-contained system.

Every science is based on certain presuppositions. They are:

(1) The reality of its subject matter;

(2) The capacity of the human mind to apprehend, receive and rationalize this subject matter; and

(3) Some medium of communication by which the subject matter is brought before the mind and presented to it for apprehension.[1]

Theology, like all other sciences presupposes:

(1) The reality of its subject matter, namely, that there is a God and that he has relations with his creatures.

(2) That man has a religious nature, that is, a nature capable of understanding that God is, and something of what he is, and the relations he sustains toward man.

(3) That there are media of communication by which God and his relations are brought before our minds, and further, that man is capable of receiving and understanding these things.

From this, we conclude that theology is the science which treats of God and of the relations between God and the universe. As such, theology might well exist for its own sake. Warfield says:

> The truths concerning God and his relations are, above all comparison, in themselves the most worthy of all truths of study and examination. Yet we must vindicate a further goal for the advance of theology and thus contend for it that it is an eminently practical science. The contemplation and exhibition of Christianity as truth is far from the end of the matter. This truth is specially communicated by God for a purpose, for which it is admirably adapted. That purpose is to save and sanctify the soul. And the discovery, study, and systematization of the truth is in order that, firmly grasping it and thoroughly comprehending it in all its reciprocal relations, we may be able to make the most efficient use of it for its holy purpose.... [D]octrine is in order to life,

---

1. Benjamin B. Warfield, "The Idea of Systematic Theology," *op. cit.*, p. 53.

and the study of doctrine must be prosecuted in a spirit which would see its end in the correction and edification of life.[2]

Warfield concludes his study of the idea of systematic theology with this very moving statement regarding the student of theology:

> If such be the value in use of doctrine, the systematic theologian is preeminently a preacher of the gospel; and the end of his work is obviously not merely the logical arrangement of the truths which come under his hand, but the moving of men through their power, to love God with all their hearts and their neighbors as themselves; to choose their portion with the Saviour of their souls; to find and hold him precious; and to recognize and yield to the sweet influences of the Holy Spirit whom he has sent. With such truth as this, he will not dare to deal in a cold and merely scientific spirit, but will justly and necessarily permit its preciousness and its practical destination to determine the spirit in which he handles it, and to awaken the reverential love with which alone he should investigate its reciprocal relations. For this he needs to be suffused at all times with a sense of the unspeakable worth of the revelation which lies before him as the source of his material, and with the personal bearings of its separate truths on his own heart and life; he needs to have had and to be having a full, rich, and deep religious experience of the great doctrines with which he deals; he needs to be living close to his God, to be resting always on the bosom of his Redeemer, to be filled at all times with the manifest influences of the Holy Spirit. The student of systematic theology needs a very sensitive religious nature, a most thoroughly consecrated heart, and an outpouring of the Holy Ghost upon him, such as will fill him with that spiritual discernment, without which all native intellect is in vain. He needs to be not merely a student, not merely a thinker, not merely a systematizer, not merely a teacher - he needs to be like the beloved disciple himself in the highest, truest, and holiest sense, a divine."[3]

II. The Task of Systematic Theology

A. Modern Views of the Task

Before considering the Reformed view of the task of systematic theology, it is useful to examine briefly some of the modern approaches to theology.

1. Schleiermacher

For Schleiermacher, religion and therefore theology is essentially the feeling of dependence upon God. It is neither knowledge nor moral action but rather this sense of dependence upon ultimate reality. Dogma, therefore, is merely the intellectual expression or interpretation of this feeling of religious dependence. This being the case, the task of systematic theology is to set forth in

---

2. *Ibid.* pp. 79-85.
3. *Ibid.* pp. 86-87.

an orderly fashion the dogmas of the church at any given time in its historical development. Resting, therefore, upon feeling and experience instead of upon an objective standard, Schleiermacher has placed theology on an entirely subjective standard. Systematic theology, for him, is the historical or descriptive science of that subjective theology.

2. Ritschl

The Ritschlian view of dogmatics defines the subject as the exposition of the Christian faith or the science of the Christian faith. In treating the subject, the Ritschlians try to divorce, as much as possible, knowledge from faith. The emphasis is entirely upon the *fiducia* aspect of faith instead of the *notitia*. The content of faith is the religious - ethical experiences. This, again, is subjective. It cannot be systematized and, therefore, systematic theology or dogmatics is little more than the description of such religious - ethical experiences. Though there is in this view something more of the objective than is found in Schleiermacher's view, nevertheless the subjective is basic. As Ritschl himself stressed value judgments of the individual in religious life, so the religious experience of the Ritschlian is ultimately dependent upon the particular religio-ethical values of the individual concerned.

3. Barth and Brunner

Karl Barth defines dogmatics as a theological discipline but, as he says, theology is a function of the church.[4] With this, Emil Brunner also agrees. As he says, if dogmatics is anything at all, it is the function of the church.[5] He goes on to say that the presupposition of dogmatics is not only the existence and doctrine of the church but also the life within the church.[6] Barth describes the task of dogmatics as follows:

> The task of dogmatics is thus not merely the combination, repetition, and transcription of a number of already present 'truths of revelation,' once for all expressed and authentically defined as to wording and meaning . . . the concept truths of revelation, in the sense of Latin propositions given and sealed once for all by divine authority in wording and meaning, is theologically impossible, if it be the case that revelation has its truth in the free decision of God, made once for all in Jesus Christ, and for that very reason and in that way strictly future for us, and must become true in the church from time to time in the intractable reality of faith. Truth of revelation is the freely acting God, Himself and quite alone. Results of dogmatic work, like the dogmas underlying the creeds, which are venerable results, because gained in the common knowledge of the church at a definite time, may and should guide our own dogmatic work, but never replace it at any point in virtue of their authority. Moreover, in dogmatics it can never be a

---
4. *Church Dogmatics*, (Edinburgh: T. & T. Clark, 1957), vol. I, 1, p. 1.
5. *The Christian Doctrine of God*, Dogmatics I, p. 3.
6. *Ibid.*, p. 5.

question of the mere combination, repetition, and summarizing of Biblical doctrine.[7]

Barth's subjectivity comes out most clearly in the following statement, which occurs later on this same page, "Therefore, dogmatics as such does not inquire what the apostles and prophets have said, but what we ourselves must say on the basis of the apostles and prophets."[8] For Barth, revelation is event, and therefore, ultimately it is not the written Word, but the event behind that Word with which he seeks to deal. He says:

> The Word of God is the speech, the act, the mystery of God, and so not a substance imminent in the church apart from the event of its being spoken and believed or discoverable and demonstrable to her. Therefore, even the church is not constantly, continuously the church of Jesus Christ but such she is in the event of the Word of God being spoken to her and believed by her.[9]

From these very limited citations of "neo-orthodox" theologians, we see that it is again the church's experience that is the subject matter for systematic theology. Of necessity, this is subjective in nature. Barth wants to point to the Bible as the norm, as the witness--as the pointer to the revelation of God, but he does not want to allow that the Bible is objectively the Word of God itself. We shall have more to say about this when we treat the subject material of systematic theology.

B. The Reformed View

1. Based on the Revelation of God

The Reformers maintained that Scripture alone is to be the source of all theological thought. The task of systematic theology is to set forth in an orderly and coherent manner the truth concerning God and his relations to the world and man. In so doing, it is seeking to produce a systematic presentation of all doctrinal truths under one comprehensive system.

The truths being thus systematized are those discovered in the areas of God's revelation to man. The theologian may use all areas of God's revelation, but in particular his primary source is the Holy Scripture.

It should be kept in mind that systematic theology is a derivative from revelation. It is not revelation itself nor is it an addition to God's special revelation. The development of our understanding of the system of theology has come through the long development of the church in history. As such, it should be recognized that systematic theology is not the product of a single theologian or series of theologians. It is rather the development of the thinking of the church under the influence of the Holy Spirit down through her history. Murray says:

> It is this ceaseless activity of the Holy Spirit that explains the development throughout the centuries of what we call Christian doctrine. Individual theologians are but the spokesmen of this accumulating un-

---
7. *Ibid.*, p. 16.
8. *Idem.*
9. *Ibid.*, p. 299.

derstanding which the Spirit of Truth has been granting to the church. Christ as head of the church must not be thought of apart from the Spirit nor the Spirit apart from Christ. Hence, it is to state the same truth in terms of Christ's presence when we say that he is walking in the midst of the churches and the angels of the churches are in his right hand. In him are hid all the treasures of wisdom and knowledge and from this fullness that resides in him, he communicates to the church so that the church organically and corporately may increase and grow up into knowledge unto the measure of the stature of the fullness of Christ. It is this perspective that not only brings to view, but also requires the progression by which systematic theology has been characterized. The history of doctrine demonstrates the progressive development, and we may never think that this progression has ever reached a finale. Systematic theology is never a finished science nor is its task ever completed.[10]

2. Threefold Task of Systematic Theology

a. Constructive Task

Systematic theology involves at least a threefold task First, there is the constructive task. This, of course, is the task of building a complete system. Ultimately, the systematic theologian must go to the Bible and find out what it says about each part of his system. From this, he constructs his system. This is more than merely the gathering of Biblical statements together. It involves the integration of Biblical thought. It involves the formulation of doctrinal statements based upon principles or particular ideas revealed in Scripture. The connection between different doctrines must be seen and set forth, thus developing the fully-integrated system.

b. Demonstrative and Defensive Task

The second aspect of the task of systematic theology is what might be called the demonstrative or defensive task. It is not enough simply to set forth the system of theology. The system must also be shown to be truly Biblical in all of its parts and in its totality. The task of dogmatics is to seek for absolute truth. Though we must acknowledge that we do not attain the complete and final truth, nevertheless this is to be our goal. It is here also that the *locus* called apologetics fits in with systematic theology for apologetics is defined as the defense of the faith. Thus, not only do we need to be able to prove the Biblical character of the system but also be ready to defend the entire system.

---

10. John Murray, "Systematic Theology," *Westminster Theological Journal*, vol. XXV, 2, May 1963, pp. 138-9.

c. Critical Task

The third aspect of the task of systematic theology is the critical task. Entering as we do into church history after there has been already a great deal of systematic theology developed, it must always be the continuing task of the systematic theologian to examine critically all that has gone before. He is constantly to test the dogmas of the church by the Word of God. It should be observed at this point that the theologian does not start *de novo*. Rather, he stands upon the shoulders of those who have gone before, resting upon the works of men who have already labored in this field. Nevertheless, it is his task to do so with a critical eye so that if there have been errors in the theologies of individuals or of churches, he can detect them and seek to correct them. Sometimes there have been areas that have not been properly covered. Here again, the theologian's task is to develop fuller statements and fill in the gaps that may be missing. A rather striking example of this occurred in American Presbyterian theology. Charles Hodge, the great Princeton theologian, failed to deal with the subject of adoption. Thornwell at Columbia Seminary and his successors Girardeau and R. A. Webb, later of Louisville Seminary, all wrote on this particular area and helped to fill this gap.

III. The Method of Systematic Theology

The question of method for systematic theology is basic. For if we choose the wrong method, then we will arrive at wrong conclusions. "If a man adopts a false method, he is like one who takes a wrong road which will never lead him to his destination."[11] In the discussion of methodology that follows, we are deeply indebted to the discussion of the subject by Dr. Cornelius Van Til in his syllabus, "An Introduction to Systematic Theology." First he discusses methodology in general, and then more specifically the proper method for systematic theology. We shall follow his line of discussion.

A. Christian Theistic Methodology

Charles Hodge indicates that there are two basic approaches to methodology, either *a priori*, or *a posteriori*. The first moves from cause to effect, or from presumption to its logical conclusion. The *a posteriori* method moves from effect to cause, from facts to principles. It is the inductive method, or the empirical approach.

The Christian theistic method employs both. It has sometimes been called the method of implication. It uses both the *a priori* and the *a posteriori* methods. The *a priori* aspect of this method lies in the fact that Christianity presupposes the living God of the Bible. Based on this presupposition, certain conclusions may be reached. The *a posteriori* aspect of the method is to gather the facts of revelation, in particular, the Bible, and then move back to the principles from these facts. This is not just *a priori* and *a posteriori* methods in general, or

---

11. Charles Hodge, *Systematic Theology*, (New York: Charles Scribner's Sons, 1898), vol. 1, p. 3.

in the abstract. The Christian theistic method in particular presupposes the living self-contained, ontological, triune God. Included in our concept of this God is the idea of his incomprehensibility. This is not to say that we cannot know him, but it is to affirm that man cannot fully comprehend him. God is fully self-comprehensive. He is absolute rationality. He is the only absolute, self-contained being. God has always been. He has always known all truth. He is himself the only ultimate fact. He is, thus, the ultimate principle of all being and the principle of all knowledge.

The Biblical doctrine of the Trinity is also of significance in our considering methodology. For the problem of the one and the many has always been one of the major problems of human knowledge. All non-Christian thought that has used a supra-mundane existence has used it to furnish unity or the *a priori* aspect of knowledge. The *a posteriori* aspect of knowledge is constructed on the diversity found in the universe.

> In distinction from this, Christianity says that there was once no *a posteriori* aspect to knowledge at all. When God existed alone, there was no time universe, and there were no new facts arising. The only knowledge activity that existed was completed in the circuit of the mutually exhaustive personalities of the triune God. It is only with respect to man that we can speak of a relation of the *a priori* and the *a posteriori* elements of knowledge. Such a distinction cannot exist in God. The plurality of the Godhead cannot be compared with the arising of new facts as we see it in the creative universe. The plurality of God is as eternal as the unity of God... There is no novelty in God and there can be no novelty for God.[12]

Growing out of this concept of God, we see then that all human knowledge must be derivative knowledge. This is in contrast to non-Christian theories of how men reason. Non-Christians maintain that man reasons univocally. Man is viewed as the ultimate reference point in the area of knowledge.

> Man will therefore have to seek to make a system for himself that will relate all the facts of his environment to one another in such a way as will enable him to see exhaustively all the relations that obtain between them. In other words, the system that the non-Christian has to seek on his assumption is one in which he himself virtually occupies the place that God occupies in Christian theology.[13]

Christians, on the other hand, maintain that all human reason is analogical, which holds as the basic presupposition the fact that God is the source of all knowledge and that all facts are first preinterpreted by him. By this we are simply saying that all human thinking is a reinterpreting of God's thought after him. This may be illustrated by the difference in the way in which Christians and non-Christians use the law of contradiction.

For the non-Christian, the law of contradiction is a principle of logic that stands above God and man alike. This means that God and man are correlative.

---

12. Cornelius Van Til, *An Introduction to Systematic Theology*, op. cit., p. 10.
13. Cornelius Van Til, *A Christian Theory of Knowledge* (Nutley, NJ: Presbyterian and Reformed Publishing Company, 1969), p. 15.

God and man are under the same system of logic, which is higher than both and exists independent of both.

For the Christian, on the other hand, God exists before time and laws of logic. The law of contradiction is a part of the created temporal world. It is the expression of the internal coherence of God's nature, but is not above God. In other words, the Christian cannot use as his ultimate criterion the law of contradiction. For him, the ultimate criterion is God and his self-revelation. The law of contradiction operates only under God and not above him. The Christian can and does use the law of contradiction to deal logically with the facts of the temporal world, but he does not use it to say what can or cannot be true about God himself.

> ... the law of contradiction cannot be thought of as operating anywhere except against the background of the nature of God. Since, therefore, God created this world, it would be impossible that this created world should ever furnish an element of reality on a par with him. The concept of creation as entertained by Christians makes the idealistic notion of logic once for all impossible. The creation doctrine is implied in the God-concept of Christianity; deny the creation doctrine and you have denied the Christian concept of God.[14]

From this, we see that for all Christian thinking in any area the underlying presupposition of the living God is basic. Derived from this presupposition is the further concept that all human reason must be analogical or reinterpretative rather than original. We shall now move on to a consideration of this methodology as it applies specifically to systematic theology.

B. Theological Methodology

As we have seen, all facts in the universe have been first preinterpreted by the self-contained God, and therefore, all knowledge is analogical. As such, all knowledge is in a sense theological knowledge. That is, all facts are revelational of God, and thus any knowledge derived from the study of facts must point back to God ultimately. When we are talking about the theological method, however, we are talking about that area of human thought which deals more directly than the other sciences with our knowledge of God and his relations to us. As Dr. Van Til puts it, "The difference between theology and other science does not lie in the fact that God is any less necessary for the one than for the other, but that the difference lies only in the degree of directness with which God is brought into the knowledge situation."[15]

From the Christian point of view, every fact in the space-time universe is a revelation of God's plan, and, therefore, every fact deals with theology. Perhaps the best way to illustrate the relation of theological method to general Christian theistic methodology is to think of concentric circles. The larger circle outside contains all the facts of science save theology and the second circle inside includes all of the theological disciplines, while the third and smallest circle deals with theology proper.

---

14. Van Til, *Systematic Theology, op. cit.*, p. 11.
15. *Ibid.*, p. 14.

CHAPTER II IDEA, TASK AND METHODOLOGY

In the development of the history of dogmatics, a number of different approaches have been applied to methodology. First of all, there was, during the apostolic period, a time in which the church lived by the preached word of the apostles. This preaching was, of course, based upon the facts of the life and work of Jesus, but it is striking to see that the apostles themselves constantly referred to the Old Testament as the authoritative Word of God. They based their message upon that Word of God written and now fulfilled in Christ. The New Testament church as seen at Berea, searched those Scriptures to see if what the apostles taught was true. Being convinced of the truth of that teaching, the work of the apostles both spoken and later written, became authoritative for the church. By the end of that New Testament period, the full Scripture was the rule of faith. The Old and New Testaments were the source of the dogmas or doctrines of the Christian Church.

Of course, from the nature of the case, the recognition of the full canon of the New Testament by the entire church universal took a good deal of time. One of the early marks of the church was the use of the baptismal formula, a short confession, which slowly grew into the Apostles Creed. There are a number of statements in the New Testament that are creedal in nature, and thus, there is a Biblical basis for the use of creeds by the Church.

With the rise of the episcopate in the second and third centuries, it was natural that these men were looked upon as having the gift of determining what was true and pure. This gave rise to the traditions of these fathers which were placed beside the Scripture as being authoritative. Eventually, with the coming of the papacy, and the Medieval Church, the authority of the fathers was officially recognized as being on a par with that of Scripture. Also, with the rise of the authority of the institution of the Roman Church, there developed the idea that only what the Church said should be accepted as doctrine. This development in the Roman Catholic Church reached its climax in 1870 with the declaration of the infallibility of the Pope in matters of doctrine. Thus, the Church of Rome teaches that it is the task of the systematic theologian to study not only Scripture but also tradition, and to elucidate the truth of what the church has decreed. Though there is in the Roman view the affirmation that the Scripture is the ultimate authority, nevertheless, since she places the church between the Bible and the people, she, in effect, subordinates the Bible to the church. In other words, the ordinary Christian is not capable of understanding the Bible without the authoritative interpretation of the church. Thus, the church is the final authority of what is to be believed and practiced.

With the coming of the Reformation, there was a return to the Bible as the only infallible rule of faith and practice. The Reformers, however, were not unaware of the development of dogma throughout the history of the church. These dogmas were subjected to the critical study in the light of the Word. What could be received from the historical development was thus accepted. This approach allows for a recognition that God's Spirit does and has moved in the life of his Church. Of course, it is also critical for the church in that there is the recognition that the church may err and that her teachings must constantly be examined in the light of the Word.

Following the Reformation, there came the period of the *Aufklarung*. Out of this period have grown various different methods of dealing with theology.

Though they differ one from another in many ways, they have a common subjectivism. Man has become the ultimate instead of God, and the knowledge of God is sought in the human will, intellect, emotions, or in his mystical experience. Immanuel Kant in his *Critique of Pure Reason* virtually denies the possibility of revelation. He divides the realms of knowledge into the phenomena and the noumena. The only area that man knows lies in the phenomena. There can be no real knowledge of the noumenal realm. This is ultimately a denial of the possibility of the Christian God. Kant, however, was aware that he needed some sort of higher authority. This he found in his moral imperative, growing out of practical reason. In essence, this means that he sought a God out of the phenomenal area. In other words, the moral man makes his own God after his own image. This method may be called the ethical--subjective method.

Hegel represents one who would seek his knowledge of God from the intellect of man. He posits the dialectical method of developing a system of absolute truth. God is seen as a logical part of this system.

Schleiermacher emphasized the feeling of dependence. In other words, he found the knowledge of God in the religious experience of the church. This method may be spoken of as the mystical-subjective method.

Though Ritschl sought to avoid the pure subjectivism of Schleiermacher by ascribing revelational significance to the Scripture and especially the New Testament, he nevertheless fails to escape subjectivism because he allows the individual to judge what is of religious value. In all of these modern, subjective methods of dealing with theology, there is the attempt to get away from the Bible as the final authority, and to become more scientific. Faith in the Scripture is not scientific, thus Scripture is rejected as the final source of theological thought. The source of religion is to be found elsewhere.

In the modern reaction to old-line modernism as led by Karl Barth, we again find affirmations about the authority of Scripture, yet as this theology is further examined, it also is found to be basically subjective. Barth will affirm that *das Wort Gottes* is the only source of knowledge of God, but he does not hold that the Bible is that word. Barth maintains that the real word of God is one that is behind the Scripture, and Scripture is the reliable witness to that word. It is interesting to note that while he posits a word behind the Scripture, yet he identifies that word with the questions of where and how the Word of God is to be found, and of what it is and how it is knowable. He says:

> All of this on the presupposition that its promised and commissioned identity with church proclamation (in view of the fact that in the latter we have to do with man's work) in reality stands in question, that church proclamation must become what, because of its promise and task, it is, and that from this becoming what it is, there grows up for the church, alongside the commission of proclamation itself, the commission of dogmatics, i.e., the commission of testing, criticizing and revising its actual proclamation from time to time. We next saw how the Word of God concretely confronts church proclamation in the form of Holy Scripture as the witness given to the church concerning God's revelation. *Church proclamation in agreement with Scripture is the fulfillment of the concept of dogma, after knowledge of which dogma strives.* ... The whole meaning of the correspondence between holy

Scripture and proclamation and so to the whole meaning of the path of knowledge and dogmatics actually consists in our having to do with the Word of God both in Holy Scripture and in proclamation, with the difference that in the former (Holy Scripture) we have simply to discover it so far as it affects the task of dogmatics, whereas in the latter (proclamation), at least in connection with the task of dogmatics, we have not so much to discover it as to inquire into it, to investigate proclamation in relation to it - but in either case we have to do with the Word of God...And if correspondence really does take place between the Bible and proclamation and so a path to dogmatic knowledge becomes visible, even that may not be left looking like an accident or as a result of general didactic considerations; it must rise out of the matter, out of the fact that the Bible and proclamation are or may become the Word of God.[16]

Barth considers that there are three forms of the Word of God, namely, God's language, God's act, and God's mystery. He speaks thus of these three forms of the Word:

... of proclamation, of the Bible, and then in the third (but in fact the first and decisive) place of revelation, as the source of the Word of God in the Bible and in proclamation, as of the primary form of the Word of God, by connection with which, by participation in which the Bible and proclamation may also become the Word of God; of the Word of God so far as it simply is the Word of God without any becoming, of the event of the Word of God in virtue of which the Bible and proclamation become the Word of God. The Bible and proclamation are the Word of God in virtue of the Word of God revealing itself.[17]

He then describes the fact that dogmatics must investigate the nature of this revelation, this underlying, this primary revelation of the Word of God, which lies behind the Bible and proclamation.

From the concept of revelation, we must arrive at the extent to which the Bible and proclamation are to be regarded as the Word of God, the nature of the correspondence which holds between the two, and the way in which the second is to be measured by the first . . . and revelation must constitute the starting point and proclamation the goal.[18]

Barth has written extensively in the field of what he calls *church dogmatics*. He has intentionally chosen this as his title, since he considers the task of dogmatics to be the study of the proclamation of the church. It is interesting to observe that in his work, *The Word of God and the Word of Man*, he states "... in the truest sense, there is no such thing as Reformed doctrine, except the timeless appeal to the open Bible and to the spirit which from it speaks to our spirit."[19] He goes on to speak, however, of Reformed doctrine as:

... the ideas which took shape in *our* minds as a result of the *unavoidable necessity* to regard reformed Christianity *respectfully* in terms of its concrete beginnings *and* to *criticize* that Christianity in accordance

---

16. Barth, *op cit.*, pp. 330-332.
17. *Ibid.*, p. 333.
18. *Ibid.*, p. 335.
19. *Op. cit.*, p. 229.

with the character of those beginnings. It may be our doctrinal task to make a careful revision of the theology of Geneva or the Heidelberg Catechism or the Canons of Dort, or, if we credit ourselves with the necessary authority and insight, it *may* be our task to draw up a new creed, a *Helvetica tertia*, in the same way that our fathers substituted *a posteriori* for *a priori*. Both are real possibilities for the Reformed Churches.[20]

In the long run, Barth's view of the Bible-- as something that can become the Word of God for us, as it speaks to us in the event of revelation--is a subjectivizing of the Bible. Though he has sought to escape the subjectivism of Modernism, he has himself remained subjective in his methodology.

Having discussed some of the different views of theological methodology, let us return now to the more positive presentation of the true Reformed view of methodology. This may be called the genetico-synthetic method. It has also been called the theological method or the method of authority. We have already pointed to this method in our earlier reference to the fact that the Christian theologian begins with his presupposition of the living God of the Bible. As one analyzes the subjective, empirical method of the various modern theologians, it is clear that they are seeking to deal with the phenomenal world, the world of experience. It is a method of starting with the results and going back, or trying to go back, to the source. The true Christian approach to methodology, as we have already indicated, begins with God the preinterpreter of all facts, including theological facts. This methodology then begins with the source of theology and moves out to the river, rather than moving from the river to the source. Along with the presupposition that God is the source of all our thought and being goes the presupposition that God has spoken, that God has revealed himself, and that he has done so authoritatively and truly, and that this revelation has been set down in the Scriptures, or the Word of God written. The theologian then takes the Scripture itself as the *principium theologiae*. From this, he develops his dogmas or doctrines. In that it is a synthetic method, seeking to arrive at the system of truth, it is the task of systematic theology to show how the dogmas of the church have grown out of Scripture as an organism. This is to be seen not on the basis of a few proof texts, but from the Scripture as a whole in its full breadth and depth. "The various dogmas are not isolated propositions but they form a unity. There is really but one dogma, that is borne out of the Scripture... the method of a dogmatician can and may not be other than systematic."[21]

In the application of the synthetic method the theologian will not merely receive isolated doctrines from Scripture, but rather the divine truth as a whole revealed in facts and words. The facts are the embodiments of the truths that are revealed, and the truths illumine the facts and stand out on the pages of Holy Writ. The teachings of Scripture are seen in their grand unity, since the Bible indicates in the various ways how its separate doctrines are inter-related. Bearing all these data in mind, the dogmatician will seek to construct his system in a logical way, supplying whatever links may be missing in the Confession of the

---
20 *Ibid.*, p. 231.
21 Herman Bavinck, *Gereforemeerde Dogmatiek* (Kampen: Kok, 4th ed., 1928), Vol I, p. 71.

Church from the Bible as the fountainhead of religious truth, and calling attention to the various deviations from Scripture in the historical development of the Truth. It will be his constant endeavor to set forth all the treasures of wisdom and knowledge that are hidden in Christ and revealed in Scripture.[22]

Having seen the basic principles of methodology for systematic theology, we shall seek to carry out the actual outworking of this methodology in succeeding chapters.

---

22 Louis Berkhof, *Introductory Volume to Systematic Theology* (Grand Rapids: William B. Eerdmans Publishing Company, 1932), p. 72.

Chapter III The Source or First Principle of Theology

I. Definition of *Principia* in Theology

It has been customary in the fields of Philosophy and Theology to speak of the *principia*. The Latin *principium* is a translation of the Greek word *arche*,[1] which means "beginning" or "source". Aristotle used it to refer to the primary source of all being, of actuality, and of knowledge (*principium essendi, existendi*, and *cognoscendi*). Instead of simply speaking of "principle" in English, we can come closer to approximating the meaning of the original by speaking of "first principle," or "primary source." The Krauth-Fleming *Vocabulary of the Philosophical Sciences* states:

> The word is applied equally to thought and to being; and hence principles have been divided into those of being and those of knowledge, or *principia essendi* and *principia cognoscendi*...*Principia essendi* may also be *principia cognoscendi* for the fact that things exist is the ground or reason of their being known. But the converse does not hold; for the existence of things is in no way dependent on our knowledge of them.[2]

Berkhof observes that in ancient philosophy the greater attention was given to the *principia essendi*, while in modern philosophy the *principia cognoscendi* receive the greater attention.

II. *Principia* of the "Non-Theological" Sciences

A. The *Principium Essendi*

The Bible opens with the declaration that God is the source of all being. He is the self-contained, ontological, triune God. He is independent, non-derived, a self-contained being. He has always been. He IS. He is the eternal source of his own being.

God is the creator of all else that is and, therefore, ultimately he is the source or *principium* of all being. Nothing is, which he has not made (Genesis 1:1; John 1:1-2). The being of all of creation rests ultimately in God. He is the primary source of the being of any object or fact that exists. Thus the *principia essendi* of the subject of non-theological science is God.

Any truth that may be derived from the study of any particular subject matter ultimately comes from God. He has always known himself exhaustively, and he has eternally contained within himself the full knowledge of every fact that ever shall come into being. So it is that God is the *principium essendi* of all scientific knowledge. That is, he is the primary source of being and of knowledge. It should be pointed out that his knowledge is a self-conscious knowledge. This is in contrast to pantheism with its impersonal, unconscious Absolute, a being who has no knowledge of himself. Such an impersonal absolute as posited by pantheism can never be the principle or source of our knowledge.

---

1. ἀρχή
2. As cited in Berkhof, *op cit.*, p. 93.

B. The *Principium Cognoscendi Externum*

The *principia* related to knowing consist of two types. First, there is the external or the objective source of knowledge. Secondly, there is the internal or subjective source of our knowledge.

As we have already indicated, God is the ultimate source of the being of all that exists and therefore of all knowledge. When one studies the universe, he is not considering God directly. Rather, he is considering that which God has made. One of the implications of the Biblical doctrine of creation is that everything that God has made is revelational of God. Psalm 19:1 asserts that "the heavens declare the glory of God." All that God has made reveals to us something of his thought--the absolute truth.

Created reality is a revelation of the truth, and not the ultimate source of the truth itself. Such revelation is incomplete. It is not fully comprehensive in scope. Only God has the full comprehensive knowledge of all truth in and of himself. Man as a finite creature can never know the infinite, creator God exhaustively. Because of sin man is not able to interpret revelation properly or to come to a full, true picture of all that God has revealed.

God's beautiful creation, replete with Divine Wisdom, is the *principium cognoscendi externum* of all non-theological sciences. It is the external means, by which the knowledge that flows from God is conveyed to man. This view of the matter is, of course, absolutely opposed to the principle of idealism, that the thinking man creates and constructs his own world: not only the form of the world of thought (Kant), but also its material and contents (Fichte), and even the world of being (Hegel).[3]

C. The *Principium Cognoscendi Internum*

It is not enough that God has revealed himself. There must also be the receiver of this revelation. Bavinck says "Science always consists in the logical relations between subject and object."[4] Only when the subject is adapted to the object can science result. God in making the human mind made provision for this. The human mind was made with the capacity for knowledge and is thus able to discover the truth in the revelation contained in the world. Human reason, therefore, is the *principium cognoscendi internum* of science. It is by reason that man appropriates the truth revealed in creation.

It should be observed that the rationalists see the source of knowledge in human reason, assuming that the reason will ultimately be able to write a formula that could predict everything that will take place in the universe. The empiricist, on the other hand, sees the source of knowledge in the phenomena. The empiricist regards the human mind as a *tabula rasa*. That is, the human mind gathers knowledge which it inscribes upon the *tabula rasa* from experience. Ultimately, empiricism results in skepticism, for if there is no relation between the

---

3. *Ibid.*, p. 94.
4. *Gereformeerde Dogmatiek, op cit.*, Vol. I, p. 186.

facts, then all happens by chance, and where chance is in the system there can be no system.

In the last analysis, it is only on the basis of the Christian epistemology that science can be preserved. For if God has created all that exists, and if he has placed in the universe the truth that is there, then human reason is not the ultimate source of the truth nor is that truth in the final analysis based upon the facts themselves. Ultimately, the truth is based upon God and his plan. Man's thinking is thus derivative and not original. It is man's duty to think God's thoughts after him. And since God has made both the facts of the universe and made man in his own image, with a mind capable of dealing with those facts, man is able to come to true knowledge of the truth. In other words, man has the capability of arriving at truth as he studies the universe which God has made. God has made his mind with this capability, and God has placed the truth to be learned in the facts of his universe. We have already noted that this truth will not be comprehensive or final, but it will be true.

III. *Principia* in Theology

A. God is the *Principium Essendi* of Theology.

Just as God is the *pricipium essendi* of non-theological science, so he is also the *principium essendi* of theology. God is the source of all being, and, therefore, the source of all knowledge. If this is true of knowledge in general, it is especially true of the knowledge of God himself.

> God possesses a complete and in every way perfect knowledge of himself. He knows himself in the absolute sense of the word, not only as he is related to his creatures, nor merely in his diversified activities and their controlling motives, but also in the unfathomable depths of His essential Being. His self-consciousness is perfect and infinite; there is no sub-conscious life in Him, no subliminal region of unconscious mentality. And of that absolute, perfectly conscious self-knowledge of God, the knowledge which man has of the divine Being is but a faint and creaturely copy or imprint. All human knowledge of God is derived from him, Matt. 11:27; I Cor. 2:10 f.[5]

All our knowledge of God thus has its origin in God himself. He knows himself perfectly and absolutely. All human knowledge is derived from him. Just as man's existence is dependent on the voluntary creation by God, so also his knowledge is dependent on the voluntary act of God's revealing of himself. God in the act of creation has voluntarily revealed something of his nature. Any and all the truth that may be derived from the study of creation is derived from the Creator. Thus every bit of man's knowledge is derivative, reinterpretive, or analogical.

---

5. Berkhof, *op. cit.*, pp. 95-6.

B. The *Principium Cognoscendi Externum*

In speaking of the non-theological sciences, the *principium cognoscendi externum* was found to be the revelation of God in creation. This we customarily call "general revelation." For theology, however, the *principium cognoscendi externum* is to be found in God's special revelation. From the very beginning man's special relationship to God was to be understood in the light of God's special revelation to him. That is, even before the fall, though man could read the world of nature truly, and therefore know that he was the creature of God-- made for the glory of God, made to use the universe around him for the glory of God-- nevertheless he did not see in the general revelation the personal covenant relationship that God intended for him to understand. Thus from the beginning, even before the creation of the woman, God revealed to Adam that he had been created a covenant creature. This covenant relation was revealed in the special revelation, known as the covenant of works. Man thus needed the special revelation for his full understanding of his relation to God before the fall. This special revelation was the *principium cognoscendi externum* of Adam before the fall just as much as it is for us now after the fall.

With the fall of Adam came the noetic effects of sin. That is, the mind of man has been blinded, and his reason perverted, so that he is now blind to the revelation of God in the world about him. The consequence is that though he sees the glory of God revealed in general revelation, and though he knows that he is a creature of the living and true God, yet he persists in his sin, suppressing that knowledge, and denying its validity.[6] God has graciously entered into a new covenant with his elect, namely, the covenant of grace. He has revealed this new covenant unto man in the special revelation that he has granted to us since the fall. A distinguishing characteristic of this new special revelation is that it is now redemptive in character. It has pleased God further to embody that revelation in an objective record, namely, the Scriptures.

The question of whether Scripture is the only source of knowledge in theology has been raised. Since God has revealed himself both in general and in special revelation, why should we not derive our theology from both? Since the fall man is unable to derive a true theology from general revelation without the light of special revelation. Therefore, the Bible is referred to as the *principium unicum* from which the theologian must derive his knowledge. What may be learned from general revelation comes only as it is seen in the light of the Bible.[7]

We shall have much more to say about the nature of the Bible and of its authority and inspiration in a later section. We may affirm, however, that it is only on the basis of a Bible that is free from error that we can expect to find a pure and true theology. With the entrance of sin, and thereby, of error into the world, one of man's most basic needs was the re-insertion by God of the truth into the world. This he has done in the Gospel. Jesus declared that he is the Truth (John 14:6), and he further affirmed that the Word of God is the Truth (John 17:17).

---

6. Rom. 1:20-23.
7. Abraham Kuyper agrees with this position. See his *Encyclopedia of Sacred Theology* (New York: Charles Scribner's Sons, 1898), p. 347.

Before leaving the subject of the external source of our knowledge, we should at least mention the fact that the church of Rome places human tradition on a par with Scripture.

Many modern theologians also elevate their reason to a par with or above Scripture. We shall have occasion to deal with these erroneous views more fully as we treat the doctrine of Scripture more extensively later.

C. The *Principium Cognoscendi Internum*

Just as in the case of non-theological sciences, the *principium cognoscendi internum* was found to be human reason, so in the case of theology, the *principium cognoscendi internum* is found to be response of faith. Bavinck describes it thus: "Even if there is a knowledge of God through nature, this does not mean that there are two principles in dogmatics. Dogmatics has only one *principium externum*, namely, the Scriptures, and only one *principium internum*, namely, the believing reason."[8] He treats this subject of the *principium internum* in great detail. We shall have occasion to look further into this. Bavinck concludes a section dealing with the significance or meaning of the *principium internum* by saying:

> God is thus the *principium essendi* of religion and theology; the objective revelation in Christ set down in Scripture is its *principium cognoscendi externum*; and the Holy Ghost, who is poured out on the congregation regenerates and leads it into the truth, is its *principium cognoscendi internum*. By this witness of the Holy Spirit, the revelation comes to realization in mankind and attains its goal. For it is God's good pleasure to recreate humanity according to his image and likeness. Objective revelation is thus not enough; this must itself in a certain sense be forwarded and completed in the subjective illumination. Indeed, the former is only the means, this is the purpose. The *principium externum* is *instrumentale*; the *principium internum* is the *principium formale* and *principale*.[9]

Bavinck thus holds that both faith and the internal witness of the Holy Spirit are involved in the *principium internum*. We shall want to deal with this more fully later. Essentially, however, as we think of the matter, we can state that faith is the internal principle. As we shall see from a further study, the faith of man is the consequence of the mighty working of the Holy Spirit in his heart.

---

8. Bavinck, *op. cit.*, p. 64.
9. *Ibid.*, p. 471.

Chapter IV Revelation (*Principium Cognoscendi Externum*)

Introduction

As we have indicated earlier, the Christian presupposes the truth of Christianity, and thus moves from this basic presupposition in his thinking about all truth. We have also stated that the Bible is ultimately the *principium cognoscendi externum* for Christian theology. Thus, as we begin to examine the subject of revelation, we shall turn to the Bible itself for a proper understanding of it. This approach might be condemned by some as circular. We readily admit to its circular character. This is not grounds for condemnation, however, for all reasoning is ultimately circular. Everyone reasons from the basis of his particular presuppositions.

Non-Christians falsely charge that the assumption of the truth of Christianity is irrational. Though this may appear to be the case from that perspective, the fact is that the assumptions underlying all non-Christian thought, namely, of chance and the ability of the human reason to be able to deal with all of the facts, are really irrational, and make any predication impossible. How impossible it is to assume that the universe as we know it has evolved by chance, and that rational creatures, with a sense of morality have arisen by chance from the non-rational materials of the universe. It is only the Christian presupposition that provides a rational basis to account for the facts of the universe and of mankind. All other proposals are irrational.

The fact is we have not simply arrived here in space and time by chance. What the Bible says is true. We were made by the Living and True God. This means that the character of human existence is theological. There is no neutral or non-theological vantage point. Every man ultimately recognizes that he is a creature of God. He may deny or suppress this *sensus deitatis*, but it remains with him. The Christian, of course, has had the blindness of his sinful nature removed, and he alone sees the truth concerning reality. Thus it is not irrational for the Christian, whose eyes have been opened, to move on the basis of what he knows to be true. It would be irrational for him to do otherwise.

It shall be our purpose, therefore, to examine the Bible's teaching about revelation. For that matter, it shall be our purpose to look to the Bible for its view of all the subjects that are to be studied in Systematic Theology. Our procedure is to derive from a study of the Biblical givens the concepts that it teaches, and then to build our system from these concepts and teachings.

The Bible, of course, is not a systematic presentation of theological data. Rather, it is the record of God's redemptive revelation. Or, to put it in another way, it is a record of redemptive history. It is the historical record of what God has done--his redemptive acts, and also of what he has said. In other words, we find in the Bible not only the mighty acts of God, but also his own interpretation of those acts. There is much emphasis today on the idea that revelation is event or act, and that propositions are not revelational. A study of the Bible itself reveals a combination of both. In this unit of study, it shall be our purpose to examine the historical record of God's self-revelation in order to come to the fully Biblical concept.

I. The Biblical Idea of Revelation

A. Revelation in Creation and Providence

The first chapter of Genesis presents us with one of the most magnificent revelatory acts of God. "In the beginning God created the heavens and the earth." All the truth that is discoverable in this reality has come from God as a result of his creative and providential activity. The Bible teaches us that creation is revelational. "The heavens declare the glory of God, the firmament showeth his handiwork."[1] This illustrates the idea that the word revelation conveys. It is derived from the Latin *revelatio* which denotes "unveiling" or "disclosure." The heavens unveil--disclose the glory of God.

Not only is the creating work of God revelational, but also his sustaining and governing of that creation, which we call providence. This is seen in the daily revelation of creation to us. "Day unto day uttereth speech, and night unto night showeth knowledge."[2] The same thought is expressed many times in Scripture. For example, "The heavens declare his righteousness, and all the peoples have seen his glory."[3] Paul attests the same thing to the multitudes of Lystra, "And yet he left not himself without witness, in that he did good and gave you from heaven rains and fruitful seasons, filling your hearts with food and gladness."[4] He has just announced that God is the creator of all in verse 15, and it is his sustaining grace that is a witness even to the heathen of himself. Romans 1:20 asserts the same basic principle: "For the invisible things of him since the creation of the world are clearly seen being perceived through the things that are made, even his everlasting power and divinity; that they may be without excuse." Note that this verse includes both the creation and the continuation of the universe as being revelatory. That is, both creation and providence are revelatory.

As one examines the details of the account in Genesis one he finds that the means of creation was through the speaking of God. "And God said, ..." occurs eight times. Four times the product of his creative activity is "called" by name. We see here that the revelation in creation is not only the act, but also involves the word revelation of God. This association of God's spoken revelation with creative activities is found in other passages.[5]

The significance of this is accented by the prologue of John where the term Logos is used of the Second Person of the Trinity. "In the beginning was the Word, and the Word was with God, and the Word was God. The same was in the beginning with God. All things were made through him; and without him was not anything made that hath been made."[6] The Word is the express revela-

---

1. Psalm 19:1.
2. Psalm 19:2.
3. Psalm 97:6.
4. Acts 14:17.
5. See Psalm 33:6,9; 148:5.
6. John 1:1-3.

tion of God to us. He was active in the creation, and also in providence. Hebrews 1:1-3 reads:
> God, having of old times spoken unto the fathers in the prophets by divers portions and in divers manners, hath at the end of these days spoken unto us in his Son, whom he appointed heir of all things, through whom also he made the worlds; who being the effulgence of his glory, and the very image of his substance, and upholding all things by the word of his power, when he had made purification of sins, sat down on the right hand of the Majesty on high.

Here we see that the Son of God was not only active in creation, but also in providence. And again, it is by his word that he upholds all things.

The creation of man in the image of God is a unique act of his revelation. It is the image of God in man that marks him as distinct from the rest of creation. The idea of image (*tselem*[7] in Hebrew or *eikon*[8] in Greek) is that which is a likeness. In other words, man was created expressly to be a revelation of God.

This is borne out in the New Testament. Paul says, "that which is known of God is manifest in them."[9] Again he teaches that even the Gentiles have the law of God written in their hearts.
> For when Gentiles that have not the law do by nature the things of the law, these, not having the law, are the law unto themselves; in that they show the work of the law written in their hearts, their conscience bearing witness therewith, and their thoughts one with another accusing or else excusing them.[10]

By virtue of their being made in the image of God, even the heathen bear in their inmost being something of the revelation of God and his law. Though men may deny and pervert this inner revelation, it is one of the clear concepts of Scripture, and should not be overlooked by the Christian.

In the Gospel man is to be conformed to the image of Christ--restored to the image, which had been so marred by sin, in knowledge, righteousness and holiness (Rom. 8:30; Eph. 4:24; Col. 3:10). God's revelation comes to expression in the Christian's life as he causes his glory to be seen and reflected in our lives. The ultimate revelation of God's image in man is to be seen in the Second Adam, the Word of God Incarnate, even our Lord Jesus Christ.

To summarize what we have learned about revelation from creation and providence we have seen:
1. Both creation and upholding the universe are themselves revelational acts.
2. The continued existence of this created universe gives a permanent and continuing revelation.
3. Accompanying the acts of creation and providence is the speaking of God, implying the rational character of the revelation.
4. The revelation is of the Triune God, since all three Persons of the Trinity were and are active in creation and providence.

---

7. צֶלֶם
8. εἰκών
9. Rom. 1:19.
10. Rom 2:14-15.

5. Particularly revealed are the following: the glory of God; the wisdom of God; the righteousness of God; the everlasting power of God; and the divinity of God.
6. This revelation is addressed to and available to all men, and is thus called General Revelation.
7. As suggested by the place given to creation in Scripture, revelation from it is a background for the fuller unfolding of God's special purposes for man.
8. Being the revelation of God, it is an authoritative revelation. God speaks with authority, whenever, wherever and however he speaks.
9. It is sufficient to display those things for which it is particularly designed. It is sufficient to serve as the background for the special revelation that is to follow, but it is not sufficient to reveal that further truth which God has in store for man.
10. It is clear enough for all men to read, and to be left without excuse.

B. Revelation in the Garden of Eden before the Fall

In Genesis 2:4-25 we find the expanded account of the creation of man and of his first condition. In chapter three we have the account of the temptation and the fall of man. From there onward the Bible is a record of God's redemptive revelation. Only in Genesis 2 do we find the prefallen condition treated. This is given for our understanding of the original state of man, and his fall into sin.

The most striking new feature of the revelation in this chapter is the fact that God addresses his rational creature in verbal revelation. We have already observed that verbal or spoken revelation accompanied the creative acts of God. Genesis 1:28-30 and 2:16-17 present the picture of God in direct personal communion with man, speaking to him, first of what he has given to him, and then of the probation connected with the tree of the knowledge of good and evil. We may assume that, since this record serves only as a backdrop for understanding the fall, there may have been much more direct verbal communion between God and man in Eden that is not recorded for us. The original unfallen state of man was that of fellowship with God. This was the normal condition for man. All that follows the fall must be called abnormal. It should be observed that verbal revelation was not necessitated by sin. It was part of the normal situation for a creature, made in the image of God, to have direct and personal communion with his God. This communion includes verbal communication.

One more feature of revelation is found in this chapter, namely, the use of the symbolic. This is seen in several parts of the account. First, there is the Garden itself. This is a place, particularly prepared by God--a place where God himself came and walked (3:8)--a place for the communion of God with man. Ezekiel describes Eden as the "garden of God" (28:13). In this we have the picture of the essence of the Biblical religion, namely, of fellowship between God and man. The God-centered character of this religion is thus revealed in Eden.

The second symbol to be noted is the tree of life. Rev. 2:7 reads, "He that hath an ear, let him hear what the Spirit saith unto the churches; To him that overcometh will I give to eat of the tree of life, which is in the midst of the paradise of God." Here the reference is to the tree of life in the Paradise of God. The last chapter of Scripture portrays the final glory about the throne of the Lamb, with the river of life flowing from the throne, and the tree of life beside it. Rev. 22:1-2 reads:

1. And he shewed me a pure river of water of life, clear as crystal, proceeding out of the throne of God and of the Lamb. 2. In the midst of the street of it, and on either side of the river, was there the tree of life, which bare twelve manner of fruits, and yielded her fruit every month: and the leaves of the tree were for the healing of the nations.

On the basis of these references to the tree of life, we may assume that this tree would have been the sacramental means of conveying eternal life to man, had he passed the test.

What has been said of the tree of life being a sacramental means of revelation and conveying of blessing, can also be said of the tree of the knowledge of good and evil. This tree was to be the means for man to come to the knowledge of good and evil, no matter how he used it. Without our going further into the content of the probation and fall at this time, let it suffice to say that we find God revealing his purpose and blessings in the Garden of Eden through the use of the symbolic and sacramental signs of the two trees.

As we summarize what we learn here of the nature of God's revelation, we shall call this revelation in the Garden of Eden as addressed to man preredemptive special revelation. It is special in that it is addressed to man as a special communication that could not be derived from nature. Its particular design was that of promoting the personal relation between God and man. In other words, this revelation was specifically religious in character.

In anticipation of what will be found in our further study, the modes of God's revelation already suggest what will be seen later. First, we have seen in creation the act of God as revelation. Second, we have seen in his speaking to man his word revelation. Third, it is at least suggested that God came and appeared in some theophany to man, as the Voice of the Lord God came in the Garden during the cool of the day. Thus we see the three direct modes of his revelation, namely, miracle, prophecy and theophany. These modes of revelation were not necessitated by sin, but were part of the normal condition of God's revealing himself to unfallen man. So also with the use of the sacramental. Here God graciously accommodates his revelation to the needs of his creatures, and this was part of the original, normal situation.

Before presenting our summation of findings in this section, we should notice the terminology that theologians have used to speak of revelation. We have used the terms "general" and "special" to describe the different types of revelation. The terms "natural" and "supernatural" are also used by some. Natural and supernatural describe the mode of revelation, whereas general and special are distinguished on the basis of the design. Natural revelation is that which comes through created reality, both within and without man. Supernatural revelation refers to that which is revealed outside of nature. Thus, verbal revelation is designated as supernatural.

General revelation is that which is addressed to all, and accessible to all men. Special revelation is that which is specific, and cannot be obtained through nature. Most Reformed theologians of the present period use the terms general and special instead of natural and supernatural, since the latter may suggest the idea of natural theology that Rome teaches. On the other hand, the terms natural and supernatural will be found in a number of older Reformed theologians.

Let us now summarize the findings concerning revelation in the Garden of Eden before the fall:
1. This is the period that should be described as normal for man.
2. God addressed man in a special verbal revelation, giving the creation mandate (Gen. 1:28-30) and the probation or Covenant of Works (Gen. 2:16-17).
3. God also used the symbolic or sacramental to reveal his truth to man during this period.
4. This revelation has been called preredemptive special revelation.
5. The four basic modes of special revelation are: act, word, theophany, and symbol.
6. This preredemptive special revelation was necessary to teach man his function and covenant relationship with God. These were matters that he could not have learned from nature.
7. This revelation was the authoritative Word of God.
8. The meaning of the instruction to Adam was explicitly clear. This is evidenced by Eve's repeating of the command when asked by the Serpent. In other words, the revelation was suited to the mind of man, and clear to him.
9. This special revelation was completely sufficient, therefore, to have brought men to a self-conscious choice of good, and thus to have confirmed him in his holiness.

C. Revelation after the Fall

The rest of the Biblical record treats of God's dealings with man since the fall of Adam. Of necessity, our study must be highly selective. We are not seeking to study the content of this revelation now, but to observe the modes of the revelation in order to be able to reach a conclusion about the Biblical idea of revelation.

1. From the Fall to the Flood

Immediately after the fall we find the account of God coming to the Garden and walking there. We noted in the section above that this points to the idea of theophany. That is, God came in some visible form and manifested himself to Adam and Eve. As already indicated, we believe that God must have appeared to Adam and Eve before the Fall in a theophany. That was to be expected, for Adam and Eve were then holy and good creatures, created for communion with their Maker. Now, however, the fall has taken place, and they are cut off from fellowship with God. They sensed this and attempted to hide from him. He came and sought them out.

A second observation about this revelation is that God addressed them verbally. It was the "Voice of the Lord God" who came. He "called" them, and he entered into discourse with them. Thus the verbal character of revelation is seen after the fall.

Despite the fact of the similarity between the pre and postfallen revelation, a marked change has taken place. Before the fall, man was made for communion with God, and could commune directly with him. After the fall, however, he is no longer fit for communion. He must be cast forth from the Garden of God (Gen. 3:23). The entrance of sin has destroyed the normal relations between God and man. The whole situation for man has now become abnormal. This is seen in the change that takes place in the realm of general revelation. Now the woman must suffer in that which constituted her as woman, namely, child-bearing. The man must labor by the sweat of his brow to feed himself. Labor is not a consequence of the fall. Adam had been given the task of tending the garden before the fall. It is the tediousness and difficulty of labor that is a consequence of the fall. The ground shall be cursed: "Cursed is the ground for thy sake; ... thorns also, and thistles shall it bring forth to thee..."[11]

By the fall man died spiritually. He had lost communion with God. His very being has become subject to dissolution in physical death. From all of this, we must conclude that the general revelation, which had served as a backdrop for the original special revelation in the garden, now shows the effects of sin, and again serves as a backdrop for the new special revelation which is to come.

Since the postfallen condition of man is one of alienation from God, he can no longer expect the communion of special revelation with God. But God graciously seeks him out and converses with him. Further, in Genesis 3:15 God sounds the note that he is going to act in behalf of man, and restore the fellowship with him. Even in pronouncing the words of judgment against the woman and the man, there is accompanying it the note of grace. For the woman will be able to bear children, despite her sorrow, and the man will be able to earn his living through his sweat. Thus, though there now has entered a note of judgment, the very fact of God's continued speaking with man is itself gracious. The promise of eventual victory over sin given in Genesis 3:15 is to be based on the work of the Seed of the woman--a work that shall involve his own suffering. In other words, this is the promise of the coming redemptive work of Christ. It is on the grounds of this anticipated redemption that God will continue to reveal himself to man. Hereafter all special revelation is redemptive in character, and is called redemptive special revelation.

One other act of revelation is given in the garden. It is the clothing of Adam and Eve by God with the skins of animals (Gen. 3:21). We are not told anything more of this transaction, but it may be assumed that this act is symbolic, just as the garden and the trees were symbolic of certain truths. Whether or not a blood sacrifice is involved, we are not told; but one thing seems clearly revealed, namely, that whereas Adam and Eve were not able to cover themselves,

---

11. Gen. 3:17-18.

God is able so to do. Thus, we have the symbolic revelation of God's truth continued after the fall.

The symbolic again appears in the placing of the Cherubim at the east of the Garden, and the sword to guard the tree of life. Elsewhere in Scripture the Cherubim are always associated with the throne of God, and with his direct presence (Exod. 25; 37; Ezek. 1:6; 41:18-19; Rev. 4:7-8). Because of their sin, Adam and Eve could no longer enter the garden nor directly approach the presence of God.

Let us again summarize our findings concerning the nature of revelation after the fall in the garden:
1. General revelation continues as a backdrop for the special. It now shows the effect of the fall of Adam, and the necessity of a Divine intervention, if there is to be any restoration of the original, normal order. As a backdrop, this sin-affected general revelation is necessary for us to see the special as special and redemptive in character.
2. As it was sufficient and clear before the fall to serve as a backdrop for the special, general revelation continues to be sufficient for this purpose, and continues to be clear in pointing to the need for a Saviour. It groaneth and travaileth until now.
3. God did not cut man off from continued special revelation.
4. The special revelation has assumed a new quality. It includes the element of grace or redemption, and therefore should be called redemptive special revelation.
5. The redemptive special revelation continues to show the modes of verbal and symbolic, as well as action in the clothing and then the expulsion of Adam and Eve. Theophany also continued in the coming of the Lord to speak to Adam and Eve after their sin.

2. Revelation Connected with the Flood

As we move from Eden to the flood we are treating another major period of God's revelation. It is noteworthy that the period between the fall and the flood is one of very little communication between God and man. It has been described as a "hands off" period, in which God allowed the human race to develop and display its wickedness.

The flood is an act of God's revelation, in which we again see both his judgment and mercy. After the fall, all of God's acts of revelation become double edged. Paul in II Cor. 2:16 speaks of this in connection with his own preaching: "to the one a savour from death unto death; to the other a savour from life unto life..." The flood was the judgment of God against the wicked world, and yet in this he was preserving his covenant people.

The central note in Genesis 6-9 is God's act. Many modern theologians speak of revelation as being only act or event. The emphasis is on the acts of God in opposition to the "intellectualistic conception" of verbal or propositional communication. The question that must be answered, is whether this is the Biblical representation of revelation or not.

The flood is typical of many other acts of revelation. It involves more than the act of God alone. For, before he sent the flood God announced his intent to Noah, and instructed him to build the ark. Then, following the flood, God again spoke to Noah, and interpreted it to him. The order found here is one that is frequently to be found in Scripture, namely, a word of announcement, the act itself, and then the word of interpretation. This is the case with the exodus, and also with the coming of the Messiah. God, in each of these cases, prophesied ahead what he would do, and then the fulfillment takes place, followed by God's interpretation of what he had done.

The flood itself and the actions of Noah are entirely incomprehensible without the word revelation that accompanied this mighty act of God. The flood is mute and dumb in and of itself. Thus to deny or ignore the word revelation here is to fail to see and understand the whole Biblical account of the flood.

3. Revelation During the Time of the Patriarchs

The period of the Patriarchs is one that contains a number of specific revelations of God to men. Vos observes that the form of the revelation is gaining in importance here. Before, it was said that God spoke, without any added details of how he spoke. Here there is an increased emphasis on the circumstances of the revelation. "On the whole we may say that revelation, while increasing in frequency, at the same time becomes more restricted and guarded in its mode of communication. The sacredness and privacy of the supernatural begin to make themselves felt."[12]

The first revelation to Abraham (Gen. 12:4) is given in rather indefinite language. God simply spoke to him. With his coming into the promised land there is a change. In Gen. 12:7 we read that Jehovah appeared[13] to Abram. Again in Gen. 15:13 a less definite statement is used, "the Lord said to Abram." In Gen. 15:17 we find a description of a visible manifestation of God, or theophany, in the form of a smoking furnace or flaming torch. Vos says, "The theophany here assumes the character of something fearful."[14] In Chapter 17:1 he lets himself be seen of Abram, and then in verse 22, "He left off talking with him, and God went up from Abraham," clearly referring to a theophany.

Only two appearances of God to Isaac are recorded, Gen. 26:2, 24. With Jacob there is a return of theophanies, but still with less frequency than Abraham (Gen. 28:13; 35:9). There are no theophanies recorded in connection with the life of Joseph.

The patriarchs frequently built altars in places where theophanies occurred. They thus indicated their consciousness of God's presence in that place, and often returned to them for worship (Gen. 13:4; 35:1-7). It should also be observed that these theophanies all occurred in the land of promise. This is not to say he was not Lord of all the earth, for he was, but it suggests that he was attaching his redemptive presence to that land.

---

12. Geerhardus Vos, *Biblical Theology, Old and New Testaments* (Grand Rapids: William B. Eerdmans Publishing Company, 1948), p. 82.
13. A passive form of *raah* (ראה) "to see," thus the Lord let himself be seen by Abram.
14. Vos, *op. cit.*, p. 82.

Another characteristic of revelation during this time is seen in the privacy sought. This is seen in the fact that night was often the time of the appearance of God to the patriarchs (Gen. 15:5; 12; 21:12, 14; 22:1-3; 26:24). It is also seen in the use of visions and dreams as the mode of revelation.

Visions are mentioned only twice in Genesis, namely, 15:1 (*machazeh*[15]) and 46:2 (*marah*[16]). The first of these words is used only three times more in the Old Testament, Num. 24:4, 16; Ezek. 13:7. It is derived from the root (*chazah*[17]) meaning "to see," and thus refers to that which comes to the seeing of the person. The second is derived from (*raah*[18]) meaning to see, look, behold. Again the import of the term is that which comes to the seeing of the person.[19] We shall have more to say about visions later, but suffice it to indicate that here was a revelation addressed to the seeing of the recipient. In the vision, not only the seeing, but also the hearing could be addressed. It may or may not involve the physical seeing, but could refer to an inner sight. Even if it were internal, there was a real, objective seeing. In Gen. 15 and 46 we find references to the night as the time of the visions. This again suggests the privacy of the revelation.

Along with the night occurrences of special revelation, comes the dream-form. "In dreaming the consciousness of the dreamer is more or less loosened from his personality. Hence dreams were preferably used as a vehicle of revelation where the spiritual state was ill-adapted for contact with God."[20] Heathen people received revelation through dreams (Gen. 20:3; 31:24; 40:5; 41:1). Dreams were used with God's people, especially when their spiritual condition was immature (Joseph) or at a low ebb (Jacob) (Gen. 28:12; 31:11; 37:5, 9).

In the case of both visions and dreams, the revelation is from God, and is thus no less objective than other forms of revelation. The same language is used of God's appearing and speaking as in the more direct revelation. "God has direct access to the dream-life and complete control over everything entering into it."[21]

The most striking form of special revelation found in the patriarchal period is that which came through "the Angel of Jehovah" (*malak yehowah*[22]). He appeared to Hagar (Gen. 16:6-13; 21:17-20); to Abraham (Gen. 18; 19; 22; 24:7, 40); and to Jacob (Gen. 28:13-7; 31:11-13; 32:24-30; Hos. 12:4; Gen. 48:15-16). There are two characteristic features noticeable in connection with this form of revelation. First, the Angel distinguishes himself from Jehovah by speaking of him in the third person. Second, he speaks as though he is identical with Jehovah. In other words, we have a personal manifestation of God, which is both identical with and distinct from God. As we see this phenomena from the perspective of the New Testament, we recognize immediately that the same holds true of the Incarnate Son of God. This is not the time for a full presentation of data regarding the identity of the Angel of the Lord. Suffice it to

---

15. מַחֲזֶה
16. מַרְאָה
17. חָזָה
18. רָאָה
19. For a distinction in these terms see W. J. Beecher, *The Prophets and the Promise* (Fort Worth: Seminary Book Store, 1947).
20. Vos, *op cit.* p. 85.
21. *Ibid.*, p. 85.
22. מַלְאַךְ יְהוָה

say for the present that there are good reasons to identify him as the Second Person of the Trinity.

In the revelation of the Angel of the Lord during the patriarchal period the primary object seems to have been the verbal communications that he conveys. In fact, we may say of him, as we did of the flood, that the revelational significance of the Angel's appearances would be unknown to us without his verbal messages.

The revelation of God in act is also to be found in the period of the patriarchs. The destruction of Sodom and Gomorrah reveals his continued displeasure with the sin of man. The birth of Isaac from the womb of one as good as dead (Heb. 11:12) is a display of his grace in keeping his promise of a seed to Abraham.

To summarize the period of the patriarchs:

1. We find in the period of the patriarchs the continuation of the three modes of special revelation that were noted in Eden, namely, theophany, prophecy and miracle.
2. Theophanies assume varying forms, both personal (the Angel of Jehovah) and impersonal (the Smoking Furnace-Flaming Torch).
3. As in the case of earlier periods, the verbal revelation is needed to explain the meaning of the theophanies and acts.
4. The theophany of the Angel of Jehovah prefigures the Incarnation of the Lord Jesus.
5. The use of visions, dreams and private conversations emphasizes the selectivity of God in his special revelation.
6. A study of the content of the special revelation given in this period shows that it is redemptive in character. This is especially seen in the covenant promises made to the patriarchs.

4. Revelation in the Period of Moses

a. The Place of Moses in Biblical Revelation

As we come to Moses, we come to one of the high periods of Old Testament revelation. Moses himself is a unique figure in redemptive history, and in the history of revelation.

(1) Retrospectively Considered

As one surveys the redemptive history of the Old Testament, the peculiar place of Moses is immediately seen. Looking back to the Abrahamic Covenant, it was the privilege of Moses to see the beginnings of its fulfillment. First, it was under Moses that the people of Israel became a distinct people, a nation. Second, Moses led them to the land of promise. Third, Moses brought a blessing to the other nations, both negatively in the condemnation of pagan error through the plagues, and positively in the Law which has become basic in much of western civilization.

(2) Prospectively Considered

Looking forward, there is no other figure until Christ who is so important in redemptive history. The prophets recognized this, in that they place him and his work above their own, though he was himself a prophet. According to Numbers 12:7 Moses was set over all God's house. As such he becomes a type of Christ. He was a type in the work of redemption. Thus the deliverance from Egypt becomes a foreshadow of Christ's redemption. See I Cor. 10:1-6; Heb.3:1-6. In this connection many of his acts were miraculous, as a preview of Christ's activity. Moses performed the three offices that Christ executes as our Redeemer, namely, prophet (Deut. 18:15); priest, before the Aaronic priesthood was instituted (Ex. 24:4-8), and in his intercession including his offer to vicariously suffer for his people (Ex. 32:30-33); and king in his leadership of the people, and giving of the Law. Even the attitude of the people toward him was like that of the Christian to Christ, namely, faith and trust (Ex. 14:31; 19:9). Paul speaks of Israel being baptized unto Moses (I Cor. 10:1-3).

b. The Form of Revelation in the Mosaic Period

Of particular interest to us is the form and mode that revelation took during this period. As one might expect, we find the same three primary modes of revelation continued in this period.

(1) Theophany

As in the period before, so also in this particular period we find the theophany continuing. The same sort of diversity is also found between impersonal and personal theophanic revelations.

(a) Impersonal Theophanies

When we speak of impersonal theophanies, it is not to suggest that the God revealed is any less personal. Rather, he was using an impersonal mode of revelation.

The first such to be noted is the appearance of the Angel of the Lord in the burning bush (Ex. 3:2, 4). "And the angel of Jehovah appeared unto him in a flame of fire out of the midst of a bush... And when Jehovah saw that he turned aside to see, God called unto him out of the midst of the bush." The word revelation that accompanies this appearance explains something of the meaning of the bush that burned without being consumed. For God declared his name to be "I AM that I AM" (vs. 14). This is essentially a declaration of unchangeable eternity.

A similar theophany appeared in the pillar of cloud and fire. "And Jehovah went before them by day in a pillar of cloud to lead them the way, and by night in a pillar of fire, to give them light: that they might go by day and by night: the pillar of cloud by day, and the pillar of fire by night, departed not from before the people" (Ex. 13:21-22). From this passage we learn that the pillar of cloud and fire is a theophany. For the Lord himself appeared in it. Exodus 14:10 identifies this as the Angel of the Lord, just as the burning bush was the Angel of the Lord.

Of particular significance is the permanence that this theophany assumes in Israel's life at this time. The original prefallen condition of man was one that involved direct personal communion between God and man. God came and walked and talked with man in Eden. This was the normal situation. With the fall this communion was cut off. In the period of the patriarchs there are the intermittent theophanies, but now that a whole people are being called of God, he graciously grants a public and more permanent theophany to them.[23]

The permanence of God's presence with his people is seen in the fact that God revealed himself over the Tabernacle (Ex. 33:9; 40:34f.; Lev. 9:23; Num. 9:15-23; 11:17, 25; 12:5; 17:7; 20:6; Deut. 31:15; Ps. 99:7; Is. 4:5), and in the Holy of Holies (Ex. 25:8, 22; 29:45-6; Lev. 16:2; 26:11-12; Num. 7:89). In addition to being a sign of his presence, the indefiniteness of the form both of fire and of cloud suggest the spiritual nature of God's being. "And Jehovah spake unto you out of the midst of the fire: ye heard the voice of words, but ye saw no form; only ye heard a voice."[24]

We are taught in Scripture that it was particularly the glory ($kabod$[25] or $doxa$[26]) that is revealed in the fire and cloud (Ex. 16:20; 24:17; Lev. 9:6,23,24); and thus this is called a consuming or devouring fire (Ex. 24:17; Lev. 9:23-4).

(b) Personal Theophanies

As we have seen, the Angel of Jehovah appeared by impersonal means of revelation. There are other references to him, which do not describe his appearance, and we may assume that he took personal forms in some of these. Exodus 23:20-21 reads: "Behold, I send an Angel before thee, to keep thee by the way, and to bring thee into the place which I have prepared; take ye heed before him, hearken unto his voice; provoke him not; for he will not pardon your transgressions: for my Name is in him." This sounds much like the description of the pillar of cloud and fire, but here we have a reference to the speaking of the Angel, which presumably implies a personal manifestation of him. The deity of the Angel is taught with respect to sinning against him. To do so was the same as sinning against God.

Again in Exodus 33:14 we find "my Presence shall go with thee, and I will give thee rest." This comes after the Lord has refused to send his Angel with the people, and Moses has pled their cause. Finally, God agrees to accompany them. We have no clear indication of just how this Presence was to be manifested.

These two cases introduce the reference to two special modes of God's revelation, namely, "the Name" and the "Presence" or "Face of God." The Name-bearing Angel of Exodus 23 is the Angel who is identified with God. The

---

23. See also: Exodus 14:19-24; 40:38; Num. 9:21; 14:14; Deut. 1:33; Neh. 9:12,19; Ps. 78:14.
24. Deut. 4:12.
25. כָּבוֹד
26. δόξα

Presence of God going forth must be equivalent to God's going. The Name is said to be in the place of the sanctuary. Jehovah causes his "Name" to dwell there (Deut. 12:5, 11, 21; 14:23, 24; 16:2, 6, 11; 26:2). God is said elsewhere to dwell in the sanctuary. Vos concludes that "the Name is not something in the apprehension of man; it is objective, equivalent to Jehovah himself. Still there always remains a difference in point of view between Jehovah as such and his 'Name.' The 'Name' is God in revelation. And the same distinction applies to the use of the Shekinah, the Angel and the Presence."[27]

Moses had the peculiar privilege of speaking directly with God. This is described in Exodus 33:9-11. "And it came to pass, when Moses entered into the Tent, the pillar of cloud descended and stood at the door of the Tent: and Jehovah spake with Moses... And Jehovah spake unto Moses face to face, as a man speaketh unto his friend..." It is in this same chapter that we find, "And he said, I will make all my goodness pass before thee, and will proclaim the name of Jehovah before thee; and I will be gracious to whom I will be gracious and will show mercy on whom I will show mercy. And he said, Thou canst not see my face; for man shall not see me and live... I will put thee in a cleft of the rock, and will cover thee with my hand until I have passed by: and I will take away my hand, and thou shalt see my back; but my face shall not be seen."[28] In the first instance there seems to have been some theophany medium used by God that Moses can approach and converse with directly. On the Mount, however, Moses was confronted with a more direct Presence of the Glory of God, and only permitted to view his back, but not the full Glory of his Face.

(2) Prophecy

Under the term prophecy we have included all verbal communication by God. The Mosaic period is marked by such verbal communication. God spoke to Moses from the Burning Bush (Ex. 3). He instructed him in what he was to do. He commanded the various plagues, and explained the hardening of Pharaoh's heart as part of his own purpose for the display of his power over him (Ex. 3:19-20). He gave in the greatest detail by verbal communication the instructions for the Passover (Ex. 11; 12), and so forth.

Not only did God give verbal revelation to Moses and Aaron, he also addressed the whole of Israel, so that all the people heard him speaking from Mt. Sinai. See Exodus 20:1-18. The people were so frightened by this that they asked that God mediate his word to them through Moses (Ex. 20:19; Deut. 5:22-27; Heb. 12:19-20). God graciously agreed to this, and his voice was not heard by the multitude again until the time of Christ (John 12:28-9). The need for messengers to mediate the verbal communications of God to man gave rise to the office of the prophet. Moses, as we have already noted performed this function, and in Deut. 18:15-22 he announced the establishment of the office, which would eventually culminate in The Prophet, the Lord Jesus (Act. 3:22).

In addition to oral, verbal revelation, this period records the fact that God himself wrote the Law on tables of stone (Ex. 31:18; 32:15-16; 34:1, 28). Here

---

27. Vos, *op. cit.*, p. 123.
28. Ex. 33:19-23.

is verbal revelation in the most permanent form, written by none other than God himself. Along with this we find the record that Moses wrote (Ex. 17:14; 24:4; 34:27; Num. 33:2; Deut. 31:9, 19).

The verbal revelation of God is intertwined with both theophany and miracle. Without this verbal revelation, we would not understand the appearances or the acts of God.

(3) Miracle

The Mosaic period is one of the most notable for revelation by miracle. Several terms are used to describe miracles: *Niphlaoth*[29] translated "wonders" in Ex. 3:20 and "marvels" in Ex. 34:10; *pele*[30] translated "wonders" in Ex. 15:11 and in Ex. 4:21 and in Ps. 105:5. The Greek translates these by *terateia*. The emphasis is on the unusual, special, or extraordinary. *Giburah*[31] translated "mighty acts" in Deut. 3:24 or "power" in Ps. 21:13 or "might" in Ps. 54:1 and Ps. 66:7, is translated by *dunamis*[32] in Greek. *Maaseh*[33] translated by "works" in Ps. 8:6; Ps. 103:22; Is. 5:19; and by "handiwork" in Ps. 19:1; and *maasyim* "doings" in Ps. 9:11; Ps. 77:11 is translated by *erga megaleia*[34] in Greek, because of the great, divine power which they reveal. They are called *'oth*[35] translated "token" in Ex. 3:12; 12:13 because they are a proof and sign of the presence of God. We have already observed that creation and providence are revelational. All of God's works are wonders. The works of nature are also often called wonders in Scripture (Ps. 77:13; 97:3; 98:1; 107:24; 139:14). This fact should not mislead us to think that the Scriptures make no distinction between nature and miracle. Of course, we cannot entertain the idea of a miracle being in contradiction to nature and thus impossible. The Scripture teaches that nothing is impossible with God (Gen. 18:14; Deut. 8:3f; Matt. 19:26). On the one hand, the Scripture recognizes the orderly laws of nature as established by God (Gen. 1:26, 28; 8:22; Ps. 104:5, 9; 119:90-1; 148:6; Jer. 5:24; 31:35f, 33:20, 25). On the other hand, a clear distinction is recognized, as God exercises his power over nature (Matt. 8:27; 9:5).

Miracles have as their foundation and backdrop the work of creation and providence, which is a continuing wonder of God (Ps. 33:6, 9); John 5:17). All that happens has its ultimate foundation in the will and power of God. God has revealed his displeasure with sin and the wicked by miracles of judgment as is seen in the plagues against Egypt (Ex. 5ff), the death of Nadab and Abihu (Lev. 10:1-2), the death of Korah (Num. 16:30-33), etc. In the last case the miracle is called "make a new thing", literally create a creation *beriyah yibra*[36] On the other hand, there are the miracles of grace. The Passover was both judicial and redemptive in character. So also was the crossing of the Red Sea. For the people of God, not only were there the actual acts of redemption and sustenance by

---

29. נִפְלָאוֹת
30. פֶּלֶא
31. גְּבוּרָה
32. δύναμις
33. מַעֲשֶׂה
34. ἔργα μεγαλεῖα
35. אוֹת
36. בְּרִיאָה יִבְרָא

God, there were also those which were designed to encourage their faith. In Exodus 4:1-9, Moses was given signs to prove that he had been commissioned by Jehovah, "... that they may believe that Jehovah, the God of their fathers, the God of Abraham, the God of Isaac, and the God of Jacob, hath appeared unto thee" (vs. 5). Deuteronomy ends with a statement about Moses as a prophet and miracle worker: "And there hath not arisen a prophet since in Israel like unto Moses, whom Jehovah knew face to face, in all the signs and the wonders, which Jehovah sent him to do in the land of Egypt to Pharaoh, and to all his servants, and to all his land, and in all that mighty hand, and in all the great terror, which Moses wrought in the sight of all Israel."[37]

The revelation by miracle appears to be for several purposes. First of all, it was given as a sign to attest the authority of God's messenger. Second, it may reveal the judgment of God against sin, by direct action of God to punish it. Third, there may be the direct action of God, intervening in the ordinary routine of nature and history in behalf of his own. This last design of the revelation is specifically redemptive in character. Events of the Mosaic history foreshadow the redemptive work of Christ. This was seen, in particular, with the exodus itself. The people of Israel were redeemed from bondage. This redemption was accomplished only through the sacrifice of the Passover lambs, and the mighty arm of God bringing them through the Red Sea. God then provided for his people in the wilderness with the water from the rock, which Paul identifies as the Christ (I Cor. 10:1-3), and the feeding with manna, which Christ indicates foreshadows himself as the Bread of Life (John 6:31-35). In other words, the acts of God during the Mosaic period were pictures of the acts of God in Christ Jesus as our Savior. It should again be observed that the acts were accompanied with the word interpretation.

(4) Symbolic or Sacramental Revelation

Just as the Mosaic period was marked with many theophanies, prophecies and miracles, so also it was marked with much in the realm of the sacramental or symbolic revelation. We have already observed something of this in connection with the forms of the theophanic revelation, namely, the cloud and fire, which represent certain aspects of God's nature.

The Mosaic period is of special significance in that it is the period of institution of the Aaronic priesthood, the sacrificial system, and the ritualistic form of worship. This is not the time for a study of the details of this system, but simply to observe that God continues to use the symbolic and sacramental in revealing his truth to man. The Tabernacle with all its furniture, together with the Priesthood and the ritual of worship all have symbolic meaning, pointing to the reality of the Gospel in Christ.

c. Summary of the Mosaic period

To summarize our findings concerning the Mosaic period, we find:

---

37. Deut. 34:10-12.

(1) That Moses himself bears a unique place in the economy of revelation, both with respect to the Abrahamic Covenant, and to the Christ.
(2) There is a continuation of the four modes of revelation in this period, with new matter in each area that become normative for the rest of the Old Testament.
(3) The verbal form of revelation includes the written as well as the spoken word.
(4) The organic character of the Special Revelation is seen in that all differing modes prefigure the coming of the Messiah. They are intertwined with one another in the redemptive history.

5. Revelation from Moses to the End of the Old Testament

With the close of the Mosaic period Israel became a distinct people, with their own land. There is a transitional period before they take on a unified national character under a king. With the establishment of the monarchy comes the institution of the royal office. God, in his all wise providence, just prior to the establishment of the monarchy raised up one man to serve in the threefold capacity of prophet, priest and judge, namely, Samuel.

During the transitional period of Joshua and the Judges the three primary forms of revelation continued, though in a much less prominent degree than before. Joshua met the Angel of the Lord at Jericho (Joshua 5:13ff). He experienced the miraculous aid of the Lord at Jericho (Joshua 6). The Lord spoke with him in verbal communication (Joshua 7:10f). So also with the Judges. All three were again experienced in the days of Samuel, though the sparsity of prophecy is noted at the beginning of his career (I Sam. 3:1).

With the establishment of the three offices of prophet, priest and king, the chief mode of revelation was the prophecy. There were some miracles, with the chief period being that of Elijah and Elisha. Theophanies were far less frequent. In part, this can be accounted for by the permanent symbolic forms of the Tabernacle and later the Temple, where the Lord dwelt. His presence was associated with the Holy of Holies and the Ark of the Covenant. The cloud of glory filled the Temple at its dedication (I Kings 8:9-11). With the destruction of the Temple, personal theophanies or angelophanies again appeared (Dan. 3:25; 5:5; 8:13,15; 9:21; 10:5f). It shall not be our purpose to examine these forms more in detail, but to spend some time with the most prominent mode of revelation during this period, namely, that of prophecy.

In Deuteronomy 18:15ff Moses had prophesied the office of the prophets that would be raised up. He gave there a description of the essence of the prophetic office. "I will raise them up a prophet from among their brethren, like unto thee; and I will put my words in his mouth, and he shall speak unto them all that I shall command him."[38] This agrees with the usage of the word prophet *nabi*[39]. In Exodus 7:1 Aaron was described as the prophet of Moses, "See I have made thee as God to Pharaoh; and Aaron thy brother shall be thy prophet

---

38. Deut. 18:18.
39. נביא

(*nabi*)." This relationship is more fully elaborated on in Exodus 4:15-16, "And thou shalt speak unto him, and put the words in his mouth; and I will be with thy mouth, and with his mouth, and will teach you what ye shall do. And he shall be thy spokesman unto the people; and it shall come to pass, that he shall be to thee a mouth, and thou shalt be to him as God." In other words, Aaron was described as the prophet of Moses, or his spokesman. Moses was to give him the words that he would say. Moses stood in the place of God to Aaron, that is, he had absolute authority as to what Aaron should say. So it is that the prophet is the spokesman for God. This does not always involve telling the future. It does involve being an authoritative spokesman with an authoritative message from the living God.

It should be observed that this is quite a foreign concept to the modern critical scholars, who assume the prophets to have been the "angry young men" of their time. They assume that they speak out of their historical situation and only to their historical situation. It is perfectly true that much of the prophetic message was directed to the immediate historical context. But, it is not the word of an "angry young man" disturbed by social injustices that is spoken. Rather, it is the word of the Living God who is condemning formalism and injustices. The prophetic office, as we have indicated above, really came into being with the establishment of the nation under the human monarchy. In other words, there was an integral relation between the nation and the prophetic office. The close relation between the prophets and the kings is seen throughout the rest of Old Testament history. Nathan, Elijah, Isaiah, Jeremiah were among the pre-exilic prophets who stood in close connection with the kings of their respective periods. Many of their messages were addressed to these kings. Because of the sinfulness of the kings, the prophetic message was often one of reprimand. This fact has given rise to the critical suggestion that they represent two differing parties in Israel, and two different conflicting institutions. Such a view really misunderstands the nature of the two offices. Insofar as both kings and prophets were true to God's Word, they were in perfect harmony. Even when the prophets had to condemn the kings or the people, it was as one who was truly loyal to God and to the proper concept of the monarchy and kingdom. The prophets were aware that they were to keep both the king and the people reminded that the Kingdom and the Throne were of the Lord, not of man.

The etymology of the word prophet (*nabi*) is uncertain. Various suggestions have been given, but it is not perfectly clear what the derivation of the word is. Thus it is best to rely on the usage of it in the Old Testament for our idea of it. As already noted, Ex. 4:16 and 7:1 give us a picture of its usage. This is confirmed by Jeremiah 1:5,9, "Before I formed thee in the belly I knew thee, and before thou camest forth out of the womb I sanctified thee; I have appointed thee a prophet unto the nations... Then Jehovah put forth his hand, and touched my mouth; and Jehovah said unto me, Behold, I have put my words in thy mouth." Here we see that the office of the prophet involved exactly the same function that Aaron was to perform for Moses. Taking both of these passages (Exodus and Jeremiah) we cannot help but be impressed with the fact that the Biblical idea of a prophet is that he is an official spokesman for one who is over him. What the prophet says are not his words, but those of one who has placed them in his mouth.

The prophet's business lies in the sphere of speaking. And this speaking is not ordinary speaking... It is a unique representation conveying divine authority and, in a measure, divine omnipotence, and these are based on divine communication. Jehovah touches the mouth and puts the words there, and they acquire the effect of divine words.[40]

As Vos goes on to speak of the implications of such an office, he says, "It marks the religion of the O. T. as a religion of conscious intercourse between Jehovah and Israel, a religion of revelation, of authority, a religion in which God dominates, and in which man is put into the listening, submissive attitude."[41]

Two other words *roeh*[42] and *chozeh*[43] are translated by the English term "seer". They suggest one who has special insight. Whether it is an actual vision, or a supernatural insight cannot be determined from the words by themselves. The original meanings, no doubt, refer to physical sight. Later this was broadened to include more than just the visual sight. The term *nabi* describes the prophet in terms of speaking, whereas *roeh* or *chozeh* describe him in terms of his reception of the message.

As Vos suggests, the other terms used of prophets, are really self-explanatory, and need no detailed discussion. They are: *tsaphah*[44] "outlooker;" *natsar*[45] "watchman;" *malak yehowah*[46] "messenger of Jehovah;" *raah*[47] "shepherd;" *ish haruach*[48] "man of the Spirit;" *ish elohim*[49] "man of God."

Two other points ought to be observed with regard to the passage in Deut. 18:15ff. First, prophets are to be called from God's people. On occasion God may have used a non-Israelite to deliver a prophecy, such as Balaam and the Witch of Endor, but these did not bear the office of prophet. Second, they are to be like unto Moses. That is, they are to continue that same revelation that was begun and amplified so much in Moses. Their teaching must be like his, and built on his. "The prophets were not antagonistic to the law, but contemplated by the law itself, not to reform it, but to keep it before the minds of the people."[50]

Before leaving this passage in Deut. 18, we should take note of those forms of seeking God's will that are condemned. In other words, in order to discover the Biblical idea of revelation, it is necessary to examine the Biblical teaching as to what is not revelation. Deut. 18:10-14 describes various means by which the pagans sought messages from their deities. Let us simply list these, with just a brief comment about each:

(1) Passing children through fire

It is believed by many that this refers to human sacrifice of children. The heathen practiced this (II Ki. 3:27; 17:31). It was occasionally practiced by Israelites also (II Ki. 16:3; 17:17; 21:6; 23:10; II Chron. 28:3; 33:6). Not only was it forbidden by Moses, it was condemned by the prophets (Mi. 6:7). The

---

40. Vos, *op. cit.*, p. 211.
41. *Ibid.*, pp. 211-212.
42. רֹאֶה
43. חֹזֶה
44. צָפָה
45. נָצַר
46. מַלְאַךְ יְהוָה
47. רֹעֶה
48. אִישׁ הָרוּחַ
49. אִישׁ אֱלֹהִים
50. William Henry Green, *Prophets and Prophecy* (Princeton: The Princeton Press, 1888), p.10.

idea of human sacrifice, *per se,* is not to be condemned, for this would exclude the sacrifice of Christ. But that was a God-initiated and a God-ordained act. For man to assume the prerogative of acting as God over other humans, and sacrificing them is the height of presumption and blasphemy. Further, to take life without divine authorization is murder. It is again an attack on the image of God in man, and thus an attack against God (Gen. 9:6). It is, therefore, the worst of these abominations of the heathen, and placed at the head of the list of sins in this area.

(2) The three terms: one that uses divination, one that practiceth augury, and an enchanter

All three terms describe those who attempt to discern events that are distant in time or space, which thus cannot be seen through ordinary means. Again, we face here the attempt of man, by means of his own devising, to see beyond the God-established limits of his knowledge. It is an attempt at human autonomy, and is presumptuous. Ezekiel calls it "lying divination" (13:6-7), which teaches its true character.

(3) Reference to sorcerers and charmers

This introduces the area of magic. Magic is opposed to true religion. True religion has to do with man's walk with the Living God. Magic is man's attempt to deal with other supernatural powers, or the attempt to force issues through using psychic forces, regardless of whether it is God-honoring or not.

(4) Consulters with familiar spirits, wizards and necromancers

All of these terms allude to what today is called spiritism. Any attempt to gain knowledge in this way is also condemned.

God's people are to rest upon God alone for revelation. He promised them his word through the prophets as the proper means of discovering his will. Any other approach is an abomination in his sight, for it is a rejection of his own revelation, and it is an assertion of the sufficiency of man without God.

Of particular interest in studying the Biblical idea of revelation are the modes of revelation to the prophets. We shall not deal with critical views of this matter. Excellent studies of these are found in Vos, *Biblical Theology,* and Young, *My Servants the Prophets.* Our interest is in the Biblical data. Vos suggests that the modes of revelation to the prophets may be divided as follows: the speaking of the Lord followed by the hearing; and the showing by the Lord followed by the seeing.

The most frequent expressions describing the speaking of the Lord are *'amar yehowah*[51], *dabar yehowah*[52], and *neum yehowah*[53]. The first two are in the perfect tense, and may be translated, "Jehovah has spoken." The third is a passive participle, meaning "that which has been spoken." This speaking of the Lord is objective verbal revelation. This is clear when one remembers that the Lord is contrasted with the idols which are dumb and cannot speak. This contrast would be meaningless, if God had not actually spoken (Is. 41:22-26; 43:9; Jer. 10:5; Hab. 2:18). Jehovah is said to have a mouth (Is. 58:14), and thus understood as literally speaking. Sometimes the direct reference is made of

---

51. אָמַר יְהוָה
52. דִּבֶּר יְהוָה
53. נְאֻם יְהוָה

Jehovah speaking to the particular prophet. He spake to me (Is. 8:1; 18:4). Further, the utterances of Jehovah are often located as to a definite place and time (Is. 5:9; 16:13-44; 22:14; Jer. 1:13; Ezek. 3:12). Also, it will be remembered that Samuel heard the voice so clearly that he mistook it for that of Eli (I Sam. 3:8-9).

As to whether the voice was something external or not, is not easily determined. Even if it was internal, this does not take away its objective character. Just as a vision may be seen by the inner eye, and not be the product of the seer, but brought to him by the Lord, so also with hearing. Vos says of the external voice, "Every external approach of God to his people is more or less of the nature of a sacrament."[54] The use of the external word would seem to be more needed for those in a lower spiritual state. They needed something external which they could grasp. The more spiritual prophets, on the other hand, may well have been able to receive the word internally, without the external word.

Parallel to the audible revelation is the visual. These are called visions. Visions are found in the following of the writing prophets: Isa. 6; Jer. 1:11-12; 24:1; Ezek. 1-3; 8-11; 37:1-10, 40-48; Dan. 2:19; 7; 8; 10; 11; 12; Amos 7:1-9; 8:1-3; 9:1; Zech. 1:8; 6:1-8. The following prophets do not record visions: Hosea, Joel, Obadiah, Jonah, Micah, Nahum, Habakkuk, Zephaniah, Haggai, and Malachi.

Visions apparently could involve the physical seeing, such as the case of the servant of Elisha in II Kings 6:17, whose eyes were opened to see the heavenly hosts protecting them. Elisha himself seems not to have needed this. He either saw internally, or perhaps had already had his eyes opened. A third possibility exists, namely, that of a rapturing of the person to heaven to see glories there in person. This may have been the case of Isaiah 6. Paul speaks of such an experience in II Cor. 12:1-4.

The term "vision" eventually lost its technical meaning, and came to refer to revelation, without regard to its particular mode of transmission. The book of Isaiah bears the title, "The vision of Isaiah..."

The question of whether the prophets were ecstatics is discussed very helpfully by Vos. He points out that the Greek usage of the term involved insanity or mania. Though its usage in the Greek Old Testament is toned down to astonishment or dread, it still carries the idea of being "beside oneself." Philo used it to mean the literal absence of reason or mind ($nous$[55]) from the body. "When the divine Spirit arrives in the prophet, he observes, the $nous$ takes its departure, because it would not be fitting for the immortal to dwell with the mortal."[56] In other words, the prophet was without his mind during the period of ecstasy. Vos rejects this concept as being applicable to the Biblical prophets.

> It is plain on the surface of the Biblical data that ecstasy in the Philonic or Montanist sense had no place in prophetism. The Biblical prophets coming out of the visionary state have a distinct remembrance of the things seen and heard. Biblical prophecy is not a process in which God dislodges the mind of man. Its true conception is that it lifts the human

---

54. Vos, *op. cit.*, p. 238.
55. νοῦς
56. Vos, *op. cit.*, p. 244.

mind to the highest place of intercourse with God. And it is of the very essence of Biblical religion that its exercise lies in the sphere of consciousness.[57]

Let us summarize our findings concerning the post-Mosaic period of the Old Testament:
(1) The four modes of special revelation continue through this period, with a greater emphasis on prophecy.
(2) The prophetic institution was established simultaneously with the monarchy.
(3) The prophet was essentially the spokesman of God. God put his words into his mouth, and the prophet spoke with the authority of God.
(4) The prophets were called from God's chosen people.
(5) They were to continue the revelation already begun through Moses. They were to be like unto him.
(6) Regardless of the mode of revelation, the prophets received an objective revelation from the Lord.
(7) In the prophets, there is an emphasis on the verbal form of revelation. Not only did they receive verbal revelation, but they passed it on verbally, both in preaching and in writing.

6. Revelation in the Inter-testament Period

A study of the Scripture reveals the closing of the Old Testament took place around 400 B. C. Then there is a period of silence. There are no prophets, no new special revelations during this time. Why did this happen?

To answer this, one must be aware of the close relation between redemptive history and the history of revelation. The history of revelation is an aspect of the redemptive history. From this, one can derive the principle that where there is much redemptive activity, there is much accompanying redemptive revelation. So it is, that with the redeeming of Israel from Egypt, there is a rich period of revelation. Also, with the establishment of the monarchy came the gift of the institution of the prophets. Even in the times of judgment, which were a part of God's redemptive activity, there was an emphasis on the revelation. On the other hand, with the passing of the monarchy, and the inaction of God in redemptive history, there comes a silence in revelation. This is not to suggest that God abandoned his people. Instead it was a period of waiting and general providence, raising up the Graeco-Roman world to serve as the vehicle for the spread of the Gospel--the fullness of time.

7. Revelation in the Earthly Ministry of Christ

One of the things that may be observed regarding the Old Testament is the incompleteness of all the modes of revelation. The theophanies of the Old Testament were only temporal. Even the glory cloud in the Temple did not show itself continually, and of course, with the Babylonian captivity the Ark of the

---

57. *Ibid.*, pp. 244-245.

Covenant disappeared. All of this leaves one feeling that this is an incomplete revelation of God. There must be something more to come. So also with prophecy. With the decline of the Kingdom, the prophets increasingly alluded to the coming of the Messiah and the Messianic age. With the close of the Old Testament, one is left expecting that someday the sure promises of God in prophecy will yet come to pass. The miracles of the Old Testament also remain incomplete. The deliverance of Israel from Egypt is called a redemption, and yet it is only a pointer to the great redemptive act of God in Christ. Other miracles, which overcome for the time the forces and laws of nature, have fallen. The whole of creation then awaits the day of redemption. Of course, the symbolic and sacramental of the Old Testament all foreshadow the reality. As the book of Hebrews points out, these ordinances display their weakness in that they needed constant repetition. They only served to cleanse the flesh, but not the conscience (Heb. 9:13-14).

We see, therefore, that the whole revelation of the Old Testament remains incomplete. All the strands of revelation, which together constitute a single organic whole, are in themselves incomplete. They thus point forward to a completion that is yet to come (Heb. 11:39-40). This completion or fulfillment is to be found in the Lord Jesus Christ. He spoke of himself in connection with the Old Testament as not destroying it, but coming to fulfill (a strong word, implying complete filling) (Matt. 5:17). As we survey the revelation found in the New Testament, we again must be quite selective. We shall first examine some introductory passages concerning the revelation found in Christ, and then consider the four modes of revelation as related to him.

a. Introductory Passages

(1) Christ the Logos - John 1:1-14

The prologue of John describes Christ with a very suggestive term. John used the term "*Logos*"[58] as a name for Christ. That this is the proper identification of the *Logos* is clear from verse 14 where the Logos became flesh, full of grace and truth, and from verse 17 where grace and truth are identified with Christ. According to verse 1, the *Logos* has always existed. He is distinguished from God, and then identified with him. The next verses speak of him as being involved with the creative activity of God. The term *Logos* thus refers to Christ in both his ontological as well as his functional activity. He was the Logos as the Second Person of the Trinity. He was always the *Logos*. He did not just become the *Logos* in functioning as the revealer of God. It is because he was the *Logos* that he is the appropriate Person of the Trinity to serve the *Logos* function.

This dual usage of the term *Logos* is borne out by the progression from the *Logos* in eternity to the Life, and then from Life to Light. The term Light suggests revelation. This is the function of the *Logos*, but the idea of the *Logos* is much broader than just revelation. As the *Logos* he was God. As the *Logos* he was creator. As *Logos* he was Life. Only then does the revealing function of the

---

58. λόγος

Logos appear as the Light. From this analysis it becomes clear that we must reject any idea that he became *Logos* only in the revelation.

On the basis of this passage, it is quite proper to speak of Christ as the Personal Word of God, or the Word of God Incarnate. To say this, however, we should not in any way erase the distinction that the Bible teaches between the Personal Word and the Written Word. Also, we should guard against speaking of the Personal Word as existing only as Christ Incarnate. The Personal Word is none other than the Second Person of the Trinity, eternally the Word of God.

Having made the distinction between the personal and the written Word, it is of interest to note that there are two Greek terms translated "word," *logos* and *rhema*[59]. *Logos* is clearly used of the Person. Because there may be some ambiguity as to its usage, whether personal or written, there are those who argue that any reference to verbal words is only an accommodation. In those places where it applies to the written word, it does not really mean that, but must be understood indirectly. The written words are a witness to the Personal Word. On the other hand, *rhema* has no such personal reference. It refers specifically to that which is verbal, written or spoken. For example, see: Matt. 4:4; Luke 3:2; I Peter 1:25. Thus the Scripture clearly teaches that we should distinguish between the Personal and the written Word.

(2) Christ the Express Image of God - Heb. 1:1-3

In this passage we have a summary of the fact that God has revealed himself in various ways in the past. Particular reference is made to the verbal revelation of his speaking by the prophets. Now he has spoken by his Son. Here we have reference to the verbal revelation of the Son to us, as well as the Personal revelation found in him as the "express image of his (the Father's) person."

From both John 1 and Hebrews 1 we find a new element introduced in the Biblical concept of revelation. It is the fact that the revelation is ultimately Personal. It is the Personal Word who has given us the verbal revelation. The Person who is in view is One who is both divine and human. In both of these passages we see references to both of these aspects of his being. This same emphasis on Christ as the revealer, who is both divine and human is found in the following passages: I John 1:1-2; Luke 2:27ff; John 14:9; I Tim. 3:16; and John 17:6.

b. Christ and the Four Modes of Revelation

(1) Theophany

In Eden God had come and walked with man. With the fall, man hid himself from God, but God came and sought him out. Following his expulsion from the Garden man could no longer expect that God would walk with him. Yet God, by his grace did come from time to time to appear unto man in various forms. Now in the fullness of time the Second Person of the Godhead was made flesh, and we behold the ultimate Theophany in Immanuel. Christ came into the

---

59. ῥῆμα

world to be one with us, to walk with us, to go before us, and to restore that fellowship lost by Adam in Eden. This he accomplished in the Incarnation. He has assumed our nature, and having been identified with us, though without sin, yet he suffered in our behalf in order that he might conquer sin, death, hell and Satan for us. Now he has arisen from the dead, and ascended to the right hand of God in our flesh. He is our sure hope that we too can be made fit to stand before that Throne in eternal fellowship with him. Immanuel--God with us--expresses the essence of the Biblical religion. God had promised to Abraham that he would be God to Abraham and to his seed (Gen. 17:7). John in the book of Revelation can rise no higher than to say of the final glorified state that God himself shall be with them, and be their God (Rev. 21:3). It is in Christ Jesus that God has given the ultimate and final Theophany of himself, the crown of theophanic revelation.

(2) Prophecy

Christ is the climax of prophetic revelation just as he was of theophanic revelation. There are two ways in which he is related to prophecy. First, he is the Prophet. The fact is that all the prophecy that had come in the Old Testament had been given by him. Peter speaks of the prophets of old searching their own writings which the Spirit of Christ had given them (I Pet. 1:10-11). Also it should be remembered that when Moses promised the prophetic office in Deut. 18, he spoke of a single prophet (vs. 18). Peter in Acts 3:22 cites this passage, and then goes on to say that God has given that Prophet in his Servant (vs. 26). As the Prophet, Christ gave verbal revelation in all that he spoke. The Gospels record the astonishment of the people at his teaching, "for he taught them as one having authority, and not as their scribes" (Mt. 7:28). Peter testified, "Lord to whom shall we go? thou hast the words of eternal life" (John 6:68).

Not only was Christ the Prophet, he was also the Word. By this is meant that he was the very revelation of God. He is the personal Word of God to us. He is also called the Truth (John 14:6). Man in his fall had chosen falsehood over against the truth. If there is to be any restoration of man to his original state, the truth must be reintroduced into the world. God began to do this immediately in Eden as he gave the first promise of victory over sin by the Seed of the Woman. From Eden onward there is the continuous line of prophecy which points to the ultimate revelation of the Truth, namely, Christ Jesus, the Truth. As the Truth he received no revelation from above or beyond himself. He himself is the source of prophecy. The Holy Spirit did not come over him or fall on him, but he dwelt in him without measure (John 3:34). By that Spirit was he baptized, and by that Spirit he spoke, acted, lived and died (Matt. 3:16; 12:28; Lk. 1:17; 2:27; 4:1,14,18; Rom. 1:4; Heb. 9:14). And he gave that Spirit to his disciples, as the Spirit of revelation and illumination (Mark 13:11; Lk. 12:12; Jn. 14:17; 15:26; 16:13; 20:22; Acts 2:4; 6:10; 8:29; 10:19; 11:12; 13:2; 18:5; 21:4; I Cor. 2:12ff; 12:7-11).[60]

---

60. Bavinck, *Gereformeerde Dogmatiek, op.cit.*, Vol. I, p. 306.

(3) Miracle

Not only did God come and walk with man again in Eden and thereafter in theophany, he also talked with him in prophecy, but this was not sufficient for his salvation. Man needed God to act in his behalf. He needed someone to overturn that ungodly alliance which he had fallen into with Satan by sinning against God. Man was totally helpless to do this for himself. It would require the supernatural action of God in his behalf. In other words, he needed God's miracle. We have seen that God graciously introduced miracles early in his redemptive history. A stream of miracles continues throughout the Old Testament, with special groups of them associated with the redemption from Egypt and the ministries of Elijah and Elisha.

Miracle, as with theophany and prophecy, culminated in the person of Christ. His coming into the world was by the miracle of the virgin birth. His life was marked by a number of miracles, and, of course, they all culminate in his resurrection from the dead. His miracles were signs of the divine presence and proof of the Messianic time (Matt. 11:3-5; 12:28; Lk. 13:16) and a part of the Messianic work. Miracle working was not a peripheral part of his work. It was the central aspect of his work. His incarnation, atonement, resurrection and ascension are the great saving acts of God. These are the principal acts of regaining the paradise that Adam had lost. These salvation acts were not just the means of revealing something, they were the revelation of God himself. Miracle here becomes history, and history itself is a miracle.[61]

The organic character of revelation is seen in the way in which the three primary modes of revelation all find their ultimate expression in the person of Jesus Christ. Christ as the Theophany came by miracle--came to reveal the Truth, to be the Prophet, and to perform the miracles needed for our salvation. He is thus the *Logos* in the fullest sense of that term.

(4) Sacramental

Since the sacramental mode of revelation denotes that which stands for the reality, this aspect of revelation does not appear in the person of Christ, who is the reality toward which all the former revelation has pointed.

It is significant, however, to see that Jesus himself institutes further sacramental revelation of the Gospel for future generations. Having come to fulfill all that had been typified by the former revelation, all the earlier symbolic and sacramental forms pass from use. The new sacraments of Jesus reflect the new situation, namely, that the work of redemption has been accomplished by him. Whereas both of the former sacraments, circumcision and the passover, together with the whole of the sacrificial system of the Old Testament, involved blood shed, the new sacraments of baptism and the Lord's supper point to the finality of Christ's sacrifice by not involving any blood shed. These new signs serve a two-fold purpose, namely, of looking back to the death of Christ, and forward to his return. They represent the benefits of the Gospel to us, and so continue to accompany the word in witnessing to the saving work of Christ.

---

61. *Ibid.*, p. 310.

8. Revelation during the Apostolic Age

As redemptive history moves past the work of Christ and begins to take on the character of church history, a new identification for the carrying on of revelation is found, namely, the Apostolate. The chief function of the Apostles was to bear witness to Christ (Acts 1:8; and Luke 24:48). This witness was given the full authority of Christ by his having commissioned them, and by his giving them the Holy Spirit to equip them for this office (Mk. 3:14ff; Mt. 10:18-20; Mk. 13:11; Lk. 21:13ff; Jn. 14:26; 15:26-27; 16:13).

The apostles as the authoritative witnesses to Christ, not only preached the Word, but also some of them wrote the record of Christ's life and work, and interpreted these to the Church. The verbal element of revelation was especially prominent in this period. Miracles continue as authenticating signs of the apostolic authority. Though they were markedly fewer, there were still a few cases of theophany during this period also. Christ appeared to Stephen at his death, and to Saul on the road to Damascus. Paul was transported to the third heaven (II Cor. 12:1-4). John, on the isle of Patmos, was granted the visions of heaven and the future.

The apostolic office was unique in being appointed directly by the risen Christ. It carried with it a unique authority, which could not be repeated again in the history of the Church. It was during the apostolic period that the New Testament was written and completed either by or under the authority of the apostles.

Of particular interest is the question of whether all special revelation ended with the end of the apostolic period. We have already seen that the various modes of special revelation constituted an organic unity, and that this revelation all pointed to the Lord Jesus Christ as The Theophany, The Prophet, and The Miracle. This being the case, one certainly expects that with the completion of his life and work on earth, and of the authoritative interpretation of this made during the apostolic era, all special revelation would cease. Warfield says:
> There is, of course, a deeper principle recognizable here, of which the actual attachment of the charismata of the Apostolic Church to the mission of the Apostles is but an illustration. This deeper principle may be reached by us through the perception, more broadly, of the inseparable connection of miracles with revelation, as its mark and credential; or, more narrowly, of the summing up of all revelation, finally, in Jesus Christ.[62]

He goes on to say:
> (God) has chosen rather to deal with the race in its entirety, and to give to this race his complete revelation of himself in an organic whole. And when this historic process of organic revelation had reached its completeness, and when the whole knowledge of God designed for the saving health of the world had been incorporated into the living body of

---

62. Benjamin B. Warfield, *Miracles: Yesterday and Today: Real and Counterfeit* (Grand Rapids: William B. Eerdmans, 1953), p. 25.

the world's thought--there remained, of course, no further revelation to be made, and there has been accordingly no further revelation made.[63]

Warfield quotes Herman Bavinck to the same effect:
According to the Scriptures special revelation has been delivered in the form of a historical process, which reaches its end-point in the person and work of Christ. When Christ had appeared and returned again to heaven, special revelation did not, indeed, come at once to an end. There was yet to follow the outpouring of the Holy Ghost, and the extraordinary working of the powers and gifts through and under the guidance of the Apostolate. The Scriptures undoubtedly reckon all this to the sphere of special revelation, and the continuance of this revelation was necessary to give abiding existence in the world to the special revelation which reached its climax in Christ--abiding existence both in the word of Scripture and in the life of the Church. Truth and life, prophecy and miracle, word and deed, inspiration and regeneration go hand in hand in the completion of special revelation. But when the revelation of God in Christ had taken place, and had become in Scripture and church a constituent part of the cosmos, then another era began. As before everything was a preparation for Christ, so afterward everything is to be a consequence of Christ. Then Christ was being framed into the Head of his people, now his people are being framed into the Body of Christ. Then the Scriptures were being produced, now they are being applied. New constituent elements of this special revelation can no longer be added; for Christ has come, his work has been done, and his word is complete.[64]

Scripture confirms this view of the matter in Heb. 1:1-3. Here two periods of revelation are mentioned. The first is former times, the second is the end of these days. There is a note of finality to the whole, for the revealer of this second period is none other than the Son of God, who has completed his work of redemption, and is now seated at the right hand of God.

II. Summation

In order to draw together the theological understanding of the above survey, let us summarize our findings.

A. General Revelation

There is a general revelation of God addressed to all men in the created universe around us and within us. The glory of God, his wisdom, power, righteousness and divinity are seen in this general revelation. This revelation serves as a backdrop for special revelation and as such it is fully sufficient. It is not sufficient to bring man to the self-conscious choice of good or evil. Following the fall, the world of nature exhibited the effects of the sin, and again serves as a

---
63. *Ibid.*, p. 26.
64. Bavinck, *op. cit.*, Vol. I, p. 319, as quoted in Warfield, *Ibid.*, p. 27.

backdrop for the redemptive special revelation. Again it is sufficient for this purpose, but not to bring men to salvation. This general revelation is authoritative, for God speaks with authority whenever, wherever, or however he speaks. Further, it is clear enough to leave all men without excuse.

B. Special Revelation

In order to bring men to a self-conscious moral choice, God gave him an additional special revelation. The original, unfallen state of man was the normal condition for man. Special revelation was given in this period, and was not necessitated by sin. As such it may be called preredemptive special revelation. During this "normal" period the four modes of revelation that are to be found throughout the rest of the Bible are encountered. God walked with man (theophany); he talked with him (prophecy); and he wrought for him (miracle). He used symbols of the trees and garden to convey the truth.

Following the fall, these four modes of revelation continue through every age of Biblical history. The necessity for a redemptive special revelation is seen in the totally lost condition of man after his sin. Only by the sovereign grace of God could there be any salvation, and this redemptive revelation is a manifestation of this grace. God always spoke authoritatively in his special revelation. He also spoke clearly enough to leave men without excuse, if they rejected him. At every age from Eden onward this special revelation was entirely sufficient to bring men to a saving faith. Under the old economy this faith was in the promise of a coming Messiah. With his coming, we now know that we are to trust in the Lord Jesus, and in his redemptive work upon the Cross for our salvation. These basic tenets of the Gospel have been clearly revealed in every age.

We should note again that all of the modes and aspects of revelation in the Bible find their ultimate meaning and purpose in the Lord Jesus Christ. The different modes together constitute an organic whole. Christ is the fulfillment of all that pointed forward to him, and all that follows is a consequence of his life and work on earth. With the completion of his work and of the record of it, given during the apostolic period, special revelation has ceased. We should not expect any further special revelation until the return of the Lord. At his appearing we shall see all that has gone before summed up in him, The *Logos*, The Express Image of God, The Theophany, The Prophet, The Priest, The King of kings and Lord of lords.

Chapter V The Scripture--*Principium Cognoscendi Externum* (Continued)

Introduction

As we studied the Biblical idea of revelation, one of the prominent concepts that we found in each era was the verbal form of much of God's special revelation. This verbal revelation was spoken by God to men, and in at least one case it was written by him. We also observed that the prophets were men who had the words of God placed in their mouths, and they, in turn, became official spokesmen of God. Not only did they speak the word, many of them were led by the Lord to set down in writing the revelations they had received.

Written scriptures are common to many religions. This is because one generation wants to pass to the next its principles, doctrines, traditions and laws. This is best done by committing them to writing. Thought and word, thinking and speaking stand in the most intimate relation to each other. They are not identical however, for there may be a conscious thinking, which is not expressed in words.

Language is the bearer of values and standards of mankind. It is the bond of men and people and families. It is the soul of the nation. Audible languages are the audible symbols of communication. This audible language seeks stability in the visible symbols of writing. There is, thus, great value in the written word. It gives to the thought a property of its own, namely, that of being remote from the thinker, and of remaining after the thoughts have been thought and expressed. In a sense it gives body and color to the thought as well as permanence.[1]

The revelation of God has taken place by means of the historical process. The center of that revelation came in the Person of Christ, his incarnation, his life, his death, his resurrection and his ascension. These events have occurred only once. They are not to be repeated. They have become a part of human history, and they must be passed on to mankind. Thus we see the necessity of committing the record and meaning of that revelation to writing. Only thus can it become the revelation to all mankind. The Scripture then is a means, not a goal in and of itself.

We should observe that Scripture and revelation are not identical. The revelation of God came in various modes, as we have already noted. It came in theophany and in miracle. The Scripture may give a record of the theophany or miracle, and yet it does not give all that one would see, if he were confronted with the revelation itself. Further, there were many, such as Elijah, Elisha, Thomas and Nathaniel, who were recipients of special revelation, and yet who did not write a word of Scripture. Every word that Jesus spoke was a special revelation from God; but, of course, we do not have the full account of all that he said here on earth. Thus, special revelation is broader than Scripture.

All of this is true, yet, without the Scripture, we would know nothing of God's revelation to Moses, or to Israel. We would know nothing of Christ with-

---

1. Bavinck, *op. cit.*, I, pp. 348-349.

out the Scripture. To all intents and purposes then, Scripture is for us the special revelation of God. There is no other *principium cognoscendi externum* for us. The inscripturation of the record of revelation is itself a part of the revelational process. That is, the inspiration of the writers of Scripture was itself revelational.

The Holy Spirit authored the Scripture in order to provide a means for calling his own to himself, and for the perfecting of the saints. In it God comes daily to his people. In it he speaks to his children, not from afar, but from nearby. In it he reveals himself from day to day to the believers in the fullness of his grace and truth. The Scripture is the remaining rapport between heaven and earth, between Christ and his congregation, between God and his people.[2]

It shall be our purpose to examine the means by which God has given this Scripture. That is, we shall study the Biblical concept of inspiration. Just as we assumed the truthfulness and authority of the Bible when examining the question of revelation, so we do also with the doctrine of inspiration. Only as we discover the Biblical concept of inspiration can we properly compare it with various human theories.

This particular doctrine is one of the most important for us to study. It is in this area that the historic Christian Church is being most dangerously attacked in our day. The best answer that we can give to the gainsayers is not that of our own making, but that which is derived from the Word itself.

I. The Witness of the Old Testament to Itself

The Old Testament provides us with the following important testimony concerning its own claim to inspiration.

A. The prophets were conscious of a definite calling from the Lord to the office or function of prophet (Ex. 3; I Sam. 3; Is. 6; Jer. 1; Ezek. 1-3; Amos 3:7-8; 7:15). This calling often was against their own wishes, as in the case of Moses (Ex. 3), or Jeremiah (Jer. 20:7), or Amos (Amos 3:8). In this connection, the overall conviction of Israel was that the prophets were the ambassadors of the Lord (Jer. 26:5); 7:15), that he had raised them up and sent them forth (Jer. 29:15; Deut. 18:15; Num. 11:29; II Chron. 36:15), that they were his servants (II Chron. 17:23; 21:10; 24:2; Ezra 9:11; Ps. 105:15; etc.), and that they stood before his presence (I Kings 17:1; II Kings 3:14; 5:16).

B. The prophets were conscious that the Lord had spoken to them, and that they had received the revelation from him. He taught them what they should say (Ex. 2:12; Deut. 18:18). He placed the words in their mouth (Num. 22:38; 23:5; Deut. 18:18). He spoke to them (Hos. 1:2; Hab. 2:1; Zech. 1:9, 13; 2:2, 7; 4:1, 4, 11; 5:5, 10; 6:4; Num. 12:2, 8; II Sam. 23:2; I Kings 22:28). They constantly used the formula: "thus said the Lord," or "the word of the Lord came to me," or "God said." The whole Old Testament is full of these expressions. Time and time again the prophet's message was introduced with these words. Passages in which the Lord is speaking in the first person are introduced with these

---

2. *Ibid.*, I. pp. 356-357.

phrases (Josh. 24:2; Is. 1:1-2; 8:1, 11; Jer. 1:2, 4, 11; 2:1; 7:1; Ezek. 1:3; 2:1; Hos. 1:1; Joel 1:1; Amos 2:1). It was actually the Lord who spoke through them (II Sam. 23:1-2), who spoke by their mouths (Ex. 4:12, 15; Num. 23:5), who spoke by his servants (Hag. 1:1; II Kings 17:13). All their words were clothed with the authority of God, since it was his word and not their own.

C. This consciousness of the prophets was so clear and fixed that they often designated the time and place when he spoke to them. Further, they distinguished between times when he spoke and those in which he did not speak to them (Is. 16:13-4; Jer. 3:6; 13:3; 26:1; 27:1; 28:1; 33:1; 34:1; 35:1; 36:1; 49:34; Ezek. 3:16; 8:1; 12:8; Hag. 1:1; Zech. 1:1). Thus their consciousness of his speaking was so objective, that they sharply distinguished themselves from the Lord. He was speaking to them (Is. 8:1; 51:16; 59:21; Jer. 1:9; 3:6; 5:14; Ezek. 3:26), and they listened with their ears and saw with their eyes (Is. 5:9 6:8; 21:3, 10; 22:14; 28:22; Jer. 23:18; 49:14; Ezek. 2:8; 3:10, 17; 33:7; 40:4; 44:5; Hab. 3:2, 16; II Sam. 7:27; Job 33:16; 36:10), and they took the words of the Lord into themselves (Jer. 15:16; Ezek. 3:1-3).

D. They, therefore, made a sharp contrast between what the Lord had revealed, and what had arisen from their own hearts (Num. 16:28; 24:13; I Kings 12:33; Neh. 6:8; Ps. 41:6-7). They charged the false prophets that they spoke out of their own hearts (Ezek. 13:2, 17; Jer. 14:14; 23:16, 26, Is. 59: 13), without being sent (Jer. 14:14; 29:9; Ezek. 13:6), so that they are lying prophets (Jer. 23:32; Is. 9:14; 20:6: 23: 21, 22, 26, 31, 36; 27:14; Ezek. 13:6f; Micah 2:11; Zeph. 3:4; Zech. 10:2).

E. The prophets were ultimately conscious, whether speaking or writing, of proclaiming not their own word, but the word of the Lord. Indeed, the word was not revealed to them for themselves, but for others. They had no freedom to hide it. They must speak (Jer. 20:7, 9; Exod. 3:4; Ezek. 3: Amos 3:8; Jonah 1:2). They were thus precisely prophets, speakers in the name of Jehovah and of his word. As such they knew that they must give all that they had received (Deut. 4:2; 12:32; Jer. 1:7, 17; 26:2; 42:4; Ezek. 3:10).

What is affirmed of the spoken word of the prophets is also true of their written word. The texts speaking of the writing of the prophets are relatively few (Ex. 17:14; 24:3-4; 34:27; Num. 33:2; Deut. 4:2; 12:32; 31:19; Is. 8:1; 30:8; Jer. 25:13; 30:1; 36:2, 24, 27-32; Ezek. 24:1; Dan. 12:4; Hab. 2:2), and they describe but a very small part of the Old Testament Scriptures. The inscripturation is a later, and yet necessary stage in the history of prophetism. Many prophecies were presumably never spoken, but were intended to be read and studied. Most show that they were destined for writing by the careful form they take. The recording of God's word was motivated by the thought that Israel would not be rescued, and that now and in distant generations the service of the Lord must find entrance by the Word and rational conviction. They resorted to writing because they wished to address persons beyond their hearers.

F. There was often a time lapse between the reception of a particular revelation and the preaching of it, and then its writing. The prophets claimed the same authority for their written word as for the spoken, and thus we may assume that at the moment of inspiration there was also a refreshment on the revelation itself, which often amended and completed the original revelation. The prophets were so aware of the closeness of their word with that which they received from the Lord, that they claimed for their writings the authority of God (Jer. 36:8, 10-11; 25:3). Isaiah speaks of his own writings as the book of Jehovah (Is. 34:16).

G. Not only did the prophets claim their own inspiration, but they acknowledged the Law as being divinely given. The prophets were not the creators of a new religion or a new ethical system. Rather, they spoke out of the conviction that they themselves and the people were the community of God's people. They underscored all that they said on the basis of the covenant of God with Israel, a gracious calling of Israel by God (Hos. 1:1-3; 6:7; 8:3; Jer. 11:6f; 14:21; 22:9; 31:31f; Ezek. 16:8f.; Is. 54:10; 56:4, 6; 59:21). The prophets acknowledged that the people in every age were guilty of sinning against God. The standard of righteousness was the Torah. The prophets frequently referred to the Torah by name as the objective revelation of the Lord (Is. 2:3; Micah 4:2; Amos 2:4; Hos. 8:1; 4:6; Jer. 18:18; Ezek. 7:26; Zeph. 3:4; Mal. 4:4).

H. We have already observed the unique relationship that Moses sustained in the history of revelation. He was the mediator in the Old Testament. Not only were the Ten Commandments and the Book of the Covenant (Ex. 20-23) represented as the Word of God, all of the other laws were also. It was Jehovah who gave the Torah by Moses to Israel. Throughout the Pentateuch the formula "the Lord said to Moses" or "the Lord spake to Moses" is to be found. Many chapters or sections are marked with the statement that the Lord said (Ex. 25:1; 30:11, 17, 22; 31:1; 32:9; Lev. 1:1; 4:1; 6:1; Num. 1:1; 2:1; 3:44; 4:1). Deuteronomy gives nothing but what Moses said to the people (Deut. 1:6; 2:1, 2, 17; 3:2; 5:2, 6). The people of Israel accepted the writings of Moses as the word of the Lord from the very beginning. This is seen in the allusions to the Torah by the prophets, cited above.

I. The historical books of the Old Testament were listed by the Israelites as the former prophets. This indicates that the tradition of Israel was that these books were written by prophets, or under the direction and authority of the prophets. There is testimony to the authorship of some of the historical books that confirms this tradition. Laird Harris traces this testimony as follows:

> A chain of verses in Chronicles gives us the tradition of a series of writing prophets in Israel. First Chronicles 29:29 says that the history of David was written in the books of the prophets Samuel, Nathan, and Gad. In II Chron. 9:29 the history of Solomon is said to have been written by the prophets Nathan, Ahijah, and Iddo. In II Chron. 12:15 the work of Rehoboam is said to have been written by the prophets Shemaiah and Iddo. Abijah's history was added by Iddo (II Chron. 13:22); Jehoshaphat's by Jehu the prophet, son of Hanani (II Chron. 20:34); Hezekiah's by Isaiah the prophet (II Chron. 32:32); Manasseh's by unnamed "seers" (II Chron. 33:19). The other kings are said to have their deeds recorded in the "book of the kings of Israel and Judah" (II

Chron. 35:27), although the names of the authors are not specified. We have listed here a chain of writing prophets from before the days of David to virtually the end of the kingdom of Judah. The old traditions of Israel preserved for us in the Book of Chronicles clearly include a succession of writing prophets.[3]

Harris goes on to note the fact that there seems to be an organic unity of all the historical books. The consciousness of this unity is seen in the footnote added to each that ties it with what is to follow. Deuteronomy ends with the account of the death of Moses and the rise of Joshua. Joshua ends in a similar fashion. Judges-Ruth ends with a genealogical note carrying the account to David. Samuel and Kings comprise a unit that ends with the captivity, with a note added well after the captivity had begun. So also with the books of Chronicles. Harris concludes:

> It thus appears that in every case from the Pentateuchal history to the post-Exilic writings a historical book is given a colophon or footnote that unites it in continuous narrative fashion to the succeeding book. . . . The chain of prophets evidently wrote a chain of histories from Genesis to Nehemiah, and the writings of these prophets were accepted, one by one, through the centuries until, when the spirit of prophecy departed from Israel, the canon was complete.[4]

Harris cites Jewish writings that confirm this view. Of particular interest is the statement of Josephus:

> For we have not an innumerable multitude of books among us, disagreeing from and contradicting one another, as the Greeks have, but only twenty-two books, which contain the records of all the past times; which are justly believed to be divine; and of them five belong to Moses, which contain his laws and traditions of the origin of mankind till his death . . . but as to the time from the death of Moses till the reign of Artaxerxes . . . the prophets, who were after Moses, wrote down what was done in their times in thirteen books. . . . It is true, our history hath been written since Artaxerxes very particularly, but hath not been esteemed of the like authority with the former by our forefathers, because there hath not been an exact succession of prophets since that time.[5]

It is of interest to note that the materials from the Dead Sea scrolls confirm this same view of the Old Testament.

The historical books are the commentary in facts on the covenant of God with Israel. They are not just history in our sense of the term. They are prophecy. For in the history of Israel we have the revelation of God, and his dealing with his covenant people. In the historical books, therefore, we find not only the recording of the events, but also the judgment of these events, particularly in the light of the Law.

J. The so-called poetical books remain to be commented on. They bear with the rest of the Old Testament writings the same religio-ethical character.

---

3. Laird Harris, *Inspiration and Canonicity of the Bible* (Grand Rapids: Zondervan Publishing House, 1957), pp. 166-167.
4. *Ibid.*, pp. 168-169.
5. *Against Apion*, I, 8.

They are based on the underlying revelation of God, and present the outworking of that revelation in different experiences and relations of life. The Preacher condemns the vanity of a world without the fear of the Lord. Job is concerned with the problem of the righteousness of God and the suffering of the saints. Proverbs pictures to us the true wisdom in its application to life. The Song of Solomon treats of love under God. The Psalms mirror for us the whole of human experience under God. II Samuel 23:1-3 speaks of David as the "sweet psalmist of Israel," who spoke under the influence of the Spirit of the Lord, and "His word was upon my tongue."

K. From all the foregoing, we see that the various types of Old Testament writings bear testimony to their own authority. The prophets constantly referred to their having received the Word from God. He placed his words in their mouths. The Torah of Moses was recognized as authoritative immediately. He had been thoroughly attested by the various miracles and theophanies that accompanied his ministry. Thus his verbal announcements were accepted as divinely authoritative. The laws of God were placed in the sanctuary (Ex. 25:25; 40:20; Deut. 31:9, 26; Josh. 24:25f.; I Sam. 10:25). Further, the poetic products were valued highly and approved by God (Deut. 31:19; Josh. 10:13; II Sam. 1:18). Collections of the Psalms seemed to have been made early as is seen in the five books into which our present Psalter is divided. Proverbs were collected as is witnessed by Prov. 25:1. The earlier books were cited by the later ones (Mal. 1:13-14; 2:7-8; 4:4-6). Professor John Murray speaks of this testimony:
> It is surely of the greatest weight that the long line of Old Testament prophetic witness should come to its close with so insistent an appeal for devotion to the law of Moses, the Lord's servant, and that the intertestamentary period should be bridged, as it were, by the retrospective and the prospective, the appeal to Moses, on the one hand, and the promise of the resumption of the prophetic voice in him than whom there should not have arisen a greater, namely, John the Baptist, on the other (cf. chap. 4:5).[6]

L. We have demonstrated, thus far, the fact that the Old Testament bears witness to the authority and divine origin of all its parts. In other words, the whole of the Old Testament was given by inspiration. One further question that needs to be asked, before we go on to the testimony of the New Testament, has to do with the quality of the product that is so inspired. Is it all true? Are there parts of it that are more true than others? Is there error in the Old Testament? Does one part of the Old Testament adversely criticize another portion, so that we may say that the Old Testament teaches there must have been some error within its contents?

On the surface, there are passages that give the appearance of adverse criticism. Some of the prophets seem to contradict the Mosaic law. For example, Jeremiah writes, "For I spake not unto your fathers, nor commanded them in the day that I brought them out of the land of Egypt, concerning burnt offerings

---

6. Stonehouse and Woolley, ed., *The Infallible Word* (Philadelphia: The Presbyterian Guardian Corporation, 1946), pp. 18-19.

or sacrifices: but this thing commanded I them, saying, Obey my voice, and I will be your God, and ye shall be my people: and walk ye in all the ways that I have commanded you, that it may be well unto you."[7] Murray notes regarding this passage:

> It must be replied that the argument based on this antithesis in the prophecy of Jeremiah fails to appreciate one of the basic principles of Biblical interpretation, namely, that a relative contrast is often expressed in absolute terms.[8]

That is, mere ritual, even without ethical integrity and particularly without regard to spiritual attachment and obedience to the Lord God is mockery.[9]

We may, therefore, conclude regarding the whole matter of the testimony of the Old Testament regarding itself that it does make the claim throughout to its being divinely originated. One portion cites another portion as authoritative. Finally, there is no contradiction between one part of the Old Testament and another. From this, one might well suppose that the view of inspiration held by the Old Testament is that which we call plenary verbal inspiration, resulting in an infallible Word. As we study the New Testament witness to the Old, we shall discover that this is exactly the doctrine that we find there set forth by Jesus and his disciples. That this was the prevalent Jewish view is seen from the way in which the utterances of Jesus and his disciples on the subject did not elicit any reaction from the Jews, other than acceptance of the same viewpoint.

II. The Witness of the New Testament to the Old Testament

A. Reverence for the Old Testament

The terms of the New Testament speakers and writers used to refer to the Old Testament indicate their reverence of the Word.

1. The human author is often cited. For example, Jesus refers to Moses (Matt. 8:4; 19:8; Mark 7:10; John 5:45; 7:22); to Isaiah (Matt. 15:7; Mark 13:14); to David (Matt. 22:43); and to Daniel (Matt. 24:15).

2. On the other hand the reference is often made to God as the author of Scripture (Matt. 15:4; 22: 43, 45; 24:15; Mark 12:26; Heb. 1:5ff.; 3:7; 4:3, 5; 5:6; 7:21; 8:5, 8; 10:16, 30; 12:26; 13:5).

3. Another way in which the Old Testament was cited by the New is the use of one of the terms translated Scripture or Scriptures. There are three expressions in the New Testament that are virtually synonymous. They are *graphe*[10] Scripture; *he graphe*[11] the Scripture; and *hai graphai*[12] the Scriptures.

---

7. Jer. 7:22-23.
8. *Infallible Word, op. cit.*, p. 13.
9. *Ibid.*
10. γραφή
11. ἡ γραφή
12. αἱ γραφαί

These terms are used some 50 times in the New Testament referring to the Old Testament. The following are instances in which the technical force is used:

hai graphai	Matt. 22:29	I Cor. 15:3
he graphe	John 13:18	Rom. 4:3
graphe	John 19:37	I Pet. 2:6

    4. In the Gospels the expression "that which was spoken by the prophet" or its equivalent is often found (Matt. 1:22; 2:15, 17, 23; 3:3, etc.). In connection with some of these passages, the Lord is specifically cited as speaking through the prophet (Matt. 1:22; 2:15).

    The impression received from a survey of all of these various ways of referring to the Old Testament is that there was a common conviction of Jesus and his disciples regarding the authority and unity of the Old Testament. The entire Old Testament constituted an organic whole, which had God as its primary author.

    5. The Hebrew Old Testament as it comes to us today is divided into three parts, namely, the law, the prophets, and the writings. This usage was already in vogue by the time of the New Testament. In Luke 24:44 all three portions are referred to: ". . . all things must needs be fulfilled, which are written in the law of Moses, the prophets, and the psalms concerning me." The more common usage found in the New Testament, however, is the employment of one or two of these names to refer to the whole Old Testament. (Matt. 2:23; 5:17; 7:12; Lk. 1:70; 16:16; Jn. 10:34; Acts 13:27; Rom. 16:26; I Cor. 14:31; etc.). Note in particular John 10:34, where Jesus uses the term law and quotes from the Psalms. The three terms are each appropriate for the whole of Scripture. First, the term law speaks of the authority and binding character that the Scripture sustains, because it is the very word of God. The term prophets suggests the divine origin, because those who are designated prophets are the official messengers of God, who received their message directly from him. The term Scriptures, suggests that these are writings that stand above all others. They are The Writings. Thus, it is entirely appropriate to find the phenomena of interchanging these terms to refer to the whole Old Testament. All of these terms speak of the divine character of the Old Testament.

B. No Adverse Criticism of the Old by the New

    Jesus and his Apostles never criticized the Old Testament, but accepted its whole content without any reservation. This is true of all parts and not just of the religio-ethical sections, or only those passages in which God himself actually spoke. The historical settings as represented in the Old Testament were accepted by the New Testament. For example, Jesus held that Isaiah 54 came from Isaiah (Matt. 13:14), that Psalm 110 was written by David (Matt. 22:43), that Daniel had prophesied concerning the abomination of desolation (Matt. 24:15), and that Moses had written the Law (John 5:46). Not only were the historical settings accepted, but also the historical accounts as given in the Old Testament were accepted as true. For example, the creation of man as presented in Genesis is received by Jesus as factual, and becomes the basis for his reaffirming the marriage ordinance (Matt. 19:4-5). Other events that are simply accepted are: Abel's murder (Matt. 22:35); the flood (Matt. 24:37-39); the history of the patriarchs (Matt. 22:32; John 8:56); the destruction of Sodom (Matt. 11:23; Luke 17:28-33); the burning bush (Luke 20:37); the serpent in the wilderness (John 3:14); the manna (John 6:32); the history of Elijah (Luke 4:25-26); the history of Jonah (Matt. 12:39-41); etc.

C. New Testament Viewed as Fulfilling the Old

Of particular interest is the way in which the New Testament views itself as the fulfillment of the Old. It is often stated that certain events have occurred in order that Holy Scripture might be fulfilled, *(hina plerothe hai graphai*[13]*)* (Matt. 1:22; Mark 14:49; 15:28; Luke 3:4; 24:44; John 13:18; 17:12; 19:24, 36; Acts 1:16; James 2:23; etc.). Even small particulars are seen as fulfillments of Scripture (Matt. 21:16; Luke 4:21; 22:37; John 15:25; 17:12; 19:28; etc.). All that happened to Jesus was written before in the Old Testament (Luke 18:31-32). Jesus and the apostles justified their conduct and proved their doctrine by citing the Old Testament (Matt. 12:3; 22:32; John 10:34; Rom. 4; Gal. 3: I Cor. 15; etc.). This divine authority of the Scripture was extended so far by them that even one word, indeed a tittle or a jot was clothed with it (Matt. 5:17-8; 22:45; Luke 16:17; John 10:35; Gal. 3:16).

D. The Testimony of Jesus Regarding the Old Testament

The testimony of Jesus toward the Old Testament as reflected in Matt. 5:17-18 is especially relevant in a day and age that has seen a general rejection of verbal inspiration. First, the terms "law and prophets" as used by Jesus here probably refers to the whole of the Old Testament. If, however, one insists that it refers only to the first two sections of the Old Testament, there is no reason to believe that Jesus would make any distinction or treat the third portion any differently. This passage gives Jesus' own view of the Old Testament, or at least a large portion of it. He did not come to destroy it. The word for destroy *(katalusai*[14]*)* means to abrogate, to demolish, to disintegrate or to annul. Jesus affirms here that his Messianic work will not destroy the law and the prophets, but will leave them intact. Positively, he came to fulfill. The word for fulfill *(plerosai*[15]*)* speaks of the complete filling.

In verse 18 Jesus applies his general statement to the smallest details of the law. He came to fulfill, not only in general terms, but even down to the minutiae of the law. The jot and tittle refer to the smallest letter of the Hebrew alphabet, and to the minute projection that distinguishes one letter from another. It would be similar to referring to dotting the I's and crossing the T's of the English. Professor Murray says:

> Could anything establish more conclusively the meticulous accuracy, validity and truth of the law than the language to which Jesus attaches

---

13. ἵνα πληρωθῇ αἱ γραφαί
14. καταλῦσαι
15. πληρῶσαι

his own unique formula of asseveration?... It is difficult to understand why those who assent to inspiration should stumble at *verbal* inspiration. For words are the media of thought and, so far as Scripture is concerned, the written words are the only media of communication. If the thoughts are inspired, the words must be also. . . . The indissolubility of the law extends to its every jot and tittle. Such indissolubility could not be predicated of it if it were in any detail fallible, for if fallible it would some day come to nought. And this is just saying that in every detail the law was in his esteem infallible and therefore indissoluble. It is indeed strange prejudice that professes adherence to the infallibility of Christ and yet rejects the clear implications of his teachings. Nothing could be plainer than this, that in the smallest details it is taken up by him and finds, in his fulfillment of it, its permanent embodiment and validity. By the most stringent necessity there is but one conclusion, namely, that the law is infallible and inerrant.[16]

A second passage that gives us the particular view of Jesus toward the Old Testament is John 10:33-36. Jesus has just been challenged on his claim to be one with the Father. He cited Psalm 82:6 in answer to this challenge.

It is this appeal to Scripture that is the pivot of his whole defence. This cannot be explained on any other basis than that he considered the Scriptures as the unassailable instrument of defence. For 'the Scripture cannot be broken'.[17]

The passage cited was from the portion of the Scripture that may have been omitted from Matthew 5:17ff. Here he shows the same high regard for this portion of the Old Testament as he did for the Law and the Prophets.

He appeals to Scripture because it is really and intrinsically a finality. And when he says the Scripture cannot be broken, he is surely using the word 'Scripture' in its most comprehensive denotation as including all that the Jews of the day recognized as Scripture, to wit, all the canonical books of the Old Testament. It is of the Old Testament without any reservation or exception that he says, it 'cannot be broken'. . . He affirms the unbreakableness of the Scripture in its entirety and leaves no room for any such supposition as that of degrees of inspiration and fallibility. Scripture is inviolable. Nothing less than this is the testimony of our Lord. And the crucial nature of such witness is driven home by the fact that it is in answer to the most serious of charges and in defence of his most stupendous claim that he bears this testimony.[18]

In addition to these specific passages, there is a mass of materials in the Gospels that lead us to the conclusion that he held this high view of the whole of Scripture.

His attitude is one of meticulous acceptance and reverence. The only explanation of such an attitude is that what Scripture said, God said, that the Scripture was God's Word, that it was God's Word because it

---

16. *Infallible Word, op. cit.*, pp. 22-23.
17. *Ibid.*, p. 25.
18. *Ibid.*, pp. 25-26.

was Scripture and that it was or became Scripture because it was God's Word.[19]

E. The Testimony of the Apostles Regarding the Old Testament

The testimony of the Apostles and writers of the New Testament regarding the Old is found to be in full conformity with that of Jesus. The very fact that they record for us the high view of Jesus implies that they agreed with this view. Had they held a lower view, they would scarcely be expected to teach his high view, and then set themselves in opposition to it.

There are two passages that especially show the view of the Apostles toward the Old Testament. The first of these is II Tim. 3:16. Here the Apostle has been speaking to Timothy of the "holy writings" which are able to make him wise unto salvation. This is obviously a reference to the Scriptures of the Old Testament, which he had learned from his childhood. Paul asserts, "All Scripture is God-breathed" or "Every Scripture is God-breathed." Whether taken as a whole, or as all of the parts makes little difference. The grammatical structure does not indicate which is preferable. What Paul is asserting, using either translation, is plenary inspiration. All Scripture (both Old and New Testaments) is God-breathed. The term (*theopneustos*[20]) translated "given by inspiration" is literally "God-breathed." The emphasis here is on the out-breathing of God.

> The whole emphasis is upon the fact that all Scripture proceeds from God and is therefore invested with a divinity that makes it as authoritative and efficient as a word oracularly spoken by God directly to us.[21]

It may be observed that Paul refers solely to the primary authorship here, though he frequently cites the secondary human authors in other passages. He is here asserting what is true of the whole of the Old Testament, that it is all "God-breathed" no matter who the secondary author may have been.

Peter in II Peter 1:20-21 gives us more insight into the way in which God used the secondary authors. The teaching here is both negative and positive. Negatively, he asserts that the prophecy of Scripture does not come from man. It is not the product of mere human instrument. "Men spake from God." They spake because the Holy Spirit bore (*pheromenoi*[22]) them to his destination.

Professor Murray summarizes the witness of the New Testament to the Old as follows:

> Summing up the witness of the New Testament, we find that human authorship or instrumentality is fully recognized and yet human agency is not conceived of as in any way impairing the divine origin, character, truth and authority of Scripture. It is divine in its origin because it is the product of God's creative breath and because it was as borne by the Holy Spirit that men spoke from God. For these reasons it bears an oracular character that accords it an authority as real and divine as if we

---

19. *Ibid.*, p. 27.
20. θεόπνευστος
21. *Infallible Word, op. cit.*, p. 30. For a full treatment of the meaning of this term see Warfield, "The Biblical Idea of Inspiration" in *The Inspiration and Authority of the Bible* (Philadelphia: Presbyterian and Reformed Publishing Company, 1948).
22. φερόμενοι

heard the voice of God speaking from heaven. This oracular character is a permanent feature and so Scripture has an abiding stability and application--it is unbreakable and indissoluble.[23]

F. Passages Interchanging "God" and "Scripture"

There is in the New Testament an interesting usage that confirms this high view of the Scripture that is asserted in these passages just treated. There are passages in which the Scripture is spoken of as if it were God, and then on the other hand, there are passages in which God is spoken of as if he were the Scriptures. In other words, for the writers of the New Testament there is such a close connection between the Scriptures and God that they can be brought together into such a connection as to show that in point of authority there is no distinction between the two. Sometimes the orthodox Christian today is accused of Bibliolatry, which is an unfair charge. The fact is that the acceptance of the Bible as divinely authoritative is the teaching of the Scripture itself.

Examples of passages in which Scripture is spoken of as if it were God are: Gal. 3:8, "The Scripture, foreseeing that God would justify the heathen through faith, preached before the gospel unto Abraham, saying, In thee shall all the nations be blessed." (Gen. 12:1-3); Romans 9:17, "The Scripture saith unto Pharaoh, even for this same purpose have I raised thee up" (Ex. 9:16). Actually, in both cases, no written Scriptures yet existed. It was not Scripture, therefore, which foresaw the grace of God extended to the heathen, but God. So also with Pharaoh.

> These acts could be attributed to 'Scripture' only as the result of such a habitual identification, in the mind of the writer, of the text of Scripture with God as speaking, that it became natural to use the term 'Scripture says,' when what was really intended was 'God, as recorded in Scripture, said.'[24]

Examples of passages in which God is spoken of as if he were Scripture are: Matt. 19:4-5, "And he answered and said, Have ye not read that he which made them from the beginning made them male and female, and said, For this cause shall a man leave his father and mother, and shall cleave to his wife, and the twain shall become one flesh?" (Gen. 2:24); " Acts 4:25, "Who by the Holy Spirit, [by] the mouth of our father David thy servant, didst say, 'Why did the Gentiles rage, And the peoples imagine vain things?" Heb 3:7, "Wherefore, even as the Holy Spirit saith, 'Today if ye shall hear his voice." (Ps. 2:1); etc. (See also: Acts 13:34-5 and Is. 55:3; Ps. 16:10; Heb. 1:6 and Deut. 32:43; Ps. 104:4; Ps. 95:7; Ps. 102:26.) Originally the words quoted as from God in the New Testament passages are not found so directly quoted from him in the Old. They again can be attributed to him, because of the association of all that Scripture said as coming from God himself.

---

23. *Infallible Word, op. cit.*, p. 32.
24. Warfield, *The Inspiration and Authority of the Bible, op. cit.*, pp. 299-300.

G. Difficulties Considered

There are some difficulties found in the New Testament's witness to the Old that need to be considered. Having seen the view of Jesus and his disciples, our examination of the difficulties is not to be taken as questioning this view. Rather, it is with the conviction of the truth of the high view held by Jesus and his disciples that we should approach these difficulties seeking to understand just how they can be reconciled with it. At many points we may have to admit to being unable to solve all of the problems. It is our conviction, however, that if we knew enough about all of the circumstances, and meanings of particular passages, that no contradiction or error would appear in the Scriptures, and the difficulties would be removed.

There are several types of difficulties to be mentioned. We shall look at just a sample of each, and indicate the type of solutions that have been offered.

1. Apparent error in the text.

One of the most difficult texts of this category is that found in Matthew 23:35, "That upon you may come all the righteous blood shed on earth, from the blood of Abel the righteous unto the blood of Zechariah son of Barachiah, whom ye slew between the sanctuary and the altar."

The problem here lies in the fact that the only Zechariah whose death was recorded as taking place in the sanctuary is Zechariah son of Jehoiada (II Chron. 24:20-22). If it is assumed that this is the Zechariah to whom Jesus refers (and it is likely, because this is the last martyrdom recorded in II Chronicles, which stood as the last book of the Hebrew Old Testament), then the question of the father's name is raised. One simple solution has been offered, namely, that this is the real name of his father, and that the reference in Chronicles to Jehoiada is to his more famous grandfather. This kind of loose reference in genealogies is found in the Scripture, and there is no error implied, so long as one understands the real meaning of the passage.

Commentators such as Plummer suggest that there is an error here that has crept in from the fact that the writing prophet Zechariah was the son of a Barachiah. In other words, this was just a slip of the pen, either by a copyist, or even by the evangelist. The latter possibility has to be rejected on the basis of the teaching of Scripture regarding itself. In other words, the Bible teaches that the originals were without error, and thus any solution that resorts to such a supposed error is in opposition to the Biblical teaching regarding itself. The possibility of a copyist error is very slim in this case, due to the almost universal textual evidence for our present reading. Only one manuscript omits the reference to Barachiah.

Another possible avenue for solution is found in the silence of the Old Testament regarding the death of the writing prophet Zechariah son of Barachiah. Possibly the allusion of Jesus is to him. Against this is the fact that there is no other allusion either in or out of Scripture to such a martyrdom. Others have suggested the possibility of other Zechariahs, even to the mention of the father of John the Baptist, though again there is no other record of such a martyrdom.

Without being able to settle the problem, let us conclude our treatment of it by saying that if we knew enough, we are certain that no actual error exists. Our real difficulty here is our ignorance of the full facts of the case.

2. Reference to fulfillment of prophecy, which apparently refers to other matters.

Another difficulty lies in the constant citation by the New Testament, in particular, by Matthew to the effect that certain events in the New Testament fulfill Old Testament prophecies. The difficulty is not the citation of clear cut prophecies, but the use of passages that do not seem to have been designed as prophecies as such. For example, Matt. 2:15 says," ... that it might be fulfilled (*hina plerothe*[25]) which was spoken by the Lord through the prophet, saying, Out of Egypt did I call my son" (Matt. 2:15). The reference is back to Hosea 11:1, where the prophet seems clearly to be alluding to the exodus out of Egypt. The best understanding of prophecy is not to suppose a double meaning. Nor, is this just an artificial association by Matthew. Rather, we must recognize that, under the inspiration of the Holy Spirit, we have here the ultimate meaning of the exodus itself. It was a foreshadowing of the redemptive work of Christ. Thus, in a real sense the fulfillment of the words of Hosea are not found in the type of Israel, but in the antitype, Christ.

3. The quotation of the Old Testament.

The variety of quotations of the Old Testament by the New also raises problems. There are three groups of citations as they relate to the Hebrew text and to the Greek translation. In some texts there is deviation from the LXX and agreement with the Hebrew text (Matt. 2:15, 18; 8:17; 12:18-21; 27:46; John 19:37; Rom. 10:15-16; 11:9; I Cor. 3:19; 15:54). On the other hand, there are citations that agree with the LXX and deviate from the Hebrew (Matt. 15:8-9; Acts 7:14; 15:16-17; Eph. 4:8; Heb. 10:5; 11:21; 12:6). A third group of citations vary from both the Hebrew and the LXX (Matt. 2:6; 3:3; 26:31; John 12:15; 13:18; Rom. 10:6-9; I Cor. 2:9). As one considers this phenomenon, it must again be assumed that the Holy Spirit has given to us the inspired commentary on the deeper spiritual meaning of the texts concerned. Sometimes this is most agreeable to the Hebrew text, whereas other times the Greek translation of the LXX gives the true meaning, and yet at other times, neither the Hebrew nor the LXX gives us the best meaning, but something differing from them both.

III. The Witness of the New Testament to the New Testament

A. The Witness of Christ Regarding the New Testament

Though the situation of the New Testament differs from that of the Old Testament, so that we cannot expect a confirmation of the whole New Testament

---

25. ἵνα πληρωθῇ

after it was completed, as we have in the New of the Old, nevertheless, we do find considerable claim of divine authority for the New Testament within itself.

The first and most obvious claim comes in connection with the witness of Christ. Throughout the New Testament Christ is acknowledged as divine, and thus his word is fully authoritative. He is called the Word (*Logos*[26]) (John 1:1,14), who declares unto us the Father (John 1:18; 17:6). He is the faithful witness (Rev. 1:5), the faithful and true witness (Rev. 3:14 cf. Is. 55:4). No guile was in his mouth (I Pet. 2:22). He is the Apostle and High priest of our confession (Heb. 3:1; I Tim. 6:13). He was sent by the Father (John 8:42), and he spoke nothing but what he had seen and heard (John 3:32). He spoke the words of God (John 3:34; 17:8). He gave to all a true witness (John 5:31-32; 18:37), and therefore his testimony is true (John 8:14; 14:6). He is designated as The Prophet whom Moses had foretold (Acts 2:22-23). The consequence of this divine authority of Christ was that his hearers recognized in him one who "taught them as one having authority, and not as the scribes" (Mt. 7:29). In both John 5 and John 8 we have the direct assertions of Jesus that he spoke from the Father, "If I bear witness of myself, my witness is not true. It is another that beareth witness of me; and I know that the witness which he witnesseth of me is true... But the witness which I received is not from man: howbeit he that sent me is true; and the things which I heard from him, these speak I unto the world... I do nothing of myself, but as the Father taught me, I speak these things." (John 8:28-29); "If ye abide in my word, then are ye truly my disciples; and ye shall know the truth and the truth shall make you free" (John 8:31-32); "Which of you convicteth me of sin? If I say truth, why do ye not believe me? He that is of God heareth the words of God: for this cause ye hear them not, because ye are not of God" (John 8:46-47). These statements all assert the inspired character of his own words. His words are truth.

B. The Promise of Inspiration

The promise of inspiration was given by Jesus to his Apostles, so that they could bear a faithful witness to his work. The Apostolic office was a unique office in the Church. The Apostles were given to Jesus by the Father (John 17:6); chosen by him (John 6:70; 13:18; 15:16,19); and prepared by him for their future task. That task was described by Jesus as bearing witness (Luke 24:48; John 15:27). They were ear or eye witnesses to his word and work, and had beheld the Word of Life (I John 1:1). It was their task to bear witness to Israel and to the whole world (Matt. 28:19; John 15:27; 17:20; Acts 1:8). To equip them to be faithful and true witnesses, Jesus promised the Holy Spirit (Matt. 10:20; John 14:26; 15:26; 16:7; 20:22). John 14:26 especially teaches that the Holy Spirit will give them the truth, reminding them of what they had seen and heard Jesus do. "But the Comforter, even the Holy Spirit, whom the Father will send in my name, he shall teach you all things, and bring to your remembrance all that I have said unto you." This is the promise of Jesus of divine inspiration to his Apostles. Regarding the Gospels, the Holy Spirit was not to

---

26. λόγος

give new revelation but to bear witness to the Person and Work of Christ (John 15:26; 16:13-14).

C. The Apostles Testified by the Help of the Holy Spirit

It was by the help of the Holy Spirit that the Apostles bore their testimony as recorded in Acts (Acts 1:8, 21-22; 2:14,32; 3:15; 4:8,20,33; 5:32; 10:39; 13:31). In this witness they told what they had seen and heard, and herein lay the meaning of their being Apostles. God confirmed their witness by granting to them signs and wonders (Matt. 10:1,9; Acts 2:43; 3:2; 5:12-16; 6:8; 8:6f; 10:44; 11:21; 14:3; 15:8, etc.). Though we do not have the express command of Jesus that the Apostles should write, except in Rev. 1:11, 19, etc., nevertheless, they did write with the same authority as they spoke. Their writing was a special form of their witness. Their writings were a testimony to Christ (Luke 1:2; John 1:14; 10:35; 20:31; 21:24; I John 1:1-4; I Pet. 1:12; 5:1; II Pet. 1:16; Heb. 2:3; Rev. 1:3; 22:18-19). Their written testimony was faithful and true (John 19:35; III John 12).

D. Paul's Claims for His Writings

Paul, though he had been a persecutor of the Church, was called by Christ (Gal. 1:1). He claimed that he had seen Christ personally (I Cor. 9:1; 15:8), and was given revelation and visions (II Cor. 12; Acts 26:16); had received the gospel from Jesus (Gal. 1:12; I Tim. 1:12; Eph. 3:2-8); and thus was an Apostle just as the others, especially to the Gentiles (Acts 26:16). His Apostolic witness was confirmed by God with signs and wonders (I Cor. 12:10; Rom. 12:4-8; II Cor. 11:23ff; Gal. 3:5; Heb. 2:4 etc.). Paul therefore, was conscious that there was no other Gospel than his (Gal. 1:7-8); that he was truthful (I Cor. 7:25); that he had the Spirit of God (I Cor. 7:40); that Christ spoke by him (II Cor. 13:3; I Cor. 2:10, 16; II Cor. 2:17; 5:23); that he proclaimed God's word (II Cor. 2:17; I Thess. 2:13); and that not only what he spoke, but also what he wrote was authoritative (I Thess. 5:27; Col. 4:16; II Thess. 2:15; 3;14). He clearly claimed divine inspiration in I Cor. 14:37.

E. New Testament Cited as Scripture by the New Testament

The New Testament writers bore witness to the writings of their fellow servants by quoting them as Scripture. In I Timothy 5:18, Paul quotes as Scripture a passage from Deuteronomy, and also one from Luke (10:7). Peter in a similar way refers to the writings of Paul as being "according to the wisdom given to him" and compares them with "other scriptures" (II Peter 3:15-16).

F. All Scripture "God-breathed"

If the writers of the New Testament refer to the New Testament writings as "Scripture," then they would apply to the New Testament all that they affirm of the Old Testament Scriptures. In other words, II Tim. 3:16 and II Pet. 1:21 are both applicable to the New Testament, just as much as to the Old. We have already observed that the view of the New Testament toward the Old is one of a plenary verbal inspiration. Now, we would go on to apply the same terms to the New Testament as well. This concurs with the organic character of the whole of Scripture (Heb. 1:1-2).

G. Inspired Books Recognized When Written

Without taking time or space to trace the history of the recognition of the New Testament Canon, we may assert that the same basic principle that held true for the Old Testament holds true here. As a particular writing came from the pen of an inspired writer, that book was added to the Canon by the Lord. Generally speaking, the New Testament can be shown to have been written, either by an Apostle (Matthew, John, Peter and Paul) or under the auspices of an Apostle (Mark for Peter, Luke a companion of Paul). This leaves only a small portion of the New Testament not fully accounted for, namely, Hebrews, James and Jude. The latter two may have come from the pens of Apostles, or the brothers of Jesus. Hebrews is the most difficult because its author is not known for certain. Presumably, if it was not written by an Apostle, it was written by one who was closely associated with the Apostles, and would have been recognized immediately by the Church as bearing the marks of inspiration. With the close of the Apostolic age, special revelation ceased, and the Canon of the New Testament was complete. Perhaps, one of the signs of this completion is to be found in the destruction of Jerusalem. The dating of the writing of all of the New Testament except the writings of John is usually placed before 70 A.D. It may well be, however, that these too could be placed earlier, and then the destruction of Jerusalem would become the clear sign of the closing of special revelation.[27]

IV. The Nature of Inspiration

Having examined the Bible's testimony to itself, it remains now for us to seek to draw some conclusions from this testimony. Various views have been held as to the nature of inspiration. We shall examine these various views in the light of Scripture to see just what we can say about its nature.

A.. Mechanical Dictation

The view of plenary verbal inspiration has often been represented as involving a mechanical dictation theory of inspiration. The argument is that if inspiration involves the very words used by the writers of Scripture, then this could be done only by a mechanical means. The error of this suggestion arises from the fact that all mechanical inspiration would be verbal, but it is not acknowledged that the reverse is not necessarily true. Verbal inspiration is not necessarily mechanical. Actually the terms describe two different aspects of inspiration. Mechanical has to do with the mode, whereas verbal is descriptive of the extent of inspiration.

---

27. For a full discussion of the principle of canonicity see Laird Harris, *Inspiration and Canonicity of the Bible, op. cit.*

In the history of the Church the term dictation has on occasion been used of Scripture, and this is taken to imply a mechanical dictation, which overrules all mental activity on the part of the human writer. For example, J. H. Thornwell said, "Hence the theory of 'verbal dictation,' . . . is the only theory we have ever regarded as consistent with the exigencies of the case, the only theory which makes the Bible what it professes to be, the WORD OF GOD, and an adequate and perfect measure of faith."[28] On the surface this statement sounds like mechanical dictation. Elsewhere, however, Thornwell stated his rejection of such a view: "It has been compared to *dictation*. The mistake there is that the man is passive. The analogy is good, but the resemblance is a failure."[29] One of the Reformed Confessions approaches this sort of language also, namely, the *Formula Consensus Helvetica* (1675). This Confession was recognized by only a few Cantons of Switzerland, and has never been broadly accepted by the Reformed Churches. It was written in opposition to loose views of Scripture held by Cappelus of Samur.

As we have cited from Thornwell, the error of this view is its failure to recognize that the human authors were active in their production of the Scripture. The fact that this is true is easily seen in the differences of style found between authors. Thus, the Bible does not lead us to believe in a mechanical view of inspiration.

B. Dynamic Inspiration

Schleiermacher maintained what is called the dynamic view of inspiration. This theory rejects the direct operation of the Holy Spirit in the production of Scripture. Bannerman describes this view as the illuminating of the rational or the spiritual consciousness of a man, so that out of the fullness of his own Christian understanding and feelings he may speak or write the product of his own religious life and beliefs.[30]

This is a complete subjectivizing of inspiration. Man is influenced, or inspired, but not necessarily the words that he sets down. Consequently, the Bible contains the highest sort of religious truth, and also may contain error. This view has sometimes been called a theory of spiritual insight or spiritual intuition.

The problem with this view is that it simply does not measure up to the high view of the writings themselves, which is held by Jesus and his Apostles. There is no allowance for error by them. In effect this view robs the Scripture of its supernatural character.

---

28. *Collected Writings of James Henley Thornwell*, ed. John B. Adger and John L. Girardeau (Richmond: Presbyterian Committee of Publications, 1881), Vol. III, p. 51.
29. Thornwell MS, Historical Foundation of the Presbyterian Churches, Montreat, North Carolina, quoted in *Studies in Southern Presbyterian Theology* by the author (Phillipsburg: Presbyterian and Reformed Publishing Company, 1987), p. 129.
30. *Inspiration of Scriptures: the Infallible Truth and Divine Authority of the Holy Scriptures* (1865), p. 142.

C. Organic Inspiration

That which best describes the Biblical view of inspiration has been called "organic" inspiration. It should be observed that there have been some who interchange these last two names. John L. Girardeau calls this view the dynamic theory. He describes it thus:

> It holds that both the thought and language are imparted by the inspiring influence to the inspired person, but in such a manner as not to exclude the voluntary exercise of human faculties, or the spontaneous employment of individual peculiarities in speaking and writing. . . . This theory is the same as that commonly styled the theory of verbal inspiration . . .[31]

God acted upon the writers in an organic way. He used them in their own individual personalities. He created them, prepared them, prompted them to write, repressed their sinfulness, and guided them in an organic way to the choice of the very words they wrote. Sometimes inspiration may have involved the mechanical dictation. Often it involved the refreshing of the memory (John 14:26), the selection of the proper materials (Luke 1:1-4), or the expression of their own experiences of sin and forgiveness (Ps. 32; 51).

V. Inspiration Applies only to the Autographa

Of what use is this doctrine, if inspiration applied only to the autographa (the original writings of the Biblical authors). The autographa have been lost, and thus we do not have this plenary, verbally inspired Bible. All that we have is a close approximation to it. Thus many, even orthodox men, suggest that the best that can be claimed for the Bible is that it is generally trustworthy.

Dr. Cornelius Van Til gives a good illustration contrasting these views:

> We may perhaps illustrate the difference between a general trustworthiness and the doctrine of Scripture which holds to the infallible inspiration of the autographa, though it recognizes the fact that the autographa are not in our possession, by thinking of a river that sometimes overflows its banks. Suppose we are seeking to cross such a river while the flood has gone so high as to cover the bridge. As far as the surface appearance is concerned, we cannot see whether there is a bridge. We have to drive in the water even while we are driving on the bridge. Yet, if there were no bridge, we should certainly not be able to cross that river. We can drive with comparative ease in water that is a few inches deep as long as we have a solid bottom under the water. What the idea of general trustworthiness without infallible inspiration does in effect is to say that it really makes no difference whether there is a solid bottom under the water, inasmuch as we have to drive through water in any case. But we have seen that man needs absolutely authoritative interpretation. Hence, if the autographa were not infallibly inspired, it would mean that at some point human interpretation would stand above

---

31. *Discussion of Theological Questions*, ed. George A. Blackburn (Richmond: Presbyterian Committee of Publication, 1905), pp. 295-296.

divine interpretation. It would mean that man were, after all, not certain that the facts and the interpretations given to the facts in Scripture are true.... We are actually crossing the river of life on this bridge of infallible interpretation even though it be covered (1) objectively, by the loss of the autographa, and (2) subjectively, by the inability of any sinner to interpret the truth perfectly to himself.[32]

VI. Preservation of the Original Text

As to the preservation of the original, Sir Frederick Kenyon says:
The number of manuscripts of the New Testament, of early translations from it, and of quotations from it in the oldest writers of the Church is so large, that it is practically certain that the true reading of every doubtful passage is preserved in some one or other of these ancient authorities. This can be said of no other ancient book in the world.[33]

The careful use of textual study enables us to reconstruct the original text on the order of 999 words out of every 1,000. In the New Testament there are only 375 variations that bear on the meaning of the passages, and even here there is no change of a doctrine, precept or fact.

Though the situation of the Old Testament differs from the New, there is reason for a similar confidence in it. Gleason Archer concludes his chapter on the textual criticism of the Old Testament with the following statement:
In conclusion we should accord to the Masoretes the highest praise for their meticulous care in preserving so sedulously all the consonantal text of the Sopherim which had been entrusted to them. They together with the Sopherim themselves gave the most diligent attention to accurate preservation of the Hebrew Scriptures that has ever been devoted to any ancient literature, secular or religious, in the history of human civilization.... Because of their faithfulness, we have today a form of the Hebrew text which in all essentials duplicates the recension which was considered authoritative in the days of Christ and the apostles, if not a century earlier. And this in turn, judging from Qumran evidence, goes back to an authoritative revision of the Old Testament text which was drawn up on the basis of the most reliable manuscripts available for collation from previous centuries. These bring us very close in all essentials to the original autographs themselves, and furnish us with an authentic record of God's revelation."[34]

Again Sir Frederick Kenyon says:
The Christian can take the whole Bible in his hand and say without fear or hesitation that he holds in it the true Word of God, handed down without essential loss from generation to generation, throughout the centuries.[35]

---

32. *An Introduction to Systematic Theology, op. cit.*, pp. 148-149.
33. *Our Bible and the Ancient Manuscripts*, (New York: Harper, 1940), p. 11.
34. *A Survey of Old Testament Introduction* (Chicago: Moody Press, 1964), pp. 66-67.
35. *Op. cit.*, p. 23.

Chapter VI The *Principium Cognoscendi Internum*

I. The Meaning of the *Principium Internum*

The very idea of revelation suggests that there will be a recipient of the truth revealed. Man must be capable, either by nature, or by a gracious work of renewal, of receiving the revelation. "All knowledge, and consequently also all science, requires a certain correspondence between subject and object."[1] Thus there must be a *principium cognoscendi internum* that corresponds to the *principium cognoscendi externum*. The absolute Idealist would not agree to this. He holds not to the correspondence between subject and object, but to the identity of the two.

The Neo-orthodox school in effect denies this also, for they hold that there is no revelation until it is brought into the heart by the event of faith. In other words, they deny the concept of propositional truth. Thus, the written Word cannot be the *principium externum*.

Reformed theology holds to the validity of both the subject and the object, and thus to both the *principium externum* and *internum*. In the history of thought a number of views of the nature of the *principium internum* have been held. We shall survey these different views briefly.

II. Non-Biblical Views

A. Human Understanding

From the earliest period of the Church's history there have been attempts to set forth proofs of the Christian faith that would appeal to the intellectual apprehension of man. This is found in the earliest Apologists. It is found most fully worked out in the Scholastics of the Middle Ages, with their natural theology. Man can demonstrate the reasonableness of Christianity by starting with natural theology, and then later moving by faith to supernatural theology. Protestantism was not immune to this type of approach, as is seen in the popularity of the apologetic method of Bishop Butler, and is seen today in what is known as "evidential" apologetics.

Berkhof criticizes this view as follows:

In actual practice, Apologetics has often moved in the wrong direction. (a) It has divorced itself from faith, assuming a place outside of, above, and preceding theology, and has thereby laid claim to an authority to which it is not entitled. (b) It has separated faith and knowledge in such a way as to cause religious truth to rest wholly or in part on purely intellectual grounds, something that is entirely contrary to the nature of that truth. (c) The result was that it cherished exaggerated expectations

---

1. Berkhof, *Introductory Volume to Systematic Theology* (Grand Rapids: William B. Eerdmans Publishing Company, 1932), p. 170.

with reference to its scientific labors, as if it could change the heart through the intellect, and by means of sound reasoning could cultivate piety.[2]

B. Rationalism

In the area of philosophical thought the system known as rationalism is characterized by the idea that the unaided natural reason of man is capable of dealing with all truth, including religious truth. Again there is no need for a *principium externum*. Human reason is seen as the source of all truth derived under this type of thinking.

C. Subjectivism

With Immanuel Kant a revolution took place in the area of epistemology. The autonomy of the subject of knowledge is asserted by Kant. He maintained that we can never know the *noumena* or essence of any thing. All that we can know is the *phenomena*, and here the mind has imposed its forms. In other words, the subject contributes to and produces the phenomenal world. All truth is thus subjectivized. Kant did not deny the reality of the objective world as Fichte did, but he did deny that we can know this world. Schleiermacher and Hegel represent a reaction to Fichte's skepticism. They both assert the reality of the objective. Hegel asserts an objective, logical Idealism as the nature of reality. He replaced being with becoming. The world is in the process of development. Religious truth is a part of this Absolute Ideal. The task of philosophy is to remove the husks of historical forms and to get back to the real idea. The truths of religion, including Christianity, are represented by Hegel as the necessary thought of reason, and not dependent on any outside authority such as the Scripture. If the mind comes to hold some thought to be necessary, a logical necessity, then it is real. All that is rational is real. That which forms a part of the coherent logical system is true. Ultimately, then, because we think something, it exists, and not the reverse. All reality and truth is subjectivized.

D. Devout Feeling or Intuition

Yet another view of the internal principle of theology is found in the school of Schleiermacher, who emphasized feeling or religious intuition as the organ by which religious truth is received. Schleiermacher and Hegel both were subjective in their starting points. Hegel, however, would make all theology into philosophy. Schleiermacher reversed this direction and would remove all philosophy from theology. He held that our feeling and not reason is the seat of our religious life. The subjective feelings become the source of religious life and of religious truth. Experience and the consequent feeling about it constitute the approach to truth. This has been called the religio-empirical method. Devout

---

2. *Ibid.*, p. 173.

feeling is the criterion of religious truth, and the test applied is the test of experience.[3]

This movement came in reaction to the rationalistic approach of both human understanding, and speculative reasoning. Instead of appealing to historical or rational proofs or even to the Bible for the basis of belief in religious truth, the experience of the individual is the standard. Schleiermacher analyzed the phenomena of the Christian religion as something that arises in the devout feelings of people in the Church. In other words, doctrines have been derived from religious or pious feelings, and not from the Bible.

Franz Hermann Reinhold von Frank (1827-1894) of the Erlangen school began with the subjective experience of regeneration and conversion. This is an experience of marked change and transformation in the moral life of the individual. From this experience Frank deduced the certainty of all the other important truths of Christianity. He distinguished three classes of truths: imminent, transcendent and transient. The imminent are those which are immediately involved in the experience of regeneration, namely, reality of sin, judgment, etc. The transcendent are those which must be assumed to explain the new condition, namely the reality of God, the Trinity, and the redemption wrought by Christ. The transient truths are the channels through which the transcendent truths pass to become immediately related to the Christian's life, such as, the Church, the means of grace. Frank's work developing this system is entitled, *The System of Christian Certainty*.

Though the system that Frank derived is basically orthodox, his methodology and starting point are not valid. First, he divorces regeneration and other Christian experiences from the objective revelation of the Bible. Second, since he cannot derive all of orthodox theology from his subjective starting point, he inconsistently appeals to the objective revelation. Third, this is a philosophical method, which does not fit with theology. Fourth, this method of attaining Christian certainty is not born out in actual Christian experience. It involves a modern gnosticism, which holds that certainty is not available to the simple Christian, but comes only to the one who can carry on the elaborate process of reasoning he proposed. Fifth, the basic weakness of this view is that it departs from the objective authority of the Bible, and the truly historical and objective character of the Gospel.

E. Moral Consciousness

When Kant destroyed the possibility of knowing the objective, *noumenal* world, he was faced with the serious question of how to account for religious truth. He resorted to what he called the moral imperative. We all have the sense of "oughtness." That is, we all have a moral consciousness, which is the real instrument for reaching religious truth. Ritschl replaced Kant's moral imperative with his idea of the "value judgment" as the criterion of religious truth. The emphasis here is neither on rational deduction, nor on emotional experience, but on an ethical sense. Does a certain truth satisfy the requirements of the conscience,

---

3. *Ibid.*, p. 176.

and thus answer our practical need? This method has been called the ethical-psychological or the ethical-practical method.

The idea of appealing not to reason, but to the moral consciousness of men did not begin with Kant. The apologists of old and Tertullian make this sort of appeal, as one of the corroborative evidences for Christianity. Pascal did the same. With Kant's critique of pure reason, he had to resort to practical reason as the only ground for reaching religious truth. He held that theoretical reason suggests the ideas of God, freedom and immortality to us. It is practical reason, however, that really testifies to a moral order over natural order. Thus, man must be free, there must be immortality, and there must be a final Judge of all.

Ritschl and Lipsius saw Christianity as a historical phenomenon, with religious and ethical power. It is this practical power of Christianity that is the proof of the truth of Christianity for Ritschl. For science theoretical proofs apply, but for religion the judgments of value are the only means of coming to truth. Here, as with Schleiermacher, is an attempt to divorce religion from philosophy.

To stress that Christianity is of religious value is perfectly valid, but to make value judgments the measure of the truth of Christianity is not proper. One cannot reach the certainty of truth through such a subjective means. Thus, this method also fails to give a proper *principium cognoscendi internum*.

III. Biblical View

A. Name of the *Principium Internum*

Having briefly surveyed erroneous views of the *principium cognoscendi internum*, we shall now turn to consideration of the Biblical concept of the proper *principium internum*. A careful examination of the Bible reveals that several different terms are used in connection with our coming to religious truth. For example, regeneration is named as a necessity for our seeing the kingdom (John 3:3; I Cor. 2:12-14); the pure in heart are promised the sight of God (Matt. 5:8); willingness to do his will brings knowledge of the truth (John 7:17); and the gift of the Spirit brings knowledge (I Cor. 2:13). Faith is the generally preferred term for several reasons. First, it is a most prominent concept in Scripture, as the means by which we come to proper relation to God. Second, it is a term that is descriptive of our conscious life. The *principium cognoscendi internum* has to do with the realm of conscious knowledge. Regeneration is a work of God that takes place in the subconscious.

It is the prerequisite to faith. The unregenerate cannot believe, and it is only as God gives the rebirth that a man can come to the response of faith in the Gospel. Thus, regeneration and faith are closely related. Along with this is the gift of the Holy Spirit, and his teaching work. The rebirth is the result of the Spirit's operation. Purity in heart and willingness to do the will of God are the consequences of this same work of the Holy Spirit. Thus, though a variety of terms is used in the Scripture to speak of the *principium internum*, an examination of them shows that they are really all closely interrelated.

B. The Nature of Faith

The term faith describes our conviction of the reality, the reliability, or truth of a certain event, object or person. We come to faith as an evaluation of judgment, which may be so spontaneous that we are not conscious of arriving at it. Such a judgment is made by us on the basis of evidence, or at least our conviction that there is sufficient evidence for our evaluation. This evidence may or may not be real, but once we are satisfied that it exists, we move to faith on the basis of it. Note that faith does not need to involve an element of uncertainty. Faith is psychologically nothing less than a conviction. It may be a conviction regarding a certainty. Faith then is not essentially different from knowledge as something less firm. It differs from experimental knowledge in the way in which the evidence is brought to the attention, and in the way in which we arrive at a particular conviction.

C. The Ground of *Fides Generalis*

The faith that involves the conviction of the truth of the Scripture in general is called *Fides Generalis* as distinguished from *Fides Specialis* or Saving Faith. It is *Fides Generalis* that concerns us here, for it is the instrument of receiving knowledge of God in general, and not the specific act of acceptance of Christ as Savior that is the *principium cognoscendi internum*. As we have suggested above, all faith involves a conviction based on evidence. The external ground of faith has already been examined in our study of the claim of Scripture for itself. But, the question must be asked, Can man recognize the truth and come to sound judgments with his unaided sinful reason? This is what those who hold to human understanding or the speculative reason of man as the *principium internum* hold. The Scripture itself, however, teaches that this is not true. "Now the natural man receiveth not the things of the Spirit of God: for they are foolishness unto him; and he cannot know them, because they are spiritually judged."[4] "Verily, verily, I say unto thee, Except a man be born anew, he cannot see the kingdom of God."[5]

This being the case, for sinful man to come to true knowledge of God there must be an operation of God's Spirit upon him. This particular work of the Spirit is called the internal testimony of the Holy Spirit. It is the witness of the Spirit to his own work, namely, to the Scripture. The Westminster Confession refers to this in the Chapter on Scripture, where it affirms that "our full persuasion and assurance of the infallible truth and divine authority thereof, is from the inward work of the Holy Spirit, bearing witness by and with the word in our hearts."[6]

This is confirmed by the Scripture in several groups of passages. First, there are those that teach that the Gospel is hidden from some and revealed to others. "At that season Jesus answered and said, I thank thee, O Father, Lord of heaven and earth, that thou didst hide these things from the wise and under-

---

4. I Cor. 2:14.
5. John 3:3.
6. *WCF*, I, 5.

standing and didst reveal them unto babes."[7] Again John 6:44-45 reads, "No man can come to me, except the Father that sent me draw him: and I will raise him up in the last day. It is written in the prophets, And they shall all be taught of God. Every one that hath heard from the Father, and hath learned, cometh unto me." Second, there are those which teach that we can confess Christ only by the help of the Holy Spirit. Matt. 16:17 says, "And Jesus answered and said unto him, Blessed art thou, Simon Bar-jonah: for flesh and blood hath not revealed it unto thee, but my Father who is in heaven." Again I Cor. 12:3 says, "Wherefore I make known unto you, that no man speaking in the Spirit of God saith, Jesus is anathema; and no man can say, Jesus is Lord, but in the Holy Spirit." A third group of passages teach that the natural man is unable to see the truth without the Spirit, and that the Spirit does enlighten. For example, I Cor. 2:14-16 says, "Now the natural man receiveth not the things of the Spirit of God: for they are foolishness unto him; and he cannot know them, because they are spiritually judged. But he that is spiritual judgeth all things, and he himself is judged of no man. For who hath known the mind of the Lord, that he should instruct him? But we have the mind of Christ." In Eph. 1:17-18 Paul prays, "That the God of our Lord Jesus Christ, the Father of glory, may give unto you a spirit of wisdom and revelation in the knowledge of him; having the eyes of your heart enlightened, that ye may know what is the hope of his calling, what the riches of the glory of his inheritance in the saints." Fourth, there are those passages which speak of the gift of wisdom that comes with the Spirit. Phil. 1:9-11 says, "And this I pray, that your love may abound yet more and more in knowledge and all discernment; so that ye may approve the things that are excellent; that ye may be sincere and void of offence unto the day of Christ; being filled with the fruits of righteousness, which are through Jesus Christ, unto the glory and praise of God." I John 2:20-27 reads:

> And ye have an anointing from the Holy One, and ye know all the things. 21. I have not written unto you because ye know not the truth, but because ye know it, and because no lie is of the truth. 22. Who is the liar but he that denieth that Jesus is the Christ? This is the antichrist, [even] he that denieth the Father and the Son. 23. Whosoever denieth the Son, the same hath not the Father: he that confesseth the Son hath the Father also. 24. As for you, let that abide in you which ye heard from the beginning. If that which ye heard from the beginning abide in you, ye also shall abide in the Son, and in the Father. 25. And this is the promise which he promised us, even the life eternal. 26. These things have I written unto you concerning them that would lead you astray. 27. And as for you, the anointing which ye received of him abideth in you, and ye need not that any one teach you; but as his anointing teacheth you concerning all things, and is true, and is no lie, and even as it taught you, ye abide in him.

Fifth, there are particular references to the way in which the Spirit accompanies the preached Word with his demonstrations of power. For example I Cor. 2:4-5 says, "And my speech and my preaching were not in persuasive words of wisdom, but in demonstration of the Spirit and of power: that your faith should not

---

7. Matt. 11:25

stand in the wisdom of men, but in the power of God." In I Thess. 1:5 Paul affirms, "How that our gospel came not unto you in word only, but also in power, and in the Holy Spirit, and in much assurance; even as ye know what manner of men we showed ourselves toward you for your sake." Without this accompanying work of the Spirit the preaching would be in vain, but with it men believe the truth proclaimed. A survey of these passages teaches that the reception of truth is an intellectual discrimination on the part of the individual. This comes with the demonstration of power through the renewing agency of the Holy Spirit. The faith that results is a confident assurance that the Word of God brought through man is not just the word of man, but is the very Word of God.

D. The Nature of this Internal Testimony of the Holy Spirit

The internal testimony of the Holy Spirit is the demonstration with power that the Spirit brings to bear upon the hearer of the Word. The Word of God is carried into our hearts with an irresistible conviction. This internal testimony includes the illumination of the Spirit. He is the One who enlightens our hearts to see the truth of the Word. Then, he confirms this conviction to our minds. He seals it to us, and continues to stir the conviction of the truthfulness of the Word. The object of all of this operation of the Spirit is the truth of the Word.

It should be observed in this connection, that the internal testimony of the Spirit is not itself new revelation. The revelation is complete in the Bible. This is rather the illumination by the Spirit. If this testimony is not itself revelation, then it follows that it is not the rule of faith. Again, the rule of faith is the Bible alone. Further, the internal testimony of the Spirit does not make the Bible authoritative. The Bible is authoritative because the Lord has given it as his Word. In other words, the same Spirit has authored the Bible, and it is his authorship that gives it authority. The internal testimony of the Spirit in the heart of man simply brings man to the recognition of the authority of Scripture. The internal testimony does not give us the doctrine of inspiration. This again we derive, as we have already done, from the Bible itself.

The internal testimony of the Spirit must itself be distinguished from our Christian experience. It gives us a Christian experience, but is not the experience itself. The experience is a consequence of the testimony of the Holy Spirit in our hearts.

We have already noted that the consequence of the internal testimony of the Holy Spirit is faith in the truth of the Bible--in the truth of the Gospel. This is distinguished from the saving faith or trust in Christ as personal Savior. Actually, one may be conscious of his saving faith before he is aware of the *Fides Generalis*, for the claims of the Gospel are directed to the calling of men to faith in Christ. *Fides Generalis* is implicitly involved in *Fides Specialis*, though it may not always be explicitly acknowledged. One believes in Christ ultimately because he comes to recognize the truth of the Bible's teaching concerning him.

We should distinguish between the internal **testimony** of the Holy Spirit which produces *Fides Generalis*, and the internal **witness** of the Holy Spirit, which is a joint witness with our spirits that we are the sons of God if we are Christ's (Rom. 8:16-17). The internal testimony is associated with regeneration and our introduction to the faith in the general truth of the Bible and its message.

The internal witness is a later operation of the Spirit, after he has come to dwell within our hearts, whereby he seals to us the conviction that we are joint heirs with Christ, because we are His adopted children.

DIVISION II THEOLOGY

Chapter VII The Knowability and Incomprehensibility of God

I. The Knowability of God

A. The Place of the Knowability of God in Theology

The Christian faith has always maintained that God is knowable and known by man. This is basic to any religion having to do with God. If he does not exist, or if he exists, but is unknowable to man, then there can be no such thing as religion, since by definition religion has to do with man's relations with God. The essence of the Biblical religion is that the God of Creation is known by his intelligent creatures.

Calvin opened his *Institutes* with a treatment of the "knowledge of God." In this Calvin differed from those who had gone before him. Most Protestant theologians since Calvin have begun with Scripture, or with the nature of God, thus following him in his starting point. John Frame comments on the place of the knowledge of God in Calvin, "For Calvin 'knowledge of God' was a 'foundational' concept, a concept by means of which he intended to bring all his other concepts into focus, a concept by which he sought to make all other concepts understood."[1] As Frame observes, Calvin was not just a theologian of the knowledge of God, but he saw this as one of the important perspectives by which the whole Biblical message may be summed up. This being the case, it is important to get a proper grasp of this subject.

B. Grounds for Belief that God is Knowable

1. God is represented in the Scripture as revealing himself. The very idea of revelation involves the concept that God discloses himself to his creatures. God does not reveal himself to himself. He knows himself exhaustively. Thus existence of revelation is itself a testimony that he makes himself known to man. This is particularly evident when the Biblical idea of revelation is studied, and it is found to be specifically addressed to man. In other words, it is to man in particular that the revelation is addressed, and not just to creation in general.

2. This is confirmed by the fact that man was made in the image of God (Gen. 1:26). It is this image and likeness of God that distinguishes man from all the rest of creation. Since God is a God of knowledge, we may properly assume that the image of God that man bears includes the element of knowledge. This is verified by the Scripture, for Col. 3:10 says: "And have put on the new man, that is being renewed unto knowledge after him that created him." Man

---

1. John M. Frame, *The Doctrine of the Knowledge of God* (Phillipsburg, NJ: Presbyterian and Reformed Publishing Company, 1987), p. 1.

had lost true knowledge in the fall. As originally created he had true knowledge as a part of the image of God that he bore. Knowledge to be valid must be knowledge of the truth, and God is the ultimate Truth. All the truth that exists in the universe has come from God, and apart from him there is no meaning to the universe. Thus any true knowledge of the universe involves knowledge of God. Man made in the image of God was made capable of knowledge of God. And, though man has fallen, and lost the truth, nevertheless he is redeemable, and can again be brought back to a true knowledge of God.

3. The Scripture affirms directly that men know God. In fact, the assertion is made that all men know him, not just the regenerate. Rom. 1:19-21 declares this:

> Because that which is known of God is manifest in them; for God manifested it unto them. For the invisible things of him since the creation of the world are clearly seen, being perceived through the things that are made, even his everlasting power and divinity; that they may be without excuse: because, that knowing God, they glorified him not as God, neither gave thanks; but became vain in their reasonings, and their senseless heart was darkened.

Here it is the unregenerate who are in view, and of whom it is said, "knowing God." It is not our purpose to enter into a discussion of the extent of this knowledge, but simply to note that knowledge of God is predicated concerning all men.

Frame again has some significant things to say of this knowledge. First, he indicates that the God of whom we are speaking is the God of the Bible. This God is revealed in both Testaments as "Lord."[2] In particular, God announced at critical points in redemptive history, "I am the Lord, I am he" (Is. 41:4; 43:10-13, 25; 44:6; 48:12 cf. 26:4-8; 46:3ff.; Deut. 32:39ff, 43; Ps. 135:13; Hos. 12:4-9; 13:4ff.; Mal. 3:6, which allude to Exod. 3:13-15).[3] Of importance in these passages is not only the references to "Lord", but also the emphasis on the verb "to be", which recalls the revelation of Exodus 3:14. It is striking to see how Jesus also uses this verb in identification of his own character and work (John 4:26; 8:24, 28, 58; 13:19; 18:5ff; cf. 6:48; 8:12; 9:5; 10:7, 14; 11:25; 12:46; 14:6; 15:1, 5).[4] Frame concludes, "To summarize those points: throughout redemptive history, God seeks to identify himself to men as Lord and to teach and demonstrate to them the meaning of that concept. 'God is Lord'--that is the message of the Old Testament; 'Jesus is Lord'--that is the message of the New."[5] This Lordship is covenantal--the relation of lord and servants--in nature. As such God is both transcendent--exalted above his people, and immanent--deeply involved with them. Having developed these thoughts, Frame asserts regarding Rom. 1:21:

> The 'agnostic' who says that he does not know if God exists is deceiving himself and may be seeking to deceive others. God's covenantal presence is with all his works, and therefore it is inescapable (Ps. 139).

---

2. Deut. 6:4ff; Rom. 10:9; I Cor. 12:3; Phil. 2:11. Miracles were performed that men might know that he is the Lord, eg. Ex. 7:5; 14:4, 18.
3. Frame, *op. cit.*, p. 11.
4. *Idem.*
5. *Ibid.*, p. 12.

Furthermore, all things are under God's control, and all knowledge, as we will see, is a recognition of divine norms for truth; it is a recognition of God's authority. Therefore in knowing anything we know God.[6]

The knowledge of the Christian is much more profound than that of the unbeliever. John 17:3 speaks of a much fuller knowledge of God, "And this is life eternal, that they might know thee the only true God, and Jesus Christ whom thou has sent." Such knowledge is posited only of believers. Here we have the express declaration of Christ that speaks of men knowing God. Such knowledge as is in view here is so full that it involves eternal life itself. Without our trying to plumb the depth of this statement, it is sufficient here to say that the Scripture does teach that man knows God. The knowledge here is far more than just a cognition about him, that he exists, that he is Ruler and Judge. It involves man in a personal relationship with God. (See also: Matt. 11:27; John 1: 14: I Cor. 2:9-15; 13:12; II Tim. 1:12; I Jn. 5:20.)

C. The Character of our Knowledge of God

Modern philosophy, particularly since Kant, has raised the question of whether it is possible to know God as he really is or not. According to Kant, we do not know things as they are in the *noumena*, but we know only the *phenomena*. Further, we contribute to the phenomenal realm, and thus cannot know the reality itself. Ritschl followed with his idea that postulates of faith are not theoretic judgments, or existence judgments, but value judgments. Thus our knowledge of God is said to be a subjective matter. We do not know God as he is, but only as he wills that we think of him.

Calvin uses this type of expression, "not as he is in himself, but as he is toward us "[7], and "For it does not so concern us what he is in himself, as what he wills to be to us."[8] Calvin is stressing the fact that we know God from his Word. He is not asserting that we do not know God, but rather that we do know him as he has revealed himself in his Word. Of course, it is true that we do not know God as he is to himself, that is, as he knows himself. He knows himself intuitively, and exhaustively. We know him only as he reveals himself to us. This is not to say that we do not really know God from his revelation. Calvin is asserting just this, that we do know him truly from his revelation but not exhaustively. It is not just the revelatory data that we know, but the Living God who confronts us in his Word.

The question that we must answer is whether the Bible gives warrant for saying we do not really know God. An examination of various passages will show that the Bible teaches that we do know God. For example, in Matthew 11:25-27, there is a contrast between the intuitive, immediate, all inclusive knowledge that the Son has of the Father, and the derivative knowledge that we have. The contrast is not one of different objects of our knowledge, but rather it is our kind of knowledge. Christ's is immediate, ours is derivative.

---

6. *Idem.*
7. *Institutes*, (I, x, 2).
8. *Ibid.*, (III, ii, 6).

At that time Jesus answered and said, I thank thee, O Father, Lord of heaven and earth, because thou hast hid these things from the wise and prudent, and hast revealed them unto babes. 26. Even so, Father: for so it seemed good in thy sight. 27. All things are delivered unto me of my Father: and no man knoweth the Son, but the Father; neither knoweth any man the Father, save the Son, and he to whomsoever the Son will reveal him.

Again in I John 5:20, we read, "And we know that the Son of God is come, and hath given us an understanding, that we may know him that is true, and we are in him that is true, even in his Son, Jesus Christ. This is the true God and eternal life." Here the word "true" is used to describe the God whom we know. He is the absolute Truth. To know him is to know final truth. There is nothing beyond him.

In this connection it should be observed that we speak of human knowledge as analogical. This is perfectly proper, when we use the term correctly. It should not be used to say that the object of our knowledge is an analogy of the Truth. Our knowledge is analogical, or after the likeness of the knowledge of God, but the object of our knowledge is not analogical. Our knowledge is analogical, but it is not an analogy of God that we know. We know the Living and True God.

II. The Incomprehensibility of God

A. The term "Incomprehensible"

The term "incomprehensible" comes directly from the Latin "*incomprehensibilis.*" This term has a dual meaning. On the one hand, it refers to that which is not able to be contained. This is applied in theology to the metaphysical realm. It describes the immensity of God. God is so great that the universe cannot contain him. "But will God indeed dwell on the earth? behold, the heaven and heaven of heavens cannot contain thee; how much less this house that I have built!"[9].

The second meaning of the Latin word refers to understanding, or the epistemological area. Here again the term "comprehend" can be divided into two meanings, apprehending, and comprehending fully. Generally speaking, the term "incomprehensible" is used by theologians to refer to the last meaning, namely, not able to understand exhaustively. It should be observed that this is not a term suggesting that God is unknowable. It rather suggests that there is a limit to our knowledge of him.

B. The Theological Idea of Incomprehensibility

We have seen that the Scripture teaches that we can and do know God truly. It also teaches that our knowledge is limited. He cannot be known

---

9. I Kings 8:27.

exhaustively or comprehensively by man. This is true from the very nature of our being finite creatures, whereas God is the infinite God. The finite can never fully comprehend the infinite. God's knowledge of himself and of all truth is exhaustive and comprehensive. Man, on the other hand, always knows only at a creaturely level. This is true, even when the object of our knowledge is not on the creature level. The Creator-creature distinction in knowledge shall always continue to exist.

This subject has received particular attention in recent times as is witnessed by the debate between Cornelius Van Til and Gordon H. Clark in the Orthodox Presbyterian Church during the 1940's. Though both of these men have passed on to glory, their disciples continue to debate the issues. John Frame has given the most incisive treatment that this author has seen of this matter. We shall try to summarize some of the salient points of his treatment, and would commend the reading of Frame to those who desire to get a fuller picture of this matter. Frame begins his treatment with this observation:

> Neither man was at his best in this discussion; each seriously misunderstood the other, as we will see. Both had valid concerns. Van Til wished to preserve the Creator-creature distinction in the realm of knowledge, and Clark wished to prevent any skeptical deductions from the doctrine of incomprehensibility, to insist that we really do know God on the basis of revelation.[10]

Van Til insisted that human knowledge of a fact was different from that of God. Man can only think God's thoughts after him. God knows exhaustively. Clark feared that this would lead to skepticism as to whether we know the truth or not. He insisted that the very nature of truth is identity with God's mind. Thus if man knows truth, then he must know as God knows. Frame concludes that to say God is incomprehensible is to mean that there is some discontinuity between our thoughts and God's thoughts of himself and of creation.

Frame seeks to assist us in understanding this doctrine by presenting a list of the discontinuities and continuities between our thoughts and God's. We shall give his lists in a somewhat paraphrased and abbreviated form:

Discontinuities
The ways in which divine and human thought differs.

1. God's thoughts are uncreated and eternal; man's are created and temporal.
2. God's thoughts determine what comes to pass, an expression of his Lordship. Man's thoughts do not determine what comes to pass.
3. God's thoughts are self-attesting-- simply true because he thinks them. Our thoughts are not self-attesting. They are not necessarily true.
4. God's thoughts always bring glory and honor to himself. Man's thoughts are blessed only by virtue of God's covenantal presence with us.

---

10. Frame, *op. cit.*, p. 21.

5. God's thoughts are the originals. Man's thoughts are at best only copies.
6. God knows everything exhaustively without any revelation. Man only knows by virtue of revelation.
7. God has not chosen to reveal all truth to us. We do not know all facts about God or about creation.
8. God knows without the use of organs of perception, or of reason. Man must use both.
9. God reveals truth to man by means of accommodation. Man does not know as God knows.
10. God's thoughts constitute a perfect wisdom. Man's thoughts are not perfectly organized. At times he is unable to relate some revealed truths to others coherently, and thus sees some things as "apparently contradictory."
11. Even what God has revealed is beyond our comprehension (cf. Judg. 13:18; Neh. 9:5; Ps. 139:6;147:5; Is. 9:6; 55:8ff.). The more we know, the more our sense of wonder.[11]

Continuities
The ways divine and human thought are alike.

1. Divine and human thought are bound to the same standard of truth-- the divine norm.
2. Divine and human thought may be about the same things or objects, and may affirm the same truths, while maintaining the discontinuities.
3. Both God and man may have true beliefs.
4. Just as God is omniscient, so man's knowledge has certain universal aspects. All things are potentially knowable by man, though man cannot know as God knows. Man can never know anything exhaustively.
5. God knows all things by knowing himself and his decrees. Man knows by receiving impressions from outside, which must enter our minds; if man is to know, he must know what is within his mind.
6. As God's knowledge is self-attesting, so human knowledge must involve norms that he adopts. The norms originate in God, and thus proclaim his authority. Man must choose the ones that are truly authoritative.
7. God's thoughts are ultimate creators. Human thought is also creative, in a secondary sense.[12]

Problem Areas
1. Do we have an "adequate" idea of God?
   Bavinck and Van Til say, "No." They seem to be referring to the classical theological usage, which implies more than our contemporary usage, which suggests that our knowledge of God is sufficient for our needs.

---
11. *Ibid.*, pp. 22-25.
12. *Ibid.*, pp. 25-29.

2. Do we know the essence of God?

Bavinck says, "Calvin deemed it vain speculation to attempt 'an examination of God's essence.' It is sufficient for us 'to become acquainted with his character and to know what is conformable to his nature'."[13] Frame points out that Van Til is right when he says that we know something of everything, including the essence of God, though we cannot comprehend it. "Thus Van Til teaches that with regard to knowledge of God's 'essence,' we are basically in the same position that we are in with regard to all of our other knowledge of God."[14] Frame suggests that the problem lies in our understanding of the meaning of essence. He gives some basic definitions, and then concludes that Van Til is right, though we need to be careful as we speculate regarding the nature of God.

3. Do we know "God in himself" or only "God in relation to us?"

Good theologians have shown confusion in answering this question. Bavinck, for example, makes affirmations to the effect that we do not know him as he is, and yet states that we deal with his Being as it exists. Again Frame considers the meaning of this phrase, and concludes that as we know the facts revealed in Scripture, they must be the revelation of reality and thus we must know him as he is.

Frame concludes this section with a clear statement of the Christian position in opposition to modern relativism. We shall quote this in its entirety:

> Some people have argued that because our knowledge of God comes through revelation and then through our senses, reason, and imagination, it cannot be a knowledge of God as he really is but only of how he appears to us. It is certainly true that we know God as he appears to us, but must we therefore assume that these appearances are false, that they do not tell us the truth? We would assume that only if we were to buy the Kantian presupposition that truth is always relativized when it enters our consciousness, that reality is forever hidden from us. But that is an unscriptural concept. In Scripture, reality (God in particular) is known, and our senses, reason, and imagination are not barriers to this knowledge; they do not necessarily distort it. Rather, our senses, reason, and imagination are themselves revelations of God--means that God uses to drive his truth home to us. God is Lord; he will not be shut out of his world.[15]

4. Does a piece of human language have the same "meaning" for God as for man?

Frame addresses the question of the meaning of "meaning." He suggests that it is best employed to designate that use of language that is authorized by God. Each piece of language has a multitude of uses, which we learn by degrees. Our knowing the meaning of a

---

13. Herman Bavinck, *The Doctrine of God* (Grand Rapids: William B. Eerdmans Publishing Co., 1951), p. 33.
14. *Ibid.*, p. 30.
15. *Ibid.*, p. 33.

sentence like 2 + 2 = 4 is something that we learn. In fact, we are learning more and more of the meaning of this sentence. God, on the other hand, does not have to learn the meaning of any sentence. He knows it exhaustively. "He can use our language better than any of us can."[16] Thus God's knowledge of the meaning of any sentence is more profound than ours, and is different from ours. On the other hand, it must be said that God also understands and knows our limited understanding of the meaning of any particular proposition. In this sense his knowledge and ours as to the meaning of any proposition can be said to be the same.

5. Is all language about God figurative or literal?

The question being asked here is whether our words must have different senses when talking about God. Our language refers to the finite, and when we are talking of God must it take on a different meaning from its natural use. Must it be used figuratively or analogically?

Among several points made by Frame is the following helpful statement:

> A Christian epistemology will reject the promise that human language necessarily refers primarily to finite reality, because this premise is based on what we have called a non-Christian view of transcendence--that God is not clearly revealed in creation. On a Christian basis, we must say that God made human language for his own purposes, the chief of which was to relate us to himself. Human language is (perhaps even chiefly, or 'primarily') a medium by which we can talk to one another about God.[17]

The result of such a Christian epistemology is that we can see that there are some words that speak directly of God, whereas others are used in a figurative sense. In this connection Frame introduces Van Til's idea that all of our knowledge is analogical, by which he means, we rethink God's thoughts after him. Such analogical thought may be either literal or figurative.

6. Does God's "thought-content" always differ from man's?

The term "thought-content" is itself ambiguous. This ambiguity is part of the cause of the misunderstandings and controversy between Van Til and Clark. If it is referring to the object of thought, then both God and man may think about the same object. If, on the other hand, it refers to all of the attributes of a particular object, then God's content is different from man's.[18]

7. Is there a "qualitative difference" between God's thoughts and ours?

The phrase "qualitative difference" is difficult to define, and thus Frame feels that it is better to avoid its use.

Frame summarizes his consideration of the incomprehensibility of God as follows:

---

16. *Ibid.*, p. 34.
17. *Ibid.*, p. 35.
18. For a fuller discussion see Frame, *op. cit.*, pp. 37-38.

The lordship of God must be recognized in the area of thought, as well as in all other aspects of human life. We must confess that God's thoughts are wholly sovereign and therefore sharply different from ours, which are the thoughts of servants. God's being, too, is quite beyond our comprehension, but we must not interpret God's incomprehensibility in such a way that we compromise the knowability of God or the involvement of God with us in the process of thinking and knowing. God is revealed, and we know him truly, but it is in that revelation and because of that revelation that we stand in wonder.[19]

C. Biblical Teaching

There are a number of Biblical passages that clearly assert this concept of the incomprehensibility of God: "Great is the Lord, and greatly to be praised; and his greatness is unsearchable"[20], "Great is our Lord and of great power: his understanding is infinite"[21]; "Such knowledge is too wonderful for me; it is high, I cannot attain unto it"[22]; "O the depth of the riches of the wisdom and knowledge of God; how unsearchable are his judgments, and his ways past finding out."[23]

D. Incomprehensibility as an Attribute of God

1. Incomprehensibility is not an essential attribute of God. That is, God is not incomprehensible to himself, and the Persons of the Godhead are not incomprehensible to one another. "The Spirit searcheth all things, yea, the deep things of God."[24] Incomprehensibility then is not an intrinsic attribute of God. It has reference only to the knowledge that the creature may have of God. It is out of the very nature of the Creator-creature relation that God is incomprehensible to his creatures. It is God's godhood or divinity that makes him incomprehensible to all finite creatures.

2. We must distinguish the incomprehensibility of God from our inability to know the universe exhaustively. Our finite understanding is not capable of a full and exhaustive understanding of all of the created universe. There is a difference between the incomprehensibility of God and that of the created universe. God is absolutely incomprehensible, whereas created reality is relatively incomprehensible. God's incomprehensibility is original or primary, that of the created universe is derived or secondary. Ultimately the incomprehensibility of the universe is derived from the fact that the God of all wisdom has created it all. It is therefore revelatory of the attributes of God. Thus the universe reflects the incomprehensibility of God in that it is also incomprehensible to man.

---

19. *Ibid.*, pp. 39-40.
20. Psalm 145:3.
21. Psalm 147:5.
22. Psalm 139:6.
23. Romans 11:33-36.
24. I Cor. 2:10.

3. The incomprehensibility of God is absolute. That is, God remains incomprehensible, even with our increased knowledge of him. He is eternally incomprehensible to the created mind. The Creator-creature distinction always exists. The more we know of him, the more we understand that he is incomprehensible. Paul exclaims on this, after he himself has received deep insight into the revelation of God concerning his eternal decrees, "O the depths of the riches of God both of the wisdom and knowledge of God. How unsearchable are his judgments, and his ways past tracing out!"[25]

4. The revelation of God is incomprehensible in the same sense that the created universe is incomprehensible. We must be careful not to assume that because he has not revealed all things to us that there are areas which he cannot reveal to us, for he has revealed unto us much respecting himself and his own internal relations. To assume that some areas are beyond the realm of revelation would be to assume that they were more ultimate than his essential being and Trinitarian relationships, which he has revealed. This would be blasphemous, for these are the most ultimate of truths. The incomprehensibility of revelation arises from the Creator-creature distinction.

> The incomprehensibility of God, therefore, lies at the basis of all proper thought respecting God. For the incomprehensibility of God is the correlate of his specific divinity. It is a correlate of his godhood. There is ineffable mystery in God's being, perfections, counsel, and will; and the recognition of this belongs to that reverence which is the soul of godliness. He dwells in light that is inaccessible, full of glory, and the clouds of darkness around about him, and his footsteps are not known. We cannot by searching find out God, the Almighty and Perfect, so that if this sense of mystery does not condition our thinking about God, it is because we are not governed by the profound apprehension of his majesty, an apprehension which is a reflection in us of his incomprehensibility and greatness.[26]

---

25. Rom. 11:33.
26. John Murray "Class Lectures in Systematic Theology" as recorded by a student.

Chapter VIII The Revelation of God in the Names of God[1]

Introduction

In this chapter we shall examine something of the revelation of God that can be discovered by a study of the names that are given God in the Bible.

I. Significance of the Names of God

The original meaning of the term *shem*[2] "name" is probably sign, or distinguishing mark. The Greek *onoma*[3] and the Latin *nomen* may be derived from *gno*[4], indicating that by which an object may be known. A name is thus an appellation by which a person or object may be known. In Biblical usage names are not just arbitrarily given, but are often actually descriptive of the persons named. For example, Adam named the animals in accord with their nature (Gen. 2:19-20). Frequently the Bible gives the meaning of the name, and the reason for its being assigned a person; e.g., Eve, Gen. 3:20; Cain, Gen 4:1; Seth, Gen. 4:25; Noah, Gen 5:29; Babel, Gen. 11:9; Ishmael, Gen. 16:11; Esau and Jacob, Gen. 5:29; Moses, Exod. 2:10; Jesus, Matt. 1:21; etc. On other occasions names were changed, or a surname was added to indicate a new function or relation; e.g. Abraham (Gen. 17:5); Sarah (Gen. 17:15); Israel (Gen. 32:28); Mara (Ruth 1:20); Peter (Mark 3:16); etc. Jesus received a name that is above every name following his Resurrection (Phil. 2:9; Heb. 1:4). In the New Jerusalem a new name is given to believers (Rev. 2:17; 3:12, 22:4).

The names of God are revelatory of him. This is especially evident when it is recognized that God has assigned the names by which he is called. Men do not give him his name, but God gives himself a name. The names by which he designates himself are, therefore, God's revelation of himself. He is actively and objectively making himself and his relations to the creation known. Since God is truth, all that he reveals is also true. Thus for God to call himself by a name, this must be a revelation of what he is. That is, "God is what he calls himself, and he calls himself what he is" (Bavinck). This is not to say that any one name is the description of his full essence. He has so many attributes, that many names may be used to speak of him. On the other hand, when God reveals himself by various names, so it is proper for man to refer to him by these designations.

---

1. The substance of this chapter by the author first appeared in *The Encyclopedia of Christianity* (Marshalltown, DE, 1972), Vol. IV, p. 356-366.
2. שֵׁם
3. ὄνομα
4. γνῶ This etymology is suggested by Bavinck in *The Doctrine of God*, op. cit., p.83.

II. Classification of the Names of God

In the history of dogmatics, various approaches have been taken in the discussion of the names and attributes. Some, such as Calvin, Hodge, Pieper, Barth, do not treat the names of God separately, but discuss particular names only as they throw light on the attributes of God. Mastricht divides the material between the names and the virtues of God. Brake distinguishes between names, essence, and attributes. Abraham Kuyper follows Mastricht in the twofold division, but under names, he treats both proper or appellative names, and also what he calls "*wezensnamen.*" Under the latter he discusses the concepts of Spirit, Love, Light and Life. Bavinck sought to deal with the nature of God under the following heads: *Nomina propria* or *appellativa, nomina essentialia,* and *nomina personalia.* Under the first the appellatives by which God is designated as an independent and personal Being, and by which he is addressed are treated. The second category include all of the various additional attributes of God. The Trinitarian names and personal properties are considered under the third category. It is with the first category only that this particular chapter deals.

III. Old Testament Names

A. *El* (אֵל); *Elohim* (אֱלֹהִים); *Eloah* (אֱלוֹהַּ) - God

The simplest name for God is the word *El*[5]. Its exact etymology is uncertain. There are several suggestions: 1. from *'el*[6] a preposition meaning "to" or "towards" thus indicating the One to whom the soul aspires; 2. from *ul*[7] "to be strong" or "to be in front"; 3. from *alah*[8] meaning "to be strong, powerful," a term often associated with the sacred tree; 4. from *alam*[9] meaning "to bind." Any of these derivations would suggest possible concepts for God, such as Mighty One, Leader, or Governor. Regardless of which of the suggestions is adopted, all carry with them the idea of the overwhelming majesty of God. It is of interest to observe that these are not terms that suggest any identification of God with any part of creation. Rather, the thought is of the Mighty One who is behind creation, a Power which man cannot master. This emphasis is seen in passages such as, Psalm 19:1 "The heavens declare the glory of God (*el*)"; and Nehemiah 9:32 "Now therefore, our God (*elohim*), the great, the mighty, and the terrible God (*el*)..."

This is a very common word for deity in the Hebrew. It is used in contrast to that which is human. "...thou art man (*adam*[10]) and not God (*el*)" Ezek. 28:2. The two terms are mutually exclusive. Hosea 11:9 says, "I am God (*el*) and not man (*ish*[11])..." Again in Numbers 23:19 we find the same contrast, and the absolute difference in ethical qualities spelled out. "God (*el*) is not a man

---

5. אֵל
6. אֶל
7. אוּל
8. אָלָה
9. אָלַם
10. אָדָם
11. אִישׁ

CHAPTER VIII THE NAMES OF GOD   109

(*ish*), that he should lie..." Hosea 11:9 also stressed the holiness of God in contrast to man.

It is such a general term to designate deity that it is used to refer to false gods, or even to idols (Gen. 35:2; Is. 44:10, 15; Ex. 34:14; Ps. 81:10). Since it is such a broad term, it is frequently associated with an epithet, such as, "the living God" (*el hay*[12]), "the eternal God," (*el olam*[13]), or "God Most High" (*el shaddai*[14]). The specific identification with Jehovah is made in passages such as Deuteronomy 5:9, "... for I Jehovah thy God (*elohim*) am a jealous God (*el*) ..." This is the general usage in prose literature, whereas it often stands alone in poetic writings.

Closely associated with *el* are *eloah*[15], another singular form, and the plural *elohim* which occurs far less frequently than the other two forms. The etymology of these words is just as uncertain as that of *el*. They are probably derived from the same root as *el*, and thus carry the meaning of the Mighty One.

The plural form *elohim* is the most commonly used of these names for God in the Old Testament. It occurs some 2,550 times. It is the first name for God that appears in Scripture. "In the beginning God (*elohim*) created the heavens and the earth" (Gen. 1:1). Though it is plural in form, it is generally treated as a singular noun when referring to the Living God. Various suggestions have been given to account for the use of the plural. Some have suggested that it is derived from a more primitive polytheism, but there is no suggestion of this in the Biblical representation of the Hebrew religion. Parallels with plural usage in Babylonian, pre-Israelite Palestine, and Egypt are cited as suggesting that the Hebrews simply adopted this form of expression from these peoples. Again, if we take seriously the Biblical presentation, this must be rejected. For, as we have said above, the names of God found in the Bible are God's own revelation of himself. If there is borrowing, it is more likely to have been from the true religion by the false, rather than the opposite. All the human race knew of the true God (*elohim*) as they came from the flood. It is not surprising that as sinful men began to corrupt the true religion there would be some similarities to the true in the false.

The significance of the plural form in the Hebrew usage seems to be that of a plural of majesty or of intensification. This is the God above all other gods. He is the God of all power and might. He is the God behind all of the creation (Gen. 1:1). When we realize, however, that the God who reveals himself in the Old Testament is the Triune God, it is not inconceivable to see in the plural a suggestion of that triune nature. This is not to say that the doctrine of the Trinity may be proved by the plural form. It is to say, on the other hand, that when the triune character of God is fully revealed in the New Testament, it is not contradictory to the revelation of the Old Testament. This plural usage prepares us for the fuller revelation of the Three Persons of the Godhead. This is especially true of passages that suggest inter-divine consultation, such as, Gen. 1:26, "And God said, Let us make man in our image, after our likeness..."

---

12. אֵל חַי
13. אֵל עוֹלָם
14. אֵל שַׁדַּי
15. אֱלוֹהַּ

This word, as in the case of *el*, is such a general designation for deity that it may be used of false gods as well. In such cases the plural has a polytheistic reference or, as in the case with Aaron and the golden calf, a clear borrowing from the true religion (Exod. 32:4, 8).

B. Jehovah or Yahweh (יְהוָה) — Lord

This is the second name of God used in the Scriptures. It first occurs in Genesis 2:4, where it is joined with *elohim*. It is the most frequently used name for God. It occurs some 6,823 times in the Old Testament.

It has been translated in various ways. The King James version translates it with the word LORD in capital letters. When it stands in conjunction with *adonai*[16] meaning "Lord", then the King James translators use GOD in capital letters for *yehowah*[17]. The American Standard Version (1901) uses Jehovah throughout, and thus avoids this problem. Many of the more modern writers use Yahweh. Justification for translation as LORD is found in the fact that the New Testament translates it by the term *kurios*[18] meaning "Lord." The question of proper pronunciation is one that cannot be settled, for the Jewish practice was not to pronounce it. In their reading of Scripture they substituted *Adonai* for it, or *Elohim*, when it was accompanied by *Adonai*. This not only occurred in the reading, but the four consonants of the tetragrammaton were pointed with the pointing for either *Adonai* or *Elohim*. The pointing of *Adonai* with the tetragrammaton gives rise to the pronunciation Jehovah. Yahweh has come as an attempt to reconstruct the original pronunciation, as it must have been derived from the verb "to be."

God Most High was used from the second chapter of Genesis onward. Abraham, in particular, refers to God by this name. As he returned from the battle with the kings, Melchizedek, priest of God Most High (*el elyon*[19]), came and blessed Abram saying, "Blessed be Abram of God Most High (*el elyon*)." Later, when the King of Sodom sought to reward Abram, he refused and said, "I have lifted up my hand unto Jehovah, God Most High (*yehowah el elyon*)..." (Gen. 14:19, 22). Here he acknowledges the God of Melchizedek, who is called the Most High, and the possessor of heaven and earth, to be his own God, whom he knows by the name Jehovah (*yehowah*). Abraham and Isaac after him built altars to Jehovah and called on his name (Gen. 12:8; 13:4; 26:25).

It is particularly in connection with the revelation given to Moses that we find the meaning of this name set forth. The passages in view are Exodus 3:6, 13-15; 6:2-3. Of special note are the words of verses 14-15, "And God said unto Moses, I am that I am (*ehyeh asher ehyeh*[20]); And he said, Thus shalt thou say unto the children of Israel, I AM (*'ehyeh*[21]) hath sent me unto you. And God said moreover unto Moses, Thus shalt thou say unto the children of Israel, Jehovah, the God of your fathers, the God of Isaac, and the God of Jacob, hath sent me

---

16. אֲדֹנָי
17. יְהוָה
18. κύριος
19. אֵל עֶלְיוֹן
20. אֶהְיֶה אֲשֶׁר אֶהְיֶה
21. אֶהְיֶה

CHAPTER VIII THE NAMES OF GOD

unto you: this is my name for ever, and this is my memorial unto all generations."

It is generally believed that the tetragrammaton is derived from *hayah*,[22] the verb "to be." This passage serves to confirm this view, as God used a form of the verb to describe himself. The phrase has been translated variously: I AM that I AM or I WILL BE that I WILL BE or I AM who I AM. Regardless of which is the best translation, it speaks of the aseity of God. God possesses being, eternity and immutability in contradiction to the absolute non-existence of other gods, and the derivative existence of created reality. God is , all else that exists becomes. This is one of the most profound statements that can be made about God. He is the same yesterday, today and forever. Of particular interest is the fact that this is not just an abstraction. It is a revelation of God in the concrete, for he goes on to identify himself as the God of Abraham, Isaac and Jacob. In other words, he is and continues to be the God of the Covenant. He will be faithful to the promises of the Covenant.

The passage in Exodus 6:2-3 raises a question of earlier usage of the name Jehovah; "and God spake unto Moses and said unto him, I am Jehovah: and I appeared unto Abraham and Isaac, and unto Jacob, as God Almighty; but by my name Jehovah I was not known to them." On the surface this sounds as though the name Jehovah had not been used at all before this. The fact is, however, this name had appeared 164 times in Genesis (14:22; 15:7; 24:3; 28:13, 16; 32:9, *et al.*). This has been used by the modern critical scholars as a basis for distinguishing between different documents in the book of Genesis. Such a view is destructive of the unity of the Scripture, and of the truthfulness of the Word. A study of the passage answers this view. It should be observed that the word "name" does not occur in connection with "God Almighty" (*el shaddai*), but the word "as". That is, it was in the character of, or nature of God Almighty that God had appeared to the patriarchs, but in the character that the name Jehovah implies he was not yet known. What had not yet been revealed was the significance of that name. This significance is even more than the idea that God IS. In Exodus 34, the character of Jehovah is revealed as redemptive. It was not sufficient that the name Jehovah be proclaimed to Moses but his character was also revealed: "Jehovah descended in the cloud, and stood with him there, and proclaimed the name of Jehovah. And Jehovah passed by before him, and proclaimed, Jehovah, Jehovah, a God merciful and gracious, slow to anger, and abundant in lovingkindness and truth; keeping lovingkindness for thousands, forgiving iniquity and transgression and sin; and that will by no means clear the guilty...for thou shalt worship no other God: for Jehovah whose name is Jealous, is a jealous God" (vs. 5-7a, 14). The redemptive significance of God's name Jehovah had not been known by the Patriarchs, but it was to be revealed to the enslaved Israelites, who were redeemed from Egypt, and saved by the mighty hand of Jehovah. With the event of the exodus, the usage of the name Jehovah jumped to 1,800 times in the rest of the Hexateuch, as compared with 125 times for Elohim. The Patriarchs, no doubt, knew the meaning of the name, but had not yet seen the salvation of the Lord. Thus Jacob exclaims in Genesis 49:18, "I have waited for thy salvation O Jehovah." What God was going to do through

---

22. הָיָה

Moses was to bring salvation to the enslaved Israel, and reveal his redemptive character. Thus this name as given to Moses was to encourage Israel's trust in the promises of redemption and deliverance.

Jehovah is the proper name *par excellence* of God in the Old Testament. God's nature in the highest sense of the word is revealed in this Name. It is the name by which he is to be distinguished as the God of Israel. It was sometimes referred to as "the Name" (*hashem*[23]). Blasphemy of the Name was punishable by death (Lev. 24:11, 16).

The high view of this name is taught by the Law (Exodus 15:3); the Prophets (Isaiah 42:8; Hosea 12:5); and the Psalms (83:18). It is never used of any other god. It does not occur in the Hebrew in the construct state, in the plural or with suffixes. There are modified forms of the name. One of the most common is *yah*[24] or *yahu*[25]. It occurs alone some 50 times in Scripture, as in the case of Exodus 15:2, "Jah is my glory and song." (See also Ps. 68:4; 89:8; 94:7, 12; 118:14; Isaiah 12:2; 26:4; 38:11.) It is a part of the exclamation "Hallelujah" or "Praise ye Jehovah" (Ps. 104:35; 105:45; 106:1, etc.). Hallelujah occurs some 25 times in the Psalms.

C. Adonay (אֲדֹנָי) — Lord

The name *adonay*[26] comes from the root *adan*[27] meaning master, ruler, owner, lord. The simpler form *adon*[28] may be used of human lordship. It may be used as an expression of veneration or respect. The slave speaks this way to the master (Gen. 13:12; Ex. 21:5). The wife may use it in speaking to her husband (Gen. 24:12). The form *adonay*[29] is used in connection with God. When so used it speaks of his sovereign power. The reference is to his nature, rather than lordship over land. His lordship over the whole earth is specifically indicated by the use of this word: "The mountains melted like wax at the presence of Jehovah (*yehowah*), At the presence of the Lord (*adonay*) of the whole earth" (Psalms 97:5). "Behold, the ark of the covenant of the Lord (*adonay*) of all the earth passeth over before you into the Jordan" (Joshua 3:11). (See also Micah 4:13; Zechariah 4:14, 6:5)

Isaiah introduced his vision of the Lord in the Temple with a reference to *adonay*. The seraphim sing praise to this same high and exalted God under the name *yehowah*. Isaiah then goes on to speak of having seen "the King, Jehovah of hosts" (*hamelech yehowah tsbaoth*[30]). In all of this passage the exalted glory of God is before us, and it is interesting to see the variety of names used to refer to him.

This word occurs some 340 times in the Old Testament. It was used by the Jews in reaching the Scriptures to substitute for *yehowah*. As a word suitable

---

23. וְהַשֵּׁם
24. יָהּ
25. יָהוּ
26. אֲדֹנָי
27. אָדַן
28. אָדוֹן
29. אֲדֹנָי
30. הַמֶּלֶךְ יְהוָה צְבָאוֹת

for personal communion between a man and wife, it is most appropriate for personal communication between men and God.

D. Compound Names with El (אֵל)

1. El Shaddai (אֵל שַׁדַּי) -- God Almighty

Not only are there individual words that serve as names for God, but there are a number of phrases by which he is designated. Most of these are phrases using either *el* or *yehowah*, with an additional word that is descriptive of some aspect of God's nature. These composite titles include the full wealth of the meaning of the terms *el* or *yehowah* plus the addition of the other word.

The name *el shaddai* is characteristic of the patriarchal period. It occurs in its full form (*el shaddai*) six times in the Pentateuch and once in Ezekiel (Gen. 17:1; 28:3; 25:11; 43:14; 48:3; Exodus 6:3; Ezek. 10:5). A shorter form, *shaddai* by itself appears in Job some 30 times, in Psalms 68:14; 91:1; in the prophets three time (Isaiah 13:6; Joel 1:15; Ezek. 1:24); and once in Ruth (1:21).

Several possible etymologies of *shaddai* have been suggested. First, it may be derived from the relative *she*[31] and *day*[32], meaning "sufficient." The meaning then would be he that is sufficient. Another suggestion is that it comes from *shadah*[33] meaning "breast," suggesting the idea of God as the source of our needs as a mother is to her babe. The sufficient God would be the translation of the phrase *el shaddai*. The more commonly accepted etymology is that it is derived from *shadad*[34] meaning "to overpower" or "to destroy." The idea is the God who is all-powerful. This is the way in which the phrase has been translated in the LXX, where it is rendered by *pantokrator*[35] "the almighty." The emphasis is on the power of God, not only as Creator, but as the Sovereign controller of the universe.

2. El Elyon (אֵל עֶלְיוֹן) -- Most High God

This is a name that is translated the "Most High God." *Elyon*[36] is derived from *alah*[37] meaning "to go up." It is used of persons and things to show their exaltation. Thus it is a reference to the Exalted God. This name is sometimes used in parallel with *el shaddai*. The two names occur in Psalms 91:1, "He that dwelleth in the secret place of the Most High (*elyon*) shall abide under the shadow of the Almighty (*shaddai*)." The word *elyon* occurs most frequently with *el* (Gen. 14:18; Psalm 78:35). It occurs with Jehovah (Psalms 7:17; 97:9), and with Elohim (Psalms 56:2; 78:56). It may also occur alone (Deut. 32:8; Ps. 18:13). In Genesis 14:19 the additional phrase describing him as "possessor of heaven and earth" is used. The basic concept of Deity, including his transcen-

---

31. שֶׁ
32. דַּי
33. שָׁדָה
34. שָׁדַד
35. παντοκράτωρ
36. עֶלְיוֹן
37. עָלָה

dent exaltation and also his sovereign rule and control of the universe, is conveyed here.

3. El Olam (אֵל עוֹלָם) — Everlasting God

This is a less common name for God. The word *olam*[38] is variously translated in the English, "everlasting," "evermore," "old," "old time," "ancient time," "beginning of the world." From this we see that no one word is adequate to translate it. The everlasting God is perhaps the best translation in connection with the name of God. It certainly speaks of his eternity, "...from everlasting to everlasting, thou art God" (Psalms 90:2b). Paul uses the same title in the New Testament, "Now to him that is able to establish you according to my gospel and the preaching of Jesus Christ...according to the commandment of the eternal God...(*tou aioniou theou*[39])." (Romans 16:25-26).

4. El roi (אֵל רֳאִי) — God that Sees

This title occurs only once in the Old Testament. It was spoken by Hagar after she had been found in the wilderness by the Angel of the Lord. Out of the gracious treatment by the Lord, Hagar "called the name of Jehovah that spake unto her, Thou art a God that seeth..." (Gen. 16:13). The thought here seems to be that God sees us wherever we may be. Nothing can be hid from him. (Psalm 139:1-2). "The eye of Jehovah is upon them that fear him, upon them that hope in his lovingkindness" (Psalms 33:18).

5. El gibbor (אֵל גִּבּוֹר) — Mighty God

This particular name occurs as such in Isaiah 9:6, where the reference is to the Messiah. The question has been raised as to whether it really is a title of divinity, since both *el* and *gibbor*[40] may be at times used of men. A study of the Old Testament usage of these two words reveals that wherever they are found in conjunction with each other they clearly refer to deity. First, there is a passage in Isaiah 10:21 in which the exact title is used, with a clear reference to deity. The other usages are: Deuteronomy 10:17; Nehemiah 9:32; Psalms 24:8; Jeremiah 32:18; and Zephaniah 3:17. In Deuteronomy, Nehemiah and Jeremiah the adjective *haggibor*[41] is used in close connection with *haggadol*[42] meaning "the great." It is the greatness and dread majesty of God that is being emphasized in these passages. The word *haggibor* is used elsewhere in clear reference to the Messiah: Psalms 45:4; 89:20. The thought is that of one who has power to accomplish his task. As a title for God and his Messiah this word speaks of his might and power. He is a man of war who conquers all his enemies.

---

38. עוֹלָם
39. τοῦ αἰωνίου θεοῦ
40. גִּבּוֹר
41. הַגִּבּוֹר
42. הַגָּדֹל

E. Compound names with Jehovah (יְהֹוָה)

1. Jehovah-tsabaoth (יְהֹוָה צְבָאוֹת) -- Jehovah of Hosts

There are other compound phrases in which the name Jehovah appears. Strictly speaking these are not names of God, but are phrases that express certain truths about him.

Just as in the case of names involving El and Elohim, so also with Jehovah, the full significance of the name "Jehovah" is implied in compound names using this title. One of the most important of these compounds is Jehovah-sabaoth (*yehowah tsabaoth*[43]), which is translated Jehovah or LORD of Hosts. This title occurs first in I Samuel 1:3. It is used most frequently in the prophets. It should be observed that this name is used only after the people have experienced defeat, or are threatened by defeat. Jeremiah used it some 88 times, and it occurs 14 times in Haggai, 55 in Zechariah and 25 in Malachi. It was a name of God that reminded Israel that God was sufficient and able to save, despite the failures of Israel.

The question has been raised about the exact meaning of the "hosts." Jacob referred to the angels of God by this term (Genesis 32:2). David also referred to angels under this name (Psalms 103:21; 148:2). The armies of Israel, as his servants were also designated by this term (I Sam. 17:45). In the sense that all of creation is his, and all the multitude of the hosts of creation serve him, they may all be included. In particular, the angels who serve him as ministering spirits to do his bidding wherever he sends them are most likely intended by the phrase. As a name suggesting the power of God, and given most frequently in times of need on the part of Israel, this is a most comforting name.

2. Jehovah-jireh (יְהֹוָה יִרְאֶה) — Jehovah Will Provide

After the Angel of the Lord had provided the ram to be offered in the stead of Isaac, Abraham called the name of that place Jehovah-jireh (*yehowah yir'eh*[44]), which means Jehovah provides. It is a very suggestive title, in that it speaks of the essential character of the Gospel, namely, that God provides the Savior for sinners (Gen. 23:14).

3. Jehovah-nissi (יְהֹוָה נִסִּי) — Jehovah is my Banner

Exodus 17:15 reads, "And Moses built an altar, and called the name of it Jehovah-nissi (*yehowah nissi*[45])." This was in celebration of the victory that the Lord had given to Israel over the Amalakites (Genesis 17:8-15). The word *nissi* means banner or standard. Though this is the only place where this title as such appears, Isaiah picks up the figure to encourage his readers with the coming of the Messiah. "And it shall come to pass in that day, that the root of Jesse, that standeth for an ensign of the peoples, unto him shall the nations seek; and his

---

43. יְהֹוָה צְבָאוֹת
44. יְהֹוָה יִרְאֶה
45. יְהֹוָה נִסִּי

resting place shall be glorious" (Is. 11:10). Weak though we may be, we are "more than conquerors" in Christ (Romans 8:37).

4. Jehovah-rapha (יְהוָה רָפָא) — Jehovah Your Healer

After he had healed the bitter waters in the wilderness, God announced to Israel that he is the God who heals. "If thou wilt diligently hearken to the voice of Jehovah thy God...I will put none of the diseases upon thee, which I have put upon the Egyptians: for I am Jehovah that healeth thee (*yehowah rophe'eka*[46])" (Exodus 15:26). The healing power of God was celebrated throughout the Old Testament (Ps. 30:2; 103:3; 107:20; 174:3: Isaiah 30:26: 57:19; Jeremiah 6:14; 8:11; 30:17; 17:14). One of the most prominent aspects of Jesus' ministry was that of healing (Matthew 12:15; 14:14).

5. Jehovah-shalom (יְהוָה שָׁלוֹם) — Jehovah is Peace

Gideon named that altar which he erected in Ophrah Jehovah-shalom (*yehowah shalom*[47]), which means, "Jehovah is peace" (Judges 6:24). Paul in Ephesians 2:14 speaks of Christ as our peace. It is only the Gospel of grace in Christ that can bring peace to the sinner, but that peace is a peace that passeth all understanding. It is a peace that can meet all adversity and tribulation. "The peace of God, which passeth all understanding, shall guard your hearts and your thoughts through Christ Jesus" (Phil. 4:7).

6. Jehovah-roi (יְהוָה רֹעִי) — Jehovah my Shepherd

David gave us the title for our Lord and his intimate relationship to his own, which is one of the favorite figures found in the Scripture. It is Jehovah-rohi (*yehowah roi*[48]), "The Lord is my Shepherd." The richness of this relation is seen in all the various phases of life coming under his gracious care. Again in Ezekiel 34:15 God claims to himself the prerogative of being the good shepherd, "I myself will be the shepherd of my sheep..." (John 10:11, 14). The tender care of God for his people, and even his sacrifice of himself is implied in this term, "the good shepherd layeth down his life for the sheep" (John 10:11).

7. Jehovah-tsidkenu (יְהוָה צִדְקֵנוּ) — Jehovah our Righteousness

Jeremiah gives us this name of God in a messianic passage. "Behold, the days come, saith Jehovah, that I will raise unto David a righteous Branch...and this is his name whereby he shall be called: Jehovah our righteousness (*yehowah tsidkenu*[49]) (23:5-6). This is to be the name of the Messiah. Paul picks up this thought in I Corinthians 1:30, "But of him are ye in Christ Jesus, who was made unto us wisdom from God, and righteousness and sanctification and redemp-

---
46. יְהוָה רָפָא
47. יְהוָה שָׁלוֹם
48. יְהוָה רֹעִי
49. יְהוָה צִדְקֵנוּ

tion." That God is righteous is the clear teaching of Scripture. This name goes further to say that he is our righteousness. That is, he is the provision for sinners to become righteous before God. This provision is made in the Gospel of Christ.

8. Jehovah-meqaddishkem (יְהוָה מְקַדִּשְׁכֶם) — Jehovah who Sanctifies You

This is a name closely related to *Jehovah-tsidkenu*. It is translated, "Jehovah who sanctifies you." It occurs in the Pentateuch in connection with various laws that God gave his people (Exodus 31:13; Leviticus 20:3; 21:8, 15, 23; 22:9, 32). The context of Leviticus 20:7-8 teaches that what God demands in sanctification, he provides. "Sanctify yourselves therefore, and be ye holy; for I am Jehovah your God. And ye shall keep my statutes, and do them: I am Jehovah who sanctifieth you." The New Testament throws the additional light on this name, in that it ascribes sanctification to each of the Persons of the Godhead. God the Father sanctifies (Jude 1); Christ "is made unto us . . . sanctification" (I Cor. 1:30); and we are sanctified through the Spirit (I Peter 1:2). We are responsible for our own sanctification, and yet as we seek it, it is the gracious gift of God to us.

9. Jehovah-shammah (יְהוָה שָׁמָּה) — Jehovah is There

This is the last name of God introduced in the Old Testament. It occurs in Ezekiel 48:35. It is actually used to describe the city that Ezekiel saw in his vision. "It shall be eighteen thousand reeds round about: and the name of the city from that day shall be, Jehovah is there (*yehowah shammah*[50]). It is the glory of the final consummate state that God shall be with his people. John repeated the same idea regarding the New Jerusalem. The glory of that city is that the Lord is there. "And I saw no temple therein: for the Lord God the Almighty, and the Lamb are the temple thereof. And the city hath no need of the sun, neither of the moon, to shine upon it: for the glory of God did lighten it, and the lamp thereof is the Lamb." (Revelation 21:22-23). This is the essence of the Covenant promise made of old to Abraham (Genesis 17:7), and which reaches its culmination in these visions of the future.

F. Compounds with Israel

God in his grace has condescended to be named as the God of Men. We find this with the patriarchs, as he is called the God of Abraham, of Isaac and of Jacob. Such titles are based on his gracious covenant relationship with these men, and with his people.

1. Jehovah the God of Israel (יְהוָה אֱלֹהִים יִשְׂרָאֵל)

This is a title that occurs in Deborah's song (Judges 5:3). The prophets continued to use it. It is combined in Psalm 59:5 with God of hosts (*elohim tse-*

---

50. יְהוָה שָׁמָּה

baoth[51]). "Even thou, O Jehovah God of hosts, the God of Israel... (*yehowah elohim tsebaoth elohe yisrael*[52])." The prophets make frequent use of this title (e.g. Isaiah 17:6; Zephaniah 2:9).

2. The Holy One of Israel (קְדוֹשׁ יִשְׂרָאֵל)

This was a favorite of Isaiah. It is found some 29 times in this book. It was also used by Jeremiah and the writers of the Psalms. It speaks of his holiness, and his covenant relation with Israel. This title is applied to the Messiah. "Thus saith Jehovah, your Redeemer, the Holy One of Israel (*qedosh yisra'el*[53])..." (Isaiah 43:14; 48:17). The New Testament applies the attribute to Christ in a way that is reminiscent of Isaiah's title (Acts 3:14; 4:30).

3. The Mighty One of Israel (אֲבִיר יִשְׂרָאֵל)

The word *abir*[54] meaning strong or mighty occurs in compounds either with Jacob or with Israel as a designation of God. The emphasis is on the Divine strength in behalf of the oppressed. Jacob first used it in Genesis 49:24. Other occurrences include Deuteronomy 32:11; Psalms 132:2, 5; Isaiah 1:24; 49:26; 60:16. Its use in connection with Jacob or Israel identifies God as the God who cares for and defends his people.

IV. New Testament Names

A. Theos (Θεός) — God

The most frequent name for God in the New Testament is *theos*[55]. It occurs over 1,000 times. Though this word in Greek concept was used to designate various idea, such as, the polytheistic gods, or with the impersonal, metaphysical forces and powers that bring order out of chaos, it still served the writers of the New Testament as a word to translate the Hebrew *El* and *Elohim*. As thus used in the New Testament it is a designation of essential Deity. It is applied to Christ as well as to the Father (John 20:28; Romans 9:5).

B. *Kurios* (Κύριος) - Lord

The next most common name for God in the New Testament is *Kurios*[56]. It is used to translate Jehovah (*yehowah*) and *'adonai*. It is found some 600 times in the New Testament. It is derived from a root meaning to be strong. It was used in Greek literature to designate one with legal power of disposal, without the same emphasis on arbitrariness as *despotes*[57]. It has been suggested that

---

51. אֱלֹהִים צְבָאוֹת
52. יהוה אֱלֹהִים צְבָאוֹת אֱלֹהֵי יִשְׂרָאֵל
53. קְדוֹשׁ יִשְׂרָאֵל
54. אֲבִיר
55. Θεός
56. Κύριος
57. δεσπότης

the use of *kurios* in the LXX to refer to the Lord is due to the emphasis on the legal or legitimate authority of God, and not just his power and lordship. Jesus gives an example of the usage of this term which carries the full idea of sovereign lordship and rule, "In that same hour he rejoiced in the Holy Spirit, and said I thank thee, O Father, Lord (*kurie*[58]) of heaven and earth, that thou didst hide these things from the wise and understanding, and didst reveal them unto babes: yea, Father; for so it was well pleasing in thy sight" (Luke 10:21 cf. Matt. 11:25).

This word, which thus carried the full weight of the Old Testament name *kurios*, was also applied to Jesus. Paul speaks of this in connection with his humiliation and subsequent exaltation, "Wherefore also God highly exalted him, and gave unto him the name which is above every name; that at the name of Jesus every knee should bow, of things in heaven and things on earth and things under the earth, and that every tongue should confess that Jesus Christ is Lord (*kurios Iesous Christos*[59]), to the glory of God the Father." The name to which Paul referred with the definite article is *kurios*. This is saying that Jesus is Jehovah. Peter had affirmed the same thing in Acts 2:36, "Let all the house of Israel therefore know assuredly, that God hath made him both Lord and Christ, this Jesus whom ye crucified." In Revelation John speaks of him as King of Kings and Lord of Lords (17:14; 19:16). No more exalted language is known to the human tongue to praise God.

C. *Despotes* (δεσπότης) - Lord

A second term used for Lord is *despotes*[60]. It is far less frequently used in the New Testament. It is used some 10 times for other than God, referring to the Lord of a house, etc. (II Tim. 2:21). The idea of ownership and thus of authority is conveyed by the word. It is used of God some five times (Luke 2:29; Acts 4:24; II Peter 2:1; Jude 3; Rev. 6:10). The passages in Peter and Jude are references to Jesus as Lord.

D. Father, Son and Holy Ghost

In the great commission as recorded by Matthew we find the unique expression of the singular word "name" referring to the three names of the three Persons of the Godhead. "Go ye therefore, and make disciples of all the nations, baptizing them into the name of the Father and of the Son and of the Holy Spirit" (28:19). This name of God was revealed only after the clear revelation of the triune character of God as seen in the Incarnation and the promised Spirit. It is a succinct statement of the doctrine of the Trinity. There is one name, one God, who exists in three Persons. More than that, this name reveals something of the relations the three Persons sustain to one another. The first is Father, the second is Son, and the third is Holy Spirit.

---

58. κύριε
59. κύριος Ἰησοῦς Χριστός
60. δεσπότης

E. Descriptive Names

The New Testament follows the Old in using various terms that are descriptive of God. Some of these are "Almighty" (*pantokrator*[61]). This word corresponds to the Old Testament *El shaddai* or *tsebaoth*. See II Cor. 6:18; Rev. 1:18; 11:17; 15:3; 16:7; 19:6; 21:22; 16:14; 19:15.

Most High (*hupsistos*[62]) is found in Luke 1:32, 35, 76, 2:14; Acts 7:48; Luke 6:35; 8:23; Acts 16:17; Heb. 7:1. It is equivalent to the Hebrew *El elyon*.

Jesus made frequent use of "Father" (*pater*[63]) as he addressed the First Person of the Trinity (Mt. 6:9; 11:25; John 17:25; II Cor. 6:18). We are taught to pray to "Our Father," and this is one of the most intimate of the names given to us. Paul speaks of the crying "Abba, Father" (Romans 8:15; Galatians 4:5). Though many take this expression as teaching the idea of a universal fatherhood of God, the context where this concept is taught indicates that it is used almost exclusively in the religious sense of those who are adopted children of God in Christ. To suggest that we may be children of God without Christ is to deny the real significance of this name as it is used in Scripture.

---

61. παντοκράτωρ
62. ὕψιστος
63. πάτηρ

Chapter IX The Being and Attributes of God

I. The Theistic Proofs

A. The Validity of Theistic Argument

One is struck by the fact that the Bible makes no attempt to prove the existence of God. He is presupposed as existing. The Bible simply opens with the assertion that in the beginning God created the heavens and the earth. Thereafter, the heavens and the earth will be pointers to the Maker, but no attempt is made to give a demonstrable proof of his existence.

In the history of human thought, however, men have sought to prove the existence of God in a logical and systematic way. Various approaches have been developed along this line. Before examining these "proofs", it seems appropriate first to consider their validity. Can we actually prove the existence of God in this way? If not, then is there any value in these theistic arguments?

We have seen earlier that God has not left himself without a witness. He reveals himself to us in the world around us, and in our own beings (Romans 1:20-21). All men, then, are confronted with the revelation of God, the evidence of his being and perfections. Since this is true, it is not improper for us to gather in a systematic fashion all of this evidence, and then to present this orderly evidence for all to see even more clearly his handiwork. Such a treatment of general revelation is similar to that which is used in systematizing of the data of special revelation. This may be called the theistic argument. It is the reasoned presentation of the testimony of general revelation. Such a presentation may well bring about conviction in the heart and mind of the viewer that God has made and does preserve his universe - that God does exist.

Of course, it may be objected that we cannot win men by argument. We cannot constrain faith through argumentation. This is perfectly true. Due to sin the heart of man is deceitful above all things and desperately wicked. It cannot, and will not acknowledge the truth of God unless it is operated upon by the gracious work of the Holy Spirit in regeneration. Though this is true, it does not invalidate the witness of God's general or special revelation. Thus, if the evidence is true, and the argument is properly presented, it is valid, regardless of the response that it receives.

It might be further objected that since men are depraved, and since the theistic argument cannot persuade, it is a waste of time to use it. In answer to this, it should be pointed out that it is our duty to seek to set forth to the best of our ability the glory of God. The orderly presentation of the witness of general revelation is thus God-honoring whether or not it elicits a response in man. The validity of an argument based on the truth is not measured by the response that sinful men give to it. The validity is measured by its adherence to the truth itself.

B. The Proper Method in Theistic Argument

The Christian cannot assume a "neutral" position. His thinking must always be conditioned by his knowledge that Christianity is true. He must read general revelation in the light of special revelation. Natural revelation does not contain any message of redemption. It has to do with the power, wisdom, goodness, righteousness, and divinity of God. Theistic argument, therefore, should never be abstracted from the Gospel message of special revelation.

The idea of a natural theology that stands independently from the special redemptive revelation of the Bible has been one of the errors into which men fall when they treat the theistic proofs abstractly, and not as a part of systematic theology.

C. The Use of Theistic Argument

1. For the Unbeliever

Theistic argument may be used to present to the non-Christian the evidence of God's glory that is to be seen in general revelation. It is designed to bring him under conviction of the truth that God exists, and that he is a creature of God, who has sinned and needs salvation. This conviction can only come with the working of God's Spirit in his heart, but it is the duty of the Christian to bear true witness to him, whether or not he will receive it. That witness may begin with any aspect of God's revelation, and should ultimately present the claims of Christ. The Christian sees the manifestation of God's glory everywhere, and thus he can begin to talk about God at any point. It is our duty to be instant, in season and out of season, to do the work of an evangelist.

2. For the Believer

Theistic argument can enrich the faith of the believer as he learns better to see the glory of God all around him. The whole earth is full of his glory, and theistic argument, which is the systematic presentation of this witness, should be used to assist us to praise him.

As we become increasingly aware of the presence of God in all the world around us, there will be an increasing sensitivity to the real essence of piety, namely, the pervasive sense of God's presence and majesty around us.

In addition to this, our awareness of God's presence becomes a source of great comfort for us. God is with us. This should encourage us in our witnessing for him. Wherever we go, God's self-witness has already been there. Thus our witness comes to complement what God has already begun, and he in turn, complements all we say in his general revelation addressed to the sinner.

D. The Theistic Arguments

Thornwell suggests that there is an ascending, progressive order for the theistic proofs, namely, the rational proofs from causality, from order, and from being, and then the moral arguments, and finally, the religious argument.

1. The Cosmological Argument

This argument is based on the idea that every effect must have a cause. An infinite succession of finite and changeable objects is a contradiction. There must have been a first cause for the universe. In another form, an infinite number of effects cannot be self-existent. Our minds demand some sufficient cause for the world. Thus we are forced to assume the existence of a self-existent first cause. This type of argument was posited by the Greeks, and continued to be used by the Schoolmen until the time of Kant. He maintained that the law of cause and effect is only in our minds.

The Bible gives warrant for this type of reasoning in that it teaches that the only explanation of the world is to be found in the creative work of God (Romans 1:19-20). The creation witnesses to the divinity and power of God. In other words, the Bible asserts that the universe does present us with evidence of the handiwork of God. This is not to endorse all of the rationalistic argumentation that has been presented in the history of thought along this line, but it is to say that there is in the created universe a revelation of God himself. In other words, on the basis of the presupposition of the existence of the Living God, we find that the universe serves as a witness to this presupposition.

2. The Teleological Argument

This argument may be stated in the syllogistic form: design supposes a designer. The world is seen to have design in it, and thus there must have been a mind behind it. Hodge states the argument:

> Such is the nature of design, that it of necessity implies an intelligent agent; and, therefore, wherever, or whenever we see evidence of design we are convinced that it is to be referred to the operation of mind. On this ground we are not only authorized, but compelled to apply the argument from design far beyond the limits of experience, and say: It is just as evident that the world had an intelligent creator, as that a book had an author.[1]

The validity of this argument lies in the fact that the universe does evidence the hand of the all-wise God. It displays order and design. Again, presupposing the Living God as creator, then this argument confirms that presupposition. It fails in being a demonstrable proof of an infinite Author of the universe. "It proves intelligence, but it does not prove that that intelligence may not be derived."[2]

3. The Ontological Argument

This argument is one that is derived from the *sensus deitatis* that all men possess. Anselm developed it thus: That which exists in reality is greater than

---

1. Hodge, *op.cit.*, Vol. I, p. 217.
2. Thornwell, *op.cit.*, Vol. I, p. 62.

that which exists only in the mind. We have an idea of an infinitely perfect being. Actual existence is one of the attributes of an infinitely perfect being. If God did not exist, we could not conceive of him, and since we can and do conceive of him, then he must actually exist. Descartes developed the argument thus: We are finite and yet we have the idea of an infinitely perfect Being. Since we only know the finite, then the idea of an infinite Being could not have originated with us. It must have come from God, whose Being then is a necessary assumption.

Though this argument is derived from the universal consciousness that all men have of God, it fails as a demonstrable proof because "we cannot pass from thought to existence, unless the thought begins with existence."[3] On the other hand, starting as we do with the presupposition of the existence of God, then this argument is valid as a witness to the truth of God.

4. The Moral Argument

Even after he had destroyed the rational theistic proofs, Kant still felt the impact of the moral imperative that we all have. From this he concluded that there must be a God, for our sense of "oughtness" must be in response to a moral God. Again, this is based in truth. We all do have the *sensus deitatis*, which involves the idea of moral responsibility. Paul says in Romans 1:32 that sinners know the judgment of God. Modern psychology has found all men to have a sense of guilt. This sense of guilt is there because man is guilty of sinning against God. Again, this argument is valid, when the Living God of the Bible is presupposed as existing, but it is not a demonstrable proof if one starts from some other presupposition.

5. The Religious Argument

The fact that religion is a universal phenomenon has been used as an argument for the existence of God. "If it is the nature of man to worship, there must be a being to be worshipped ..."[4] This is like the former arguments. It is a fact that man was created in the image of God for fellowship with God. Again, the validity of this argument must be admitted when the presupposition of the Christian God is accepted, but this is not so on the basis of other presuppositions.

We are not able to demonstrate by the theistic proofs that God exists, nor can reason reach out for him by means of syllogism. For whatever can be so demonstrated and proven, of necessity, belongs to the world of human understanding and experience, and therefore is not God.

> He that cometh unto God must believe that he is, and that he is a rewarder of them that diligently seek him. . . . One who would speak of the knowledge of God can not approach his object either with a question as to whether or not he is, or with an outright denial of his existence. Without faith it is impossible to find him. Nor is there need of

---
3. *Ibid.*, p. 65.
4. *Ibid.*, p. 71.

proof to convince man that God is, for he reveals himself and does not leave himself without witness in the consciousness of any man. And it is only as evidence of revelation that the so-called proofs for the existence of God have significance and value.[5]

II. The Being of God

A. The Uniqueness of His Being

When we treat the Being of God we are concerned with the simple fact that God IS. He IS in the most absolute and ultimate sense of existence. With him there is no becoming. He IS necessarily and eternally. He alone IS in this way. He did not begin to be. He always has been and IS. His existence is of himself. He is of himself existent and of himself sufficient. All other beings ultimately have their existence as the result of creation. They have become. Only God has not become, but has always been. This is what he asserted in Exodus 3:14, "I AM that I AM." It is from the verb "to be" that the tetragram ($YHWH$)[6] is derived. Whenever this name is used of God it refers to his eternal existence. There is no more ultimate truth about God than this, God IS. God is absolute, ultimate, independent and unoriginated Being. The Scripture asserts the uniqueness of his Being: "I am the first and the last; and beside me there is none else."[7] "Is there a God besides me? Yea there is no God; I know not any."[8] "I am the Lord and there is none else."[9] "For I am God and there is none else; I am God there is none like me."[10] This is a theme that is found repeatedly in the Scriptures. When we speak of the Being of God, therefore, we are speaking of someone who is unique in his Being. He alone is self-contained and self-sufficient.

B. The Being and Personality of God

In Exodus 3:14 God speaks of his Being in the most ultimate terms, "I AM." This teaches us that God is not merely an abstraction or an impersonal idea. God is personal. This ultimate proposition, I AM, reveals to us that God is the ultimate, absolute, self-conscious Being. This is the essence of personality, namely, a seat of self-consciousness. I AM asserts that God is Personal.

C. The Being and Essence of God

If there is any distinction between being and essence, it is that essence is more abstract, and being is more vital. Essence is derived from the Latin *esse* meaning "to be". In theology we may at times speak of the Godhood of God, when we are thinking of his essence. We should not think of being as an at-

---
5. Herman Hoeksema, *Reformed Dogmatics* (Grand Rapids: Reformed Free Publishing Association), p. 43.
6. יהוה
7. Isaiah 44:6.
8. Isaiah 44:8.
9. Isaiah 45:18.
10. Isaiah 46:9.

tribute that is added to the essence of God. The essence of God refers to what God is in respect to his Being.

As we try to formulate our idea of the essence or being of God, we are faced with the question of whether it is possible to define deity. Ordinarily a definition involves a comparison of the thing defined with other entities, or it is a delimiting of the object being defined. It is customary to place the object that is being defined in a class, and then to distinguish it from other objects in that class by its specific characteristics. Strictly speaking, God cannot be defined, for he is unique. He does not fit into a class with others, nor can he be compared with others. "To whom then will ye liken me, or shall I be equal? saith the Holy One."[11] "Any definition or description of God that fails to take into account this incomparability of God would thereby destroy the very idea of God. But what cannot be compared cannot be defined. Nor is it possible to find the *genus* of such a definition in God himself."[12] Attempts have been made to do the latter. That is, it has been suggested that there is a *genus*, such as, spirit or love or being or independence. As Hoeksema comments:

> But all these attempts, in as far as they purpose to offer a definition of the Most High, suffer shipwreck on the rock of God's simplicity. God is One. He is his virtues; and all his virtues, even though they are differentiated in his revelation to us, are one in him. ... To say that we can define God is to deny his very Godhead.[13]

To conclude that we cannot define God is not to say that we are unable to say anything about him. To suggest this would be to give ourselves over to agnosticism. We are not driven to this conclusion because God has graciously seen fit to reveal himself to us. On the basis of this revelation, we are able to speak about him, and to describe his nature.

> Without claiming to be able to give a logical and comprehensive definition of God's essence, we may rather clearly circumscribe our conception of God as it is based on revelation, so as to express who and what he is, both in himself and in relation to the world, and that too, in distinction from and in opposition to all such conceptions of God as are not based on revelation, and are therefore necessarily false.[14]

Thus, we must again turn to the Bible as the source of our knowledge of God. Since it is the infallible Word of God, its teachings must be true. Any description that we give of God, or for that matter of any doctrine, must always be subject to correction by the Word.

III. The Attributes of God

A. The Being or Essence of God and His Attributes

Before we begin to consider the various attributes of God, it is proper to see how the attributes are related to the Being of God. In the Middle Ages two different views were taken. First, there were those who maintained that the at-

---
11. Isaiah 40:25.
12. Hoeksema, *op. cit.*, p. 48.
13. *Idem.*
14. *Idem.*

tributes referred to distinct elements in the Being of God. This was the view known as Realism. The Nominalists, on the other hand, held that the attributes are merely the different ways in which we think about God. This has carried down into modern times. Schleiermacher, for example, held that the attributes of God were just different ways in which our feeling of dependence comes to expression in our consciousness. The question for us is, what is the proper Biblical understanding of this matter?

1. The Bible Does Not Present God as a Distinctionless Monad.

The Bible gives a revelation of an inexhaustible fullness of God. The attributes of God represent real distinctions and differentiations that are to be found in the fullness of God's Being.

2. If God Has Attributes, How Are They Related to His Being?

Are we to conceive of his essence or being as existing separate from the attributes, or is his being to be found described by his attributes? "God's Essence is pure perfection, simple goodness, and the implications of all possible perfections and virtues."[15]

The Bible suggests that this is the proper approach to the matter by the fact that there are several statements in which God is identified with a particular attribute. "God is a Spirit"[16]; "God is Light"[17]; "God is love"[18], "God is a consuming fire."[19] The first of these is in the metaphysical sphere, whereas the last three belong to the ethical realm. It is of significance that the same kind of predication is used of both areas. Though other attributes are not placed in the same sort of proposition in the Bible, nevertheless, these four give sufficient ground for identifying him with the sum of his attributes.

It remains the task of theology in harmony with Scripture to bestow equal honor upon each divine attribute. Now, Christian theologians have always been more or less conscious of this calling. On the whole, their teaching has been that God is simple, exalted above all composition, and that there is no real distinction between his being and his attributes. Every attribute is identical with God's being. He is what he has . . . Whatever God is he is completely and simultaneously. 'God has no properties but merely is essence, God's properties are really the same as his essence: they neither differ from his essence, nor do they differ materially from one another.'[20]

---

15. *Ibid.*, p. 59.
16. John 4:24.
17. I John 1:5.
18. I John 4:8, 16.
19. Hebrews 12:29.
20. Herman Bavinck, *The Doctrine of God*, translated, edited and outlined by William Hendriksen (Grand Rapids: Wm. B. Eerdmans Publishing Company, 1951), pp. 120-121.

Bavinck observes that this doctrine of the simplicity of God has preserved the Christian Church from a polytheism that would see a different god in each of the different attributes.

Gnosticism sought to account for the different attributes with the various emanations or aeons. God was defined as the Unknowable, from whom the various emanations came. Christian theology by identifying the attributes with the essence has avoided the philosophical error of seeking by subtraction to arrive at the essence as distinguished from the attributes. The result is an essence that is an empty abstraction without content or reality.[21]

On the other hand, when theology speaks of God as essence, it arrives at this concept not by subtraction or elimination but by the opposite process, namely by addition, i.e., by ascribing to God all creaturely perfections in an absolute sense and by viewing him as absolute reality, the sum-total of all essence, 'most pure and simple actuality.' The essence which theology ascribes to God is at once the richest, most complete, and most intensive essence and the most determined and concrete, the absolute, only, and simple essence.

The doctrine of the simplicity of God does not deny the reality of the distinction between attributes. Rather, since God is all that he has, he is thus a God of infinite fullness. "God's essence is infinitely rich; hence it cannot be seen at a glance."[22] Since we are finite, and he is Absolute Essence, it is necessary for us to receive our revelation of him by means of many names and attributes. No one name or attribute fully describes him, and so we need a multiplicity of names to speak of the One God. Each name gives us some knowledge of what he really is in his infinite fullness.

B. Classification of the Attributes of God

Various suggestions have been given as to the best way of classifying the attributes of God. We shall note some of these, and indicate the advantages and disadvantages of each.

1. Absolute and Relative Attributes

It has been suggested that the attributes of God should be divided between those which speak of his eternal nature as contrasted to those he sustained to creation. The attributes referring to the former were called absolute attributes. The latter were designated as relative attributes. Among the absolute attributes are eternity, infinity, immutability, immensity, spirituality, holiness, righteousness, and love. The relative attributes refer to his relation to creation, such as, omniscience, omnipresence, omnipotence, mercy, and grace.

One problem that arises from this type of classification is the question of just how we are to understand the relative attributes to be related to God. For, as we already noted, we cannot conceive of his Being without his attributes. These "relative" attributes seem to be present only after he has created. Are we to understand that God takes on new attributes after he creates? One suggestion of a

---

21. Based on Bavinck, *op. cit.*, pp. 123-124.
22. *Ibid.*, p. 131.

solution is to see the relative as the expression of the absolute attributes in relation to the creation. For example, immensity is one of the essential attributes of God, whereas this is expressed in the created universe by what we call omnipresence. So also with knowledge and omniscience, etc. As we try to deal with the proper terminology here, we must recognize that the real problem before us is that of the relation between eternity and time. Our difficulty in giving a satisfactory definition here lies in the inherent incomprehensibility that eternity holds for us as temporal creatures.

2. Attributes Derived by Elimination, Eminence, and Causality

A second suggestion for classifcation of the attributes is derived from a process of elimination. First, we exclude those limitations which we find in creation. These limitations are not ascribed to God. Second, we ascribe to God in a superlative way all of the virtues we find in the creation. Finally, the causality of all things is ascribed to God. Though the results of this procedure are valid, there is no guarantee that we shall discover all of the attributes of God. It is a scholastic approach to the matter, with the basic weakness of not starting with God, but with man.

3. Incommunicable and Communicable Attributes

One of the most commonly used divisions of the attributes is derived from the difference between those attributes which are exclusively God's, and those which are reflected in the creation. The former include such attributes as infinitude, eternity, immutability, immensity, omnipresence, omnipotence, and omniscience. None of these attributes can be ascribed to any creature. On the other hand, there are attributes which are reflected in the creature, which have been called communicable attributes. For example, man as created had knowledge, righteousness and holiness. Man had these characteristics because God is truth, righteousness and holiness. It may be questioned if God communicated his attributes to man. It is better to hold that man was made in the image of God, and not that God communicates his attributes to us. To speak of God's attributes as communicated suggests the idea that man actually participates in God's own attributes. The Creator-creature distinction prevents us from making this identity. This is not to deny at all the fact that creation displays the glory of God, or that man is made in the image of God, and as such displays attributes that are analogous to those found in his Maker.

4. Metaphysical and Ethical Attributes

Another proposal for classifying the attributes is to distinguish between those which speak of the metaphysical aspects of God's nature, such as, omnipresence, omniscience, and omnipotence, as contrasted with others which refer to his ethical nature. Among the latter are attributes such as, righteousness, holiness, love, goodness, mercy, and truth.

The chief problem with this division, however, comes from the Biblical propositions about God. On the one hand, the Bible speaks of God in the metaphysical term, "God is Spirit," but on the other hand, it uses ethical terms to describe his Being, "God is love," "God is light," "God is consuming fire." Thus, the Bible itself does not make the sharp distinction between the metaphysical and the ethical.

C. The Attributes Considered

From all of this, we must conclude that no entirely satisfactory division of the attributes has yet been devised. For our purposes, we shall follow the order found in the first paragraph of Chapter II of the Westminster Confession of Faith. This is the order suggested by Charles Hodge, Thornwell, and Beattie.

1. Essential Attributes

Essential attributes are those which pertain to the essence of God, and thus qualify all the other attributes. Note that this is the way in which the Westminster Shorter Catechism arranges the attributes. God is a Spirit, infinite, eternal, and unchangeable in all his other attributes and perfections.

a. Spirituality

(1) Incorporeality

To say, as the Scripture does, that God is Spirit, is to say for one thing, that he has no body. Indirectly, this is implied in the Second Commandment, which forbids us to make any graven image or likeness of him. God has no physical, measurable form. Hence, we are not to make any image of him, either physically, or in our imagination.

(2) Invisibility

The invisibility of God is declared in the Scripture: "No man hath seen God at any time"[23]; "Who only hath immortality, dwelling in the light which no man can approach unto; whom no man hath seen nor can see; to whom be honor and power everlasting."[24] This is not to deny that God has revealed himself in visible form, such as, the theophanies and the incarnation; and yet he in his essence is invisible. Paul in Romans 1:20 speaks of the invisible things of God as being revealed by the things that are made. That is, we come to an understanding of the Invisible God and some of his invisible attributes through our observation of his handiwork. His invisibility differs from that of creatures, such as, angels and the spirits of men. The creaturely spirits are not necessarily and absolutely invisible as God is. They have locality. They are not omnipresent, but have a specific locus. Thus, the angels appeared in various visible

---

23. John 1:18.
24. I Timothy 6:16. See also: Romans 1:20; Colossians 1:15; I Timothy 1:17.

forms. God's invisibility, on the other hand, is one of his essential attributes. We cannot see his immensity, spirituality, eternity, or infinity. To assume that he could become visible would be to go counter to one of his essential attributes, in the same way that it would be to suggest that he could be finite or temporal.

(3) Immortality

Not only does I Timothy 6:16 speak of the invisibility of God, it also says that he has immortality. Just as with the invisibility, immortality in God is higher than that which is found in the creatures. God has life in and of himself. This life is absolute and underived. It is eternal and indestructible. All other life has come by the decree of God, and continues only by the will of God. Creatures, thus, do not possess immortality intrinsically. Their immortality is one that is derived from God, and exists only by the Sovereign will and grace of God. God alone can say, as Jesus did, "I am the Life."[25] To see that spirituality involves the possession of life, leads us to the further conclusion that he is active. He has the power of self-motion and self-determination.

> The grounds of its action, in reference to God, are solely within himself. He is not moved or impelled from without: the springs of his energy are all within, in the fullness and depths of his own being. He never rests, never slumbers, never grows weary, never relaxes his activity. To live is his blessedness as well as his glory. Ceaseless action is the very essence of his nature.[26]

In seeing that God is eternally active, we must go further and say that his activity is of the highest order, namely, the activity of thought and will. "He is to himself an inexhaustible fountain of knowledge and action."[27] He does not act out of blind fate or principle, but he acts out of wisdom and knowledge. "He knows what he does, and does it because he knows it to be right and wise."[28] "It is in this Being of knowledge and liberty, this Being of pure spiritual life, that we recognize the God who made the heavens and the earth, and in whom we live and move and have our being, and who we are bound to worship with our whole souls."[29]

(4) Simplicity

From all of this we see that God is essentially One. That is, he has no parts. His nature is simple, and not composite. This grows out of his absolute spirituality.

---

25. John 14:6.
26. Thornwell, *op. cit.*, p. 183.
27. *Ibid.*, p. 184.
28. *Ibid.*, p. 185.
29. *Idem.*

(5) Self-consciousness or Personality

As we have already noted, God's activity in his spirituality involves thinking and willing. This, of course, involves a self-conscious Being. That is, he is personal.

He is absolute, self-existent Personality. Everywhere in Scripture he meets us as *the Ego*, in whom consciousness and Self-consciousness are absolutely one and identical."[30] Though his personality exists in the Triune subsistences of the Trinity, he never speaks to man as a plural subject. He speaks within himself as plural (Genesis 1:26), but "to us he reveals himself and speaks as the absolute."[31]

One of the implications of his being Personal is the fact that personal creatures may have communion with him. The spirituality of God, then, lies at the very root of all true religion, namely, the communion between God and creature. The spirituality of this communion implies that there should be no worship of God through idols or images. The impossibility of images representing God is seen from the fact that every image is itself a dead material entity, which by its nature cannot properly represent the Living Spirit. Further, as a mechanical, unmoving idol it cannot possibly represent the infinite, self-moved God. "A Spiritual God can only be worshipped in spirit and in truth. A free Personal God can only be worshipped with a free personal will."[32]

b. Immutability

From the idea that God is, we may derive the fact that he is unchangeable. When he says to Moses, "I AM that I AM" or "I Will Be what I Will Be," he is asserting that basic difference that exists between the Creator and the creature. The creature is constantly changing, becoming something new. God eternally IS. In him there is no shadow of turning.[33] "I am Jehovah, I change not; therefore ye sons of Jacob are not consumed."[34] "Of old hast thou laid the foundations of the earth: and the heavens are the work of thy hands. They shall perish, but thou shalt endure; Yea, all of them shall wax old like a garment: as a vesture shalt thou change them, and they shall be changed: But thou art the same and thy years shall have no end."[35]

Our problems with this concept arise from the representations in the Scripture of apparent change in God. He repents (Genesis 6:6; I Samuel 15:11; Amos 7:2, 6; Joel 2:13; Jonah 3:9; 4:2); he changes his purpose (Exodus 32:10-14; Jonah 3:10); he becomes angry (Numbers 11:1,10; Psalms 106:40; Zechariah 10:3); he turns away from his anger (Deuteronomy 13:17; II Chronicles 12:12; 30:8; Jeremiah 18:8.10; 26:3). With the creation of the world he sustains new relations to it. With the entrance of sin, the new relations of wrath and displeasure are displayed, whereas in the Gospel God reveals grace and mercy to the

---

30. Hoeksema, *op cit.*, p. 59.
31. *Ibid.*
32. Thornwell, *op cit.*, p. 188.
33. James 1:17.
34. Malachi 3:6.
35. Psalms 102:25-27; Hebrews 1:11-12.

sinner. Our best understanding of these apparent changes in God is that they are changes in relations, but are not changes in his nature or purposes. It may be shown that the same attribute of his nature, which on the one hand demands goodness be displayed to the good, demands wrath to be shown to the sinner, and in turn pours out mercy on the objects of his grace. It is because he is holy and good that he reveals all of these various relations to the world. Instead of suggesting change in him, these different relations actually reveal his unchanging character.

> Moreover, being immutable in his existence and essence, he is also unchangeable in his thoughts and will, in all his purposes and decrees: he is not a man that he should repent. He does not cast off his people, Romans 11:1. He perfects what he begins, Psalms 138:8; Philippians 1:6. Summing it up in one word: he, Jehovah, changes not, Malachi 3:6; with him there can be no variation, neither shadow that is cast by turning.[36]

c. Infinitude

This is a term that suggests the negative of being finite. "Infinitude is not a negative but a positive concept. Applied to God it does not indicate that he is not a distinct being, but it indicates that the limitations of finite creatures do not apply to him."[37] Bavinck goes on to speak of two different areas in which infinitude applies. "If we wish to convey the thought that God is exalted above the limitation of time, infinitude coincides with eternity; if we wish to indicate that God transcends the limitation of space, infinitude is the same as omnipresence."[38] Even here, however, we must avoid the error of applying the mathematical idea of infinitude as an endless expansion in either the time or space dimension. God is incorporeal, as we have already seen, and the attributes of expansion should not be ascribed to him.

(1) Eternity

As we come to the attribute of eternity we are confronted with a very deep and profound mystery. Our difficulty here lies in the fact that we who are finite, temporal creatures simply cannot think in terms of eternity. We are called upon to recognize God's eternity, and yet we are not able to comprehend its significance, because all of our categories are temporal. We can state some things that eternity is not, and thus guard against certain errors that men have made in defining it. First, eternity is not endless time.

> Deism, however, defines eternity as time extended infinitely in both directions; according to it the difference between eternity and time is quantitative, not qualitative; gradual, not essential, the distinction is ... merely that it excludes a beginning and an end; past, present, and future are terms that should be applied to God as well as to man.[39]

---

36. Bavinck, *op cit.*, p. 146.
37. *Ibid.*, p. 153.
38. *Ibid.*, p. 155.
39. *Ibid.*, p. 154.

As Bavinck goes on to point out, pantheism makes the mistake of confusing time and eternity. The Bible indicates that this sort of identification of time and eternity as an extension of time is not valid when it speaks of the "beginning" (Genesis 1:1; John 1:1). Beginning is a part of the temporal creation. Genesis tells us that God created in the beginning, thus starting time and history. John speaks of the fact that at the beginning, God already was. His Being was, therefore, not conditioned by the beginning. Time was a part of God's creative work. Time cannot be considered as existing outside of the creation. To think of God as existing in time would be to deny his eternity.

Second, we must say that eternity is distinguished from time in that it does not involve a succession of moments. Here we see again the significance of the title "I AM". God eternally is. His Being, knowledge, and will are eternally present. There is no history with God. Psalms 90:3 says, "Even from everlasting to everlasting, thou art God."[40] "He is without beginning and end, and also without succession of moments; he cannot be measured or counted in his duration." God's eternity should be conceived of as an eternal present. With him all is present. That he is not in any way conditioned by time is affirmed by both the Psalmist (90) and I Peter 3:8, "One day is with the Lord as a thousand years, and a thousand years as one day." Taken with the statement "I AM " this is an assertion that he inhabits eternity, and is not in any way conditioned by time, either in his being or thinking. The same is asserted in Revelation 1:4 when it speaks of God as "him who is and who was and who is to come." This is not speaking of succession of moments, but of the fact that he eternally was, is, and shall be the same. "Jesus Christ is the same yesterday, and today, yea and forever."[41]

Third, we must recognize that the eternity of God is to be distinguished from the eternal life of creatures. The everlastingness of the life of the elect is a created everlastingness, whereas God's eternity is an attribute of his Being. Our everlasting life is given to us, but his is inherently part of his nature.

Fourth, we should observe that though God is not conditioned by time, nevertheless he fills it with his all-pervasive presence. This is a part of his omnipresence. Time receives its meaning and reality from the creative hand of God, and from his presence in it. It is not, however, a mode of his eternal Being, or an aspect of eternity. It is a part of creation, as distinguished from eternity, which is one of God's attributes, a part of his nature.

> Time is the concomitant of created existence; it has no origin in itself; eternal time in the sense of time without beginning is inconceivable. God, the eternal, is the only, absolute cause of time. In and by itself, moreover, time is not able to exist or to endure: it is a continuous becoming, and must needs rest in an immutable essence. It is God, who by virtue of his everlasting power, bears the time, both in its entirety and in its separate moments. In every second the pulsation of his eternity is felt. God stands in a definite relation to time; with his eternity he fills time; also for him time is object; by virtue of his eternal consciousness he knows time in its entirety and in the succession of all its

---
40. *Ibid.*
41. Hebrews 13:8.

moments ... He never becomes *subject* to time, measure, number: he remains eternal, and inhabits eternity.[42]

He uses time for the display of his eternal thoughts and excellencies. He thus proves himself the "King of the ages" (I Timothy 1:17).

(2) Immensity

When we think of the infinitude of God in relation to space we use the term immensity. It means that he is above all of creation. He is not circumscribed or contained in space. "But will God indeed dwell on the earth? Behold, the heaven and heaven of heavens cannot contain thee; how much less this house that I have builded?"[43] "The Lord of heaven and earth, dwelleth not in temples made with hands."[44] Just as in the case of eternity there was a qualitative difference between it and time, there is a qualitative difference between God's immensity and space. God's immensity is uncreated, and space is created. Created space, therefore, cannot be the place of his residence.

He is essentially above space, so that the essential characteristics and laws of space do not apply to him at all. Essential to space are the attributes of distance (*locus extrinsecus*) between one point and another, one line and another, one body and another; and extension, dimension, the space occupied by the bodies themselves (*locus intrinsecus*); and, therefore, form and measurableness. These are not applicable to God. He is not contained in space: one cannot measure the distance from God to the world, or to any point in the world; nor does he occupy space: he has neither dimension nor form."[45]

From this we conclude that God is transcendent. That is, he is infinitely exalted above all of time and space. It should be remembered that all of the attributes relate to the whole Being of God. Thus, he is transcendent in all of his attributes. "His transcendence implies that he is essentially, i.e., with his whole Essence, above the world, and above all its moments and relations."[46]

(3) Omnipresence

Lest our idea of the transcendence of God lead us to think of God only in terms of the "Wholly Other One", we should recognize that the Bible also represents God as intimately related to the world of space that he has made. "He is not far from every one of us; For in him we live, and move, and have our being."[47] There are differences in the manner of his presence in different parts or times of the spatio-temporal world. Scripture teaches that though he created heaven, it has become his dwelling place (Deuteronomy 26:15; II Samuel 22:7; I Kings 8:32; Psalms 11:4; 33:13; 115:3,16; Isaiah 63:14; Matthew 5:34; 6:9; John 14:2; Ephesians 1:20; Hebrews 1:3; Revelation 4:1ff., etc.). He is said to descend from heaven to the earth (Genesis 11:5,7; 18:21; Exodus 3:8). He

---

42. Bavinck, *op. cit.*, p. 157.
43. I Kings 8:27.
44. Acts 17:24.
45. Hoeksema, *op cit.*, p. 75.
46. *Ibid.*, p. 56.
47. Acts 17:27-28.

walked in the Garden (Genesis 3:8). We have already seen the many occasions of his appearances in special ways to his people. He is said to have dwelt in a particular sense with his people Israel (Exodus 19:6; Deuteronomy 7:6; 14:2; 26:19; Jeremiah 11:4; Ezekiel 11:20; 37:27); in the Land of Canaan (Judges 11:24; I Samuel 26:19; II Samuel 14:16; II Kings 1:3,16; 5:17); in Jerusalem (Deuteronomy 12:11; 14:23; II Kings 21:7; I Chronicles 23:25; II Chronicles 6:6; Ezra 1:3; 5:16; 7:15; Psalms 135:21; Isaiah 24:23; Jeremiah 3:17; Joel 3:16; Matthew 5:34; Revelation 21:10); in the Tabernacle and later the Temple, which was called his house (Exodus 40:34,35; I Kings 8:10; 11:2; II Chronicles 5:14; Psalms 9:12; Isaiah 8:18; Matthew 23:21) and above the ark (I Samuel 4:4; II Samuel 6:2; II Kings 19:15; I Chronicles 13:6; Psalms 80:1; 99:1; Isaiah 37:16). In Christ the fullness of the Godhead bodily dwelt (Colossians 2:9). The Holy Spirit now dwells in the Church as his Temple (John 14:23; Romans 8:9,11; I Corinthians 3:16; 6:19; Ephesians 2:21; 3:17). In the consummation he will dwell with his people (I Corinthians 15:28; Revelation 21:3).

Omnipresence expresses the idea that God is present in all of space. We must avoid the error of pantheism of identifying God with space. He is in it, but he is not encompassed by it. He is in no way restricted by the limits of space. It is also incorrect to think of space as being within God, as though God were "the space in which the universe exists." Space is a mode of created existence. "But the relation of God to space is such that God, the Infinite, having the ground of his existence in himself, is present in every point of space *repletively*, and sustains space by means of his immensity."[48] As we have already observed, his presence with his creatures differs according to his own pleasure. As Bavinck puts it, "His immanence varies with the character of their essence; in some he dwells 'by means of his nature'; in others 'by means of his justice'; in others 'by means of his grace'; in others 'by means of his glory'. There is endless variety, in order that all may reveal God's glory."[49]

The infinitude of God, then, teaches us that he is both transcendent and immanent.

> He is the immeasurable One, transcendent above all space, the Wholly Other: and yet he is, not only with his power, but also essentially, in all creation, in every creature, and in every point of creation existing in space, and that too, with his whole infinite Being. He is the immanent One; and as the immanent One, he is transcendent ... The heaven of heavens cannot contain God; yet in him we live and move and have our being. He is the immense, the omnipresent, the immeasurable God, to Whom we may never ascribe limit or form.[50]

Bavinck quotes a very suggestive passage from Augustine that teaches us the implications of the mystery of his omnipresence for our own lives.

> Do not, therefore think that God is present in certain places: he is with thee such a one as thou shalt have been. What is that which thou shalt have been? Good, if thou shalt have been; and he will seem evil to thee, if thou shalt have been evil; but a Helper, if thou shalt have been good;

---

48. Bavinck, *op cit.*, p. 162.
49. *Ibid.*, p. 163.
50. Hoeksema, *op cit.*, p. 75.

an Avenger, if thou shalt have been evil. There thou hast a Judge in thy secret place. When thou dost wish to do something evil, thou retirest from the public into thy house where no enemy may see thee; from those places in thy house which are open and visible to the eyes of men thou removest thyself into thy chamber; even in thy chamber thou fearest some witness from another quarter; thou retirest into thy heart, there thou meditatest: he is more inward than thy heart. Whithersoever, therefore, thou shalt have fled, there he is. From thyself whither wilt thou flee? Wilt thou not follow thyself whithersoever thou shalt flee? But since there is One more inward even than thyself, there is no place whither thou mayest flee from God angry but to God reconciled. There is no place at all whither thou mayest flee. Wilt thou flee from him? Flee unto him.[51]

See Psalms 139 for the account of the Biblical writer who experienced just this.

2. Attributes That Are Chiefly Intellectual

a. Omniscience

The Bible presents God as knowing all things. "For the Lord is a God of knowledge, and with him actions are weighed."[52] Job asks, "Shall any man teach God knowledge?"[53] The Psalmist tells us, "He that teacheth man knowledge, shall he not know? The Lord knoweth the thoughts of man, that they are vanity."[54] Much of the Book of Proverbs speaks of the wisdom of God, for example: "By wisdom hath he founded the earth, and by understanding he established the heavens. The depths are broken up by his knowledge, and the clouds drop down the dew."[55] Isaiah says, "With whom took he counsel, and who instructed him ..."[56] The implication is that none could counsel him. "Hast thou not known, hast thou not heard? The everlasting God, Jehovah, the Creator of the ends of the earth, fainteth not, neither is weary: there is no searching of his understanding."[57] The Psalmist is amazed at the knowledge of God, "Thou searchest out my path and my lying down, and art acquainted with all my ways. For there is not a word in my tongue, But, lo, O Jehovah, thou knowest it altogether ... Such knowledge is too wonderful for me; It is high, I cannot attain unto it."[58] "How great are thy works, and thy thoughts are very deep."[59] "For my thoughts are not your thoughts, neither are your ways my ways, saith Jehovah. For as the heavens are higher than the earth, so are my ways higher than your ways, and my thoughts than your thoughts."[60] Paul exclaimed, "O the depth of the riches both of the wisdom and knowledge of God."[61] All things are viewed as under the

---

51. Bavinck, *op cit.*, pp. 163-164.
52. I Samuel 2:3.
53. Job 21:22.
54. Psalms 94:10-11.
55. Proverbs 3:19-20.
56. Isaiah 40:14.
57. Isaiah 40:28.
58. Psalms 139:3-6.
59. Psalms 92:5.
60. Isaiah 55:8-9.
61. Romans 11:33.

purview of his knowledge. "He that planted the ear, shall he not hear? He that formed the eye, shall he not see?"[62] His eyes are said to run to and fro throughout the earth (II Chronicles 16:9). Even the least significant thing comes within his knowledge (Matthew 6:8,32; 10:30). The most hidden objects, including the reins and heart (Jeremiah 11:20; 17:9-10; 20:12; Psalms 7:10; I Kings 8:39; Luke 16:15; Acts 1:24; Romans 8:27); thoughts and meditations (Psalms 139:2; Ezekiel 11:5; I Corinthians 3:20; I Thessalonians 2:4; Revelation 2:23). Wickedness and sin are known by him (Psalms 69:6; Jeremiah 16:17; 18:23; 32:19). He knows the future (Isaiah 41:22ff; 42:9; 43:9-12; 44:7; 46:10). He knoweth all things (I John 3:20).

Theologians have sought to distinguish between the knowledge God has of himself and that he has of the world. The first is called his natural knowledge, and the latter his free knowledge. God's natural knowledge of himself is a part of his essence. It is not communicable to the creatures. The free knowledge of God also comes out of his eternal thought. It includes all that is capable of realization. It is his knowledge of his preinterpretation of every fact that shall ever come to pass in his creation and providence. Thus, it is also eternal and a priori in nature, and does not depend on any vision of the events themselves.

> God is the creator of all things: all things have been thought before they were called into being. This world could not be known to us unless it existed, but it could not have existed unless it had been known of God.' he has the ground of his existence in himself, hence, his consciousness and knowledge cannot be dependent upon or determined by anything outside of himself . . . his knowledge is simple, undivided, immutable, eternal; he knows all things instantaneously, simultaneously, eternally; all things are eternally present in his mind.[63]

b. Wisdom

Along with omniscience God is said to be all-wise. The distinction between knowledge and wisdom is recognized in most languages. They are rooted in different capacities of the soul.

> The source of *knowledge* is study; of *wisdom*, discernment. *Knowledge* is discursive, *wisdom* intuitive. *Knowledge* is theoretical; *wisdom* practical, teleological; it makes knowledge subservient to an end. *Knowledge* is a matter of the mind apart from the will; *wisdom* is a matter of the mind made subservient to the will.[64]

God is said to have created the world in wisdom (Proverbs 8:22ff; John 1:1-3; I Corinthians 1:24; Colossians 1:15ff; Revelation 3:14). His ruling and governing of all things is according to wisdom (Hebrews 1:3). The plan of salvation is declared to be the wisdom of God (I Corinthians 1:24,30).

---

62. Psalms 94:9.
63. Bavinck, *op cit.*, pp 188-189.
64. *Ibid.*, p. 195.

c. Freedom

The freedom of God may be placed here as one of the intellectual attributes, for as Jesus taught, to know the truth is to make one free. God's full and comprehensive knowledge of all truth thus implies the most complete and absolute freedom for himself. This attribute may also be considered one of the essential attributes, for it refers to the fact that he is not dependent in any way upon any one outside of himself for his existence. In other words, the independence or *aseity* of God implies that God is of and in and through himself. The eternal ground and fountain of his Being is within himself. He was not caused in any way by any being outside of himself. He is, therefore, self-sufficient. From this independence we may deduce his Lordship and Sovereignty. He is called Lord (*adonai*[65]) in the Scripture. He is the Lord of Whom, and through Whom, and unto Whom are all things. This independence is true of God of his whole nature, and of all of his attributes. "In his essence he is the '*ehyeh 'asher 'ehyeh*." [66]

He has life in himself (John 5:26).

He is independent in his counsel, mind and will. And he is the Lord of heaven and earth, the absolute Lord, Who has within himself the power and the prerogative to rule all things according to the counsel and purpose of his own will (Ephesians 1:5,11).[67]

3. Attributes That Are Chiefly Moral

a. Holiness

The term "holiness" translates the Hebrew *qadosh*[68], which is from the root *qadash*[69]. The root meaning is to cut or to separate. The Greek *hagios*[70] carries the same meaning. As One who is separate from the world, holiness may be understood as referring to the transcendence and uniqueness of God. In other words, it is a reference to the majesty of God, to his deity, to that which distinguishes the Creator from the creature. This may be the import of such passages as these: "Holy, Holy, Holy is the Lord of hosts; the whole earth is full of his glory"[71]; "God alone is God, and there is none beside him."[72] "For thus saith the high and lofty One that inhabiteth eternity, whose name is Holy: I dwell in the high and holy place ..."[73]; "Who shall not fear thee, O Lord, and glorify thy name? For thou only art holy."[74]

A second idea involved in holiness is purity. This is found frequently in Scripture. "For I am the Lord your God: ye shall therefore sanctify yourselves, and ye shall be holy, for I am holy"[75]; "Ye shall be holy, for I the Lord your God

---
65. אֲדֹנָי
66. אֶהְיֶה אֲשֶׁר אֶהְיֶה, Hoeksema, *op cit.*, p. 69.
67. *Ibid.*
68. קָדוֹשׁ
69. קָדַשׁ
70. ἅγιος
71. Isaiah 6:1-5.
72. Isaiah 40:18.
73. Isaiah 57:15.
74. Revelation 15:4.
75. Leviticus 11:44.

am holy"[76]; "Sanctify yourselves therefore and be ye holy: for I am the Lord your God"[77]; "Thou art of purer eyes than to behold evil, and canst not look upon iniquity"[78]; "But as He which hath called you is holy, so be ye holy in all manner of conversation; because it is written, Be ye holy; for I am holy."[79] The idea of separation is still found in this usage, for God as holy is separate from all sin and impurity, from all that is inconsistent with his nature.

The two aspects of holiness complement each other. His majesty and purity go together. It is both his majesty and his purity that the Seraphim extoll about his throne in Isaiah 6. Hoeksema defines the holiness of God as:

... that wonder of the divine nature according to which God is absolute, infinite, eternal, and ultimate ethical perfection. Himself being the standard, motive, and purpose of all the activity of his personal nature, so that he is eternally consecrated to himself alone as the only Good.[80]

Dabney says:

Holiness, therefore, is to be regarded not as a distinct attribute, but as the resultant of all God's moral attributes together. And as his justice, goodness, and truth are all predicated of him as a Being of intellect and will, and would be wholly irrelevant to anything unintelligent and involuntary, so his holiness implies a reference to the same attributes. His moral attributes are the special crown; his intelligence and will are the brow that wears it. His holiness is the collective and consummate glory of his nature as an infinite, morally pure, active and intelligent Spirit.[81]

Again, Hoeksema draws some very pertinent implications from the Biblical concept of the holiness of God.

1. That holiness is primarily a divine attribute. God is holy: he is the Holy One in the absolute sense of the word.

2. That especially in his holiness God is GOD, the One that is of and by himself, and that is distinct from all creatures. The reason for this is that holiness denoted that he is the sole Good, the implication of all perfections, and that as such he seeks himself, is consecrated to himself, the absolutely Self-centered One.

3. That as the Holy One, he is also the absolute Sovereign. Being ultimate goodness in himself, and consecrated unto himself, he seeks himself and his glory also in all creation, and is its absolute Lord, with the sole prerogative to declare what is good and to impose his will upon every creature.

4. That especially the revelation of his holiness as divine holiness is his glory.

---

76. Leviticus 19:2.
77. Leviticus 20:7.
78. Habakkuk 1:13.
79. I Peter 1:15-16.
80. Hoeksema, *op cit.*, p. 100.
81. Robert L. Dabney, *Syllabus and Notes of the Course of Systematic Theology and Polemic Theology Taught in Union Theological Seminary* (Richmond: Presbyterian Committee of Publication, 1927), pp. 172-3.

b. Righteousness

Directly related to the holiness of God is righteousness. The Hebrew *tsaddiq*[83] from the root *tsadaq*[84] means "to be right or straight." The hiphil means "to make right," and piel and hiphil can both mean "to pronounce right." The Greek adjective *dikaios*[85] and related words refer to one who is just or righteous. "He is the Rock, his work is perfect: for all his ways are judgment: a God of truth and without iniquity, just and right is he."[86] "Righteous art thou, O Lord, when I plead with thee: yet let me talk with thee of thy judgments: ..."[87] "the Lord is righteous in all his ways, and holy in all his works."[88] "If ye know that he is righteous, ye know that every one that doeth righteousness is born of him."[89] Here we see that there can be the reflection of the righteousness of God in men, who are born of his Spirit. The righteousness of God is said to be declared in the Gospel of the Lord Jesus in Romans 3:24-26. Again Hoeksema defines the attribute of God's righteousness: "Righteousness in the absolute sense is according to his own infinite, perfect judgment in harmony with his holiness, or, the infinite ethical perfection of his Being."[90]

4. Attributes Chiefly Emotive

a. Love

In I John 4:8 God is specifically identified as love, "God is love." The essence of this love is described more fully in verse 10, "Here is love, not that we loved God, but that he loved us, and sent his Son to be the propitiation for our sins." John 3:16 also speaks of this love, "For God so loved the world that he gave his only begotten Son, that whosoever believeth in him should not perish, but have everlasting life."

There are two Hebrew words translated love. They are: *chashaq*[91] and *'ahab*[92]. The first of these has as it root meaning "to bind, to join together." Along with this is the idea of delight, and thus the meaning of the term is that of a bond of fellowship. This is the usage found in Deuteronomy 7:7, "The Lord did not set his love upon you, nor choose you, because ye were more in number than any people; for ye were the fewest of all people."

The second term refers to the action of love, rather than the essence of it. The root meaning of the word is "to breathe after, to long for, to desire strongly." This word is used in Deuteronomy 6:5, "And thou shalt love the Lord thy God with all thy heart, and with all thy mind, and with all thy soul, and with all thy

---

83. צדיק
84. צדק
85. δίκαιος
86. Deuteronomy 32:4.
87. Jeremiah 12:1.
88. Psalms 145:17.
89. I John 2:29.
90. *Op. cit.*, p. 130.
91. חשק
92. אהב

strength." God is to be the only object of our longing and desire. The Psalmist expresses this thought thus, "Whom have I in heaven but thee? and there is none upon earth that I desire besides thee."[93] The same is presented in Psalms 42 in the picture of the hart panting after the waterbrook. "As the hart panteth after the water brooks, so panteth my soul after thee, O God. My soul thirsteth for God, for the living God . . ."[94] All of these usages are of man's attitude toward God. The word is also used of God's attitude toward man. "And because he loved thy fathers, therefore, he chose their seed after them, and brought thee out in his sight with his mighty power out of Egypt"[95], " . . . in his love and in his pity he redeemed them; and he bare them, and carried them all the days of old."[96] From these two terms, which are translated by the one English word "love", we may conclude that there is a twofold usage in the Old Testament. It denotes the bond of fellowship of two parties for one another, and the longing or desire that two parties have for one another.

There are two terms in the New Testament also, namely, *agapao*[97] and *phileo*[98]. There is a clear difference of level between these two words. *Agapao* is the highest term for love, whereas, *phileo* refers to an affection on a human level. *Agapao* is the only one of these words that needs to be considered in connection with God. Colossians 3:14 identifies love as the "bond of perfectness." Hoeksema says:

> By 'bond of perfectness' I understand a bond or union that is characterized by perfection in the ethical sense of the word, such as, truth, righteousness, justice, etc. Love, then, according to this phrase, is a bond that can exist only in the sphere of moral perfection. There is no love in the sphere of darkness. They that love darkness cannot love one another in the true sense of the word.[99]

Hoeksema goes on to say:

> Love is profoundly ethical, and is a bond that unites the ethically perfect only ... Love is also the fulfillment of the law (Romans 13:10); and the love of God is the first and great commandment, while the love of the neighbor is like unto it. For this reason the Lord emphasizes that he that loves him does keep his commandments, while he that loves him not will not keep his sayings (John 14:23-24).[100]

An examination of I Corinthians 13 reveals this same ethical character of love. Love "rejoiceth not in unrighteousness, but rejoiceth in the truth."[101]

This being the case, we can understand something of the concept that "God is love" conveys. For one thing, God alone is absolute perfection. God loves himself with a complacent love. The object of his love is the absolute perfection and goodness of his own being. The love of God is perhaps more understandable when we remember that he exists in three persons. These three persons

---

93. Psalms 73:25.
94. Psalms 42:1-2.
95. Deuteronomy 4:37.
96. Isaiah 63:9b.
97. ἀγαπάω
98. φιλέω
99. Hoeksema, *op cit.*, p. 103.
100. *Ibid.*
101. I Corinthians 13:6.

contemplate one another within the Godhead in eternal love, as the perfect subject beholding and delighting in the perfect object. Hoeksema concludes with this definition:
> And, the love of God is the infinite and eternal bond of fellowship that is based upon the ethical perfection and holiness of the divine nature, and that subsists between the Three Persons of the Holy Trinity.[102]

It should be observed that love is emotive in character. B. B. Warfield said, "Enough for us that a God without love and emotional life, would be without all dignity that attaches to a personal spirit - whose very being is movement - and that is as much as to say no God at all."[103] There are two basic aspects of the love of God that we should note.

First, there is the love that is *ad intra*. This is the love of complacency of which we have already been speaking. It is the love that God has within his Being. It is a delight and satisfaction in his infinite perfection, and the mutual and reciprocal delights that the Three Persons of the Trinity sustain with One another (John 15:9; 17:24). Second, there is the love of God that is *ad extra*. This is the love that he shows toward that which is outside of himself, and distinct from his Being. This love may be complacent in character as he delights in his handiwork. "The glory of the Lord shall endure forever; the Lord shall rejoice in his works."[104] "And God saw everything that he had made, and behold, it was very good ..." (Genesis 1:31). On the other hand, man having fallen into sin is not deserving of the love of God, and yet he is said to love us. This, then, is called the love of benevolence. It is his sovereign good pleasure to move in a saving way, even toward sinful, hell-deserving creatures. This is the love referred to in I John 4:9-10, "This is love, not that we loved God, but that he loved us and sent his Son to be a propitiation for our sins." This love is not essential to his nature, but is the consequence of his sovereign will, the free exercise of his unsearchable riches in grace.

b. Gracious, Merciful and Long-suffering

These three terms are grouped together in describing God's character in several places in Scripture, and we shall consider them together.
> And Jehovah descended in the cloud, and stood with him there, and proclaimed the name of Jehovah. And Jehovah passed by before him, and proclaimed, Jehovah, Jehovah, a God merciful and gracious, slow to anger, and abundant in lovingkindness and truth, keeping lovingkindness for thousands, forgiving iniquity and transgression and sin. And that will by no means clear [the guilty], visiting the iniquity of the fathers upon the children, and upon the children's children, upon the third and upon the fourth generation.[105]

"But thou, O Lord, art a God merciful and gracious, Slow to anger, and abundant in lovingkindness and truth."[106]

---

102. Hoeksema, *op. cit.*, p. 107.
103. *The Saviour of the World* (New York: Hodder and Stoughton, 1914), p. 117.
104. Psalms 104:31.
105. Exodus 34:5-7.
106. Psalm 86:15.

"Jehovah is merciful and gracious, Slow to anger, and abundant in lovingkindness."[107]
"Gracious is Jehovah, and righteous. Yea, our God is merciful."[108]

These closely related attributes are expressions of the goodness of God as manifested to his people, especially as sinners. Grace is a term that is used to speak of the goodness displayed to those who deserve nothing but evil. The word grace is used of favor that one finds with another. "Ascribed to God, however, its object is never creation in general or heathendom, but only his people."[109] It was granted to Noah (Gen. 6:8); to Moses (Exod. 33:12, 17, 34:9); to Job (Job 8:5; 9:15); to Daniel (Daniel 1:9); to the lowly and those in misery (Prov. 3:34; Dan. 4:27), especially to Israel as a people.

The keynote of history and law, of the psalms and of the prophets is always: 'Not unto us O Jehovah, not unto us, but unto thy name give glory,' Ps. 115:1. He does all things for his name's sake . . . Hence, again and again God's grace is extolled and magnified, Ex. 34:6, II Chron. 30:9, Neh. 9:17, Ps. 86:15, 103:8, 111:4, Jon. 4:2, Joel 2:13, Zech. 12:10. In the N.T. grace becomes even deeper and richer in content. . . . Ascribed to God *grace is his voluntary, unrestrained, unmerited favor toward guilty* sinners, granting them justification and life instead of the penalty of death, which they deserved. As such it is a virtue and attribute of God, Rom. 5:15, I Pet. 5:10, which is made manifest in sending Christ, who is full of grace, John 1:14 ff., I Pet. 1:13, and in the bestowment of all manner of spiritual and natural blessings, all of which are the gifts of grace . . .[110]

c. The Wrath of God

As we consider the "emotive" attributes of God, we must also look at the retributive justice of God, expressed in his wrath. The writer to the Hebrews described God thus: "For our God is a consuming fire."[111] This is an expression of God's holy righteousness against sin. God does not hold the guilty innocent (Exod. 20:7; Nah. 1:3). His judgment is represented as impartial.

Hear now my reasoning, And hearken to the pleadings of my lips. Will ye speak unrighteously for God, And talk deceitfully for him? Will ye show partiality to him? Will ye contend for God? Is it good that he should search you out? Or as one deceiveth a man, will ye deceive him? He will surely reprove you, If ye do secretly show partiality. Shall not his majesty make you afraid, And his dread fall upon you? Your memorable sayings are proverbs of ashes, Your defences are defences of clay.[112]

The punishment of the wicked is often ascribed to God's righteousness.

---

107. Psalm 103:8.
108. Psalm 116:5.
109. Bavinck, *The Doctrine of God, op. cit.*, p. 207.
110. *Ibid.*, p. 208.
111. Heb. 12:29.
112. Job. 13:6-12.

CHAPTER IX BEING AND ATTRIBUTES OF GOD

Thou hast rebuked the nations, thou hast destroyed the wicked. Thou hast blotted out their name for ever and ever. The enemy are come to an end, they are desolate for ever. And the cities which thou hast overthrown, the very remembrance of them is perished. But Jehovah sitteth [as king] for ever. He hath prepared his throne for judgment. And he will judge the world in righteousness, he will minister judgment to the peoples in uprightness. Jehovah also will be a high tower for the oppressed, A high tower in times of trouble.[113]

Which is a manifest token of the righteous judgment of God; to the end that ye may be counted worthy of the kingdom of God, for which ye also suffer: if so be that it is a righteous thing with God to recompense affliction to them that afflict you, and to you that are afflicted rest with us, at the revelation of the Lord Jesus from heaven with the angels of his power in flaming fire, rendering vengeance to them that know not God, and to them that obey not the gospel of our Lord Jesus: who shall suffer punishment, even eternal destruction from the face of the Lord and from the glory of his might, when he shall come to be glorified in his saints, and to be marvelled at in all them that believed (because our testimony unto you was believed) in that day.[114]

The Bible speaks of the wrath of God. The Hebrew uses *aph*[115] and *qetseph*[116] usually translated by "wrath" or "anger" and *chemah*[117] generally translated by "fury", while the New Testament uses *thumos*[118] and *orge*[119] translated by "wrath." Wrath is thus indicated by words which are based on roots meaning to burn, and thus designate a strong emotion of wrath. "For a fire is kindled in mine anger, And burneth unto the lowest Sheol, And devoureth the earth with its increase, And setteth on fire the foundations of the mountains."[120]

Behold, the day of Jehovah cometh, cruel, with wrath and fierce anger. To make the land a desolation, and to destroy the sinners thereof out of it. For the stars of heaven and the constellations thereof shall not give their light. The sun shall be darkened in its going forth, and the moon shall not cause its light to shine. And I will punish the world for their evil, and the wicked for their iniquity. And I will cause the arrogancy of the proud to cease, and will lay low the haughtiness of the terrible. I will make a man more rare than fine gold, even a man than the pure gold of Ophir. Therefore I will make the heavens to tremble, and the earth shall be shaken out of its place, in the wrath of Jehovah of hosts, and in the day of his fierce anger.[121]

The same attribute of holiness that is disclosed in his gracious and merciful goodness displayed to his own, is manifested in wrath and anger against his

---

113. Ps. 9:5-9.
114. II Thess. 1:5-10.
115. אַף
116. קֶצֶף
117. חֵמָה
118. θυμός
119. ὀργή
120. Deut. 32:22.
121. Isaiah 13:9-13.

enemies. The wrath and judgment of God are always expressed in accord with his holiness, and for his own glory.

Chapter X The Doctrine of the Trinity

I. Terminology

A. Trinity

The term "trinity" is not itself a Scriptural term. It is not found in the Bible. It is a term that was first used by Tertullian to describe the Biblical doctrine of the three persons of the Godhead. For theology, it is not essential to limit oneself to the actual language of Scripture, so long as the doctrines of Scripture are strictly maintained.

B. Person

Though we have spoken of God as being personal, and it is proper so to do, we usually do not refer to him as a person. The preferred usage is to reserve the term "person" to distinguish between the three seats of self-consciousness found in the Godhead, namely, the Father, Son, and the Holy Spirit. The Greek term is *hypostasis*[1] and the Latin is *persona*.

C. Properties and Attributes Distinguished

In the last chapter the term "attribute" was used to describe the nature of Deity. Theologians use the word "property" to describe the distinguishing character of the Persons of the Trinity. Properties, thus, distinguish one person from another, whereas the attributes apply to all of the Godhead.

D. Ontological and Economical Trinity Distinguished

The word "ontological" as applied to the Trinity refers to the eternal and immanent distinctions within the Godhead. It is a good term to suggest the necessary character of these distinctions. The term "economical trinity", on the other hand, is not an accurate expression. It is better to refer to the economic relations which the persons of the Godhead sustain to one another in the economy of redemption. The danger of the term "economical trinity" is that we may get the impression that the eternal and immanent relations of the ontological Trinity are somehow suspended or modified by the economy of redemption. This is not the case, and thus it is preferable not to use this expression.

II. The Biblical Witness to the Trinity

A. The Old Testament Witness

Though we do not find the doctrine of the Trinity as fully developed in

---

1. ὑπόστασις

the Old Testament as it is in the New, nevertheless, it must be remembered that it is the triune God who is revealed in both, and thus we find indications of his triune character in the Old. One of the most striking evidences of the truth of the trinity is the fact that all of the New Testament writers were trinitarians. When it is remembered that most of these had been raised in the Jewish faith, it is a most remarkable testimony. A study of the Old Testament shows that it was preparatory for such an acceptance of the Trinity upon the clear revelation of it in the incarnation and outpouring of the Holy Spirit.

1. The Plurality of God

Though it is not a conclusive proof of the Trinity, the fact that one of the most common names of God is *Elohim*, which is a plural name, suggests a plurality within the Godhead. It is often argued that this is nothing more than a plurality of majesty as is found used by modern kings. Against this is the fact there is no usage of a plurality of majesty by the Hebrews recorded concerning the Kings of Israel or Judah. Though the full doctrine of the trinity cannot be deduced from these plural references in the Old Testament, once this doctrine is revealed in the New Testament, the real significance of this plurality becomes clear.

2. The Threeness of the Persons Suggested

There are passages in the Old Testament that actually suggest the plurality to be found in the Godhead is a trinity. For example, Psalms 33:6 says, "By the word of the Lord were the heavens made, and all the host of them by the spirit of his mouth." Again Psalms 147:18 reads, "He sendeth out his word and melteth them: He cause his spirit to blow, and the waters flow." Creation and providence are ascribed to the Word of the Lord: Genesis 1:3; Psalms 33:6,9; 147:18; Joel 2:11. The Word is personified as Wisdom: Job 28:23-27; Proverbs 8:22ff. On the other hand, creation and providence are ascribed to the Spirit of Jehovah: Genesis 1:2; Psalms 33:6; 104:30; 139:7; Job 26:13; 27:3; 32:8; 33:4; Isaiah 40:7,13, 59:19. Bavinck says:

> *Elohim* (God) and the *cosmos* (the universe) do not stand over against one another in dualistic fashion; but the world, created by God has his Word for its objective, and his Spirit for its subjective principle. God first thought the universe; hence, the latter is called into being by means of God's omnipotent Word; once realized, it does not have a separate existence, i.e., apart from God or opposed to him, but it rests in his Spirit.[2]

The threefoldness of God is suggested in the Aaronic benediction (Numbers 6:24-26), which has its counterpart in the apostolic benediction (II Corinthians 13:14). The clearest references to the threefoldness are found in Psalms 33:6; Isaiah 11:1-5; 48:16; 53:9-12; 61:1 and Haggai 2:4-6.

---

2. *Doctrine of God, op cit.*, p. 256.

3. The Separate Persons Mentioned

a. The Son

The Angel of the Lord is seen as One who is distinguished from the Lord, and yet also identified with him. (See Genesis 16:6-13; 18; 21:17-20; 22:11-19; 24:7,40; 28: 13-17; 31:11-13; 32:24-30; 48:15-16; Exodus 3:2ff; 13:21; 14:19; 23:2-23; 32:34; 33:2ff; Joshua 5:13-14; Judges 2:1-14; 6:11-24; 13:2-23; etc.) The promised Messiah is to be called the "Mighty God" (Isaiah 9:6). He is to be "the branch of Jehovah (Isaiah 4:2). He is described as the Lord Jehovah, who comes as the shepherd feeding his flock (Isaiah 40:10-11). He is called "Jehovah our Righteousness" (Jeremiah 23:6).

From these passages there is sufficient evidence in the Old Testament that there are distinct persons in the Godhead. Further, it may be seen that the Messiah shall be one of those persons. David calls him his Lord, and this is cited by Jesus as evidence of his own deity (Psalms 110:1; Matthew 22:41-45).

b. The Holy Spirit

Mention is made of the Spirit of the Lord throughout the Old Testament. Genesis 1:2 speaks of his being involved with creation. God's Spirit is the source of gifts throughout the Old Testament. He is the source of courage (Judges 3:10; 6:34; 11:29; 13:2,5; I Samuel 11:6). He is the source of physical strength (Job 32:8; Isaiah 11:2); of holiness (Psalms 51:12; Isaiah 63:10); of prophecy (Numbers 11:25, 29; 24:2-3; Micah 3:8). He is especially related to the Messiah (Isaiah 11:2; 42:1; 61:1). He is promised to be poured out on all flesh (Joel 2:28-29; Isaiah 32:13; 44:3; Ezekiel 36:26-27).

4. Summary of the Old Testament Witness

Though we do not find the doctrine of the trinity as fully revealed in the Old Testament as it is in the New, there is enough evidence for it that with its fuller revelation in the New Testament time, the disciples immediately became trinitarians. Once we have the New Testament revelation of the doctrine, we can go back to the Old Testament and see how much of it falls into place. There is nothing in the Old Testament that forbids the concept of the trinity, and much is there which points to it.

B. The New Testament Witness

1. The Unity of God in the New Testament

The New Testament is the proper development of the doctrines of the Old Testament. One of the most insistent teachings of the Old Testament is the unity of God. This is also affirmed in the New Testament (John 17:3; I Corinthians 8:4).

2. The New Testament Teaching on the Creation

The New Testament adds further insight regarding the creation as it was related to the respective persons of the trinity. The name Father is used of the creator (Matthew 7:11; Luke 3:38; John 4:21; Acts 17:28; I Corinthians 8:6; Hebrews 12:9). All things are said to be of him (I Corinthians 8:6). The Son or Logos is the one through whom the Father created (John 1:3; I Corinthians 8:6; Colossians 1:15-17; Hebrews 1:3). The Holy Spirit adorns and finishes the work of creation (Matthew 1:18; 4:1; Mark 1:12; Luke 1:35; 4:1,14; Romans 1:4).

3. The Direct Revelation of the Trinity in the New Testament

The New Testament is full of the revelation of the trinity. For one thing, the birth and baptism of Christ reveal the Trinity (Matthew 1:18ff; Luke 1:35; Matthew 3:16-17; Mark 1:10-11; Luke 3:21-22). The teachings of Christ refer to the trinity. He constantly refers to the Father (John 2:16; 4:24; 5:17, 26; Matthew 11:27). He is the eternally begotten and beloved Son of the Father (Matthew 11:27; 21:37-39; John 3:16). He is equal to the Father in glory and power (John 1:14; 5:26; 10:30).

The Holy Spirit is the One who qualifies Christ for his task as Messiah (Mark 1:12; Luke 4:1,14; John 3:34). Jesus calls him another comforter (paraclete) whom he will send from the Father (John 15:26). Jesus specifically refers to the trinity in the Great Commission and the baptismal formula, "baptizing them in the name of the Father, and of the Son, and of the Holy Spirit" (Matthew 28:19). The "name" is singular, and yet it encompasses all of the three persons. The three are placed on a par with one another in this statement.

The economy of redemption is divided between the three persons as follows:

> The good pleasure, foreknowledge, election, power, love and kingdom pertain to the Father, Matthew 6:13; 11:26; John 3:16; Romans 8:2,9; Ephesians 1:9; I Peter 1:2. Reconciliation, mediatorship, redemption, grace, wisdom, and righteousness pertain to the Son, Matthew 1:21; I Corinthians 1:30; Ephesians 1:10; I Timothy 2:5; I Peter 1:2; I John 2:2; etc. Regeneration, rejuvenation, sanctification, and communion pertain to the Holy Spirit, John 3:5; John 14:16; Romans 5:5; 8:15; 14:17; II Corinthians 1:21-22; I Peter 1:2; I John 5:6; etc.[3]
> The apostles place the three names on a par with equal prominence (I Corinthians 8:6; 12:4-6; II Corinthians 13:14; II Thessalonians 2:13-14; Ephesians 4:4-6; I Peter 1:2; I John 5:4-7; Revelation 1:4-6).[4]

---

3. *Ibid.*, p. 265.
4. Note: Much of the material here has been derived from Bavinck, *Doctrine of God, op. cit.*, pp. 263-266.

III. The Formulation of the Doctrine of the Trinity

We have seen some of the testimony of the Scriptures to the doctrine of the Trinity. We shall now seek to give the results of this survey in a systematic statement. The best simple statement of the doctrine of the trinity is found in the Westminster Shorter Catechism, Question 6. "There are three Persons in the Godhead, the Father, the Son and the Holy Ghost, these three are one God, the same in substance, equal in power and glory."

A. God is One

The unity or oneness of God is clearly taught in the Scripture. "Hear, O Israel: Jehovah our God is one Jehovah" (Deuteronomy 6:4). God is numerically and specifically one. He is not three beings with the same specific nature, but he is one being with one numerical essence. God is one, and there is none beside him (Deuteronomy 4:35).

B. God is Three

God is three just as truly as he is one. This is not to say that he is one and three in the same sense, for this would be contradictory. By a series of negatives and an affirmative, we can clarify the meaning of the unity and trinity of God.

1. The trinity teaches that he is **not** a distinctionless monad.
2. He is **not** one who became three by promotion, growth or development.
3. He is **not** one and three.

4. **Positively**, we may affirm that God **is** one **IN** three and three **IN** one. Thus the unity or oneness of God does not exist before his tri-unity. The unity is NOT more basic or more important than the trinity. This is not to deny that the unity was revealed more clearly at first. But that is not the question here. God has eternally existed as the Triune God, and thus neither unity nor trinity is more basic. Ultimately, then, it is just as unthinkable to ask why God is Triune as it is to ask why he exists. He is triune simply because he is triune. He is triune eternally and necessarily. God is, and God is the Father, and the Son, and the Holy Spirit.

There is great mystery in this truth. We cannot think of the one living and true God without being surrounded by the glory of the three persons. For the believer this is not a mystery that causes perplexity and doubt. Rather, it is a mystery that causes us to be filled with adoration and worship. Our God is One who is beyond our apprehension and understanding.

IV. The Trinitarian Distinctions

The distinctions or properties of each of the persons of the trinity are not differences of essence or being, but rather, they are distinctions within the Being of God. They are real. They are eternal and necessary. The particular property of each person is his exclusive property, and is never communicated to one of the other Persons. The Father alone is Father. He is eternally Father, and never began to be Father. Fatherhood or paternity is the exclusive property of the first person of the trinity.

The second person of the trinity alone is the Son. He is eternally the Son, and never began to be the Son, though he is eternally begotten of the Father (John 3:16). The property of sonship is the exclusive property of the Son. Together with the Father he "spirates" the Holy Spirit.

The third person of the trinity alone is the Holy Spirit. He is eternally the Holy Spirit, and never began to be the Holy Spirit. Procession is the exclusive property of the Holy Spirit. He eternally proceeds from the Father and Son (John 15:26; Acts 2:33). The exact nature of either the eternal generation of the Son or the eternal procession of the Spirit is a mystery to us. The use of these terms by theologians is derived directly from the Scripture.

It is of interest to observe the treatment of these concepts by the Nicene theologians (325 A. D.). They sought to define the eternal generation of the Son as follows: first, it was not by creation that Christ is the Son of God. Second, it is not temporal, but eternal. Third, it is not after the manner of human generation. Fourth, it is not by division of essence. After giving these four negations, the following positive speculations are suggested: first, the Father is the beginning, the fountain, the cause, the principle of the being of the Son. Second, the Son thus derives his essence from the Father by eternal and indefinable generation of divine essence from the Father to the Son. Calvin was the first one to challenge these last two speculations. He taught that the Son was *a se ipso* with regard to his deity. He did not derive his essence from the Father. There is no warrant in the Scripture for the subordination of the Son in his essence to the Father. The same may be said of the Holy Spirit. He is *a se ipso* as regards his essence.

The relations of the Persons may be set forth in a tabular form:

Person	Name	Exclusive Property	Relation to other Persons
First	Father	Paternity	Eternally generates the Son Eternally spirates the Spirit
Second	Son	Sonship	Eternally begotten of the Father Eternally spirates the Spirit
Third	Holy Spirit	Procession	Eternal procession from both the Father and the Son

There is an order in the mode of subsistence of the Three Persons, which cannot be reversed, and properties that cannot be interchanged, an order of relationship. This is not to be construed as subordination, however. These distinctions between the Persons are not distinctions of essence, but of person. They are "the same in substance, equal in power and glory." The essence of God involves infinite, eternal, and unchangeable being and perfection. The fact that we recognize each of these persons as deity implies that there can be no subordination of essence.

The economic relations reveal appropriate distinctions, which rest upon these eternal personal distinctions. It is the Father who is usually thought of as the source of creation. The Son is the one who has come to do the bidding of the Father in the Covenant of Grace, and the Holy Spirit is sent by both the Father and the Son to apply the work of redemption accomplished by the Son.

The Godhead is more comprehensive than the distinctions by which the individual Persons are distinguished. Thus, it is not strictly correct to say "God is the Father;" or "God is the Son;" or "God is the Holy Spirit." Of course, Scripture does use the name "God" as a personal name of the Father, but in the full theological sense the name "God" is more inclusive than any one of the Persons. It should be observed, on the other hand, that since each Person of the trinity is divine, it is proper to say: "The Father is God," or "The Son is God," or "The Holy Spirit is God." Shedd summarizes this as follows: "A trinitarian person includes all that is in the unity, but not all that is in the trinality of God; all that is in the essence, but not all that is in the modes of the essence.[5] If we make God the subject of the sentence, then we may say, "God is Father, Son, and Holy Spirit."

---

5. W. G. T. Shedd, *Dogmatic Theology* (Grand Rapids: Zondervan Publishing House, n.d., reprint of 1888 edition), Vol. I, p. 280.

Chapter XI The Decrees of God

I. The Place of the Decrees in God's Works

A. Immanent Works

God is described throughout Scripture as the living and acting God. He is the God of creation, preservation, government, redemption, regeneration, and sanctification. God never slumbers nor sleeps (Psalms 121:3-4). He faints not, nor grows weary (Isaiah 40:28). Jesus speaks of him as being continually active (John 5:17). From this we may deduce the fact that as the Living God he is by nature active. If this is so, then the work of creation did not mark the beginning of his activity. He is eternally active, from everlasting to everlasting.

Among those activities of his, which are eternal may be included the intrapersonal relations between the persons of the trinity, namely, the eternal generation and procession of the second and third persons. Also, the love and fellowship that has eternally existed between the three persons are among his immanent works. The Father is said to give the Son the gift of having life in himself (John 5:26). The fellowship and communion between the three persons is suggested by the words of Jesus in Matthew 11:27 and John 17:24. Paul speaks of the Spirit of God as searching all things, even the deep things of God (I Corinthians 2:10). All of these works are properly immanent works. They are all within the Godhead, and do not bear directly on anything that exists outside of God. Their presence suggests to us the absolute sufficiency of God. He is "not served by men's hands as though he needed anything, seeing he himself giveth to all life, and breath and all things."[1] "God does not need the universe in order to be perfect; he does not need to create and preserve in order not to be idle; in himself he is absolute activity.[2]

B. Works Relating to the Created Universe

1. Works Which Are Immanent until Outwardly Realized

We may distinguish from the immanent works of God those works which have relation to the created existence. These may in turn be divided between the internal and external works. By the first group we refer to the decrees or plan of God. This eternal counsel of God has three characteristics. First, they are derived from the fullness of God's immanent knowledge. It should be observed that the possible and the actual do not coincide. Second, all of the decrees of God are based upon his free sovereignty. That is, God is not under any necessity bound to act as he has. He decrees out of his own freedom. Third, the fact that God decrees implies the execution of the decree in time. Thus, though there was no necessity in God's nature that required the creation, once he had decreed it, it became necessary. This may be called a consequent necessity.

---

1. Acts 17:25.
2. Bavinck, *Doctrine of God, op.cit.*, p. 338.

2. Works That Are Outgoing or Emanant Acts

Once God decreed then there is necessarily the execution of the decree. This execution takes place in the works of creation and providence. Under the latter term is included the covenant relationship established with man in Eden, and after the fall, re-established through Christ. In other words, redemption falls under the category of providence. It is a special act of providence. It should be observed that the economic relations of the Persons of the trinity are dependent upon the decree. These relations exist because he has willed they should, and were not inherent in the nature of God as triune.

In the remainder of this chapter we shall be discussing the decrees or counsel of God. The execution of the decrees comprises the rest of the system of theology.

II. The Biblical Idea of the Decrees

A. The Old Testament Teaching

The Old Testament clearly affirms that God's creation and providence are according to his word of wisdom (Psalms 33:6; 104:24; Job 38; Proverbs 8; etc.). God is said to know and declare beforehand (Isaiah 41:22-23; 42:9; 43:9-12; 44:7; 46:10; 48:3ff; Amos 3:7). He is represented as prophesying the future (Genesis 3:14ff; 6:13; 9:25ff; 12:2ff; 15:13ff; 25:23ff; 49:8; etc.). The days of men are said to be ordained by him, "Thine eyes see mine unformed substance; And in thy book they were all written, Even the days that were ordained for me, When as yet there was none of them" (Psalms 139:16). Again, the Psalmist says, "My times are in thy hand" (Psalms 31:15); and "Seeing his days are determined, The number of his months is with thee, And thou hast appointed his bounds that he cannot pass" (Job 14:5).

All things are represented as happening according to his counsel (Isaiah 14:24-27; 45:7; 46:10-11; Daniel 4:17, 24). The counsel of God may be secret (Deuteronomy 29:29; Job 15:8), but as history unfolds, we see the execution of the decree, "for all things happen in accordance with that eternal and irresistible decree."[3] "The counsel of Jehovah standeth fast forever, The thoughts of his heart to all generations"[4]; "There are many devices in a man's heart; But the counsel of Jehovah shall stand."[5]

In addition to these general statements of the Old Testament, we find in the development of the covenant the idea of election and reprobation as specific decrees. This will be treated more fully later, but suffice it to mention the fact of God's choosing of Abraham and then Isaac, and then Jacob while passing others by. The choice is not on the basis of worth, but is an act of God's sovereign grace.

---

3. *Ibid.*, p. 341.
4. Psalms 33:11.
5. Proverbs 19:21.

B. The New Testament Teaching

The New Testament uses a number of terms to suggest the idea of the decrees of God. *Eudokia*[6] which translates both *ratsah*[7] and *chephetz*[8] means "good pleasure". *Chephetz* is found in Isaiah 46:10, "Declaring the end from the beginning, and from ancient times things that are not [yet] done. Saying, My counsel shall stand, and I will do all my pleasure." *Eudokia* is found in Luke 12:32, "Fear not, little flock; for it is your Father's good pleasure to give you the kingdom," and in Matthew 11:26, "Yea, Father, for so it was well-pleasing in thy sight." It is also found in Ephesians 1:5,9, "Having foreordained us unto adoption as sons through Jesus Christ unto himself, according to the good pleasure of his will ... making known unto us the mystery of his will, according to his good pleasure which he purposed in him."[9]

The term "counsel" (*etsah*[10]) also found in Isaiah 46:10 is translated by the Greek word *boule*[11]. Thus we read in Acts 2:23, "Him being delivered by the determinate counsel and foreknowledge of God, ye have taken and by wicked hands have crucified and slain." The phrase "determinate counsel" is a translation of the Greek phrase *te horismene boule*[12]. Acts 4:28 uses it again speaking of the deed of Herod, Pilate, and the Gentiles as doing "whatsoever thy hand and thy counsel foreordained to come to pass." Again, it is found in Ephesians 1:11 which gives us the basic teaching about all things being done according to God's plan. "In whom also we were made a heritage, having been foreordained according to the purpose of him who worketh all things after the counsel of his will." This note of God's determination is sounded in a number of places. Luke 22:22 reads, "For the Son of man indeed goeth, as it hath been determined: but woe unto that man through whom he is betrayed." Again, Acts 17:26 speaks of a determination of world history, "And he made of one every nation of men to dwell on all the face of the earth, having determined their appointed seasons, and the bounds of their habitation."

Along with these terms for counsel and good pleasure is the term *protesis*[13] meaning purpose. It is found in Ephesians 1:11, which has already been quoted. It is also found in Romans 8:28, "For we know that to them that love God all things work together for good, even to them that are called according to his purpose." Again, it is used in Romans 9:11, "For the children being not yet born, neither having done anything good or bad, that the purpose of God according to election might stand, not of works, but of him that calleth." It is also in Ephesians 3:11, "According to the eternal purpose which he purposed in Christ Jesus our Lord," and in II Timothy 1:9, "Who saved us, and called us with a holy calling, not according to our works, but according to his own purpose and grace, which was given us in Christ Jesus before times eternal."

---

6. εὐδοκία
7. רָצָה
8. חֵפֶץ
9. See also Luke 2:14; 10:21; Philippians 2:13; II Thessalonians 1:11.
10. עֵצָה
11. βουλή
12. τῇ ὡρισμένῃ βουλῇ
13. πρόθησις

Romans 8:29 uses another term, namely, *proginoskein*[14] or foreknowledge. The word "to know" (*yada*[15] or *ginoskein*[16]) has a breadth of meaning. It can mean simply to know, but it also can have a much fuller sense, including the idea of a "knowing in love," or a "setting of affection upon," or an "election." For example, Genesis 18:19 speaks of God's choice of Abraham unto the purpose of his teaching the faith. "For I have known him, to the end that he may command his children and his household after him, that they may keep the way of Jehovah, to do righteousness and justice; to the end that Jehovah may bring upon Abraham that which he hath spoken of him." Psalms 1 ends with the statement, "For Jehovah knoweth the way of the righteous, but the way of the wicked shall perish." The ground of the reward of the righteous is the love that God had for their ways. He certainly knew the way of the wicked also, but he did not love it. Amos 3:1-2 reads, "Hear this word that Jehovah hath spoken against you, O children of Israel, against the whole family which I brought up out of the land of Egypt, saying, You only have I known of all the families of the earth ..." Here again it is the note of knowing with love and affection. The word *yada* then often denotes more than mere prescience. It denotes a knowing before in love. This is the meaning of the word in Romans 8:29, "For whom he foreknew, he also foreordained to be conformed to the image of his Son, that he might be the first-born among many brethren." This is borne out by the entire context of Romans 8 and 9. Romans 9:11 specifically speaks of the purpose of election as not being dependent upon works. Romans 11:2 uses the term in this same way. "God did not cast off his people which he foreknew ..."[17] "That this is a distinctive knowledge, and therefore a knowledge in love, and not simply prescience, is evident from the fact that the objects of this foreknowledge are the people of God, while all men are, of course, the objects of the foreknowledge of God in general."[18]

Romans 8:29 also uses the word *proorizein*[19], meaning foreordination. This term is also found in Acts 4:28; I Corinthians 2:7; Ephesians 1:5,11. The word *ekloge*[20] meaning "election" is found in a number of passages, including Mark 13:20; Acts 9:15; 13:17; 15:7; Romans 9:11; 11:5,28; I Corinthians 1:27-28; Ephesians 1:4; I Thessalonians 1:4; II Peter 1:10; James 2:5. Bavinck summarizes regarding these terms:

> We differentiate as follows: '*prothesis*' indicates that in the work of redemption God does not act arbitrarily, but according to a fixed and definite plan, an immutable purpose; '*ekloge*' shows that this purpose of redemption does not include all men, but is a 'purpose according to election,' Romans 9:11, so that not all but many are saved; '*prognosis*' reveals the fact that in this purpose according to election the persons are not the objects of God's 'bare foreknowledge' but of his 'active delight'; while '*pro-orismos*' refers to the means used by God to bring his 'known

---
14. προγινώσκειν
15. ידע
16. γινώσκειν
17. See also I Peter 1:2.
18. Hoeksema, *op. cit.*, p. 160.
19. προορίζειν
20. ἐκλογη

ones' to their appointed destiny. The term '*prothesis*' indicates the certitude of the events; '*prognosis*' directs attention to the singleness of the persons; while '*pro-orismos*' points out the order (or succession) of the means.'"[21]

It should be observed that the New Testament includes under the idea of God's decrees all actions, including evil, and reprobation. The perdition of Judas is a revelation of God's will (John 17:12). The heathen are said to be given up by God to their lusts and uncleanness (Romans 1:24). Esau was passed by and thus rejected by God (Romans 9:13). The wicked were hardened (Romans 9:18) and Pharaoh was raised up (Romans 9:17) as a part of God's plan. So also was the fact that some were vessels of wrath fitted for destruction (Romans 9:22). Christ is represented not only as a Saviour, but his coming was also for the falling of some (Luke 2:34); for judgment (John 3:19-20); for a stone of stumbling and a rock of offense (I Peter 2:7-8).

III. The Doctrine Formulated and Analyzed

A. God Has From Eternity Had an Unchangeable Plan for His Creation

1. The Decrees Are Eternal

That the decrees of God are eternal is expressly affirmed in the Scriptures (Isaiah 46:10; 48:3,5; Ephesians 1:4; 3:9,11; II Timothy 1:9; I Peter 1:20). The understanding and knowledge of God is eternal, because of his nature as the all-knowing God. He himself exists before his decree only in order of production, not in time. His decree is the expression of his will. The eternity of God is a necessary aspect of his being, while his decree is eternal because he wills it so.

2. The Decrees of God are Unchangeable

It follows from the nature of God as unchangeable that his decrees are also unchangeable. There is no change or purpose in God, nor is there any frustration of his plan from without. Since his wisdom is infinite, there can be no unforeseen contingency that will arise, and since he is infinite in power there can be no deficiency in power to execute his plan. "The counsel of Jehovah standeth fast forever, the thoughts of his heart to all generations" (Psalms 33:11).

B. God's Decrees Include All Things and Events of Every Kind that Come to Pass

That the plan of God is all-inclusive is explicitly stated in Scripture. "Being predestinated according to the purpose of him who worketh all things after the counsel of his own will."[22] Jesus included the minutiae of life in the decree," Are not two sparrows sold for a farthing? and one of them shall not fall

---
21. Bavinck, *op. cit.*, p. 343.
22. Ephesians 1:11.

on the ground without your Father. But the very hairs of your head are all numbered."[23]

All sorts of actions are included, whether physical or moral, good or evil. All actions of man are foreordained (Ephesians 2:10); even wicked actions are included. "Jehovah hath made everything for its own end. Yea, even the wicked for the day of evil."[24] "Him, being delivered up by the determinate counsel and foreknowledge of God, ye by the hand of lawless men did crucify and slay."[25] Contingent acts are under his direction (Proverbs 16:33); the means as well as the ends are a part of his plan (Psalms 119:89-91; Ephesians 1:4); the duration of man's life (Job 14:5; Psalms 39:4); and the place of his habitation (Acts 17:25).

The fact that sin is foreordained raises problems in our minds about the decrees. Strictly speaking, the decree of God is positive, even in regard to sin and evil, since, by definition, the decree is the eternal purpose of God. The execution of the decree, however, may well be permissive. This is the case with regard to sin. God is not the active agent in man's sin. It is man who sins, and who is thus held accountable for his wickedness (Acts 2:23). "God cannot be tempted with evil, neither tempteth he any man."[26] " ... God is light and in him is no darkness at all."[27]

In the case of the hardening of the heart of Pharaoh, the Bible speaks on the one hand of God hardening it, and on the other hand, of Pharaoh hardening his own heart. Paul treats the case of Pharaoh as an illustration of the doctrine of reprobation. Rom. 9:14-18 reads:

> What shall we say then? Is there unrighteousness with God? God forbid. 15. For he saith to Moses, I will have mercy on whom I have mercy, and I will have compassion on whom I have compassion. 16. So then it is not of him that willeth, nor of him that runneth, but of God that hath mercy. 17. For the scripture saith unto Pharaoh, For this very purpose did I raise thee up, that I might show in thee my power, and that my name might be published abroad in all the earth. 18. So then he hath mercy on whom he will, and whom he will be hardeneth.

Let us consider the fact that the Bible says that God hardened the hearts of Pharaoh and of the Egyptians. This expression occurs nine times in Exodus.[28] How are we to understand these expressions that seem so harsh to our ears? Calvin's commentary on Exodus 4:21 is most helpful.

> Now, therefore, God exhorts him to perseverance; and although he might perceive after three or four miracles that obstinacy of the king was indomitable, still that he should not turn back, nor be discouraged, but should continue even unto the end. . . . Thus he shows Moses the reason why he should not stop until he had performed all the miracles; because the tyrant must be gloriously conquered, and overwhelmed in so many hard-fought engagements, that the victory might be more

---
23. Matthew 10:29-30.
24. Proverbs 16:4.
25. Acts 2:23. See also Acts 4:27-28.
26. James 1:13.
27. I John 1:5.
28. Exodus 4:21; 7:3; 9:12; 10:20, 27; 11:10; 14:4, 8, 17.

splendid. In the meantime he declares that the king of Egypt would not be thus obstinate contrary to his will; as if he could not reduce him to order in a moment; but rather that he would harden his heart in order that he might violently overwhelm his madness. . . . Since the expression seems harsh to delicate ears, many soften it away, by turning the act into mere permission; as if there were no difference between doing and permitting to be done; or as if God would commend his passivity, and not rather his power. As to myself, I am certainly not ashamed of speaking as the Holy Spirit speaks, nor do I hesitate to believe what so often occurs in Scripture, that God gives the wicked over to a reprobate mind, gives them up to vile affections, blinds their minds and hardens their hearts. But they object, that in this way God would be made the author of sin; which would be a detestable impiety. I reply, that God is very far from the reach of blame, when he is said to exercise his judgments; wherefore, if blindness be a judgment of God, it ought not be brought in accusation against him, that he inflicts punishment.[29]

The hardening by God is his righteous judgment against the sinner. The hardness of heart is the sinfulness of man. To those who would accuse God of being the author of sin, or of being unfair in holding us accountable for our sins, Paul answers the question, "Thou wilt say then unto me, Why doth he still find fault? For who withstandeth his will? Nay, but, O man, who art thou that repliest against God?"[30]

We see from these passages that the Bible does teach that God's decree comprehends all actions, including evil and sin, though he is never to be accused of being the author of sin.

C. God's Decrees Are Not Conditioned by Anything Outside of Himself

All has been determined according to the counsel of his own most holy and wise will. As we have already observed the decrees are immanent within the Godhead. Thus they cannot be dependent in any way upon anything that is not within God. All which lies outside of God is created, and is the consequence of the decree of God, not the cause of it. There may be mutual dependence of parts of the decree on other parts of the decree, but the decree is in no way dependent on anything outside of God (Ephesians 1:5,11).

D. The Decree is Efficacious, and Includes the Means of Its Execution as well as the Goal

What God has decreed will certainly come to pass. The decree provides that the event will be actuated by causes completely consistent with the nature of the event in question. For example, the acts of a free

---

29. John Calvin, *Commentaries on the Four Last Books of Moses Arranged in the Form of a Harmony* (Grand Rapids: William B. Eerdmans Publishing Company, 1950), Vol. I, pp. 101-102.
30. Rom. 9:19.

moral agent are included in his plan. This is possible on the following grounds: first, he decrees that the agent shall be free. Second, he decrees all of his antecedents, and all of the antecedents to any particular action. Third, he decrees that all the present conditions of the act be what they are. Fourth, he decrees that the act be spontaneous and the free act of the moral agent. Fifth, he decrees the future with certainty (Psalms 33:11; Proverbs 19:21; Isaiah 46:10).

IV. Objection to this Doctrine Examined and Answered

A. It Is Objected that God Is Made the Author of Sin

This objection may be answered by the following arguments:
1. God cannot be the author of sin, since his very nature is holy. He always reveals himself as opposed to sin.
2. The nature of sin is a want of conformity unto or a transgression of the law of God. How can God, the lawgiver, find himself in either case?
3. The nature of man is that of a responsible free moral agent. As such he always originates his own actions. Grace and goodness are always attributed to God in the Bible, while sin and evil to the heart of evil man.
4. The Bible explicitly states that God is holy and that he is not the author of sin (Psalms 92:15; Ecclesiastes 7:29; James 1:13; I John 1:5).

B. It is objected that the decrees are inconsistent with the moral freedom of man. How can God have decreed whatsoever comes to pass, and man have any freedom as a moral agent?

Though this may appear to be an insurmountable difficulty for man, the Bible sees no inconsistency here. It places the two side by side throughout (Genesis 50:19-20; John 6;37,40,44; Acts 2:23; 4:27-28). There is no indication that the inspired writers saw any contradiction here. They simply put them together, without any attempt to harmonize the two. This should restrain us from assuming a contradiction, even if we cannot harmonize the two. Especially is this the case when we realize that Jesus, who knew both as God and man, and thus knowing both the solution and our difficulty, does not give us any answer to the problem. He too places the two side by side (Matthew 11:25-30).

C. It is objected that the doctrine of the decrees removes all motive for human exertion

In answer to this objection two basic thoughts must be kept in mind. First, the decree of God is not addressed to man as a rule of action, and cannot be such a rule, since the contents are not revealed to man. The revealed will is his Word, and it is the obligation of man to obey it. Second, the decree includes the means as well as the ends, and the means to reach God's ends for man include the use of all the means that God has given us (Philippians 2:13; Ephesians 2:10).

Chapter XII Predestination

I. Definition

It is customary to use the word "decrees" for the over-all plan of God for all of his creation, and to use "predestination" in a more limited sense. There is nothing inherent in the term to restrict its usage thus, but it is the generally recognized usage of theologians. The degree of limitation of the term differs with the theologians. Predestination may be applied to the purposes of God regarding all his moral creatures, both men and angels. Sometimes it is restricted to man, and includes both election and reprobation. Or it may be used in the most restrictive sense of applying only to the elect, and not referring to the reprobate. The *Westminster Standards* use it to refer to just the elect of both men and angels. The word "foreordination" is used of the non-elect men and angels. John MacPherson comments on this usage:

> It is to be noticed that nowhere throughout this chapter is the term predestination used in reference to evil, while foreordination is used of good and evil alike. Now there is nothing in the words to vindicate such a distinction in their use; but evidently the Westminster divines wished to make it clear that they regarded God's proceedings in regard to the elect, and in regard to the reprobate respectively, as resting upon entirely different grounds. In the one instance, we have an act of grace, determined purely by God's good will; in the other, an act of judgment, determined by the sin of the individual.[1]

It seems to the present writer that the most precise procedure is to use "predestination" regarding the moral creatures, as including both election and reprobation. These latter terms are so clear that there is no doubt as to their meaning, and it is generally best to use the clearest terms. We shall take up the two parts of predestination, namely, election and reprobation, separately. Following the lead of Bavinck, we shall treat reprobation first, and then election. In this way we shall see the true glory of election, for it will be portrayed against the background of reprobation.

II. Reprobation

A. The Biblical Idea of Reprobation

Under the decree of reprobation are included the two ideas of preterition or passing by, and condemnation. "The Bible does not make frequent mention of reprobation as an eternal decree."[2] On the other hand, it does teach that "sin, unbelief, death, and eternal punishment are the object of God's government as well as all things."[3] The evidence for this is found in the historical development of

---
1. *The Confession of Faith with Introduction and Notes* (Edinburgh: T. & T. Clark, 1907), p. 48.
2. Bavinck, *Doctrine of God, op cit.*, p. 395.
3. *Ibid.*, p. 394.

the human race. God rejected Cain (Genesis 4:5); He sent Ishmael away (Genesis 21:12; Galatians 4:30). The account of Ishmael given in Romans 9:7 speaks of the choice of Isaac, and the passing over of Ishmael, which is the idea of preterition. Esau is also represented as passed over:

> And Jehovah said unto her, Two nations are in thy womb, And two peoples shall be separated from thy bowels. And the one people shall be stronger than the other people. And the elder shall serve the younger.[4]

Thus Esau is the object of God's hatred:

> I have loved you, saith Jehovah. Yet ye say, Wherein hast thou loved us? Was not Esau Jacob's brother, saith Jehovah. Yet I loved Jacob. But Esau I hated, and made his mountains a desolation, and [gave] his heritage to the jackals of the wilderness.[5]

> "Even as it is written, Jacob I loved, but Esau I hated."[6]

He is described in Hebrews as a profane person, who was unable to receive a blessing, even when he desired it.

> Lest there be any fornication, or profane person, as Esau, who for one mess of meat sold his own birthright. For ye know that even when he afterward desired to inherit the blessing, he was rejected; for he found no place for a change of mind [in his father], though he sought it diligently with tears.[7]

God permitted the nations to walk in their own ways, "Who in the generations gone by suffered all the nations to walk in their own ways."[8]

He is represented as rejecting his own people, or certain definite individuals at times (Deuteronomy 29:28; I Samuel 15:23,26; 16:1; II Kings 17:20; 23:27; Psalms 53:5; 78:67; 89:38; Jeremiah 6:30; 14:19; 31:37; Hosea 4:6; 9:17). This negative act of rejection is described in positive terms, such as, hatred (Malachi 1:2-3; Romans 9:13); cursing (Genesis 9:25); hardening (Exodus 7:3; 4:21; 9:12; 10:20,27; 11:10; 14:4; Deuteronomy 2:30; Joshua 11:20; Psalms 105:25; I Samuel 2:25; John 12:40; Romans 9:18); blinding and deafening (Isaiah 6:9; Matthew 13:13; Mark 4:12; Luke 8:10; John 12:40; Acts 28:26; Romans 11:8). God's control even of the wicked deeds of man and Satan is spoken of in various terms. He is said to put a lying spirit in the mouth of false prophets (I Kings 22:23; II Chronicles 18:22). He used Satan to move David to number Israel (II Samuel 24:1; I Chronicles 21:1). He permitted Satan to test Job (Job 1). Nebuchadnezzar and Cyrus are called his servants (II Chronicles 36:22; Ezra 1:1; Isaiah 44:28; 45:1; Jeremiah 27:6; 28:14). Assyria is called the rod of his anger (Isaiah 10:5ff). He delivered Christ into the hands of his enemies (Acts 2:23; 4:28). He sent Christ to serve for the falling and rising of some, for a savor of death and life, and for a stone of stumbling and rock of offense (Luke 2:34; John 3:19; 9:39; II Corinthians 2:16; I Peter 2:8). He is represented as giving men up to their own lusts (Romans 1:24), and as sending a working of

---

4. Genesis 25:23.
5. Malachi 1:2-3.
6. Rom. 9:13.
7. Hebrews 12:16-17.
8. Acts 14:16.

error (II Thessalonians 2:11). He raised up Pharaoh to show his power (Romans 9:17), and Shemei to curse David (I Samuel 16:10).

Lest we think that this presents God as arbitrary, the Bible associates Divine judgment with sin. Divine hardening implies human hardening (Exodus 7:13,22; 8:15; 9:35; 13:15; II Chronicles 36:13; Job 9:4; Psalms 95:8; Proverbs 28:14; Hebrews 3:8; 4:7). Jesus used parables *not only in order* that unbelievers would not hear, but *also because* they neither see nor hear (Matthew 13:13; Mark 4:12).[9] Romans 1:24 speaks of God's having given men up to sin. This is his judicial act of punishment of wicked men for their sins.

B. Formulation of the Doctrine

1. Preterition

We have already defined reprobation as including two ideas, namely, that of passing by, and of condemnation. The first of these is called preterition. As we examine the Biblical data, we find that God is represented as passing by some in the operation of grace. The nations of Acts 14 were permitted to walk in their own ways. Ishmael was passed over in favor of Isaac, so also was Esau. In connection with Jacob and Esau, Romans 9 clearly asserts that the election of Jacob and the passing by of Esau was according to the purpose of God, and not on the basis of the works of either. Thus, we must conclude that the decree to pass by is a sovereign decree of God, according to his own good pleasure.

2. Condemnation

Having passed some by with his gifts of grace, they are left to their own ways. As we have already noted, this is a part of God's judicial punishment of their sins (Romans 1:24). The positive terms connected with the rejection by God such as hardening, hatred, blinding and deafening, may be understood as part of this same judicial treatment of the wicked. The grounds of the condemnation rests upon their sinfulness. In preterition God has simply passed some by, and now they have demonstrated their character as wicked, and consequently, fall under the wrath and curse of God.

Professor John Murray comments on the relation of these two aspects of the decree as follows:

> There have been and are those who wish to make the decrees of reprobation a purely judicial act of God. This is generally motivated by revulsion from the thought of any sovereign discrimination between men on the part of God. The differences in the ultimate destiny of men are supposed to find their whole explanation in the determinations that arise from men themselves, that in the matter of salvation the differences among men rest upon differences in men themselves. The Westminster divines, on the contrary, show peculiar care to stress the sovereign good pleasure of God in the decree of reprobation as in the decree of election - 'God was pleased, according to the unsearchable

---

9. Bavinck, *op. cit.*, p. 395.

counsel of his own will, whereby he extendeth or withholdeth mercy, as he pleaseth.'

The insistence upon the absolute sovereignty of God does not, however, obliterate a very important distinction. The decree of reprobation, as we noted, includes two sides, the passing by and the ordaining to dishonor and wrath. It will be observed that the words 'to pass by' are not in any way modified, whereas the words 'to ordain them to dishonor and wrath' are modified by the words 'for their sin.' The distinction is all important. The precision of the Confession is masterly. It is not because men are sinners that they are passed by. If that were the case, then all men would be passed by. It is, however, because the non-elect are sinners that they are ordained to dishonor and wrath. To state the matter otherwise, sin is not the ground upon which some are passed by and are therefore non-elect; but sin is the ground of the dishonor and wrath to which they are ordained. The passing by rests upon the sovereign good pleasure of God - he may extend or withhold mercy as he pleases. But dishonor and wrath presuppose ill-desert. Wrath is always the wages of guilt and guilt is the consequence of sin. In other words, dishonor and wrath have always their judicial ground in sin and condemnation.

The construction of this section (of the *Westminster Confession*, Chapter III, Section VII), however, requires one further observation. The words, 'God was pleased,' govern 'to ordain them to dishonor and wrath, for their sin' as well as 'to pass by.' This would seem to perplex the simplicity and force of the distinction noted above, and it has sometimes escaped the notice of some Reformed commentators on the *Confession*. But again the jealousy with which the divines maintained the principle of God's sovereign will comes to light. The sovereign good pleasure of God alone is operative in the passing by. But in the ordination to dishonor and wrath *both* the sovereign good pleasure *and* the judicial condemnation of God are operative. The ground of dishonor and wrath is truly sin and sin *alone*, but the reason why *they*, the non-elect, are ordained to such dishonor and wrath, when others equally sinful and hell-deserving are not, is the sovereign will of God. We thus discover that, while the distinction between the ground of passing by and the ground of ordaining to dishonor and wrath is distinctly and eloquently drawn, the sovereign will of God is not denied its proper sphere of operation in the eternal condemnation of the reprobate. And sober analysis of the question will again vindicate the construction that the divines chose to adopt.[10]

A careful study of the passages referring to election and reprobation indicate clearly that they are according to the good pleasure of God, and not based on his foresight of good or evil in man. The *Westminster Confession* is explicit in this:

---

[10]. "The Theology of the Westminster Standards," *Calvin Forum*, X, 6, January 1944, pp. 111-115. Note that this is a different article from that which appears in Murray's *Collected Writings*, Vol. IV, under the same title.

CHAPTER XII PREDESTINATION

> Those of mankind that are predestinated unto life, God, before the foundation of the world was laid, according to his eternal and immutable purpose, and the secret counsel and good pleasure of his will, hath chosen in Christ, unto everlasting glory out of his mere free grace and love, *without any foresight of faith or good works, or perseverance in either of them, or any other thing in the creature, as conditions, or causes moving him thereunto*; and all to the praise of his glorious grace.[11]

The *Confession* here is asserting that the election of some to life, and the passing by of others, is unconditional. That is, there is nothing in us that causes God to elect some of us and to pass by others. Rather, as Scripture clearly states: "All have sinned and come short of the glory of God."[12] "There is none righteous, no, not one."[13] "They that are in the flesh cannot please God."[14] In other words, all of us are sinners, there is no good in any of us, and it is utterly impossible for us to change ourselves to do good, and thus, if any are to be saved, it must be because God out of his compassion has looked upon us in mercy and drawn us unto himself.

Horatius Bonar succinctly argues: "The real question in all this is just, 'Are all men so depraved that they will not be saved unless God must put forth his power to save every one that is saved; and surely he is at liberty to choose whom he is to save.'"[15] If it is argued that the doctrine of reprobation means that God made men in order to damn them it should be answered that such is a profane argument. It does an injustice to God's holy nature. Bonar says again:

> God did *not* make the angels 'who kept not their first estate,' to damn them. He did *not* make Lucifer for the purpose of casting him out of Paradise. He did *not* make Judas for the purpose of sending him to his own place. God made man, every man, and everything to *glorify Himself*. This every creature, man and angel, must do, either actively or passively, either willingly or unwillingly, - actively and willingly in heaven, or passively and unwillingly in hell. This is God's purpose; and it shall stand. God may have many other ends in creation; but this is the chief one, the ultimate one, - the one which is above all the others, and to which all the rest are subordinate. In this sense then plainly, God did not make men either to destroy them or to save them. He made them for his own glory.[16]

Again, in the face of the argument that reprobation means that God cannot have foreordained the damnation of some, Bonar argues:

> Whatever is right for God to do, it is right for him to decree. If God's casting sinners into hell be not wrong or unjust, then his purposing to do so from all eternity cannot be wrong or unjust. So that you must either deny that there is a hell, or admit God's right to predestinate who

---

11. *Westminster Confession of Faith*, III, 5.
12. Romans 3:23.
13. Romans 3:10.
14. Romans 8:8.
15. *The Five Points of Calvinism in a Series of Letters*, by Horatius Bonar, Andrew Fuller, John Calvin, John Gill, Thomas Goodwin, and Jonathan Edwards (Evansville: Sovereign Grace Book Club, n.d.), p. 35.
16. *Ibid.*, p. 37.

are to dwell there forever. There is no middle way between Calvinism and Universalism.[17]

Thornwell speaks in the same vein:

In fact, every passage of Scripture which teaches that any will be finally lost, teaches at the same time, by necessary implication, if the doctrine of election be true, that they were eternally reprobated or left out of the number of the elect. The two doctrines stand or fall together.[18]

G. B. Strickler, another Southern Presbyterian theologian, affirms the same:

Many men are not saved; God foreknew they would not be saved; he foreknew it because he had no purpose to save them, to overcome their inexcusable love of sin and thus inexcusable opposition.[19]

Girardeau argues for the doctrine of reprobation on the basis of it being the logical consequence of election.

Such are the proofs of the doctrine of reprobation which are derived from the word of God, and they are too solid to be shaken by appeals to human sentiment, or even to human reason. It is admitted that the chief weight of the argument consists in the Scriptural evidence in favor of unconditional election. That being proved, reprobation cannot be denied. ... The two doctrines stand or fall together. They are opposite sides of the same truth.[20]

This raises the question that has been debated as to whether election and reprobation are equally ultimate. The equal ultimacy of the two sides of the decree is asserted by Dr. Cornelius Van Til, but denied by men like James Daane and G. C. Berkouwer.[21] As Van Til points out:

Since I take my point of departure in God and his plan, I think of this plan as back of reprobation as well as back of election. God's plan is a unity. His act of election of some is itself the act of not electing others ... The precise point is that, if we deny the equal ultimacy of election and reprobation, we deny that God's plan controls whatsoever comes to pass. We then make men the ultimate as well as the proximate cause of their destiny.[22]

Again, Van Til argues for equal ultimacy:

All Reformed men should abhor the idea that God, conceived of as abstract and neutral power apart from Christ, creates men in order to send them to their ultimate death *(ad mortem)*; of course, the *proper* work of Christ is, as Calvin says, to save the world. Of course, God has no pleasure in the death of the wicked. Even so, if God is God and man is man, the creature of God, if God's counsel does control whatsoever comes to pass, then unbelief or sin, however much the proximate and responsible,

---

17. *Idem.*
18. "Election and Reprobation" in *Collected Writings, op cit.*, Vol. II, p. 144.
19. "Reprobation", unpubl. MS Sermon at Union Theological Seminary Library, cited in the author's *Studies in Southern Presbyterian Theology, op cit.*, p. 309.
20. *Calvinism and Evangelical Arminianism: Compared as to Election, Reprobation, and Related Doctrines* (Columbia: W. J. Duffie and New York: The Baker and Taylor Company, 1890), p. 174.
21. *Divine Election* (Grand Rapids: Wm. B. Eerdmans Publishing Co., 1960), p. 189.
22. *The Theology of James Daane* (Philadelphia: Presbyterian and Reformed Publishing Company, 1959), pp. 67, 69.

is not the ultimate reason for reprobation. That reason must ever be the sovereign good pleasure of God. He could have prevented sin from coming into the world at all. That is the point to which Calvin leads back all objectors to the idea of the all-inclusive plan of God. Sin is therefore in the world by his good pleasure. It serves the ultimate purpose of his good pleasure. . . . As the convex and concave side of a disc are equally aspects of one disc so election and reprobation are equally aspects of one decree. It cannot be otherwise. God's decree is one; it is eternal. It precedes all that happens in time. . . . Created objects are by the very fact of creation eliminated from ultimacy, and the devil accordingly is also denied ultimacy, because he is a creature.[23]

Admittedly this doctrine is one of sobering thought. Girardeau concludes his discussion of it with these solemn words:

It is indeed suited to appall the stoutest heart and blanch the boldest face. It reveals more strongly than anything else, except the Cross on which Jesus bled and died, God's infinite abhorrence of sin--the opposite of his nature, the menace of his government, the dynamic of the universe. And it is enough to fill us with horror of sin to know that even infinite mercy has rescued not one of the fallen angels from their doom, and only some of our guilty and ruined race from the everlasting damnation which is its due.[24]

III. Election

A. The Biblical Idea of Election

1. The Election of Israel

The Bible uses the idea of election in several ways. First, there is the election of the nation or people of Israel. This election was for special privileges and special service to God (Deuteronomy 4:37; 7:6-8; 10:15; Hosea 13:5).

2. The Election of Individuals to Office

Not only does God elect the people of Israel, but he also distinguishes between individuals by electing certain persons to particular offices. For example, Moses was called to bring the people out of Egypt (Exodus 3). The priests were chosen of God and set aside for special service (Deuteronomy 18:15). So also were the kings chosen by God (I Samuel 10:24; Psalms 78:70); and the prophets (Jeremiah 1:5). In the New Testament the Apostles were specially selected for their office (John 6:70; Acts 9:15).

3. The Election of Individuals to Salvation

In addition to these examples of election, the Bible uses the concept sote-

---

23. *Ibid.*, pp. 70-72.
24. *Op. cit.*, p. 177.

riologically. That is, it is used in regard to those who are elected to the privileges of salvation, namely, to become children of God, and heirs of salvation. This is the usage of the term that is especially in view here. Examples of soteriological election are found throughout the Scripture. Abraham is a classic example of it in the Old Testament. "Many are called, but few are chosen."[25] "Even so then at this present time also there is a remnant according to the election of grace."[26] "Even as he chose us in him before the foundation of the world, that we should be holy and without blame before him in love."[27] "Knowing, brethren, beloved of God, your election."[28] "Peter, an apostle of Jesus Christ, to the elect who are sojourners ... according to the foreknowledge of God the Father ..."[29] "Wherefore, brethren give the more diligence to make your calling and election sure ..."[30]

B. The Nature of Election

Since election is a particular aspect of the Decrees of God, the characteristics of the two are identical. It is important to note them specifically again in connection with election, so that we may better understand the plan of salvation as revealed in the Bible.

1. The Source of Election is God's Sovereign Good Pleasure

Just as the Triune God is the Author of the decrees, in general, so he is Author of the specific decree of election. Paul in Romans 9:11 expressly teaches that election is not according to the works of man, but according to the good pleasure of God. "For the children being not yet born, neither having done anything good or bad, that the purpose of God according to election might stand, not of works, but of him that calleth, it was said unto her, The elder shall serve the younger. Even as it is written, Jacob I loved, but Esau I hated."[31]

The language of the Bible in this connection is that he has elected according to his good pleasure (Ephesians 1:8). This means that Christ as the Mediator is not the moving or meritorious cause of election. He is the meritorious cause of the salvation of the elect, but not of the election itself. Election precedes the coming of the Son as is seen in John 3:16; Romans 5:8; I John 4:9.

2. The Decree is Immutable

Since God himself is unchangeable in his being and nature, his decrees are also unchangeable. This means, just as the *Westminster Confession* says, that the number of the elect has been settled and will not change. This unchanging character of the decree of election is of great comfort to the elect, for it assures

---

25. Matthew 22:14.
26. Romans 11:5.
27. Ephesians 1:4.
28. I Thessalonians 1:4.
29. I Peter 1:1-2.
30. II Peter 1:10.
31. Romans 9:11-13.

them of the certainty of their salvation. "And we know that to them that love God all things work together for good, even to them that are called according to his purpose. For whom he foreknew, he also foreordained to be conformed to the image of his Son, that he might be the first born among many brethren: and whom he foreordained, them he also called: and whom he called, them he also justified: and whom he justified, them he also glorified."[32] "For the gifts and the calling of God are not repented of."[33] "Howbeit the firm foundation of God standeth, having this seal, the Lord knoweth them that are his ..."[34]

3. Election is Eternal

As with all of the decrees of God, election is eternal. We have already observed the distinction that may be made between God's own eternity and the eternity of the decrees. The same distinction holds true here. Election is eternal because of the eternal will of God. The eternity of election excludes any idea that it takes place in time. "Even as he chose us in him before the foundation of the world, that we should be holy and without blemish before him in love: having foreordained us unto adoption as sons through Jesus Christ unto himself, according to the good pleasure of his will."[35]

4. Election is Unconditioned by Man

We have already affirmed this when we saw that the decree of election was the expression of the sovereign good pleasure of God. Romans 9:11, cited above, is explicit to the effect that the election was not based on what either Jacob or Esau did. Other examples of this same idea are found throughout the Scripture. "And as the Gentiles heard this, they were glad, and glorified the Word of God: and as many as were ordained to eternal life believed."[36] "Who saved us, and called us with a holy calling, not according to our works, but according to his own purpose and grace, which was given us in Christ Jesus before times eternal."[37] The teaching of these passages as to the unconditional character of the election is clear. If it should be argued that the election is based on foreseen faith, Ephesians 2:8-10 precludes this idea.

> For by grace have ye been saved through faith; and that not of yourselves, it is the gift of God; not of works, that no man should glory. For we are his workmanship, created in Christ Jesus for good works, which God afore prepared that we should walk in them.

5. Election is an Efficacious Decree

We have already observed that what God wills he will do. Romans 8:28-30 clearly affirms that the decree of election made in eternity past will be

---

32. Romans 8:28-30.
33. Romans 11:29.
34. II Timothy 2:19.
35. Ephesians 1:4-5.
36. Acts 13:48.
37. II Timothy 1:9.

brought to a consummation in eternity future. The elect shall be glorified. Jesus affirms the same thing in John 6:37, "All that which the Father giveth me shall come unto men, and him that cometh unto me I will in no wise cast out." Again he said, "My sheep hear my voice ..." (John 10:27a). This is an assertion of fact. The irresistible character of the decree does not mean that there cannot be sinful resistance to a certain degree. Saul of Tarsus is a good example of such. The conquest of the sinner is not by means that are inconsistent with man's free agency. Rather, God exerts such an influence on man as to make him willing. This influence comes with a rebirth by the Spirit of God, and the gift of faith.

6. Election is Gracious in Character

In speaking of the gracious character of election, we are saying that it is not a matter of debt or obligation, but it is purely free and sovereign grace. The decree of election cannot be charge with injustice. Injustice can be charged only when one party has a claim on another. If God owed salvation to all, and failed to give it to all, then he could be accused of injustice. Actually, the case is the opposite. The sinner has absolutely no claim on the blessings of God. He has even forfeited the blessings that had first been bestowed upon him in Eden. God would have been perfectly just if he had not saved any. The decree to elect some to salvation is an act of his sovereign grace. "What shall we say then? Is there unrighteousness with God? God forbid. For he saith to Moses, I will have mercy on whom I have mercy, and I will have compassion on whom I have compassion. So then it is not of him that willeth, or of him that runneth, but of God that hath mercy."[38]

C. The Purpose of Election

Two purposes of election may be found in the Scriptures. First, the proximate purpose is the salvation of the elect. "But we are bound to give thanks to God always for you, brethren beloved of the Lord, for that God chose you from the beginning unto salvation in sanctification of the Spirit and belief of the truth."[39] "But ye are an elect race, a royal priesthood, a holy nation, a people for God's own possession, that ye may show forth the excellencies of him who called you out of darkness into his marvelous light: who in time past were no people, but now are the people of God: who had not obtained mercy, but now have obtained mercy."[40] It should be observed that along with salvation is the goal of service and holiness.

The final or ultimate goal of election is the glory of God. "Having foreordained us unto adoption as sons through Jesus Christ unto himself, according to the good pleasure of his will, to the praise of the glory of his grace, which he freely bestowed on us in the Beloved."[41] "In whom also we were made a heritage, having been foreordained according to the purpose of him who worketh all things after the counsel of his will; to the end that we should be unto the praise

---
38. Romans 9:14-16.
39. II Thessalonians 2:13.
40. I Peter 2:9-10. See also Ephesians 2:10; I Peter 1:15; Romans 8:29-30.
41. Ephesians 1:5-6.

of his glory ... ye were sealed with the Holy Spirit of promise, which is an earnest of our inheritance, unto the redemption of God's own possession, unto the praise of his glory."[42]

IV. Misrepresentations of the Doctrine Answered

A. It is suggested that the doctrine of reprobation teaches that God created some only for the purpose of damning them.

In answer to this misrepresentation, let it be said, first of all, that God created all of his creatures in holiness. He gave them the opportunity to stand, and warned them to do so. Second, once they had fallen into sin, he offered salvation to all who would receive it. Third, he has not made the case of any of the non-elect any worse. He sincerely warns them by conscience and the Word. Fourth, it is a monstrous dream to fancy one of the reprobate as penitent. They remain in their sins because this is their own preference. God simply passes them by, and leaves them to demonstrate the true nature of their character.

B. It is suggested that the decree of reprobation is the ground of the condemnation of the reprobate.

In answer to this argument it should be observed that the decree is the decision to pass some by. In the execution of the decree God's action toward them is purely passive. They are left to the full and free exercise of their own wills. Since their natures are sinful the will is always inclined toward sin. As a consequence of their sin, they are condemned. Thus, the ground of the condemnation is the sin of the reprobate.

C. It is suggested that God does not treat all men fairly or justly in electing some and passing by others.

This objection fails to recognize that all men, if treated in justice or fairness, would be cast into hell forever. For all are sinners, and every sin deserves his wrath and curse. But God in his sovereign good pleasure elected some unto everlasting life. This election was based entirely on grace, and in no way conditioned by our works.

V. Supralapsarianism Compared with Infralapsarianism

A. Background

From the time of the Reformers there have been differences in the conception of the order of the decrees in God's mind. Originally, as indicated by Dr. K. Dijk[43] the question was one of whether or not sin was a part of God's plan. In this form the Supralapsarian view maintained that the fall of Adam was in the

---

42. Ephesians 1:12-14.
43. *De Strijd over Infra- en Supralapsariame in de Gereformeerde Kerken van Nederland.*

decree of God, whereas the Infralapsarian view held it to be just a part of his foreknowledge, not a part of his plan. This latter view was held by Bullinger.

The history of this dispute indicates clearly that much more is involved than a mere question regarding order. Dijk was therefore quite correct when he opposed the opinion that the actual point at issue lies in the 'order.' At least that was not the original problem. Only in the later development of the doctrine of election the element of succession began to play an important role.[44]

Berkouwer feels that, even after the idea of succession entered into the problem, the question of Bullinger, as to whether sin could have been a part of the counsel of God, continued to live.

B. Supralapsarianism

The Supralapsarian view may be described as one which holds that God logically decreed to elect before he decreed to create and to permit the fall. The thought here is that God saw the final end of his glory first, and then proceeded to work out the means of attaining that glory, namely, to provide Christ an elect body, and in this connection to reprobate others, and then to create, to permit the fall, to justify, etc. Bavinck points out the advantage of the supra- view:

> Accordingly, supralapsarianism undoubtedly has in its favor the fact that it refrains from every attempt to justify God, and that both with respect to reprobation, and with respect to election it rests in God's sovereign incomprehensible, yet wise and holy good pleasure.[45]

Hoeksema, who adopts the supralapsarian view, suggests a modification in stating it as follows:

1) God wants to reveal his own eternal glory in the establishment of his covenant.

2) For the realization of this purpose the Son becomes the Christ, the image of the invisible God, the firstborn of every creature, that in him as the first begotten of the dead all the fullness of God might dwell.

3) For that Christ and the revelation of all his fullness the church is decreed and all the elect. In the decree of God Christ is not designed for the church, but the church for Christ. The church is his body, and serves the purpose to reveal the fullness there is in him.

4) For the purpose of realizing this church of Christ, and, therefore, the glory of Christ, the reprobate are determined as vessels of wrath. Reprobation serves the purpose of election as the chaff serves the ripening of the wheat. This is in harmony with the current thought of Scripture: and we find it expressed literally in Isaiah 43:3,4: 'For I am the Lord thy God, the Holy One of Israel, thy saviour: I gave Egypt for thy ransom, Ethiopia and Seba for thee. Since thou was precious in my sight, thou hast been honourable, and I have loved thee; therefore will I give men for thee, and people for thy life.'

---

44. Berkouwer, *op. cit.*, pp. 256-257.
45. *Op. cit.*, p. 387.

5) Finally, in the counsel of God all other things in heaven and on earth are designed as means to the realization of both election and reprobation, and therefore, of the glory of Christ and his church.[46]

C. Infralapsarianism

Infralapsarianism sees the order of the decrees with election and reprobation following the decrees to create and to permit the fall. The great advantage of this view is that it is closer to the historical order of the events as they have taken place. That is, historically, creation was first, then the fall, and then the distinction is made between men by God. Generally speaking, Bavinck considers this the more "modest" or "moderate and less offensive" of the two views. Most of the Reformed creeds seem to be more infra than supra. After considerable debate in the Netherlands over this matter, the Synod of Utrecht in 1905 gave a short synopsis of the debate, saying, "That our Confessions, certainly with respect to the doctrine of election, follow the infralapsarian presentation," but this "does not at all imply an exclusion or condemnation of the supralapsarian presentation."[47]

Berkouwer's judgment of Utrecht is that it "did not intend to give a definite solution to this problem, but, rather, warned its members to speak as little as possible of such matters which go beyond the understanding of simple believers, and it gave the concrete advice to adhere as closely as possible in preaching and catechetical teaching to the presentation given by the Confessions."[48] The same thing may be said of the *Westminster Confession*. Though the Confessions may be more infra in tone than supra, this does not mean that the Confessions have clearly settled the issue. Berkouwer considers this to be a good thing, because the Bible itself does not give us sufficient materials to be dogmatic about this subject.

> It can therefore be said that in spite of the contrast between supra and infra the Church has been kept from making a definite confessional statement with respect to succession in the decrees of God. If that had actually been done in the so-called infra presentation, it would have been illogical not to reject the supra. And that this did not happen is the bright spot in the struggle between supra and infra, for now we can take a responsible attitude toward the *Confession* with its 'infra presentation' and at the same time understand that the problem of succession in the theological supra and infra is a self-created and therefore insoluble problem which does not touch upon the essential faith of the Church.[49]

VI. Addendum

Moses Hoge, the first teacher of theology at Hampden-Sydney, later Union Seminary of Virginia, wrote an excellent treatise in defense of Calvinism. He concluded this pamphlet with a warm and moving appeal to the conscience of

---
46. *Op. cit.*, p. 165.
47. As quoted in Berkouwer, *op. cit.*, p. 255.
48. *Ibid.*, p. 256.
49. *Ibid.*, p. 265.

Christians, urging them to live more godly lives. Here we see the heartfelt religion of the true Calvinist.

And was the Father of mercies mindful of you in the counsels of eternity -- Did your compassionate Redeemer bear you upon his heart in Gethsemane, and upon Calvary -- and can you ever forget such love?

When wandering from God and happiness, did your blessed Saviour seek you -- find you in the high way to ruin, and arrest your headlong course; while others, as good by nature as you, are permitted to go on? Did he forgive your sins, heal your souls, make you heirs of glory, because he loved you with an everlasting love? Do you believe and confess that sovereign unmerited grace hath thus distinguished you from your acquaintances -- from all mankind who are yet in their sins -- and will not you distinguish yourselves by the fervency of your love, and the holiness of your conversation?

Strange: that every reflection upon such amazing love does not melt your hearts, and set your souls on fire. When you grow remiss and conversation is vain, and your life unfruitful -- do you then believe and realize this love and grace? No: if the everlasting unmerited love of God, and the sovereign distinguishing grace of Christ were known and heartily believed, you would not fold your arms with the slothful -- the melting, and the constraining influence of such amazing love and grace would bear you away in an unremitted course of cheerful and devout obedience to the laws of your God and the gospel of your Lord and Saviour Jesus Christ.

Hoge's final word was to the intellectually orthodox man, who has not yet committed himself to Christ.

But my unhappy friends, who are Calvinists in speculation only, not in heart, what shall I say to you?

Will orthodoxy save you -- will good sentiments deliver you from the wrath to come? The design of the truths revealed in the word of God, is to lead the sinner to a living faith in Jesus Christ, and thus to promote holiness in heart and holiness in life. But if these purposes are not accomplished, what will your knowledge of the truth avail? To have just sentiments of the faith once delivered to the saints, is, indeed, a privilege for which you ought to be very thankful; but it is a privilege which, if unimproved, will sink you deeper in ruin. . . .

You profess to believe that Christ is all, and the sinner nothing in the great concerns of salvation. And yet in heart you go about to establish a righteousness of your own: and self in some form, is still an idol to which you offer homage which is due only to Christ. . . .

Trust then no longer to this or any other refuge of lies. Be assured that according to your own choice, your eternal state will be decided. If Jesus and his salvation be your hearty choice, heaven is yours. But unless you make this happy choice, you are undone forever. Nor is there anything to hinder you from doing this, but guilty opposition in heart to Jesus Christ for grace and salvation with which the saints in glory will forever encompass his holy throne.[50]

---

50. Moses Hoge, *Strictures upon a Pamphlet lately published by Jeremiah Walker: titled, "The Fourfold Foundation of Calvinism Examined and Shaken"*, as quoted in my *Studies in Southern Presbyterian Theology, op. cit.*, pp. 91-93.

DIVISION III ANTHROPOLOGY

Chapter XIII Creation

I. Introduction

We have adopted the synthetic method of arrangement of the materials of Systematic Theology, with its seven *loci*. Within this system there are differences as to just where certain matters belong. It is quite common to include Creation and Providence under the *locus* on Theology, and then to treat the creation of man as a new head under Anthropology. It seems preferable to limit Theology to the Being and Nature of God, the Trinity and his immanent works, and to place all of his external works in subsequent *loci*. The next division, which is Anthropology, begins with the first of the external works of God, namely, creation, and then moves on to man and his fall. This is the order followed by Bavinck and Hoeksema.

II. Presuppositions

1. The Bible, being divinely inspired, is infallible and without error.

2. Though the Bible is not a textbook of science, being God's Word, it must speak truly when it speaks about any subject, including matters studied in science.

3. Since God is Truth, and all truth has come from him, whether in the Written Word, or in the created universe, all truth must ultimately be in accord. In other words, there is no real reason for any conflict between the Bible and science.

In natural science man seeks to observe the facts of the universe around him and to discover the truth about the universe from his observations. All facts that are observed in the universe have had their origin in God. He has preinterpreted all facts before the foundation of the world. The true scientist, therefore, seeks to reinterpret the facts after God.

4. The only reason that there is ever conflict, or apparent conflict, is because man has not made the proper interpretation, either of the Bible or of the universe, or of both. Actually, no contradiction exists. It is our duty as God's servants to seek to come to the truth in both realms, and thus to see how gloriously his wisdom and power are revealed in both nature and the Bible.

5. The true doctrine of creation is known only by revelation. It is understood only by faith, Heb. 11:3.[1] This being the case, we look to the Scripture for the doctrine of creation.

III. Views of the Origin of the World

Every human culture has sought to answer the question of the origin of the world and of man. This grows out of the fact of human existence. Charles Hodge states the ground for this as follows:

> The question concerning the origin of the universe has forced itself on the minds of men in all ages. That the mutable cannot be eternal, would seem to be self-evident. As everything within the sphere of human observation is constantly changing, men have been constrained to believe that the world as it now is had a beginning. But if it began to be, whence did it come?[2]

Natural man, because of unbelief, has sought to explain the origin and existence of the universe without God. The various theories for the origin of the world may be classified under four categories.

A. Atheistic Theories

Those theories which deny any existence of God or any spiritual entity as the source of the world are classified as atheistic.

1. Atomistic

One of the earliest forms of atheistic views of the origin of the world is found in the Greek "atomistic" philosophy. Matter was considered to be eternally existent. It was endowed with eternal properties of motion, diversity, and the tendency to aggregation. All that exists in the world is to be accounted for by the movement of this eternal matter, etc.

2. Evolution

The most commonly accepted theory of today is that of evolution. In purely naturalistic evolution matter is eternal. It contains within itself the germ of development. The world is in a constant state of evolving. Ultimately, the universe is seen as something that never began and that will never cease. It is in a continuing process. "Nothing is, and everything becomes."

Criticism: Both of these views deny the existence of God, and assert eternity of matter. This is an irrational assumption. The irrationality is seen in the assumption that the present form of the universe, with all its complexity, has all come to be through pure chance. The probabilities against each evolutionary step are so great that the acceptance of a chance evolution must be on the basis of a blind

---
1. Bavinck, Herman, *Gereformeerde Dogmatiek, op cit.*, Vol.II, p. 371.
2. Hodge, Charles, *Systematic Theology, op cit.*, Vol. I, p. 550.

faith. It is impossible to account for the evidence of order in the universe, or for the production of an intelligent creature, such as man, on this basis. It can be held only on the basis of faith assumptions that are totally groundless.

The only tenable view of evolution would be one that posits it as the way in which God created. The question that has to be asked regarding this is whether it is compatible with the Scriptural teaching about creation. We shall examine this question more fully later.

3. Phenomenalism

With the rise of modern subjectivism has come a skepticism about the reality of the world around us. All we know is what we experience through our senses, and we cannot be sure that there is any reality beyond ourselves.

Criticism: This view conveniently avoids the question of the origin of the universe by denying its existence. The consequence of such a view is skepticism about all facts.

B. Dualism

From Greek philosophy comes dualism, which posits the eternity of both spiritual and material substances. The spiritual is called God, and he is seen as using the matter to create or form the world. God is limited by the imperfect and evil nature of the matter he must use to create the world. Thus, the world is imperfect.

Criticism: This view denies the sole, absolute, eternal, and independent nature of God, by making matter co-eternal and co-existent with him. Further, it limits him in the creation, and in his control over the universe. Thus, the final outcome of history is in question.

C. Pantheism

Atheism posits matter and energy, dualism assumes two eternal substances, while pantheism seeks to identify everything with God. Both the infinite and the finite are recognized, but they are correlated as different modes of God's existence. The material world is the manifestation of the spiritual reality of God. God is everything, and everything is God.

Criticism: By identifying God with the universe, creation is ruled out, along with any idea of God's sovereignty over the world. Ultimately, under this view, there can be no ethic, no religion, no creator, no creature.

D. Theism

Theism posits the idea of a Creator God, who creates all else beside himself, without the use of any material. This is the Biblical view of the origin of the universe. Let us now examine the Biblical idea of creation more fully.

IV. The Biblical Idea of Creation

A. The Words Used

The Hebrew uses three words to describe creative activity. They are *bara*[3], *asah*[4], and *yatsar*[5]. *Bara*, translated by *ktizein*[6] in Greek, has as its root idea "cutting off", "separation". In Joshua 17:15, 18 it refers to the cutting down of trees. From the concept of splitting comes that of forming. These (*bara*, *ktizein*) terms are used in three different senses. First, there is the absolute sense, creation without any pre-existent material (Genesis 1:1). Second, there is what may be called secondary creation. This is the forming of something from material already existing (Genesis 1:21, 25; 5:1; Isaiah 45:7, 12; 54:16; Amos 4:13; I Corinthians 11:9; Revelation 10:6). Third, these terms are even used to refer to that which comes into existence under providential guidance (Psalms 104:30; Isaiah 45:7, 8; 65:18; I Timothy 4:4).

The word *asah* translated by *poiein*[7] meaning "to make" or "to create" has the same threefold application. Primary creation is seen in Genesis 2:4; Proverbs 16:4; Acts 17:24. The secondary creation, which is the more frequent usage of these terms is found in Genesis 1:7, 16, 26; 2:22; Psalms 89:47. The third form of providential creation is found in Psalms 74:17.

The third word, *yatsar*, translated by *plassein*[8] meaning "to form" is found with a similar threefold usage. Primary creation is referred to by this term in Psalms 90:2. Secondary creation is found in Genesis 2:7, 19; Psalms 104:26; Amos 4:13; Zechariah 12:1. The providential creation is found in Deuteronomy 32:18; Isaiah 43:1, 7, 21; 45:7.

All three of the words are found in Isaiah 45:7. "I form (*yotser*[9]) the light, and create (*ubore*[10]) darkness; I make (*oseh*[11]) peace, and create evil; I am Jehovah, that doeth all things." From the Genesis account we learn that the light and darkness are part of the secondary creative activity of God. Peace and evil would be the products of his providence.

Of particular interest is the first verse of Genesis, for here we have the first assertion regarding creation. Is it a reference to absolute creation, or to a secondary creation? Some have suggested that *bereshith*[12] be taken in the construct sense, with the translation then, "in the beginning of." This leads to making the first verse a dependent clause, either by emending *bara* to the infinitive construct form *bero'*[13], and thus reading "In the beginning of the creating of God," that is, "When God began to create ..." It is not necessary to emend *bara* for it is possible to follow the construct with a finite verb. The translation then

---

3. בָּרָא
4. עָשָׂה
5. יָצַר
6. κτίζειν
7. ποιεῖν
8. πλάσσειν
9. יֹצֵר
10. וּבוֹרֵא
11. עֹשֶׂה
12. בְּרֵאשִׁית
13. בְּרֹא

would be, "In the beginning of, God created ....," that is, "When God began to create." Ordinarily, however, when a construct is followed by a finite verb, the construct form is clear, or else the context demands the construct. Neither case exists here in Genesis 1:1. Thus, the preferred reading is that of the absolute and not construct, "In the beginning, God created..."

Dr. E. J. Young notes the alliteration in the Hebrew of the first two words, namely, *bereshith bara*[14]. This serves to link these two words. The creative act was in the beginning.

What then is the significance of *bara*? This question can be answered only by a survey of its usage in the Old Testament, and such a survey will confirm the time-honored and oft-noted view. In the Qal stem *bara* is employed exclusively of the divine activity. The subject of the verb is always God and never man. The idea of novelty or extraordinariness of result seems frequently implied. The word is employed with the accusative of the product but the material used, if any, is never mentioned. ... The word *bara*, therefore, has a more restricted usage than does the English word "create". If, in Genesis 1:1, Moses desired to express the thought of absolute creation there was no more suitable word in the Hebrew language at his disposal. And when this word is taken in close conjunction with *bereshith*, we may paraphrase the thought, 'The beginning was by means of a creative act'. The beginning and unique creation -- namely, that of heaven and earth -- are here joined together. Hence, we may understand the writer as asserting that the heaven and earth had a beginning and that this beginning is to be found in the fact that God created them.[15]

B. Relevant Passages on Creation

1. Hebrews 11:3, "By faith we understand that the worlds (*tous aionas*[16]) have been framed (*katertisthai*[17]) by the word of God (*rhemati theou*[18]), so that what is seen hath not been made (*gegonenai*[19]) out of things which appear."

The assertion of this verse that the Biblical idea of creation must be accepted by faith is our starting point. It is a clear teaching of the Bible, but, as with all Biblical doctrine, it cannot be demonstrably proved to the non-believer. The Christian simply believes what the Bible says on this subject, namely, that God is the creator of heaven and earth. Further, this verse teaches that the creative activity of God was by the power of his fiat command, by his word. Though the Greek *logos*[20] could have been used, there would be danger of con-

---

14. בְּרֵאשִׁית בָּרָא
15 "The Relation of the First Verse of Genesis One to Verses Two and Three," *Westminster Theological Journal*, XXI, (May, 1959), pp. 138-139.
16. τοὺς αἰῶνας
17. κατηρτίσθαι
18. ῥήματι θεοῦ
19. γεγονέναι
20. λόγος

fusing this with the Personal Logos. *Rhema*[21] signifies more explicitly the verbal word of God. "God said, Let there be ..." is the language of Genesis 1. The emphasis here, then, is on the command of God.

This verse also suggests the idea that has been expressed by the phrase *creatio ex nihilo* (creation out of nothing). Bavinck reviews the words used in various languages (Hebrew, Greek, Latin, Dutch, English) to speak of creation, and finds that none of these words inherently mean to create out of nothing. Bavinck sees Heb. 11:3 as clearly asserting the idea of original creation. "A formless matter is hereby excluded; the visible world has not proceeded from the visible, but must rest in God, who called all things into being by his word."[22] "The term 'creation out of nothing' is then also not literally derived from Scripture, but appears first in II Maccabees 7:28, where it is said that God *ex ouk onton epoiesen*[23] (Vulg. *fecit ex nihilo*) heaven and earth and man. . . . The Scripture . . . does not use the term, but clearly teaches the matter."[24] Though the concept expressed by this phrase is true, it may not be the best phrase to describe the Biblical teaching on creation. Hoeksema says of this expression:

> As a definition this is very defective and incorrect. For, in the first place, such a definition could not be applied to all the various acts of God that constitute the one mighty work of creation. But, in the second place, the real idea of the work of creation is not expressed in this definition. It leaves, after all, the impression that the origin of things must be sought in nothing. The idea of a creation *ex nihilo* is entirely foreign to Scripture. The Word of God explains the origin of things according to the counsel of God from his omnipotent will, and tells us that God calls the things that are not as if they were.[25]

Berkhof says, "However, in view of the fact that the expression 'creation out of nothing' is liable to misunderstanding, and has often been misunderstood, it is preferable to speak of creation without the use of pre-existing material."[26] We have been using the term absolute creation to express this thought.

   2. Romans 4:17, "(As it is written, a father of many nations have I made of thee) before him whom he believed, even God, who giveth life to the dead, and calleth the things that are not, as though they were."

Though this verse is not speaking directly to the creation, but of the fact that God could give Abraham a son, it nevertheless bases the hope of Abraham for a son on the fact that God is able to call into being from things that were not.

   3. Revelation 4:11, "Worthy art thou, our Lord and our God, to receive the glory and the honor and the power: for thou didst create all things, and because of thy will they were, and were created."

---

21. ῥῆμα
22. Bavinck, *op. cit.* II, p. 381.
23. ἐξ οὐκ ὄντων ἐποίησεν
24. Bavinck, *op. cit.*, p. 379.
25. Bavinck, *op. cit.*, p. 170.
26. *Systematic Theology, op cit.*, p. 133.

Here, as in the last two verses considered, the idea of the power of God in creation is emphasized. The will of God is seen as the cause of all that was created. In other words, the work of creation is but the execution of God's decree to create.

4. Psalms 33:6, 9. "By the word of Jehovah were the heavens made, and all the host of them by the breath of his mouth. ... For he spake, and it was done; he commanded, and it stood fast."

The emphasis that is repeated in these verses is the power of God's command. He spake, he commanded, and it was done. The sovereign majesty and power of God is displayed here.

5. Psalms 104:24, "O Jehovah, how manifold are thy works: In wisdom hast thou made them all: The earth is full of thy riches."

This verse stresses the wisdom of God that is to be seen in the creation. With all of the manifold variety in the universe, we have a great display of the riches of God and of his divine wisdom. Also, implied in his making the world in wisdom, is the idea that he has planned all that is to take place in creation. As we have said before, he has already preinterpreted every fact that is found in the universe. As man studies it, therefore, he is to seek to reinterpret God's thoughts after him, and thus to come to truth and wisdom. The failure of the non-Christian to acknowledge the created nature of the universe bars him from ever coming to the ultimate truth about himself or reality.

6. Isaiah 40:25, 26, 28, 29, "To whom then will ye liken me, that I should be equal to him? saith the Holy One. Lift up your eyes on high, and see who hath created these, that bringeth out their host by number; he calleth them all by name; by the greatness of his might, and for that he is strong in power, not one is lacking. ... Hast thou not known? Hast thou not heard? The everlasting God, Jehovah, the Creator of the ends of the earth fainteth not, neither is weary; there is no searching of his understanding. He giveth power to the faint; and to him that hath no might he increaseth strength."

The prophet is concerned to present the uniqueness of God as the Creator. Ultimately, the most basic thing that can be said of all of the universe is that it has been made by God. It is the God of the Bible who has made it. No other god can claim this prerogative. This great fact is basic to all Christian thought about metaphysics, epistemology and ethics. In other words, it is the creation that underlies the Christian world and life view, and it is the creation that distinguishes the Christian *Weltanschauung* from all others.

C. Treatment of Genesis 1

1. The interpretation of Genesis 1:1-2, "In the beginning God created the heavens and the earth. And the earth was waste and void; and darkness was upon the face of the deep: and the Spirit of God moved upon the face of the waters."

As we have already seen, verse one sets forth the fact that God did in the beginning create in the most absolute sense, that is, without using any pre-existent material. The expression "the heavens and the earth", *hasshamayim we'eth ha'arets*[27], includes all things outside of God himself. "Verse one is a narrative complete in itself."[28] Verses 2-31 then constitute another narrative complete in itself. Verse one is an introductory statement, asserting that God created everything, and then beginning with verse two, we have the detailed treatment of the fashioning of the earth into the present condition. The three-fold condition described in verse two is that which the earth had at the end of verse one. There is no necessity to suggest that this condition was less than what God desired it to be. It has been suggested that the condition described by desolation and waste (*tohu webohu*[29]) is that of chaos. Isaiah 45:18 contrasts the void (*tohu*[30]) with the place "to be inhabited." "For thus saith Jehovah that created the heavens, the God that formed the earth and made it, that established it and created it not a waste, that formed it to be inhabited..." Young says of this verse, "Isaiah 45:18 is often treated as though it taught that God did not create the earth as *tohu*. This is a misinterpretation. The prophet is simply stating the purpose of creation. It should be noted that this very chapter of Isaiah (v.7) speaks of God as 'forming darkness' *qotsar hoshde*."[31]

In other words, Genesis 1:2 is not affirming that the world was a disorderly and confused mass, but simply that it was not habitable. "In so far as the words *tohu webohu* are concerned we must conclude that they simply describe the earth as not habitable. There is no reason why God might not have pronounced the condition set forth by the first circumstantial clause of verse two as 'good'."[32] The clause "and the Spirit of God moved upon the face of the waters" describes the condition of the earth at this stage as under the control of God. "The threefold statement of circumstances in itself seems to imply order. The material of which this earth consists was at that time covered with water, and darkness was all about. Over the waters, however, brooded God's Spirit. There is something of the awesome in the description."[33] This is not to be the final condition of the earth, for God will prepare the earth for man, and finally place man upon it.

Before moving on to the next verse, it should be observed that verse one speaks of the whole of created reality under the term "heavens and earth". From the second verse on the account becomes geocentric. That is, the earth is the center of the picture. Even the sun, moon and stars are mentioned only in relation to the earth.

2. The Six Days

In treating the six days we shall not try to go into a detailed treatment of each day. Rather, it shall be our purpose to note the various views held about the

---

27. הַשָּׁמַיִם וְאֵת הָאָרֶץ
28. Young, *op. cit.*, p. 143.
29. תֹהוּ וָבֹהוּ
30. תֹהוּ
31. Young, *op. cit.*, p. 144.
32. *Ibid.*, p. 145.
33. *Idem.*

over-all account. As we do this, we are immediately confronted with the question of the antiquity of the earth, and the length of the days of creation. Until the 19th century the generally accepted view was that the days of creation were 24 hour days, and that the earth was young. One of the impacts of the theory of evolution on science has been to assume the immense antiquity of the universe and the earth. With the general testimony of science favoring the great antiquity of the earth, and the uncertainty as to the teaching of the Bible on this subject, many orthodox Christians have accepted this idea. Nigel Lee says:

> As regards the primordial creation, time itself was apparently created with and at the beginning of the creation of the universe as recorded in the first verse of the Bible. . . .After this, the earth remained in its pristine condition without form and void, when darkness was upon the face of the deep (Gen. 1:1-2a). *How long* this condition obtained, we are not told. It may have been millions of years, or it may have been less than a second. God has kept this secret and not revealed it to us . . . What is the precise length of these seven 'days' of formation week according to the *Genesis* account itself. It is our firm conviction that this question cannot be answered.[34]

Warfield observes, "The question of the antiquity of man has of itself no theological significance."[35] He argues for the unity of the human race, regardless of its antiquity. It is this that has theological significance. Though we may have strong convictions regarding this question, Lee is probably correct in saying that we do not have enough information to settle it definitively. We should refrain from judging fellow Christians, who differ with us on this particular question.

a. Literal Days

Berkhof says, "The prevailing view has always been that the days of Genesis 1 are to be understood as literal days."[36] Arguments favoring this view are as follows:

(1) The basic meaning of the word *yom* denotes a natural day. It is one of the rules of exegesis to take the primary meaning of a word, unless the context demands otherwise.

(2) The expression "and there was evening and there was morning" used of each of the creation days seems clearly to point to literal days.

(3) The Fourth Commandment (Exodus 20:9-11) bases the command to labor six days and rest one, on the fact that God has done the same. The word *yom* is used in reference both to God's activity and man's activity. Exegetically there is no reason to give this word a different meaning in this passage.

---

34. *The Origin and Destiny of Man* (Philadelphia: Presbyterian and Reformed Publishing Co., 1974), pp. 6-8.
35. Warfield, "On the Antiquity and Unity of the Human Race," *Studies in Theology* (New York: Oxford University Press, 1932), p. 235; also in *Biblical and Theological Studies* (Philadelphia: Presbyterian and Reformed Publishing Co., 1952), p. 238.
36. Berkhof, *op. cit.*, p. 153.

(4) The Sabbath of God's rest was a literal day. Some have maintained that the Sabbath rest of God is eternal, that he will never again create. If the Sabbath is eternal, then, the other days would also be eternal days.
(5) The last three days are presumably three literal days, since the sun, moon and stars have been set the heavens, which gives the means for measuring the length of the days. Though it is difficult to show how the first three days were measured, it is presumed that they would have been of the same length as the last three.
(6) On the theory of long periods, Adam would have been in paradise for a long time, and should thus have produced a race while there on the "sixth day". This is not the representation of Scripture.
(7) Long periods would necessitate the distortion of the concept of the creative work of God. "And God said, Let there be light, and there was light." The impression is that there were immediate results to his command. Psalms 33:9 says, "For he spake, and it was done, he commanded, and it stood fast."
(8) Long periods of time would require death and decay to have been part of the creation before the advent of sin. The Genesis account does not introduce death until after the fall, and along with the fall came the cursing of nature as a consequence of man's sin.
(9) Long periods would present a strange view of God's work. For, on the basis of the Biblical records, the earth and man are to be dated on the order of the 6,000 or even 10,000 to 15,000 years in age. Also, on the basis of the Word, it would appear that the end of the world is not too far distant. If this is the case, and the theory of billions of years occurring before the creation of man were true, then "the Lord in that case builds a foundation of thousands of feet deep in order to build a very little house on top of it of one story high."[37]
(10) It is interesting to observe that Henry M. Morris holds to a short history of the earth, with the upper range at 15,000 years.[38] Dr. John W. Klotz in *Genes, Genesis, and Evolution* concludes that the age of the earth is on the order of thousands, and not millions or billions of years. He accepts the Genesis account as speaking of literal days.[39]

b. Long Periods of Time

The arguments for the long periods of time are as follows:
(1) The text does not demand literal days. For example, the word *yom*[40] is used in different ways in the Bible. In Genesis 1:5 it is used to designate the period of light as contrasted with darkness, without any specific reference to time. In Genesis 1:16 it seems to refer to the period of daylight as measured by the sun. In Genesis 2:4 it is used to refer to the whole period of creation. "These are the generations of the heavens and of the earth when they were created, in the day that Jehovah God made

---
37. Hoeksema, *op. cit.*, p. 181.
38. *Evolution and the Modern Christian*, pp. 63-64.
39. P. 116.
40. יוֹם

earth and heaven." In other words, this usage is of a period that is characterized by the total creative activity of God. It was at least a week in length, if not a much longer period. Psalms 90:4 says, "For a thousand years in thy sight are but as yesterday when it is past, and as a watch in the night." II Peter 3:8 says, "But forget not this one thing, beloved, that one day is with the Lord as a thousand years, and a thousand years as one day." These passages certainly teach that God does not live in time, and that he is above it. If a thousand years is compared to a day, there is no reason that a million or a billion could not also be so compared in the same way. The point of all this evidence is that a case cannot be made from the word *yom* for a literal day.

(2) Even if literal days are accepted for the last three, the first four could not have been measured by the sun, since it is not even mentioned until the fourth day.

(3) The expression "morning and evening" simply refers to the beginning and end of each day, or period, not to a literal morning or evening. This would certainly be true of the first three days, since there was no sun.

(4) The Sabbath of the Lord is an eternal Sabbath of rest. If this is so, then the other days were also long periods of time.[41]

(5) The long periods fit better the findings of science, and the dating of the age of the earth by various scientific methods.

c. Framework Hypothesis

On the basis of the parallelism between the first three days and the second three days, it has been suggested that there is no chronological order intended. This has been set forth by Professor Arie Noordtzij of the University of Utrecht in 1924, under a work entitled: *Gods Woord en der Eeuwen Getuigenis*.

Young summarizes this view as follows:

> The Holy Scripture, so he tells us, always places the creation in the light of the central fact of redemption, Christ Jesus. When we examine the first chapter of Genesis in the light of other parts of Scripture, it becomes clear that the intention is not to give a survey of the process of creation, but to permit us to see the creative activity of God in the light of his saving acts, and so, in its structure, the chapter allows its full light to fall upon man, the crown of the creative work....
>
> That the six days do not have to do with the course of a natural process may be seen, thinks Noordtzij, from the manner in which the writer groups his material. We are given two trios which exhibit a pronounced parallelism, all of which have the purpose of bringing to the fore the preeminent glory of man, who actually reaches his destiny in the sabbath, for the sabbath is the point in which the creative work of God culminates and to which it attains. . . . What is significant is not the concept 'day', taken by itself, but rather the concept of 'six plus one'.

---

41. See Hebrews 4:1-11.

Inasmuch as the writer speaks of evenings and mornings previous to the heavenly bodies of the fourth day, continues Noordtzij, it is clear that he uses the terms 'days' and 'nights' as a framework (*kader*). Such a division of time is a projection not given to show us the account of creation in its natural historical course, but, as elsewhere in the Holy Scriptures, to exhibit the majesty of the creation in the light of the great saving purpose of God. ... Why then, we may ask, are the six days mentioned? The answer, according to Noordtzij, is that they are only mentioned to prepare us for the seventh day.[42]

As Young goes on to point out, Noordtzij was answered by Professor G. C. Aalders of the Free University of Amsterdam. Aalders held that two basic considerations must guide the interpreter of Genesis one, namely:
(1) In the text of Genesis itself ... there is not a single allusion to suggest that the days are to be regarded as a form or mere manner of representation and hence of no significance for the essential knowledge of the divine creative activity.
(2) In Exodus 20:21 the activity of God is presented to man as a pattern, and this fact presupposes that there was a reality in the activity of God, which man is to follow.[43]

After a full treatment of the whole chapter, Young draws the following conclusions:
1. The pattern laid down in Genesis 1:1-2:3 is that of six days followed by a seventh.
2. The six days are to be understood in a chronological sense, that is, one day following another in succession. This fact is emphasized in that the days are designated, one, two, three, etc.
3. The length of the days is not stated. What is important is that each of the days is a period of time which may legitimately be denominated *yom* ("day").
4. The first three days were not solar days such as we now have, inasmuch as the sun, moon and stars had not yet been made.
5. The beginning of the first day is not indicated, although, from Exodus 20:11, we may warrantably assume that it began at the absolute beginning, Genesis 1:1.
6. The Hebrew word *yom* is used in two different senses in Genesis 1:5. In the one instance it denotes the light in distinction from the darkness; in the other it includes both evening and morning. In Genesis 2:4b the word is employed in yet another sense, "in the day of the LORD God's making."
7. If the word "day" is employed figuratively, *i.e.*, to denote a period of time longer than twenty-four hours, so also may the terms "evening"

---
42. "The Days of Genesis", *Westminster Theological Journal*, Vol. XXV, No. 1, (Nov., 1962), pp. 3-5.
43. From *De Goddelijke Openbaring in de eerste drie Hoofdstukken van Genesis*, p. 233, as cited by Young, *op. cit.*, p. 5.

and "morning", inasmuch as they are component elements of the day, be employed figuratively.

8. Although the account of creation is told in terms of fiat and fulfillment, this does not necessarily exclude all process. In the second work of the third day, for example, the language suggests that the vegetation came forth from the earth as it does today....

9. The purpose of the six days is to show how God, step by step, changed the uninhabitable and unformed earth of verse two into the well-ordered world of verse thirty-one.

10. The purpose of the first section of Genesis, (1:1-2:3), is to exalt the eternal God as the lone creator of heaven and earth, who in infinite wisdom and by the Word of his power brought the earth into existence and adorned and prepared it for man's habitancy. The section also prepares for the second portion of Genesis, the Generations, which deals with man's habitancy of God's world.

11. Genesis one is not poetry or saga or myth, but straight-forward, trustworthy history, and inasmuch as it is a divine revelation, accurately records those matters of which it speaks. That Genesis one is historical may be seen from these considerations. (1) It sustains an intimate relationship with the remainder of the book. ... (2) The characteristics of Hebrew poetry are lacking. ... (3) The New Testament regards certain events mentioned in Genesis one as actually having taken place. We may safely allow the New Testament to be our interpreter of this mighty first chapter of the Bible.[44]

V. The Formulation of the Doctrine

A. The Author of Creation is God--the Triune God

That God is the Creator is readily seen from the Scripture. It is of interest to note that all three Persons of the Trinity are associated with his creative activity. The following passages show the various usages of Scripture in this regard:

1. There are passages which refer the creation to God absolutely, without distinction of person (Genesis 1:1, 26).
2. God the Father is spoken of as creator (I Corinthians 8:6).
3. God the Father is said to have created through the Son (Hebrews 1:2).
4. God the Father is said to have created through the Spirit (Psalms 104:30).
5. Creation is ascribed to the Son (John 1:1-3).
6. Creation is ascribed to the Holy Spirit (Genesis 1:2; Job 33:4).

---

44. Young, "The Days of Genesis II", *Westminster Theological Journal*, Vol. XXV, No. 2, May, 1963, pp. 169-171.

From these passages we may conclude that the Bible does not present an abstract speculation about the source of creation. Rather, it identifies the author of creation as the personal, triune God.

B. The Nature of the Creative Act

1. Creation Was a Free Act of God

We have already seen that the Bible teaches the decrees of God are free. Since creation is a part of the execution of his decrees, its necessity lies only in his sovereign free decree. Thus, creation is a free act of God. Pantheism and emanation make the origin of the universe to be an evolutionary process of deity, and thus necessary. The Bible teaches that only those actions which are inherent in his nature are necessary actions. For example, the intra Trinitarian relations are necessary. To say that the creation is necessary would be to affirm that it is equally eternal with God.

The only necessity that can be ascribed to actions which are not inherent in his nature is that necessity which grows out of his having decreed them. They are necessary because he has decreed them so, and thus are not necessary in an absolute sense, but only in a consequent sense. The Bible clearly teaches that God created according to the counsel of his will (Ephesians 1:11; Revelation 4:11), and that he is not dependent on his creation in any way (Job 22:2-3; Acts 17:25).

2. Creation Was a Temporal Act of God

Both Genesis 1:1 and John 1:1 speak of creation as occurring in the beginning. Time was not in existence when God created the world. Time began with creation. Augustine thought it more correct to speak of creation as "*cum tempore*" than "*in tempore*". In the sense that God is not in time, all of his actions may be said to be in eternity. This terminology is misleading, however, for it gives the impression that there was no beginning. The Bible clearly affirms there was a beginning. Thus, it seems proper to speak of creation as temporal, understanding it to mean that time itself began with creation.[45]

3. Creation Was Without External Means

We have already observed that the Bible speaks of creation in the absolute sense. We have noted the objection of Hoeksema to the expression *ex nihilo*, though we would observe that the *Westminster Confession and Catechisms* use the English equivalent of this, that God has created "out of nothing". What is affirmed is that no pre-existent material was used. That is, there was no matter existing before God created it. He called it into being by Divine command. He simply commanded, and where there had been nothing prior to that command, there now exists the universe. This concept of creation by the word of his power

---

45. See Psalms 90:2; 102:25; Matthew 19:4, 8; John 1:1-3.

is beyond our comprehension, and should cause us afresh to glorify and worship him as God.

4. Creation Was All-Inclusive

In Genesis 1:1 we observed the absoluteness of the creative work of God. The terms "heavens and the earth" also speak of the all-inclusiveness of the work. The *Westminster Confession* speaks of "The world and all things therein whether visible or invisible" as being created by God. The terms "heavens and earth" include all that we mean by the word "universe". Under the categories of "visible and invisible" may be understood both those forces and powers that lie within the physical universe, and also the spiritual realms. Both of these have been created by God. When it is said that God created light on the first day, and one remembers that physicists find light to be but a small portion of a much larger group of electro-magnetic waves, we may assume that this whole scale of energy was a part of that creative act.

Just when we are to understand that the creation of the angelic hosts took place is not clear. Evidently, it was accomplished before the end of the sixth day. Perhaps it belongs in the first day, before the ordering of the earth was begun. The angels are not a race, as mankind is. Each is a separate creation. They are rational creatures, with moral obligations. They were all created with freedom of will, and though originally inclined to good were changeable. As with the rest of creation, they were created for the praise and glory of God. As moral creatures they were obligated to obey God's commands. Some rebelled and fell into sin, as is indicated by Jude 6, and Revelation 12. No plan of salvation was provided for them, as is the case for men.

5. Creation Was Progressive in Character

As one studies the account in Genesis one, it is evident that there is an orderly progression from the first act of primitive absolute creation to the placing of man on the earth, and the resting of God from his creative work. In addition to the straight line development from the first to the seventh day, there also seems to be a parallelism between the first three and the second three days. This may be seen best by the use of a table as follows:

Day	Event	Day	Event
1	Absolute creation. Creation of light.	4	Sun, moon and stars placed in the firmament for signs, seasons, days and years.
2	Firmament separated from seas beneath.	5	Waters swarm with living creatures. Birds fly in heaven, after their kind.
3	Seas collected. Dry land appeared. Earth put forth herbs, grass, trees after their kind.	6	Earth brings forth living creatures, cattle, creeping things, beasts, after their kind. Man made after the image of God.

7 God rested and blessed the Sabbath.

What we are to make of the apparent parallelism between the first trio of days and the second trio is difficult to determine. This much can certainly be said, the orderliness of God's activity is displayed. Broadly speaking, the progress shown here is similar to that suggested by scientists who hold to an evolutionary development of the earth and life on it. We have already noted the irrationality of a chance evolution, but suggested that it would be possible to hold to a theistic evolution. Many believe that the days of Genesis one are long periods of time, and that the progressive order of the six days is the broad outline of God's evolutionary development of the earth, and the life on it. It should be observed, however, that the Genesis account places certain limits on an evolutionary hypothesis, namely, in the mention of multiplying "after their kind". The evolutionary hypothesis would hold that one "kind" has evolved from another. This seems to be counter to the teaching of Scripture. Further, the more detailed account of the creation of man and woman given in Genesis two seems to preclude human beings from this evolving process, even if it occurred in the rest of the plant and animal kingdom.

It should be observed that nothing in the Bible forbids the idea of an evolutionary development of plants or animals within their respective "kinds". The fact is that man is able to control such development in selective breeding of both plants and animals. He is able to induce mutations through various means, and to produce varieties of the particular plant or animal. No doubt there has been such evolution taking place within the "kinds" down through the ages, and this has given rise to the idea that evolution would account for the whole development of life from the simple to the complex. The problem of the evolutionist, however, is not just one missing link between animals and man, but missing links between each of the "kinds". Since there is a demonstrable kind of evolution in both the plant and animal kingdoms, it behooves the Christian to use care in condemning all evolution as false. He may very well speak of a limited evolution, namely, that within the Genesis "kinds". Of course, here, as with all events, the Christian must insist that such evolution is not by chance, but under the control of God, who orders all things according to the counsel of his will (Ephesians 1:11).

6. The Result of the Act of Creation Is a Dependent Creation

As a consequence of the creative work of God, there is now a created reality that is distinct from the Being of God. By its nature, as created, it is dependent upon the Creator, who has made it, and who now upholds and preserves it. Only God is independent and self-contained. The universe and all that is in it are dependent upon and derived from God.

Man as a part of this creation only comes to the knowledge of God through creation.

> We are not self-existent and self-sufficient beings, existing in abstraction from creation, and viewing God in his eternal being and independence by some kind of super-intuition and perception. We are dependent beings, and it is only by creation and in the context of creation that we think and entertain a conception of God. When *we* think, and particularly when we think of God we think as beings conditioned by creation. In other words, when *we* think of God, we cannot think of God aright without thinking of our relation to him. Even if the thought of our relation to him is not in the forefront of consciousness at a particular time, it must always be in the immediate background conditioning our whole attitude in thinking of him. To be quite specific, any thought of God by us must be conditioned by a profound apprehension of his transcendent majesty and glory; in a word, that he is God and that there is none else beside him. . . . So far then as we are concerned, we can never think of God without thinking of God as God and ourselves as his creatures. In other words, the thought of creation, the thought of our dependence upon God, is implicated in any true thought *we* entertain with respect to God. Without the concept of creation, then, we cannot think even one right thought of God.[46]

Since the universe and all that is in it came from the hand of the perfect and holy God, it could be nothing but good as first created. This is just how it is described in the Bible (Genesis 1:4, 10, 12, 18, 21, 25, 31). There are two negative implications derived from this fact: "first, that evil and sin are not eternal; second, that sin and evil were not resident in God's created handiwork. Sin had an origin, and it originated subsequent to creation."[47]

It is true that the creation was mutable, but this does not take away the fact that it was originally good. It was the rebellion of the highest creature of the universe that brought the whole of creation under the curse, and thus marred and disfigured it. Ultimately, in the plan of redemption the whole of creation is to be restored (Romans 8:21).

---

46. John Murray, "The Significance of the Doctrine of Creation," *Collected Writings* (Edinburgh: Banner of Truth Trust, 1976), Vol. I, pp. 325-6.
47. *Ibid.*, p. 327.

7. The Purpose of the Creation Was for the Manifestation of the Glory of God

That the creative work of God was for the manifestation of the glory of God is clearly asserted in the Scripture. "The heavens declare the glory of God, the firmament showeth his handiwork."[48] "... [W]hom I created for my glory ..."[49] "Thy people also shall be all righteous; they shall inherit the land for ever, the branch of my planting, the work of my hands, that I may be glorified."[50]

As we recognize the design of the universe and of ourselves to be for the glory of God, we see everything in a different way from the non-Christian. All that we are and do is to be governed by the fact that man's chief end is to glorify God and to enjoy him forever. This is the basis for a Christian *Weltanschauung*, or world and life view.

---

48. Psalms 19:1.
49. Isaiah 43:7.
50. Isaiah 60:21. See also Ephesians 1:5, 6, 9, 12, 14; 3:9, 10; Colossians 1:16.

Chapter XIV Angels, Their Creation, Nature and Functions

Introduction

Today in modern theology, the idea of angels is dismissed as part of the primitive mythology. The Bible teaches that God not only created the earth with man as its highest creature, but also created other intelligent, moral creatures, which are known as angels. Though this is true, the Bible does not give us a great deal of information regarding the angels. First, we shall consider the names given to the angels. Next, we shall examine what is taught in the Bible concerning this subject, beginning with their origin. Then we shall examine what the Bible teaches concerning the nature of the angels, and their functions.

I. The Biblical Terms

The word angel is an Anglicizing of the Greek word *aggelos*[1], which in turn translates the Hebrew *malak*[2]. Both of these words mean messenger. The term is used in various ways in Scripture.

First, it may refer to an ordinary messenger, Job. 1:14; Luke 7:24; 11:52. Prophets were sometimes designated by this word, Isaiah 43:19; Mal. 3:1. Priests were also so called, Mal. 2:7. Ministers of the New Testament were sometimes called angels, Rev. 1:20. The impersonal theophany of the pillar of cloud was called the angel of the Lord, Ex. 14:19. Other impersonal agents were: pestilence, II Sam. 24:16-17; winds, Ps. 104:4; plagues, called evil angels, Ps. 78:49. Paul spoke of the thorn in the flesh as an angel of Satan, II Cor. 12:7. The Second Person of the Trinity is called the Angel of his presence, the Angel of the Covenant, Is. 63:9; Mal. 3:1.

Finally, of course, the term is used of the spiritual beings, we know as angels. "Good angels are designated in Scripture as to their nature, dignity and power as 'spirits,' Heb. 1:14; 'thrones, dominions, principalities, powers, mights,' Eph. 1:21, and Col. 1:16; 'sons of God,' Luke 20:36; Job 1:6; 'mighty angels,' and 'powerful in strength,' II Thess. 1:7; Ps. 103:20; 'holy angels,' 'elect angels,' Luke 9:26; I Tim. 5:21; and as to the offices they sustain in relation to God and man, they are designated as 'angels or messengers,' and as 'ministering spirits,' Heb. 1:13-14."[3]

The context in the Bible must determine whether the word is referring to an angel, to a human or to another messenger.

---

1. ἄγγελος
2. מלאך
3. A. A. Hodge, *Outlines of Theology* (Grand Rapids: William B. Eerdmans Publishing Company, 1949), p. 249.

II. The Creation of the Angels

The Bible does not, in the Genesis account, give any detail concerning the creation of the angelic beings. That the angels were a part of his creation is clearly stated in the Fourth Commandment, where it says he created the heavens and the earth and all that in them is.[4] This is implied also in Genesis 1:1, where the statement is made that in the beginning God created the heavens and the earth. "His (Moses) words suggest that the angelic creation is to be conceived of as occurring at the time of God's forming the heavenly systems, though it is true that angels are not specifically noted in Genesis 1:1."[5] It is certainly clear from the second chapter of Genesis, where the fallen angel, Satan, is found already fallen that there must have been some interval after the creation of the angels in which this fall took place. This clearly implies that the creation of the angels is prior to the creation of the world and of man. Job says that the "sons of God" rejoiced over the creation of the world, which also implies that they were already in existence. "Whereupon are the foundations thereof fastened? or who laid the cornerstone thereof; When the morning stars sang together, and all the sons of God shouted for joy."[6] Hoeksema cautions, "From this passage the conclusion has been drawn that the angels were created on the first day, although it must certainly be said that the text offers no strict proof for this contention and that if we may conjecture that there is a parallel between the creation of the earth and that of heaven and heavenly beings, it would seem more natural to suppose that the angels were created on the sixth day."[7] With the declaration that all of the creation was good, this must also have included the angelic beings. Their fall must have taken place after the end of the creation week. Further, if we posit that the fall of Adam was not immediate, there could be an interval of time for the fall of the angels prior to the fall of Adam.

How many angels were created is not specifically taught. The Bible does teach that they are a very great host.[8]

III. The Nature of Angels

As we consider the nature of the angels, it must be affirmed from the outset that they are to be distinguished from God in that they are created. We have already observed that very little is said about their creation, but the fact is clearly asserted in the Scripture. Psalm 148:2 and 5 says, "Praise ye him all his angels, Praise ye him all his hosts. . . . Let them praise the name of Jehovah; For he commanded, and they were created." Again in Colossians 1:16 it is affirmed, "For in him were all things created, in the heavens and upon the earth, things visible and things invisible, whether thrones or dominions or principalities or powers; all things have been created through him, and unto him." The angels are said to dwell in heaven, and to be around the throne of God. They must, there-

---

4. Exodus 20:11.
5. Barton Payne, *Theology of the Older Testament* (Grand Rapids: Zondervan Publishing House, 1962), p. 285.
6. Job. 38:7.
7. *Reformed Dogmatics, op. cit.*, p. 249.
8. I Kings 22:19; Dan. 7:10.

fore, be spiritual beings. This is implied by the language of Scripture regarding them.[9]

The purely spiritual nature of angels has been a point of debate, both among Jews and Christians. Many Jews and early Christian fathers ascribed to them some sort of fiery or airy bodies. Even some of the Protestant theologians have followed this line of thought. Though the Bible does not give a great deal of instruction regarding angels, it does seem to teach their spiritual nature. See Matt. 8:16; 12:45; Luke 7:21; 8:2; 11:26; Acts 19:12; Eph. 6:12; Heb. 1:14. They have no flesh and bones, Luke 24:39, do not marry, Matt. 22:30, can be present in great numbers in a very limited space, Luke 8:30, and are invisible, Col. 1:16. All of these passages imply the spiritual nature of angels.

The fact that angels appeared to men in various forms does not disprove their essential spiritual nature. "The purpose of these appearances is obvious, to bring the presence and functions of the angelic visitant under the scope of the sense of God's servants, for some particular purpose of mercy."[10] The appearances were manifested in three different circumstances. They occurred in dreams, or to persons under the inspiration of the Spirit, or to men under ordinary circumstances. It is only the last of these that call for explanation. In passages such as Gen. 18 and 19, the angels occupied real material bodies, for a time. Whence these bodies? Dabney considers the various possible cases:

> Say some, they were the actual bodies of living men, which the angels occupied, suppressing, for the nonce, the consciousness and personality of the human soul to which the body belonged. Some, that they are material, but glorified substances, kept in heaven, ready for the occasional occupancy of angels on their missions; as we keep a Sunday-coat in our wardrobes. Some, that they were aerial bodies, composed of compacted atmosphere, formed thus for their temporary occupancy, by divine power, and then dissolved into air again. And still others, that they were created by God for them out of matter, as Adam's body was, and then laid aside. Where God has not seen fit to inform us, I think it best to have no opinion on this mysterious subject. The Scriptures plainly show us, that this incorporation is temporary.[11]

When we see the breadth of speculation on this subject, we see the wisdom of Dabney in cautioning against taking a firm position where the Scripture itself has not given us an answer.

In addition to their being spiritual beings, the Bible clearly indicates that they are rational, moral creatures. Passages such as II Samuel 14:20; Matt. 24:36; Eph. 3:10; I Pet. 1:12; II Pet. 2:11 explicitly represent the angels as rational. It must be observed, however, that they are not omniscient, though they may well have superior knowledge to that of men. The latter stems from the fact that they, as spiritual beings, are created to serve in the presence of God himself. Further, the unfallen angels have not suffered the noetic effects of sin that men now live under. Turretin classifies their knowledge into four classes: natural, experimental, supernatural, and revealed. Dabney thinks that a better arrange-

---

9. Ps. 148:1-2.
10. Dabney, *Systematic Theology, op. cit.,* p. 266.
11. Ibid., pp. 266-267.

ment of their knowledge would be threefold: concreated, acquired and revealed. That their knowledge is great is clear. In Daniel and Revelation they appear as man's teachers.

As intelligent creatures they are, of course, moral creatures, responsible for their decisions and actions. They are rewarded for obedience to God, or punished for disobedience. The Bible speaks of "holy angels" referring to those who have remained obedient, Matt. 25:31; Mark 8:38; Luke 9:26; Acts 10:22; Rev. 14:10. In contrast, the fallen angels are spoken of as lying and sinning, John 8:44; I John 3:8-10.

Both the holy and the fallen angels are immortal. The holy angels are not subject to death. The fallen angels, though cast into hell, and suffering death, will not cease to exist, but will continue in that suffering forever.

As beings that do not marry, they do not reproduce themselves into a race. There are according to Scripture great numbers of angels that have been created. "They form the army of God, a host of mighty heroes, always ready to do the Lord's bidding, Ps. 103:20; Col. 1:16; Eph. 1:21; 3:10; Heb. 1:14; and the evil angels form the army of Satan, bent on destroying the work of the Lord, Luke 11:21; II Thess. 2:9; I Pet. 5:8."[12]

As created, all of the angels must have been good. This is implied in Gen. 2:1. John 8:44, II Pet. 2:4 and Jude 6 all presuppose the original good condition of angels. Those who remained in their original state are called "elect angels." This implies that they received grace to enable them to retain their holy positions, and also to be confirmed in holiness, so that now they are not capable of sinning. In addition to their being called holy, they are called angels of light, II Cor. 11:14. They are always before the face of God, Matt. 18:10, and are called exemplars in doing the will of God, Matt. 6:10.

IV. The Orders of the Angels

That there is a great host of angels is clear from explicit statements of Scripture. Deut. 33:2 speaks of Jehovah coming from Sinai, "from the ten thousands of holy ones." Psalm 68:17 speaks of "The chariot of God are twenty thousand, even thousands upon thousands: The Lord is among them, as in Sinai, in the sanctuary." The demons spoke of their numbers as being "legion, for we are many."[13] Jesus spoke of being able to call upon twelve legions of angels, if he so desired.[14] Rev. 5:11 reads, "And I saw, and I heard the voice of many angels round about the throne and the living creatures and the elders; and the number of them was ten thousand times ten thousand, and thousands of thousands." Berkhof concludes, "In view of all these data it is perfectly safe to say that the angels constitute an innumerable company, a mighty host."[15]

Though they do not constitute a race as man does, there are indications in Scripture that they are organized in some way. We see some evidence of this in the different names ascribed to them. First, there are cherubim. These are first mentioned in Gen. 3:24, where they were set to guard the entrance of the garden

---

12. Berkhof, *Systematic Theology, op. cit.*, p. 145.
13. Mark 5:9, 15.
14. Matt. 26:53.
15. Berkhof, *op. cit.*, p. 146.

against the intrusion of sinful men, after they were cast out of it. They are portrayed in the holy of holies as gazing upon the mercy seat, Ex. 25:18; Ps. 80:1; 99:1; Is. 37:16; Heb. 9:5. In Ezekiel they are seen associated with the chariot throne of God. They again appear in the description of the throne of God in Rev. 4. They seem to have the special place of serving at the very throne of God.

Patrick Fairbairn says:
> They were symbolical of the highest properties of creature life, and of these as the outgoing and the manifestation of the divine life; but they were typical of redeemed and glorified manhood, or prophetical representations of it, as that in which these properties were to be combined and exhibited.
>
> They were appointed immediately after the fall to man's original place in the garden, and to his office in connection with the tree of life.
>
> The other and more common connection in which the cherub appears is with the throne or peculiar dwelling-place of God. In the holy of holies in the tabernacle, Ex. 25:22, he was called the God who dwelleth between and sitteth upon the cherubim, I Sam. 4:4; Ps. 80:1; Ezek. 1:26-28; whose glory is above the cherubim. In Rev. 4:6, we read of the living creatures who were in the midst of the throne and around about it.
>
> What does this bespeak but the wonderful fact brought out in the history of redemption, that man's nature is to be exalted to the dwelling-place of the Godhead? In Christ it is taken, so to speak, into the very bosom of the Deity; and because it is so highly honored in him, it shall attain to more than angelic glory in his members.[16]

In addition to cherubim, there is another name used only once, namely, the seraphim. "They are also symbolically represented in human form, but with six wings..."[17] Berkhof distinguishes between the cherubim and seraphim.

> In distinction from the Cherubim, they stand as servants round about the throne of the heavenly King, sing his praises, and are ever ready to do his bidding. While the Cherubim are the mighty ones, they might be called the nobles among the angels. While the former guard the holiness of God, they serve the purpose of reconciliation, and thus prepare men for the proper approach to God.[18]

Other names that seem to be references to angelic beings, are found in Col. 1:16: principalities, powers, thrones and dominions. They seem to point to different ranks among the angels.

Two specific angels are mentioned by name, Gabriel and Michael. Gabriel appears in Dan. 8:16; 9:21; Luke 1:9, 26. He may be among the seven angels that are said to stand before the throne of God, Rev. 8:2. He seems to have the special task of mediating and interpreting the revelation of God on special occasions.

Michael is the second specifically named angel. He is mentioned in Dan. 10:13, 21; Jude 9; Rev. 12:7. He is called the archangel in Jude 9, which indi-

---

16. Patrick Fairbairn, *The Typology of Scripture* (Grand Rapids: Zondervan Publishing House, n.d.), Part II, Chapter, 1, section 3.
17. Berkhof, *op cit.*, p. 146.
18. *Idem.*

cates that he occupies a higher place among the angels. He is seen as fighting the battles of the Lord against his enemies. The title archangel may also belong to Gabriel and others, though we do not have this explicitly stated in the Bible.

V. The Service of the Angels

Berkhof distinguishes between the ordinary and the extraordinary service of the angels.

A. The Ordinary Service

The ordinary service consists in their praising of God night and day, Job 38:7; Is. 6; Ps. 103:20; 148:2; Rev. 5:11. They are seen as speaking and singing to the praise of God at the birth of Christ.

They rejoice over the conversion of sinners, Luke 15:10; and watch over believers, Ps. 34:7; 91:11, and protect the little ones, Matt. 18:10. They are present in the Church, I Cor. 11:10; I Tim. 5:21.

B. The Extraordinary Service

Since the fall of man, God has used the angels in extraordinary ways.
> They often mediate the special revelations of God, communicate blessings to his people, and execute judgment upon his enemies. Their activity is most prominent in the great turning points of the economy of salvation, as in the days of the patriarchs, the time of the law giving, the period of the exile and the restoration, and at the birth, the resurrection, and the ascension of the Lord."[19]

We may expect their extraordinary services to begin again with the return of the Lord.

The Law was "ordained through angels by the hand of a mediator."[20] They served as instruments of good to God's people, "Are they (angels) not all ministering spirits, sent forth to do service for the sake of them that shall inherit salvation."[21] On the other hand, they are used in executing judgment on God's enemies, "And immediately an angel of the Lord smote him, because he gave not God the glory: and he was eaten of worms, and gave up the ghost."[22] They will assist in the final judgment, separating the good from the bad, and gathering the elect to meet the Lord.[23]

---

19. *Ibid.*, p. 148.
20. Gal. 3:19b. See also Acts 7:53; Heb. 2:2.
21. Heb. 1:14. See Acts 12:7; Ps. 91:10-12.
22. Acts 12:23. See also II Kings 19:35; I Chron. 21:16.
23. Matt. 13:30, 39; 24:31; I Thess. 4:17.

C. The Question of Guardian Angels

The early Christian fathers[24] held to the idea of a particular angel assigned to each individual as a guardian angel. They also held to the idea of two angels, one good, and one evil either prompting good or evil.[25] The Jews, other than the Sadducees, held to this idea, as do the Moslems. The Greeks and Romans had similar ideas.

The doctrine of guardian angels is a part of Roman Catholic teaching. "We are assisted in our struggle against evil by our *guardian angel*.... each of us has an angel who has particular charge of us throughout life....This angel of ours, who is called our guardian angel, protects us in both soul and body; he encourages us to live a purposeful and persevering life, guided by the will and law of God; he makes use of our instinct of self-preservation to warn us of danger, and he shares his wisdom with us when our own fails us. He is also a messenger between God and us, offering up our prayers and requests for us."[26]

Reformed thinkers reject the idea of guardian angels. Warfield argues against the popular interpretation of Matt. 18:10 and Acts 12:15 as teaching the notion of guardian angels.

> But the real difficulty of explaining these passages by the aid of the notion of 'guardian' angels is that this notion does not in the least fit their requirements. Where should a 'guardian angel' be, except with his ward? That is the essential idea of a 'guardian angel' ; he is supposed to be in unbroken attendance upon the saint committed to his charge. But neither in Matt. 18:10, nor in Acts 12:15 are the angels spoken of found with their wards; but distinctly elsewhere.[27]

After reviewing various possible explanations of the meaning of these two passages, Warfield indicates that he favors the idea that "angel" in each of these passages may be a reference to the spirit or soul of the person. He says, "It is perhaps unwise to draw conclusions too definite from such a survey. There has been suggested no explanation of these two unique phrases-- 'the angels of these little ones' and 'Peter's angel'--which has not difficulties in its way."[28] The idea of disembodied spirits has fewer difficulties to face than the other proposals. "It satisfies all the conditions of the passages themselves--which cannot be said of any of its rivals. It is rooted in a natural extension of the common meaning of the term employed. And it presupposes no conceptions which cannot be shown to have existed in the circles out of which Christianity arose-- which again cannot be said of its chief rivals."[29]

---

24. Origen in *De Oratione*, 11 says "But also the angel of each, even of those who are little in the Church, always beholding the face of the Father that is in the heavens and gazing on the Godhead of him that created us, prays with us and works with us, as far as possible, for things for which we pray." Chrysostom in *Homilia in Numeros*, 20:3 also taught this, "All Christians at the moment of baptism, receive each, an angel from God."
25. Hermas 11:6.
26. N. G. M. Van Doornik, S. Jelsma, A. van De Lisdonk, edited by John Greenwood, *A Handbook of the Catholic Faith, A Triptych of the Kingdom*, translated from the Dutch (Garden City, New York:Image Books, A Division of Doubleday and Company, Inc. 1956), pp. 173-174.
27. *Selected Shorter Writings of Benjamin B. Warfield*, edited by John E. Meeter (Nutley, New Jersey: Presbyterian and Reformed Publishing Company, 1970), Vol. I, p. 256.
28. *Ibid.*, p. 266.
29. *Idem*.

VI. The First Estate and Probation of the Angels

A. The First Estate of the Angels

That all of the angels as created were holy is implied in the nature of God as holy. All that he created was good. The Bible speaks of the angels as holy. Passages dealing with the wicked angels speak of their sinning and being cast down,[30] and of not keeping their first estate.[31]

Dabney says of the fall of the angels, that we must infer much from the Scripture, since not much is explicitly stated.

A holy, intelligent creature, would owe service to God, with love and worship, by its natural relation to him. And while God would be under no obligations to such a creature, to preserve its being, or bestow a happy immortality, yet his own righteousness and benevolence would forbid his visiting external suffering on that creature, while holy. The natural relation then, between such a creature and God, would be this: God would bestow perfect happiness, just so long as the creature continued to render perfect obedience, and no longer.[32]

B. The Probation and Fall of the Non-elect Angels

The Bible indicates that there are two groups of angels. First, there are the elect, who have been confirmed in their holiness, since they are spoken of as sharing with saved men in the heavenly mansions. On the other hand, there is another class of angels, who have irrevocably fallen into spiritual death. By analogy from the probation in Eden, the angels were placed under a probation. "The elect kept it, the non-elect broke it; the difference between them being made, so far as God was the author of it, not by his efficacious active decree and grace, but by his permissive decree, in which both classes were wholly left to the freedom of their wills."[33] This sounds as though Dabney is suggesting that the decree to elect was conditioned on the response of the angels to the probation. Surely, if God is sovereign, and has foreordained, whatsoever comes to pass, then this must hold true for the probation of the angels as well as for that of man. Granted that the execution of the decrees is by permission, the act of election and reprobation by God must not have been contingent on the acts of the angels, but must have been the sovereign act of God.

The presumption is that the probation of the angels was completed before the fall of Adam, since Satan certainly had fallen by this time. The nature of the fall of Satan is not conclusively taught in Scripture. Some have, on the basis of Mark 3:29 assumed it to be the blasphemy against the Holy Spirit. Others, on the basis of I Tim. 3:6 take it to have been pride.[34] Dabney says:

---

30. II Pet. 2:4.
31. Jude 6.
32. Dabney, *Systematic Theology*, p. 269.
33. *Ibid.*, pp. 269-270.
34. Isaiah 14:12ff has been taken as referring to Satan. This is a debatable exegesis of this passage. See commentaries of J. A. Alexander and E. J. Young.

It may very possibly be that pride was the sin, for it is one to which Satan's spiritual nature and exalted state might be liable. The great difficulty is how, in a will prevalently holy, and not even swayed by innocent bodily wants and appetites, and where there was not in the whole universe a single creature to entice to sin, the first wrong volition could have taken place.[35]

C. Satan and the Fallen Angels

1. Satan a person

That Satan is represented as a person is clear from the Scripture. He is seen speaking, reasoning, hating, lying. He is the object of God's judgment. In the temptation of Jesus, he clearly appears as a person speaking to the Lord. Also, Jesus calls him the father of unbelievers.[36]

2. His relation to fallen spirits and to the world

Other evil spirits are called the angels of the devil, Matt. 25:41. He is called the prince of the devils, Matt. 9:34, and the prince of the powers of the air, and the prince of darkness, Eph. 6:12.

He is called the god of this world (II Cor. 4:4), and the spirit that worketh in the children of disobedience, (Eph. 2:2). Berkhof says:

> This does not mean that he is in control of the world, for God is in control, and he has given all authority to Christ, but it does convey the idea that he is in control of this evil world, the world in so far as it is ethically separated from God. . . . . He is superhuman, but not divine; has great power, but is not omnipotent; wields influence on a large, but restricted scale, Matt. 12:29; Rev. 20:2, and is destined to be cast into the bottomless pit, Rev. 20:10.[37]

---

35. Dabney, *op cit.*, p. 270.
36. See Matt. 4:1-11; John 8:44.
37. Berkhof, *Systematic Theology*, p. 149.

Chapter XV God's Work of Providence

Having seen that God created the universe, the next question that faces us is how this creation continues in its existence. The idea of the preservation of the created universe, together with its governance is designated by the term "providence." This particular term is not itself Biblical, but both preservation and governance are clearly Biblical concepts. Actually the literal significance of the word "providence" is not a proper description of God's care of the universe. It comes from the Latin *provideo*, which means "to see ahead." As such, the term suggests that God merely knows beforehand what will come to pass. Actually, God does not just see or know beforehand. He brings things to pass. "He knows them not by a certain prescience, but eternally from his counsel."[1] Hoeksema observes:

> However, the term has obtained a place in theological parlance; and, for want of a better term, we may well continue to use it. It denotes the almighty and omnipresent power of God whereby he causes all things to continue to exist and where he in and through all creatures executes his counsel and guides them in such a way that they must all, without exception, lead to the end he had determined for them in his counsel.[2]

I. The Crisis of the Doctrine of Providence in Contemporary Thought[3]

The twentieth century, with its two world wars and all of the atrocities that were involved with them, has come to sense of the meaninglessness of life which is widely held in our day. Humanism has turned from the optimism of the 19th century to pessimism, which it calls a new realism. The 20th century seems to have room for only one realistic world and life view, namely, nihilism. Are not atheism and meaninglessness the only logical conclusions to be drawn from the realism of this 20th century? With such thinking the idea of the providence of God is severely questioned in our times, especially in the light of daily events. Existentialism forces the problem of dread to our attention with anxiety as the essence of existence, and our existence is thought of as suspended in nothingness.[4]

The Bible reveals the reason for the radical estrangement of man expressed in his dread and anxiety. It is the sickness unto death which stems from man's sinfulness. The Bible also knows that victory over this dread is not the result of autonomous human thinking, but comes only as the gift of God's grace in the gospel of Christ.

The Bible does not avoid the questions of fear and uncertainty, but faces them head-on. Psalm 73 shows the Psalmist struggling with the problem of the prosperity of the wicked. Job presents the personal confrontation with the problem of human suffering. God's wisdom and goodness come into question.

---

1. Hoeksema, Herman, *Reformed Dogmatics, op cit.*, p. 228.
2. *Idem.*
3. Thoughts in this section have been drawn from G. C. Berkouwer, *The Providence of God* (Grand Rapids: Wm. B. Eerdmans Publishing Company, 1952), Chapter 1.
4. See Heidegger, *Sein und Zeit*, I, p. 191, and *Was ist Metaphysik?*, p. 23ff.

Ecclesiastes speaks of the apparent meaninglessness of life. The Bible bares the problem. This Biblical realism should warn us against oversimplification of the problems of men. We of the Church should not lose contact with those who are in distress and the storm. The Bible is not a witness to the darkness of the night, but a witness to the light in the night.

All too often the Church has failed to deal with the reality of man's distress. The result has been an increasing estrangement of the world from the Church. The increased place of science in modern thought has been the means of teaching men unbelief. Nature is reduced to natural causes. God and the faith are relegated to the prescientific era, which is no longer relevant. Along with this secularism of science have come the philosophies that teach that religion is but the projection of man's desire. In this way the truths of religion are discarded, but their tenacity among the masses are thus accounted for. Marx posited that it was a way for man to make the unbearable bearable, as he spoke of religion as the opium of the people. Feuerbach saw it as the egotistical wish projection, thus making theology nothing more than anthropology. Nietzsche saw Christianity as a Platonism for the people. Faith is the projection of an ideal, supernatural world, which devaluated earthly reality. Freud simply saw it as the result of human imagination. All of these see religion as an escapism. They call for man to face reality and accept life void of illusions. He must find his own way to freedom.

The development of modern human thought brings the crisis regarding the doctrine of providence. With the coming of the Enlightenment, the concept of God was humanized and caricatured. He was seen as a shrewd master-worker managing the affairs of this world. Deism was influential in destroying the right view of God. It sought to dehumanize God, to remove all anthropomorphisms from our thinking about him. The result was a God, who is only a sterile intellect. In place of this barren concept Ritschl substituted a God of love. God was made in the image of human love. God was incapable of wrath. This view of God still underlies much of modern liberal thought. With the catastrophes of the 20th Century, this eternal philanthropist was exposed as a delusion. This brought on the crisis of faith of our day. This crisis has been addressed by the crisis or existential theologians with less than orthodox theology. The result is a generally misunderstood doctrine of providence in the Church today.

The one-sided, optimistic God concept of Ritschlian liberalism is in absolute contradiction to the God of the Bible. With the era following the Enlightenment, the Biblical view of God and sin was abandoned, and the result was a "genial providence" --grace without judgment, love without justice, forgiveness without redemption. The cataclysms of the 20th century unmasked this view of reality, but with the departure from the Bible there has been a failure to return to the true view of providence.

II. Different Views of Providence

A. That Providence is only Foreknowledge

Some of the Church fathers limited providence to God's foresight of events. Others included not only foresight, but also the foreordination by God.

Essentially this is the identification of the decrees of God with providence. Buswell considers providence in the same chapter with the decrees.[5] Both creation and providence are the outworking of the decrees of God, but they are not identical with them. As the Westminster Shorter Catechism says, the decrees are executed in the works of creation and providence.

B. The Deistic View of Providence

The Deists held that God was not concerned about the world, except in a general way. When God created the world, he set it in motion with its inherent powers and laws. He no longer governs or sustains it, but allows it to operate by itself. This concept was held by Pelagianism. It was adopted by the Socinians, and infects Arminianism, because of its denial of the sovereignty of God and his decrees. It was set forth in philosophical form by the Deists of the 18th century. Today, this view is seen in the theory of evolution, with the emphasis on the uniformity of nature.

C. Atheistic - Fatalism

The idea of providence for atheism is contradictory, and yet there are those who, while denying the existence of God, hold to a blind determinism or fatalism. The thought is that there are influences which determine our destinies. Astrology is an example of such atheistic fatalism. Such a view, of course, makes life meaningless and hopeless.

An example of this pagan view of providence was the way in which Hitler appealed to providence as bringing him to power in the Third Reich. Here the pagan was borrowing Christian language for propaganda purposes, but not at all meaning the Biblical doctrine of providence. For him it was fate, or fortune that governed history.

D. The Biblical Theistic View of Providence

The Biblical view of providence is that God has not left his creation alone, but continues to preserve and sustain it, and also to govern and control all that takes place in it.

III. Knowledge of Providence

Though the world may at times refer to it, any view of providence not informed by the special revelation of God, will, because of the noetic effects of sin, be a false view of it. We have affirmed that the doctrine of creation is known only through revelation. The same is true of providence. Rome, with its doctrine of natural theology, maintains that we can come to a true knowledge of providence from nature. Such a view assumes that the natural man is able to interpret the world properly, without the regenerating work of the Holy Spirit.

---

5. Buswell, Oliver J., *Systematic Theology* (Grand Rapids: Zondervan Publishing House, 1962), Vol. I, p. 170.

The true doctrine of providence is a distinctively Christian doctrine. The plan of salvation itself is seen as the special providence of God. In the Cross, the Christian sees the special providence of God, resulting in forgiveness and regenerating grace. He has experienced it, and now he looks at all of history as being under the hand of his gracious Heavenly Father. Abraham Kuyper says, "The Reformed Confession and Church is among all the Christian confessions and churches, the only one which definitely does not place providence alongside of the way of salvation, but defines them both as one unit."[6] This comment apparently was made in connection with remarks on the Belgic Confession, Article XIII, which speaks of providence thus:

> We believe that the same God, after he had created all things, did not forsake them, or give them up to fortune or chance, but that he rules and governs them according to his holy will, so that nothing happens in this world without his appointment ... And as to what he doth surpassing human understanding we will not curiously inquire into it further than our capacity will admit of; but with the greatest humility and reverence adore the righteous judgments of God which are hid from us, contenting ourselves that we are disciples of Christ, to learn only those things which he has revealed to us in his Word without transgressing these limits.[7]

Hoeksema affirms the same idea, as based on the first question of the Heidelberg Catechism.

> Already in the first question and answer of the Heidelberg Catechism this truth is presented as a rich source of comfort for him that belongs with body and soul, in life and death to his faithful Savior, Jesus Christ. For there we read that this faithful Savior 'so preserves me that without the will of my heavenly Father not a hair can fall from my head; yea, that all things must be subservient to my salvation.' Beautiful is this answer of the Heidelberg Catechism because it connects at once the providence of God with the doctrine concerning our salvation.[8]

If providence is thus related to salvation, then knowledge of it can only come through the same means by which we know of God's saving work--special revelation.

Berkouwer warns of the danger of separating our view of providence from the Christian faith. He wisely observes:

> History illustrates the results of a confession of Providence without Christ, whether in the form of a religiously clothed national socialism or in the conclusions of a consistent natural theology. Phantoms of gods and idols and deified creature appear on the stage of human existence. It may be a vague conjecture or a reasoned conclusion, a final or first cause, a prime-mover or ultimate principle, a mysterious X, a sphinx, or a 'Guidance' which embraces men with protecting arms.

---

6. Kuyper, Abraham, as cited by Berkouwer in the English translation of *The Providence of God*, p. 48. It is referenced to Kuyper's *E Voto*, but is not found there. There is no footnote in the original Dutch edition for this citation.
7. The Belgic Confession, Philip Schaff, *The Creeds of Christendom* (Grand Rapids: Baker Book House, 1966), Vol. III, pp. 396-397.
8. *Op. cit.*, p. 227.

Whatever it may be, it is confusion without Christ, a groping in the darkness. One may still talk of the comfort derived from a non-Christian idea of Providence, but in any such concept there is no real thankfulness in prosperity and, certainly, no real patience in adversity. This Providence is an imposter, acceptable in prosperity; but, in times of terror, when she withdraws her friendly arms of protection, she fails to inspire either confidence or faith. For this reason, the soteriological orientation of the Providence doctrine in the confessions is decisive.[9]

As we shall see, the Bible has much to say about providence. We shall examine the content of this revelation in the following sections of this chapter.

IV. Providence as Sustaining

A. The Biblical Teaching Regarding Preservation

There are a number of passages which convey the idea that God not only created, but also sustains his creation. Col. 1:16-7 says, "All things were created by him . . . by him all things consist." Here we see the close relation of creation and providence. "After creating the world, God did not withdraw from it, neither entirely nor half nor in the least degree, but he remains in contact with the world and sustains everything in it, the greatest and the least, by his divine power."[10]

Hebrews 1:3 speaks of the sustaining work of Christ, "who being the effulgence of his glory, and the very image of his substance, and upholding all things by the word of his power . . ." This phrase, "upholding all things by the word of his power" indicates the fact that the created universe needs his continued preservation. Nehemiah records the prayer of the Levites, which describes this sustaining work of God. "Thou art Jehovah, even thou alone; thou hast made heaven, the heaven of heavens, with all their host, the earth and all things that are thereon, the seas and all that is in them, and thou preservest them all; and the host of heaven worshippeth thee."[11] Notice that the preserving work of God is seen as including all of his creation, the heavens, the earth, the sea and all that in them is. This is the thrust of Jesus' teaching in Matt. 10:29-30, "Are not two sparrows sold for a penny? and not one of them shall fall on the ground without your Father; but the very hairs of your head are all numbered." Jesus draws the implication from this that we are of more value than the sparrows, and thus the doctrine of providence should be comforting to us.

God's work of providence is as incomprehensible as is this work of creation. Elihu said, "God thundereth marvelously with his voice; Great things doeth he, which we cannot comprehend."[12]

Many passages speak of the activity of God in connection with the world and universe. Elihu speaks of it in Job 37 and 38. The Psalmist celebrates it.

---

9. Berkouwer, *op. cit.*, p. 50.
10. Pieper, Francis, *Christian Dogmatics* (St. Louis: Concordia Publishing House, 1950), Vol. I, p. 482.
11. Nehemiah 9:6.
12. Job 37:5.

"The heavens declare the glory of God, the firmament showeth his handiwork."[13] The whole of Psalm 104 celebrates his activity in the earth. The Psalmist directs us toward our proper response to the providence of God as he expresses his adoration of him. "O Jehovah, how manifold are thy works! In wisdom hath thou made them all: The earth is full of thy riches."[14]

Berkouwer rightly observes, "The so-called nature Psalms, then are not dedicated to the glory of nature. Neither do they point a way to God through nature in itself. In them the majestic might of God is sung (Cf. Ps.74: 12-17, and especially Psalms 19, 33, 89, 104 and 148).[15]

B. The Relation of Sustenance to Creation

The question has been raised as to the relation of this sustaining work to the creative activity of God. Some have posited the idea that the sustaining work of God, by the Word of his power is a continuation of the creative activity of God, which was also done by the word of his power. That is, God is perpetually creating the universe from moment to moment, otherwise it would return to non-existence. Thus, sustentation is a perpetual re-creation. The argument for this is as follows:

    1. God alone is self-existent, thus creation has no ground of existence or of continuance in itself.

    2. All creatures exist in successive instances of time, which have no connection. Thus "successive existence is momentarily returning to nothing, and is only kept from it by a perpetual recreation."[16]

    3. The following Scriptures are cited as teaching this: Neh. 9:6; Job 10:12; Ps. 104:27-30; Acts 17:28; Heb. 1:3; Col. 1:17; and Is. 10:15.

The Lutheran theologian, Francis Pieper, quotes Luther, "We Christians know that creating and preserving is one and the same thing with God (*idem est creare et conservare*)" (St. L. I:1539).[17]

Bavinck calls providence a *creatio continua*, a work just as great, mighty and omnipresent as creation. They are one deed, the difference being only a thought distinction. "Creation and sustenance are, thus, not to be distinguished objectively and materially as works of God, in God's essence, but only in thought."[18] Though Bavinck speaks of sustenance as a continuing creation, he indicates that he does not mean to say that God is continually calling the world out of nothing. This was unique to creation as distinguished from providence. Both creation and sustenance are alike in that they involve the word of God's power. Berkouwer says, "Creation calls out of nothing into existence; sustenance calls to continued existing."[19]

Abraham Kuyper also dealt with this subject. He said, "We must definitely insist that providence is a *creatio continuata*, to be understood in the

---

13. Psalm 19:1.
14. Psalm 104:24.
15. Berkouwer, *op. cit.*, p. 61.
16. Dabney, Robert L., *Systematic Theology, op. cit.*, p. 278.
17. *Op. cit.*, p. 484.
18. Idem.
19. Bavinck, *op. cit.*, p. 566.

sense that from the hour of original creation until now, God, the Lord has done the same thing as in the moment of creation: He has given all things power of existence through his power."[20] He did not hold that sustenance was continuous successive creative acts of calling into being from nothing. He distinguishes the two as follows: "Creation refers to what comes into existence; Providence to what, already existing, is continuously upheld by God's power."[21]

Berkouwer, after considering what Bavinck and Kuyper wrote, discusses the question of whether it is really best for us to speak of sustenance as a continuing creation. He concludes:

> Thus, though Reformed theologians use the term continuous creation in order to emphasize the greatness and divinity of the work of sustaining, they, nevertheless, reject the idea in the sense of renewed acts of creation out of nothing.... We may better reserve the term creation out of nothing for the original creation and follow the example of the Heidelberg Catechism which describes sustenance simply as the power of God which upholds all things.[22]

Berkouwer backs his position with reference to Biblical passages speaking to the matter of sustenance. Psalm 102:25 says, "Of old didst thou lay the foundation of the earth." It has been noted that the Hebrew does not have a separate word for sustenance, and the concept of the continuation of the world is indicated by the word *bara*. "This does not weaken the distinction between them, but does underscore the Scriptural testimony to the unity of God's word, and the implied dependency of all creation."[23] "I form the light and create darkness."[24] Berkouwer concludes:

> To see the work of God in nature and history---this is to understand that God is as magnificent in his work today as in the first day of creation. The word *bara* indicates 'Divine origination'; not only the Divine origination of creation out of nothing but also the Divine origination of each moment. Thus, we have the grandeur of the Divine work of sustaining, without losing the continuity of created reality within perpetually repetitive creative acts.[25]

That creation is seen as something completed may be learned from the fact that God is represented in Scripture as looking upon creation as something done and now standing. "I have made the earth, and created man upon it: I even my hands, have stretched out the heavens; and all their hosts have I commanded."[26] Again Isaiah affirms that God sits above the circle of heaven, and stretched out the heavens as a curtain.[27] The concept of a finished work is also implied in Isaiah 51:13, where he is called ". . . Jehovah thy Maker, that stretched forth the heavens and laid the foundation of the earth. . ." The Psalmists speak in the same way, "The heavens are thine, the earth also is thine:

---

20. Kuyper, Abraham, "Locus de Providentia" in *Dictaten Dogmatiek*, (no date), p. 37f, cited by Berkouwer, *op. cit.*, p. 69.
21. *Ibid*.
22. *Op. cit.*, p. 70.
23. *Ibid.*, p. 72.
24. Isaiah 45:7
25. Kuyper, *op. cit.*, p. 72.
26. Isaiah 45:12.
27. Isaiah 40:22.

The world and the fulness thereof, thou hast founded them."[28] ". . . The world is also established, that it cannot be moved."[29]

The New Testament like the Old Testament sees the creation as a distinct act, taking place as the world began, thus indicating that creation of the world was not formed of previously existing matter.[30] Berkouwer concludes:

> The Scripture compels us to make the distinction between creation and sustenance. We do not suggest that the relation between the distinct acts of creation and sustenance within the work of Divine power is conceivable. To ask that it be humanly conceivable is to ask the forbidden. At this point we reach what Bavinck, for lack of words, called 'mystery.'[31]

C. The Question of Common Grace

Abraham Kuyper points out that sustenance is more than simple preservation. He held that the doctrine of providence is generally treated very superficially by theologians. He insists that creation is not just dead matter, but is living, and constantly changing. Since creation is moving towards God's predetermined goal, his sustenance must be involved in the entire process. This being the case, sustenance and governance should not be separated, but rather seen as closely related. Ruling must not be abstracted from the presently existing world, nor sustenance from its final purpose.

The Noahic Covenant is a promise of the continued sustenance of the world unto the end of history. "I will not again curse the ground any more for man's sake . . . While the earth remaineth, seed time and harvest, and cold and heat, and summer and winter, and day and night shall not cease."[32] Kuyper saw the Noahic Covenant as the historical point of departure for the doctrine of common grace. In the Noahic Covenant "God has performed an act of preserving grace reaching out through the entirety of human existence."[33] Klaas Schilder differed sharply with Kuyper on this. He saw no grace in this activity. "This continuation and development manifest no grace. Neither do they manifest condemnation or judgment." They are the substratum upon which both grace and judgment rest.[34] According to Schilder the purpose of history is not to realize salvation, but rather to fulfill the twofold aspects of Christ's work, namely, Savior-Redeemer and Savior-Judge. The consummation will be in this double end: blessing and judgment. History receives its meaning in this twofold end. Sustenance is not primarily for salvation, but gives the basis upon which both salvation and judgment come to fruition.

When the Christian Reformed Church in 1924 adopted a position that affirmed common grace, saying that God is favorably disposed to all men, as well as the elect, Herman Hoeksema broke with the Church. His view is that there is

---

28. Psalm 89:11.
29. Psalm 93:1b.
30. See Mark 10:6; Heb. 1:10; II Pet. 3:4; Mt. 19:4, 8.
31. Berkouwer, *op. cit.*, p. 73.
32. Genesis 8:21-22.
33. Kuyper, Abraham, *Gemeene Gratie* (Kampen: J. H. Kok, 1931), Vol. I, p. 94.
34. Schilder, Klaas, *Christus en cultuur* (Kampen: J. H. Kok, 1948), p. 63.

only pure wrath toward the non-elect. There can be no measure of grace offered to the reprobate. There can be no serious offer of the Gospel to the non-elect.[35]

Neither Schilder nor Hoeksema see passages such as Mt. 5:45 or Luke 6:35 as teaching common grace. Schilder maintains that neither teaches a favorable disposition of God to the reprobate. Hoeksema agrees with this general position, saying, "all the Scriptures witness that God does not love, but hates his enemies, and purposes to destroy them---except those whom he chose in Jesus Christ." God is "kind to the unthankful and evil," but , "He is not kind to the reprobate unthankful and evil."[36]

Schilder maintained that we can never conclude the disposition of God from his gifts. Both Van Til and Murray take exception to this position.[37] Though it may be true that the gifts are inseparable from the disposition of God, it must be admitted that ultimately even the goodness of God to the non-elect works to their greater condemnation. On the one hand, it must be recognized that God says that he takes no pleasure in the death of the wicked, and yet on the other hand, it is also clear that the reprobate wicked shall be cast into hell for eternity. It may be best not to insist on using the term "common grace", but to call it "general benevolence." God certainly treats all men with blessings, which certainly reflects his goodness and benevolence. This does not necessarily mean that he is bestowing grace upon the reprobate, however.

Berkouwer is critical of Schilder for his not doing justice to the Biblical concept of "longsuffering." He finds a classic example of longsuffering in the case of Jonah and Nineveh. He also finds longsuffering in II Peter 3:4, when men would scoff at believers for their view of the progress of history toward the end.

> How clear it is that the Providence of God as sustenance is no flat dogmatic theory. It is actual in the passing of each night into day.... We cannot make a logical scheme of the speech of Scripture. No one can comprehend God in his holy wrath and grace, in his ruling and sustaining, in his tolerating and sparing. But let no one in the face of these incomprehensible realities sacrifice God's longsuffering to his wrath, or his wrath to his longsuffering.[38]

As we conclude this section on providence as sustenance, Berkouwer's closing remarks on the subject are fitting: "He who knows God in his grace and forbearance with the world knows that the confession of sustenance is not a theological refinement, but a call to preach."[39]

V. Providence as Government

Not only does God preserve the creation, he also governs it. Berkhof defines the government as "that continued activity of God whereby he rules all

---

35. As presented by Berkouwer, *op. cit.*, p. 82 with reference to Hoeksema, Herman, *The Protestant Reformed Church in America*, 1936, and *The Wonder of Grace*, 1944.
36. Hoeksema, *The Protestant Reformed Church in America*, p. 317, as cited by Berkouwer, *op. cit.*, p. 82.
37. Van Til, Cornelius, *Common Grace*, 1947, p. 32; Murray, John, "Common Grace," in *Westminster Theological Journal*, Nov. 1942.
38. *Ibid.*, p. 89.
39. *Idem.*

things teleologically so as to secure the accomplishment of the divine purpose."[40] This grows out of the nature of God as God. He, as the all-wise God, has a plan and goal for his creation, which he carries out. "The idea that God would create this vast universe teeming with life in all its forms, and exercise no control over it . . . is utterly inconsistent with the nature of God."[41] The doctrine of providence as government grows out of the decrees of God. The fact that God has decrees covering all of the history of the universe logically means that he will execute his decrees. The Scriptures teach that his providential government is universal, including all of his creatures and all their actions.

The external world, rational and irrational creatures, things great and small, ordinary and extraordinary, are all equally and always under the control of God. The doctrine of providence excludes both necessity and chance from the universe, substituting for them the intelligent and universal control of an infinite, omnipresent God.[42]

It is because this is true that the Christian should refrain from references to luck or fortune. Rather, he should acknowledge that events occur by the providence of God.

It is clear that the doctrine of providential government is Biblical from the many passages that speak of the rule of God as King and Sovereign over the universe. "He ruleth by his power forever; his eyes behold the nations: let not the rebellious exalt themselves."[43] "He doeth according to his will in the army of heaven, and among the inhabitants of the earth."[44] "He changeth the times and the seasons; he removeth kings and setteth up kings."[45] "The Most High ruleth in the kingdom of men and giveth to whomsoever he will."[46] "I am the Lord, and there is none else; there is no God besides me: I girded thee, thou hast not known me."[47] "A man's heart deviseth his way: but the Lord directeth his steps."[48] "Promotion cometh neither from the east, nor from the west, nor from the south. But God is the judge: he putteth down one, and setteth up another."[49] "He maketh of one every nation of men to dwell on all the face of the earth, having determined their appointed seasons, and the bounds of their habitation."[50] "Jehovah sat as King at the Flood; Yea, Jehovah sitteth as King for ever. Jehovah will give strength unto his people; Jehovah will bless his people with peace."[51] "He sendeth out his commandment upon earth; his word runneth very swiftly. He giveth snow like wool; he scattereth the hoar-frost like ashes. He casteth forth his ice like morsels: Who can stand before his cold? He sendeth out his word, and melteth them: He causeth his wind to blow and the waters

---

40. Berkhof, Louis, *Systematic Theology, op cit.*, p. 175.
41. Hodge, Charles, *Systematic Theology, op cit.*, Vol. I, p. 583.
42. *Ibid.*, p. 582.
43. Psalm 66:7.
44. Dan. 4:35.
45. Dan. 2:21.
46. Dan. 4:25.
47. Is. 45:5.
48. Prov. 16:9.
49. Ps. 75:6-7.
50. Acts 17:27.
51. Ps. 29:10-11.

flow. He showeth his word unto Jacob, his statutes and ordinances unto Israel."[52] "Jehovah will reign for ever, Thy God, O Zion, unto all generations."[53]

The concept of the rule of God fills the Scriptures from beginning to end. Berkhof treats of this government under three heads:[54]

    1. It is the government of God as King of the universe. As the creator of all things, he is also the ruler of all. The representation of God as sitting enthroned as King, and the earth as his footstool connotes this universal kingship of God. "The God that made the world and all things therein, he, being Lord of heaven and earth . . ."[55] He is called "the King, immortal, invisible, the only God."[56] Again in Rev. 19:6 it is said that, "the Lord our God, the Almighty, reigneth."

    2. It is a government adapted to the nature of the creatures which he governs. This is seen in the fact that he has established laws of nature, and administers his government in the natural world through the use of these laws. In the rational world, he also uses laws of the mind, and also the direct operations of the Holy Spirit. When dealing with his moral creatures, he uses a variety of means to persuade and lead. He also operates directly by the Holy Spirit on the intellect, will and heart.

    3. The extent of this government is universal. This is the explicit teaching of Scripture: "For the kingdom is Jehovah's; and he is the ruler over the nations."[57] "Jehovah hath established his throne in the heavens; and his kingdom ruleth over all."[58] ". . . and I (Nebuchadnezzar) blessed the Most High, and I praised and honored him that liveth for ever; for his dominion is an everlasting dominion, and his kingdom from generation to generation; and all the inhabitants of the earth are reputed as nothing; and he doeth according to his will in the army of heaven, and among the inhabitants of the earth; and none can stay his hand, or say unto him, What doest thou?"[59]

This rule includes not only the general, but also the particulars of the universe. The most insignificant things are included. "Are not two sparrows sold for a penny? and not one of them shall fall on the ground without your Father: but the very hairs of your head are all numbered."[60] What appears to be accidental and by chance is under his control. "The lot is cast into the lap; But the whole disposing thereof is of Jehovah."[61] The good deeds of men as well as the evil deeds are all under his rule and control. "For it is God who worketh in you both to will and to work, for his good pleasure."[62] "Who in generations gone by suffered all the nations to walk in their own ways."[63] This is not to deny or negate the human responsibility for all of our actions. Paul in Philippians 2:12 had just called upon his readers to work out their own salvation with fear and

---

52. Ps. 147:15-19.
53. Ps. 146:10.
54. Berkhof, *op. cit.*, pp. 175-176.
55. Acts 17:24a.
56. I Tim. 1:17.
57. Ps. 22:28.
58. Ps. 103:19.
59. Dan. 4:34b-35.
60. Mt. 10:29-30.
61. Prov. 16:33.
62. Phil. 2:13.
63. Acts 14:16.

trembling. It is they, not God who do the work, though it is under his providential government. The classic example of the sovereignty of God and the responsibility of man in connection with sin was the crucifixion of our Lord. Peter says, "Him being delivered up by the determinate counsel and foreknowledge of God, ye by the hand of lawless men did crucify and slay."[64] Here we see that the crucifixion was ordered by God's decree and providence, and yet the responsibility falls upon the wickedness of men. We must admit that we are not able to fathom how both of these facts are true. The Bible does not solve this problem for us, but simply states the two facts side by side. We must bow our minds to the Lord in this matter and walk by faith and not by sight.

Having seen the passages cited above, which ascribe providential government to the Triune God, the question may well be asked how it is related to the Messianic Kingship of Christ. Jesus affirmed in Mt. 28:18, "All authority has been given unto me, in heaven and on earth." He is further described in terms of absolute king. "And he put all things in subjection under his feet, and gave him to be head over all things to the Church."[65] ". . . until the appearing of the Lord Jesus Christ: which in its own times he shall show, who is the blessed and only Potentate, the King of kings and the Lord of lords."[66] "And he (Christ) hath on his garment and on his thigh a name written KING OF KINGS, AND LORD OF LORDS."[67]

Abraham Kuyper treated this subject. He made a distinction between the essential rule, grounded in the original creation and exercised by God as Creator, and the temporary rule of grace, which is grounded in the Mediatorial work of Christ, and exercised by Christ. This rule is mediating in character, having as its purpose the reconstruction of the essential rule, which had been temporarily disrupted by sin. "This mediating kingdom shall some day disappear, leaving the essential rule forever remaining, after the fashion of I Cor. 15."[68] Kuyper saw the point of contact between the kingdoms as the person of the Mediator, who is King in the rule of grace, and at the same time the Second Person of the Trinity. This connection is expressed in Scripture by reference to Christ "sitting at the right hand of God." The Scripture refers to Christ having power over all things, which could only be true because he is the Second Person of the Trinity. Kuyper was opposed to the idea that the giving of all things to the Son means an abdication by the Father of his work as ruler. He therefore opposed the idea of a Christocracy. Berkouwer says:

> This protest against what Kuyper calls the abdication of God is quite justified. It is not as though, after Jesus' ascension 'the Providential rule of God Triune is suspended temporarily and given over to the Mediator . . .' The majesty of the Mediator is never shoved into the place belonging to the majesty of the Divine Being.[69]

---

64. Acts 2:23.
65. Eph. 1:22.
66. I Tim. 6:14b-15.
67. Rev. 19:16.
68. Berkouwer, *op. cit.*, p. 118.
69. *Ibid.*, p. 119.

In saying this Kuyper recognizes that the problem of the relation between the two rules has not been solved. Berkouwer calls for us simply to allow the Scripture to speak on the subject. "In the ruling of Christ we encounter 'God in Christ.'"[70] God's rule now has a mediating character through Christ sitting at the right hand of God. The change which took place is only in the mode of God's rule. "After Christ ascended, the same activity that was formerly immediate became mediate through him who sits on God's right hand."[71]

VI. Providence as Concurrence

Just as there is mystery regarding the relation of the providential governance and Christ's kingship, so also there is mystery regarding how both God and the creature act. The Bible teaches that both occur simultaneously. This relationship has been called concurrence. Berkhof defines it as "the cooperation of the divine power with all subordinate powers, according to the pre-established laws of their operation, causing them to act and to act precisely as they do."[72] He draws two implications from this doctrine:

1. That God is immediately operative in every act of the creature. The creature does not act out of its own inherent powers, which is what Deism teaches.
2. That the second causes are real causes and not simply God's acts, which Pantheism teaches.

The Bible gives a number of passages that teach the idea of concurrence. A classic case is that of Joseph being sold into Egypt. It was the action of the brothers, while also being the act of God. The brothers were guilty of sinning against Joseph, while God was overruling their sin to save their lives. "And he said, I am Joseph your brother, whom ye sold into Egypt. And now be not grieved, nor angry with yourselves that ye sold me hither: for God did send me before you to preserve life."[73] "As for you, ye meant evil against me; but God meant it for good, to bring to pass, as it is this day, to save much people alive."[74] Another clear case of concurrence is the speaking of Moses to Pharaoh. It was both God's word and his own word. "And Jehovah said unto him, Who hath made man's mouth? or who maketh a man dumb, or deaf, or seeing, or blind? is it not I Jehovah? Now therefore go, and I will be with thy mouth, and teach thee what thou shalt speak."[75] The basic idea of concurrence is stated in Proverbs 21:1, "The king's heart is in the hand of Jehovah as the watercourses: He turneth whithersoever he will." The application of this principle is seen in the case of the king of Assyria recorded in Ezra 6:22, " . . . for Jehovah had made them joyful, and had turned the heart of the king of Assyria unto them, to strengthen their hands in the work of the house of God, the God of Israel." Even in matters of sin, God is represented as concurring. "And David said . . . let him curse; for

---

70. *Idem.*
71. *Ibid.*, p. 120.
72. Berkhof, *op. cit*, p. 171.
73. Gen. 45:4-5.
74. Gen. 50:20.
75. Ex. 4:11-12.

Jehovah hath bidden him."[76] "And Jehovah said unto him, Wherewith? And he said, I will go forth, and will be a lying spirit in the mouth of all his prophets. And he said, Thou shalt entice him, and shalt prevail also: go forth, and do so. Now therefore, behold Jehovah hath put a lying spirit in the mouth of all these thy prophets; and Jehovah hath spoken evil concerning thee."[77] We have already noted the verse in Acts 2:23 speaking of the crucifixion as being the preordained work of God, and also the work of wicked men.

Berkhof warns against three errors regarding this doctrine of concurrence:

1. That it is a general communication of power, but not determining the specific action. Such a view ultimately means that man is in control.

2. That God does his part and man his part. "Each deed is in its entirety both a deed of God and a deed of the creature."[78] There is nothing that is independent from the will of God. He is thus involved in every act of the creature. God has so ordered it that the creature itself acts, thus carrying out his will.

3. That the work of God and creature are co-ordinate. God's will always has the priority. "It is God who worketh in you, both to will and to work, for his good pleasure."[79]

Having seen these erroneous views, let us now look at the characteristics of Divine concurrence.

1. It is predetermining in a logical sense, not necessarily a temporal sense. As we have already noted every act in the universe has underlying it the act of God. This movement from God is not on the action, but on the creature itself. God thus enables and prompts, while the creature acts freely. The Bible affirms this. "And there are diversities of workings, but the same God, who worketh all things in all."[80] Again in Ephesians 1:11, we have the classic statement that God "worketh all things after the counsel of his will." From these passages, we see clearly that God is in control of and working all things to his predetermined end.

2. It is also a simultaneous concurrence. Not only is God the one moving us to an act, he must sustain and accompany every act at every moment if it is to continue. Paul affirms that it is in God that we live and move and have our being.[81] "This divine activity accompanies the action of man at every point, but without robbing man in any way of his freedom. The action remains the free act of man, an act for which he is held responsible."[82]

3. It is an immediate concurrence. This grows out of the fact that God's action must accompany every act of the creature, if the act is to occur.

The relation of Divine concurrence with sin remains a major problem. Pelagians, semi-Pelagians and Arminians reject the idea that God's concurrence

---

76. II Sam. 16:11.
77. I Kings 22:22-23.
78. Berkhof, *op. cit.*, p. 172.
79. Phil. 2:13.
80. I Cor. 12:6.
81. Acts 17:28.
82. Berkhof, *op. cit.*, p. 173.

is predeterminative, since this logically means that God becomes the author of sin. Reformed theologians, while being aware of this have been unwilling to deny God's absolute control over the free actions of his moral creatures as clearly taught in Scripture. (See passages cited above.) Having affirmed this position, Berkhof again summarizes the teachings of Reformed theology on this subject:

1. Sinful acts are under the divine control, occurring according to his predetermined purpose, but only by permission, so that he is not the efficient cause of sinful acts (Gen. 45:5; 50:19-20; Ex. 10:1,20; II Sam. 16:10-11; Is. 10:5-7; Acts 2:23; 4:27-28).

2. God often restrains the sinful works of the sinner (Gen. 3:6; Job 1:12; 2:6; Ps. 76:10;Is. 10:15; Acts 7:51).

3. God overrules evil for good (Gen. 50:20; Ps. 76:10; Acts 3:13).[83]

Berkouwer questions whether this resort to permission is satisfactory. He cites Calvin as rejecting the idea of permission. "Calvin, therefore, considers the idea of Divine permission as an obscuration of the Scriptural insight."[84] If permission is used to describe the decree, then we must agree with Calvin. If, on the other hand, a clear distinction is made between the decree and the execution of the decree, then the term permission may be used. In other words, God decrees actively all that is to come to pass. In the execution of the decree in providence, God permits the sinner to act contrary to his preceptive will, though the act will be according to his secret, decretive will. The creature is morally responsible for all of his acts. He is the efficient agent in his acts. When he is enabled by the grace of God to do good, then because it was not in his nature or ability to do it, he must acknowledge that it was by God's grace. On the other hand, when he sins by the permission of God, he must assume the full guilt and blame, since it stems from his own sinful nature and desires.

We must agree with Berkouwer that the whole question of how the actions of God and the creature are related remains a mystery for us. Though he questions whether concurrence should be a third aspect of providence or not, it is helpful in speaking to the problem of how providence operates.

VII. Extraordinary Providence - Miracles

If all of history is the outworking of the providence of God, which we observe to take place under general laws and principles, how do we account for the miracles that are recorded in Scripture? Theologians have made the distinction between ordinary providence and extraordinary providence. The ordinary providence is that in which God uses the second causes in accordance with the laws of nature. Extraordinary providence is that in which he works immediately, or without the use of second causes in their ordinary operations. "The distinctive thing in a miraculous deed is that it results from the exercise of the supernatural power of God."[85]

---

83. *Ibid.*, p. 174.
84. *Ibid.*, p. 149, citing Calvin's *Institutes*, I, 18, 4.
85. Berkhof, *op. cit.*, p. 176.

Hoeksema is critical of the distinction between the natural and the supernatural works of God.

> From the Word of God it is evident that all the works of God are wonders, because they are, as works of God, marvelous. For this reason the question whether anything is natural or supernatural, which has so often been discussed in the connection with the idea of a miracle, is quite irrelevant and is based upon an erroneous notion of the relation between God and the world. The question does not properly belong in Reformed theology. It is really a deistic notion. For whoever believes in the Reformed conception of the providence of God will certainly understand and confess that the distinction between the natural and supernatural is false. . . . Nature works nothing by itself. . . . Everything is both natural and supernatural because everything is the work of God's sustaining and governing hand.[86]

There are several words in the Hebrew and Greek that denote miracles. The Hebrew term *pala*[87], which means to separate, to make wonderful, extraordinary, is translated by Greek *thauma*[88], meaning marvelous work. Another Hebrew word is *mophet*[89] often used with *othoth*[90] in the phrase *othoth umophethim*[91] meaning "signs and wonders", and translated by Greek *semeia kai terata*[92]. Miracles are also called "mighty works" *geburoth*[93] in Hebrew or *dunameis*[94], and *erga megaleia*[95] in Greek.

Some have sought to define miracle as conflicting with the laws of nature. This is the view generally held by Roman Catholic theologians. Kuyper rejects this view. "A miracle , thus is no occasional intervention by God into the course of natural things, 'for nothing operates through any power apart from God.' A miracle 'means nothing more than that God at a given moment wills a certain thing to occur differently than it had up to that moment been willed by him to occur.' "[96] Berkouwer points out that this definition was not a denial of miracles, but a denial of the idea that they were done in opposition to nature. "Miracles are not occasional interferences by God in a fixed order of nature. They are new extraordinary ways of God's rule over all things."[97] Exodus 34:10 confirms this concept of miracle. "And he said, Behold, I make a covenant: before all thy people I will do marvels, such as have not been wrought in all the earth, nor in any nation; and all the people among which thou art shall see the work of Jehovah; for it is a terrible thing that I do with thee." (See also Num. 16:30; Jer. 31:22; Is. 48:6ff.) Walter Chantry in his excellent little book entitled *The Signs of the Apostles* defines miracles in virtually the same way. "Miracles

---

86. *Op. cit.*, p. 241-242.
87. פלא
88. θαῦμα
89. מופת
90. אות
91. אותות ומופתים
92. σημεῖα καὶ τέρατα
93. גבורה
94. δυνάμεις
95. ἔργα μεγαλεῖα
96. Kuyper, *E Voto*, I, p. 240 as cited by Berkouwer, *op. cit.*, p. 213.
97. Berkouwer, *op. cit.*, p. 214.

then, are the extraordinary works of God's power which demand the awed attention of men."[98]

There are only three major periods of miracles in the Bible. They are the time of Moses and the Exodus, the time of Elijah and Elisha and the time of Christ. Moses was concerned that he would not be believed when he went to Egypt. God gave him the power to perform the miracle of turning his rod into a serpent and then back. This first of the Mosaic miracles was given as a sign to Israel and the Egyptians, "that they may believe that Jehovah, the God of their fathers, the God of Abraham, the God of Isaac, and the God of Jacob hath appeared unto thee."[99] Again God gave him the power of changing his hand to a leprous hand and back again. "And it shall come to pass, if they will not believe thee, neither hearken to the voice of the first sign, that they will believe the voice of the latter sign."[100] In other words, the miracles wrought by Moses were signs to confirm his authority as God's spokesman. Deuteronomy ends (34:10-12) with a reference to his signs, "And there hath not arisen a prophet since in Israel like unto Moses, whom Jehovah knew face to face, in all the signs and wonders, which Jehovah sent him to do in the land of Egypt..."

Not only was this true of Moses, it was also true of Elijah. The miracle on Mt. Carmel was for the explicit purpose of letting it be known that Jehovah is God, that Elijah was his servant and spokesman.[101]

Psalm 74:9 speaks directly to the effect that miracles were signs of true prophets. "We see not our signs: There is no more any prophet; Neither is there among us any that knoweth how long." Chantry comments, "In other words, the absence of signs is equivalent to the absence of a prophet, which in turn is the same as having no authoritative answer to their question, 'How long will God be absent from us?'... Where miracles are performed we should expect to hear the inspired Word of God spoken. Where their is no prophet, there are no signs."[102]

When we turn to the New Testament, we find that miracles serve precisely the same purpose as they did in the Old. John spoke of the miracles as "signs."[103] Jesus called upon men to believe in him because of the works he did (John 10:37-38). Peter opens the sermon at Pentecost with reference to the fact that "Jesus of Nazareth was a man approved of God unto you by mighty works and wonders and signs which God did by him in the midst of you, even as ye yourselves also know."[104] The Apostles appealed to the miracles they did as evidence that they were authoritative messengers from God. (See Gal. 3:5; Rom. 15:18-19). Hebrews 2:1-4 speaks pointedly of the attestation of wonders and signs to the apostolic authority. Verse 4 reads, "God also bearing witness with them, both by signs and wonders, and by manifold powers, and by gifts of the Holy Spirit, according to his own will." Chantry concludes, "Miracles are God's

---

98. (London: The Banner of Truth Trust), 1973, p. 14.
99. Exodus 4:5.
100. Exodus 4:8.
101. I Kings 18:36.
102. *Op. cit.*, p. 18.
103. See John 2:11 and 20:30-31.
104. Acts 2:22.

attestation to the divine mission of those who bring his fresh revelations to us."[105]

The question often asked today is whether miracles continue now or not. Rome and neo-Pentecostals affirm that they do. When we recognize the Biblical purpose of miracles is to attest to the authority of the prophets and apostles, it is clear that the close of the Apostolic age brings the cessation of miracles. Berkouwer observes that sacraments, like miracles, are signs. There is a difference, however. The sacraments add no new revelation, whereas miracles were associated with inspired revelations of prophets and apostles. Berkouwer observes:

> That men later began to yearn wistfully for special signs and new revelations of the Divine presence is indication of a serious devaluation of Word and sacrament and an emasculation of the power of faith. Men often thought that a God without special signs was a distant God. They lost their perspective for the reality of salvation in Christ, yes, of Christ himself.[106]

Although the Bible does not explicitly speak of the cessation of miracles, the fact that they are signs of the apostles, means that with the close of the Apostolic age, and the completion of the canon of the New Testament, miracles have ceased. The sign of the end of special revelation may well have been the destruction of Jerusalem and of the Temple in 70 A.D. This event certainly ended the old economy with its sacrificial system. That age had been marked with special revelation, and signs of that revelation: thus, the sign of the end of that age may well be the sign of the close of special revelation and of the signs that attested it.[107]

---

105. *Op. cit.*, p. 26. It is because of this linking of miracle to revelation that the subject of miracle has been treated as a mode of special revelation earlier in this text.
106. *Op. cit.*, pp. 242-243.
107. See Chapter XLI for a fuller treatment of the cessation of miracles.

Chapter XVI The Creation of Man

Introduction

The origin and nature of man is one of the most fascinating matters to man. This grows out of the fact that the subject matter is man himself. Berkouwer says:

> Man has always been concerned, in scholarly fashion as well as in the popular consciousness, with the many aspects of man's humanity, and thus with man himself. And yet we can scarcely deny that in our time the attention given to this problem has a new urgency, seriousness, and concentration. The intensive contemporary interest is closely tied in with the actual manifestations of man's nature in the events of the twentieth century. Our concern with the nature of man does not grow from a purely abstract and theoretical interest, but is related to the fact that we have learned to 'know' man, in our age, in direct and often alarming or catastrophic manner.[1]

Berkouwer goes on to suggest that the difficulty of our knowing man, grows out of the fact that it involves self-knowledge.

> Every view of man's nature affects not only others, but also the man doing the viewing. No man can abstract himself from his own nature, and it is precisely this fact which gives such an existential character to every judgment about 'man' and to every view of man's nature. When we inquire as to the source of our knowledge about man, we are asking about the source of our knowledge about *ourselves*. And, while it appears at first glance simple enough to include both under the same word 'knowledge', on closer examination we are faced with a rather strange situation -- a man may sometimes obtain a good insight into the lives of others without ever coming to a true self-knowledge.[2]

Due to the deceitfulness of his own heart, and to the fact that man is unable to approach himself objectively, the only reliable source of man's knowledge of man must be Divine revelation. Thus, we turn again to the Bible for its idea of our origin and nature.

---

1. G. C. Berkouwer, *Man, The Image of God* (Grand Rapids: Wm. B. Eerdmans Publishing Co., 1962), p. 12.
2. *Ibid.*, p. 18.

I. The Distinctive Features in the Origin of Man

A. Genesis 1:1-2:3

From our study of the account of creation in Genesis 1, we have seen that there is a progressive preparation of the earth for the creation of man. Man is represented in the passage as the climax of all of God's creative activity. A study of this passage reveals that there is a uniqueness to the creation of man. At each earlier stage of the production of non-human life the formula of God's command and fulfillment is given. "And God said, Let the earth put forth grass, herbs yielding seed, and fruit-trees bearing fruit after their kind. . . . And the earth brought forth grass, herbs yielding seed after their kind, and trees bearing fruit . . ."[3]; "And God said, Let the waters swarm with swarms of living creatures, and let birds fly above the earth in the open firmament of heaven. And God created the great sea-monsters, and every living creature that moveth wherewith the waters swarmed after their kind, and every winged bird after its kind . . .";[4] "And God said, Let the earth bring forth living creatures after their kind, cattle, and creeping things, and beasts of the earth after their kind: and it was so."[5] As we come to the creation of man, however, there is a difference in the language used to describe this act.

Genesis 1:26 reads, "And God said, Let us make man in our image after our likeness: and let them have dominion over the fish of the sea, and over the birds of the heavens, and over the cattle, and over all the earth, and over every creeping thing that creepeth upon the earth." Calvin says, "Hitherto God has been introduced simply as commanding; now, when he approaches the most excellent of all his works, he enters into consultation."[6] This divine consultation implies that man is to be unique and elevated above all the rest of creation.

Genesis 1:27 says, "And God created (*wayibra'*) man in his own image, in the image of God created (*bara*[8]) He him; male and female created (*bara*) He them." We have already noted the uniqueness of the usage of the word (*bara*) in the Old Testament. It is of interest to note the view of Gerhard Von Rad concerning this term.

> To express divine creation, the Hebrew language already had a verb, which, as the Phoenician shows, could designate the artistic creation. But the Old Testament usage rejects even this comparison. The verb was retained exclusively to designate the divine creative activity. This effective theological constraint which extends even into the language is significant . . . It means a creative activity, which on principle is without analogy. It is correct to say that the verb *bara'*, 'create', contains the idea both of complete effortlessness and *creatio ex nihilo*, since it is never connected with any statement of the material.[9]

---

3. Genesis 1:11, 12.
4. Genesis 1:20.
5. Genesis 1:24.
6. *Commentary on Genesis*, Loc. cit. (rev. ed.)
7. וַיִּבְרָא
8. בָּרָא
9. *Commentary on Genesis*, p. 57.

Von Rad comments on verse 27, thus:
> The use of the verb *bara* in verse 27 receives its fullest significance for that divine creativity which is absolutely without analogy. It occurs three times in the one verse to make clear that here the high point and goal has been reached toward which all God's creativity from verse 1 on was directed.[10]

We have seen earlier that this word may be used of secondary creation, but in the Qal form the word is used only of God, and has the unique emphasis that he stresses here.

Without entering into the full significance of the image at this point, we should observe that the expression "after the image of God" teaches again the special place of man in creation. His exemplar is not earthly, but heavenly--God himself. This is said only of man.

Another feature of this passage is the dominion with which man is invested. This dominion is not the image, but is a consequence of his being made in the image of God. Man is thus made to be the vice-regent of God to administer the affairs of God on earth, because he has been made in the image and likeness of God.

B. Genesis 2:7

The second chapter of Genesis presents a second account of the creation of man. It is not in conflict with the first chapter, which presents the original creation and the ordering of the earth in a progressive way culminating in the creation of man. In the second chapter man is also central and is introduced first. The rest of the earth is presented as being made for him. The teaching of the two chapters then is the same, in that man is the central creature of both.

Verse 7 reads, "And Jehovah God formed (*wayitser*[11]) man (*haadam*[12]) of the dust of the ground (*aphar min haadamah*[13]) and breathed into his nostrils the breath of life (*nishmat hayim*[14]); and man became a living soul (*nephesh hayyah*[15])." This verse gives us some detail about the creation and thus the constitution of man. The first thing to be noted is that man is made of the dust of the earth (*aphar min hadamah*[16]). This was not a commanding of the earth to form man, or to bring him forth, as in the case of other living beings. God is represented as acting directly in the formation of man. Animals have the same constituent of dust, but the manner of formation was not the same. Further, it should be observed that the designation of this creature *adam*[17] (man) is a reminder of his earthly origin *adamah*[18] (earth). Man is called "earth" as it is said to him,

---

10. *Ibid.*, p. 55.
11. וַיִּיצֶר
12. דָּאָדָם
13. עָפָר מִן דָאֲדָמָה
14. נִשְׁמַת חַיִּים
15. נֶפֶשׁ חַיָּה
16. עָפָר מִן דָאֲדָמָה
17. אָדָם
18. אֲדָמָה

"dust (*aphar*[19]) thou art" (3:19). Not only is this generic name of man a reminder of his earthly beginnings, but also the phrase used to describe him after God has breathed into him the breath of life, and he becomes a living soul (*nephesh hayyah*). This also is a term which describes his animation in the same terms as that of other living creatures.[20] Delitzsch says, "Man has his name '*adam* from no other source than from the earth, ('*adamah*) because it is not this which is his characteristic dignity, that God created him after His image; but this, that God created him the earthly one, -- taken from the earth in respect of his natural constitution, -- after His image."[21]

Reference to the dust of the earth is a reference to the fine dust of which the earth is made, or its constituent elements. When this passage is coupled with Genesis 3:19, where it is said, "for dust thou art and unto dust shalt thou return," and with the ever-present reality of the fact of the corruption of our bodies back to dust, it emphasizes the fact that the constituent elements of our bodies are earthly. Delitzsch again has a suggestive comment about the particular earth used for the creation of man. "And it was earth of Eden, the land of delight, and therefore of the same source and ground whence sprang the trees of paradise, and whence the beasts of paradise were formed."[22]

It was not until God breathed into the body of man the breath of life that he became a living soul. Apparently, this in-breathing was itself a part of the creative activity of God. It is this which constituted man as man. We have already noted that the expression "living soul" (*nephesh hayyah*) does not distinguish man from other living creatures. In other words, this is not a term that speaks of the man having a human soul as distinguished from animals. Rather it is a description of the genus of all animate beings, including both man and animals. There is no idea of the body which God had fashioned as having any animation prior to this in-breathing, thus ruling out the idea that this is the description of the addition of a soul to a body that had been evolved from the animals.

The creative act that constituted man as a living soul was also the act that constituted man as a moral, rational and spiritual being, for he is immediately treated as such. This is not to say, however, that this divine in-breathing is necessarily the imparting of the moral and spiritual nature. Though the language of Genesis 2:7 implies something higher than other living creatures, it is Genesis 1:26-27 which states this difference much more clearly in reference to man's being made in the image of God.

II. The Origin of the Soul of the Individual

There have been three views regarding the origin of man's soul. The first is that of pre-existence; the second, traducianism; and the third, creationism. We shall survey the arguments for each. It should be noted, however, that the Bible does not speak of this subject directly. This, no doubt, accounts for the large measure of uncertainty about the subject among theologians. The history of the subject is interesting. Origen (c. 185 - c. 254) was the only theologian to hold to

---
19. עָפָר
20. See Genesis 2:19; 1:20; 1:24, where "living soul" נֶפֶשׁ חַיָּה is used of fishes, birds and quadrupeds.
21. *A System of Biblical Psychology* (Grand Rapids: Baker Book House, 1966), p. 83.
22. *Ibid.*, p. 93.

the pre-existence of the individual soul. He seems to have borrowed this from Plato's doctrine of the transmigration of the soul. Tertullian was the first theologian to set forth traducianism, namely, that the souls are generated with the bodies in the act of procreation by the human parents. This view was gradually accepted in the West, whereas the East turned to creationism. Augustine hesitated to accept creationism, but was not strongly in favor of traducianism either.[23] The scholastics moved toward creationism, and Aquinas said, "It is heretical to say that the intellectual soul is transmitted by way of generation."[24] Since the Reformation, Protestantism has been divided on the subject. Luther favored traducianism, and Calvin favored creationism. Generally speaking, Lutherans have followed Luther, and Reformed theologians have followed Calvin, though there have been a number of more recent Reformed theologians who are less settled on the matter. For example, Jonathan Edwards favored traducianism, as does J. Oliver Buswell. Dabney felt it was a mystery that we could not answer. The modern Dutch School with its emphasis on the unity of man rejects creationism, but does not adopt traditional traducianism. For them it is a mystery also.

A. Pre-Existence

The idea that the soul of individuals pre-existed was held by Origen in the Third Century. As we have already noted, he borrowed this idea from Plato. This theory has never had many advocates. Scotus Erignea and Julius Miller in *The Christian Doctrine of Sin*, have argued for pre-existence. In modern times the theosophists, and the other cults hold to this doctrine. Also philosophers such as F. C. S. Schiller of Oxford, and F. R. Tennant of Cambridge have held it. Generally speaking, however, pre-existence has not been held by any orthodox theologians.

Several arguments may be listed against this theory:

1. There is no Biblical evidence for it.

2. It is based on heathen dualism, and makes the soul the real essence of man, and thus makes the body just the prison for the soul, or something that is accidental to man. Man is complete without the body.

3. It destroys the unity of the human race, for the souls are all pre-existent, and not derived from our first parents. They are individual creatures, just as the angels are, and not a race.

4. There is no support for this view in the consciousness of man. He has no recollections of a pre-existence. Also, he does not feel that the body is the prison for the soul. Rather, he dreads death, the separation of body and soul (II Corinthians 5:4).

---

23. See Warfield, *Studies in Tertullian and Augustine* (New York: Oxford University Press, 1930).
24. As cited in Berkhof, *Systematic Theology, op. cit.*, p. 196.

B. Traducianism

The idea that the souls of individuals are propagated along with the bodies through the act of procreation has been held by a number of theologians. In the ancient church Tertullian, Rufinus, Apollinarius, and Gregory of Nyssa held this view. Augustine was inclined toward it, and Leo the Great called it a teaching of the catholic faith. During the Middle Ages it gave way to creationism. Luther adopted it, and most Lutherans since then have held it. Among the Reformed, in addition to Edwards and Buswell, H. B. Smith, Shedd, A. H. Strong and Gordon H. Clark favor it.

The arguments favoring this theory are:

1. The Genesis account of creation is said to favor it. Adam received his soul directly by in-breathing (Genesis 2:7), but no new mention of a soul is made in connection with Eve (Genesis 2:23).

2. God ceased his creative activity after making man (Genesis 2:2).

3. The descendants are described as having been in the loins of the fathers (Genesis 46:26; Hebrews 7:9-10).

4. The fact that certain traits are passed on to the children implies that they derive the seat of personality, the soul, from the parent.

5. Traducianism accounts best for the inheritance of moral and spiritual corruption.

A number of arguments can be presented against traducianism:

1. The philosophical problem of the nature of the soul as being simple, and thus not capable of division raises difficulties in accounting for its propagation. Also, there is the problem of whether the soul comes from the father or the mother, or is some sort of combining of the two. If it is said to originate in the physical seed, then this leads to materialism.

2. The idea that God ceased to act creatively is not fully consistent with the doctrine of regeneration, which posits that God makes a new heart for us.

3. If associated with a realistic view of the transmission of sin, then there is a difficulty with the incarnation. For, if we were realistically in Adam and sinned there, then Christ, the descendent of Adam must also have sinned in him, and be guilty with him.

C. Creationism

Creationism holds that each individual soul is immediately created by God. As God's immediate creation it must be pure, but it is then united to a depraved body, and thus contracts the corruption of sin.

Arguments for creationism:

1. Biblical passages that seem to favor this view:
Numbers 16:22 "And they fell upon their faces, and said, O God, the God of the spirits of all flesh . . ."
Psalms 33:15 "He fashioneth their hearts alike; he considereth all their works."
Isaiah 57:16 "For I will not contend for ever, neither will I be always wroth; for the spirit shall fail before me, and the souls which I have made."
Jeremiah 38:16 "As the Lord liveth, that made us this soul . . ."
Zechariah 12:1 "The burden of the word of the Lord for Israel, saith the Lord, which stretcheth forth the heavens, and layeth the foundation of the earth, and formeth the spirit of man within him."

2. It is in accord with the Biblical representation of man as body and soul, in which these two entities are distinguished, and presumably then having different origins (Ecclesiastes 12:7; Isaiah 42:5; Zechariah 12:1; Hebrews 12:9).

3. It is more tenable from a philosophical point, which maintains that the soul is by nature indivisible.

4. It avoids the problems with the incarnation and Christology.

Objections to creationism:

1. The most telling argument is that of the relation of sin to the soul. If God created the soul with depravity, then he is the creator of sin. If, on the other hand, he places a pure soul in a depraved body, he is indirectly the author of moral evil.

2. It fails to account for the passing on of personality traits to the child. Under this view the parents generate only the body, not the soul, and thus not the personality of the child.

3. It assumes that God did continue his creative activity, contrary to Genesis 2:2.

4. The verses cited favoring creationism are not conclusive, since they do not specify immediate creation. It could refer to secondary creation through the human parents.[25]

Dabney makes a rather wise observation after having considered the various arguments for both views. He says, "Now, since we have no real cognition by perception, of spiritual substance, but only know its acts and effects, we should not be surprised at our ignorance of the precise agency of its production,

---

25. Note: Most of these arguments have been derived from Berkhof's treatment in his *Systematic Theology*. He himself prefers a form of creationism.

and the way that agency acts."[26] He goes on to say, "May not this insoluble question again teach us to apprehend a great truth, which we are incompetent to comprehend; that there is such a reality as spiritual generation instanced in the eternal generation of the Word, in the infinite Spirit, and in the generation of human souls from the finite?"[27]

The Dutch School as represented by Dooyeweerd and Berkouwer reject both creationism and traducianism on the ground that both are based on a dualistic concept of man. This school has stressed the "whole man" idea, and insist that the body and soul are not separate substances or entities. Berkouwer says:

> It is to be regretted that the dubiousness of the Scriptural evidence did not cause earnest questioning whether or not we actually did have a Scriptural witness here which would evoke an echo in the heart; for it is precisely the emphasis on the authority of Scripture which should have led to the recognition of the limit of the type of reflection in which the problem of the origin of man is replaced by the problem of the origin of the soul. And we need not be surprised that in the measure that the Scriptural witness regarding the origin of the whole man is appreciated, the importance of the apparent dilemma seems to fade, and that consciousness of the whole man in his mysterious relationship to God opens the way for us to rise above this historic dilemma. In this light the continuing hesitation of Augustine becomes a meaningful sign in the history of Christian thought.[28]

Without agreeing fully with the Dutch School about the idea that there are not two separable entities, nevertheless, the thrust of these remarks seems to be valid. The Bible is not really clear on the subject. It lies in a mystery, and it appears best not to be too dogmatic in such cases.

---

26. *Systematic Theology, op. cit.,* pp. 320-321.
27. *Idem.*
28. *Ibid.,* p. 307.

Chapter XVII The Image of God

Introduction

Modern scientists have sought to determine the distinguishing characteristic of man. Various suggestions have been made. For example, man has been called the only tool-making animal. Now, however, it has been found that some animals do in a simple way make tools. Another distinguishing character has been the idea of using language. Here again various efforts have and are being made to teach animals some sort of means of communicating their thoughts to us. Very interesting experiments have been done with chimpanzees, and with dolphins in this area. Again, language as the distinguishing characteristic of man seems to be blurred.

In the last chapter on the creation of man, we found that the Bible teaches the distinguishing character of man is that he was made in the image of God. We shall examine just what is involved in the concept of the image of God more fully in this chapter.

I. Importance of the Concept

The terms "image" and "likeness of God" occur rather infrequently in the Scriptures, namely, in Genesis 1:26-27; 5:1; 9:6; I Corinthians 11:7; Ephesians 4:24; Colossians 3:10; James 3:9. Compare also: Romans 8:29; II Corinthians 3:18; 4:4; Colossians 1:15. This infrequency of reference might cause one to minimize the teaching. Actually, the most fundamental truth regarding the nature of man lies in the declaration that he has been made in the image of God. This is seen in the emphasis laid upon the idea in the first mention of man in Genesis 1:26-27. Further, if the divine image underlies the rationality and moral responsibility of man, then we see its importance in the history of redemption. First, only a moral creature can sin. Second, special redemptive revelation can be addressed only to a rational creature, and third, the fact that man was made the image of God brings the possibility of the incarnation into view. Of course, it was a step of infinite condescension and humiliation for our Saviour to assume our nature, yet it was not degradation, for our nature was created as His image, and was thus consonant with the Divine nature. All of this serves to point up the great significance of the image of God for us.

The fundamental character of the creation of man in the image of God is to be seen in the usage of the term in this connection. It is not said that man has the image of God in him. The Biblical usage is rather that man is created in the image of God, and in I Corinthians 11:7 it is said that "he is the image of God." Thus, we ought not to speak of the image of God in man, as though it were something distinct from man himself. Instead, we should speak of man as the image of God, or as being made in the image of God. The image is not something that is outside of God, after which man is fashioned, but rather, man is fashioned after God himself. Man is the image of God.

II. The Biblical Idea of the Image

In Genesis 1:26-27 the affirmation that man is made in the image or likeness of God is made three times. Verse 26 uses two different words to speak of this concept, namely, image (*tselem*[1]), and likeness (*demuth*[2]).

A. A Study of These Two Words

The question naturally arises as to whether there is any intended difference between these words.

1. The History of the Interpretation of these Two Terms Reviewed.

a. Pre-Reformation

The pre-Reformation period saw a division of the two into sharply different concepts. Irenaeus held that *imago* referred to the bodily form, whereas, *similitudo* was the likeness of man to God because of the spirit being breathed into his nostrils. Augustine thought of the image as referring to the intellectual faculties, and the likeness to the moral qualities. The Roman Catholic theologian Bellarmine considered the image as including the natural abilities of man that were not lost in the fall, while likeness referred to the *donum superadditum* which was lost with the fall. The LXX inserts "and" (*kai*[3]) between the two words, and thus gives rise to a sharper division than is implied in the Hebrew text. This coupled with the fact that likeness is not used after the fall, gave arguments for the sharp distinction that grew up in the pre-Reformation period.

b. The Reformers

Generally speaking, this division between these words was rejected by the Reformers. A study of the usage of the terms in Genesis indicates a certain interchangeability of the two. In Genesis 1:26 both words are used to describe the intention of God to make man in this way, after his image, and in his likeness. When we move on to verse 27, however, only one of these words is used to describe the fulfillment of this intention, namely, *betsalmo*[4] and *betselem*.[5] There is no reason to hold that the fulfillment is less comprehensive than the intention. Thus, it may be assumed that the one term of verse 27 covers what was covered by the two terms of verse 26.

There is a similar usage of *demuth* in Genesis 5:1 to include both terms. Note that the verb in this verse is *bero*[6], and thus the reference evidently is to the

---

1. צֶלֶם
2. דְּמוּת
3. και
4. בְּצַלְמוֹ
5. בְּצֶלֶם
6. בְּרֹא

original creation that was described in Genesis 1:26-27. Here, then, *bidemuth*[7] includes both terms of 1:26.

The LXX generally translates the Hebrew words as follows: *tselem* by *eikon*[8]; and *demuth* by *homoiosin*[9]. In Genesis 5:1, however, *demuth* is translated by *eikon*, and in Genesis 5:3 *demuth* is translated by *idea*[10] and *tselem* by *eikon*. Apparently, the translators of the Greek Old Testament did not see a sharp distinction between the two Hebrew terms.

2. A Comparison of the Two Terms Themselves

a. *Tselem* is derived from a root which means "to cut off". It is used to describe a sculptured or pictured image (Numbers 33:52; I Samuel 6:5; Ezekiel 23:14). On the basis of this sort of usage, it has, at times, been suggested that this word really refers to the physical image. Irenaeus held such a view. The word is used in Genesis 5:3 to speak of the likeness of Seth to his father Adam. This may well refer to the physical likeness, but it seems to be more inclusive than just this. Seth is like Adam in that he has a human nature, including the spiritual as well as the physical aspects. If we exclude the limitation of the word from being just the physical aspect, so also we should exclude it from being limited to just the spiritual aspect of man. According to Genesis 1:26-27, it is the man who is the image of God, and not just his body or his soul.

b. *Demuth* is a word that means likeness or similitude. It is used in various ways. It may refer to the concrete representation, such as, pictures or blue-prints (Ezekiel 23:15; II Kings 16:10). It is used in drawing the parallel between the voice of the mountains and of the multitude (Isaiah 13:4). Again, Isaiah uses it to say that nothing can be compared to God (Isaiah 40:8). We must conclude, from this brief survey, that this is a more abstract term than *tselem*. Its thrust is that of similarity or likeness.

Why were there two different words, if there was no intended distinction? Leupold simply says, "So we shall have to regard the second phrase, 'according to our likeness', as merely supplementary to or explanatory of the first."[11] Bavinck agrees with this:

> The likeness is a closer definition, a strengthening and a complement of image. Likeness is itself weaker and broader than image. An animal has some traces of likeness and oneness with, but yet is not the image of man. Image expresses the idea that God is the archetype and man is the echtype; likeness adds to it that image is in agreement with the original in all parts.[12]

---

7. בִּדְמוּת
8. εἰκών
9. ὁμοίωσιν
10. ἰδέα
11. H. C. Leupold, *Commentary on Genesis*, (Grand Rapids: Baker Book House, 1950), 1:26.
12. *Gereformeerde Dogmatiek, op. cit.*, Vol. II, p. 493.

Aalders says:
> So far as we are able to define the words more precisely, 'image' brings out the fact that man is found in such a conformity with the Divine essence, as exists between a person and a picture of that person. The word 'likeness' strengthens this, by laying emphasis that the conformity between the image and the original is close.[13]

It seems clear from the usage of the terms that man is not equated with God. The Creator-creature distinction is preserved, and yet there is a very close relationship of this highest creature with his Maker. He is his image and likeness. This is the basic characteristic of man, distinguishing him from all the rest of creation.

3. Examination of the Prepositions Used, Namely *Be*[14] and *Ke*[15]

In Genesis 1:26 these two prepositions are used, *be* with *tselem* and *ke* with *demuth*. What is the precise import of these prepositions? Normally, *be* is translated by "in" and *ke* is translated by "according to". It should be observed, however, that they may be used somewhat interchangeably. For example, in connection with these same nouns, the usage is reversed from that found in Genesis 1:26-27 in Genesis 5:1, 3. In Genesis 5:1 *be* is used with *demuth* and in Genesis 5:3 *be* is used with *demuth* and *ke* with *tselem*. In this connection the LXX translates both by *kata* with the exception of Genesis 9:6, where *en* is used. On the basis of this interchanging of the prepositions, we conclude that no sharp distinction is meant by the use of the two prepositions in either Genesis 1 or Genesis 5.

B. The Relation of the Image to the Dominion over Creation

Though some have sought to identify the image with the dominion, the generally accepted view is that the dominion is the consequence of man's being made in the image of God. It is because he is the image of God that he exercised dominion over the world. The structure of Genesis 1:27-28 suggests that the dominion is something conferred on the man, who is already the image of God.

C. The Relation of the Image to Man's Being Male and Female

The close proximity of the reference to the image of God, and of the reference to man's being made both male and female has given rise to the suggestion of some relation of the two. Contemporary theologians have been interested in this aspect. Barth finds the image in the fact that man is created male and female. The I-Thou relation on the creaturely level reflects the I-Thou relation within the Godhead.

---

13. *Het Boek Genesis*, p. 47.
14. בְּ
15. כְּ

God created him in his own image in the fact that he did not create him alone, but in this connection and fellowship. For in God's action as the Lord of the covenant, and even further back in His action as the Creator of a reality distinct from Himself, it is proof that God himself is not solitary, that although he is one in essence He is not alone, but that primarily and properly He is in connection and fellowship. It is inevitable that we should recall the Triune Being of God at this point. God exists in relationship and fellowship. As the Father of the Son and the Son of the Father he is himself I and Thou, confronting himself and yet always one and the same in the Holy Ghost. God created man in His own image, in the image which emerges even in His work as the Creator and the Lord of the Covenant. Because He is not solitary in Himself, and therefore does not will to be so *ad extra*, it is not good for man to be alone, and God created him in his own image, as male and female. ... God is in relationship, and so too is the man created by him. This is his divine likeness. When we view it in this way, the dispute whether it is lost by sin finds a self-evident solution. It is not lost. But more important is the fact that what man is, indestructible as he is, man with the fellowman, he is in hope of the being and action of the One who is his original in this relationship.[16]

Brunner has a similar view. He starts with the thesis that God is love. His nature is community. Man must be able to love and must also be in community. "He cannot realize his nature without the 'Other;' his destiny is fellowship in love." Brunner distinguishes between the formal image, the responsibility, the existence for love, and the material image, his existence in Christ, his existence in love. His sexuality is not the image of God, but reflects it. Man could not be the image of God, unless he were created a pair.[17]

Horst and W. Vischer see the male and female relationship not so much as a reflection of the intertrinitarian relations, as the designed relation between God and man. Passages such as Hosea and Jeremiah are cited as demonstration of this. Von Rad observes that "It is therefore noteworthy that procreative ability is carefully removed from God's image and shifted to a special word of blessing."[18]

Though the statement regarding man's being male and female is very closely related to the image, it is highly doubtful that sexuality can itself be identified with the image. For one thing sexuality exists in both the plant and animal worlds, and these are not called the image of God. Further, the passage teaches that man is the image of God. That is, the whole man, not just some of his attributes or qualities. On this basis, we should reject the identification of either the body or the soul, or man's sexuality as the image. Rather man is the image of God.

The suggestion has been made that reference to the sexuality points to the whole of the human race as the image. The idea of love and communion grow-

---

16. *Church Dogmatics* (Edinburgh: T. & T. Clark, 1957), Vol. III, 2, p. 324.
17. *The Christian Doctrine of Creation and Redemption* (Philadelphia: Westminster Press, 1952), pp. 63-65.
18. Gerhard von Rad, *Genesis op. cit.*, p. 59.

ing out of man as a bisexual creature is a consequence of this fact, and not the constituent element of it. A further consequence is the procreative ability, which is removed from the image to the area of command and blessing.

Again, as we read the passage carefully, we see the thrust is that man is the image and likeness of God. It is the whole man, and not just part. It has frequently been the attempt of theologians to identify some particular aspect of man's nature as the image. For example, the body has been so identified, by Von Rad; or the spirit by Hodge, and Bavinck. Some want to identify the image more particularly with the intellectual or moral qualities of man, or his personality. Others have identified it with the *donum superadditum* of Paradise, which was lost in the fall.

None of these partial identifications take into account the simple language of the passage, which equates man as the image of God. The image is not a part of man, or an added feature to his basic nature. His basic nature is to be the image of God. Man is the image of God in the essence of his being. Because he is the image of God, he can know God and have communion with him. Just as the dominion over the earth is a consequence of man's being the image of God, so also are other human attributes consequences of his being the image. Since man is the image of God, it is to be expected that he be rational, that he have a will, freedom, personality, etc., corresponding to those attributes of God. The same may even be said of the body. Man has a body because he is the image of God. God sees and hears, and man who is his image also sees and hears, but he must have organs with which to do so. Of course, since he is not identical with God, but only his image, the necessity of his having a body is one of the differences of man from God. Moral excellence in his original condition was also a consequence of the image.

III. The Image in Relation to Christ

The Bible speaks not only of man being made in the image of God, but also of Christ as the image (*eikon*) of God,[19] and the "image of the invisible God."[20] It further teaches that believers are "to be conformed to the image of his Son, that he might be the first born among many brethren."[21] The question may be asked of the original image of God in man, was it the image of Christ? A careful reading of Genesis 1:27 indicates otherwise. Kuyper says:

> Hence we maintain the tried explanation of the Church's wisest and godliest ministers, that by these words the Father addressed the Son and the Holy Spirit. And then the unity of the Three Persons expresses itself in the words: 'And God created man after his image.' Hence this image can not be the Son.[22]

Kuyper goes on to define his understanding of the image.

> That image must be, therefore, a concentration of the features of God's Being, by which he expresses himself. And since God alone can rep-

---
19. II Cor. 4:4.
20. Col. 1:15.
21. Rom. 8:29.
22. Kuyper, Abraham, *The Work of the Holy Spirit*, translated from the Dutch by Henri de Vries (Grand Rapids: Wm. B. Eerdmans Publishing Co., 1946), p. 221.

resent his own Being to himself, it follows that by the image of God we must understand the representation of his Being as it eternally exists in the divine consciousness.[23]

The idea that the divine image in man is the image of Christ has been held by various theologians. This view originated with Origen. Tertullian and Ambrose in the West, and Chrysostom and Basil in the East supported this view. Augustine opposed it, as did Reformed theologians such as Calvin, Voetius and Coccejus. Despite the fact that Reformed theologians have rejected this as erroneous, it is popular to hold that the "image" is the image of Christ.

The Bible teaches that the redeemed are to be renewed and transformed to the image of Christ. "We all are changed into the same image from glory to glory, even as by the Spirit of the Lord."[24] Again, Romans 8:29 says, "That we are predestinated to be conformed to the image of his Son." We are taught to increase to the stature of the fullness of Christ. The image to which we are to conform is not that of the Second Person of the Trinity, but to that of the Messiah, the Incarnate Word.

The Second Person of the Trinity is the image of the Father. He has taken on human nature in the capacity of Messiah. It is this that we are called upon to imitate.

> Mere similarity of sound should not lead us to make this mistake. Every effort to translate Gen. 1:26, 'Let Us make man in or after the image of the Son,' is confusing. Then 'Let Us' must refer to the Father speaking to the Holy Spirit; and this cannot be. Scripture never places the Father and the Holy Spirit in such relation. Moreover, it would put the Son outside the greatest act of creation, viz. the creation of man. And Scripture says: 'Without Him was not anything made that was made'; and again: 'Through Him are created all things in heaven and on earth.'[25]

To hold that the image that Adam had prior to the fall was the image of the Messiah, involves importing into Eden the concept of the fall, and sin thus necessitating the Messiah. Had Adam not fallen, he would have remained in the unmarred image of the Triune God, without any concept of a Mediator of the Covenant of Grace. Paul teaches that we have two different images. "And as we have borne the image of the earthy, we shall also bear the image of the heavenly."[26] This passage is somewhat difficult to interpret, but it seems to point to the fact that we have borne the image that Adam had, namely, the image of God, and now in Christ we shall bear the image of Christ.

We thus maintain that man as created was created in the image of the Triune God, and not of the Messiah.

IV. The Effects of Sin on the Image

Various passages in the Scripture refer to man, even in his fallen state as the image of God (Genesis 5:3; 9:6; James 3:9; I Corinthians 11:7; compare

---
23. *Idem.*
24. II Cor. 3:18.
25. Kuyper, *op. cit.*, pp. 244-245.
26. I Cor. 15:49.

Psalm 8). As we study these passages, we see that the usage of the term "image" does not distinguish between man as unfallen and fallen, but between man and other creatures. The Scriptures do not hesitate to speak of the terrible effects of sin on man, and yet they do not apply this language to the image. The implication is that the fact that man is the image is not directly affected by sin. The image though not lost has been terribly marred, and thus man suffers the loss of some of the consequences of being the image of God, such as the loss of moral excellence, and the darkening of his reason, and the corruption of all his members. He still remains, however, the image of God.

V. Man Renewed in the Image of God

The plan of salvation provides for the rebirth, and the renewal of the whole man so that he becomes conformed to the image of the Son of God (Romans 8:29). We have already observed that though the moral excellence of man was lost in the fall, this was not the image itself, but rather one of the consequences of the image in man's unfallen state. It is one of the glories of the Gospel that God confers the restoration in Christ of what was lost by sin. So Ephesians 4:24 and Colossians 3:10 speak of the renewal of knowledge after the image of him, and the creating of righteousness and true holiness after God. In other words, the rebirth involves the planting afresh in the heart of man these principles of knowledge, righteousness and holiness. In sanctification the whole man is renewed in all of these principles, until we are conformed to his image.

Some Reformed theologians in the past have spoken of the moral excellence as the "narrow image" and the human nature as the "broad image." Though this may be a convenient way in which to refer to these two aspects of the image, it may lead to erroneous thinking about the image. On the one hand, the impression may be given that there are two images of God in man, the broad and the narrow images. John Murray warned against this, and suggested that we refer to the broad and the narrow aspects of the one image. Since the Bible does not use this terminology, but explicitly speaks of man as the image, it is better to use this simple language, while recognizing the moral excellence as particular aspects of this image.

VI. Inferences of Man's Being the Image of God

A. The Moral Agency of Man

Since man is the image of the Personal, Living God, who is in his essence a moral being, so man must be a moral, personal creature. Personality implies rationality and free agency, or the power of self-determination. As a rational creature with this power of self-determination, man is responsible to his Maker for all of his actions. Thus, he is a moral agent. As we have seen, man remains the image of God, even in his fallen condition, and thus remains responsible to God, despite the marring of the image due to sin. That this is the case is seen in the way in which God holds him accountable for his sins.

B. The Moral Excellence of Man

As originally created man possessed moral excellence, namely, knowledge, righteousness and holiness. To say that man was created with this moral excellence is to affirm more than just a metaphysical resemblance of man to God. It affirms that there was an ethical resemblance. Moral excellence is the proper exercise of the moral agency. Thus, man in his primitive condition had true knowledge, and was the true interpreter of reality. He had true righteousness, which was more than just the absence of sin. It involved a positive conformity to the Divine Will. He was holy in the purity of his character.

C. The Dominion over the Creatures

We have already observed that the dominion is not the image, but a consequence of man being the image of God. The dominion is a function of man, and not a quality of his nature. It was specifically commanded to man, upon the completion of his creation. This has been called the "creation mandate".

Dominion was assigned to man over the whole world (Genesis 1:26-27; Psalms 8; I Corinthians 15:24-28; Hebrews 2:5-8). This dominion was the rationale for the "creation mandate" to fill the earth and subdue it (Genesis 1:28). Being by nature equipped to have dominion over the earth, man has sought to fulfill this function, even as a sinner. It is a part of the Gospel promise that the full obedience of all will come to pass in the Second Adam (I Corinthians 15:24-28), who thus fulfills what the first Adam failed to do when he sinned.

Chapter XVIII Man, His Nature - Biblical Psychology

Introduction

Having considered the creation of man, and the fact that the distinguishing characteristic of man lies in his being made in the image of God, it is now important for us to examine more about his nature. As we have already observed it is difficult for man to be able to come to a proper understanding of man, since he cannot be objective regarding himself. This is particularly true because of the noetic effects of sin, that cause man's thinking to be blinded and thus false. For this reason, it is imperative that we go back to the Bible as the only source for the truth about man.

Modern man has entitled the study of man and his nature "psychology." By the nature of the case with man as the object of study, the study has proved to be largely experimental in nature, and anything but a precise science. It has been based on humanistic assumptions, and though it has been able at times to come to certain hypotheses that seem to be operable, it is essentially false in its view of man.

One of the most serious errors that Christians are prone to make is to think that they can borrow the alleged findings of non-Christian psychology and simply "baptize" it with some Biblical ideas. What we desire to do in this chapter is to examine some of the Biblical givens regarding the nature of man, and seek to come to some conclusions on the basis of this examination. Because of the large body of material we shall not be able to handle all of it, and thus some of the conclusions will only be tentative.

The title Biblical Psychology has been questioned. Berkouwer observes, "Theological investigations of man cannot seek a solution along the lines of a scientific anthropology, or a Biblical psychology and physiology, as if the intention of Scripture were to give us information about the various aspects of man, or the details of the composition of man."[1]

If we define the idea of Biblical Psychology as being a full science of man derived from the Bible, we must agree with Berkouwer, there is no real Biblical Psychology, for the Bible does not provide the exclusive data for making such a textbook on Psychology.

If the Bible is not a textbook of science, and in particular of psychology, just what is the proper place of the Bible in connection with the study of psychology? How can we have a chapter entitled "Biblical Psychology?"

The Bible is first of all the Word of God written. As such it has been given under the inspiration of the Holy Spirit so that all that was set down by the human authors was also the Holy Word of God. This inspiration has produced a book, which though it has come through the pen of the human authors, has nevertheless been preserved as God's infallible Word--a Word that is without error, and wholly authoritative. From this fact the Church has concluded that the Bible is the only infallible rule of faith and practice.

---

1. *The Image of God, op. cit.*, p. 30.

This is not to say that there is no place for extra-Biblical study. We learn a great deal from the area of general revelation about a great many things which are not covered by the teaching of the Bible. Further, it is not to say that we do not learn truth outside of the Bible, for the whole realm of general revelation is itself the revelation of God, and reflects his truth also. The problem with man lies in his inability to interpret both the areas of general and special revelation properly. This problem has arisen, not primarily because man is a finite creature, but rather as a result of the noetic effects of sin. The unfallen man, being finite, could never fully comprehend all that God had made and revealed, but he did understand what he saw truly. With his rejection of the true interpretation of reality that God had presented in connection with the tree of the knowledge of good and evil, man became a false interpreter of the universe, and also of the special revelation of God in the Bible. This is nowhere more clearly seen than in the interpretations of the modern sinful man of himself in the area of psychology.

For the present, it should be said that even the sinful man is dealing with the area of General Revelation when he is treating natural science. Though we as Christians must oppose his presuppositions--his so-called neutral method, and final conclusions, nevertheless, we must acknowledge that the non-Christian mind has brought to light much that we acknowledge to be true, not on his basis, but on ours. This is not less true in the field of psychology than it is in the field of chemistry or physics.

The great advantage that we as Christians have over the non-Christian is the fact that we have and acknowledge the Bible as God's infallible Word, and thus we have an additional source of information that the non-Christian rejects. Thus, though we are ready to acknowledge and declare that the Bible is not a textbook of psychology, nevertheless, we do believe that it teaches something about man, and that what it teaches is fully authoritative.

The term psychology comes from *psuche*[2] meaning "soul", "mind", or "life," and *logos*[3] meaning "word," or "wisdom." The Oxford Dictionary defines it simply as: "The science of the nature, functions and phenomena of the human soul or mind." Delitzsch defines Biblical psychology thus: "Under the name of Biblical Psychology I understand a scientific representation of the doctrine of Scripture on the psychical constitution of man as it was created and the ways in which this constitution has been affected by sin and redemption."[4]

I. Biblical Terms

The wealth of material referring to one aspect or another of human nature is extensive in the Bible. Since this is not intended to be an exhaustive study of the subject, it will be our purpose only to examine some of the terms that bear on the subject, and to summarize the findings of word studies on this subject. As we enter into this survey, we shall consider those terms that refer to the spiritual

---

2. ψυχή
3. λόγος
4. Franz Delitzsch, *Biblical Psychology, op cit.*, p. 16.

aspect of human nature first, and then look at expressions that come from the physical side of man.

A. Old Testament Terms Chiefly Spiritual

1. Soul, *nephesh*[5]

The word *nephesh* is related to the Akkadian *Naptistu* and the Ugaritic *nps*, both meaning throat or neck. This usage may appear in such passages as Isaiah 5:14, "Sheol hath widened its throat (KJV self, ASV soul) and opened its mouth without limit...", and Jonah 2:6 (vs. 5 Eng.) "Water encompassed me up to the (*nephesh*) neck (KJV, ASV soul), The deep surrounded me, reeds entwined my head." Other possible cases are Psalm 105:18; 124:4-5; Prov. 23:7a; Jer. 4:10; Ezek 24:21, 25.

The neck and throat representing the breathing space, it became natural for the word to shift in meaning to refer to the breath. Death was referred to as the result of the breathing out of the *nephesh* or breath. See Job 41:21, Is. 3:20; Ps. 29:9.

From the idea of breath the word became used to refer to the sign of life or the life-power, the life spirit. See Gen. 1:30, "And to every beast of the earth, and to every bird of the heavens, and to everything that creepeth upon the earth, wherein there is life, [I have given] every green herb for food. And it was so."; 2:7, "And Jehovah God formed man of the dust of the ground, and breathed into his nostrils the breath of life; and man became a living soul."; Job. 12:10, "In whose hand is the soul of every living thing, And the breath of all mankind?". The New Testament *psuche* has the same usage, Rev. 8:9. In this usage there is a variety of application:

a. It was used of animal life in general at least 32 times, 5% of the total Old Testament uses.

b. It is used of God 21 times, nine of which are in Jeremiah.[6] This represents 3% of the total. It is used once of foreign gods in Isaiah 46:2.

c. The most common usage is of man as living.

1). So long as a man lives his soul is in him, II Sam. 1:9; Acts 20:10.

2). The soul leaves man at death, Jer. 15:9; 38:16; Job 11:20; 31:9; Gen. 35:18. It is poured out in Psalm 140:8; Is. 53:12. It is said to depart in Gen. 30:18; Jer. 15:9.

---

5. נֶפֶשׁ
6. Jer. 5:9, 29; 6:8; 9:9; 12:7; 14:19; 15:1; 51:14.

3). The soul is spoken of as returning when a life is restored, I Kings 17:21ff.

4). The soul is identified as the life, Ex. 4:19; Mt. 2:13; Rom. 11:3; Judges 5:18; Acts 15:26.

    d. Sometimes *nephesh* is used to refer to the totality of the person, Gen. 44:30; 49:6; Ex. 23:9 (heart); Prov. 12:10.

    e. Of particular interest is the breadth of applications in which *nephesh* is used regarding various aspects of man's nature. Some of the specific feelings associated with the soul are as follows:

1) It is the seat of pleasure, Deut. 23:24.

2) It is the seat of hunger and thirst, Psalm 107:5; Prov. 6:30; it is satisfied with bread, Lam. 1:11, 19.

3) The desire for various objects is ascribed to the *nephesh*:

    a) food, Deut. 12:15; Micah 7:10; Rev. 18:14.
    b) wages, Deut. 1215.
    c) fatherland, Jer. 22:27.
    d) evil, Prov. 21:10.

4) It is the seat of desire for God and for holiness, Ps. 25:1; 42:2, 3; 119:81.

5) It is the seat of love, I Sam. 20:17; Is. 42:1; Mt. 12:18; 22:37.

6) It is also the seat of hatred, II Sam. 5:8; Is. 1:14; Jer. 5:9; 6:8; Ps. 11:5.

7) It is the seat of joy, Ps. 35:9; 71:23; 86:4; Is. 61:10.

8) It is the seat of grief, Ps. 119:25, 28; Mt. 26:38.

9) It rests, Ps. 62:2; Mt. 11:29.

10) It experiences unrest and anxiety, Is. 15:4; John 10:24.

11) It has patience, Job 6:11.

12) It is impatient, Num. 21:4.

13) It experiences bitterness or vexation, I Sam. 30:6; Acts 4:2; II Pet. 2:8.

f. The use of *nephesh* as the seat of knowledge is relatively rare in the Old Testament, but it is found in Ps. 139:14; Prov. 2:10; 19:2; 24:14.

g. It is the seat of the will, Gen. 23:8; Deut. 21:14; II Kings 9:15; Job. 7:15; Ps. 27:12; 47:3.

h. It was often used in connection with *awah*[7] (desire), expressing the soul's desire:

1) hunger, Deut. 12:15, 20.

2) desire of the king for extension of power, II Sam. 3:21, "And Abner said unto David, I will arise and go, and will gather all Israel unto my lord the king, that they may make a covenant with thee, and that thou mayest reign over all that thy soul desireth. And David sent Abner away. And he went in peace."

3) worshipper's longing for Jehovah, Is. 26:8-9, "Yea, in the way of thy judgments, O Jehovah, have we waited for thee. To thy name, even to thy memorial [name], is the desire of our soul. With my soul have I desired thee in the night. Yea, with my spirit within me will I seek thee earnestly. For when thy judgments are in the earth, the inhabitants of the world learn righteousness."

i. It is used of the intention of a group, suggesting the idea of corporate personality, II Kings 9:15.

j. All of these human feelings and desires are used anthropathetically of God, Isaiah 1:14; 42:1; Jer. 12:7; Matt. 12:18.

k. The use of *nephesh* to express the seat of feelings, gives rise to the fact that it appears as something distinct from its possessor--something in the man--located within, Job 30:16, "And now my soul is poured out within me. Days of affliction have taken hold upon me"; Ps. 42:6; 131:2.

l. It is not surprising to find the speaker address his soul as distinguished from himself, Ps. 42:5. 11; 103:1-2, "Bless Jehovah, O my soul. And all that is within me, [bless] his holy name. Bless Jehovah, O my soul, And forget not all his benefits"; Lk. 12:19.

m. The reflexive use of the soul in the Bible seems to be one of emphasis--the intensive use, I Sam. 18:1; Prov. 6:16; Jer. 12:7. Briggs cites some 123 cases of this usage. In this usage, the emphasis is on the entire personality, Job 16:4, "I also could speak as ye do. If your soul were in my soul's stead, I could join words together against you, And shake my head at you."

---

7. אָוָה

n. As the soul is identified with the life, so it was also identified with the blood, which when lost meant death, Gen. 9:4; Lev. 17:11; Deut. 12:23-4.

Observations on *Nephesh* for Biblical psychology

a. *Nephesh* is used as the center of knowing, feeling and willing, and corresponds with the idea of a person.

1) To swear by the soul is to swear by self, Jer. 51:14.

2) "My soul" is equivalent to "my person", I Sam. 20:3; Gen. 49:16; 12:13; Ps. 66:16; Lk. 1:46.

b. *Nephesh* is not limited to the spiritual, immaterial aspect of man, but includes the total man. Num. 5:2, "Command the children of Israel, that they put out of the camp every leper, and every one that hath an issue, and whosoever is unclean by the dead (*lanaphesh*[8])." (*NKJ*, "*dead* body" compare Lev. 1:2; 2:1 and 5:2 and 22:5). Soul is equivalent to person in Gen. 46:15, "These are the sons of Leah, whom she bare unto Jacob in Paddan-aram, with his daughter Dinah. All the souls of his sons and his daughters were thirty and three"; Ex. 1:5; Acts 2:41, "They then that received his word were baptized. And there were added unto them in that day about three thousand souls"; 7:14; 27:37; I Pet. 3:20.

2. Spirit - *ruach*[9], pneuma, - *pneuma*

a. Statistics on the usage of *ruach*

Ruach is used 378 times in Hebrew, and 11 times in the Aramaic portions of Daniel, thus making a total of 389 times. It is found in the various portions of the Old Testament as follows:

Pentateuch	6
Historical	105
Poetic	40
Wisdom Literature	75
Prophetic	163
Total	389

b. Root meaning of the word *ruach* - wind

Ruach is used 117 times of the total 389 to mean wind, including everything from a gentle breeze in Jeremiah 2:24; 14:6; Hosea 8:7, to stormy winds in Psalm 48:8 and Jonah 1:4.

---

8. לָנֶפֶשׁ
9. רוּחַ

In 37 cases God is the agent behind the wind. The emphasis is on its force and strength (Amos: 4:13). God is the creator and controller of the wind (Job 28:25).

In Ezek. 37 it is used to refer to life-giving qualities.

It is sometimes used to refer to a quarter or side of the world (Jer. 49:36; Ezek. 42:16-19).

c. *Ruach* also denotes "spirit"

1) *Ruach* is used of God as a powerful influence, which creates and controls. There seems to be a play on the dual sense of the word in II Kings 2:16, speaking of the wind that carried Elijah up, "Lest peradventure the spirit of the Lord hath taken him up and cast him upon some mountain, or into some valley." (See also Gen. 1:2: I Kings 18:12; Ezek. 2:21; 3:12, 14, 24, *et al*.)

2) The Spirit of God is seen as operating in men, producing various psychical and physico-psychical effects, such as, physical strength, courage, prophet ecstasy, etc.

Judges 3:10, "And the Spirit of the Lord came upon him, and he judged Israel."

Isaiah 61:1, "And the spirit of the Lord God is upon me, because the Lord hath anointed me to preach good tidings . . . "

The sense of evil, or a guilty conscience is attributed to the Spirit of God, or to an evil spirit from the Lord. I Sam. 16:1-4. 15, 16, 23. It is the spirit from the Lord which gives the power to see evil in one's life. Gen. 6:3; Prov. 20:27, the spirit of man is the lamp of the Lord.

3) The Spirit of God is called Holy.

This occurs only rarely in the Old Testament. Psalm 51:11, " . . . take not thy Holy Spirit from me." Isaiah 63:10-11.

d. Usage in reference to man

1) The Spirit of God is viewed as the source of man's life. This is implied in Gen. 2:7, though it is *nishma*[10], not *ruach* that is used here. Job 33:4 reads, "The Spirit of God has made me, and the breath of the Almighty giveth me life." Again Job 27:3 says, "As long as my breath (*nishmathi*[11]) is in me, and the spirit (*ruach*) of God is in my nostrils . . ." See also: Gen. 6:17; 7:15; Hab. 2:19; Ezek 37:5; Ps. 31:6; Zech. 12:1.

J. G. S. S. Thompson suggests that it is the same spirit in man that is called on the one hand the Spirit of God, and on the other hand

---

10. נִשְׁמָה
11. נִשְׁמָתִי

the spirit of man. Ps. 104:29, "Thou dost hide thy face, they are troubled, Thou dost take away their breath (*ruach*), they die and return to their dust. Thou dost send forth thy Spirit, they are created: and Thou dost renew the face of the earth." Thompson says, "It is this spirit of God, or spirit of man that distinguishes him from the animal world." [12]

It may appear from these passages that there is some interchangeability of the terms Spirit of God and spirit of man, but as we have already noted, it is the image that man bears that distinguishes him from the animals. Psalm 104 cited above is not just speaking of man, but of the creatures as a whole. The apparent interchangeability of these terms is not to teach us that the Creator-creature distinction is in any way erased. We must conclude that the spirit of God and the spirit of man are closely related, but they are not one and the same. The one is the source, the other the resultant, which corresponds to the first.

2) The spirit of man

The spirit of man is used in connection with various different activities of man.

a) It is identified either as the seat of, or directly as strength, courage, anger, distress, etc.
Judges 8:3, "Then their anger was abated."
Job 7:11 "I will speak in the anguish of my spirit."
Prov. 18:14 "The spirit of man will sustain his infirmity; but a broken spirit who can bear?"
Feelings and affections are seen in such passages as II Kings 19:7; Gen. 14:8; I Sam. 1:15.

b) It is seen as the seat of intellectual activities. Job 20:3, "I have heard the reproof which putteth me to shame, and the spirit of my understanding answereth me."
Job 32:8, "There is a spirit in man; and the breath of the Almighty giveth them understanding."
Abilities to plan and to build the tabernacle are seen as given by the Spirit. See Ex. 28:3; 31:3; 35:31; Deut. 34:9.
Joseph's ability to interpret dreams was due to his having the spirit of God, Gen. 41:38.
Moses was granted the gift of the spirit of God for his function of judging, Num. 11:17.

c) The spirit of man is the seat of disposition and the will or the character of the man.
Exod. 35:21, "And they came every one whose heart stirred him up, and every one whose spirit made him willing." Note the coordination of the spirit and the heart. Prov. 16:2, " All the ways of a man are clean in his own eyes, but the Lord weighs the

---

12. "The Spirit in the Old Testament," *Christianity Today*, March 1957.

spirits."
I Kings 10:5 "... the Queen of Sheba's spirit was no more in her."
Gen. 45:27 "... the spirit of Jacob their father revived."
I Sam. 30:12 "... and his spirit came again to him."
We might term this low spirits or high spirits.
Courage - Joshua 5:1 "Their hearts melted, neither was there spirit in them any more because of the children of Israel."
Anger - Judges 8:3 "Then their anger was abated toward him."
Anguish - Exod. 6:9 "... but they hearkened not unto Moses for anguish of spirit and for cruel bondage."
Troubled - Gen. 41:8.
Jealous - Num. 5:14.

e. Relation of the Spirit of God to the spirit of man

1) Source of the physical life, Job 33:4.

2) Source of man's mental life, Gen. 41:38; Job 32:8; Exod. 28:3; 31:3; 35:31; Deut. 34:9.

3) Source of man's moral life. As the Holy Spirit, he strives with the conscience of man, Gen. 6:3; He may send an evil spirit, I Sam. 16:14; 18:10.

4) Source of man's renewed life.
It is the Spirit of God who is the Author of the rebirth of the sinner, so that he enters into a newness of life. Ezekiel describes the work of the Spirit in the rebirth, "A new heart also will I give you, and a new spirit will I put within you; and I will take away the stony heart out of your flesh, and I will give you a heart of flesh. And I will put my Spirit within you, and cause you to walk in my statutes, and ye shall keep mine ordinances, and do them."[13] As Jesus said to Nicodemus, no one can see the kingdom, except he be born again by the Spirit of God. This rebirth involves the planting of a new spirit in us, and also the gift of the Holy Spirit to us.

f. Relation of the *ruach* to the *nephesh*

1) In some passages *ruach* and *nephesh* appear to be virtually identical. They are interchangeable terms, "With my soul I have desired Thee in the night, yea with my spirit within me I will see thee early..."[14]

2) Passages in which there are differences. Snaith suggests that as a psychological term, *ruach* denotes a dominant disposition. There is an

---
13. Ezek. 36:26-27. Cf. Ezek 11:19-20; John 3:5-6.
14. Is. 26:9.

idea of power implied by *ruach*, which is not found with *nephesh*. "A man can control his *nephesh*, whereas his *ruach* controls him."[15] Prov. 16:32 says, "He that is slow to anger is better than the mighty. And he that ruleth his spirit (*berucho*[16]), than he that taketh a city."

Oehler maintains that,

> ... the substance of the human soul is the divine spirit of life uniting itself with matter; the spirit is not merely the cause by reason of which the *nephesh* contained beforehand in the body becomes living, as Gen. 2:7 has by some been understood. For the *aphar*[17] (dust) as such, in the structure of dust, there is, according to the Old Testament, as yet no *nephesh*, even latently. This is first in the *basar*[18], in the flesh: but the earthly materials do not become flesh until the *ruach* has become united with it, 6:17; 7:15; Job 12:10; 34:14f.... The soul sprang from the spirit, the *ruach*, and contains the substance of the spirit as the basis of its existence, the soul exists and lives also only by the power of the *ruach*; in order to live, the soul which is called into existence must remain in connection with the source of its life.[19]

Withdrawal of the *ruach* weakens and eventually causes the death of the soul. Individuality lies in the soul, not in the spirit. Man is not the spirit, but he has it, while he is the soul. Thus only *nephesh* can serve as reflexive sense, not *ruach*. Also the soul stands for the whole person (Gen. 12:15; 17:14; Ezek. 18:4). A man who has fainted has his *ruach* return to him (I Sam. 30:12), whereas the *nephesh* departs at death (Gen. 35:18) and is restored in the renewal of life (I Kings 17:22).

The impulse to act is from the *ruach* (Exodus. 35:21), but the subject of the act is the *nephesh*, eg. the soul that sinneth (Ezek. 18:4).

Thus the Old Testament does not teach a trichotomy of body, soul and spirit. It teaches the idea of the whole man included in the *basar* and *nephesh*, which spring from the union of the *ruach* with the *aphar*, "My soul longeth, yea, even fainteth for the courts of Jehovah; My heart and my flesh cry out unto the living God."[20] (Is. 10:18; Ps. 16:9). "The *ruach* forms in part the substance of the soul individualized in it, and in part, after the soul is established, the power and endowments which flow into it and can be withdrawn from it."[21]

J. Barton Payne concludes his comparison of *ruach* and *nephesh* by saying,

> Soul, *nephesh*, is generally felt as being a more personal individual term than *ruach*, spirit. Man has a *ruach*, but he is a

---
15. Norman Snaith, *The Distinctive Ideas of the Old Testament* (London: Epworth Press, 1944), p. 150.
16. בְּרוּחוֹ
17. עָפָר
18. בָּשָׂר
19. Gustave Friedrich Oehler, *Theology of the Old Testament*, translated by George E. Day (Grand Rapids: Zondervan Publishing House), pp. 150-151.
20. Ps. 84:2.
21. Oehler, op. cit., p. 151.

nephesh: he thinks with his *ruach*, but the thinker is the *nephesh*. Roughly speaking then, man's constitutional elements may be plotted as follows:

aphar, dust   }
+   } = *basar*, flesh   }
nishman, breath }   +   } = *nephesh*, soul, self
                      ruach, spirit   }

At death the flesh returns to dust (Gen. 3:19; Ps. 103:14; Job 34:14, 15), for man is but dust and ashes (Gen. 18:27). . . . At death the spirit returns to the presence of God Himself (Eccl. 12:7). In this regard, *ruach* and *nephesh* are often used interchangeably (Isa. 26:9; and compare Ex. 6:9 with Num. 21:4). Both leave the body at death, and they then exist in a state separate from that of the body (Gen. 35:18) . . ."[22]

g. Conclusions from the study of Nephesh and Ruach

The following chart compares what has been found regarding these two terms.

Nephesh	Ruach
Root Meaning	
throat, neck, breath	wind (with force)
Principle of Vitality	
of animals and of man, spirit of life,	spirit of man derived from the Spirit of God
leaves at death	
returns in life	
related to the blood	
Psychical Usage	
seat of knowledge	intellectual
seat of emotion	feeling, usually strong
seat of will	will and character as controlling power of the whole personality
whole personality	not used as personality
corporate personality	not used of corporate personality
reflexive usage - self	not used reflexively

From this comparison, it must be concluded that though the terms are not identical in their meaning, they are closely parallel in usage, and at times synonymous. As Oehler suggests the *ruach* gives the impulse to act, whereas the *nephesh* is the acting agent. He suggests that the *ruach* forms the substance of the *nephesh*. In other words, they are not two separable entities, but are different aspects of the spiritual nature of man.

---

22. *Op cit.*, p. 225.

B. The New Testament Terms *Psyche* and *Pneuma*

1. Soul, *psyche*[23]

a. Statistics

Psyche is used 104 times in the New Testament, of which 58 are translated by soul, and 40 by life.

b. Usage

1) Two uses of *psyche* in the New Testament refer to God. They are both citations of Old Testament passages. Mt. 12:13; Heb. 10:38.

2) Animal life is referred to by this word, much as living souls in the Old Testament refers to animal life. Rev. 8:9; and 16:3.

3) Twice the word is found in an adjectival form, referring to that which is living. I Cor. 15:45; II Pet. 2:14.

4) In the majority of cases it is used regarding man, and here the same basic ideas are those found in the Old Testament:

> a) Principle of vitality of man's life, Mk. 3:4; 10:45; Acts 15:26; 27:22; Rom. 16:4; Phil. 1:27; John 13:27; Rev. 12:11.
>
> b) Personal reflexive usage, Mk. 13:34; Lk 1:46; John 10:24; Acts 2:27; James 5:20; I Peter 1:19.
>
> c) An element of human nature that experiences:
>
>> (1) Intellectually, Acts 3:23; 14:22; Phil. 2:2.
>> (2) Emotional, affections, Mark 12:30; Acts 14:2; Rev. 18:14.
>> (c) Will, Eph. 6:6; Col. 3:23.
>
> The following are examples of the usage, some of which overlap different categories listed above:
> Mark 12:30, Love the Lord with all the soul.
> Luke 1:46, My soul doth magnify the Lord.
> Luke 2:35, piercing the soul.
> Acts 3:23, every soul that hearkeneth not to that prophet.

---

23. ψυχή

Acts 14:2, But the Jews that were disobedient stirred up the souls of the Gentiles, and made them evil affected against the brethren.
Eph. 6:6, doing the will of God from the heart (soul).
Heb. 12:3, fainting of your souls.
Rev. 18:14, And the fruits which thy soul lusted after are gone.

Man is a soul at times, and has a soul at other times.

d) New and prevalent usage in the New Testament
A new usage in the New Testament stresses the future of the soul, and not its present status.
Mk. 8:35-37 "For whosoever would save his life (*psyche*) shall lose it; and whosoever shall lose his life (*psyche*) for my sake and the gospel's shall save it. For what doth it profit a man, to gain the whole world and forfeit his life (*psyche*)."
Luke 21:19 " In your patience ye shall will your souls."
I Pet. 1:9 ". . . receiving the end of your faith, even the salvation of your souls."
Men cannot injure the soul, but God can hand it over for destruction, Matt 10:28, "And be not afraid of them that kill the body, but are not able to kill the soul; but rather fear him who is able to destroy both soul and body in hell."
It is used in the Synoptics eleven times to refer to life after death.

e) Pauline usage
Paul's usage of soul and spirit is in contrast to that of the Old Testament. The Old Testament has 756 usages of *nephesh* and 378 of *ruach*, approximately 2 to 1.
Paul used *psyche* 13 times and *pneuma*[24] 146 times, approximately 1 to 10.
He uses *psyche* in the three ways that *nephesh* is used in the Old:

(1) Vitality
I Cor. 14:7; 15:45; Rom. 11:3; 16:4; Phil. 2:30; I Thess. 2:8; II Cor. 1:23.
(2) Seat of experience, feeling, will thought
Col. 3:23; Eph. 6:6; Phil. 1:27.
(3) Used for Person
Rom 2:9; 13:1; II Cor. 12:15; Acts 27:37.

---

24. πνεῦμα

This usage may allow the idea that Paul thought of the *psyche* as the seat of personality, but does not require it.

Peter used the word to refer to the whole man "Christ the Shepherd and Bishop of your souls." I Pet. 2:25.

c. Conclusion

Though the word *psyche* is not used as frequently, or in as large a proportion of times in the New Testament as *nephesh* in the Old, yet there are examples of its usage in the New Testament that indicate it still carried the same meanings as *nephesh*. The New Testament uses some additional terms to express the same concepts. Also, more prominent in the New Testament is the idea of rebirth.

2. Spirit, *pneuma*

The word *pneuma* is like *ruach* used to convey several different ideas.

a. Wind

John 3:8, "The wind bloweth where it will..."

b. Breath

II Thess. 2:8 "And then shall be revealed the lawless one, whom the Lord Jesus will slay with the breath of His mouth."

c. Spirit of God

The term is used of the Spirit of God according the following divisions.
29 times to refer to the Spirit of God or of the Lord.
102 times to the Spirit of Truth, of Holiness, etc.
89 times to the Holy Spirit.

1) Cause of extraordinary gifts, I Cor. 12:4, "Now there are diversities of gifts, but the same spirit."

2) Cause of the conception of Jesus
Mt. 1:18, "And she was found with child of the Holy Spirit." Compare Luke 1:35.

3) Seat of intellectual activity in God
I Cor. 2:11, "Even so the things of God no one knoweth save the Spirit of God."

4) Operative in the external world
Acts 8:39, "And when they came up out of the water, the Spirit of the Lord caught away Philip."

5) Spirit of power
Luke 4:14, "And Jesus returned in the power of the Spirit into Galilee."
Acts 1:8, "Ye shall receive power, after that the Holy Spirit is come upon you . . ."

6) Produces in man ethical results
Rom. 8:4, "Who walk not according to the flesh, but according to the Spirit."

d. Spirit of Man

1) Seat or principle of life
Luke 8:55, "And her spirit returned and she arose immediately." Mt. 27:50; Lk. 23:46; John 19:30; Acts 7:59; James 2:26.

2) Seat of Emotion
Mk. 8:12, "And He sighed deeply in his spirit."
Lk. 1:47, "My spirit hath rejoiced."
Jn. 11:33, "groaned in his spirit."
Jn. 13:21, "troubled in spirit."
Acts 17:16, "spirit provoked."
Acts 18:25, "fervent in spirit."

3) Seat of the will
Jn. 4:23-4, " worship in spirit and truth."
Rom. 1:9, "I serve in my spirit."

4) Seat of the intellect
Rom. 8:6 "The Spirit himself beareth witness with our spirit."
I Cor. 2:11, "For what man knoweth the things of man, save the spirit of man which is in him?"
Mt. 5:3; Mk. 2:8; Lk. 1:80.

From this survey, it will be observed that the usage of *pneuma* is very close to that of *ruach* in the Old Testament.

e. Pauline usage of the word *pneuma*

1) *Pneuma* as Spirit of God
Rom. 8:14; I Cor. 2:11; 3:11; II Cor. 3:3 God is spirit. Paul interchanges God with Spirit of God, and also with Spirit of Christ. Rom. 8:9; Gal. 4:6; Phil. 1:19. The essential feature of the Spirit of God is his activity -- the activity of creating, redeeming, sustaining and

sanctifying man. Without the Spirit there is no Christian life at all, Rom. 8:9.

2) Influence of the Holy Spirit on the Christian
116 cases of *pneuma* being used of supernatural influences on the believer.

3) The Holy Spirit creates the Christian spirit. The results of the work of the Spirit are:

    a) Spirit of Adoption, Rom. 8:15.
    b) Power, I Cor. 2:4
    c) Faith, I Cor. 4:13
    d) Wisdom, and Revelation Eph. 1:17.
    e) Meekness, I Cor. 4:21.
Compare the gifts of the Spirit, I Cor. 12 and the fruit of the Spirit, Gal. 5:16-25 and Rom. 8:1-4.

    The Spirit of God and the spirit of Christians are not mixed. I Cor. 2:11 contrasts the two to show the inadequacy of the human spirit. In Rom. 8:16 both the Spirit of God and the spirit of the believer are called as witnesses of the sonship of believers. See also Rom. 8:12-114, 23, 26, for contrasts between the two. The Spirit of God is a resident dwelling in man, his home, his temple. The spirit of man is energized by the Spirit of God, but never mixed. There is fellowship and communion, but never absorption.

4) Natural Personal spirit
    I Cor. 2:6-16. The natural man has a spirit of his own, which is not able to receive the things of God. I Cor. 15:45 does not give us warrant to assume that the natural man had only a *psyche* and no *pneuma*.

    The Christian does not have two spirits, both the natural and the Christian. Regeneration involved the renewing of the *pneuma*, so that it takes on a new character, Rom. 8:10. But, after this renewal, the spirit is the seat of feeling, etc., and thus the language common to any spirit of man is also usable regarding the Christian's spirit. I Cor. 16:18; II Cor. 2:13; 7:13.

    The spirit is the directing and controlling element in man. Spirit is never used of animals. It is capable of evil, I Cor. 7:34; II Cor. 7:1. It is very close to the *psyche* in its activities.

        It is not only true that Paul's usage and the Old Testament usage agree at several points, but it is also true that altogether they cover the same field. Between Paul and the Old Testament there are no striking differences, only development and variation of emphasis. The framework of Paul's belief about the Spirit is exactly the Old Testament framework. It begins with the divine nature, passes on to divine activity, to the power that invades men, to the element in regenerated men that receives it, and to the results in belief and practice that ensue from the spirit invasion.[25]

Paul's more prominent usage of *pneuma* than *psyche* can be accounted for by his conversion experience. He had the sense of the power of God's Spirit in his life, and the word *pneuma* best conveys this concept. Thus his anthropology is neither Jewish nor Greek. It is Christian.

II. Terms primarily physical

A. Heart in the Old Testament (Leb[26]) (*Lebab*[27]) [28]

Von Meyenfeldt has made a major study of the Old Testament word for heart. We shall summarize the usages of this term as he has listed them.

1. The Heart of Man

1) The Biotic sense

   a) Chief organ of life, I Sam. 25:37; II Kings 9:24; Psalm 37:15.
   b) Place of honor, Song of Solomon 8:6.
   c) Inmost part, I Sam. 25:37; Nahum 2:10, midst of the sea Jonah 2:3; midst of heaven, Deut. 4:11.

2) Subject of Life Power

   a) The living- by projection, Ps. 22:26.
   b) The bearer of life, Gen. 18:5; Judges 19:5; Ps. 104:15.
   c) Personal reflexive sense, Ps. 4:4; Deut. 7:17; Ps. 22:26.
   There is no reference in the Old Testament of the relation of the heart to the blood.

2. The Heart in the Emotional (Sensitivity) Sense

1) Seat of pain, Gen. 6:6; Jer. 4:19.
2) Seat of joy, Prov. 14:10; 15:13; Eccl. 7:3.
3) The agent in sensuality, Deut. 17:17; Job 31:9; Hos. 4:11.
4) Other feelings:
   Anxiety I Sam. 4:13.
   Dismay Isa. 21:4.

---

25. W. David Stacey, *The Pauline View of Man* (1956), p. 138.
26. לב
27. לבב
28. The material in this section is drawn from Von Meyenfeldt, *Het Hart (Leb, Lebab) in Het Oude Testament*, 1950.

Hate Lev. 19:17.
Courage Ps. 31:24.
Haughtiness Deut. 17:20; II Kings 14:10; Jer. 48:29.
Pity Is. 15:5.
Anger Deut. 19:6.
Mind Prov. 14:30.
Work of grace in the heart Jer. 31:33; Ezek. 36:26; 18:31.

3. The Heart in the Noetic Sense - Seat of the Intellectual

1) Perception, Jer. 44:21.
2) Memory, Is. 33:18.
3) Knowledge, Prov. 15:7.
4) Insight, Deut. 8:5; 5:29; Prov. 15:28.
5) Consciousness, Jer. 5:21, Is. 32:4.
6) Critical Judgment, Eccl. 2:1; 2:3, 15.
7) Juridical Feeling, I Kings. 3:9.
8) Organ for wisdom, Exod. 35:26; Job 12:3.
9. Organ for foolishness, Prov. 12:23.

4. The Heart in the Volitional Sense

1) Plotter, I Kings 8:17-18; 10:2.
2) Deciding subject, Gen 8:21; Is. 63:4; Dan. 1:8.
3) Seat of ideals, I Sam. 13:14; Jer. 3:15.
4) Seat of desires, Jer. 22:17; Job 17:11; Psalms 21:2; Deut. 30:17.
5) Mainspring, Ex. 25:2; 35:5.
6) Forge of the deed, I Kings 3:6; 8:39; Jer. 17:10.
7. Standard of deeds, Deut. 29:18; I Sam. 2:1f; 13:14.

5. The Heart in the Ethical Sense

1) Conscience, Gen. 20:5-6; I Sam. 24:5; Job 27:6.
2) Ethical realization, Prov. 15:21.
3) Character, Prov. 15:30; Eccl. 7:7.
4) Keeper of human commands, Prov. 3:1; 6:21; 7:3.
5) Disposition towards other people, Exod. 14:5; Deut. 15:7.
6) Haughty disposition, Deut. 17:20; II Kings 14:10; Jer. 48:29.
7) Unsocial disposition, Deut. 15:9.
8) Love, I Sam. 10:26; II Sam. 14:1; Prov. 26:23; 31:11; II Chron. 7:16.
9) Care, I Sam. 9:19; Jer. 32:41.
10) Pity, Is. 15:5.
11) Malicious joy, Ps. 35:25; Prov. 24:17.
12) Hate, Lev. 19:17; Prov. 26:25.
13) Work of grace in heart, Jer. 31:33; Ezek. 18:31; 36:26.

6. Characteristics of the heart

The heart is representative. This means that the heart has the place of honor among the organs. The representative may be separated from that which is represented. The heart does not designate just the physical part of man. It represents the whole person. The deepest sense of the use of heart is that it is the genuine, the authentic or the essential. There is no use of the heart as existing independently.

The heart has a predominantly religious usage. Religion is seen as the relation of the whole person to God. If the heart is involved, then the real person is concerned.

B. Heart, *kardia*[29], in the New Testament

By the time of the writing of the New Testament *kardia* was used as the seat of the will, of thought and of emotion. It approximates the idea of personality, and is used virtually as a reflexive pronoun.

1. Physical sense 145 times

-made of flesh, II Cor. 3:3.
-seat of the will, Mk. 3:5; Mt. 5:8; Rom. 6:17; I Cor. 4:5; Heb. 10:22.
-seat of intellect, Mk. 2:6-8; Lk. 2:35; Rom. 1:21; Eph. 1:18; Heb. 8:10; John 12:40.
-seat of feeling, Lk. 24:32; Rom. 1:24; Col. 3:16; John 14:1.

2. Meaning Person

The inward man as a whole, Lk. 16:15; Mt. 12:34; Rom. 8:27; Heb. 13:9; I Pet. 3:4; James 4:8.

3. Meaning conscience

Rom. 2:15; Heb. 10:22; I John 3:19-20.

4. Ethical judgments belong to the heart, Rom. 1:21; 2:15.

5. The Spirit of God related to the heart, in the same way He is related to the spirit of man.
II Cor. 1:22; 5:5, where the whole person is represented by the heart.

6. The love of God is shed abroad in our hearts, Gal. 4:6; Grace rests in our hearts, Col. 3:16.

7. The circumcision of Christ is the circumcision of the heart, Rom. 2:29.

---

29. Καρδία

8. The Heart of the believer is the seat of the Spirit of God, II Cor. 1:22; Gal. 4:6.

9. The seat of sin in the unbeliever is the heart, Mk. 7:21.

10. Christ dwells in the heart. Eph. 3:17.

Summation regarding the heart

The heart itself does not have a moral quality. From the heart spring both good and bad. Clearly the heart is not a higher principle of man, but the intending, purposing self, which decides within itself, or is moved from without, which can turn to either good or bad. For Paul, the seat of evil is not so much the heart as the flesh.

According to the *Christelijke Encyclopedie*, "Just as bodily the blood flows from out of the heart to all members, so in a metaphorical spiritual sense the entire soul life comes forth from out of the heart." According to Kittel, the "heart is the centre of the inner life of man and the source or seat of all forces and functions of soul and spirit."[30]

Bavinck says that the heart is the seat and source of the life and understanding of the mind, and also of the desire and the will. While the spirit is the principle of life, the soul the subject of life, the heart forms the central organ thereof. The heart is the innermost kernel of man. It is so deep and dark, that it is not penetrable for others and ourselves, Jer. 17:9, and is only known by Him, who trieth the heart and reins, Jer. 17:10. The heart is the seat of the hidden life of man, hidden not only from others, but often and in part always from himself.

John Frame's comments are helpful in understanding the significance of the heart as the primary center of man's constitution.

The knowledge of God is a heart-knowledge (see Exod. 35:5, I Sam. 2:1; II Sam 7:3; Pss. 4:4; 7:10; 15:2; Isa. 6:10; Matt. 5:8; 12:34; 22:37; Eph. 1:18; etc.). The heart is the 'center' of the personality, the person himself in his most basic character. Scripture represents it as the source of thought, of volition, of attitude, of speech. It is also the seat of moral knowledge. In the Old Testament *heart* is used in contexts where *conscience* would be an acceptable translation (see I Sam. 24:5).

The fact that the *heart* is depraved, then, means that apart from grace we are in radical ignorance of the things of God. . . . Only the grace of God, which restores us from the heart outward, can restore to us the knowledge of God that belongs to God's covenant servants - the knowledge that is correlative with obedience.

---

30. *Theological Dictionary of the New Testament*, Gerhard Kittel, ed., translated by Goeffrey W. Bromiley (Grand Rapids: Wm. B. Eerdmans Publishing Co., 1965), Vol. III, p. 611.

One implication of this fact is that the believer's knowledge of God is inseparable from godly character. The same Spirit who gives the first in regeneration also gives the second. And the qualifications for the ministry of teaching (theology) in Scripture are predominantly moral qualifications (I Tim. 3:1ff; I Peter 5:1ff). Thus the quality of theological work is dependent not only on propositional knowledge or on skills in logic, history, linguistics, and so forth (which, of course, believers and unbelievers share to a large extent); it is also dependent on the theologian's character....

A second implication is that the knowledge of God is gained not only through one 'faculty' or another, such as the intellect or the emotions, but through the heart, the whole person. The theologian knows by means of everything he is and all the abilities and capacities that have been given him by God. Intellect, emotions, will, imagination, sensation, natural and spiritual gifts or skills - all contribute toward the knowledge of God. All knowledge of God enlists *all* our faculties, because it engages everything we are.[31]

C. Words for Mind

1. *Nous*[32] in classical Greek meant intellect or reason and mind, including feeling. In the LXX *nous* is used 6 out of 11 times to translate *leb*, once to translate *ruach* (Is. 40:13). Paul quotes this verse twice and uses *nous* and not *pneuma*.

2. Other words used in the NT with the idea of thought, intellectual activity:

nous	23 times
noein[33]	13
noema[34]	6
anoetos[35]	6
dianoia[36]	11
dianoema[37]	1
eunoia[38]	1
eunoein[39]	1
nouthesia[40]	3
nouthetein[41]	8

---

31. John M. Frame, *The Doctrine of the Knowledge of God* (Phillipsburg, NJ: Presbyterian and Reformed Publishing Company, 1987), pp. 322-323.
32. Νοῦς
33. νοεῖν
34. νόημα
35. ἀνόητος
36. διάνοια
37. διανόημα
38. εὔνοια
39. εὐνοεῖν
40. νουθεσία
41. νουθέτειν

Eight of these terms are used in the Gospels, mostly in Luke. The basic ideas are:

1. to perceive, Mk. 8:17; Eph. 3:4.
2. to understand, Mk. 12:34; I Tim. 1:7.
3. to consider what to do, Lk. 1:51; Mk. 12:30; II Tim. 2:7.

A man perceives that he may understand, and consider what to do. The first commandment summarizes the NT idea of the doctrine of the mind, that one understands and takes counsel as to how God would have him live.

I John 5:20 summarizes the NT doctrine of the mind. "The Son of God . . . hath given us an understanding that we may know him that is true."

There is no doctrine of an impartial mind.

In Paul there are two classes. First, there are those who have the mind of Christ, I Cor. 2:16, renewed in the spirit of their mind, Eph. 4:23. The Christian mind is expounded in II Thes. 2:1-3; Eph. 4:20-24.

The second class is that of non-believers, who are described as having the mind of the flesh. The sinful mind is expounded in Rom. 1:28-32; Eph. 4:17ff.

Paul's use of *nous* is not that of the analytical approach of the Greek mind as a part of man, but rather the synthetic approach of the Hebrew mind, representing the whole man. It ceases to be a faculty, and becomes one aspect of the whole man. It ceases being academic and theoretical and becomes practical.

D. Conscience

1. Terms used

The idea of conscience is clearly in the Old Testament, though no specific word for it is found in the Hebrew. Adam and Eve certainly felt pangs of conscience after the fall. So also with David before Nathan (Ps. 51:4).

The LXX uses the word *suneidesis*[42] meaning "fellow knowledge" of self, with the idea of making a moral judgment upon a conscious act.

Suneidesis is used 30 times in the NT, by Paul 20 times, by Peter 3 times and in Hebrews 5 times.

Hebrews - good conscience, Heb. 13:18.

The other four usages refer to the idea that the blood of Christ cleanses and perfects the conscience, Heb. 9:9, 14; 10:2, 22.

Peter - I Peter 3:21, affirmation of a sincere confession.
I Peter 2:12 and 3:16 refer to the Christian conscience, when he suffers wrongly but with a clear conscience.

Paul's Use:

1. Universal - Rom. 2:14-15

---

42. συνείδησις

2. Functions

    a. Obligatory - urges man to do what he regards as right, and restrains him from doing wrong, Rom. 13:5.

    b. Judicial - passes judgments on man's acts and decisions, II Cor. 1:12; I Cor. 4:4.

    c. Executive - executes its judgment in the heart, to condemn, causing disquietude, shame, distress, remorse. On the other hand, it commends, when it judges the act to be righteous, I Cor. 4:4.

To act in face of a doubtful conscience is sin, Rom. 14:23. Conscience may be dulled so as to cease to function, I Tim. 4:2; Tit. 1:15.

2. Summary regarding conscience

    a. Every man has a conscience (II Cor. 4:2), that is, he knows that there is a difference between right and wrong, and that it is right to do right, and wrong to do wrong. The conscience does not tell what is right or what is wrong. The conscience is an arbiter of one's own conduct, Rom. 2:15. As it relates to knowledge, it is a function of the mind, Titus 1:15. When one obeys for conscience sake it is just because he knows that it is right, and not because he fears the results of doing it, Rom. 13:5; I Cor. 10:25-27.

    b. If one does what he thinks is right, he has the approval of a good conscience, Acts 23:1; I Tim. 1:5, 19; 3:9; II Tim. 1:3; I Pet. 3:16, 21; Heb. 13:18.

    c. If he does what he thinks to be wrong, he has the disapproval of an evil conscience, Heb. 10:22. The conscience either defends or accuses him, Rom. 2:15.

    d. Persistent sin sears the conscience, I Tim. 4:2, and stains the mind and conscience, Tit. 1:15. When the heart is hardened, the conscience atrophies.

    e. While every man's conscience is authoritative for him, it is not infallible, for one man's conscience may allow what another's forbids, I Cor. 8:7. Such differences arise from the difference of knowledge, Rom. 2:12, and differences of insight, I Cor. 8:7-13; 10:22-23.

    f. Christians are to seek to commend themselves, not only to themselves but also to others, Acts 24:16; II Cor. 4:2.

3. The Relation of God to the Conscience

a. God is the Creator of the conscience that is a part of every man, whether it acts under the Law of Moses or under general revelation, Rom. 2:15; 8:2; 9:4; Gal. 4:6.

b. The believer should live before God in all good conscience, Acts 23:1; cf. Acts 24:16; II Tim. 1:3; I Pet. 2:19. He is answerable not to some impersonal ethical ideal, or even to his own conscience, but to God.

c. Scripture enjoins obedience to those with authority over us for conscience sake, because they are God-ordained authorities, Rom. 13:1-7. When their authority clashes with God's commandments, then God is to be obeyed over against earthly authorities, Act. 4:19; 5:29; Rom. 2:12ff.

d. The final judgement will be in accord with the law that each man knows, Rom 2:12.

4. The Relation of Christ to Human Conscience

a. The conscience is cleansed by the blood of Christ, Heb. 9:14; 10:2.

b. Faith and conscience are related, I Tim. 1:5, "But the end of the charge is love out of a pure heart and a good conscience and faith unfeigned" and I Tim. 3:9, "Holding the mystery of the faith in a pure conscience."

c. Christ is lord over the conscience, I Pet. 3:15ff, "But sanctify in your hearts Christ as Lord: being ready always to give an answer to every man that asketh you a reason concerning the hope that is in you, yet with meekness and fear: having a good conscience . . .".

d. Believers have a good conscience toward God through the resurrection of Christ, who is now at the right hand of God, I Pet. 3:21.

e. The *Logos* in John 1:3-5 is said to lighten every man, which may refer to the God-implanted conscience that is in every man.

5. Relation of the Holy Spirit to the Conscience

The Holy Spirit bears witness with our consciences, Rom. 9:1, cf. Rom. 8:16; 2:15.

E. Physical Terms used in a Psychical Sense

1. Flesh - Hebrew terms *basar, she'er*[43].

---

43. שְׁאֵר

a. *Basar* is used to differentiate man from God, Gen. 6:3; II Chron. 32:8; Job 12:10, Ps. 56:4; 65:2; Is. 31:3; 40:6ff.

b. The part for the whole, I Kings 21:27; Lev. 13:38; 17:15ff.

c. Psychical uses:

"My heart and my flesh (basar) cry out to the living God," Ps. 84:2; Ps. 63:1, "Jehovah, my God, Thee would I seek, my soul thirsteth for Thee. My flesh (*basar*) fainteth for Thee, in a dry and weary land where no water is."
Parallel with soul in Prov. 11:17, "The merciful man doeth good to his own soul, but he that is cruel troubleth his own flesh" (*she'er*). Both the soul and the flesh seem to be used in the reflexive sense here.

d. It denotes the physical substance of man and animals, Job 7:5; Gen. 6:12; 7:15f; 8:17.

e. The whole body is designated by flesh, Lev. 6:3; 16:4.

f. The male sex organs, Ex 28:42, to cover the flesh of their nakedness.

g. The unity of one family, one flesh, Gen. 2:23, as a result of sexual union. The near of kin are literally the near flesh.
The proper Hebrew term for body (*giwiyyah*[44]) occurs 14 times in the Old Testament, but is never used in a psychical sense.

2. Head (*rosh*[45]), (*kephale*[46]).

a. Derision is expressed by the shaking of the head, II Kings. 19:21; Job 16:4; Ps. 44:14; Jer. 18:16.

b. The bowed head is a sign of weakness, Gen. 40:13; II Kings 25:27; Job 10:15; Psalm 83:2; or humiliation, Ps. 3:3; 27:6; 110:10.

c. Blessing is conveyed by the laying of the hand upon the head, Gen. 48:13ff. Consecration is done by the anointing of the head with oil, Ps. 23; 133:2.

d. Responsibility for trouble, Josh. 2:19; II Sam. 1:16; 3:29; Judges 9:57; Ps. 7:16; Prov. 25:22.

---

44. גְּוִיָּה
45. ראשׁ
46. κεφαλή

e. The head stands for the whole person. "I will make thee a keeper of my head." I Sam. 28:2.

3. Face (*panim*[47])

The face or features of a person revealed the person.

a. Not friendly, the face of Laban toward Jacob, Gen. 31:2.
b. Determination, Is. 50:7.
c. Hardened, defiance, Jer. 5:3; Ezek. 2:4.
d. Impudent, Prov. 7:13; 21:29.
e. Ruthless, Deut. 28:50; Dan. 8:23.
f. Fierceness like a lion, I Chron 12:8.
g. Cheerful, Job. 29:24.
h. Kindly, Prov. 16:15; Eccl. 8:1.
i. Fear, Is. 13:8; Ezek. 27:35.
j. Humiliation, II Sam. 19:6; II Chron. 32:21.
k. Anguish, Jer. 30:6.
l. Innocence, hold up the face, II Sam. 2:22.
m. Downcast face, anger, Gen. 4:5-6.
n. Reflexive, "He set his face to seek Jehovah," II Chron. 20:3.
o. To enjoy personal contact, II Kings 14:8, 11.
p. Moses' face shone, Ex. 34:29.
q. God's face, his revelation, Ex. 33:14; Deut. 4:37.

4. Parts of the head or face.

a. Mouth, (*peh*[48])

1) Speaks in and of itself, Gen. 45:12.
2) Speaks wisely or foolishly, Ps. 37:30; Is. 9:17.
3) Offers praise or blame, Ps. 63:5; Job 9:20.
4) Linked with false speaking, Ps. 55:21.

b. Palate (*chek*[49])

1) Tastes, Job 12:11.
2) Pronounces moral judgments, Job 6:30.
3) Speak truth, Prov. 8:7.
4) Sin, Job 31:30.

---

47. פָּנִים
48. פֶּה
49. חֵךְ

c. Tongue (*lashon*[50])

1) Speaks, Job 27:4.
2) Sings, Ps. 119:172.
3) Plans, Ps. 52:2.
4) Be contentious, Is. 54:17.
5) Speak with justice and knowledge, Ps. 37:30.
6) Responsible for boastfulness, Ps. 12:4.
7) Slanders, Ps. 140:11.
8) Deceives, Ps. 52:4.

d. Lips (*saphah*[51])

1) Speaks, Job 27:4.
2) Exults, Ps. 71:23.
3) Betrays fear by quivering, Hab. 3:16.
4) Preserves knowledge, Prov. 5:2; Mal. 2:7.
5) Bestows praise, Ps. 63:3.
6) Disputes, Job. 13:6.
7) Capable of truthfulness, Job 33:3; Prov. 8:7.
9) Capable of deceitfulness, Ps. 12:3-4.

e. Eye (*ayin*[52])

1) Sees, Gen. 45:12.
2) Find favor in one's eyes, Gen. 33:8.
3) Pride or humility, Ps. 18:27; 131:1; Prov. 30:13; Job 22:29.
4) Favor or disfavor, Ps. 101:6; Amos 9:4, 8.
5) Desire and hope, Gen. 3:6; Num. 15:39; II Chron. 20:12; Ps. 25:15.
6) Disappointment, Job 11:20.
7) Capable of pity, Gen. 45:20.
8) Subject of moral judgment, - good or evil eye, Prov. 22:9; Deut. 15:9.
9) Refers the individual as a whole, Job 24:15, "No eye shall see me."

f. Nose, or nostril (*aph*[53])

1) Breathes, Gen. 2:7; 7:22; Is. 2:22.
2) Anger, Prov. 14:17, 29; 15:18.
3) Pride, Ps. 10:5.

---

50. לָשׁוֹן
51. שָׂפָה
52. עַיִן
53. אַף

g. Forehead (*metsach*[54])

1) Determination, Is. 48:4; Ezek. 3:3-7.
2) Impudence, Jer. 3:3.

h. Ear (*'ozen*[55])

1) Hears, II Sam. 22:45.
2) Seeks knowledge, Prov. 18:15.
3) Shows understanding and discrimination, Job 13:1; 12:11; 34:3.

5. Peripheral parts of the body.

a. Arm (*ezroa, zeroa*[56])

1) Bared for action, Ezek 4:7; Is. 52:10; 53:1.
2) Strength, offense or defense, I Sam. 2:13; Job 22:8-9.
3) Power to lend support.
4) Stands for the whole person, Job 26:2; Is 17:5.

b. Hand (*yad*[57])

1) Right hand, the place of honor, I Kings 2:19; Ps. 45:9; 110:1.
2) Grief, shame, II Sam. 13:19.
3) Prayer, Prov. 1:24.
4) Repugnance, Zeph. 2:15.
5) Exultation, Ezek. 25:6.
6) Power, Num. 20:20.
7) Lay on hands, I Chron. 18:3; Exod. 7:4; II Kings 13:14-17.
8) Ethical, no rebellion in my hand, I Sam. 24:12.
9) Filled with blood, Is. 1:15.
10) Innocence, clean hands, Ps. 24:4.

Hands are seen as the measure of one's vitality, or as a guide to one's mood, purpose or character.

c. Neck (*tsawwar*[58])

1) Outstretched neck, pride, Ps. 75:5.
2) Stiff neck, stubbornness, Ex. 32:9.

---

54. מֵצַח
55. אֹזֶן
56. אֶזְרֹעַ, זְרֹעַ
57. יָד
58. צַוָּאר

d. Knees (*berek*[59])

1) Trembling knees, weakness, Psalm 109:24.
2) Despondency, Job 4:4.
3) Panic, Ezek. 7:17.
4) Worship, bowing of the knees, Is. 45:23.

e. Foot (*regel*[60])

1) Stamping of the foot, anger, Ezek. 6:11.
2) Foot on the neck, victory, Josh. 10:24.
3) Foot of pride, Ps. 36:11.

6. Internal Organs

a. Bones (*atsmoth*[61])

1) The entire person, Isaiah 66:14, "And ye shall see it, and your heart shall rejoice, and your bones shall flourish like tender grass. . . "
Hab. 3:16, "Rottenness entereth into my bones, and I tremble in my place."
Jer. 23:9, "My heart within me is broken, all my bones shake; I am like a drunken man . . ."

2) Bones are vexed, Psalm 6:2, "O Jehovah, heal me; for my bones are troubled, my soul is sore troubled."

3) Bones may be impatient, Jer. 20:9b, "I will not make mention of him, nor speak any more in his name, then there is in my heart as it were a burning fire shut up in my bones, and I am weary with forebearing, and I cannot contain."

4) Bones may be ruined by envy, Prov. 14:30, "Envy is rottenness to the bones."

5) Bones experience goodness, Prov. 15:30, "Good tidings make the bones fat."

6) Bones and souls give thanks to God, Psalm 35:9-10, "And my soul, my bones shall say, Jehovah, who is like unto thee. . ."

7) Elisha's bones seemed to have vitality, even after his death, though Ezekiel sees the valley of dry bones as dead and lifeless, II Kings 13:21.

---

59. בֶּרֶךְ
60. רֶגֶל
61. עֲצָמוֹת

b. Blood (*dam*[62])

We have already seen that the blood was associated with the soul, because it contained the life. No specific passages attribute psychical ideas to the blood, other than the identification of the blood and soul, Lev. 17:11; Deut. 12:23.

c. Inward part of the physical frame, the chest region (*qereb*[63])

1) Locale of feeling, Is. 16:11.
2) Place of the spirit, Zech. 12:1.
3) Seat of spiritual life, Psalm 51:12; Is. 26:9.
4) Seat of divine wisdom, I Kings 3:28.
5) The heart is the center of the chest.
6) Seat of ethical actions, Psalm 5:9.
7) Seat of thought, Psalm 49:11.

The chest parallels the bowels (*meim*), Is. 16:11, the heart, Prov. 14:33; and in the plural, the soul Ps. 103:1.

d. Belly, lower internal area, the abdomen (*beten*[64]), Greek, (*koilia*[65])

1) The place of physical appetites.
2) That which feels, Hab. 3:16.
3) Thinks and wills, Job 15:35.
4) Recipient of the spiritual, Prov. 22:18.
5) Searched by the Spirit, Prov. 20:27.
6) Eye, soul and belly are correlated in Psalm 31:9.

e. Intestines, (*meim*[66])

1) Physical organs, Gen 15:4; 25:23.
2) Correlated with other organs, heart, Psalm 37:31; Isaiah 51:7; chest, Jer. 31:33.
3) Law in them, Ps. 40:8, "Thy law is within my inward parts."
4) Used of God, Isaiah 63:15; Jer. 31:20; or men, Isaiah 16:11.

f. Liver (*kabed*[67])

1) Seat of desire and pleasure, Prov. 7:23.
2) Extreme pain, Lam. 2:11.

---

62. דָּם
63. קֶרֶב
64. בֶּטֶן
65. κοιλία
66. מֵעִים
67. כָּבֵד

g. Kidneys (*kelayoth*[68]) Greek (*nephroi*[69])

1) Special organ in sacrificial ritual, Lev. 3:4.
2) Seat of affections, Prov. 23:16.
3) Suffering, Ps. 73:21.
4) Overcome with affliction, Job 16:13.
5) Seat of rejoicing, Prov. 23:16.
6) Chastening, Ps. 16:7.
7) Longing, Job 19:27.

After this survey of the Hebrew view of man, it must be concluded that man is represented as an organic totality, constituted of spirit and a somato-psychic aspect. As such, he is a reasoning, feeling, willing creature of God. All of these functions have been found related to various aspects of his being, to the spirit, the soul, the flesh, the heart, and the various parts of the body.

Berkouwer concludes his consideration of the various terms used of man thus:

> We can say that in our times, under the influence of Biblical research, a fairly general consensus of opinion has arisen among theologians. They are increasingly conscious of the fact that the Biblical view of man shows him to us in an impressive diversity, but that it never loses sight of the unity of the whole man, but rather brings it out and accentuates it.
>
> No part of man is emphasized as independent of other parts; not because the various parts are not important, but because the Word of God is concerned precisely with the whole man in his relation to God. Thus the various terms and concepts it makes use of give us no exactly expressed or scientifically useful definitions, but rather are related always to the same basic reality of humanness; so that despite the various shifts in terminology, we never receive the impression that we are dealing with an important shift in the portrayal of man.[70]

In addition to these various metaphysical terms, we also find that the Bible uses the term "I" ego, or *ani, anochi*[71] of man. The most common reference is to the whole personality. It may be used of the parts of the body. The personality as a whole is described under such statements as "I am awake, I am studying, I think."

Paul in Rom 7:15 speaks of "that which I do I know not, for not what I would, that do I practice; but what I hate, that I do." Again in verse 20, he says, "But if I do what I would not, that I do, it is no more I that do it, but sin which dwelleth in me." Paul seems to speak of a deeper "I" which has been reborn, and which does not sin. Of course, it is Paul who sins, but the sin has not come from his deepest self. Thus "I" here is not the person in his totality, but in his innermost essence. We use the same concept, when we say, "In the depth of my soul, is the wish that I were other than I am."

---

68. כְּלָיוֹת
69. νεφροί
70. Berkouwer, *Image of God, op. cit.*, p. 200.
71. אֲנִי, אָנֹכִי

We must distinguish between the essential subject of psychical actions, and that with which we act. Older psychology sought order in the division of the functions, namely, the functions of knowing, feeling and willing. Though these are legitimate divisions, we have seen that the soul may be said to have more than just these three functions. On the one hand, it may be asserted that the soul has just one function, namely, to live. On the other hand, the living soul has a large number of separate functions.

The Bible in the creation account indicates that there were three primary areas of duty for man, namely, the prophetic, priestly and kingly. As a prophet he understands and interprets the word of God. As a priest he dedicates himself to God, and as king he rules in the name of God over the creation, which God has placed under him.

Though there are three offices given to men to perform, it should be observed, that they are inseparable. For example, a person may determine that he will study and learn more about the creation, which is primarily the prophetic office. The act of deciding to do this is an exercise of the kingly office, and since the whole of what he does is dedicated to the glory of God, he is also acting as a priest.

Psychology is interested in understanding what we experience in the inner man--the conduct of the "I", and the relations of various actions to one another. Since these functions have reference to the outside world, psychology is interested in how the "I" relates to the outside world. Among the subjects that it considers are the following:

How do we perceive things?
What is thinking?
How do we know things in our memories?
What do we know of feeling?
What is the relation between feeling and thinking?
What do we know about willing?
How does the conscience function?

The whole field of Biblical psychology is so vast, that it has not yet been adequately dealt with. Just this brief survey of some of the Biblical givens demonstrates its breadth, and the difficulty we have in comprehending it.

Basic in all Biblical understanding of man, is the fact that he has been made the image of God, and that he is thus a personal being, who thinks, wills and acts responsibly in all that he does.

Chapter XIX Man in the Covenant of Works

Introduction

We have treated the creation of man, and something of his nature as created. In this chapter we shall examine more fully his primitive condition before the fall, and the probation or covenant of works. As a part of this consideration we shall include a treatment of the freedom of men. This will prepare us for the study of the fall and the succeeding plan of salvation.

I. The Special Providence of God toward Man in the Physical Realm

A. The Garden of Eden

Genesis 2:8 says, "And Jehovah God planted a garden eastward, in Eden; and there he put the man whom he had formed." Ezekiel 28:13 describes Eden as the "garden of God" (*gan elohim*[1]). From this we learn that it must have been the place of God's presence, the place where man could have realized his chief end of glorifying God, and enjoying him forever. As to the geographic location of the Garden, we have no certain knowledge. It has usually been assumed that it was in the area of Mesopotamia. The effects of the fall, and then of the flood, have so obliterated all traces of the Garden, that we find no remains of it. Not the geographical location, but the reality of God's presence there is the important thing. As the Garden of God it provided Adam with a perfect environment. Nothing in that environment can be blamed for the sin of Adam.

B. Adam's Employment

Genesis 2:15 reads, "And Jehovah God took the man, and put him into the garden of Eden to dress it and to keep it." Here we see that man was given a task in the Garden. In other words, labor as such is not inconsistent with the original state of the holiness of man. Rather, in labor man found a sense of satisfaction in his active service to God. God himself is active, and man, who is the image of God, is not content with idleness, but seeks to be active also. The "dressing of the Garden" was, on the one hand, man's direct service to God. On the other hand, it was no doubt the exercise of his own dominion over the world. In other words, it was both the priestly service of Adam to God, and the kingly function of man's own rule over the creation, which he had been commanded to exercise by God.

---

1. גַּן אֱלֹהִים

C. Provision for his Subsistence

Genesis 2:16 says, "And Jehovah God commanded the man, saying, Of every tree of the garden thou mayest freely eat." Here we see the gracious provision of God for Adam. The whole world of nature was under man's dominion, and now the fruit of the earth was specifically granted to him for his food supply.

D. The Marriage Institution

Not only did God provide a happy environment for Adam, a task to keep him busy, and food for his body, he also provided him with a companion to be a help unto him. With the creation of woman, we have the establishment of the marriage relationship. "Therefore shall a man leave his father and his mother, and shall cleave unto his wife: and they shall be one flesh."[2] Since marriage was thus established in Eden before the fall, we know that it is a holy institution. It should be observed that God has made man, male and female, and thus the sexuality of man is not evil but good. Further, the one God-ordained area for the proper fulfillment of this aspect of our nature is in the marriage union. Through marriage God has ordained that the race be propagated in a holy and lawful manner. With the possibility of the birth of children, came also the possibility of the exercise of human authority, for the parents would have exercised such in the raising of the children. Thus it is that the family as an institution was the basic social institution of human society. As an institution of authority it was the precursor of civil authority. As the institution of training and education it was the precursor of the school. As the place of worship and fellowship with God, it was the precursor of the Church.

II. The Special Providence of God in the Spiritual Realm

A. Communion with God

As already suggested, the Garden of Eden was the Garden of God, and thus God provided Adam with the privilege of personal communion with himself. That such was the case is clear from the fact that God spoke to Adam directly. He did so in giving him the probation (Genesis 2:17). No doubt he communicated with him when he gave him Eve and the marriage institution. The suggestion of Genesis 3:8 is that God was accustomed to coming to the Garden during the cool of the day and of conversing with Adam and Eve. They heard him coming and knew who it was, and sought to hide from him because of their sin. The fact that Adam was made the image of God, and thus communed directly with him in Eden teaches us that he was made for the priestly function of worship and communion with God.

---

2. Genesis 2:24.

B. The Sabbath

To meet the physical and spiritual need of man for rest and direct communion with God, God gave him the Sabbath. God himself set the example of rest at the end of the six days of creation. Man needs a weekly time for rest. The emphasis of the creation account of the Sabbath, as well as the Fourth Commandment is that it is to be a day of rest. As such, the Sabbath stands for the eternal rest and communion with God which man would eventually have. As a holy day, set apart from other days, it is also the day of worship. This is clearly seen in the way in which the Second Adam observed it. "And he came to Nazareth, where he had been brought up: and, as his custom was, he went into the synagogue on the sabbath day, and stood up for to read."[3] The essence of the Sabbath then is not so much rest from secular labors and recreations, but more importantly the setting of the whole day aside for communion with God.

Though it comes from the period following the expulsion from the Garden, there is a hint in Genesis 4:3 that the first family observed the Sabbath as a day of worship. The phrase "And in the process of time" is literally "And it was in the end of days" (*wayehi miqqets yamim*[4]). This may well refer to the end of the week. It was at the end of days *(miqqets yamin*[5]*)* that Cain and Abel brought their sacrifices. It may well be that Adam and Eve had made this their practice, and that Cain and Abel were simply following the family custom of worshipping on the Sabbath day. Presumably, just as the Sabbath was to become a special day for worship after the fall, it would have been so used by unfallen man also.

C. The Covenant of Works or the Covenant of Life

1. The Biblical Idea of "Covenant"

The first usage of the word "covenant" (*berith*[6]) is found in the account of the deliverance of Noah.[7] Here it is used in connection with what is called the Covenant of Common Grace. This was the promise given to Noah on his departure from the ark. In this case we find that the Covenant had parties, namely, God and the whole earth. The promise of this covenant was that God would not again judge the whole earth by flood. He guarantees this promise by entering into a covenant with the world. This covenant was sealed by the sign of the rainbow. Even here, the bow was set in the sky for the Lord to see and to be reminded of the covenant. In other words, this was an example of a covenant in which God was the initiator, the one who saw the seal and was reminded, and the one who would fulfill the promise. This was a completely unconditional covenant. Thus we must conclude that a covenant is not always "an agreement between two or more persons." In this case it is a sovereign Divine disposition in administration. It was such in its inception, determination, disclosure, sanc-

---

3. Luke 4:16.
4. וַיְהִי מִקֵּץ יָמִים
5. מִקֵּץ יָמִים
6. בְּרִית
7. Genesis 6:18; 9:9-16.

tion and fulfillment. As Noah came out of the ark, he had offered sacrifices to God, which was the occasion of the giving of this covenant.

As we examine other covenants in the Bible we find that it may be used of conditional covenants. Even here, however, it should be kept in mind that such conditions are not reached by bargaining on the part of man, but rather, are the Divinely instituted conditions. Man's proper response to a Divine covenant is to receive it and accept it as a proper expression of his submission to the Holy Will. As a creature he has no bargaining rights with God. Generally speaking all covenants are ratified with a sacrifice of blood.

Palmer Robertson in his excellent study of Biblical covenants, *The Christ of the Covenants*, defines a covenant as "a *bond in blood sovereignly administered*. Where God enters into a covenantal relationship with men, he sovereignly institutes a life-and-death bond. A covenant is a bond in blood, or a bond of life and death, sovereignly administered."[8]

The terminology in the Old Testament translated "to make a covenant" is literally "to cut a covenant." "The original record of the inauguration of the Abrahamic covenant, laden as it is with internal signs of antiquity, first introduces the concept of 'cutting a covenant' to the biblical reader (cf. Gen. 15). At the other extremity of Israel's history, Jeremiah's prophetic warning to Zedekiah at the time of Nebuchadnezzar's siege of Jerusalem literally bristles with allusions to a 'cut-covenant' theology (cf. Jer. 34.)."[9] The cutting procedure is seen in Genesis 15, where Abraham sacrifices the animals, and then cuts the pieces, laying them over against one another. Then, God symbolically passed through between the cut pieces. The result was the cutting of a covenant. The symbolism is that the persons entering into the covenant take upon themselves the pledge of death if they break the covenant. This is what is referred to in Jeremiah 34:18-20, where the leaders of Israel by their transgressions have brought upon them the curse of the broken covenant. As a bond in blood, a covenant "involves commitments with life-and-death consequences."[10]

2. The Covenant of Works - Covenant or Law?

A. A. Hodge describes the different ways in which this Covenant has been designated.

> 1st. It has been called the Covenant of Nature, because it expresses the relations which man in his natural state as newly created and unfallen sustained to the Creator and Moral Governor of the universe. It is adjusted to the natural or unfallen man, just as the Covenant of Grace is adjusted to unnatural or fallen man. 2d. It has been called a legal covenant, because its 'condition' is perfect conformity to the law of absolute moral perfection. 3d. It has been called the Covenant of Works, because its demands terminate upon man's own being and doing. 4th. It has been called a Covenant of Life, because the promise attached to well-doing was life.

---

8. O. Palmer Robertson, *The Christ of the Covenants* (Grand Rapids: Baker Book House, 1980), p. 4.
9. *Ibid.*, p. 8.
10. *Ibid.*, p. 14.

It was also essentially a gracious covenant, because although every creature is, as such, bound to serve the Creator to the full extent of his powers, the Creator can not be bound as a mere matter of justice to grant the creature fellowship with himself, to raise him to an infallible standard of moral power, or to crown him with eternal and inalienable felicity."[11]

Palmer Robertson calls it the Covenant of Creation.

It has sometimes been suggested that Adam was not really under a covenant relation, but just under a commandment or law of God. Thomas Ridgely distinguishes between the two as follows:

A law is the revealed will of a sovereign, in which a debt of obedience is demanded, and a punishment threatened, in proportion to the nature of the offense, in case of disobedience. And here we must consider that as a subject is bound to obey a law; so he cannot justly be deprived of that which he has a natural right to, but in case of disobedience; therefore obedience to a law gives him a right to impunity, but nothing more than this: whereas a covenant gives a person a right, upon his fulfilling the conditions thereof, to all those privileges which are stipulated or promised therein."[12]

A good illustration of the difference is found in the case of Mephibosheth. He had a natural legal right to his life and the estate which descended to him from his father, Jonathan, because he had behaved himself peaceably and not rebelled against David. This legal right did not entitle him to the special privileges of David's own table. These privileges grew out of the covenant between David and Jonathan. In the case of Adam, it was not just escape of punishment that was involved, but the possibility of eternal life, which would have been granted if he had kept the covenant of works. This will be more evident as we examine the covenant itself.

Thornwell held a similar position to that of Ridgely. He posited that man as created was a servant and not a son.

The relation in which he stood to God may be more accurately defined as that of a servant, and the law of his life as obedience. Obedience, as expressive of perfect conformity with the will of God, comprehends the whole scope of his existence.... He was a creature; a servant under the moral law as the rule and guide of his obedience; bound to glorify God in perfect conformity with its requisitions, and authorized to expect the continuance of his present happiness in the sense of God's approbation as long as he persevered in the way of faithfulness."[13]

The question of whether the Adamic relation should be called a covenant has been raised. Professor John Murray preferred to call it the "Adamic Administration." Robertson has demonstrated the legitimacy of calling it a covenant.

---

11. *Outlines of Theology, op cit.*, pp. 310-11.
12. Thomas Ridgely, *A Body of Divinity, Wherein the Doctrines of the Christian Religion, Are Explained and Defended. Being the Substance of Several Lectures on the Assembly's Larger Catechism* (Glasgow: John Bryce, 1770), p. 189.
13. *Op. cit.*, Vol. I, p. 248.

First of all, some scriptural precedent exists for the omission of the term 'covenant' in discussing a relationship which unquestionably is covenantal. Nowhere in the original account of the establishment of God's promise to David does the term 'covenant' appear (II Sam. 7; I Chron. 17). Yet this relationship clearly is covenantal. God's commitments to David were covenantal in nature despite the absence of any formal application of the term 'covenant' in the original context of the establishment of the relationship. Subsequent Scripture specifically speaks of God's 'covenant' with David (cf. II Sam. 23:5; Ps. 89:3)."[14]

It is of interest to note that Hoeksema rejects the idea that the covenant relationship between God and Adam was founded upon this command of Genesis 2:17, but goes back to his being made the image of God, and thus his representative on earth with the three-fold office of prophet, priest and king. Hoeksema does not like the term "Covenant of Works". We are inclined to agree that the Covenant with Adam did involve him from his creation as the Image of God. We do not, however, see any objection to seeing in the probation a particularization of the Covenant, which was designed to bring man to a self-conscious choice, and realization of his covenant relation with God. In other words, we would affirm with Hoeksema that man as created was created a covenant creature, but we would go on to say that this covenant comes to explicit expression in the probation given to Adam before the creation of Eve. The fact that the probation was given before Eve's creation indicates that it was closely related to that which constituted man as man. It was not just an appendage added after the creation. Rather, it was given before the completion of the creation of man, male and female.

Again Robertson holds this same position.

> By creation God bound himself to man in covenantal relationship. After man's fall into sin, the God of all creation graciously bound himself again by committing himself to redeem a people to himself from lost humanity. From creation to consummation the covenantal bond has determined the relation of God to his people. The extent of the divine covenants reaches from the beginning of the world to the end of the age.[15]

3. The Covenant of Works Examined

a. The Parties of the Covenant

God and Adam are the two parties of the Covenant of Works. Adam acted in behalf of the human race. This may be seen from the following facts:

(1) All that was said to Adam in punishment for his having broken the covenant applied to the whole race. The penalty of death passed to all

---

14. *Op. cit.*, p. 18. See Robertson's further arguments from Jeremiah 33:20, 21, 25, 26, and Hosea 6:7, pp. 19-24.
15. *Ibid.*, p. 25.

his posterity.[16] The other parts of the curse also fell on all mankind, namely, the hardness of work, and the pain of childbirth, etc.

(2) The solidarity of the race, and the representative character of Adam is clearly taught in Romans 5:12,18; I Corinthians 15:22.

(3) The plan of salvation is based on the same representative principle. Christ is compared to Adam as the Second Adam, or the Last Man (Romans 5:12-21; I Corinthians 15:22, 45-59).

(4) This principle of representation is seen to be operative in many of the institutions of human society, such as family, church and state.

b. Conditions of the Covenant

As we have already suggested, the covenant relationship was more inclusive than the particular probation of Genesis 2:17. Adam as first created was to be the office-bearer for God. He was to be God's prophet, priest and king. In these offices he was to carry out the will of God. In order to make him a self-conscious covenant-keeper, God placed him under probation with regard to the tree of knowledge of good and evil. Perfect obedience was the condition of the test. It was a specific condition of specific obedience to a positive command of God. It was an obedience that would demonstrate the completeness of man's obedience to the will of God under the two-fold circumstance of probation and temptation. The probation was a divine testing of man. This test concerned the tree of the knowledge of good and evil. This tree was the divinely appointed instrument to lead man through the probation to the knowledge of being faced with evil and rejecting it, and thus to a knowledge of good contrasted with evil. The temporal character of the test is seen in the temporal character of the tree.

A. A. Hodge speaks very pointedly as to why the command not to eat of the tree of knowledge of good and evil was selected as the test of covenant obedience.

> Perfect conformity of heart, and perfect obedience in act to the whole will of God as far as revealed.--Deut. 27:26; Gal. 3:10; James 2:10. The Command to abstain from eating the forbidden fruit was only made a special and decisive test of that general obedience. As the matter forbidden was morally indifferent in itself, the command was admirably adapted to be a clear and naked test of submission to God's absolute will as such. The forbidden tree was doubtless called the tree of the knowledge of good and evil, because through the disobedient eating of it mankind came to the thorough experience of the value of goodness and the infinite evil of sin.[17]

The same tree was used of Satan as a means of temptation of man. In the temptation sinless man was confronted by a superhuman intelligence. The thought of sin did not originate in man, but in Satan, who introduced it to man.

---

16. Romans 5:12, 18, 19.
17. *Op. cit.*, p. 312.

In the face of the double circumstance of probation and temptation, man had one duty, namely, obedience to God. He had the full ability to obey, and yet, he was mutable, and had the power of will to disobey.

c. The Promise of the Covenant

The mention of the tree of life, and the banishment of man from Eden following the fall so as not to be able to partake of this tree imply that the promise of the covenant was life. This may also be inferred from the fact that the threat of the covenant was death in the event of disobedience. Also, after the fall, God provides in the Covenant of Grace through Christ the gift of eternal life. From all of these facts it may safely be inferred that the promise of the Covenant of Works was life. Paul in his comparison of Christ and Adam emphasizes the contrast of death and life. "For if, by the trespass of the one, death reigned through the one; much more shall they that receive the abundance of grace and of the gift of righteousness reign in life through the one, even Jesus Christ."[18]

Thornwell, whom we have already noted maintained that man as created stood only in the relation of a servant to God, held that the promise of the covenant extended to him the possibility of being adopted as the son of God. He saw this as the provision of the grace of God in this Covenant. "Surely, our God is love; creation shows it as well as the cross! Surely, our God is grace; the first covenant proves it as truly as the second!"[19] He then speaks of how this grace was manifested. "In order that the change from the condition of a servant to that of a son might take place, it was necessary that the man should prove himself faithful in the first relation. Adoption was to be the reward of grace, but still it was to be a reward."[20]

Girardeau, Thornwell's successor at Columbia Seminary, rejected his mentor's position. He says, "The strongest point made by those who deny that Adam sustained the filial relation to God, is that moral government and moral discipline are incompatible with each other, if directed to the same individual. Adam certainly was under moral government; therefore, he was not under moral discipline."[21] He argues that discipline is a part of moral government, and that the premise that the two cannot be addressed to the same person cannot be proved. The classic example is Christ, who was both Son and servant. So also, believers are both children of God and also his servants. It is his feeling that Thornwell based his argument too much on the nature of moral government and of discipline, rather than on the examples of the Scripture itself, where it is clear that both Christ and believers are viewed as being sons and servants. The question is whether a son can lose sonship, which must be posited, if Adam originally possessed the filial relation. Girardeau describes Adam's original condition as that of a "son who was not yet confirmed, but whose relative status was contin-

---

18. Romans 5:17.
19. *Op. cit.*, p. 266.
20. *Idem.*
21. *Discussions of Theological Questions*, *op. cit.*, p. 433.

gent upon the preservation of filial integrity."[22] Girardeau describes his understanding of Adam's situation:

> The case of Adam in innocence was out of analogy to the sinner, however conditioned, whether unredeemed or redeemed. He was neither subject to the penal measures of retributive government, nor the corrective discipline of fatherly government. He was, as innocent, an accepted servant and son of God, neither exposed to the curse of the Judge, nor to the chastisements of the Father. . . . He was, as subject and servant, under obligation to render perfect obedience to the moral law as the rule of God's retributive government. . . . But he was also under a discipline which was intended to perfect him in the discharge of filial obedience to the law as the rule of God's fatherly government. In both respects his obedience was contingent. He might, in one respect, have secured the reward of justification as a subject and servant; and, in the other, the reward of confirmation as a son. In the first case, he would have been confirmed in God's rectoral regards; in the second, he would have been confirmed in God's parental regards.[23]

It is of interest to note that Robert Smith Candlish, the successor of William Cunningham at New College in Edinburgh held to a similar position to that of Thornwell regarding Adam. He was supported by Hugh Martin, while Thomas J. Crawford opposed him. John MacLeod in his *Scottish Theology* presents both arguments, and seems to favor that of Candlish.

> Martin and Candlish found no difficulty in denying a universal Fatherhood of God with a corresponding Divine sonship of man. Crawford pleaded for such a Fatherhood and sonship. Candlish maintained that the sonship which believers receive in adoption is an entirely new relation for any one of the race of man. . . . Crawford seems to us to do less than justice to the truth that the sinner in his sin is a child of wrath, is of his father the devil, and the child of disobedience. And his defence of the common teaching of Reformed divines, that in a certain diluted sense fallen man is still a son, though an apostate son, of God, might stress more than it did the exiguous character of the content of this universal Divine sonship for which he pleads.[24]

d. The Threat of the Covenant

The threat of the Covenant is expressly stated in Genesis 2:17, "But of the tree of the knowledge of good and evil, thou shalt not eat of it: for in the day that thou eatest thereof thou shalt surely die." If life is essentially being in communion with God, then death is a separation from him. Death has three different aspects. Man by his fall incurred all three of these. First, there is the judicial aspect, which places the subject under the wrath of God. Man came under this by his disobedience. This is clear from the fact that when confronted by God, he

---

22. *Ibid.*, pp. 437-438.
23. *Ibid.*, p. 440.
24. John MacLeod, *Scottish Theology* (Edinburgh: The Publication Committee of the Free Church of Scotland, 1943), p. 273-274. See also, R. S. Candlish, *The Fatherhood of God and the Sonship of Believers*, and Thomas Crawford, *The Fatherhood of God*.

was placed under the judicial sentence of God. Thornwell speaks pointedly of the judicial consequences of sin.

> All misery, all pain, all suffering, all that interferes with the comfort and sanctification of existence, all that is contradictory to well-being, is penal in its origin. Not a pang would ever have been felt, not a sigh would ever have been heaved, not a groan would ever have been uttered, not a tear would ever have been shed, if sin had not invaded the race. All physical evil is penal; all misery is penal; all is death.[25]

Closely allied to this judicial aspect of death is the spiritual aspect. At the moment that Adam sinned he lost communion with God. As Isaiah says, "Your iniquities have separated between you and your God, and your sins have hid his face from you, so that he will not hear."[26] The fact that they had died spiritually is seen first in the act of rebellion and disobedience, and secondly, in their seeking to hide from God. Thus, the words of God were literally fulfilled. In the day that he ate, Adam died spiritually. He was separated from God by his sin. Thornwell says:

> Spiritual life breathes only in the smile of God; the moment that He frowns in anger death invades the soul. It is the judicial consequence of sin, and hence every sin, like a puncture of the heart, is fatal to spiritual life. Hence the universal dominion of sin is a part of the curse--its reign is hopeless in so far as human strength is concerned. One sin entails the everlasting necessity of sin.[27]

The third aspect of death is what we call physical death. Here again the idea of separation is basic. For in physical death the body and soul are separated from one another. It was announced to Adam that he would have to suffer physical death, "for dust thou art, and unto dust shalt thou return."[28] The Bible teaches that the *nephesh* departs from the body at death.[29] It also teaches that the *ruach* departs at death.[30] When a person is restored the soul returns[31] or spirit returns.[32] The New Testament speaks of the *psychai* of the dead as being separated from the bodies[33] and also of the *pneuma* as departed.[34] We have already observed that this interchangeability of these terms suggests the dichotomous view of man. The point here, however, is that death is the separation of the spiritual aspect of man from the physical. When it is remembered that man became a living soul with the divine inbreathing,[35] we see that death is a reversal of this process. It is thus foreign to the nature of man. Man is incomplete without the combination of body and soul. To rend these two, therefore, is to attack the essence of man's nature. Thus it is that even when he need not fear death, the Christian nevertheless does not desire it, but rather shrinks from it.[36] As we

---
25. *Op. cit.*, p. 294.
26. Isaiah 52:2.
27. Thornwell, *Collected Writings, op. cit.*, p. 296.
28. Genesis 3:19.
29. Job 11:20; 31:39; Isaiah 53:12; Jeremiah 15:9.
30. Psalms 146:4; Ecclesiastes 12:7.
31. I Kings 17:21.
32. Luke 8:55.
33. Revelation 6:9.
34. I Peter 3:19; Hebrews 12:23.
35. Genesis 2:7.
36. II Corinthians 5:4.

noted, the body was involved in being the image of God. This separation prevents him from being able to reflect God fully.

It should be observed that man as a sinner is under all three of these aspects of death. If he passes through physical death in the state of spiritual death, then he shall finally fall under the judicial penalty of God, of eternal separation from God. "And cast ye out the unprofitable servant into the outer darkness: there shall be weeping and gnashing of teeth."[37] The concept of outer darkness is that of full separation from God. It will be unending, "And these shall go away into eternal punishment ..."[38] On the other hand, the Gospel gives us the remedy for all aspects of death. Because man is spiritually dead[39] it is necessary that he be made alive again, if he is to have communion with God. Thus, the rebirth is necessary.[40] The fact that God provides such a rebirth by the power of the Holy Spirit is cause for praise to God.[41] Though we as Christians must pass through physical death, unless the Lord comes, the Gospel provides victory over this phase of death also in the resurrection of Christ, and our own promised resurrection.[42] Of course, the judicial sentence is also removed in the fact that Christ paid our penalty. So it is that God can be both just and the justifier of sinners.[43]

4. Our Relation to the Covenant of Works

a. Negatively

(1) The special command of the original probation is not our present obligation, but the obedience exemplified by it is our perpetual obligation (Genesis 17:1; Matthew 5:20).

(2) As individuals we do not go through the probation in terms of the covenant of works.

(3) We are not able to attain life in terms of the covenant of works. We forever forfeited this ability in Adam.[44]

b. Positively

(1) We are still under the consequences of the Covenant of Works in our natural state as sinners. Our sinful natures are inherited from Adam as he broke the Covenant. We are subject to the various aspects of the curse, women to pain in childbirth, the earth is cursed, we must sweat in our labor, and finally, we are subject to death.

(2) The Covenant of Grace is Related to the Covenant of Works.

---

37. Matthew 25:30.
38. Matthew 25:46.
39. Ephesians 2:1.
40. John 3:3, 5.
41. Ephesians 1:19.
42. I Corinthians 15:50-58.
43. Romans 3:24-26.
44. Romans 8:7.

(a) Christ rendered the full obedience that was demanded of man, though it was not specifically to the command of Eden. It was the same quality of obedience that was to have been exemplified in the Covenant of Works.[45]

(b) A condition of the Covenant of Grace was that the Head of the Covenant had to bear the full condemnation of the broken Covenant of Works.

IV. The Free Agency of Man

In connection with the Covenant of Works, which presented man with the probation by which he was to stand or fall, it is appropriate to consider the freedom of man. We shall look at various unbiblical views of the will of man, and then seek to set forth the Biblical views.

A. Different Views Examined

1. Necessity

a. Fatalism

This view holds that all events are determined by blind fate. There is a blind law of sequence to which both God and man are subject. Things are as they are, and must be as they are. They are without any rational cause. This view, of course, denies any liberty of action. It reduces the acts of men to the same category as those of irrational animals.

b. Mechanical Theory

This view denies that man is the efficient cause of his own acts. It assumes that the inward state of man, and consequently, his acts, are determined by outward circumstances. Modern psychology holds that man's responses are predetermined by heredity and environment. This again rejects the doctrine of the free agency and moral responsibility of man.

c. Immediate Agency of God

A view such as pantheism holds that God is the soul of the world. All operations of nature, and the acts of man are ascribed to His immediate agency. God, then, is the only Agent. All activity is but a mode of Divine activity. This view, of course, denies any moral agency or freedom to the creature.

---

45. Romans 5:12-21.

2. Contingency

This is the view that defines the liberty of the agent as that of pure indifference. The will, at the moment of decision, is indifferent to all the conflicting motives, and decides without any regard to motivation. The will is viewed here as independent of feelings, of reason and of God. It acts, therefore, without cause or motivation.

3. Certainty

The view known as "Certainty" holds that a man is free not only when outward acts are determined by his will, but also when his volitions are truly and properly his own. They are determined by nothing outside of himself, but proceed from his own views, feelings, and immanent dispositions. They are, therefore, the real, intelligent and conscious expression of his character. Thus, if the character is determined, the volitional expression of it can be certainly known.

Hodge says that the will is not determined by any law of necessity. It is not independent or indifferent or self-determined, but it is always determined by the preceding state of mind. A man is free so long as his volitions are the conscious expressions of his own mind, or so long as his activity is determined and controlled by his reason or feelings.[46]

B. The Biblical View of the Will

1. Man Does Really Act

The Bible teaches that man does truly act. His moral agency is real. It is not just an illusion, but a reality. This is seen in the Bible by the fact that man is held responsible and accountable for his actions. This could hardly be the case if the actions were not his own.

2. Man Acts Responsibly

The acts of man are worthy of blame or approval, of condemnation or justification. He acts responsibly, because he is a free agent, because the acts are his own.

3. Man's Acts Are the Result of Volition

In acts for which man is responsible, his responsibility rests upon the fact that his acts are the result of volition. If he does not will to act, then the act is contrary to his will, and he does not really act. Psychologically, it is impossible to do anything against the will. When Paul speaks in Romans 7 of doing what he would not, he is not saying that he has not willed to act. Rather, he is indicating that he has within his being two principles. The one would do one thing, whereas he succumbs to the other principle and goes contrary to what he knows

---

46. Charles Hodge, *Systematic Theology, op. cit.*, Vol. II. p. 288.

he should do. He is not disclaiming responsibility, but cries out in desperation as to how to escape his dilemma.

4. The Exercise of Volition Arises from the Power of Volition

We exercise our wills because we have the power of volition. The possession of this power does not explain why we exercise it in any particular way. The volitions of a particular person find their roots in the character of the person. It is his complex of motives, aims, purposes, convictions, not just his metaphysical constitution that determine his will.

5. The Freedom Consists in This, that the Underlying Character, Which Determines the Volition Is Our Own

It is true that the volition is causally determined, but the determination lies within ourselves. There is motion, but it is self-motion. We are free, not because we are autonomous, but because we are individuals, and self-moved.

In the fall, man's disposition was mysteriously changed from holiness to depravity. The act of disobedience in the eating of the forbidden fruit was the expression of man's changed disposition. Both before and after conversion, we are free - before, free to sin; after, free to do good.

Psychologically speaking, man's free agency means that nothing can make man will against his own will. He does what he desires to do. The *Westminster Confession* says, "God endued the will of man with that natural liberty that it is neither forced nor by any absolute necessity of nature determined to good or evil" (XI, par.1). Man's liberty, therefore, consists in: negatively, the absence of compulsion, and positively, the self-determination of volitional acts. Man is responsible for his actions, because they express his own volitions. He is responsible for his volitions, because they express his own inclination and character. It is of interest to note that David confesses not only his sinful actions, but also his sinful nature in Psalms 51.

6. Man's Freedom Includes the Whole Area in Which He Is Responsible

Man's freedom is not restricted only to volitional acts. Included are his thoughts, desires and inclinations, as well as his volitional actions. Even his character is his responsibility, and thus belongs within the area of his freedom. The depravity of the sinner is the responsibility of the sinner. On the other hand, the holiness of the saint is also his own holiness. Both the depravity and the holiness belong in the area of man's freedom. Neither is the consequence of volitional decision or act, but each is the disposition of nature that belongs to each individual.

7. The Power of Contrary Choice Is Not the Essence of Free Agency

The free agency includes all the area of man's responsibility. The actual power of contrary choice is not the essence of the free agency. Freedom involves the idea that what we are and do is our own character and our own action. Man had the power of contrary choice in the Garden of Eden. Adam was a good being, but he was mutable. He was able to choose either good or evil. When he fell into sin, he died to God and to good. The natural man does not have the power to do anything that pleases God. "Because the mind of the flesh is enmity against God; for it is not subject to the law of God, neither indeed can it be; and they that are in the flesh cannot please God."[47] Though he cannot do good, the natural man is free in his depraved state to do what he wants to do. The glorified saint, on the other hand, will be confirmed in his righteousness, and will not be able to choose sin. God cannot lie, nor in any way contradict his own holy character, yet He is an absolutely free agent.

8. Liberty and Ability Are to Be Distinguished

A. A. Hodge distinguishes between liberty and ability as follows:
a. Liberty consists in the power of the agent to will as he pleases, from the fact that the volition is determined only by the character of the agent willing.

b. Ability consists in the power of the agent to change his own subjective state, to make himself prefer what he does not prefer, and to act in a given case in opposition to the coexistent desires and preferences of the agent's own heart.

c. Thus man is as truly free since the fall as before it, because he wills as his evil heart pleases. But he has lost all ability to obey the law of God, because his evil heart is not subject to that law, neither can he change it.[48]

9. The Certainty of a Volition Is Not Inconsistent with the Liberty of the Agent

A. A. Hodge continues his discussion with the following observations:

a. God, Christ, and saints in glory, are all eminently free in their holy choices and actions, yet nothing can be more certain than that, to all eternity, they shall always will according to righteousness.

b. Man is a free agent, yet of every infant, from his birth it is absolutely certain that if he lives he will sin.

---

47. Romans 8:7-8.
48. A. A. Hodge, *Outlines, op. cit.*, p. 289.

c. God, from eternity, foreknows all the free actions of men as certain, and he has foreordained them, or made them to be certain. In prophecy he has infallibly foretold many of them as certain. And in regeneration his people are made 'his workmanship created unto good works, which God has before ordained that we should walk in them.'

d. Even we, if we thoroughly understand a friend's character, and all the present circumstances under which he acts, are often absolutely certain how he will freely act, though absent from us. This is the foundation of all human faith, and hence of all human society.[49]

10. Man is responsible for his outward actions.

Hodge continues:
Man is responsible for his outward actions, because they are determined by the will; he is responsible for his volitions, because they are determined by his own principles and feeling (desires); he is responsible for his own principles and feelings, because of their inherent nature as good or bad, and because they are his own and constitute his character.[50]

Jesus clearly held men responsible for their actions, "A good man out of the treasures of his heart bringeth forth that which is good, and a wicked man out of the evil treasures of his heart bringeth forth that which is evil."[51]

Hodge comments on this verse:
The act derives its moral character from the state of his heart, whether that state be innate, formed by regenerating grace, or acquired by himself, because 1st. Of the obliging nature of moral right, and the ill desert of sin; 2nd. Because a man's affections and desires are himself loving or refusing that which is right.[52]

---

49. *Ibid.*, p. 291.
50. *Ibid.*, p. 293.
51. Luke 6:45.
52. *Outlines, op. cit.*, p. 293.

Chapter XX Sin, Its Origin and Nature

Introduction

The greatest problem in theology is that of the origin of sin. How is it possible to account for the presence of sin in a world made by a holy, all-powerful God? Various different attempts have been given to answer this question.

Just as the question of the nature of man raised problems since man cannot view himself objectively, so also considering the question of the origin of sin has its unique problem. As we inquire after some first cause for sin, we are in danger of attempting to vindicate our own sinning.

> The question of *sin's origin* has a qualitatively different character from the question of any other kind of origin.... But obviously this question is not a subject for a merely theoretical dispute. The man who says that it is must certainly be standing on very dangerous grounds. Yet, throughout the course of history men have tried to construct abstract and causal answers to this question of sin's origin and have failed to realize that in so doing they have violated the very limits of objectivity. A remarkable relation exists between seeking for the origin of sin and an *exculpation or exoneration of one's own person*. Whoever reflects on the origin of sin cannot engage himself in a merely theoretical dispute; rather he is engaged, intimately and personally, in what can only be called the *problem of sin's guilt*.[1]

Berkouwer goes on to say, "Thus, when we take interest in the causality of sin we are not engaged in an *a priori* innocent activity."[2] We must be warned not to fall into this type of reasoning, lest we find ourselves trying to avoid our guilt as sinners. Adam did just this as he sought to shift the blame from himself to the woman and even to God. "The woman Thou gavest me . . ." It is the tendency of sin to make excuse or seek an explanation for our sin in some first cause, rather than confessing guilt. Examples of this penchant may be seen in Israel's complaint against God for bringing them out of Egypt.[3] Again, in later generations, Israel sought to excuse herself by saying that the fathers had eaten sour grapes, and the teeth of the children were set on edge.[4] Ezekiel responded against this kind of thinking with the words, "The soul that sins shall die."[5] Israel could not blame her sins on her forefathers. Neither may we shift blame for sin from ourselves to any other cause.

---

1. G. C. Berkouwer, *Sin*, translated by Philip C. Holtrop (Grand Rapids: William B. Eerdmans Publishing Company, 1971), p. 14.
2. *Ibid.*, p. 15.
3. Num. 14:2.
4. Ezek. 18:2.
5. Ezek. 18:4.

I. The Origin of Sin

A. The Problem

The Bible presents a Holy and Good God who created a world which could be described as "very good" as it came from his hands. And yet, in a very short time this good world was brought under the influence of sin and evil. Almost at the moment that it had come from him in its purity and glory, it was robbed of its splendor, and stood foul and impure before his sight. Sin devastated the whole of creation. Its righteousness was turned to guilt, its holiness to impurity, its glory to disgrace, its blessedness to misery, its harmony to disorder, its life to death, its light to darkness. From whence came that evil, and what is the origin of sin? The Scripture justifies God and maintains that in no case can God be considered the author of sin. He is always presented as holy and righteous, far from sin and godlessness. "For I will proclaim the name of Jehovah: Ascribe ye greatness unto our God. The Rock, his work is perfect; For all his ways are justice: A God of faithfulness and without iniquity, Just and right is he."[6] "Therefore hearken unto me, ye men of understanding: Far be it from God, that he should do wickedness, and from the Almighty, that he should commit iniquity."[7] "To show that Jehovah is upright; He is my rock, and there is no unrighteousness in him."[8] God is light in whom there is no darkness nor shadow of turning.[9] He tempts no one to evil (James 1:13). He forbids all sin in his law (Exodus 20), and in the conscience of man.[10] He hates sin and his judgment is revealed against all unrighteousness.[11] He judged and condemned it in Christ.[12] The Bible always blames the sin upon the creature and not upon God. Yet there is the fact that God has created the world so that sin was possible. He made man good, but changeable. He placed the tree of the knowledge of both good and evil in the Garden, and put man to the test thereby. "It was his will to walk with men in the dangerous way of freedom, rather than to elevate him above the possibility of sin and death at once by an act of force."[13]

B. History of Thought

The origin of evil is, after that of being, the greatest riddle of life and the most difficult theological question of the understanding. All great thinkers have sought to explain this question. It is so universal that many have sought to explain it as natural. Others have seen it as something voluntarily entered into by the free choice of man, either in this life or in some previous existence.

Various efforts of explanation have been given in the history of the Church. The Gnostics sought the explanation of evil in matter, a product of the Demiurge. The human soul upon contact with matter became corrupted. This,

---

6. Deut. 32:3-4.
7. Job 34:10.
8. Psalms 92:15. See also Isaiah 6:3; Habakkuk 1:13.
9. I John 1:5.
10. Romans 2:14-15.
11. Romans 1:18.
12. Romans 3:24-26.
13. Bavinck, *Gereformeerde Dogmatiek, op. cit.*, Vol. III, p. 2.

of course, rules out any responsibility for sin in man. Origen sought to find that responsibility in his theory of the pre-existent state of the soul. We have already noted that some of the more modern philosophers have also held to this view of the soul, namely, Muller, Lessing, Schelling, and J. H. Fichte. Other than these, the view of the pre-existence of the soul has not been widely held in the Church. Irenaeus held to a voluntary transgression of Adam in Eden. As the Church developed, the Eastern Church inclined to discount the relation of Adam's sin to that of his posterity, whereas the Western Church held to a relation. "The teachings of the Eastern Church finally culminated in Pelagianism, which denied that there was any vital connection between the two, while those of the Western Church reached their culmination in Augustinianism which stressed the fact that we are both guilty and polluted in Adam. Semi-Pelagianism admitted the Adamic connection, but held that it accounted only for the pollution of sin."[14] The Reformers adopted the view of Augustine. The Socinians adopted Pelagianism, and Arminianism adopted semi-Pelagianism. With the rise of Rationalism other suggestions have been offered. Berkhof summarizes these views thus:

> The idea of sin was replaced by that of evil, and this evil was explained in various ways. Kant regarded it as something belonging to the supersensible sphere, which he could not explain. For Leibnitz it was due to the necessary limitations of the universe. Schleiermacher found its origin in the sensuous nature of man, and Ritschl, in human ignorance, while the evolutionist ascribes it to the opposition of the lower propensities to a gradually developing moral consciousness. Barth speaks of the origin of sin as the mystery of predestination. Sin originated in the fall, but the fall was not a historical event; it belongs to superhistory (*Urgeschichte*). Adam was indeed the first sinner, but his disobedience cannot be regarded as the cause of the sin of the world.[15]

C. Biblical Data Regarding the Origin of Sin

1. God's Decree All-Inclusive

We have already observed that the decrees of God are all-inclusive. We noted in particular that they included evil. We must conclude that the decrees of God made the entrance of sin into the world a certainty. Yet we must affirm with the Scriptures that God is not the Author of sin. He may be said to decree positively all that takes place, but in the execution of the decree he may be passive. Such is the case with sin. God cannot sin (Job 34:10). Thus, though he may plan that it take place, he does not actively carry it out. This is done by the creature by the permission of God.

---

14. Berkhof, *op. cit.*, pp. 219-220.
15. *Ibid.*, p. 220.

2. God Is Not the Author of Sin

One thing that is absolutely clear from the Bible is that God is not the author of sin. The Old Testament is explicit on this matter. Jehovah is "A God of faithfulness and without iniquity, Just and right is he."[16] "As for God, his way is perfect: The word of Jehovah is tried; He is a shield unto all them that take refuge in him. For who is God, save Jehovah? And who is a rock besides our God."[17] "And also the Strength of Israel will not lie nor repent; for he is not a man, that he should repent."[18] "Thou that art of purer eyes than to behold evil, and that canst not look on perverseness . . ."[19] In addition to these clear statements, the Old Testament teaches that sin is an abomination to God. It is the object of his wrath, judgment and abhorrence. God is the fountain of all goodness, the complete counterpart to the origin of sin.

I John 1:5 affirms "God is light, and in him is no darkness at all." Here John affirms that God in his nature is light and holiness. James 1:13 affirms specifically that God cannot tempt man to sin. "Let no man say when he is tempted, I am tempted of God; for God cannot be tempted with evil, and he himself tempteth no man."

The Cross is the clearest demonstration of the antithesis of God to sin. Once our sins were imputed to him, Christ, the beloved Son of God, became the object of the full wrath of God. This shows the depth of the opposition of God to sin.

Having said all of this, we continue to face the problem. For the Bible sets forth a God who is all-powerful and sovereign. The Bible teaches that God has foreordained whatsoever comes to pass.[20] It even indicates that sin falls under his sovereign decree in passages such as Acts 2:23, which says that the crucifixion was foreordained by the "determinate counsel and foreknowledge of God." How can God have foreordained the most heinous of all sins and yet not be the author of sin?

We must affirm that God has decreed all things, including sin, and yet he is not the agent in the act of sin. The decree itself is a positive act of God, but the execution of the decree is by permission. Acts 2:23 affirms that the crucifixion took place by the hand of wicked, lawless men. In other words, though it was foreordained by God, sinful men were responsible for the sin itself.

Even when we recognize that this is the case, we are still left with the question of why God has ordained that sin should take place in the first place. Ultimately, we have no answer to this question. All that we can say is that it is for the glory of God, but that still does not answer why this is so.

---

16. Deut. 32:4.
17. Psalm 18:30-31.
18. I Sam. 15:29.
19. Hab. 1:13a.
20. Eph. 1:11.

3. Sin As It Originated in the Creaturely World

a. The Angels

The Bible indicates that sin originated in the angelic world. God created all things good, including the angels.[21] Of the angelic hosts we are told that a large number fell into sin. We are not told just when this fall took place. Jesus says of the Devil that he was a murderer from the beginning.[22] John speaks of him as sinning from the beginning.[23] Just when this beginning was we are not sure. Presumably, it refers at least to the beginning of human history. We do not know a great deal about the fall of the angels. Jude 6 describes it thus: "And angels that kept not their own principality, but left their proper habitation, he hath kept in everlasting bonds under darkness unto the judgment of the great day." We know that it was a great number from the account of the casting out of the legion of demons from the demoniac of Luke 8:30. I Timothy 3:6 suggests that the sin of the devil was that of pride, "Not a novice, lest being puffed up he fall into the condemnation of the devil." The sins of the kings of Babylon[24] and of Tyre[25] are given in such exalted terms that many feel these are descriptions of the fall of Satan. Whether they are directly referring to Satan or not may be questioned, and yet the sins of these men were of the same nature as his. We see in Revelation 12:7-9 a description of the warfare in heaven, and the casting out of Satan.

How a creature who was created holy and good, and who dwelt in the presence of God could turn to sin is something that is not explained. All we know is that this is the case. At this point, all that we can do is acknowledge the mystery of the origin of evil. Perhaps there is some comfort in thinking that it did not have its beginning in man but in Satan, but this does not explain it for us.

b. In Man

The Bible teaches that it was Satan who first introduced sin into the world. The world as made by God was good. It was not due to any inherent limitation of the world or man that he sinned. It was his own voluntary act. The suggestion of sin was given by Satan in the form of the serpent. The temptation by Satan was the occasion, but NOT the cause of man's fall. No external power, influence, proposal, or suggestion can itself cause a rational being to sin. The sin of our first parents as a movement of apostasy began and came to fruition in man's own bosom. The sin was not the tempting, but their voluntary acquiescence to it. This is confirmed by James 1:12-15.

A careful study of the temptation of Eve by Satan reveals how he may often tempt us to sin. In Genesis 2:16-17 we see how graciously God had given the whole of the Garden, and all of the trees in it, except for the one, to Adam and Eve. The emphasis there is certainly on the goodness and graciousness of

---

21. Genesis 1:31.
22. John 8:44.
23. I John 3:8.
24. Isaiah 14:12ff.
25. Ezekiel 28:2ff.

God to man. Satan's opening remark, however, suggests that God has not been fair with man, that he has not given them all that they deserved to have. In these first words there was an appeal to the pride of man. There is the attempt to bring man to assert his autonomy and reject God as his Creator and Lord. With Eve's answer we see the process beginning in her thinking. She is beginning to emphasize the irrationality of the demand, and adds that they were not even to touch the tree. Satan's next move was to question the veracity of God. By such an attack he is revealing his true apostasy, and when Eve listens, it reveals that she has also moved to open rebellion. Satan attacked the hard part of the commandment, namely, the threat of death. In doing so, he was attacking the veracity of the Word of God. This is where he still tempts men away from the truth. Satan seals the matter with the open assault on the Sovereignty of God and on his Deity, by suggesting that man could be his equal. Here again it is the pride of the personal creature that is appealed to. From here on, it was the woman who looked at the fruit, saw it to be good to eat, and who rationalized that it was proper to eat of it.[26] There is a parallel in the temptations of Christ.

Somehow the morally upright character of man was changed so that he succumbed to this temptation. The overt act of transgression was determined by the changed character of man. This act presupposes such a change in nature. It presupposes a disbelief of God's Word, and a coveting of God's divine prerogatives. "The essence of that sin lay in the fact that Adam placed himself in opposition to God, to have God determine the course of his life; and he actively attempted to take the matter out of God's hand, and to determine the future for himself."[27] In other words, it was an assertion of man's autonomy against God.

II. The Nature of Sin

A. Inadequate Views of Sin

1. Dualistic View

One of the classic non-Biblical approaches is that of dualism. "Dualism proposes a primordial antithesis between two original principles (viz. light and darkness) in terms of which every form of good and evil is ultimately deduced."[28] Even Augustine, in his earlier writings, adopted Manicheanism, which sought to answer the question of the origin of evil by positing that it was there with the origin of things. On the surface, it might appear that this solves the question in a reasonable way.

> The Church has protested the eternalizing of evil and has renounced the idea which assigns to evil an ur-reality apart from God's good creation. She has taken issue with any concept of an ur-darkness in opposition to God's light.[29]

Growing out of the Greek dualism, Gnosticism posited that sin and evil were inherent in matter itself. Matter is posited as eternally existing opposite to

---
26. Compare with I John 2:16-17.
27. Berkhof, *op. cit.*, p. 222.
28. Berkouwer, *op. cit.*, p. 67.
29. *Ibid.*, p. 68.

God. Philosophically this is one of the weaknesses of the theory, for it is positing two eternal beings existing beside each other. Evil is thus not under the control of God. Further, this view removes evil from the ethical realm, and makes it purely physical. Actually, this does away with the idea of sin as a moral evil.

2. Privation

Leibnitz in his *Theodicy* maintained that God had created the best possible world. Sin was not to be ascribed to God. Sin is defined as simply negation or privation of good. No cause was needed for such privation. The fact that the world is a limited and finite world, of necessity involves it in evil. Leibnitz was seeking to justify God in the presence of evil in the world. He does not avoid making God responsible for evil, for God created the limited world, with its necessary evil. Again, this view tends to make evil just a part of the nature of things, and thus fails to do justice to the moral character of evil and sin.

3. Sin as Illusion

Spinoza held that if man had enough knowledge, he would not have a sense of sin. In other words, our sense of sin is a result of our limitation of knowledge. Modern Christian Science holds a similar view. Evil is considered the result of our imagination. Matter and evil are not real. If we would exercise mind over matter, we could do away with all evil and sin. Such a view fails to take into account the effects of sin. It would reduce all of our human experience in this life to an illusion.

4. Sin Due to Man's Sensuous Nature

Schleiermacher held that as man becomes God-conscious, he becomes aware of his own opposition to him in his lower sensuous nature. This is close to the old Greek view, for the body is considered sensuous in nature, and the soul in contact with the physical has become sensuous with it. The attempt is made to hold that God is not the author of sin, since it is a lack that occurs only in man. But, as we consider the fact that God created man a physical and thus a sensuous creature, he is thus author of his sinfulness.

5. Sin a Want of Trust in God Due to Ignorance

Ritschl sees man's sin as due to ignorance. The man who is ignorant of God fails to trust in him, and thus opposes his Kingdom. It is not an attitude toward the law of God, but the attitude toward the establishment of the Kingdom, which is the highest good. Since he does not know about God, and his purpose to establish the Kingdom, he resists it. For Ritschl, then, sin is essentially ignorance, and may be forgiven without any atonement required.

6. Sin Is Selfishness

Taking the two great commandments as the basis, men such as Jonathan Edwards, Julius Muller, and A. H. Strong held that sin was essentially selfishness. That is, it is the choice of self rather than God as the object of our love. Berkhof describes this as the best of these views, and yet unsatisfactory.

> Though all selfishness is sin, and there is an element of selfishness in all sin, it cannot be said that selfishness is the essence of sin. Sin can be properly defined only with reference to the law of God, a reference that is completely lacking in the definition under consideration.[30]

B. The Biblical View of Sin

1. The Terms Used for Sin

The most common term in the Old Testament is *chata*[31] which is translated by *harmartia*[32] in the New Testament. The root meaning is "to miss something". The idea is that sin is missing the mark. This is the way in which Romans 1:21 describes sin, "Because that, when they knew God, they glorified him not as God, neither were thankful." The point is that they missed the goal of their knowledge. So also Romans 3:23 says, "For all have sinned and come short of the glory of God."

A second Old Testament term is *avon*[33] from the root *avah*[34]. The meaning of this root is "to bend or curve". Thus, we have the idea of making crooked or distorting. Proverbs 12:8 speaks of the perverse heart. Related to this is *avel*[35] from the root *aval*[36] meaning "to turn away, to distort". This in turn came to mean "to be wrong, to be evil". The Piel is translated "to do evil, to act wickedly". The noun *avel*[37] is translated by *adikia*[38] meaning "unrighteousness", and by *anomia*[39] meaning "lawlessness".

Other words are: *aven*[40] from *un*[41] which means "to be nothing, to be vain". It can also be used of falsehood or deceit. *Ra*[42] or *roa*[43] from *raa*[44] means "to break in pieces, to destroy". The noun speaks of the morally bad, like *kakon*[45]. *Pesha*[46] from *pesha*[47] means rebellion. *Abar*[48] used with the law or covenant means transgression.

---

30. *Op. cit.*, p. 230.
31. חטא
32. ἁμαρτία
33. עָוֹן
34. עָוָה
35. עָוֶל
36. עָוַל
37. עָוֶל
38. ἀδικία
39. ἀνομία
40. אָוֶן
41. אוּן
42. רַע
43. רֹעַ
44. רָעַע
45. κακόν
46. פֶּשַׁע
47. פָּשַׁע

The Greek also uses several words for sin. *Harmartia* is the most common term. *Parabasis*[49] or *paraptoma*[50] means "transgression" and *opheilema*[51] "debt."

2. Propositions Regarding Sin

a. Sin is a real evil.

It is a real evil in opposition to those views which speak of it as mere privation, negation, ignorance, limitation, or illusion. Sin is not the absence of something, but a positive reality.

b. Sin is a specific evil.

Sin is a specific evil as distinct from other evils that are a consequence of sin. For example, the curse on the earth as a consequence of sin is an evil, but it is not itself sin. So also with the pain of childbirth, or the sweat of man's labor as a consequence of sin.

c. Sin is specifically a moral evil.

Sin is the coming short, or missing the mark of the moral imperative of God. It is not merely a thing that is unbecoming, or unwise, or unsocial. It is wrong.

d. Sin is the violation of law.

Sin is a moral evil because it is the violation of law. The word "ought" has meaning only in relation to a norm of right, a law. Sin cannot be reduced to lower terms than to that of disobedience to the law.

e. Sin is the violation of the law of God.

The law which sin violates is the law of God. The authority of the imperative is God's authority. This authority rests in his own perfection. The law of God is not an expression of man's nature, or of the nature of the universe. It is the expression of God's nature. It should be observed here that there is no antithesis between love and law. Both reflect the nature of God. Love does not replace the law in the Bible. Rather, it is the fulfilling of the law (Romans 13:10).

---

48. עָבַר
49. παράβασις
50. παράπτωμα
51. ὀφείλημα

Chapter XXI The Effects of Sin

Introduction

Having considered the origin and the nature of sin, and the probation under which Adam was placed, we shall now examine the fall itself, and the consequences of sin.

I. The Fall

We have seen that the nature of sin is essentially a transgression of the law of God. The sin of Adam and Eve was just this. They sinned by eating the forbidden fruit. The specific command under which they were living was the command not to eat of the tree of knowledge of good and evil.

Dabney comments:
> The sin of Adam consisted essentially, not in his bodily act, of course; but in his intentions. Popish theologians usually say that the first element of the sin of his heart was pride, as being awakened by the taunting reference of the Serpent to his dependence and subjection, and as being not unnatural in so exalted a being. The Protestants, with Turrettin, usually say it was unbelief; because pride could not be naturally suggested to the creature's soul, unless unbelief had gone before to obliterate his recollection of his proper relations to an infinite God; because unbelief of the mind usually dictates feeling and action in the will; . . .[1]

Paul makes a distinction between the sin of Eve and that of Adam. "And Adam was not beguiled, but the woman being beguiled, hath fallen into transgression."[2] What does this difference mean? John Gill discusses this question as follows:
> That Adam sinned as well as Eve, is most certain; for though it is said, *Adam was not deceived*; the meaning is, that he was not first deceived, that he was not deceived by the serpent, but by his wife; and when she is said to be, *in the transgression*, the sense is, that she was in the transgression first; but not only in it; for Adam was also; hence we read of Adam's *transgression*. Rom. 5:14. And if he was with his wife when she eat (sic) of the fruit, as seems from the letter of the text Gen. 3:6 he sinned in not attempting to detect the sophistry of the serpent; in not defending his wife from his assaults; in not persuading her not to eat of the fruit; in not warning her of her danger; yea, in not using his conjugal authority, and laying his commands upon her not to eat; for if he was present and silent, he must be criminal and accessory to her sin;

---

1. *Op. cit.*, p. 310.
2. I Tim. 2:14.

but perhaps he was not with her. But his sin lay in hearkening to his wife, to her solicitations and requests, upon which it is put, Gen. 3:17. . . . . Though some think that he was not deceived by her; that he knew what he did, and what would be the consequence of it; he sinned with his eyes open; knew full well the sense of the law, and what would be the effect of it; but what he did was in complaisance to his wife, and from a vehement passionate love and affection for her; because he would not grieve her; and that she might not die alone, he chose to eat and sin and die with her: but then this was all very criminal; it was his duty to love his wife, as his own flesh; but then he was not to love her more than God: and to hearken to her voice more than to the voice of God.[3]

II. The Immediate Effect of the First Sin

The immediate effect of the fall was the instantaneous displeasing of and alienation from God, along with the depraving of his own soul. Adam had by his sinning broken the covenant of works, and thus fell under the curse of the covenant, namely death. A. A. Hodge indicates that this involved three aspects: the mortality of the body, the corruption of the soul and the sentence of eternal death.[4] We have already considered the alienation from God as a spiritual death.

For Adam and Eve the first noticeable effect was a sense of shame.

Both are equally guilty; both experience the same result. Here is one of the saddest anticlimaxes of history: 'they eat, they expect marvelous results, they wait--and there grows upon them the sense of shame' (Procksch). They now have a knowledge of good and evil, but not as a result of having remained steadfast in the good but from the low level of sin, as it has been aptly put. The immediate gain of the experience of sin is so utterly sordid. . . . The good Lord with definite purpose lets this effect be felt first in order that the baseness and utter worthlessness of all of sin's achievements may be made apparent. . . . That the sense of shame should concentrate itself around that portion of the body which is marked by the organs of generation, no doubt has its deeper reason in this that man instinctively feels that the very fountain and source of human life is contaminated by sin.[5]

Bavinck speaks of this moment as follows:

After that sin, man could no longer go on as though nothing had happened. . . . This is evident from the fact that immediately after the fall Adam and Eve tried to conceal themselves from God and from each other. And the eyes of them both were opened and they knew that they were naked (Gen. 3:7). Suddenly, in an instant they stood over against each other in a different relationship. They saw each other as they had never before seen each other. They dared not and could not freely and

---

3. John Gill, *Body of Divinity* (Atlanta: Turner Lassetter, 1950), pp. 317-318.
4. A. A. Hodge, *Outlines of Theology, op. cit.*, p. 323.
5. H. C. Leupold, *op. cit.*, p. 154.

unreservedly look into each other's eyes. They felt themselves guilty and impure . . .[6]

Another immediate effect of sin was the fear of meeting God. This constituted a fear of judgment. Adam and Eve were keenly aware that they had disobeyed God, and that they were justly under His wrath and curse. They did not want to meet the Maker, who had made them and dealt with them so graciously to this point, for now they have become odious to him. They, therefore, sought to hide themselves from him as their Judge. The reason for this fear of their Maker is that they have experienced spiritual death, which we have already discussed. It was because of this change in their spiritual relationship to God that they had the sense of guilt which manifested itself in the sense of shame. The attempt to cover themselves from each other is not to be taken as an evidence that they for the first time discovered their sexuality. The original creation command had included the command to be fruitful and multiply. Thus, unfallen man was to enter into the marital union and to propagate the race. The sense of shame was the result of a sense of guilt that involved them in their inmost being.

The inability of man to hide from God or to clothe himself is evidence that he had lost all ability to change his character. Prior to the fall he had been good, but with the ability to change. Now that he has chosen evil, he cannot reverse the process. This can only come as a work of God.

The first sin did not stand alone. It was only the first of on-going rivers of sins which proceeded from it. Adam and Eve as confronted by God, fail to confess and repent, but make excuses for their sin. Their sin produced in a generation the first murder, and the floods of sins continue to engulf the whole earth, wherever man resides.

III. The Curse

A. Upon Adam and Eve

The curse as announced to Adam and Eve indicates a change that has taken place in their natures. The woman is cursed in the pain of childbearing. Thus, in that which constituted her woman she received the effects of sin. So also with man, who had been created for service and labor to the glory of God. Whereas, prior to the fall he had been given the task of tending the Garden, and this was his joyful service, now he must labor with the sweat of his brow. Labor, the thing for which he had been created, has now become tedious to him. It should be observed that in both cases, there is an element of the grace of God to be seen. For the woman will be able to bear children despite the pain, and the man will be able to obtain food despite the sorrow of his labor.

B. Upon the Earth

The earth itself is said to be cursed. This is seen in the curse placed on the ground. "And unto Adam he said, Because thou has hearkened unto the

---

6. Herman Bavinck, *Our Reasonable Faith* (Grand Rapids: William B. Eerdmans Publishing Co., 1956), p. 230.

voice of thy wife, and hast eaten of the tree, of which I commanded thee, saying, Thou shalt not eat of it: cursed is the ground for thy sake; in sorrow shalt thou eat of it all the days of thy life; thorns also and thistles shall it bring forth to thee ..."[7] This speaks of an upset of nature itself as a consequence of sin. The enormity of the sin of man is seen in the fact that the whole creation has been disrupted by his sin. Paul speaks of the fact that the whole of creation is awaiting the day of redemption. "For the creation was subjected to vanity, not of its own will, but by reason of him who subjected it, in hope that the creation itself also shall be delivered from the bondage of corruption into the liberty of the glory of the children of God. For we know that the whole of creation groaneth and travaileth in pain together until now."[8] This will come to a consummation in the destruction of the present creation. "But the day of the Lord will come as a thief; in the which the heavens shall pass away with a great noise, and the elements shall be dissolved with fervent heat, and the earth and the works that are therein shall be burned up."[9]

IV. The Effect of Sin on the Human Race - Total Depravity and Inability

A. Total Depravity

1. Definition

When we assert that the fall of man introduced the condition of total depravity into the human race, we need to define what is meant by this term. In the negative this is not asserting that Adam immediately became as wicked as he could be. What is meant is:

    1st. His apostasy from God was complete. God demands perfect obedience. Adam was now a rebel in arms.

    2d. That the favor and communion of God, the sole condition of his spiritual life, was withdrawn.

    3d. A schism was introduced into the soul itself. The painful reproaches of conscience were excited, and could never be allayed without an atonement. This led to fear of God, distrust, prevarication, and, by necessary consequence, to innumerable other sins.

    4th. Thus the whole nature became depraved. The will being at war with the conscience, the understanding became darkened; the conscience, in consequence of constant outrage and neglect, became seared; the appetites of the body inordinate, and its members instruments of unrighteousness.

    5th. There remained in man's nature no recuperative principle; he must go on from worse to worse, unless God interpose.

        Thus the soul of man being essentially active, although one sin did not establish a confirmed habit, it did alienate God and work confusion in the soul, and thus lead to an endless course of sin.[10]

---

7. Genesis 3:17-18a.
8. Rom. 8:20-22.
9. II Peter 3:10.
10. A. A. Hodge, *op. cit.*, pp. 323-324.

2. Extent of the Depravity

The depravity of man is all-inclusive of all mankind descending from Adam by ordinary generation. Romans 3:9-23 clearly affirms this. There is none righteous, none that seeketh God, none that doeth good. All have sinned and come short of the glory of God.

We shall consider the relation of Adam's sin to the race, and its transmission in the next chapter. For the present, on the basis of the Biblical passages cited, it is sufficient to assert that all of Adam's posterity by ordinary generation has been affected by his sin. Again, A. A. Hodge sets this forth succinctly:

> 1st. The judicial charging of legal responsibility upon all at their creation whom he represented in the Covenant of Works.
>
> 2d. The consequent birth of each of his descendants in a state of exclusion from the life-giving communion of the divine Spirit.
>
> 3d. The consequent loss of original righteousness, and the inherent and prevailing tendency to sin which is the invariable moral condition of each of his descendants from birth.
>
> 4th. The absolute moral inability of men to change their natures or to fulfil their obligations.[11]

3. Intensiveness of the Depravity

This depravity extends to all aspects of our nature. Though there is some singling out of particular aspects of our nature, such as heart, or mind, a consideration of the total teaching of Scripture indicates that the whole man is depraved. His body is spoken of as the body of sin. It is out of the heart that all manner of sins proceed. His understanding is blinded.

This is clearly taught in the Bible. We have an early witness to the total depravity of man in Genesis 6:5 and 8:21. "And Jehovah saw that the wickedness of man was great in the earth, and that every imagination of the thoughts of his heart was only evil continually." "And Jehovah smelled the sweet savor; and Jehovah said in his heart, I will not again curse the ground any more for man's sake, for that the imagination of man's heart is evil from his youth." In these passages we have the following teachings.

> a. First, there is the **intensity** of the sin. "The Lord God saw that the wickedness of man was *great*."
>
> b. Second, the **totality** of the evil is affirmed. Every imagination is evil. As we consider that the imagination refers not to the carefully thought out plan, but the most rudimentary of our thoughts, we see how penetrating sin is.
>
> c. Third, the **inwardness** of sin is mentioned, in that it is every imagination of the thoughts of the heart. The combination of these terms is

---

11. *Ibid.*, p. 324.

almost unparalleled in the Scripture. It is used only one other time in II Chronicles. Any one of the terms would be sufficient to suggest the inwardness of sin, but all three press it to the very utmost of what is rudimentary in our being.

d. Fourth, evil in man is exclusive. His thoughts were *only* evil *continually. Every* imagination was *only* evil.

e. Fifth, the habitual character of evil is stressed by the term continually.

f. Sixth, the sinfulness of man is said to be innate. Man is a sinner "from his youth" (8:21). It is not something that he acquires from his environment, but he is born this way.

Other passages of the Old Testament reaffirm this same doctrine, such as, Psalms 38 and 51.

Romans 3:9-23 in the New Testament sets forth the same teaching about sin. The Apostle here is quoting from the Old Testament in the Psalms and Isaiah. "There is none righteous, no not one; There is none that understandeth; There is none that seeketh after God; They have all turned aside, they are together become unprofitable; There is none that doeth good, no, not so much as one." The Apostle asserts the inwardness first, in his emphasis on the understanding, and then as a consequence of this, the actions of man are seen to be evil. Having reflected on the inwardness of our sin, he turns next to treat the physical organs. The throat, the tongue, the mouth, the feet. Thus the whole man, both inwardly and outwardly is wicked. The final indictment of verse 18 is that "there is no fear of God before their eyes." This, in Biblical terms, is an assertion that there is a complete lack of godliness. For the Scripture sees the "fear of the Lord" as the beginning of godliness.

Verses 9, 19, and 23 all indicate that this indictment is of the whole human race, and not of just one segment or of one generation. This is a description of our character, yours and mine. It is against this background that Paul develops the doctrine of justification by faith. It is when this is seen that the Gospel really appears as good news.

Other passages that should also be noted in this connection are: John 3:6, where we are referred to as being born of the flesh: Ephesians 2:1, 2 where we are described as dead in trespasses and sin; and Romans 8:5-8 where we are described as being at enmity with God and unable to please him. We see from these passages that it is a matter of our natural condition to be sinners. Further, we see that we are by nature opposed to God and good. Having asserted it is a part of our natural condition, we should not think of this as man's normal condition. Sin is abnormal. The normal condition was that of the unfallen state. Ever since the fall man has been abnormal.

Aspects of our fallen natures under the indictment of God are:
- **the understanding**, I Corinthians 2:14, "Now the natural man receiveth not the things of the Spirit of God: for they are foolishness unto him; and he cannot know them, because they are spiritually judged."; II Corinthians 4:4, "In whom

the god of this world hath blinded the minds of the unbelieving, that the light of the gospel of the glory of Christ, who is the image of God, should not dawn upon them."; Ephesians 4:18, "Being darkened in their understanding, alienated from the life of God, because of the ignorance that is in them, because of the hardening of their heart.";
- **the will**, John 5:14, "Afterward Jesus findeth him in the temple, and said unto him, Behold, thou art made whole: sin no more, lest a worse thing befall thee."; Romans 8:7, "Because the mind of the flesh is enmity against God; for it is not subject to the law of God, neither indeed can it be.";
- **the feeling or affection**, I John 2:15-17, "Love not the world, neither the things that are in the world. If any man love the world, the love of the Father is not in him. For all that is in the world, the lust of the flesh and the lust of the eyes and the vainglory of life, is not of the Father, but is of the world. And the world passeth away, and the lust thereof: but he that doeth the will of God abideth forever.";
- **the conscience**, Titus 1:15, "To the pure all things are pure; but to them that are defiled and unbelieving nothing is pure; but both their mind and their conscience are defiled."; cf. I Timothy 4:2.

B. Total Inability

1. Definition

a. Negatively

To understand what we mean when we speak of the inability of man, it may help first to speak of those ideas not intended. First, it is not a reference to any limitation due to our finitude, or creaturehood. Second, it does not deny the possibility of certain natural or civil virtues that we may exercise, even as natural men. Such natural virtues exist because the law of God is written on our hearts, and thus are constitutional with us. Third, the inability is something that man did not have in his original state. Fourth, as we have already noted, it is not the same as the loss of liberty. Liberty does not rest in the ability of contrary choice, but rather in the fact that the agent is self-moved to do as he pleases.

b. Positively

This inability is that which has come as a consequence of sin. It is the inability of the sinful character to change from its sinfulness to that which is opposite. Two features of the inability are seen, first, the fact that man as totally depraved cannot desire to do that which is good. Second, he is unable to change himself to choosing or doing good. His mind is at enmity against God, and he cannot change this enmity.

2. Biblical Basis

a. Matthew 7:17-18; "Even so every good tree bringeth forth good fruit; but the corrupt tree bringeth forth evil fruit. A good tree cannot bring forth evil fruit, neither can a corrupt tree bring forth good fruit." Jesus is using the parabolic saying about the trees to illustrate the case with men. It speaks of the inability of the sinner to bring forth anything but evil fruit.

    b. John 6:44-65; In this passage Jesus says, "No man can come unto me, except the Father that sent me draw him; and I will raise him up in the last day." And again, "And he said, For this cause have I said unto you, that no man can come unto me, except it be given unto him of the Father." Both of these verses teach the inability of man to come to Jesus in saving faith without the help of the Father. In other words, Jesus is asserting the necessity of divine intervention if a man is to come to God. The emphasis is on our inability, and the gracious character of the plan of salvation. On the basis of such an unambiguous statement by Jesus, it is difficult to understand how some evangelicals maintain that God cannot save us until we give him permission.

    c. Romans 6:16, 20; 7:1; "Know ye not, that to whom ye present yourselves as servants unto obedience, his servants ye are who ye obey; whether of sin unto death, or obedience unto righteousness?" These verses affirm the bondage of a man to sin. The implication is that he cannot break this bondage in himself.

    d. Romans 8:7-8; "Because the mind of the flesh is enmity against God, for it is not subject to the law of God, neither indeed can it be; and they that are in the flesh cannot please God." The first portion of this passage may have reference to the law of God, but the second part affirms plainly the inability of the natural man to please God at all. This teaches the inability of the sinner to do anything to please God.

3. Man's Accountability

Having shown that the natural man is totally unable to do spiritual good, it must be asserted that this in no way diminishes his responsibility for his deeds. He sins because he wants to sin. He acts out of his freedom to do what he wants to do, and thus God holds him totally accountable for all that he does. That this is the case may clearly be seen from the fact that in the day of judgment, men are to be called into account, and to be judged on the basis of their deeds.

It is when we face the full implication of the total, heart depravity of man, and his personal desire to remain in his sins, that the grace of God stands in amazing contrast. Some suggest the idea that the doctrine of election is unfair, because God does not give all men an equal chance to be saved. The fact is, that all men do have an equal opportunity. All men everywhere are called upon to repent and receive Christ as Savior. None will want to do this, unless by the grace of God their hearts are changed by the efficacious grace of God. The point that is amazing is not that God has passed some by in his plan of salvation, but that he has elected any to salvation. By nature we are all sinners, justly deserving the wrath and curse of God. The natural man is in bondage to his sin, and is unable to break this bondage. As such, he is thus unable to please God, or to make himself over so as to please him.

The consequence of the Biblical doctrine of sin is the fact that all men are under the judgment and condemnation of God. In other words, all are hell-deserving, and all would eventually end up there, were it not for God's sovereign grace by which he has determined to save some from the wrath to come through a Redeemer. We shall be considering this Redeemer and his work in the next *locus* of our study.

Chapter XXII Original Sin

Introduction

In this chapter, we shall examine the idea of original sin, and also how sin and its effects are transmitted to the human race. Theological opinion on these subjects has varied, even among Reformed thinkers. Something of an overview of these opinions will be given.[1]

I. Original Sin

The term "original sin" has been used by theologians to refer to the sin and corruption that have come to all men, descended by ordinary generation, from Adam. There is some ambiguity in its usage.

A. History

Berkouwer says as he begins his treatment of original sin, "We now enter an area in which a strenuous and emotional debate has been constantly waged throughout the entire history of the Church and her theology. This debate is still going strong in our own day."[2] It is because of this history that we need to survey this debate.

The early church fathers have little to say about original sin. The Greek fathers spoke of a physical corruption in the human race, which did not involve guilt. This view eventually developed into Pelagianism, which denies the existence of original sin. A. A. Hodge defines Pelagianism thus:

    (a) Moral character can be predicated only of volitions.
    (b) Ability is always the measure of responsibility.
    (c) Hence every man has always plenary power to do all that it is his duty to do.
    (d) Hence the human will alone, to the exclusion of the interference of any internal influence from God, must decide human character and destiny.[3]

In the western church, especially in Tertullian, sin was seen as propagated with the propagation of the soul. Sin was viewed as hereditary, but man was not totally depraved. Augustine developed the doctrine of original sin more fully. Augustinianism holds:

    (a) Man is by nature so entirely depraved in his moral nature as to be totally unable to do anything spiritually good, or in any degree to begin or dispose himself thereto. (b) That even under the exciting and suasory influences of divine grace the will of man is totally unable to

---

[1]. See George P. Hutchinson, *The Problem of Original Sin in American Presbyterian Theology* (Nutley, NJ: Presbyterian and Reformed Publishing Co., 1972) for a full treatment of the various views held by American Presbyterian theologians.
[2]. Berkouwer, *Sin*, p. 424.
[3]. *Outlines of Theology*, op. cit., p. 338.

act aright in co-operation with grace, until after the will itself is by the energy of grace radically and permanently renewed. (c) Even after the renewal of the will it ever continues dependent upon divine grace to prompt, direct, and enable it in the performance of every good work.[4]
Original sin then includes both corruption and guilt.

In reaction to the absolutism of Augustinianism, a semi-Pelagian view was developed. Though it admitted that all men are tainted by sin, they are not viewed as totally depraved, nor is the freedom of the will lost. Original sin does not involve man in guilt. Semi-Pelagianism holds: "(a) Man's nature has been so far weakened by the fall that it can not act aright in spiritual matters without divine assistance. (b) This weakened moral state which infants inherit from their parents is the cause of sin, but not itself sin in the sense of deserving the wrath of God. (c) Man must strive to do his whole duty, when God meets him with co-operative grace, and renders his efforts successful. (d) Man is not responsible for the sins he commits until after he has enjoyed and abused the influences of grace."[5] Semi-Pelagianism became generally dominant in the Middle Ages.

Anselm agreed with Augustine. Thomas Aquinas "held that original sin, considered in its material element, is concupiscence, but considered in its formal element, is the privation of original justice. There is a dissolution of the harmony in which original justice consisted, and in this sense original sin can be called a languor of nature."[6]

The Reformers were generally of the Augustinian view. This was true of both Luther and Calvin. Calvin held that original sin is not something purely negative, and that sin is not limited to the sensuous nature of man.

The Socinians at the time of the Reformation were Pelagian, denying original sin. When the Arminians broke with the Reformed, they adopted the semi-Pelagian view of original sin. Modern evangelicalism tends to be semi-Pelagian. Modern humanism, of course, agrees with Pelagius that man is essentially good, and that he does evil, because of environment, etc.

The problem for those who reject the idea of original sin is that there is nothing that "offends our reason more than to say that the sin of the first man has made other men guilty, namely those men who are so far removed from this source that they would seem to be incapable of participating within it."[7]

On the other hand, there is a danger for those who profess the doctrine of original sin, namely, that they fall into the shifting of guilt from themselves to others. "Our confession of original sin may not function and cannot function as a means of *excusing ourselves* or of *hiding behind another man's guilt*."[8]

B. Original Sin Defined

Augustine was the first to use the expression "original sin." He used it to refer to the native depravity of every sinner. Reasons for the selection of the term "original" include the fact first, that we are all born in this state; second, it

---

4. *Ibid.*, p. 339.
5. *Ibid.*, p. 338.
6. Berkhof, *Systematic Theology, op. cit.*, p. 245.
7. Bavinck, *Gereformeerde Dogmatiek, op. cit.*, vol. III, p. 78, as cited by Berkouwer, *Sin*, p. 425.
8. *Ibid.*, p. 435.

is derived from the first sin of Adam; and third, this sinful nature is the source or origin of all our actual sins.

The Westminster Assembly defines original sin in a broad sense to include both the imputation of the guilt of Adam's first sin, and the inherent depravity consequent to it.

> The sinfulness of that estate whereinto man fell, consisteth in the guilt of Adam's first sin, the want of that righteousness wherein he was created, and the corruption of his nature, whereby he is utterly indisposed, disabled, and made opposite unto all that is spiritually good, and wholly inclined to all evil, and that continually, which is commonly called Original Sin, and from which do proceed all actual transgressions.[9]

Others, including Calvin, restrict its usage to the moral corruption with which we each are born. "Original sin, therefore, appears to be an hereditary depravity and corruption of our nature, diffused through all the parts of the soul, rendering us obnoxious to the Divine wrath, and producing in us those works which the Scripture calls 'works of the flesh.' "[10] In our treatment we shall include both the imputation of guilt and the depravity derived from it.

C. Biblical Basis

The fact of the universality of sin is clearly taught, as we have already seen in passages such as Genesis 6:5 and Rom. 3:9-23. "All have sinned and come short of the glory of God." The people of Judah complained that God was being arbitrary in punishing them, saying that the fathers had sinned, but the children were unjustly paying for it. Ezekiel replied against this false charge, "Yet ye say, The way of the Lord is not equal. Hear now, O house of Israel: Is not my way equal? are not your ways unequal? When the righteous man turneth away from his righteousness, and committeth iniquity, and dieth therein; in his iniquity that he hath done shall he die."[11] "The non-arbitrariness of God's activity is thus underscored and every stress is laid on the demonstrable relation between God's judgment and Israel's own personal guilt. There is no inconsistency between man's individual and collective culpability."[12]

Confession of original sin is coupled with confession of guilt. David's confession included this, "Behold, I was brought forth in iniquity; and in sin did my mother conceive me."[13] This is a part of David's confession of his own guiltiness, not a blame shifting. "The Bible, both in this and other places, clearly asserts that we are born in sin, and that it exists within us as a disease fixed in our nature. David does not charge his parents, nor trace his crime to them, but sees himself before the Divine tribunal, confesses that he was formed in sin, and that he was a transgressor ere he saw the light of the world."[14] It is worthy of noting that Calvin refuses at this point to get into the question of how the sin is

---

9. Larger Catechism, Q. 25.
10. Calvin, *Institutes of the Christian Religion*, II, I, 8.
11. Ezek. 18:25-26.
12. Berkouwer, *Sin*, p. 427.
13. Psalm 51:5.
14. Calvin, *Commentary upon the Book of Psalms*, ad loc.

transmitted from parents to children, but was satisfied to know that we were encompassed in Adam in his sin, and thus the whole race is corrupted and sinful.

The question of how we are related to Adam and how his sin affects us is spoken to by Paul in Romans 5 and I Cor. 15. We shall consider these passages in the next section as we look at the doctrine of the imputation of sin.

II. The Doctrine of Imputation

A. The Imputation of Adam's Guilt

1. Meaning of the Term "Impute"

A careful study of the Biblical terms *chashab*[15] and *logizomai*[16] reveals that the term "impute" means simply "to attribute to". That is, it is to reckon or to lay to one's account. The term itself does not include any indication of what is imputed. It may be either sin or righteousness. Further, it does not mean that the person to whom something is imputed has any personal claim on that which is imputed. That is, either sin or righteousness may be imputed to those who are not personally either sinner or righteous.

2. Theological Usage of the Idea of "Imputation"

a. Regarding Sin

"To impute sin, in Scriptural and theological language, is to impute the guilt of sin . . . the judicial obligation to satisfy divine justice."[17] In the Bible there are two imputations of sin. They are first, the imputation of the sin of Adam to his posterity, and second, the imputation of our sins to Christ. The consequence of both is that both are morally accountable. In neither case is the nature of the person changed. That is, it is not the imputation of Adam's guilt to us that makes us sinners. This is the consequence of our inherited corrupt nature. To say that our sins are imputed to Christ, that he bore our sins, is not to say that he committed them, but to say that he was reckoned a sinner, and thus had to pay the penalty for them.

b. Regarding Righteousness

Just as our sins are imputed to Christ, and he bore their penalty, so also the Scriptures speak of the righteousness of Christ as being imputed to us. Hodge says:

> When it is said that the righteousness of Christ is imputed to believers, it does not mean that they wrought out that righteousness, that they were the agents of the acts of Christ in obeying the law; not that the merit of His righteousness is their personal merit; not that it constitutes

---

15. חשב
16. λογίζομαι
17. C. Hodge, *Systematic Theology, op. cit.*, vol. II, p. 194.

their moral character; it simply means that His righteousness, having been wrought out by Christ for the benefit of His people, in their name, by Him as their representative, it is laid to their account, so that God can be just in justifying the ungodly.[18]

In this connection Hodge goes on to indicate that there is confusion because righteousness may be used to describe both personal and judicial righteousness. He suggests that a man may be personally unrighteous, and yet legally righteous.

If this were not so, no sinner could be saved. There is not a believer on earth who does not feel and acknowledge himself to be personally unrighteous, ill-deserving, meriting the wrath and curse of God. Nevertheless, he rejoices in the assurance that the infinitely meritorious righteousness of Christ, his full atonement for all sin, constitutes Him legally, not morally, righteous in the sight of divine justice. When, therefore, God pronounces the unrighteous to be righteous ... He simply declares that their debt to justice has been paid by another.[19]

3. The Ground for Imputation

The ground for the imputation of Adam's guilt to his posterity lies in the union that we have with him. The sin of the angels is not imputed to men, since there is no bond of union between these two groups. There is a twofold bond that exists between Adam and his posterity, namely, the natural and the federal.

The fact of natural union accounts for the inheritance of a corrupt nature, but does not account for the imputation of the guilt of Adam's first sin. As a consequence of our inherited corruption we become guilty, because out of that nature come forth sinful actions. How can we account for the fact, however, that the effects of the curse, including death, fall upon those who have not yet sinned. It must be by the fact of imputation, which in turn rests, not on the inherited nature, but on the relation to Adam as our representative.

Romans 5:12-21 is the most extensive commentary on the sin of Adam and its consequences in the human race to be found in the Bible. Here it is asserted, "Therefore, as through one man sin entered into the world, and death through sin; and so death passed unto all men, for that all sinned."[20] The statement that "all sinned" is not an assertion that all sin in their own lives at some time, but rather that in Adam all sinned. The question of the nature of our union with Adam has been raised. The fact that Paul in this passage, and in I Corinthians 15 stresses the parallel between Adam and the consequences of his act, and Christ and the consequences of his act makes this a very important question.

The meaning of the "all sinned" of verse 12 is elucidated by verse 14, where it is asserted that death reigned even in those who had not sinned in the same way that Adam did. The Pelagian interpretation tries to identify the "all sinned" of verse 12 as actual sins, but the context teaches that this is not so. Professor Murray points to five occasions in verses 13-19 that assert that death reigned because of the one sin of Adam, not the actual sins of the posterity: "by

---

18. *Ibid.*, p. 195.
19. *Idem.*
20. Romans 5:12.

the trespasses of the one the many died" (verse 15); "the judgment was from one unto condemnation" (verse 16); "by the trespass of the one death reigned through the one" (verse 17); "through one trespass judgment came upon all men unto condemnation" (verse 18); "through the disobedience of the one man the many were constituted sinners" (verse 19). Murray says, "This reiteration establishes beyond doubt that the apostle regarded condemnation and death as having passed on to all men by the one trespass of the one man Adam."[21] In addition to this exegetical reason for interpreting this phrase of verse 12 this way, there is also the fact of experience, for it is not true that all die because of their own sin. Infants who die in infancy have not sinned themselves, and yet they are under the curse of Adam's sin.

It should be observed that verse 12 begins a comparison that is not completed until verse 18 and 19. The parenthesis explains the doctrine set forth. Verse 18 begins again the comparison and completes it. "So then as through one trespass the judgment came unto all men to condemnation; even so through one act of righteousness the free gift came unto all men to justification of life." The teaching of the passage is that there is a union and solidarity of the race with Adam, and of the redeemed race with Christ. The principle of solidarity is found throughout the Scriptures. In the family, church, and state God does not just deal with the individual. He often deals through the representative of the people.

In answer to the question of the nature of this union, three basic views have been suggested.

a. Seminal

This is the view that holds that Adam is the natural root of all mankind, and therefore acted as their representative. Such a view is seen in the Scripture as in the case of Levi being in the loins of Abraham when he paid tithe to Melchizedek.[22] This is the view held by the earlier Reformed theologians, and is suggested by the language of the Westminster Confession, "They being the root of all mankind, the guilt of sin was imputed."[23] Though this is a true position, it is not entirely adequate to explain the emphasis of Paul as he stressed the one sin and the one man. We were in his loins when he committed other sins, and they would be just as applicable to us if the seminal union were the only consideration. There must be something beyond this.

b. Realistic

According to this view every individual was really in Adam, and sinned in him. Adam included all of human nature within himself. Each person is an individualized portion of that human nature. Thus since the whole of humanity was in Adam, each individualized portion of it, as it comes to personal existence,

---

21. *The Epistle to the Romans*, I, p. 184.
22. Hebrews 7:9-10.
23. Chapter VI, par.3.

is guilty of that in which it participated in Adam. This is a view held by W. G. T. Shedd.[24]

This view is subject to the following criticism:

(1) In his attempt to avoid an arbitrary imputation, Shedd has impersonalized humanity in Adam. How could the individual, who was not yet separate and personal, be held accountable for what humanity as a whole did? To hold this is also arbitrary.

(2) The parallelism between Adam and his descendants and Christ and his own is lost in this view.

(3) There is a very difficult problem of the relation of Christ to sin, if all Adam's descendants were really within him, and participated in his guilt. How can even the Virgin Birth avoid this difficulty, unless it is posited that the guilt is transmitted only by the father to the child?

c. Representative

This view contemplates mankind as related to Adam under his federal headship. That is, he was our head and representative. Thus, what he did he did not only for himself, but for all his posterity descending from him by ordinary generation. Involved in the imputation are both the guilt of Adam's sin, and also the depravity of it. This same principle is carried over to the work of Christ. He acted for us in his death, so that the benefits of his work are imputed to us.

This view of the matter is backed by I Corinthians 15:22, 45-49. Paul here comprehends all of God's dealing with man under the twofold headship of Adam and Christ. Adam is the first man, and there is none before him. Christ is the second Man. There are none between Adam and Christ, and none after him, for he is the last Man also. The conclusion is that the relation of these two to humanity must be directly parallel. Thus Paul teaches that as in Adam all die, so in Christ all shall be made alive. Adam is seen, then, as the type of Christ.

This same typology and parallelism is seen in Romans 5:12-21. Since Christ is our vicarious representative, so it must be assumed that Adam was our vicarious representative in Eden. This explains the emphasis on the one man, and on the one sin.

4. The Nature of the Imputation

a. Mediate Imputation

In seeking to answer the question of just how we are involved in the sin of Adam, the attempt has been made to suggest that the imputation of his sin was mediate and not immediate. This is a view set forth by La Place (or Placaeus) of the French theological school of Saumur in the 17th century. "La Place taught

---

24. W. G. T. Shedd, *Dogmatic Theology* (Grand Rapids: Zondervan Publishing, n.d.), vol. II. and *Theological Essays* (New York: Scribner, Armstrong and Co., 1877).

that we derive a corrupt nature from Adam, and that that corrupt nature, and not Adam's sin is the ground of the condemnation which has come upon all mankind ... He did not deny the imputation of that sin, but simply made it dependent on our participation in his corrupted nature. We are inherently depraved, and therefore are involved in the guilt of Adam's sin."[25] Hereditary depravity is the medium through which Adam's guilt is imputed to us.

b. Immediate Imputation

In contrast to mediate imputation is the view that holds that the guilt of Adam's first sin was immediately imputed to his posterity by reason of the union sustained to him. The hereditary depravity is a consequence of their being involved in this first sin through immediate imputation.

c. Biblical Teaching Favors Immediate Imputation

(1) Romans 5:12, 15, 16 teach the immediate conjunction between the sin of Adam and the death of all. There is no hint in these passages of an intervening hereditary corruption as the grounds of this imputation of Adam's guilt to all.

(2) The same is true of the judgment which is immediately related to the sin of Adam in Romans 5:16, 18. "Since both death and condemnation are brought into immediate conjunction with the one sin of the one man, we would expect that the sin of all would be brought into immediate conjunction with the one sin of the one man."[26]

(3) Paul explicitly relates the sin of all and the one sin immediately in Romans 5:12, 19. We have already seen that the "all sinned" of Romans 5:12 has to do, not with actual transgressions, but with the fact that in Adam all sinned. This is an immediate relation, and the interjection of hereditary depravity would break the thrust of the passage. Romans 5:19 speaks of the fact that through the one act of disobedience the many were constituted sinners. If hereditary depravity must be assumed, then it could not be said that Adam's sin constituted us sinners. The mediate imputation would hold that man is already constituted a sinner by his inherent depravity before there is any imputation of Adam's sin.

III. The Sin against the Holy Spirit

One other subject that needs to be considered before finishing with the discussion of sin, is that particular sin designated as the unpardonable sin, or the sin against the Holy Spirit.

---

25. C. Hodge, *op. cit.*, p. 205.
26. John Murray, "Unpublished class notes on Systematic Theology."

It was in immediate connection with the claim of Jesus to cast out demons in the power of the Spirit of God that we have the wicked suggestion that he was doing this by the power of evil spirits. Jesus in response warns against the sin against the Holy Spirit. This context should be kept in mind as we seek to understand what the sin against the Holy Spirit is. Remember that the Jews were suggesting that his work done by the Spirit of God was the work of Satan. He showed them the unreasonableness of this line of argument. He then warns against sinning against the Spirit. In effect he said to them that their sin was the unreasonable and absurd rejection of the Son of God as Saviour in opposition to the plain and unanswerable testimony of the Spirit. This is the historical interpretation of this sin, based on the context.

This understanding of the unpardonable sin then essentially identifies it with the rejection of Christ. This is warranted because it is the work of the Spirit to bear testimony of him (John 16:8-10). Thus when a person who has known the Gospel, and come under some conviction of the Gospel finally rejects it, he is, in effect, rejecting the testimony of the Holy Spirit. Abraham Kuyper cites not only the passages found in the Synoptics describing this sin, but also I John 5:16-18 and Heb. 6:4-8. On the basis of the last passage he suggests that "the sin against the Holy Spirit can be committed only by persons who, beholding the beauty and majesty of the Lord, turn the light into darkness and deem the highest glory of the Son of God's love to belong to Satan and his demons."[27] Again he says, "To commit this sin two things are required, which absolutely belong together:

> First, close contact with the glory which is manifest in Christ or in His people.
> Second, not mere contempt of that glory, but the declaration that the Spirit which manifests itself in that glory, which is the Holy Spirit, is a manifestation of Satan.

He who desecrates, despises, and slanders the Spirit, who speaks of Christ, in his Word, and in his work, as though he were the spirit of Satan is lost in eternal darkness. This is a willful sin, intentionally malicious. It betrays *systematic* opposition to God. That sinner can not be saved, for he has done despite unto the Spirit of all grace. He has lost the last remnant in the sinner, the taste for grace, and with it the *possibility* of receiving grace."[28]

J. A. Alexander makes the following observation in his commentary on Mark. He points out that Mark 3:30 says, "Because they said, He hath an unclean spirit." On this he comments:

> Lest there should be any doubt as to the bearing of this fearful sentence (vs. 29), Mark specifically mentions what occasioned it, only exchanging the name *Beelzebub* for *unclean spirit*, which is really its meaning. It appears then that in charging him with being possessed, they either did commit, or were in danger of committing the unpardonable sin of blasphemy against the Holy Ghost. It cannot consist therefore in mere obstinate unbelief or final impenitence, for these are chargeable on all who perish, and could not be described in such terms as a peculiar sin

---

27. Kuyper, *Work of the Holy Spirit, op. cit.*, p. 611.
28. *Ibid.*, p. 612.

distinguished from all others, and according to Matthew (12:31), even from the sin of speaking a word against the Son of God. There are two other explanations which have been extensively received and are entitled to attention. One of these is founded upon Matthew's statement, and supposes a distinction between Jesus, as the Son of man, i.e. a divine person in the form of a servant (Phil. 2:7), and under that disguise liable to be mistaken, so that men might speak against him and blaspheme him, not indeed without aggravated guilt, but without incurring this tremendous condemnation; and on the other hand Jesus as the Son of God, with the manifest tokens of divinity afforded by his miracles of mercy. But as this does not account for the Holy Spirit being put in opposition to the Son of man, and as Mark omits this opposition altogether, most interpreters agree that the unpardonable sin consists in obstinate rejection of the truth, and willful apostasy from God, in opposition to one's own convictions, and with malignant hatred of the gospel, the expression of which is the blasphemy against the Holy Ghost, as the illuminating Spirit by whom truth is carried home to the heart and understanding of believers, and to whom such apostasy and unbelief are therefore more especially insulting.[29]

Professor G. C. Berkouwer has a very interesting chapter on the sin against the Holy Spirit. He indicates that there have been various views as to what comprised this sin. First it has been suggested that it is a violation of the third commandment. The Heidelberg Catechism question 100 reads, "No sin is greater or more provoking to God than the profaning of his name." Berkouwer then points out the fact that such profaning is a blasphemy of the Holy Spirit, who is one of the persons of the Godhead. He answers the question as to whether this is the unpardonable sin, by indicating that the Gospels have an explicit reference to blasphemy against the Holy Spirit.

A second possible commandment is the seventh commandment. The grounds for suggesting that the seventh commandment may be involved in the unforgivable sin is to be found in I Cor. 6:18,19, "Every sin that a man doeth is without the body; but he that committeth fornication sinneth against his own body. Or know ye not that your body is a temple of the Holy Spirit which is in you, which ye have from God?" This passage suggests that the sin against the body involved in adultery is a sin against the Spirit of God who dwells in the body. In answer to this, it should be observed that where the sin against the Holy Spirit is dealt with in the Gospels there is no mention of the sin of adultery.

Berkouwer seeks to come to the answer as to just what the sin against the Holy Spirit is by going to other passages and studying the meaning of them. In connection with I John 5:16-17, he concludes that though there may be a tie between the forgiving and not forgiving motif in the Gospels and the life and death motif in John, the exact nature of this is not clear. Hebrews 10:26-29 and Hebrews 6:4-8 are more helpful. Both of these passages make mention of the Spirit of God, though not in an exclusive sense. The Gospels on the other hand isolate the sin against the Spirit in distinction from sins against the Son of man. Many theologians have, on the basis of these Hebrews passages, identified the

---

29. J. A. Alexander, *Commentary on the Gospel of Mark*, p. 80.

rejection of Christ and the Gospel as the unforgivable sin. Berkouwer feels that this is too simplistic. He then returns to the Gospel passages themselves and deals with them.

Only when we look at the incontestable evidence of Christ which is nevertheless contested can we possibly understand the warning which Christ gives. The pharisees exemplify the abysmal apostasy of man's heart and necessitated this stern rebuke. Hence the distinction between blasphemy as against Christ and blasphemy as against the Spirit. Hence, too, we understand why, in the rest of the New Testament, where the burden is to see Christ crucified and risen, *we never once come upon the distinction between Christ and the Spirit.* This latter revelation is no longer concerned about the concealment of Christ's Messianic secret. For the mystery has now been revealed in the *proclamation of the full light of Christ.*

From that standpoint it is plain why Hebrews points us to a deliberate and willful sinning as the conscious rejection of what *has occurred and is now manifest.* There is now a flagrant and purposeful outraging of the Son of God, a crucifying of Him anew, and a deliberate despising of His blood. Against the curtain of what has happened, it is now evident why this distinction between the Christological and the pneumatological falls away. That which men now commit against the Son of God is sewed up with the blasphemy against the Spirit of *grace.* Everything *now* is concentrated on the resistance or antipathy in which evil men respond to this decisive act in Christ. There are many who blaspheme the crucified Lord and despise Him in His deepest humiliation; yet for all of these there is still forgiveness. . . . But when the Son arose on Easter morning and the message of the cross was preached abroad and confirmed by the Spirit in the resurrection of Christ and Pentecost, a *new era* was given birth and men no longer could differentiate their sinning against Christ from their sinning against the Spirit. Sin was now qualified for all time as the renunciation of salvation in Christ and the light which shines in darkness (I John 2:8). Therefore the whole counsel of God must now be proclaimed (cf. Acts 20:27; I Cor. 2:2), and men must be adjured to come to faith and repentance. From this time forth (as we read in Hebrews) any despising of Christ's blood is the very same thing as blaspheming of the Spirit of *grace.*[30]

---

30. Berkouwer, *Sin*, pp. 340-341.

DIVISION IV CHRISTOLOGY

Chapter XXIII The Plan of Salvation

I. Classification of Various Views of Salvation

All who can plausibly be called Christian believe that man has sinned and needs salvation. There is a great deal of variety as to how various different branches of Christendom have interpreted the plan of salvation. In this connection we refer the student to Warfield's *Plan of Salvation* in which he surveys the whole field at some length.

A. A Diagram Relating the Various Views of Salvation

```
                        Professing Christendom
           ┌───────────────────┴───────────────────┐
    Naturalism or                                Supernaturalism
    Pelagianism
                    ┌──────────────────────────────┤
              Sarcerdotalism                    Evangelicalism
        ┌──────────┼──────────┐                      │
      Roman      Greek     Anglican                  │
                                                     │
           ┌──────────────────────────────┐          │
      Universalism                    Particularism
        ┌──────┬───────┐                             │
   Lutherans Remonstrants Wesleyan                   │
        ┌──────────────┬──────────────┐
   Amyraldianism  Infralapsarianism  Supralapsarianism
```

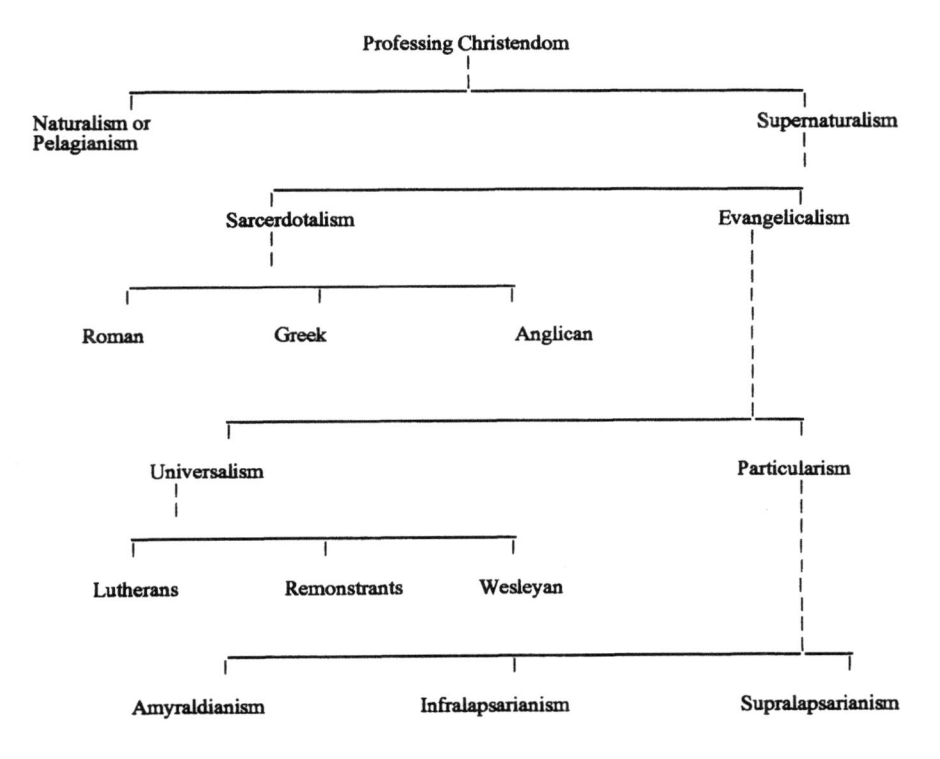

B. Description of These Various Views

1. Naturalism or Pelagianism

This is the most anti-Biblical of all the views. It maintains that Adam's sin was without any consequences on the race. Man is not affected by sin as far as his ability is concerned. Thus he is able to turn to God with his own natural ability. He does not need help from God. He does not even need Christ as an example, though this may assist him to turn to God. This is the view held by Pelagius and by the Modernists in the 20th Century. It is not officially espoused by any Christian Church, but held by individuals. The Unitarian and Universalist sects hold to this concept of man. They make very little of a salvation concept.

2. Supernaturalism

Broadly speaking, all the Church confesses that God saves. This is the characteristic of supernaturalism as contrasted with naturalism. God is the Author of the plan of salvation. There is a wide variety of understanding of the way in which the plan of salvation is to be understood within Christendom.

a. Sacerdotalism

The Sacerdotalists maintain that God saves mediately through the Church and its sacraments. The Church is the sole depository of saving grace. *Extra ecclesiam nulla salus.* The Church mediates the salvation placed in her hands by means of the sacraments. Thus, the sacraments become indispensable, if one is to be the recipient of grace. This is most consistently held by the Roman and the Eastern Orthodox branches of the Church. It is less consistently held by the high Anglicans. The Sacerdotalists consider the order of the Divine decrees to be the following:

(1) Decree to create;
(2) Decree to permit the fall;
(3) Decree to make satisfaction for the sin of all by the sacrifice of Christ;
(4) Decree to institute the Church as the repository of salvation, and to make the sacraments the means of dispensing grace;
(5) Decree to predestinate to salvation all those He foresees will receive the sacraments and continue in them;
(6) Decree to sanctify all those who will persevere in their use of the sacraments.

b. Evangelicalism

In contrast to the Sacerdotalists who hold that God saves mediately through the Church and its sacraments, the Evangelicals hold that God's saving work is applied directly to the souls of men. Evangelicals do believe that God uses means, and that ordinarily salvation is not outside of the Church, but they do not believe that God has committed his saving grace and power to any human organization. There is a great variety of difference within the Evangelical group. The question that reveals the difference best is, "What distinguishes between men who are saved and lost? Is this the work of God or man?"

(1) Universalism

This term is used here to describe the view that God does not make the difference between men. His saving operations are exerted in and on behalf of all men equally and indiscriminately. The diversity between the saved and lost arises from man and not from God. There are several different opinions of how this difference arises.

(a) Lutheranism

The Lutheran position may be briefly summarized as follows: First, God's general benevolence, which is an expression of his *voluntas generalis* (general will), is directed to the whole fallen race, and intends the salvation of all. In order to carry out this intent, he sent his Son to provide satisfaction for the sins of all. He further provides the means of grace for all men. That is, he gives all the opportunity of salvation. The difference between the saved and the lost lies in the resistance or non-resistance to the offered grace. God exercises his *voluntas specialis*, namely, to predestinate unto salvation all those whom he foresees will repent and believe the Gospel.

The Lutheran order of the decrees is as follows:

(1) Decree to create;
(2) Decree to permit fall;
(3) An antecedent, universal, conditional decree emanating from the love of God for all, willing and intending salvation for all;
(4) Decree to send Christ to render salvation for all, making salvation possible for all;
(5) Decree to give the means of grace to all;
(6) Special consequent conditional decree of predestination to eternal life of all whom God foresees will not resist his grace, and who will believe in Christ;
(7) Decree to sanctify and glorify all those thus predestinated.

(b) Remonstrant Arminianism

The position of the Remonstrants is briefly as follows: First, all men fell in Adam, and derive from him a physical and moral corruption, by which they are inclined to sin. They deny that this corruption is of the nature of sin, since man is responsible only for his voluntary acts. Man has not lost the ability to do good, and thus he has a natural ability to cooperate with God in his salvation. This ability, however, is not sufficient in itself, and thus God has given to all men sufficient grace to enable them to repent, believe, and persevere unto the end. Those who do exercise this ability and cooperate with this divine grace are converted and saved.

The order of the decrees for the Remonstrants is as follows:

(1) Decree to create;
(2) Decree to permit the fall;
(3) Decree to give Christ to make atonement for all, and to procure sufficient grace for all;
(4) Decree to give sufficient grace to all men;
(5) Decree to save those who by native ability freely cooperate with this grace;
(6) Decree to predestinate to life all whom God foresees will cooperate to the end;
(7) Decree to sanctify and glorify all those thus predestinated.

(c) Wesleyan Arminianism

Wesleyan Arminianism, otherwise known as Evangelical Arminianism, differs from Remonstrant Arminianism in that it acknowledges the depravity and moral corruption of man since the fall of Adam. Thus man is not held to have natural ability to cooperate with God's grace. Christ, who sustains a relationship for all men, similar to that of Adam, has removed the guilt of Adam's sin in his work. Every infant that comes into the world is freed from condemnation on the basis of Christ's work. Those who improve, or make good use of this universal grace will be saved. The distinction between men, lies entirely with men, as to whether they improve the grace given them.

The Wesleyan Arminian order of the decrees is as follows:

(1) Decree to create;
(2) Decree to permit the fall;
(3) Decree to send Christ to make satisfaction for the sins of all, to procure remission of original guilt and sufficient grace for all;
(4) Decree to remit the guilt of Adam's sin to all, and to give to all sufficient grace;
(5) Decree to save all those who improve this sufficient grace;
(6) Decree to predestinate to eternal life, all whom God foresees will improve the grace and persevere in it;
(7) Decree to sanctify and glorify those thus predestinated.

(2) Particularism

The difference between the universalists and the particularists is seen in the answer given to the question of who determines the diversity between the saved and the lost, God or man. Another way of putting this matter is to ask whether the distinction is by God's sovereign good pleasure, or solely because he foresees what man will do in his own autonomy. Perhaps even more pointedly, the question may be put: Do the saving operations of God actually save? Or, do they simply provide the opportunity or possibility of salvation, leaving the decision to man?

Particularists hold that the saving operations of God do actually save. They are, therefore, directed toward those whom God sovereignly determines shall benefit from them. This determination takes place in God's sovereign decrees. In other words, God makes men to differ, not only in the issues of salvation, but also in his decrees behind the salvation. The ground of this differentiation by God is not to be found in foresight of man's action, but only in his own sovereign good pleasure.

The differences that exist between particularists lie in just where they introduce the electing decree. Some see it before the decree to permit the fall, whereas others place it following this decree. We have already discussed the advantages of both supra and infralapsarianism. We shall here just list the order of the decrees, without further detailed treatment of them.

(a) Supralapsarianism

(1) Decree to elect, or to create;
(2) Decree to create, or to elect;
(3) Decree to permit the fall;
(4) Decree to send Christ to atone for the sin of the elect, and secure their salvation;
(5) Decree to give the Holy Spirit to the elect, so that he may apply the redemption purchased by Christ to them;
(6) Decree to sanctify and glorify the elect.

(b) Infralapsarianism

(1) Decree to create;
(2) Decree to permit the fall;
(3) Decree to elect;
(4) Decree to send Christ to atone for the sin of the elect, and secure their salvation;
(5) Decree to give the Holy Spirit to the elect, so that he may apply the redemption purchased by Christ to them;
(6) Decree to sanctify and glorify the elect.

(c) Amyraldianism (Post-redemptionist, Hypothetical Universalism)

(1) Decree to create;
(2) Decree to permit the fall;

(3) Decree to send Christ to make satisfaction for the sins of all, if they believe;
(4) Decree to elect;
(5) Decree to send the Holy Spirit to the elect, to enable them to believe, and to insure their actual salvation;
(6) Decree to sanctify and glorify the elect.

Chapter XXIV The Counsel of Peace

Introduction

As we enter now into the discussion of the plan of salvation, we find that there are a number of Reformed theologians who hold to an inter-Trinitarian Counsel of Salvation, and the *Pactum Salutis*. In order to avoid confusion, that has arisen out of the older designations "Covenant of Redemption" and "Covenant of Grace," it is best to use the term "Counsel" instead of "Covenant." Hoeksema has a very helpful treatment of the whole subject. He makes the point that the idea of a covenant in the Bible is not that of a pact or agreement. "It is the relation of the most intimate communion of friendship in which God reflects his own covenant life in his relation to the creature, gives to that creature life, and causes him to taste and acknowledge the highest good and the overflowing fountain of all good."[1]

Hoeksema gives this definition of the Counsel of Peace:
> [W]e would define the counsel of peace *as the eternal decree of God to reveal his own Triune covenant life in the highest possible sense of the word in the establishment and realization of a covenant outside of himself with the creature in the way of sin and grace, of death and redemption, to the glory of his holy name.* In other words, the counsel of peace, which we can also simply call the counsel of the covenant, is the eternal will, the eternal decree of God to reveal himself as the God who lives in himself a perfect covenant life of friendship, and that by receiving a people in his covenant communion and making it partaker in a creaturely way and according to the measure of the creature in his own covenant life, and thus to cause it to taste that the Lord is good.[2]

As we study the Biblical data for this counsel, we observe that each of the Persons of the Godhead sustains particular relations to one another in connection with the plan of salvation. We speak of these as the economic relations of the Trinity as established by this counsel.

I. Biblical Data to be Considered

A. The Fact of Election

Passages such as Ephesians 1:3-5, "Blessed be the God and Father of our Lord Jesus Christ . . . even as he chose us in him before the foundation of the world . . ." and Romans 8:29, "For whom he foreknew, he also foreordained to be conformed to the image of his Son . . ." speak of election as being pre-

---

1. *Reformed Dogmatics, op. cit.*, p. 322.
2. *Ibid.*, p. 330.

eminently the work of the First Person of the Trinity. It is God the Father who elects.[3]

B. The Commission

God the Father is represented in Scripture as sending his Son.[4] The Son is sent to accomplish the salvation of the elect. Christ spoke of his purpose to carry out the commission given him by his Father. "Jesus saith unto them, My meat is to do the will of him that sent me, and to accomplish his work." "For I am come down from heaven, not to do mine own will, but the will of him that sent me. And this is the will of him that sent me, that of all that which he hath given me I should lose nothing, but should raise it up at the last day."[5]

C. Promises

1. Promises to the Son

The Scripture speaks of promises made to the Son on the basis of his completing his work. Christ makes claim to these promises. "Therefore will I divide him a portion with the great, and he shall divide the spoil with the strong; because he poured out his soul unto death, and was numbered with the transgressors: He bare the sin of many, and made intercession for the transgressors."[6] "I glorified thee on the earth, having accomplished the work which thou hast given me to do. And now, Father, glorify thou me with thine own self with the glory which I had with thee before the world was. I manifested thy name unto the men whom thou gavest me out of the world: thine they were, and thou gavest them to me; and they have kept thy word." "And the glory which thou hast given me I have given them; that they may be one, even as we are one. . . . Father, I desire that they also whom thou hast given me be with me where I am, that they may behold my glory, which thou hast given me: for thou lovest me before the foundation of the world."[7]

2. Promises Concerning the Holy Spirit

The Holy Spirit's relation to the Church is seen as a gift to Christ for the completion of his saving work. It is closely related to the promises of reward to Christ. "And I will pray the Father, and he shall give you another Comforter, that he may be with you for ever, even the Spirit of truth: whom the world cannot receive; for it beholdeth him not, neither knoweth him; ye know him, for he abideth with you, and shall be in you." "But the Comforter, even the Holy Spirit, whom the Father will send in my name, he shall teach you all things, and bring to your remembrance all that I said unto you." "But when the Comforter is

---

3. I Pet. 1:2.
4. John 3:16; 17:18-19; Romans 8:3; Galatians 4:4; Hebrews 2:10.
5. John 4:34; 6:38-39; Cf. Psalms 40:7-8; Hebrews 2:14-15.
6. Isaiah 53:12; Acts 2:33-36.
7. John 17:4-5, 22, 24; Cf. Ephesians 1:20-22; 4:8; 5:24-27; Philippians 2:6-9; Titus 2:14; Hebrews 2:9; 12:2; Psalms 2:7-9.

come, whom I will send unto you from the Father, even the Spirit of Truth, which proceedeth from the Father, he shall bear witness of me."[8] "And behold, I send forth the promise of my Father unto you: but tarry ye in the city, until ye be clothed with power from on high."[9] "And being assembled together with them, he charged them not to depart from Jerusalem, but to wait for the promise of the Father, which said he, ye heard from me." "But ye shall receive power, when the Holy Spirit is come upon you . . ."[10] "But this is that which hath been spoken through the prophet Joel: And it shall be in the last days, saith God, I will pour forth of my Spirit upon all flesh."[11] "Being therefore by the right hand of God exalted, and having received of the Father the promise of the Holy Spirit, he hath poured forth this, which ye see and hear."[12]

II. Inferences from the Biblical Data

These Biblical data imply that the plan of salvation involved certain clearly defined economic relations for the different persons of the Godhead. These relations included arrangements, undertakings, and promises. In other words, there must lie behind the historic revelation of the plan of salvation certain intra-Trinitarian economic relations, whereby some functions would be carried out by the Father, others by the Son, and yet others by the Holy Spirit.

There are actions in the plan of salvation that are executed exclusively by the different Persons of the Trinity. For example, the Father alone elects in Christ, and sends the Son into the world to save. The Son alone came to give his life a ransom for many. The Spirit alone was poured out at Pentecost to regenerate and to indwell the hearts of the elect.

---

8. John 14:16, 17, 22; 15:26; Cf. 16:7.
9. Luke 24:49.
10. Acts 1:4, 8.
11. Acts 2:16-17.
12. Acts 2:33.

Chapter XXV The Covenant of Grace

Introduction

We have already observed something of the basic idea of a covenant as the term is used in the Scripture. We noted that in the case of Noah the term is used of a unilateral arrangement on the part of God with man. As such it was a sovereign administration of grace, divinely conceived, revealed and carried out. There is no idea of a bargain, or a mutual contract being established in the Noahic Covenant. It should be further observed that the Bible uses the term "covenant" in connection with revelations of God. That is, it is used of what is historical in character. This is one reason for preferring the term "counsel of peace" for the inter-Trinitarian relations to the term "covenant".

The term "Covenant of Grace" is used to refer to the gracious plan of salvation that God has given us in Christ. It may be a misleading term, if we are led to believe that there is just one gracious covenant. Actually, the Bible presents a series of covenants that may be described as gracious in character. They are all a part of the progressive revelation of the ultimate Covenant of Grace. Specifically, we find the following gracious covenants: 1) The pre-diluvian Noahic covenant (Genesis 6:18). This is the first mention of the word covenant (*berith* [1]) in the Scripture. 2) The postdiluvian Noahic covenant of common grace (Genesis 9:9-17). 3) The Abrahamic Covenant (Genesis 15, 17). 4) The Mosaic Covenant, which is mentioned as a covenant in various places (e.g. Exodus 24:5-6). 5) The Davidic Covenant (II Samuel 17; Psalms 89:3). 6) The New Covenant that is associated with the coming of Christ, and which was ratified in his blood (Jeremiah 31:31; I Corinthians 11:23ff.; Hebrews 8:8ff.). We may thus think of the grace of God coming in progressive revelations in a series of gracious covenants. They climax in the New Covenant, which is everlasting. It is in terms of it that God will be glorified eternally in his people. There cannot be any further developments for covenant revelation could not reach a higher fruition than that reached in Christ and the shedding of his blood, his resurrection, and ascension to the Tabernacle not made with hands, eternal in the heavens. Recognizing the progressive revelation of the covenant of grace, we may nevertheless speak of the whole plan of salvation under the term "Covenant of Grace". To do so is to assume the unity that exists in all of the successive revelations of the gracious covenants. We shall have more to say on this subject as we consider the dispensational interpretation of the covenants.

I. The Covenant of Grace Analyzed

Berkhof defines the covenant of grace "as that gracious agreement between the offended God and the offending but elect sinner, in which God

---

1. בְּרִית

promises salvation through faith in Christ, and the sinner accepts this believingly, promising a life of faith and obedience.[2]

A. Parties of the Covenant

As we have already noted, the Biblical idea of covenant does not coincide with our idea of a mutual contract, but involves God's unilateral binding of himself to carry out his purposes. Such binding on God's part may or may not be tied to conditioned responses in men. The Noahic covenant was made by God with all living creatures on earth. It was unconditional. The Covenant of Grace is between the two parties of God and the elect sinners. It is conditioned, first, on Christ's undertaking our salvation, and second, on the believing reception of Christ's work by the elect, which takes place as a result of the activity of the Holy Spirit.

B. The Content of the Covenant of Grace

As suggested by the definition of Berkhof, the Covenant of Grace is a promise of reconciliation between God and man on the basis of Christ's work. This promise was first suggested to Adam and Eve in Genesis 3:15, "And I will put enmity between thee (Serpent) and the woman, and between thy seed and her seed; and he shall bruise thy head, and thou shalt bruise his heel." The essence of the promise is stated to Abraham when he was given the covenant in Genesis 17:7, "And I will establish my covenant between me and thee and thy seed after thee throughout their generations for an everlasting covenant, to be a God unto thee and to thy seed after thee." Implied in these passages is the victory that Christ, the Seed of the woman, shall gain over sin and Satan. Also implied is thus the reconciling of the sinful enmity between God and man by the removal of man's sin. On the basis of this reconciliation God will accept the sinner as righteous (justification), adopt him into his family, and sanctify him unto holiness. This is to be accomplished by the coming of Christ, and the application of his work by the Holy Spirit. Ultimately, man is to be received up into glory with God.

C. The Character of the Covenant of Grace

1. It is Trinitarian

a. The Father elects and then establishes the Covenant with the elect.

b. The Son meets the requirements of a Mediator, and provides the means of effectuating the promises of the Covenant.

c. The Holy Spirit applies the blessings of the Covenant to the elect.

---

2. *Systematic Theology, op cit.*, p. 277.

2. It Is Eternal and Unbreakable

Being based on the eternal counsels of God, the work of Christ and of the Holy Spirit, this Covenant is a sure promise. God remains true to his promise, and will bring the Covenant to full realization in the elect. Man may fail to meet the covenant requirements of faith, and thus break the covenant, but God is faithful in all that he covenants.[3]

3. It Is a Particular Covenant

We have already suggested this in that we have defined the Covenant as between God and the elect. Though the provisions of the Covenant of Grace are sufficient for the salvation of all, it was not the purpose of God that all should be saved thereby. He has designed it specifically for the elect, whom he has chosen according to his own good pleasure.

4. It Is a Gracious Covenant

This is implied in the name applied to the Covenant. By grace is meant the favor of God that is given to those who deserve his wrath. In other words, it is unmerited or undeserved favor. God elected some of a hell-deserving race for salvation. He did this on the basis of his own good pleasure, and not on the basis of any foreseen goodness of men. He entered into the agreement with the Son to send him for the salvation of this sinful world (John 3:16). The Son agreed to meet the requirements as Mediator of the Covenant. He came to assume our place, and to suffer the penalty of our sins in his own body that we might have life through him. This life is offered as a free gift, to be received by faith alone. The Holy Spirit was poured out upon the Church at Pentecost, and continues to apply the redemption accomplished by Christ to the elect.

5. It Is a Conditional Covenant

The Covenant of Grace is conditional in two ways. First, there was the necessity of meeting the requirements of the Covenant of Works so that God could be both the Just and the Justifier of sinners. This demanded either that sinners themselves meet these requirements or that a Substitute for sinners do so. Since sinners are by their sins unable to change themselves, and not even desirous of doing so, it had to be done for them. Thus, the Mediator of the Covenant assumed the obligations of the sinners, and fulfilled all of the requirements of the broken covenant for them. This involved his active obedience of life as well as his passive obedience unto death. One of the most significant aspects of the gracious character of the Covenant is that God has himself provided the fulfillment of this aspect of the covenant conditions. In other words, he has entered into the Covenant of Grace to open the way of salvation to sinners, and

---

3. Genesis 17:19; Hebrews 13:20; 9:15.

he has also kept the Covenant for us. This is the good news that we declare in the Gospel.

A second condition of the Covenant is the fact that there is the required response of faith on the part of the elect. Though God has elected, and has thus determined who are to be saved, yet this does not remove the responsibility of man to respond to the Gospel. God applies the Covenant by means of the preaching of the Word calling us to repentance and faith. The invitation is given to all. The refusal to accept the Gospel is the fault of the sinner. The acceptance of the Gospel by the elect, on the other hand, is the responsibility of the sinner. The gracious character of the Gospel is seen in that God enables the elect to believe through the effectual calling of the Holy Spirit.

II. The Unity of the Covenants of Grace

We have already observed that the plan of salvation is successively revealed by a series of gracious covenants culminating in the New Covenant. It shall now be our purpose to examine the unity of these covenants. The importance of this question is seen in the light of the popularity of Dispensational theology. Those who hold to this type of theology divide Bible history into seven or more dispensations. A dispensation is defined in the *New Scofield Reference Bible* as follows:

> A dispensation is a period of time during which man is tested in respect to his obedience to some specific revelation of the will of God.
>
> Three important concepts are implied in this definition: (1) a *deposit* of divine revelation concerning God's will, embodying what God requires of man as to his conduct; (2) man's *stewardship* of this divine revelation, in which he is responsible to obey it; and (3) a *time-period*, often called an 'age', during which this divine revelation is dominant in the testing of man's obedience to God.
>
> The dispensations are progressive and connected revelation of God's dealings with man, given sometimes to the whole race and at other times to a particular people, Israel. These different dispensations are not separate ways of salvation. During each of them man is reconciled to God in only one way, i.e. by God's grace through the work of Christ that was accomplished on the cross and vindicated in his resurrection. . . .
>
> The purpose of each dispensation, then, is to place man under a specific rule of conduct, but such stewardship is not a condition of salvation. In every past dispensation unregenerate man has failed, and he has failed in this present dispensation and will in the future. But salvation has been and will continue to be available to him by God's grace through faith.[4]

It will be observed that in this note from the *New Scofield Bible* some of the points of previous criticism brought against the earlier edition of the *Scofield*

---

4. *New Scofield Bible*, (New York: Oxford University Press, 1967), p. 3.

Bible are denied. In particular, the idea that the seven dispensations were seven different ways of salvation is clearly denied here.

It is of interest to note that the *New Scofield Bible* also sets forth eight major covenants.

A covenant is a sovereign pronouncement of God by which he establishes a relationship of responsibility (1) between himself and an individual . . . , (2) between himself and mankind in general . . . , (3) between himself and a nation . . . , or (4) between himself and a specific human family. . . .

There are eight major covenants of special significance in explaining the outworking of God's purposes with man. They are: the Edenic (Genesis 2:16); the Adamic (Genesis 3:15); the Noahic (Genesis 9:16); the Abrahamic (Genesis 12:2); the Mosaic (Exodus 19:5); the Palestinian (Deuteronomy 30:3); the Davidic (II Samuel 7:16); and the New Covenant (Hebrews 8:8).[5]

It appears, at first glance, that the *New Scofield Bible* sets forth a position that is really in accord with the Covenant theology of the Westminster Standards. A careful study of the Mosaic Covenant and the Mosaic Dispensation reveals, however, that there is still a wide difference. It is the position of the historic Reformed Faith as set forth in the Westminster Standards that the Covenant of Grace is essentially the same in all its different stages. That is, there is a unity of the various gracious covenants. In other words, under this view the Mosaic Covenant and Mosaic dispensation were of grace, and their governing principle was one which, of itself, provided for salvation by grace through faith. Thus, not only was it true that men were saved during this dispensation by grace, as the dispensationalist readily admits, but that the very covenant under which Israel lived during this time was one which in its essence provided for this very salvation which the saved enjoyed. To put it in yet another way, this view asserts that the salvation that the elect enjoyed was not in spite of the Mosaic covenant, but in terms of its provisions. That this is not the view of this *New Scofield Bible* is seen in the note on the Mosaic Covenant. "The Christian is not under the conditional Mosaic Covenant of works, the law, but under the unconditional New Covenant of grace ..."[6]

The question that must be settled is whether or not the Mosaic Covenant is represented in the Scripture as a covenant of works or a covenant of grace. There are three passages that speak especially to the subject, namely, Galatians 3:17-22 and Hebrews 8:7-13; 10:16-17.

A. Galatians 3:17-22

In Galatians 3:17 Paul treats the very question that we are here discussing. He asserts that the Mosaic Covenant did not disannul the Abrahamic. That is, it did not in any degree abrogate or set aside the Abrahamic (*ouk akuroi*[7]). What Paul is asserting is that the Law is in no way inconsistent with or

---

5. *Op. cit.*, p. 5
6. *Op. cit.*, p. 95.
7. οὐκ ἀκυροῖ

contradictory to the principles of grace seen in the Abrahamic Covenant. In other words, Paul is saying that the Sinaitic dispensation was not for the purpose of setting the law in opposition to grace. This is contrary to the dispensational understanding of the law. "Law is in contrast."[8]

Galatians 3:19 confirms the interpretation we have set forth. "What then is the law? It was added because of transgressions . . ." That is, the Mosaic law or administration was an addition, not a parenthesis or a suspension of the Abrahamic Covenant. There is no suggestion that it introduces a new principle contrary to the grace of the Abrahamic administration. Rather, it is seen as an enlargement on, an extension of, or a supplement to the Abrahamic. It is foreign to Paul's thought that the Mosaic period was an intrusion of an entirely antithetical principle to the grace of the Abrahamic Covenant. This is just what the Dispensational view asserts. "The Mosaic Covenant is contrasted with the New Covenant and the Abrahamic Covenant which are based on Grace . . . Law and Grace are opposites and permit no admixture . . "[9]

Again, in verse 21 Paul seems to answer this type of teaching. "Is the law then against the promises of God? God forbid: for if there had been a law given which could make alive, verily righteousness would have been of the law." The term law (*nomos*[10]) as used throughout this passage seems clearly to refer to the Mosaic law. It might possibly be limited to the Ten Commandments, but is more likely inclusive of the whole of the Mosaic administration. Thus, Paul is asserting that the Mosaic economy is not against the promises, and, therefore, not against the Abrahamic Covenant of promise. If it is not against it, then it is in harmony with it. If it is in harmony with it, then Paul is teaching that the Mosaic economy was an extension, an enlargement or an expansion on the Abrahamic, not a contradiction to it in any way.

When Paul gives as his reason that the law was not against promise because it could not make alive, he is asserting that the law did not give a way of justification unto righteousness. If we remember that Paul is dealing with the error of the Judaizers, which was to the effect that the Mosaic economy displayed an example of how men could earn justification by works, then we see the import of this passage. Paul is saying that the Mosaic economy establishes the grand thesis of this epistle, namely, justification by grace, and grace alone. The Dispensationalists have made the same erroneous interpretation as the Judaizers of old, and this passage corrects the error.

As Paul continues in verse 22 he appeals to the whole of the Old Testament Scripture as proving justification by grace alone. How foolish this appeal would have been if the whole of the Mosaic economy had been teaching salvation by works. The Judaizers would appeal to this for such a proof, and the Dispensational view is of the same order.

---

8. *Op. cit.*, p. 1268.
9. C. F. Lincoln, *Covenant, Dispensational and Related Studies*, (unpublished syllabus), p. 24.
10. νόμος

B. Hebrews 8:7-13; 10:16-17

The writer to the Hebrews cites Jeremiah 31:31-34 in his comparison between the Old and the New Covenants. The Old Covenant is the Mosaic, and the New is the Gospel of Christ. What is the contrast? If the Dispensational view were correct, we would expect this contrast to lie in the principle of law and legalism against grace in the New Covenant. The legal principle would be the great defect of the Mosaic Covenant and dispensation.

It is true that the writer of Hebrews makes a contrast, but this particular matter is not a part of it. The faultiness of the Old Covenant is set forth to demonstrate the need for a New and better Covenant. An examination of Hebrews reveals the contrast to lie in the difference between the two orders of priesthood, Aaronic and Melchizedekian, and the Levitical sacrificial system. As one examines the Mosaic economy he cannot help but be struck with the fact that the priesthood and sacrificial system contained therein was not the legal principle of that economy. These are admittedly the gracious principles of that economy. The writer of the Hebrews finds the weakness of the Mosaic administration not in its legalism, but in the imperfections and shortcomings of the gracious provisions of that economy (7:1, 27; 8:3; 9:22ff.).

A consideration of the Levitical economy in its relation to the New Covenant is most revealing (Hebrews 9:23-24). The import is plain. The Levitical sacrifices were patterned after the heavenly Exemplar. That is, Christ, his priestly ministry, and sacrifices are the reality of which the Levitical economy is the shadow. In other words, the Levitical economy was derived from nothing less than the New Covenant itself. Its defectiveness arose from the fact that it was but a shadow and a pattern. It was not the reality. It is in the New Covenant that the reality, the fullness of grace is to be found. This being the fact, the Mosaic economy has its affinities with the New Covenant, and not with the Covenant of Works. The Old Covenant of Moses was a shadow of the New. It was an anticipation of the New. The New reaches its fullness and highest point in the priestly and heavenly ministrations of Christ, who was a priest after the order of Melchizedek. The guiding principles of the Old Covenant must be grace and not works, since it is patterned after the New Covenant, and not the Covenant of Works.

From our survey of these passages we see the unity of the gracious covenants of the Old Testament. There is a continuity of the principle of grace running from Genesis to the New Testament.[11]

---

11. The material of this section has been largely drawn from class notes of Professor John Murray, Westminster Theological Seminary.

Chapter XXVI The Person of Christ

Introduction

As we come to the Person of Christ in our study of Soteriology, it should be noted that we here limit our consideration to his Person as the Mediator of the Covenant of Grace. Those topics which have to do with his inter-Trinitarian relations belong under the *locus* of Theology. The essential requisites of the Mediator of the covenant are set forth in the *Westminster Larger Catechism*, Questions 38-42. We may summarize these requisites as follows: the Mediator should be truly God; he should be truly man; he should be one Person. It shall be our purpose in this chapter to examine each of these topics.

I. Christ Was Truly God

The Scriptures clearly teach that Christ was truly God. We have already seen that he is the Second Person of the Trinity in our study of the doctrine of the Trinity.

It is appropriate to examine some of the Scriptural proofs of the Deity of Christ at this point.

A. The Old Testament Witness to the Deity of the Messiah

1. Exodus 3:1-14

In this passage, God appeared to Moses in the burning bush. In particular, he identified himself with the name, "I AM that I AM." On the basis of Jesus' own claim that he was the "I AM" who revealed himself in the Old Testament, it is proper to view this passage as messianic. It should be observed that it is the Angel of Jehovah who appears in the burning bush. When he speaks, he speaks in the capacity of God. Thus we see the distinction from God, and the identity with God that can be understood only as we understand that there are distinct persons in the Godhead.

The special significance of this name "I AM" for our purposes is to recognize that Jesus applied it to himself. In John 8:58 he said, "Verily, verily, I say unto you, Before Abraham was born, I am." John also records another occasion when he used these same words to refer to himself. It was at the time of the betrayal. "When therefore he said unto them, I am he, they went backward, and fell to the ground."[1] It would appear that they could not stand before him in his deity. He was thus giving himself into their hands voluntarily.

The use of this expression by Jesus in reference to himself was to claim divine prerogatives for himself. He claimed eternity and the character of the un-

---

1. John 18:6.

changeableness of God as his own. The Jews responded in John 8 with the attempt to stone him. He did not suggest that they had in any way misunderstood him.

The essential picture to be found in the burning bush is that of the unchanging God. The bush burns, and yet is not consumed. Here is a God of activity, and yet an unchanging God.

The name that God gave to Moses in verse 14 makes this same point, "And God said unto Moses, I AM THAT I AM: and he said, Thus shalt thou say unto the children of Israel, I AM hath sent me unto you."[2]

2. Psalm 2:7

The second Psalm introduces the decree of anointing. "I will tell of the decree: Jehovah said unto me, Thou art my son; This day have I begotten thee." The question is how this declaration is to be understood.

a. It is possible to interpret it as a reference to the eternal and immanent relationship that has always existed between the first and second Persons of the Godhead. This is possible grammatically. The reference to the decree is not necessarily a reference to what was determined by decree, but can refer to a decree of identification. Thus, the meaning would be that the person with whom the decree is concerned is the Son of God. The Person is identified as the Son of God, and he is repeating what God has said in identifying him in this relation to God. If the passage is interpreted in this way, then the second clause, "This day have I begotten thee," is in accord with the analogy of II Sam. 7:14, "I will be his father, and he shall be my son..." The second clause then is simply a corollary to the first, and refers to a continuous relation of father and son.

b. It is possible to interpret both clauses as referring to the messianic sonship. They then have reference to the messianic identity or to the messianic investiture. The pervasive thought of the Psalm is this: verse 2 speaks of the anointed one, and verse 6 speaks of the messianic investiture. Verses 8-9 speak of the inheritance that is promised, and thus refers to the messianic kingdom. Verses 10-11 inculcate the proper attitude in reference to the messianic kingdom. Verse 7 may thus refer to the decree by which Christ was inaugurated into the messianic office, or, it could speak of his investiture and coronation as God's Son. The first clause may refer to the messianic relation, and the second to the investiture.

c. It is possible to see the first clause referring to the ontological relation within the Trinity, and the second to the messianic appointment or investiture. Psalm 89:26-27 seems to have this sort of structure and import: "He shall cry unto me, Thou art my Father, My God, and the rock of

---

2. For a treatment of this name see Chapter VIII The Names of God.

my salvation. I also will make him my first born, the highest of the kings of earth."

In seeking to come to some conclusion about these various possible interpretations of Psalm 2:7, we need to consult the New Testament usage of the passage. It is quoted in Hebrews 1:5; 5:5; and Acts 13:33.

Hebrews 1:5

In this verse both Psalm 2 and II Sam. 7:14 are quoted. The question is whether there is any indication in the context of Hebrews which gives preference to either the ontological or the messianic interpretation of these passages.

Hebrews 1:2 speaks in ontological terms, as do also verses 3, 6 and 8. The language of this whole passage in Hebrews 1 is full of the ontological relationship, and the assumption may be that the quotation in verse 5 has the same import. On the other hand, there are also messianic references in the passage. Verse 2 speaks of his being appointed heir of all things. Verse 3 speaks of the economy of providence and of the end of his economic work as a redeemer, namely, the purging of our sins and sitting down at the right hand on high. Verse 4 also alludes to the messianic investiture. His status is in virtue of his finished messianic work.

The coordination of Psalm 2:7 with II Sam. 7:14 is itself a strong argument in favor of the messianic interpretation of Psalm 2:7. II Samuel 7:14 is clearly a reference to messianic office and functions, first of Solomon and then of Christ.

The rest of the chapter also has references that are clearly messianic, such as, verse 8, which refers to the kingly scepter, and verse 9 to his anointing above his fellows.

The weight of the evidence seems to tip toward interpreting Psalm 2:7 in the messianic way.

Hebrews 5:5

Here again the context is clearly one of the messianic appointment, as reference is made to the priestly office. Psalm 110:4 is also cited in this context. The first phrase of Psalm 2:7 seems more fitted to reference to a relationship, and the second clause more to a reference to appointment. The first clause seems to give an address of identification, whereas the second seems to speak of investiture. Thus, the first clause may refer to the ontological relation, and the second to the messianic investiture. The first then would indicate the ground on which the second rests. "Thou art my Son, and therefore, I have appointed thee to this unique honor."

Acts 13:32-33

Here again the context refers to his being raised up, and thus to his messianic work. This would again favor our understanding Psalm 2 as being a reference to the messianic appointment.

Conclusion:

The New Testament usage of Psalm 2:7 clearly establishes a messianic reference by this verse. The second clause seems unquestionably to have such a reference. The first clause, on the other hand, may well refer to the ontological, intra-trinitarian relationship, which lies behind the messianic relation. If this is the proper interpretation, then the following implications may be drawn:

> 1) The messianic office rests on the eternal Sonship of Christ. Only an eternal Son would be qualified for the dignity of the office of Messiah.
> 2) The messianic office and function are expressive of the eternal and immanent relation. In other words, the commission of the economic sphere is appropriate to the super-economic sphere. The messianic office is consonant with and expressive of the eternal relation which the Son sustains to the Father in the Trinity.

3. Psalm 45

This Psalm has long been seen as messianic. It is cited in the book of Hebrews (1:8-9, quoting vss. 6-7). Though the whole Psalm is of interest, we shall treat only those verses that have direct reference to the person of the Messiah.

Verse 2 is a general statement of the glory of the Messiah. It should be observed that his fairness is greater than that of the children of men. The suggestion is that his person is more than merely human. Alexander says of the last half of the verse:

> It is only by supposing that the person here meant is the chief among ten thousand and altogether lovely, that the beauty predicated of him includes every moral and spiritual attraction, and that the grace of his lips has reference to his prophetic character and office, that the sentence can be made to seem coherent, and the promise at its close appropriate.[3]

Verse 3 pictures the King as the warrior. As he girds himself for battle, his glory and majesty are seen. Of particular interest in this verse is the title used of him, "Mighty one" (*gibbor*[4]). This is the same word used by Isaiah (9:6). In fact, when the context of this verse with verse 6 is taken into consideration, there may well have been an allusion to this Psalm by Isaiah in his use of the title "mighty God." The words "thy majesty and thy glory" are "constantly employed to denote the divine majesty (Ps. 96:6; 104:1; 111:3), as distinguished from that of mortals (Job 40:10), or as bestowed upon them by a special divine favour (Ps. 21:6). . . . The use of these expression, together with the epithet of Mighty or Hero, which is one of the characteristic titles of Messiah in prophecy (Isa. 9:6), confirms the previous conclusion that he is here the object of address."[5]

---

3. Joseph Addison Alexander, *The Psalms* (New York: Baker and Scribner, 1850), Vol. I, p. 381.
4. גִּבּוֹר
5. J. A. Alexander, *The Psalms, op. cit.*, Vol. I, p. 382.

Of particular interest are verses 5 and 6. Here we have the person addressed as God. Attempts have been made to avoid this construction. For example, *elohim*[6] is taken as a genitive instead of a vocative. This is grammatically possible. The reading then would be, "Thy throne of God is for ever and ever." It is possible to render the phrase, "Thy throne is God for ever and ever." Even if these are possible interpretations of the passage, the sense then is not clear. The more natural understanding is to take it as a vocative, "Thy throne, O God, is for ever and for ever." Such usage is to be found elsewhere in the Scripture, e.g. Psalms 43:1; 44:4; 48:9,10, etc. Further, this is the understanding of the LXX and also of the Book of Hebrews (1:8). It has some times been argued that the term *elohim* is applied to men without any implications of deity. It is true that it is sometimes used thus, but not of single individuals. Rather it has reference to the magistracy as representing the tribunal of God. Further, in the Korahite version of the Psalms the word *elohim* is the prevailing and almost only name used for deity, instead of Jehovah. It is to be expected that its usage here then refers to deity and not just to man.

When this address as God is taken with the reference to "God, thy God," anointing him, we have something of the revelation of the Trinity. Here is One who may be addressed as God, who is in turn anointed by One who is his God. Again, the reference to his being anointed "with the oil of gladness above thy fellows" suggests the fact that he will be numbered with men. He will be both God and man.

4. Psalm 110

This is one of the clearest messianic passages of the Old Testament. It is openly attested to as messianic by Jesus himself. He defended his deity by reference to it.

> Now while the Pharisees were gathered together, Jesus asked them a question, saying, What think ye of the Christ? Whose son is he? They say unto him, The son of David. He saith unto them, How then doth David in the Spirit call him Lord, saying, The Lord said unto my Lord, Sit thou on my right hand, Till I put thine enemies underneath thy feet?' If David then calleth him Lord, how is he his son? And no one was able to answer him a word, neither durst any man from that day forth ask him any more questions.[7]

Alexander introduces his comments on this Psalm thus:

> This is the counterpart of the Second Psalm, completing the prophetic picture of the conquering Messiah. The progressive development of the messianic doctrine lies in this, that the Kingship of Messiah, there alleged and confirmed by a divine decree is here assumed at the beginning, and then shown to be connected with his Priesthood, which is also solemnly proclaimed, and its perpetuity ensured by a divine oath.[8]

---

6. אֱלֹהִים
7. Mt. 22:34-46, Cf. Mk. 12:35-37; Lk. 20:41-44.
8. J. A. Alexander, *The Psalms, op. cit.*, Vol. III, p. 101.

The opening word after the title is *neum*[9] meaning "declaration" or "revelation." It is a passive participle used as a noun. It is employed in the Old Testament as a standing formula in prophecy to indicate the person speaking. The phrase *neum yehowah*[10] is often translated, "thus saith the Lord." More literally it would be "A *revelation* of Jehovah." It may be translated simply as "Jehovah saith." Its usage here does raise our anticipation of a prophetic statement.

Though the king of Israel was said to sit upon the throne of Jehovah as the representation of his kingdom, Jehovah here directs the person addressed to sit at his right hand. This is the place of highest honor. "Here the sitting at the right hand signifies not merely an idle honour, but reception into the fellowship of God as regards dignity and dominion, exaltation to a participation in God's reigning."[11] It is because he possesses in his person the divine nature that he is able to sit at the right hand of God. The idea of the Psalm is not that he is there as inactive, but rather that it is through him that the Lord will conquer his enemies. The allusion here is to his messianic rule based upon his saving work accomplished on earth. It was this to which Christ referred in Matthew 28:18, "All authority hath been given unto me in heaven and on earth." This session of Christ at the right hand of God shall last until the total subjection of all his enemies has been accomplished. At that time he shall deliver his whole kingdom unto the Father, that God may be all in all (I Cor. 15:24-28). This is said to be the most quoted verse of the Old Testament in the New. It underlies all the passages representing Christ as sitting at the right hand of the Father.[12]

The dignity of the One who thus rules from the throne of God is nothing less than divine dignity. He can sit there because he is none other than the Son of God. He himself is nothing less than God himself.

5. Isaiah 4:2

"In that day shall the branch of Jehovah be beautiful and glorious, and the fruit of the land shall be excellent and comely for them that are escaped in Israel."

Here we have the term "branch" (*tsemach*[13]) introduced as a description of the Messiah. There may be in II Samuel 23:4 an earlier allusion to this concept in the reference to salvation which the Lord must cause to grow or sprout forth. Here it is a reference of a more personal nature. This term is picked up by Jeremiah (23:5; 33:15) though here it is a Branch that is to be raised unto David. Zechariah uses the term as a proper name (3:8; 6:12). (See also Psalm 132:17.)

The phrase "branch of Jehovah" (*tsemach yehowah*) has been given various interpretations. First, it may refer to that which the Lord causes to sprout. This seems to be backed by the parallels in Jeremiah (23:5; 33:15), where it is said that the Lord will raise a branch to David. God will cause him to sprout. A second view is to take it as "He who is sprouted from the Lord." This may sim-

---

9. נְאֻם
10. נְאֻם יהוה
11. Delitzsch, *Commentary on the Psalms* (Edinburgh: T. and T. Clark, 1873), Vol. III, p. 189.
12. See Mt. 26:64; Acts 7:55-6; Rom. 8:34; I Cor. 15:25; Eph. 1:20-22; Phil. 2:9-11; Heb. 1:3, 13; 8:1; 10:12-13; I Pet. 3:22; Rev. 3:21.
13. צֶמַח

ply mean that God is the source of the branch, or more strongly that the branch is the "offspring" of Jehovah. If the latter is taken as proper, then it is a clear allusion to the deity of this One.

The parallel clause that follows suggests a definite reference to the Divine as contrasted to the human. The "fruit of the land" has its origin in the land. That this phrase is a reference to the Messiah, and not just to the fruitfulness of the land itself, is seen in the fact that there is no barrenness to which such fruitfulness is contrasted. Rather, the contrast here is between the sprout from Jehovah, and the fruit from the land. This is similar to passages such as Romans 1:3-4 and 9:5, where the two natures of Christ are contrasted and set side by side.

It is of interest to note the fact that the expression "branch of Jehovah" is not paralleled in Jeremiah where the reference is to David. That is, we do not find the expression "Branch of David" there. Instead, we find the fact that God is to raise up a branch to David. Thus there remains in the term an allusion to the divine origin of the branch to be raised up to David. A similar double reference to both the deity and humanity of the Christ is found in the promise of the virgin birth, and the child whose name is to be Immanuel. The same is true of Isaiah 9:6 where reference is made to the child born and the son given, whose name is to be the Mighty God. Micah, the contemporary of Isaiah, had also prophesied the two-sided nature of the Messiah, for he told of his place of birth, and then went on to refer to him as feeding his flock in the strength of Jehovah.

From all of this, it must be concluded that the concept of the deity of the Messiah was not unknown to the Old Testament. On the other hand, he was also to be of humble origin, to be a man.

6. Isaiah 9:6-7

This passage is one of the most explicit in the Old Testament in its witness to the Deity of Christ. "For unto us a child is born, unto us a son is given; and the government shall be upon his shoulder: and his name shall be called Wonderful, Counsellor, Mighty God, Everlasting Father, Prince of Peace" (vs. 6).

The opening phrases a child born and a son given may well refer to the miraculous birth announced in Isaiah 7:14, the birth of Immanuel. The thought is not that he shall accomplish all that is promised as a child, but that he shall be born as human beings are, that he shall be truly human.

The birth of this Child is a gift of God. He is a child, but he is also a son. . . . Why, then, inasmuch as it is so obvious that any male child born is a son, is this child also designated son? He is of course a son of David, a legitimate heir to David's throne, for he is to bear the government with all its responsibilities, and this he will do upon David's throne. . . . If this child is to be a legitimate ruler upon David's throne, it is redundant to say that he is a son of David. When, however, Isaiah does call him son, it must be with a larger reference in mind. It is the fact of sonship itself which here receives the emphasis, as is also the case in the second verse of Hebrews 1, 'God has spoken in a Son.' The Child to be born is a Son, a unique Son, a Son par excellence.[14]

As we come to the names or titles given him, we find that various attempts have been made to avoid their implications as to the deity of the Messiah.

Kimchi, a Jewish scholar, renders the passage thus: "The God, who is called and who is Wonder, Counsellor, the mighty God, the eternal Father, calls his name the Prince of Peace."[15] Calvin was one of the first to point out that the word order is against this type of translation. The words "his name" cannot be separated from the name itself by the subject of the sentence. If the question is asked, "What is the subject of the verb *wayiqra*[16], it may be answered by reference to common Hebrew usage, which leaves it indefinite. In English it may be translated, "One will call," or "One has called," or frequently, "his name shall be called." This avoids the difficulty of the word order mentioned above.

As to the number of titles there has been a good deal of difference of opinion. The Vulgate, for example, gives six: *Admirabilis, Consiliarius, Dues, Fortis, Pater futuri saeculi, Princips pacis*. The King James and American Standard versions give five names. On the other hand, there are good reasons to believe that they should be taken as four names. If this is the case, then a remarkable symmetry is seen. Each name would include two Hebrew words: *pele yoets*[17], *el gibor*[18], *avi ad*[19], *ser shalom*[20].

Further, each pair would include both a divine and a human reference. In the first two titles the first words refer to the divine, whereas the last two titles find the divine reference in the last words.

Wonderful Counsellor (*pele yoets*[17])

This is the first of these names. The first word is really a noun, "A wonder." It may be taken in construct with *yoets*, "A wonder of a Counsellor." It could also be taken as in conjunction with *yoets*, but not necessarily in the construct state. Then, it would be seen as an appositional genitive. The force then is "wonder - counsellor." (See Gen. 16:12 for an example of this construction, "a wild ass - a man.") Hengstenberg favors this construction.[21] He says, counsellor (*yoets*) designates the attribute which is here concerned, while wonder (*pele*) points out the supernatural, superhuman degree in which the King possesses this attribute, and the infinite richness of consolation and help which are to be found in such a King. As a counsellor, he is a wonder, absolutely elevated above everything which points up the divine implications involved in this word by citing the following verses: Isaiah 25:1, "I will exalt thee, I will praise thy name, for thou hast done wonders;" Ps. 77:14, "Thou art the God that doest wonders;"

---

14. Young, *The Book of Isaiah* (Grand Rapids: William B. Eerdmans Publishing Company, 1965), Vol I, pp. 329-330.
15. Cited by Young, *Isaiah*, Vol. I, p.332, fn 73 from Louis Finkelstein, *The Commentary of David Kimchi on Isaiah* (1926), p. 62.
16. וַיִּקְרָא
17. פֶּלֶא יוֹעֵץ
18. אֵל גִּבּוֹר
19. אֲבִי עַד
20. שַׂר שָׁלוֹם
21. *Christology of the Old Testament* (Edinburgh: T. and T. Clark, 1856), Vol. II, p. 87.

Judges 13:18, "Why askest thou thus after my name? -- it is wonderful," (*pele*). That is, "my whole nature is wonderful, of unfathomable depth, and cannot, therefore, be expressed by any human name."[22] Rev. 19:12 speaks of Christ having a name that no man knows, thus intimating the immeasurable glory of His nature. "That which is here, in the first instance, said of a single attribute of the King applies, at the same time, to all others, holds true of His whole nature; the King is a Wonder as a Counsellor, because His whole person is wonderful."[23]

> The Old Testament usage of this word (wonder) compels us to the conclusion that it here designates the Messiah not merely as someone extraordinary, but as one who in his very person and being is a Wonder; he is that which surpasses human thought and power; he is God himself. To designate the child with the word *pele* is to make the clearest attestation of His deity.... The position of this word as the first in the series is striking. His name shall be called Wonder. We are brought head on, as it were, with God himself as we hear the names of the child. It is our first encounter with him. All the following designations are influenced by or stand under the shadow of this first majestic name. This child who is born for us is Wonder.[24]

The Mighty God (*el gibbor*[18])

On the surface this title seems to predicate deity of the person so designated, but there have been many who would teach otherwise. For example, George Adam Smith says, "We should hesitate, therefore, to understand by these names a God in the metaphysical sense of the word."[25] He renders this title "god-hero" and understands it as just exalted language regarding a man. Some have suggested that it refers to Hezekiah in the language of court flattery. As such it is seen as a play on the meaning of the name Hezekiah, "the strength of Jehovah." It has been pointed out that men are sometimes called by the name "god" in the Bible. For example, Esau is so designated in Gen. 33:10. Actually, however, the word there used is *elohim* and not *el*. Further, the word *el* is nowhere used to designate any other than God. What is true in general of the Old Testament holds true of Isaiah.[26]

The word *gibbor* which may be translated "mighty" or "hero" etc., is also found referring to just men in the Old Testament. But, whenever it is joined with *el* it always designates deity. There are no exceptions to this. Of particular significance is the fact that the phrase occurs in the next chapter (10:20) as a clear reference to God, "A remnant shall return, even the remnant of Jacob; unto the mighty God." In both Deuteronomy 10:17 and Nehemiah 9:32 the expression "the great, the mighty, the terrible God" is found. In Jeremiah 32:18 it is "the great the mighty God." In Psalm 24:8, the word is found with Jehovah, "Who is the King of glory? Jehovah strong and mighty, Jehovah mighty in

---
22. *Idem.*
23. *Idem.*
24. Young, *op. cit.*, pp. 334-5.
25. *Commentary on Isaiah* (New York: A. C. Armstrong and Son, 1888), Vol. I, p. 135.
26. See Isaiah 31:3.

battle." In Zephaniah 3:17 *gibbor* is found in conjunction with both Jehovah and God, *elohim*.

"Jehovah thy God is in the midst of thee, a mighty one who will save."

From all of this, it may be concluded that when *gibbor* is found in conjunction with *el* deity is predicated of the person thus indicated. The question of whether the word *gibbor* is to be taken as an adjective, or as an appositional genitive may be raised. Grammatically it is possible to take it either way. As an adjective it would be translated "mighty God," and as an appositional genitive, "God, the mighty One." On the basis of the other usage of this word elsewhere in the Scripture, the weight is in favor of the adjectival usage.

It is also interesting to observe that *gibbor* is used in at least two passages to designate the Messiah. They are Psalm 45:3 and Psalm 89:19. We have already observed that deity is predicated of this Person.

From all of this we have a striking combination of data that leads us definitely to the conclusion that in Isaiah 9:6 *el gibbor* predicates deity of the child born, of the son given. We do not need to go outside of the Old Testament usage to demonstrate that the Messiah brings with him the divine attributes and prerogatives with which he exercises his office. Along with this deity is the fact that he shall be born and thus be a true human.

The Father of Eternity (*avi ad*[19])

It is difficult to be sure of the exact significance of this title. Four suggestions have been given:

a. The first is to take eternal (*ad*) as an adjective, so that it would be rendered "eternal Father." If we adopt this view, then it has to be understood in such a way as not to impinge on the fatherhood of the first person of the Trinity. Every title in this passage bears on the government of this Child who is born to exercise it. Thus the title "eternal Father" should be understood as descriptive to his government, and not a reference to his hypostatic designation in the Godhead. It is descriptive of his office and function. There would be no difficulty in applying this title to him if this is kept in mind.

b. A second interpretation is to take it as a reference to his being the Father of eternal life. That is, he is the source of eternal life.

c. Third, it may be rendered, "The One who is forever Father." The force here would be that of his being the eternal benefactor. This is to be the character of his rule. It is to be that of eternal care, mercy and love. The phrase "good shepherd" carries something of the same idea.

d. It has sometimes been interpreted as referring to the ownership of eternity. That is, "the possessor of eternity." This is a rather questionable interpretation. The precise import of it is not perfectly clear.

As we remember that the whole passage is referring to the specific office of his kingship, either the first or third interpretations could be adopted and be seen as fully in accord with the whole. There is a reflection on the fatherly character of his government and rule. Young says:

> The word 'Father' designates a quality of the Messiah with respect to his people. He acts toward them like a father. 'Thou, O Lord, art our father, our redeemer; thy name is from everlasting' (Isa. 63:16). 'Like as a father pitieth his children, so the Lord pitieth them that fear him' (Ps. 103:13).
>
> The quality of fatherhood is defined by the word eternity. The Messiah is an eternal Father...What tenderness, love and comfort are here! Eternally--a father to his people.[27]

The Prince of Peace (*sar shalom*[20])

The context of this prophecy is that of war and oppression, and now the prophet rises to the climax of the titles of the Messiah. He is to be the Prince of Peace. "He establishes peace; he seeks it and pursues it. In active vigor he is the true David, and in love of peace the real Solomon. As under David, so his kingdom will increase, and as under Solomon so will it prosper. Like the three utterances of the Aaronic blessing, the names of the Messiah die away in the word 'peace.' "[28] Just as the cessation of war does not really bring peace, the cause of war must also be removed, namely, sin. Only when this cause is removed can real peace exist. In order for there to be real peace, it must exist not only between men and men, but even more importantly between God and man. The enmity that exists between God and man must be removed. It is our sin that keeps us separated from God and him at enmity with us. The removal of this cause of enmity is the work of the Messiah. Paul celebrates the Gospel of justification by faith in these words, "Therefore being justified by faith, we have peace with God through our Lord Jesus Christ" (Romans 5:1). "For he is our peace..." (Eph. 2:14a).

> He is the Prince who has procured that peace. He procured it by removing the handwriting of ordinances that was against us and nailing it to his cross. He has satisfied the claims of absolute justice so that God in perfect justice can declare that the sinner stands in a right relationship with himself. Being at peace with the sinner, God could pardon that sinner, and give to him the peace which is a divine gift...When the peace of God is in the human heart, then there will be manifest in the world peace among men.
>
> True peace comes to us because a Child was born. That Child and he alone is the Prince of Peace. Would we have peace, it is to him that we must go.[29]

As we consider the prophecy as a whole, we find One who is to be born into this world, and yet One who bears Divine titles. In each title the supernatural and transcendent character of wisdom, might, mercy and peace is in the foreground. We have a series of designations which assert the divine and eternal

---

27. Young, *op. cit.*, p. 339.
28. *Idem.*
29. *Ibid.*, p. 340.

attributes that are to be brought to bear on the Kingdom which he administers, so that it will be established and ordered with judgment and justice from henceforth and forever. None other than a Divine Person can rule over such a kingdom.

Conclusion of the Old Testament Teaching on the Messiah

With just the few passages that have been examined, it is clear that the Old Testament concept of the Messiah included the idea that he would be of a divine nature.

B. The New Testament Witness to His Deity

Only a few passages can be looked at in detail. We shall seek to indicate the overall teaching of the different portions of the New Testament, with an examination of only a few passages. The passages chosen bear on recent errors that have arisen in Christological thought.

1. The Gospels

The Prologue of the Gospel of John clearly asserts the Deity and the pre-incarnate existence of Christ.

a. John 1:1-3, 14, 18.

Verse 1 "The Word was with God" (*ho logos en pros ton theon*[30])

There are two elements expressed by this phrase. First, the *Logos* is distinguished from God. He was with God. Second, he is in eternal coordination with God. The same is repeated again in verse two. Here our attention is directed particularly to the truth that he was in the beginning with God. He did not come to be with God. Thus there was not only a fellowship with God, but this fellowship was in eternal association with him.

"And the Word was God" (*kai theos en ho logos*[31])

A climax is reached in this phrase. It expresses the eternal identity of the *Logos* with God. In the preceding clause he was distinguished from God, and now he is identified with God. There must be two personal distinctions. It is with God that he eternally is, but it is in his identity as God that he is with God. Not he alone is God, yet he is all that God is. He must have possessed all the attributes and predicates which make God to be what he is. "John would have us realize that what the Word was in eternity was not merely God's coeternal

---

30. ὁ λόγος ἦν πρὸς τὸν θεόν
31. καὶ θεὸς ἦν ὁ λόγος

fellow, but the eternal God's self."[32] No higher predication can be made than this. John asserts that this Person has the same character as the Person he had previously asserted him to be with.

The name "*Logos*" is used only here and in verse 14 separately. In I John 1:1 the title "Word of Life" is used, and in Rev. 19:13 the construction "Word of God" is found. All of these usages are hypostatic, referring to the same Person. It is of interest to note that John does not use this name in the narrative section. His general usage is "Jesus," and occasionally "Jesus Christ." Here he designates this Person, whom he generally calls "Jesus" as "the *Logos*." The real question is whether this title of Logos belongs to him in virtue of the pre-incarnate activity, or whether it belongs in virtue of the supermundane and eternal pre-existence of the Christ? It is exceedingly difficult to answer this question. One thing that is clear, however, is that John here in the prologue has the eternal and supermundane existence of the Person in view. Whatever the particular implications of the title Logos may be, it need not prejudice the simple statements of John 1:1-3.

Verse 14 reads:

"And the Word became flesh, and dwelt among us (and we beheld his glory, glory as of the only begotten from the Father), full of grace and truth."

In this verse John identifies the Logos as the One who was incarnate. The significant thing is that John does not conceive of him as divesting himself of any of his dignity and glory when he became flesh. The meaning of the word *monogenes*[33] is important to determine, for it can make a difference in the proper formulation of the doctrine of the Trinity, especially as the relation of Christ to the Father is described. This word occurs in just four cases in the Gospel of John, and once in I John 4:9 with reference to Christ (John 1:14, 18; 3:16, 18; I John 4:9). There are only four other non-Christological passages (Luke 7:12; 8:42; 9:38; Heb. 11:17).

As Vos suggests, the problem regarding the word is that of the inherent meaning of the word, and its reference. He indicated that in some cases the second part of the word has lost any distinctive thrust, and is practically equivalent to *monos*[34]. The force of the word may then be to add a note of tenderness or poignancy over a child, as it is reflected that the child was begotten and thus highly valued.

The usage of the word in the Septuagint falls into the category just described. It is the translation of *yachid*[35] meaning "only." Only one reference occurs where the parentage is in view, Judges 11:34, "she was *monogenes* to him," which is translated, "she was his only child" in the American Standard Version. The word may carry with it the sense of uniqueness. It is of interest to note that this is the way that Warfield understands it in commenting on John 1:18. He says:

> Jesus Christ was obviously more than man; he was obviously God. His actually observed glory, John tells us further, was a 'glory as of the only

---

32. Warfield, *Biblical Doctrines* (New York: Oxford University Press, 1929), p. 192; also *Person and Work of Christ* (Philadelphia: Presbyterian and Reformed Publishing Company, 1950), p. 53.
33. μονογενής
34. μόνος, Geerhardus Vos, *The Self Disclosure of Jesus* (Grand Rapids: Wm. B. Eerdmans Co., 1954), p. 212-213.
35. יָחִיד

begotten from the Father.' It was unique; nothing like it was ever seen in another, and its uniqueness consisted precisely in its consonance with what the unique Son of God, sent forth from the Father, would naturally have; men recognized and could not but recognize in Jesus Christ the unique Son of God. . . . The visible glory of the incarnated Word was such a glory as the unique Son of God, sent forth from the Father, who was full of grace and truth, would naturally manifest.[36]

Warfield does not discuss "only begotten" here, but simply paraphrases it by the word "unique." This is in accord with the Septuagint usage of the word.

Vos, on the other hand, raises a question regarding its meaning.

Monogenes, therefore, can be equivalent to 'only,' excluding all others from the same relationship. The important question is, whether the attrition of use had so obliterated all feeling for the ending *-genes* as to render the term incapable of conveying the thought, where desired, that there was not only a single son, but that back of his existence as son, there lay also a single begetting. For this there is no proof, nor would it be easy, from the nature of the case, to furnish such proof. The etymology of the word remained so perspicuous as to keep its original force within the limits of possible resurrection.[37]

Vos goes on to compare "only begotten" with "beloved." He sees the word *monogenes* as giving the reason for the belovedness of the Son. Such is the case in John 3:16. He then develops his study of the particular use by John. He feels that there are reasons to believe that John used this word, with particular emphasis on the second half of the word in order to teach something about Christ's pre-incarnate condition. The context of John 1:14 uses the word *egeneto*[38] (became) and *egennethesan*[39] (born) in verses 12 and 13. The context in I John 4:9 also includes the term *gegennetai*[40] (begotten) in verse 7. The central theme of the whole passage is centered around that which is begotten of God.

The proximity of the very idea of begetting or being born in both of these cases suffices to create a strong presumption in favor of the significance of *-genes*. To this must be added that in both 1:14 and 1:18 the idea of *endowment by derivation* seems to be alluded to.[41]

There are two reasons given for determining the standard of Christ's glory, first, it is a glory of the only begotten, and second, it is a glory received from the Father. Vos paraphrases the thought: "such a glory as the Only begotten would have in virtue of his begetting or birth, and such as he would derive from the Father." Again he says, "The Monogenes can declare God, because he alone through his derivation from God possesses the likeness to and acquaintance with God required for such a task."[42]

---

36. *Person and Work of Christ, op. cit.*, p. 55.
37. *Self Disclosure of Jesus, op. cit.*, p. 213.
38. ἐγένετο
39. ἐγεννήθησαν
40. γεγέννηται
41. *Self Disclosure of Jesus, op. cit.*, p. 217.
42. *Idem.*

If we conclude from this study that the word *monogenes* may thus mean more than just "unique," we are still faced with the question of whether the second part of *monogenes* is to be considered as derived from *ginnesthai*[43] (to be born) or from *gennan*[44] (to beget). Either interpretation is linguistically possible. The usage in I John (3:9; 5:1, *et al.*) gives us reason to interpret it as "beget." This is especially the case in 3:9 where it is associated with *sperma*[45] (seed) of God.

Vos concludes: "The idea of a divine generation being thus prominent in the First Epistle of John, this cannot but create a presumption in favor of finding this same idea in the Gospel in 1:13, 18 and 3:3, 5, 6, 7, 8, and in the three passages where *monogenes* occurs....The emergence of *monogenes* in both contexts where this idea of the 'begetting' of believers occurs fixes the meaning of the word, with tolerable certainty, as 'Only begotten.' "[46]

As Vos goes on to point out, this term is one of the mainstays of the venerable doctrine of the eternal generation of the Son by the Father. He then presents the arguments favoring eternal generation. First, the text "God only begotten" *monogenes theos* in John 1:18 favors it, especially when seen in the context of John 1:1, where Deity is affirmed of the *Logos*. Of course, there is some question as to whether this is the genuine reading. If it is, then it might be possible to translate it differently, such as, "one who is both only begotten and God." God would then be derived from the pre-existent state, whereas the only begotten character would be derived from the incarnation. If this were the intended reading, however, we would have expected the reversal of the order, with a reference to God first, and then to the incarnation, which is the order of reality, and also of the Prologue itself in verse 14.

John 5:26 and 6:57 are used to support the idea that Christ receives the communication of life from the Father. It is debatable as to whether one can be dogmatic about these verses applying to the intra-Trinitarian relations. The Reformed understanding that there is no subordination in the Godhead suggests that these passages may better be understood as applying to the messianic Sonship instead of the intra-Divine.

John 3:16, 18; I John 4:9 teach that the Son sent into the world was already the only begotten One.

> Therefore, it may be argued, Christ is *Monogenes* apart from and previous to his mission into the world. This is certainly the only natural interpretation....The idea that God *sent* his Son, that he *gave* his only begotten Son, is robbed of its force if the *Monogenes*-filial character is regarded as beginning with the incarnation.[47]

A fourth argument favoring the eternal generation is the parallel that is found throughout John between the sonship of Jesus and that of the believer. Both are unique in character. Both are the results of Divine action. Of course, the virgin birth is such also, and yet it does take place as an earthly event,

---

43. γιννέσθαι
44. γένναν
45. σπέρμα
46. *Self Disclosure of Jesus, op. cit.*, p. 218.
47. *Idem.*

whereas the eternal generation would be a mysterious supernatural relation, just as the rebirth of believers is.

On the other side of the argument, it is pointed out that *monogenes* is introduced in the Prologue of John only after the incarnation has been mentioned (1:14). It may be answered that the Prologue is not necessarily in a chronological order.

Second, the comparison between the begetting of Christ, and the rebirth of the believer may both refer to historical events, and thus this term would refer to messianic Sonship, and not to eternal Sonship.

Vos feels that if the term is only understood as referring to the incarnation, then it may be difficult to demonstrate a pre-existent sonship of Christ.

> If not directly and explicitly, at least indirectly and impliedly, the divine sonship is carried back into the pre-existent state....The self-sacrifice of God consisted in the fact that he let his Son go out into the world. . . He was God's Son apart from and previous to that (the incarnation).[48]

b. The Works of Jesus - Matt. 9:2-6

As we view the work of Jesus, we see him performing works that are completely in accord with this first impression of him as being divine. For example, in Matthew 9:2 he said to a man sick of the palsy, "Son, be of good cheer; thy sins are forgiven." When this statement was questioned, he goes on to say, "But that ye may know that the Son of man hath authority on earth to forgive sins (then saith he to the sick of the palsy), Arise, and take up thy bed, and go unto thy house" (9:6). Here is a demonstration of his saving work, and the fact that it included the divine authority both to forgive and to heal the sick. Such authority belongs only to God alone.

c. Claims of Jesus Matt. 11:27; 14:33

He claimed equality with the Father, "All things have been delivered unto me of my Father: and no one knoweth the Son save the Father; neither doth any know the Father, save the Son, and he to whomsoever the Son willeth to reveal him" (Matthew 11:27). He performed many miracles that revealed his deity. On the occasion of his walking on the water and quieting the waters, the disciples responded by worshipping him. "And they that were in the boat worshipped him, saying, Of a truth thou are the Son of God" (Matthew 14:33). It is of interest to note that when men sought to worship them, Paul and Barnabas refused it (Acts 14:14-15), but Jesus accepted it here as his proper due.

d. Confession of Peter Matt. 16:16ff

In Matthew 16:16ff. we have the great confession of Peter that Jesus was the Christ, the Son of the Living God. Jesus accepts this confession and praises Peter for it. He then goes on to speak of building his Church, which certainly

---

48. *Ibid.*, p. 225.

was a divine prerogative. His resurrection was itself a declaration of his deity (Romans 1:4). Following the resurrection he claims all authority in heaven and in earth (Matthew 28:18). He promised that he would come back in glory as the Son of man (Matthew 25:31; Mark 8:38). Many other passages could also be cited to show his deity.

e. Other Passages

We have already noted the Prologue of John. This Gospel is full of references to his deity. In addition to the Prologue, the following passages in John may be cited as presenting the divinity of Christ: John 2:24-25; 3:16-18, 35-36; 4:14-15; 5:18, 20-22, 25-27: 11:41-44: 20:28. John presents a similar witness in his epistles. For example, I John 1:3; 2:23; 4:14-15; 5:5, 10-13, 20 speak of his deity.

The question has sometimes been raised as to whether Jesus himself was conscious of being the Messiah, and as such the Son of God. Our only way of studying his consciousness is in his words and actions as recorded in the Gospels. Vos has made a very penetrating study of this subject in his book, *The Self-Disclosure of Jesus*. Berkhof says, "For those who accept the Gospel testimony there can be no doubt as to the fact that Jesus was conscious of being the very Son of God."[49] He cites the following passages as bearing witness to the consciousness of Christ as being the very Son of God: Matthew 11:27 (Luke 10:22); Matthew 21:37-38 (Mark 12:6; Luke 20:13); Matthew 22:41-46 (Mark 13:25-27); Luke 20:41-44); Matthew 24:36 (Mark 13:32); Matthew 28:19. A special group of passages in which Jesus speaks in the first person of God as "My Father" include: Matthew 7:21; 10:32-33; 11:27; 12:50; 15:13; 16:17; 18:10, 19, 35; 20:23; 25:34; 26:29, 53; Luke 2:49; 22:29; 24:49. Again, it is in the Gospel of John that this messianic consciousness is especially seen: John 3:13; 5:17-27; 6:37-40, 57; 8:34-36; 10:17-18, 30, 35, 36.

2. The Epistles and Revelation

We have already noted the witness of John in his first epistle in connection with his gospel testimony. An examination of the epistles of Paul reveals that he held the same exalted view of Christ: Romans 1:4, 7; 9:5; I Corinthians 1:1-3; 2:8; II Corinthians 5:10; Galatians 2:20; 4:4; Philippians 2:6; Colossians 2:9; I Timothy 3:16. The writer of the Epistle to the Hebrews also attests his deity: Hebrews 1:1-3, 5, 8; 4:14; 5:8. The book of Revelation is full of passages that present Christ as the high and exalted One on the Throne of God, for example: 1:5; 1:11; 5:12; 17:14; 19:16.[50]

C. Summary on the Deity of Christ

Charles Hodge presents an excellent summary of the teaching of the Scripture on the Deity of Christ.

---

49. Berkhof, *op. cit.*, p. 317.
50. Philippians 2 will be considered in connection with the Kenosis heresy.

The Scriptures, with equal clearness, declare that Christ was truly God. ... All divine names and titles are applied to him. He is called God, the Mighty God, the Great God, God over all; Jehovah; Lord; the Lord of Lords and the King of kings. All divine attributes are ascribed to him. He is declared to be omnipresent, omniscient, almighty, and immutable, the same yesterday, today, and forever. He is set forth as the creator and upholder and ruler of the universe. All things were created by him and for him; and by him all things consist. He is the object of worship to all intelligent creatures, even the highest; all the angels (*i.e.,* all creatures between man and God) are commanded to prostrate themselves before him. He is the object of all religious sentiments; of reverence, love, faith and devotion. To him men and angels are responsible for their character and conduct. He required that men should honour him as they honored the Father; that they should exercise the same faith in him that they do in God. He declares that he and the Father are one; that those who had seen him had seen the Father also. He calls all men unto him; promises to forgive their sins; to send them the Holy Spirit; to give them rest and peace; to raise them up at the last day; and to give them eternal life. God is not more, and cannot promise more, or do more than Christ is said to be, to promise, and to do. He has, therefore, been the Christian's God from the beginning, in all ages and in all places.[51]

III. Christ Was Truly Man

A. The Old Testament Witness to His Humanity

From the first promise of the Gospel, salvation is represented as coming through the Seed of the woman (Genesis 3:15). This speaks so clearly of the humanity of the Christ that little more needs to be said. We may observe that the Seed promise is continued and appears again in the Old Testament prophecies. God promised to give to Abraham a seed, and through this Seed would all the nations of the earth be blessed. "Seed" is a collective term as well as an individual term. Thus, it could refer to the children of Israel, and to the seed that would be as innumerable as the sand of the seashore, and also could refer to the One Seed, which is the Christ (Galatians 3:16).

Of the tribes of Israel Judah is singled out as the one through which the Seed promise is to be fulfilled (Genesis 49:8-10). Of this tribe a particular family is chosen, namely, David's (II Samuel 7; Psalms 89). Thus, we see the humanity of the Messiah is clearly presented in the Old Testament. Not only was he to be human, but we have the particular nation, tribe and family of which he was to be born.

We are further told of his birth. He was to be born of a woman, but because of the uniqueness of his person and work, it must be a special birth, namely a virgin birth (Isaiah 7:14). As a man he was to be the epitome of what

---

51. *Systematic Theology, op. cit.,* Vol. II, p. 382.

the first man should have been and failed to be, namely, the obedient servant of the Lord. It is precisely under this picture that he is represented by the prophecy of Isaiah. Further, we see there his suffering as the Servant, and finally his death as a sacrifice to pay the price of sin (Isaiah 53). Along with this we see him performing the various offices that man should perform unto God, namely, that of being a prophet, priest and king. Man as created was to have performed all these functions, but in his sin he failed in all three, and thus needed One who would come and restore these functions to him. This we see Christ doing in his human nature as the Second Adam.

B. The New Testament Witness to His Humanity

The New Testament opens with the account of the birth of Jesus. True, it is a unique and special birth, and yet it is the birth of a human child, born of a woman (Matthew 1; Luke 2; Galatians 4:4). We find in both Matthew and Luke the human genealogies of Jesus. He is of the house of David, of the family of Abraham, of the seed of Adam. We see him as a boy who grew "in wisdom and stature, and in favor with God and men" (Luke 2:52). We see him subject to the affections of the human body, pain, pleasure, hunger, thirst, fatigue, suffering and death. He could be seen and felt. He had flesh and blood (Hebrews 2:14), and after the resurrection, flesh and bone (Luke 24:39). In addition to the human body, he had a true human soul. This is seen in that he increased in wisdom. He thought, reasoned and felt. He was joyful and sorrowful. He was ignorant of the time of the day of judgment. He must, therefore, have had a finite human intelligence. Thus, having a true body and a reasoning soul he was truly man. One of the most common titles of Jesus was that of "Son of Man". This expression is found some eighty times in the Gospels.

III. Christ Was One Person

A. There is a complete absence of any evidence of a twofold personality in Christ. This is in sharp contrast to the personal distinctions found in the Trinity. There we find the I-thou relationship clearly exists. Christ affirms that he and the Father are one, and yet addresses the Father as a separate person. The Father addressed the Son as a distinct person. The Holy Spirit is referred to as a different personality distinct from either Father or Son, being sent by both (John 15:26). This sort of distinction within the Person of Christ is never found. There is no record of the human speaking to the divine within him, or vice versa.

B. The individual personality of Christ is seen in the use of the singular personal pronouns regarding him. Never is there a plural term used to describe him, as though there were two persons.

C. He was One Person with two distinct natures. We have already seen that the Bible represents Christ as being both God and man. The union of these two natures is called the Hypostatic Union.

1. Definition and Principles

a. A nature is defined as a substance (hypostasis).

b. Attributes, properties and powers necessarily imply a substance of which they are manifestations.

c. Attributes cannot exist apart from a substance.

d. Where there are incompatible attributes there must be more than one distinct substance present.

e. The attributes of one substance cannot be transferred to another. For example, matter cannot be endowed with the attributes of the mind, or vice versa, otherwise matter would cease to be matter, and mind would cease to be mind.

2. Christ Had Two Distinct Natures

a. He is revealed as having all the attributes of Deity. He is declared to be God over all (Romans 9:5). He is said to be omniscient, almighty and eternal. Thus, he must be truly God.

b. He is set forth as possessing all the attributes of humanity, with body and soul. Thus, we must conclude that he was truly man.

c. The Chalcedon Creed declared him to be: "truly God and truly man, consisting also of a reasonable (rational) soul and body; of one substance with the Father as regards his Godhead, and at the same time of one substance with us as regards his manhood ..."

3. The Union of the Two Natures Was without Mixture

The properties of the two substances are incompatible, and non-transferable. No new nature was produced by the union. Thus, two distinct natures were united in the One Person of Christ.

4. Christ's Person was *Theanthropic*

Christ's person may be described as *theanthropic*, but not his natures, for this would mean that he would be neither God nor man. After the incarnation the person has both a divine and a human nature. The Biblical representation is constantly that he is both God and man. The union of the two natures was a personal or hypostatic union. It was not just the indwelling of the Person by the Spirit of God, as in the case of the Spirit dwelling within believers. It was not just a moral or sympathetic union. Rather, it was the union of the two natures in the one person.

5. The Human Nature Must Have Been an Impersonal Nature

There are not two personalities in Christ, but two natures in the One Person. Just as the personality of the man resides in the soul and not in the body, so in the case of Christ, it was the Divine Person, who assumed an impersonal human nature. In other words, he did not unite himself with a human person, but with a human nature.

D. Consequences of the Hypostatic Union

1. The Communion of Attributes

When we speak of the communion of the attributes of Christ, this is not to say that there is any transference of the attributes of one nature to the other. Rather, it is a recognition that in the One Person there are two distinct natures. Thus, the One Person has all the attributes of both natures. What is true of either nature is true of the Person. This helps explain many difficult passages of Scripture, such as the following:

a. There are passages in which the subject and the predicate both refer to the Person as a whole. Christ is called Redeemer, Lord, Prophet, Priest, King, Judge, etc.

b. There are passages in which the Person is the subject, but in which the predicate is true only of the divine nature, e.g. "Before Abraham was I am," "I and the Father are one," etc. It is possible to have the Person designated by a human name and the predicate be true only of the divine nature. "What and if ye shall see the Son of man ascend up where he was before?" (John 6:62). " ... of whom is Christ as concerning the flesh, who is over all, God blessed for ever. Amen" (Romans 9:5).

c. There are passages in which the Person is the subject, but the predicate is true only of the human nature, e.g. "I thirst," "Jesus wept," "My soul is sorrowful even unto death." Some passages refer to the Person with divine titles, but the predicate is true only of the human nature. "The Church of God, which He purchased with his blood" (Acts 20:28). "The Lord of glory was crucified" (Revelation 11:8; I Corinthians 2:8).

d. There are passages where the subject is designated by a divine title, but the predicate is applicable, not to either nature, but to the whole Person, the God-man. "The Son also himself shall be subject to him who put all things under him" (I Corinthians 15:28). "The Father is greater than I" (John 14:28). This is true of Christ as the Mediator, but not in his essence as God.

e. Concluding Observation

It is the genuine union of the two natures in Christ that accounts for this varied usage of Scripture as to the subject and predicate designations. In all that he did it is the God-man, the One Person, Christ Jesus, who acted, not one nature or the other. Hebrews 1:1-4 gives an illustration of the interchange of these terms concerning him.

> God, having of old time spoken unto the fathers in the prophets by divers portions and in divers manners, hath at the end of these days spoken unto us in [his] Son, whom he appointed heir of all things, through whom also he made the worlds; who being the effulgence of his glory, and the very image of his substance, and upholding all things by the word of his power, when he had made purification of sins, sat down on the right hand of the Majesty on high; having become by so much better than the angels, as he hath inherited a more excellent name than they.

2. The Acts of Christ Are the Acts of the Person

As we have suggested above all the acts that Christ performed, whether they be acts of one or the other of the natures, were the actions of the one person, the God-man. This is true because the one person had within himself the two distinct natures. Thus, if he as a person does that which is true only of the divine nature, it is his personal act. So also with actions that are purely human in character. These also are his personal acts. Thus, he may suffer and die in his human nature, and yet, because that human nature was united to the divine nature, in the Person of Christ, it was given infinite value, being done by the Person of Christ, who was both God and man.

3. The God-man Christ Jesus Is the Proper Object of Worship

Because of the union of the two natures in the One Person, we worship one who is both God and man. The humanity of Christ is not the ground of that worship, and yet, because it is now a part of his person, who is over all, God blessed forever, it becomes the object of adoration of saints and angels. So it was that Thomas, as he examined the wounds in his hands and feet acknowledged him as Lord and God.

4. Because He Is Both God and Man, He Can be the Mediator between God and Man

This means that he can be the representative of both. He knows the holiness and majesty of God first hand, being very God of very God. He also knows the feelings of our infirmities, being truly man, truly human. Thus, he can be our sympathetic High Priest.

As God he is ever present, almighty and infinite in all his resources to save and bless; and as man, or being also a man, he can be touched with a sense of our infirmities, was tempted as we are, was subject to the law which we violated, and endured the penalty which we had incurred.[52]

5. The Human Nature of Christ Was Exalted

He ascended up to heaven in the human nature which he had assumed at the incarnation, and in which he had been resurrected from the dead. It is of great comfort to us to know that because he has taken our human nature to the throne of God, we can be made fit to stand before that throne. We know that he is preparing a place there for us, and that we can be prepared for a heavenly abode. We are told that he shall come again in like manner to receive us unto himself.

---

52. Hodge, *op. cit.*, p. 396.

Chapter XXVII The Work of Christ

Introduction

We have already observed the fact that man as created was created a covenant creature in personal relation with God, and with covenant functions to perform. These functions constitute his office under God. They are three-fold, namely, prophetic, priestly, and kingly. As Hoeksema points out, these three functions constitute one basic office.

> There is one fundamental thought in them all, one idea that lies at the basis of all three. And this fundamental notion we may briefly express by saying that by office is meant the position of servant-king in relation to God. We might also express the same idea by describing an office-bearer as the official representative of the invisible God in the visible world. More fully defined, by office is meant the position in which man is authorized and qualified to function in the name of God and in behalf of God's covenant and kingdom to serve him and to rule under him.[1]

There is thus a two-sidedness to this office. On the one hand, man is the servant of the Lord, and on the other hand, he is to rule over the rest of creation. "From the viewpoint of his volitional life, he was priest; and from the viewpoint of his active life in relation to the world, he was king under God."[2]

By sin man became a rebel, and became the office-bearer of the devil. In all three offices he became false.

> He became the friend-servant of the devil, the slave of sin. As such he was prophet of the devil, and loved the lie; he was priest of the devil, and consecrated himself in enmity against God to the service of sin and iniquity; and he was king under Satan, and the latter became the prince of this world through him.[3]

If God was to reverse this trend he must reverse this whole pattern. This is just what is promised in the Seed promise of Genesis 3:15 where God tells Satan of the enmity that he will introduce between him and the human race. To bring this to pass there must be a renewal of the three offices in their proper function. Thus it is that Christ is found performing the three offices that man had perverted. In so doing, he restored the redeemed to his proper office again. We shall consider the work of Christ under these separate functions.

---

1. Hoeksema, *Reformed Dogmatics, op. cit.*, p. 363.
2. *Ibid.*, p. 364.
3. *Idem.*

I. Christ as Prophet

A. The Biblical Concept of the Prophet

The Hebrew word *nabi*[4] comes from the root *naba*[5] meaning "to boil forth." In the niphal this word means "to speak under divine influence." The passive form of the verb is used to suggest that the prophet is one who is moved to speak by the inspiration of God. He was thus the official ambassador or messenger of God. This is the meaning of the term as described in Exodus 7:1, "I make thee as a god to Pharaoh, and Aaron thy brother shall be thy prophet." In this connection consider also Exodus 4:16, where it is said of Aaron, "He shall be to thee instead of a mouth." Jeremiah is described as God's mouth, "Thou shalt be as my mouth."[6] Again, in his description of a prophet God said, "I will put my words in his mouth; and he shall speak unto them all that I shall command him. And it shall come to pass, that whosoever will not hearken unto my words, which he shall speak in my name, I will require it of him."[7] The prophet was thus the official spokesman of God. A distinction should be made between prophets and teachers, however. Prophets received their message directly from God by inspiration, whereas teachers are not so inspired. Thus the minister of today carries out the prophetic function in teaching the Word, and yet is not a prophet in the technical sense of the word. Since the entire Word of God was given by inspiration it may all be called prophetic in character. The prediction of the future was only an incidental aspect of the prophetic function.

In Deuteronomy 18:15ff there is a general description of the office of the prophet. This passage is twofold in its emphasis. On the one hand, there is the reference to the single Prophet who is to come, namely, the Messiah (Acts 3:23). On the other hand, there is reference to the whole office, and the possibility of false prophets arising also. The import of the message regarding the true prophets and the true Prophet is that of their being the true spokesmen of God. Thus it is that Jesus says of Himself, "The word which ye hear is not mine, but the Father's which sent me."[8] Luke records the fact that the followers of Christ considered him to be a prophet, "And they said unto him, The things concerning Jesus the Nazarene, who was a prophet mighty in deed and word before God and all the people."[9]

B. How Christ Executes the Office of a Prophet

1. Christ is the *Logos*

Underlying the prophetic function of Christ is the fact that he is revealed to us in the Bible as being the eternal *Logos*.[10] As such he is the revealer of the

---

4. נָבִיא
5. נָבָא
6. Jer. 15:19.
7. Deut. 18:18-19.
8. John 14:24.
9. Luke 24:19.
10. John 1:1.

very nature of God. He is the truth.[11] He is the light of the world.[12] He is the wisdom of God.[13]

2. Christ the Giver of the Old Testament

In I Peter 1:10-11 we are specifically told that it was the Spirit of Christ who gave the Old Testament Scriptures, "Concerning which salvation the prophets sought and searched diligently, who prophesied of the grace that should come unto you: searching what time or manner of time the Spirit of Christ, which was in them did point unto, when it testified beforehand the sufferings of Christ, and the glories that should follow them." In addition to this inspiring of the writers of the Old Testament, he manifested himself in theophanies to the saints of Old, thus revealing the truth of God to men.

3. Christ as a Prophet in His Incarnation

While here on earth Jesus was seen to be a prophet. It is of interest to observe that he defined the purpose of his coming not only in a specifically redemptive sense, but also in prophetic and didactic terms. In Luke 4 we have the account of his reading Isaiah's description of the Messiah, "The Spirit of the Lord is upon me, because he anointed me to preach good tidings to the poor: he hath sent me to proclaim release to the captives, and recovering of sight to the blind, To set at liberty them that are bruised, To proclaim the acceptable year of the Lord" (vs. 18-19). Jesus applied this passage to himself. Again at his trial before Pilate he described his purpose of coming into the world in prophetic terms, "To this end was I born, and for this purpose came I into the world, that I should be a witness unto the truth."[14] His stay on the earth was marked by his teaching ministry.

4. The Continuation of this Office

Before he departed he promised to send the Spirit of truth to the disciples. "But the Comforter, even the Holy Spirit, whom the Father will send in my name, he shall teach you all things, and bring to your remembrance all that I said unto you."[15]; "Howbeit when he, the Spirit of truth, is come he shall guide you into all the truth..."[16] Thus we see that Christ continues to perform the prophetic office even though he has now returned to Heaven. The Church is commissioned by him to continue to teach all things that he has given us.[17] "Thus from the beginning, both in his state of humiliation and of exaltation, both before and after his advent in the flesh, does Christ execute the office of a prophet in revealing to us by his Word and Spirit the will of God for our salvation."[18]

---

11. John 14:6.
12. John 8:12.
13. I Cor. 1:24, 30.
14. John 18:37.
15. John 14:26.
16. John 16:13.
17. Mt. 28:20.
18. C. Hodge, *Systematic Theology, op. cit.*, Vol. II, p. 463.

He not only speaks the Word of God infallibly; he is himself the Personal Word. He speaks not only the truth--he is THE TRUTH. The Truth in contrast with all that is provisional, relative, derived. He is the incarnate embodiment of the truth, and therefore he is TRUTH absolute and ultimate. So he transcends the bare notion of prophet, because he brings to bear upon his exercise of the prophetic function that which he uniquely and transcendently is: the Son of God. And just as Jesus defines his purpose of coming into the world in specifically redemptive terms--'The Son of Man came to give his life a ransom for many'--and is able to define the specifically redemptive purpose of his mission in prophetic terms, he does this in terms of what he distinctly and transcendently IS.[19]

II. Christ as Priest

A. The Biblical Idea of the Priest

Hebrews 5 gives a description of the basic Biblical idea of the priest. He must be one who is appointed to act for other men in things pertaining to God. He is specifically appointed to offer gifts and sacrifices for sins. This suggests the need of reconciling God, and the making of expiation of sins, and finally, of presenting the persons and their offerings to God. Further, he is charged with making intercession for the people. The writer of the Hebrews makes the point that Christ was a true priest in all of these respects, and that he was a priest of a higher order than that of Aaron.

B. Christ our Priest

After describing the concept of the priest, the writer to the Hebrews then says, "So Christ also glorified not himself to be made a high priest, but he that spake unto him, 'Thou art my Son, This day have I begotten thee:' as he saith also in another place, 'Thou art a priest for ever after the order of Melchizedek.' "[20] Here we see the clear assertion that Christ was chosen by God and appointed to the office by him. The first quotation from the Old Testament is that of the second Psalm in which the anointing of the Son is set forth, while the second reference is to Psalm 110, where the specific office to which he was anointed is designated as the priestly office.

It is of interest to note the reference to the appointment to the priesthood after the order of Melchizedek instead of the order of Aaron. It should be observed that both orders were true priestly orders. Both were types of the priesthood of Christ. The Aaronic, however, was of a lower order than that of Melchizedek. Hebrews 7 indicates something of the difference between the two. The first thing to be noted is the fact that Melchizedek was more than just a priest. He was a king, the King of Salem, and his name meant "king of righteousness." In other words, Melchizedek represented a royal priesthood, whereas

---

19. John Murray, Unpublished Class Notes.
20. Heb. 5:5-6.

Aaron was of the tribe of Levi, and forbidden to exercise royal functions. The Aaronic priesthood was a foreshadowing of one aspect of Christ's office, but the royal priesthood of Melchizedek was a much fuller type, including two offices. Further, as indicated in Hebrews 7:3, 7-10, the Aaronic priesthood depended on the descent from Levi and Aaron, whereas it was simply said that Melchizedek was a priest of God Most High, without any reference to genealogy to prove it. This is not to say that Melchizedek was more than a human being, but it does suggest that his priestly office was of such a nature that it was not passed on by genealogy. In other words, his priesthood was such because of his unique consecration to God's service, without reference to family. So also with the Christ. His priesthood was by the special appointment of God to the office. It was a unique appointment. The appointment of the Aaronic priesthood had been a true appointment under the law, but it was of temporal character. This was witnessed by the very fact that it had to be passed from man to man in the family of Levi (Heb. 7:23). On the other hand, the priesthood of Christ after the order of Melchizedek was made with an oath, and not according to the law, which made nothing perfect (Heb. 7:17-20, 28). Further, the Aaronic priesthood was marked by having sinful men who needed personal cleansing from sin before they could perform their office, whereas Christ was not so limited by a sinful nature.[21]

The *Westminster Shorter Catechism* describes the priestly function of Christ as his once offering up of himself to satisfy divine justice, and his making continual intercession for us. This is in accord with the description of the work which we call the atonement. It is appropriate that we devote a separate section of this chapter to this subject of atonement.

C. The Atonement

1. Erroneous Theories of the Atonement

Before we examine the Biblical teaching on the atonement, it seems proper to list briefly the various erroneous theories that have been suggested to account for the death of Christ. As Hoeksema suggests, they really should not be called theories of atonement, since they deny that the death of Christ was an atonement, a satisfaction of divine justice. They are, however, popularly designated as theories of the atonement, and it is under this head that we treat them.

a. The Moral Theory

Essentially this theory says that the death of Christ was to exert a moral influence upon man. Christ, by his death, was setting a great example for men in being willing to give his life for the truth. Or, Christ shows us real love by his death, and calls us to follow his example. No idea of expiation or satisfaction is involved in this theory. This theory may be condemned on several counts. First, it fails to take into account the fact that the Bible represents man as a sinner, as under condemnation by God. Man is guilty before God, and there can be no deliverance from this guilt without a full satisfaction of God's justice being made.

---

21. Heb. 7:26-28.

Second, it denies the depravity and inability of the sinner to respond to any example of love. The Bible shows that mocking of Christ was the result of his death in the hearts of sinners, not the moral improvement of these men, when they saw his great example of love. Finally, this theory fails to reckon with the direct teaching of the Scripture to the effect that the death of Christ was an expiation of sin, an atoning sacrifice, a bearing of our sins that we who were dead in sins might be made the righteousness of God in him.[22]

b. The Governmental Theory

This theory was set forth by Grotius during the Arminian controversies in the Netherlands. He asserted that the moral government of God must be maintained by God. God must demonstrate his right to punish the sinner. It is not the satisfaction of God's justice, but rather the exhibition of God's displeasure with sin. God's mercy and grace permit him to forgive sin and cancel the debt without any satisfaction, but lest he encourage man in his sin, he demonstrates his wrath against sin in the death of Christ. This theory appears more orthodox than the moral influence view, but it also fails to teach the idea of Christ's being our representative, or of his making satisfaction to God for our sins. It is true that the death of Christ was the most awful demonstration of the wrath of God against sin, but it was not just a show of that wrath. Rather Christ is represented in the Scripture as bearing our sins upon him, and thus under the wrath and curse of God in our stead. How else could he have suffered the penalty of a sinner, since he knew no sin. Actually, to make the just suffer for the unrighteous is not a show of righteousness and justice, but of the grossest injustice. Further, this sort of demonstration of God's displeasure with sin would fail to deal with the guilt of our sin. Such guilt can only be removed by the satisfaction of God's justice.

c. The Mystical Theory

This view of Christ's work denies the necessity of a blood sacrifice. Sin is not viewed as incurring guilt but as a moral weakness or sickness. Deliverance from its power is effected by the incarnation of Christ, and not by his death. It is the union of the divine and human which is particularly emphasized here. As such, this view has a strong pantheistic tendency. It has been held by Scotus Erigena in the Middle Ages, and by Osiander and Schwenckfeld at the time of the Reformation. The school of Schleiermacher has held it since the Reformation. There is a true element in this view found in the idea of the mystical union that believers have with Christ. The Bible teaches that we were crucified with him, and are raised with him and set in heavenly places with him. The dominion of sin has been broken by his death. It should be observed, however, that this breaking of the power of sin over us is seen as a fruit of the work of Christ on the Cross, not as the ground of our justification. The Bible sets forth the vicarious sacrifice of Christ satisfying divine justice as the ground of our justification. We are then made partakers in our sanctification in the mystical union with Christ.

---

22. II Cor. 5:21.

d. The Ransom theory[23]

Briefly stated the ransom theory holds that the price paid by Christ on the Cross was a ransom price that was paid to Satan. This theory was held by some of the early church fathers, and has been presented in different ways. The first is to view Satan's rights as the rights of war, in which the conquered become the slaves of the conqueror. Since Satan conquered Adam, he became the rightful owner of Adam and his posterity. Christ is seen as having paid a ransom price to free these slaves from Satan. Christ not only paid the ransom, but also broke the bonds of Satan on himself by rising from the dead.

The second form of this doctrine emphasized the conquest of Satan by Christ more than the idea of a ransom paid to him. Satan was first victorious against Adam, but Christ came and defeated him, and thus delivered men from him.

The third form of this doctrine saw the power of Satan over man as lodged in sin. Satan went too far in bringing about the death of Christ, and thus forfeited his authority over men.

All of these views have in common the idea that Christ paid a price to Satan, and not to God. It was held by a number of theologians including: Irenaeus, Origen, Theodoret, Basil, Cyril of Jerusalem, Augustine, Jerome, Hilary, Leo the Great, and others. Charles Hodge says:

> It is true that men are the captives of Satan, and under his dominion. It is true that Christ gave himself as a ransom; and that by the payment of that ransom we are freed from bondage to the prince of darkness. But it does not follow that the ransom was paid to Satan, or that he had any just claim to his authority over the children of men.[24]

2. The Biblical View of the Atonement - Satisfaction

The view that Christ's work on the Cross was a satisfaction of divine justice not only embraces the good aspects of the erroneous theories, but more importantly, it is in accord with the Bible itself. It was first set forth by Anselm, Archbishop of Canterbury (1093-1109) in his book, "*Cur Deus Homo?*" This is the view that has been held in the Protestant creeds.

a. The Source of the Atonement

As we begin to examine the Biblical presentation of the idea of the atonement, it is first appropriate to see what it teaches as to its source and necessity.

It is obvious from passages such as John 3:16 that the source of our salvation is to be found in the sovereign love of God. When we speak of the love

---

23. The ransom theory as it has been held is critiqued at this point. The positive Biblical teaching regarding ransom is dealt with later in this chapter, pp. 391-394.
24. C. Hodge, *op cit.*, p. 565.

of God, it should be observed that there are distinctions to be made between the nature of God and his exercise of that nature. God is love. He is love in his essence. This essential character of love is seen manifested within the Trinity. When it comes to the direction of his acts of love to that which is outside of his own being, we are confronted with that which comes under his decrees, and under his sovereign good pleasure. In other words, we are saying that the love within the Trinity is a part of his necessary being, but that he is sovereign in the exercise of that love beyond his inner being. That he should set his love upon hell-deserving sinners is dependent upon his sovereign good pleasure. There is no necessity that he do so, other than his own sovereign will.

Before leaving the subject of the love of God as the source of the atonement, we should observe the fact that in the Bible there are distinctions to be found regarding the love of God. First, there is the non-differentiating love of God that is the source of his goodness that comes to all men, both good and evil. It is seen in the sunshine and rain that comes to all in general.[25] In that the coming of Christ brought benefits to all, and the atonement itself brings certain temporal benefits even to the non-elect, we see that this general loving-kindness of God is included in that love which is the source of the atonement. It must be observed, however, that the Bible also speaks of a differentiating love, which results in the election of some to life eternal. Such differentiating love is clearly seen in Eph. 1:4-5, "Even as he chose us in him before the foundation of the world, that we should be holy and without blemish before him, in love having foreordained us unto adoption as sons through Jesus Christ unto himself according to the good pleasure of his will." Here we see the sovereign election asserted. It is love that is the motivating and animating cause of this election. We cannot give this love a broader connotation than the application of the predestination itself. Thus we have here an instance of differentiating love. It is a love that predestinates to a particular end.

This idea is again suggested in Eph. 2:4-5, "God being rich in mercy, for his great love wherewith he loved us, even when we were dead through our trespasses made us alive together with Christ..." Love here is the motivating force behind the actual work of Christ in dying and in our being brought from death unto life. This love again is limited to the elect. Rom. 8:31-39 also speaks of this. Here the atonement is clearly referred to in the reference in vs. 32, "He that spared not his own Son, but delivered him up for us all, how shall he not also with him freely give us all things?" The differentiation is obvious in the context of Rom. 8:29 and 33. "Who shall lay anything to the charge of God's elect?" Again the love of God in Christ is seen in verse 35 and 39 as the ultimate source of this blessing.

A passage such as John 3:16 does not deny this differentiating character of electing love. It is not necessary for us to interpret the word "world" in this verse as the elect world in order to limit the concept here. Rather, the real thrust of this passage is to be seen in the idea of "What" God loved, and not "How many" he loved. That is, it is the corrupt world. The basic idea here is the character of his love, the quality of the love that moved God to give his only begotten Son. The differentiating character of the love is not the primary thought

---

25. Matt. 5:45-48.

here, but rather the greatness of the quality of the love that would move him to send the Son.

As we think of the greatness of the atoning work of Christ, we see that it is not just the undifferentiating loving-kindness of God toward the whole world that is the motivating force behind it, but rather it is that differentiating love that resulted in a predestination unto adoption of sinners to conformity to the image of his own Son.

b. The Necessity of the Atonement

If then the love of God is the unfathomable source of the atonement, we must yet ask, Why should the love of God take its way in fulfillment in the atonement. What was the necessity of the atonement? Why must the blood of the Lord of Glory be spilt? Anselm has stated the question in its classic form: "For what necessity and for what reason did God, since he is omnipotent, take upon himself the humiliation and weakness of human nature in order to its restoration?"

Could he not have exercised his love toward us through some work of his power? Why did he not redeem men by a fiat command of power? If we say he would not, do we not limit his wisdom? As we see the transcendence of God and our own creatureliness, then the greatness of the question presses upon us. Why did God become man? Why did the Eternal One take on the temporal qualities of the creature? And, why did he, as man, have to die? Why did the Son of God die? Further, why did the Son of God die the shameful death of the cross?

Four basic answers have been given to these questions.

(1) It Was Not Necessary

The Socinian view and that which is commonly held today in liberal and modernistic circles is that no atonement was necessary. God as a gracious and merciful God can forgive without any price or satisfaction being paid. If remission is to be gratuitous no satisfaction can be required. Such a view fails to see the true nature of the graciousness of God. For the Gospel gives us the good news that God has graciously assumed the penalty for our sins and paid it himself.

(2) Antecedent Absolute Necessity

This view has not been explicitly adopted in the history of theology, but it is implicitly found in various theologians. The idea of this view is that God, in order to preserve his own honor had to save lost mankind. He could not allow his own handiwork to perish completely. He was thus under obligation to save men, and to redeem them in a way consistent with his justice. Such a redemption could be executed only by one who was both God and man. This doctrine finds some expression in Athanasius, Anselm, and A. H. Strong.

(3) Hypothetical Necessity

This is a view held by a good many worthy theologians in the history of the church. For example, Augustine, Aquinas, Thomas Goodwin, John Ball, Thomas Blake, and Samuel Rutherford have all held it. It is maintained that there was no absolute necessity for the atonement in order to carry out God's purpose of love. God could have forgiven in some other way, had he so desired. The reason that the way of atonement was chosen is to be found in the fact that this way brings more glory to God, and works greater advantages to men.

Two arguments for this view are these: First, it appears to do greater honor to the omnipotence and sovereignty of God, and gives great honor to his wisdom in choosing this way of salvation. Second, the Bible teaches that "Without the shedding of blood there IS no remission of sins." This does not say that there "COULD BE no remission." It is presumptuous to go beyond the *de facto* statement of Scripture and posit a *de jure* necessity for what God actually determines.

In answer to this, it must be remembered that it is not going beyond the Scripture to recognize that there are some things that are not possible for God to do. For example, he cannot sin. He cannot lie or deny himself. If this is so, then the question about the necessity of the atonement must be answered on the basis of our knowledge of his perfections. Are there any matters arising from his perfections that make it inherently necessary for God to accomplish salvation by means of the atonement?

(4) Consequent Absolute Necessity

The idea of a consequent absolute necessity is to be seen first of all in contrast to the antecedent of the second view. There was no necessity resting upon God to demand that he decree to save any. His nature did not require it, nor did his honor demand it. The decree to save was according to his own good pleasure. Thus, if there was any necessity, it must be viewed as consequent to the decree to save.

This view teaches that God's decree to save was a free and sovereign decree of God. Once he had so decreed, then there was an inherent necessity that required the salvation be wrought by the satisfaction of God's justice through the shedding of blood, which could only be accomplished by one who was both God and man. This is the classic Protestant viewpoint, despite the fact that some notable Reformed theologians have held the hypothetical necessity view.[26]

Arguments in favor of this view:

(a) From the Necessity of Justification

The argument for the hypothetical necessity is based on the question of whether or not God could have forgiven sins on some other basis than a blood atonement. This fails to reckon with the fact that forgiveness does not constitute

---

26. Calvin may have held a hypothetical necessity. *Institutes, op. cit.*, II, xii, 1

a salvation that will involve eternal life, and the acceptance that is necessary for God's favor. Eternal life must be based on more than just forgiveness. It rests on righteousness. The only righteousness that would be adequate for man to be made acceptable to God is that righteousness which the Scripture describes as a God-righteousness.[27] Only the Son of God incarnate could have provided such a righteousness that would be adequate for the justification of the ungodly. Thus the righteousness necessary for acceptance of sinners with God, apart from which salvation cannot be contemplated, involves the incarnation and the obedience unto death of the Son of God.

(b) The Language of Scripture Implies a Necessity

Heb. 2:10 reads, "For it became him, for whom are all things, and through whom are all things, in bringing many sons unto glory, to make the author of their salvation perfect through sufferings." The significant word for our consideration is *prepei*[28] ("became"). It might be taken as simply referring to the appropriateness of the suffering of Christ in bringing many sons to glory, but on the basis of the text itself it appears to be stronger. "It became" or "it was becoming" that he should do this. The idea of Divine propriety is expressed by the term. The stronger idea is seen in Matt. 3:15 "It becometh (*prepon estin*[29]) us to fulfill all righteousness." Not to have fulfilled all righteousness would have violated the commission of both Jesus and John. They were under obligation so to do. Again in I Cor. 11:13 "Is it seemly (*prepon estin*) that a woman pray unveiled?" The context of this passage is that the woman has according to Divine ordinance a station that requires her to be veiled in prayer. Eph. 5:3, "Fornication and all uncleanness and all covetousness: let it not be named among you, as becometh (*prepei*) saints." There is no idea of option here. It is the requirement or demand of sainthood. Heb. 7:26, "Such a High Priest became (*eprepen*[30]) us, who is holy . . . ." This is much stronger than merely being appropriate or convenient or consistent with our need. Rather, it was the indispensable need.[31] From this study of the usage of this term, we may conclude that Heb. 2:10 is speaking at least on the level of divine proprieties. That is, the divine proprieties demanded that if some were to be brought to glory, the Son of God must suffer. It is just as necessary as the fulfilling of all righteousness by Jesus, or the requirement that saints not indulge in fornication.

Heb. 2:17, "Wherefore it behooved him in all things to be made like unto his brethren, that he might become a merciful and faithful high priest in things pertaining to God, to make propitiation for the sins of the people." The word "behooved" is *opheilen*[32]. This word and its cognates express the idea of oughtness or a debt that is owed. (See Heb. 5:3, 12.) Hence in this passage the

---

27. See Rom. 1:17; 3:21-22.
28. πρέπει
29. πρέπον ἐστὶν
30. ἔπρεπεν
31. Compare also I Tim. 2:10; Titus 2:1.
32. ὠφειλεν

thought is that it was a necessity for Christ to make propitiation for the sins of the people if he was to be their priest.

Heb. 9:23, "There was therefore a necessity that the patterns of the things in the heaven be purified with these, but the things in heaven themselves with better things than these." The teaching here is that the heavenly exemplar must be purified with the blood of Christ. The word is *anagke*[33]. In the case of the patterns, there was an intrinsic necessity that they be purified by the blood of bulls and goats. The heavenly exemplar is also said to need cleansing. The necessity does not lie in heaven itself as the dwelling place of God, but in its preparation as a place for sinners. In other words, the necessity of the cleansing of heavenly things by the blood of Christ is correlated to the necessity of an atoning sacrifice by him for the elect.

(c) Argument From the Justice of God

When we remember that sin is in its essence a contradiction to God and his holiness, we see that wherever sin is, his wrath must be revealed.[34] If the wrath of God were not revealed against all unrighteousness, then God would be denying himself. If there is to be salvation, this wrath must be removed. The only provision for the removal of the wrath is propitiation. This is pointed out in Rom. 3:25-26, where it is said that propitiation is the means by which God is able to be both Just and the Justifier of sinners. To posit only a hypothetical necessity for the atonement is to fail to see the intrinsic necessity of removal of the wrath of God as it is revealed against all unrighteousness.

(d) The Cross of Christ

The enormity of the penalty paid by Christ on the Cross is itself evidence of the necessity of the atonement. Christ's prayer in Gethsemane is to the effect that if any other way could be used, let this cup pass, and yet, if not, then let it be done. We think of the Cross as the greatest demonstration of God's love for us. Would it have been love, if any other or lesser way could have accomplished the same end?

From all of these arguments, we must conclude that the best understanding of the necessity of the atonement is that of the consequent absolute necessity.

3. The Nature of the Atonement

In order to determine the nature of the atonement, it is necessary again to examine just how the Bible represents this work. There are at least five distinct terms used in the Scripture to present the work of Christ: obedience, sacrifice, propitiation, reconciliation and redemption. We shall examine each of these briefly to determine the significance of each as it relates to his atoning work.

---

33. ἀνάγκη
34. Rom. 1:18.

a. Obedience

The idea of Christ coming to do a work of obedience speaks of his whole function as the Second Man, the Last Adam. We have already noted that man as created was to have performed the office of a Servant-King. He failed in this office, and in Christ we find this office restored. It was in the capacity of Servant that Christ discharged all the phases of his atoning work.

(1) Biblical Evidence

The classic passages on the work of Christ as Servant are found in the prophecies of Isaiah, 42:1,19; 49:6; 50:10; 52:13-53:12. Again in Psalm 40:7-8 this same thought is suggested, "I delight to do thy will, O God, and thy law is upon my heart." When Jesus came, he indicated that this was his office. For example, the reason he gave for his baptism was that "it becometh us to fulfill all righteousness."[35] Again in John 4:34, "My meat is to do the will of him who sent me." John 6:38 speaks of the reason for his coming, "For I am come down from heaven, not to do mine own will, but the will of him that sent me." In particular reference to his death, he indicated that it was done as an act of obedience, "Therefore doth the Father love me, because I lay down my life that I may take it again. No one taketh it away from me, but I lay it down of myself. I have power to lay it down, and I have power to take it again. This commandment received I from my father."[36]

Paul in Phil. 2:7-8 coordinates the servant-form with that of the divine-form, as he speaks of the incarnation, and then he goes on to stress the obedience, even unto the death of the cross. There seems to be an allusion to Isaiah 53 in this reference to the Servant and his obedience.

Again in Rom 5:19 the parallel is drawn between the disobedience of Adam and the obedience of the Second Adam. "For as through the one man's disobedience the many were made sinners, even so through the obedience of the one shall many be made righteous."

In Hebrews 2:10 the captain of our salvation is made perfect through suffering. This is further interpreted in Heb. 5:8, "Though he was a Son, yet learned he obedience through the things which he suffered."

From all of these passages, we see there is a series of references to the office of Christ as Servant, and in particular to his work on the Cross as a work of obedience.

(2) The Character of this Obedience

The first thing we ought to note about the character of his obedience is that it was an inward obedience, and not just an external conformity to the law. "I delight to do thy will O my God: yea thy law is within my heart." It was for him a whole-hearted delight, so that it was his meat to do the will of his Father.

---

35. Mt. 3:15.
36. John 10:17-18.

A second aspect of the character of the obedience is that it was progressive. As a human being it was natural that he would grow and develop. Thus we read, "He increased in wisdom and stature." This we might have expected, but the rest of the verse goes beyond what we might have anticipated, "and in favor with God and man."[37] If he grew in wisdom, as is expressly asserted here, we may assume that he also grew in obedience. For, as he came to be more and more aware of the will of the Father, there would be the increase in self-conscious obedience to it. The increase in favor with God suggests the idea that he was continually conforming to the increasing demands of the will of God. Thus as the expanding demands of God were being discharged, so there would be a corresponding increase of satisfaction on the Father's part. Hebrews 5:8 confirms this progressive character of his obedience, as it says that he learned obedience. To say that the obedience was progressive is not to suggest that there was any disobedience at any point. His obedience at every stage of life was perfect, but as he grew the demands of God became more and more extensive, until finally he was confronted with the demand of death. The climactic requirement was his death. This was implied in his words in John 10:17-18, and by Paul in Phil. 2:8.

The climactic aspect of this is seen in the very nature of death. It is a complete contradiction to the sinless, normal man. Thus it was a contradiction to Jesus, who was holy, harmless and undefiled, separated from sinners.[38] Even we who are sinners dread it and recoil from it. With Christ it was not death inflicted on a sinner, but a death undertaken by the sinless Son of God. Thus for him, death did not overtake him. He laid down his own life. "He poured out his soul" and laid down his life; he dismissed his spirit. It is when we see his death thus in its uniqueness, that we can begin to have some understanding of his reaction in Gethsemane. Mk. 14:33 tells us that he began to be amazed.

Mark's expression that he began to be amazed points to a particular experience. And what is this new experience? It is just this: that he was now looking into the abyss of damnation through which he was to pass--the abyss of damnation that was already beginning to inundate his soul--the abyss that he was to extinguish in his passion. And so there was the inevitable recoil from this awful ordeal, because it could not have been otherwise. We must reckon with the enormity of his agony and the reality of his human nature. For what was this abyss of damnation? It was the unrelieved and unmitigated judgment of God against sin, and it filled him with horror and dread. Could it have been otherwise? If he had not recoiled, there would have been unreality to the ordeal. If there had not been recoil, such stoical indifference would have been unnatural, for the tender sensibilities and sensitivities of his human nature. And the recoil, the horror and dread are the proof of the incomparable ordeal and of the reality of his human nature.[39]

---

37. Luke 2:52.
38. Heb. 7:26.
39. John Murray, Unpublished Class Notes on Soteriology, p. 16.

(3) The Relation of the Obedience to our Salvation

Hebrews 2:10 and 5:9 suggest the relation of the obedience to our salvation. Both passages speak of Christ in his office, as Captain or Author of our salvation. The Captain or Author of our salvation is made perfect through sufferings (2:10), or learned obedience so that he was able to fulfill all the demands of the Father. In other words, he was constituted a Savior by obedience. That is, our salvation was wrought by the obedience of Christ.

(4) Active and Passive Obedience

It has been customary in Reformed theology to speak of the obedience of Christ under the categories of active and passive. The active obedience refers to his positive fulfillment of all the demands of the Father's will, and particularly the fulfillment of the demands of the Law. His active obedience was more than just the compliance to the Law of God, for there were demands of the Father's will that were exclusively his.

The passive obedience refers to his submission to the penal sanctions of the Law of God. It should be observed that even in his passive obedience, he was actively obeying the demands of the Father. Thus he spoke of laying down his life as his action, and that it was the fulfillment of the will of the Father (John 10:17-18). The passive obedience is the ground for the remission of our sins, the expiation of guilt and the propitiation of the wrath of God. But salvation is more than forgiveness, expiation and propitiation. It involves also the acceptance with God as righteous. Salvation thus demands a righteousness that is adequate to constitute us righteous, namely, a righteousness of God, "But now apart from the law a righteousness of God hath been manifested, being witnessed by the law and the prophets; even the righteousness of God through faith in Jesus Christ unto all them that believe; for there is no distinction. . . . "[40] It is Christ's active fulfillment of the law that becomes the ground of our acceptance with God. It is this righteousness that is imputed to us.

The obedience of Christ was, therefore, God's provision of grace for meeting the demand of righteousness. The active obedience positively earned the righteousness that Adam had forfeited. The passive obedience met the requirements of God against the sinner. It is this latter aspect that particularly concerns us as we examine the sacrificial character of the atoning work of Christ.

b. Sacrifice

(1) Biblical Evidence that His Death was a Sacrifice

That Christ's death is represented in the Scriptures as a sacrifice hardly needs to be demonstrated. The whole of the Old Testament economy with its sacrificial system pointed to the coming Messiah, who would lay down his own

---

40. Rom. 3:21-22.

life as the Sacrifice to satisfy Divine Justice. We shall examine the significance of the Old Testament sacrifices at greater length. First, let it be noted that among the many passages that speak of the Messiah's sacrifice the most notable in the Old Testament is Isaiah 53. In the New Testament we find Rom. 3:25 speaking of him being offered as a propitiatory sacrifice. Again Rom. 8:3 speaks of his being sent as a sin offering. Gal. 1:4 says that he "gave himself for our sins." Eph. 5:2 says he "gave himself for us, an offering and a sacrifice to God for a sweet-smelling savour." Heb. 9 and 10 set him forth as offering himself as a sacrifice. I John 2:2 speaks of him as "the propitiation for our sins; and not for ours only, but also for the sins of the whole world." One of the favorite presentations of Christ in the book of Revelation is that of the Lamb that was slain (Rev. 5:6, 8, 12; 7:14; 13:8, etc.).

(2) The Biblical Idea of Sacrifice

Since Christ's death is represented in Scripture as a sacrifice, it is important to examine the Biblical idea of sacrifice in order to understand the real significance of his death. It should be observed that the Old Testament sacrifices really derive their significance from the sacrifice of Christ, and not the reverse. In other words, the types are but the shadow of the reality of the anti-type. Yet, since we have much more detail given to us regarding these sacrifices, we turn to them in order to discover the meaning of the sacrificial work of Christ.

As one considers the whole ritual of sacrifice, it appears that one of the most significant ideas seen in it is that of substitution. The worshipper comes desiring to enter into the presence and fellowship of God. His sins bar him from doing this directly. Consequently he brings a substitute for himself. As prescribed by the Mosaic law the laying on of hands was required in all kinds of blood sacrifices.[41] "This is a natural and expressive symbol of transfer from the person imposing to the person or thing upon which they are imposed. Thus it is used to designate a personal substitute or representative."[42] In particular reference to sins, the sins are said to be transferred to the sacrifice, which then bore the penalty of the sinner. "And Aaron shall lay both his hands upon the head of the live goat, and confess over him all the iniquities of the children of Israel, and all their transgression in all their sins, putting them upon the head of the goat...and the goat shall bear upon him all their iniquities unto a land not inhabited" (Lev. 16:21). In the prescriptions for the selection of a suitable sacrifice, the animal must be physically perfect. Only such an animal was suitable to be a substitute for the sinner. Only the innocent and pure life could be accepted as a substitute in the stead of the polluted one. It is of interest to observe that with the offering of Isaac, the ram is given by God to be offered in his stead.[43] The offering is called a sin offering[44] or a trespass offering (Lev. 5:6, 16, 19, etc.) because, though perfect and innocent before the laying on of hands, it becomes

---
41. Lev. 1:4; 3:2; 4:4, 15; 16:21; II Chron. 29:23.
42. A. A. Hodge, *The Atonement* (Grand Rapids: William B. Eerdmans Publishing Company, 1953), p. 134.
43. Gen. 22:13.
44. Lev. 4:3; 8:20-28.

the substitute for the sinner, and must pay the penalty for that sin, namely, death. So it was that Jesus, who knew no sin was "made sin for us."[45]

(3) Levitical Sacrifices

For a treatment of the various Levitical forms of sacrifice, the student is referred to Fairbairn's *Typology of Scripture*, and to Vos' *Biblical Theology*. We shall just summarize the basic significance of the five Levitical offerings:
   (1) Burnt offerings involved propitiation, expiation and consecration;
   (2) Meal offerings represented sanctification and service;
   (3) Peace offerings represented communion with God;
   (4) Sin offerings included propitiation and expiation, the covering of sin by the blood;
   (5) Trespass offerings added to propitiation and expiation the reparation and compensation for the trespass.

All of these sacrifices symbolized a present religious significance for the Israelite worshipper, which is the point mentioned regarding each above. They also typified the future sacrifice of Christ. Though not all of these different offerings are cited in connection with the work of Christ by the New Testament, we may safely conclude that all did point to his work. He is the Anti-type of all of them and not just of one or the other. He is clearly our sin offering (Heb. 9; 13:11-13), and made atonement for us through the shedding of his own blood, and the carrying away of our sins, as the goats of the sin offering on the Day of Atonement did (Lev. 16; Heb. 9). Not only did he propitiate God's wrath and expiate our sins, he also made preparation for us in his active obedience, thus fulfilling the trespass offering idea (Is. 53:10). On the basis of his shed blood he has entered into glory where he makes continual intercession for us, which fulfills the type of the burnt offering, with the smoke rising as a sweet savor to God. He is declared to be our peace (Eph. 2:14), and it is through his blood shed and body broken that we have communion with God (Rom. 5:1). Thus he is our Peace offering. Finally, in his resurrection we have the newness of life in which we are now to walk as we become united to him. Thus the meal offering representing sanctification and service is fulfilled in him.

There were four blood sacrifices in the Old Testament. They are: the burnt offering, the peace offering, the sin offering, and the trespass offering. Each different type of offering had its own distinguishing characteristics.[46] The sin and trespass offerings were especially provided to take care of the liability incurred by sin. They involved the removal of the guilt. They did this through the payment of the life of the victim. Such a requirement grew out of the original Edenic threat against sin as given by God to Adam before the fall, "in the day that thou eatest thereof thou shalt surely die."[47] This concept of the wages of sin being death runs throughout the Scripture.[48] Thus, when the Tabernacle is built

---

45. II Cor. 5:21.
46. See Leviticus 1-7.
47. Gen. 2:17.
48. Rom. 6:23.

as a pattern of the Heavenly places,[49] the only way of access to the Holy of Holies was through the blood sacrifice as prescribed by God.[50] This was to be done only once a year on the day of atonement. The sacrifices of the bullock for the high priest, and the two goats for the people were called sin offerings (*chataah*[51]). It is of interest to note the question of whether the significance of the shed blood is the presentation of the life to God or the death of the victim. Leon Morris presents a good treatment of this subject in his *Apostolic Preaching of the Cross*[52] (Chapter III). He concludes: "We conclude then, that the evidence afforded by the use of the term *dam*[53] in the Old Testament indicates that it signifies life violently taken rather than the continued presence of life available for some new function, in short, death rather than life, and that this is supported by the reference to the atonement."[54] Thus the worshipper transferred his sin to the animal, and the wage of that sin being death, the animal must be slain in the stead of the worshipper. In Hebrews 9:6-15, 23, 24, 28; 13:10-13 the writer clearly identifies the death of Christ as a sin-offering. On the other hand, Isaiah 53:10 says, "And when his soul shall make a trespass offering (*asham*[55]) for sin." Other than these references to the sin and trespass offerings the sacrifice of Christ is not specifically identified with the specific offerings of the Levitical system. There is an additional reference in I Cor. 5:7 to the Passover, "For our passover also hath been sacrificed, even Christ." The impression that one gets from the New Testament references to the Old in connection with the death of Christ is that his death is viewed in the light of the sin or trespass offering. That is, his death is viewed as expiatory and propitiatory in nature.

(4) Expiation and Propitiation

Before going further, it would be well to make clear the distinctions between expiation and propitiation. Both of these words translate the Greek word *hilaskesthai*[56]. Expiation has reference to the guilt of sin. To expiate is to remove or cover the guilt of sin. Propitiation has reference to the wrath or displeasure of God. To propitiate is to satisfy the divine justice and thus to appease his wrath. In the Biblical usage of the term, the justice of God is satisfied by the propitiatory sacrifice. There is current today an attack on the idea of propitiation. It is argued that propitiation of the wrath of God is foreign to the New Testament. Thus in some of the more recent translations of the New Testament, such as the *RSV* and the *New English Bible* "expiation" or other terms are used in place of propitiation, which was used in the KJV and *ASV*. C. H. Dodd is one of the chief exponents of this view.[57] Among the best defenses of the view that propitiation is the proper understanding of the sacrifice of Christ are Leon Morris' *The Apostolic Preaching of the Cross*; and Roger Nicole, "C. H. Dodd and

---

49. Heb. 9:23-24.
50. Lev. 16.
51. חטאת
52. (Grand Rapids: William B. Eerdmans Publishing Company, 1955).
53. דם
54. Morris,*op. cit.*, p. 117.
55. אשם
56. ἱλάσκεσθαι
57. See *Journal of Theological Studies* XXXII, July 1931, reprinted in *The Bible and the Greeks*.

the Doctrine of Propitiation," *Westminster Theological Journal*, May 1955. We shall give the main thrust of the arguments refuting C. H. Dodd in these two works.

The verb *hilaskomai*[58] "to propitiate" occurs twice in the New Testament, namely, in the prayer of the publican, "O God, be propitiated for me (*hilastheti moi*[59]) the sinner" (Luke 18:13); and Hebrews 2:17, "Wherefore it behooved him in all things to be made like unto his brethren, that he might become a merciful and faithful high priest in things pertaining to God, to make propitiation (*hilaskesthai*) for the sins of the people." The noun *hilasmos*[60] "propitiation" is found in the expression "propitiation for our sins" twice. I John 2:1-2, "My little children these things write I unto you that ye may not sin. And if any man sin, we have an Advocate with the Father, Jesus Christ, the righteous: and he is the propitiation for our sins (*hilasmos estin peri ton hamartion hemon*[61]); and not for ours only, but also for the whole world."[62] Romans 3:25 says that God set forth Christ "to be a propitiation (*hilasterion*[63]) through faith in his blood..." This same word is found in Hebrews 9:5 where it is translated "mercy-seat." The adjective *hileos*[64] is found in Matt. 16:22 in an idiomatic usage, "Be it far from thee," and in Heb. 8:12, "I will be merciful (propitious *hileos*) to their iniquities..." We see from this survey that there are only four texts in the New Testament that use this word in reference to the death of Christ. This should not lead us to treat the concept lightly, however, "for the idea is often present where this particular terminology is absent, as for example in passages dealing with the wrath of God."[65]

Morris presents a rather full study of the picture of the wrath of God as found in the Old Testament. He says, "To the men of the Old Testament the wrath of God is both very real and very serious. God is not thought of as capriciously angry (like deities of the heathen), but, because he is a moral Being, his anger is directed towards wrongdoing in any shape or form." But it is only fair to add that the Old Testament consistently regards God as a God of mercy, so that, though men may and do sin and thus draw down upon themselves the consequences of his wrath, yet God delights not in the death of the sinner, and he provides ways in which the consequences of sin may be averted."[66] He then gives a full study of the usage of the *hilaskomai* group of words in the Septuagint. He concludes by agreeing with Westcott and Dodd to the effect that God is not said to be propitiated in the Old Testament in the crude sense of a pagan deity.[67] But, as he goes on, men have often gone too far in this line of thought to deny the whole idea of propitiation. "Examination of this word group brought us inevitably into the circle of ideas associated with *kipper*[68] and *kopher*[69], which

---

58. ἰλάσκομαι, 1st aorist imperative ἰλάσθητι
59. ἰλάσθητί μοι
60. ἰλασμός
61. ἰλασμός ἐστιν περὶ τῶν ἁμαρτιῶν ἡμῶν
62. I John 2:2.
63. ἰλαστήριον
64. Ἴλεως
65. Morris, *op. cit.*, p. 125.
66. *Op. cit.*, p. 131.
67. *Ibid.*, p. 155.
68. כִּפֶּר
69. כֹּפֶר

further strengthens the conclusion that *hilaskomai*, etc., retain the idea of putting away the divine anger, since we see that ransom which we may not unjustly regard as a propitiation... Thus we conclude that the sense of propitiation seems to be established from passages in which *hilaskomai* and its cognates occur."[70]

As we turn to the New Testament, we again find the idea of the wrath of God revealed against all unrighteousness to be the teaching of all sections of the New Testament. This is clearly seen in Romans 1-3 which is the context of the first usage of the term *hilaskesthai* (3:25). The question here is whether the term is to be translated by "expiation" or by "propitiation." The context seems clearly to demand the idea of appeasing the wrath of God, or propitiation.

> Wrath has occupied such an important place in the argument leading up to this section that we are justified in looking for some expression indicative of its cancellation in the process which brings about salvation. More than expiation is required, for to speak of expiation is to deal in sub-personal categories, as Horace Bushnell long ago pointed out, whereas the relationship between God and man must be thought of as personal in the fullest sense.[71]

Hebrews 2:17 uses the verb *hilaskesthai*. The construction of this verse suggests the idea of expiation instead of propitiation. The accusative after the verb is sin and not God. A. A. Hodge says, "All admit that the Greek word *hilaskesthai*, and its cognates *hilasmos* and *hilasterion*, have universally and from time immemorial, the sense, when construed with God of *propitiation*, and when construed with sin of expiation in the strict sense."[72] Leon Morris, however, says, "The accusative after the verb attracts our attention, for despite much that is written these days it is a very unusual construction."[73] He then proceeds to examine the verbs *hilaskomai* and *exilaskomai*[74] (which does not occur in the New Testament, but is found in the Septuagint). He concludes that of the 116 uses of these verbs there are only eight with sin as the accusative, and that it is debatable that more than two of these clearly imply expiation. Further, the New Testament gives examples of other verbs in which the accusative after them often replaces a prepositional construction, with little or no change of meaning.

> Under these circumstances it does not seem wise to lay great stress upon the occurrence of the accusative in Heb. 2:17. In the case of none of the verbs above[75] can it be said that its meaning has been seriously modified by using the accusative instead of the prepositional construction and accordingly it may fairly be asked, Why should we believe that it is otherwise with *hilaskomai*? Thus it seems best to take the accusative in Heb. 2:17 as an accusative of general respect and to understand the meaning of the expression as 'to make propitiation with regard to the sins of the people'. This seems a better course than ignoring the usual

---

70. Morris, *op. cit.*, p. 156.
71. *Ibid.*, p. 169-170.
72. *Op. cit.*, p. 139.
73. Morris, *op. cit.*, p. 175.
74. ἐξιλάσκομαι
75. Morris, *op. cit.*, p. 176.

meaning of the verb and making it signify here nothing more than expiate'.[76]

John Owen argues in a similar fashion against the change of the meaning of the verb. He says:

In the use of this word, then, there is always understood--(1st.) An *offense*, crime, guilt, or debt, to be taken away; (2d.) A *person offended*, to be pacified, atoned, reconciled; (3d.) A *person offending*, to be pardoned, accepted; (4th.) A *sacrifice* or other means of making the atonement. Sometimes one is expressed, sometimes another, but the use of the word hath respect unto them all.[77]

When we turn to I John 2:2 we again, as in the case of Romans 3:25, find a context that demands the idea of propitiation. The righteousness of God has been mentioned, the sin of the sinner is in view, and the idea of Christ as an Advocate before the holy God virtually demands the idea of propitiation.

The point is that Christ is said to be 'an advocate with the Father', and if we sinners need an advocate with God, then obviously we are in no good case, our misdeeds prevail against us, we are about to feel the hostility of God to all that is sinful. Under these circumstances we may well speak of Christ turning away the wrath of God, and thus, *hilasmos* is a natural word in the context.[78]

In I John 4:10 we again find no reason for changing the meaning of the word from propitiation to expiation. Morris makes a pertinent comment; "Concerning the use of the term in I Jn. iv.10 we would simply observe that, if *hilasmos* be given its usual meaning, we have here one of those resounding paradoxes which means so much for the understanding of the Christian view of sacrifice, for then we would have the thought that it is to God himself that we owe the removal of God's wrath,[79] whereas, if the more colourless meaning 'expiation' is understood, the verse is much less striking."[80] The critics of propitiation have failed to see the thrust of this passage, when they suggest that the idea of propitiation is contrary to the idea of God as love. It is in this passage that the assertion that God is love is made. The love of God is manifested, not in a soft, sentimental idea of God's simply passing over our sins out of the goodness of his heart. Rather, the love of God is seen in that he undertakes the work of propitiating his own wrath for us. It may be objected that if God's love for us was prior to the death of Christ, why was any propitiation of his wrath needed. Such an objection fails to distinguish between love and being propitious. Eph. 2:3 expressly asserts that the saints were children of wrath, until his grace was actually administered to them in the Gospel. The problem that those who hold this objection have is to recognize that God can both love and at the same time have wrath. Love and hatred are incompatible, but not love and wrath. The love and anger which may be the simultaneous feeling of a human parent for his child illustrates the compatibility of the two. These two attitudes may co-exist in the

---

76. *Ibid.*, pp. 176-177.
77. John Owen, *An Exposition of the Epistle to the Hebrews* (Edinburgh: J. Ritchie, 1813), Vol. III, pp. 474ff.
78. Morris, *op. cit.*, pp. 178-179.
79. Cf. Col. 1. 21ff. for a similar statement with regard to the removal of enmity.
80. *Op. cit.*, p. 179.

mind of God for his elect. The work of Christ is the provision of God's love to remove the occasion of the wrath of God.

One final word about the work of Christ as a propitiatory sacrifice must be given. To deny the propitiatory character of the sacrifice of Christ is to deny the essence of the atonement. For the atonement means that Christ *bore* our sins. He who knew no sin was made sin for us. How can we think of him carrying our sins, without bearing the judgment for those sins? Sin and judgment are inseparable in the Scriptures. Thus to bear the sins, is to bear the judgment. That is the significance of the death of Christ. The wages of sin is death, and he paid that wage. The death referred to is spiritual, separation from God, the falling under the wrath and judgment of God. Hell is the unrelieved wrath and displeasure of God. If Jesus was in our place bearing our sins, then he must have borne the whole judgment of God upon our sin. The denial of propitiation strikes at the very heart of the vicarious identification of Christ with us. When Christ was identified with us he was made sin. This means that he bore our sins, and came into as close contact with sin as possible without becoming a sinner.

c. Reconciliation

(1) Vocabulary

There are several words found in the New Testament that speak of reconciliation. They are as follows:

katallage[81] - Reconciliation - This is the only substantive in the New Testament used to designate reconciliation.

katallasso[82] - To reconcile.

apokatallasso[83] - To reconcile.

diallasso[84] - To reconcile - Though this term is not used in the New Testament of the work of Christ, it is a synonymous term with the others, as may be seen in the Septuagint.

(2) The New Testament references

It is of interest to note that the Scriptural references to reconciliation are in terms of our being reconciled to God (Rom. 5:10) and God reconciles us to himself (II Cor. 5:18-19; Eph. 2:16; Col. 1:20-22). It is never expressly stated that God is reconciled to us. On the basis of this usage, it has been asserted that the work of Christ on the cross was not directed to God, but toward man. The enmity removed is not his, but ours.[85] It should be observed at the outset that

---

81. καταλλαγή
82. καταλλάσσω
83. ἀποκαταλλάσσω
84. διαλλάσσω
85. This view is held by William Barclay and a number of other modern scholars.

reconciliation does concern our enmity with God. It has to do with our sin, and our sin is certainly an enmity against God. But, a fuller analysis of the Scripture indicates that reconciliation involves more than just this idea.

Matthew 5:24 gives a good example of the significance of reconciliation. The passage deals with reconciliation between brothers. We have here the only New Testament usage of the word *diallasso*, which the Septuagint usage shows to be a synonym of *katallasso*. The passage reads, "First, be reconciled to thy brother." The worshipper, while bringing his gift to the altar is reminded that his brother has something against him. He is commanded to "be reconciled" with his brother. Observe the fact that the alienation here is not that of the worshipper, but of the brother toward the worshipper. Thus the command to be reconciled is not directed against his own anger, but against the anger of the brother. If we draw the parallels with our relation to God, we see then the language of Scripture that speaks of our being reconciled to God is not primarily directed toward our own anger, but toward his alienation with us.

Romans 11:15 gives another interesting insight into the usage of the term reconciliation in the New Testament. Here there is a contrast between the Jews and the Gentiles, and the change of God's attitude toward the Gentiles, which is expressed by the term reconciliation. "For if the casting away of them be the reconciling (*katallage*) of the world, what shall the receiving of them be, but life from the dead?" The term reconciliation is here speaking of the change in attitude by God and not of the Gentiles. This is evident from the fact that this term is set in contrast to the "casting away" of the Jews, and not their attitude toward God. Nowhere in this passage is attention focused on the attitude of the Jews or the Gentiles, but all the way through, it is on the attitude of God to man. Therefore *katallage* means the removal of God's alienation from the Gentiles, not their subjective alienation from God.

(a) Romans 5:8-11

As we look now to the passages that speak of the work of Christ as reconciliation, it is well to remember the fact that sin not only incurs the wrath of God, but also alienation from him. Thus reconciliation is not merely a reference to the subjective change that takes place in our hearts, but involves a change of the alienation from God. Romans 5:8-11 is one of the chief passages dealing with reconciliation. In Romans 5:8-11 the love of God toward us is being stressed. This love is seen in the fact that Christ died for us, and this while we were yet sinners.

Professor Murray observes that verse 8:
> ... enunciates the essence of what follows in the next three verses. For the clause 'Christ died for us' (vs. 8) is expanded in verse 10 in the words 'we were reconciled to God through the death of his Son.' Hence it is reconciliation through the death of Christ that was accomplished *while we were yet sinners*. How nullifying this would be if the reconciliation were conceived of as consisting in the change of our hearts from sin and enmity to love and penitence! The whole point of verse 8 is that what God did in the death of Christ took place when we were still sinners and did not consist in nor was it premised upon any change

in us. To introduce the thought of change in us is to contradict the pivot of the declaration.[86]

In verses 9 and 10 justified and reconciled are placed in parallel passages. Justified and reconciled must, therefore, belong to the same orbit; they express similar concepts. But the term justify, particularly in this epistle, has forensic meaning. It does not mean to make righteous; it is declarative in form and is the opposite to condemn. It is concerned with judicial relation. Reconcile must likewise have the same force and cannot refer to an inward change of heart and attitude.

(b) II Cor. 5:18-19

The same conclusion is derived from II Corinthians 5:19: "God was in Christ reconciling the world to himself, not imputing their trespasses unto them." Not imputing trespasses is either explanatory of the reconciliation or it is the consequence of the latter. In either case it shows the category to which reconciliation belongs and is far removed from that of a subjective change in us."[87]

In both Romans 5:10 and II Cor. 5:18, 19 we find the aorist tense used. The emphasis in both is that of a completed act. The death of Christ and the resulting reconciliation was a once for all action. Subjective reconciliation would involve a continuous process.

In II Corinthians 5:21 we are pointed to the kind of action involved in reconciliation spoken of in the preceding verses. It is that 'him who knew no sin he made to be sin for us.' This unquestionably refers to the vicarious sin-bearing of Christ and belongs to the objective realm; it has no affinity with a subjective change registered in our hearts.[88]

A further argument for this understanding of reconciliation is derived from the enmity that is contemplated in Rom. 5:10. In verse 8 the Apostle referred to our being sinners, and in verse 10 he referred to the enmity. It would be perfectly possible to interpret the enmity of verse 10 as our enmity against God in parallel with our sin against him of verse 8. But Rom. 11:28 gives us another usage of this very term. Paul speaks of Israel, "They are enemies on your account." The enmity here must refer to the alienation from God's favor. They are spoken of as rejected and disinherited (Rom. 11:15). Further, the enmity is contrasted to beloved. Certainly the beloved refers to God's attitude and relation to them, and not the subjective attitude of men. From this we see that the enmity of Romans 5:10 could very properly be understood as referring to God's alienation from us.

This sense is well suited to the thought of Romans 5:10. For what the reconciliation accomplishes is the removal of God's alienation, his holy enmity. The argument is that if God by the death of his Son removed his holy enmity against us, brought us into a state of favor, how much

---

86. Murray, *The Atonement*, a monograph in Biblical and Theological Studies Series, (Philadelphia: Presbyterian and Reformed Publishing Company, 1962), p. 18.
87. *Ibid.*, pp. 18-19.
88. *Ibid.*, p. 19.

more shall we be saved from the wrath of God by the resurrection of Christ.[89]

On this point Murray is ready to acknowledge that we cannot be absolutely dogmatic that this is the proper sense of the word enmity. If it is not, then 5:10 is parallel in meaning to 5:8.

Romans 5:11 speaks of reconciliation as something received, "Through whom we have now received the reconciliation" (*ten katallagen elabomen*[90])." This form of expression does not fit with the idea of reconciliation as a subjective change. Rather it is viewed as a gift bestowed. The idea is that we have received a status in which God is no longer alienated from us, one in which we have peace and fellowship with him.

In II Cor. 5:19 we have reference to the proclamation of reconciliation. "He hath committed to us the word of reconciliation." We have received the responsibility of proclaiming reconciliation. This is another way of referring to the Gospel that we are to proclaim. The Gospel we proclaim is the good news of what Christ has done for us, not the subjective change that takes place in us. Of course, the Gospel will produce a subjective change, but this is not the good news that we proclaim. In other words, the Gospel does have demands that arise from its preaching, but the demands are not the Gospel itself. The basic message of the Gospel is not exhortation or appeal, it is the good news of what God has done for us.

When we consider the exhortation of II Cor. 5:20, "Be ye reconciled to God," we find a passage that has been variously interpreted. Even some of the most orthodox commentators have regarded it as an appeal to us to lay aside our enmity.

This is not in itself an improper appeal as the appropriate response to the gospel proclamation. But the evidences derived from the passages dealt with do not support this interpretation. It is rather an appeal to us to take advantage of that which *the reconciliation* is and has accomplished. It is to the effect: enter into the grace of the reconciliation; embrace the truth that 'him who knew no sin he made to be sin for us, that we might be made the righteousness of God in him' (II Cor. 5:21).[91]

As we conclude this consideration of reconciliation it is appropriate to turn again to Morris. He says, "It is the consistent teaching of Scripture that man could not overcome the cause of enmity. The barrier which the sin of man had erected the wit of man could not find means to remove. But in the death of him who was "made sin" for man the cause of the enmity was squarely faced and removed. Therefore a complete reconciliation results, so that man turns to God in repentance and trust, and God looks on man with favour and not in wrath."[92]

The disruption that sin caused between God and man was healed in the work of Christ, and man may again be brought into fellowship with God. "At no point does the provision of the atonement register its grace and glory more than

---

89. Murray, unpublished mimeographed class notes, p. 27.
90. τὴν καταλλαγὴν ἐλάβομεν
91. Murray, *Atonement*, p. 20.
92. *Op. cit.*, p. 222.

at the point where our separation from God is the exigency contemplated and communion with God the secured result."[93]

d. Redemption

(1) The Old Testament Idea of Redemption

There are two terms found in the Old Testament that express the idea of redemption: *gaal*[94] and *padah*[95]. These terms can be used regarding deliverance, without any reference to the mode of the deliverance (Gen. 48:16; Is. 29:22). On the other hand they are frequently used in connection with the release by payment of a price, or buying back.

The term is used to refer to the sanctifying of the firstborn of man or beast. For clean animals no substitutionary price was paid. They were sacrificed on the altar. In the case of both man and unclean animals, which could not be sacrificed on the altar, a provision of redemption was made. (Ex. 13:11-15; Num. 18:15ff.). Again the term is used in connection with the restoration of land or property. Property was not sold in perpetuity (Lev. 25:23-4). A kinsman could purchase back property. (See Ruth 4.) This price was called a redemption (*geullah*[96]). A study of these and other usages of the words in the Old Testament indicates the following: First, redemption refers to the recovery of person or things; Second, a redemption price was necessary for such a recovery; Third, when an intermediary accomplished the redemption, he was called a redeemer (*goel*).

More important for our study, however, are the references of the terms for redemption to the salvation of God's people. Both words are used in this way. The exodus of the Israelites from Egypt was designated by this name (Ex. 6:6; 15:13; Deut. 7:8). From the exodus as redemption, we come to the following points: First, it was a deliverance from bondage to a foreign power; Second, it was accomplished by the power of God's outstretched arm; Third, the idea of a price paid is present. This is expressly asserted in such passages as Ex. 15:16; Deut. 32:6; Ps. 74:2; Is. 11:11. In Isaiah 43:3-4, Egypt, Ethiopia and Sheba are called the substitutionary ransom for Israel.

One last idea from the Old Testament should be observed. It is the fact that the mediator, who secured redemption, was called the *goel* or kinsman-redeemer. This term is referred to the Lord himself in a number of passages, such as, Job 19:25; Ps. 19:14; Is. 41:14; 43:14; 44:6, 24; 47:4; 48:17; 49:7, 26; 54:5, 8; 60:16; Jer. 50:34. In Isaiah 59:20, the reference is to the effect that the Redeemer will come to Zion. It is quoted in Rom. 11:26. Thus the work of the Messiah was specifically referred to as that of a redeemer.

---

93. Murray, *Atonement*, p. 21.
94. אָגַל
95. פָּדָה
96. גְּאֻלָּה

(2) Redemption in the New Testament

The following terms are used in the New Testament to refer to redemption:

>*lutron*[97] - a ransom. This is the most explicit of the terms. It is used only twice, but it is a statement of Christ regarding his own work (Mt. 20:28; Mk. 10:45).
>
>*lutrousthai*[98] - the verbal form of ransom (Lk. 24:21; Tit. 2:14; I Pet. 1:18).
>
>*lutrosin*[99] - another substantive form (Lk. 1:68; 2:38; Heb. 9:12).
>
>*apolutrosis*[100] - a compound form. The most frequently used form of this root (Lk. 21:28; Rom. 3:24; 8:23; I Cor. 1:30; Eph. 1:7,14; 4:30; Col. 1:14; Heb. 9:15; 11:35).
>
>*agorazo*[101] - a purchase, occurring a few times in the redemptive sense (I Cor. 6:20; 7:23; II Pet. 2:1; Rev. 5:9; 14:3,4).
>
>*exagorazo*[102] - the idea of purchase, occurring only twice (Gal. 3:13; 4:5).

A survey of the passages referring to the work of Christ in these terms shows clearly the idea of a redemption that was accomplished by the payment of a price, namely, the bloodshed of our Savior.

In Mt. 20:28; Mk. 10:45, Christ refers to his own work in terms of coming to give his life a ransom for many. Note three ideas: First, the work he came to do was that of ransom. Second, the price of the ransom was the giving of his own life. Third, this ransom price was substitutionary in character. B. B. Warfield points out that with this description of his own work given to the disciples, it is no wonder that we find the same idea repeated in the words of his followers.[103] Paul echoes these words in I Tim. 2:6. Again in Titus 2:14 the giving of Christ is represented as having a two-fold design, namely, of ransom from iniquity, and of sanctifying the ransomed possession. In Rom. 3:24, Paul speaks of being justified through the redemption in Christ, and immediately relates this to the blood shed. The idea of a ransom price is implicit. In Gal. 3:13; 4:5 Paul uses different terms, and yet the notion of a purchase from bondage is present. The bondage to the ceremonial law is in view in 4:5, and the price paid in 3:13 is his being made a curse for us and being made under the law in 4:5. The effect of

---

97. λύτρον
98. λυτροῦσθαι
99. λύτρωσιν
100. ἀπολύτρωσις
101. ἀγοράζω
102. ἐξαγοράζω
103. *Biblical Doctrines, op. cit.*, p. 361.

this price paid was deliverance from both kinds of bondage. In I Cor. 6:20 and 7:23, the idea of a purchase price is present, without any mention of the price itself. The writer of the epistle to the Hebrews also associates the blood of Christ with the securing of redemption. John in Revelation 5:9 expressly names the blood of Christ in connection with redemption (*agorazo*).

From this brief survey, it is clear that the New Testament presents the concept of redemption as that of a ransom payment for the deliverance of the lost. The price paid is the shedding of the blood of Christ. Luke 1:68; 2:38 see the deliverance as from bondage to the oppression of an alien power. This, as we noted in the earlier section, was one of the prominent ideas in the Old Testament usage of the term redemption. Remembering the stress in the Old Testament on the mighty arm of the Lord being the means of deliverance, and consequently the victory over Egypt, it is not surprising to find a note of triumph associated with redemption in the New Testament, John 12:31-33; Heb. 2:14-15. This is one of the points that modern theologians such as Gustaf Aulen have seen.[104] It is a fact that is frequently overlooked in orthodox theology. The idea of the ransom price being the instrument to deliver from the bondage to sin was prominent in the early history of the Church. It gave rise to the ransom theory of atonement, which was prominent for about ten centuries. These early theologians saw the two ideas that we have noted in our survey of the Biblical data, namely, the payment of a ransom price, and the deliverance from the power of Satan. Their error was in seeing the price as paid to Satan. Anselm in his *Cur Deus Homo* showed the error in this idea. There has tended to be an overreaction in Protestant theology to the whole ransom theory, and thus a failure to take into account the reality of Satan's power, and the work of Christ in releasing us from it. Christ represents him as "prince of this world."[105] Heb. 2:14 speaks of the work of Christ thus, "That he might destroy him that had the power of death." Again Col. 2:15 says, "He spoiled the principalities and powers, and he made a show of them openly, triumphing over them." So also in I John 3:8, "For this purpose was the Son of God manifested, that he might destroy the works of the devil." We see from these passages the note of the triumphal aspect of Christ's redemptive work. Though there is an emphasis on the demonic in contemporary theology, a careful analysis of this thought shows that it is an emphasis on what is viewed as "the mythological." The Bible, on the other hand, is stressing the reality of the demonic, and of the triumph of Jesus over this real evil.

If we are sensitive to the demands of the Kingdom of God and the glory of Christ, then we will be sensitive to the invisible kingdom of which Satan is the prince. If we are sensitive to the demands of the kingdom of God and the glory of Christ, and sensitive to the principalities and powers against which we wrestle, then the real essence of our consolation, faith, and hope will be traced back to the victory which Christ once-for-all secured, when he destroyed the god of this world and brought to nought him who had power of death.[106]

---

104. Gustav Aulen, *Christus Victor* (London: SPCK, 1953).
105. John 12:31.
106. Murray, mimeographed class notes, p. 35.

It should be remembered that the very first promise of the Gospel in Gen. 3:15 had the note of victory in it. This promise reaches its consummation in the casting out of the old serpent, the Devil (Rev. 20:10). The redemption of Israel from Egypt was the picture of this triumph as God delivered his people with a mighty Arm.

(3) Bondage from which we are Delivered

The term redemption as it suggests deliverance is a comprehensive term covering our salvation. There are various aspects of our salvation that are included in the deliverance of the redemption of Christ.

First, there is redemption from sin. Titus 2:14 says he "gave himself for us, that he might redeem us from all iniquity, and purify for himself a people for his own possession, zealous of good works." Our redemption is defined as "forgiveness of our trespasses."[107] The same thought is suggested by Heb. 9:15, "And for this cause he is the Mediator of a New Covenant, that a death having taken place for the redemption of the transgressions that were under the first covenant, they that have been called may receive the promise of the eternal inheritance." The Old Testament uses a similar statement in Ps. 130:7-8, "O Israel, hope in Jehovah; For with Jehovah there is loving-kindness, and with him is plenteous redemption. And he will redeem Israel from all his iniquities."

The bondage of sin involves three aspects, namely, guilt, defilement, and power. The redemption of Christ removes us from the bondage to sin in all three of these aspects. Romans 3:24, which is found after Paul has been stressing the guiltiness of our sin, no doubt has reference to the removal of guilt. Titus 2:14 adds to the deliverance from guilt the idea of sanctification, or the deliverance from the defilement of sin. The redemption from the power of sin is particularly the triumphal character of his work.

> It is in this connection that a strand of New Testament teaching needs to be appreciated but which is frequently overlooked. It is that not only is Christ regarded as having died for the believer, but the believer is represented as having died in Christ and as having been raised up with him in newness of life. This is the result of union with Christ. For by this union Christ is not only united to those who have been given to him, but they are united with him. Hence not only did Christ die for them but they died in him and rose with him.[108] It is this fact of having died with Christ in the efficacy of his death and of having risen with him in the power of his resurrection that insures for all the people of God deliverance from the dominion of sin.[109]

Second, not only is redemption a deliverance from sin, but there is also reference to deliverance from the law as a consequence of his redeeming work. We are redeemed from the "curse of the law."[110] We are under the curse of the

---

107. Eph. 1:7.
108. Cf. Rom 6:1-10; II Cor. 5:14, 15; Eph. 2:1-7; Col. 3:1-4; I Pet. 4:1-2.
109. Murray, *Redemption Accomplished and Applied* (Grand Rapids: William B. Eerdmans Publishing Company, 1955; London: Banner of Truth Trust, 1961), p. 54.
110. Gal. 3:13.

law for having failed at any single point in keeping the law.[111] Since no one is able to keep the law, but all have sinned and come short of the glory of God, there can be no salvation unless we are delivered from the curse of the law. This we are told explicitly was a consequence of his work. The price he paid was that of taking the curse due us upon himself. He bore the full wrath of God due to us for that curse. "That curse he bore and that curse he exhausted."[112] In addition to deliverance from the ceremonial aspect of the law he purchased our adoption as sons. This is suggested by Gal. 4:5, where it is said that we are redeemed "that we might receive the adoption of sons," the idea being that Israel, under the ceremonial law, was under it as a tutor. Now that Christ was made under the law and completely fulfilled it, God's people are not under the ceremonial aspect any longer. Instead of being under the tutor, we now are adopted as sons, and have all the privileges and liberty of sons.

One final aspect of the law being fulfilled in the work of Christ is the relation of the law to the covenant of works. We have already observed under the section on the atonement as obedience that Christ's work may be seen as fulfilling all of the obedience that Adam had failed to keep. Thus it was by his obedience that he constituted many righteous (Rom. 5:19). Christ has accomplished by his obedience, both active and passive, what Adam failed to do by his disobedience.

As we conclude this section in which we have considered the nature of the atonement, it would be well for us to summarize our findings. The obedience of Christ met the demands for righteousness. The sacrifice of Christ met the needs arising out of our guilt. He propitiated the wrath of God. Reconciliation met the need caused by the alienation from God, and redemption the needs arising from our bondage.

(4) The Perfection of the Atonement

Under this head we shall consider the uniqueness, finality and efficacy of the atonement.

(a) The Uniqueness and Finality of the Atonement of Christ

It is the clear representation of Scripture that the work of Christ on the cross was a once-for-all sacrifice. This is one of the major points of the book of Hebrews as it asserts that the sacrifice of Christ is better than the Old Testament sacrifices. They had to be repeated, whereas, Christ's was a once-for-all sacrifice, "Nor yet that he should offer himself often, as the high priest entereth into the holy place year by year with blood not his own; else must he often have suffered since the foundation of the world; but now once at the end of the ages hath he been manifested to put away sin by the sacrifice of himself."[113] Again verse 28 says, "So Christ also having been once offered to bear the sins of many..."

---

111. Gal. 3:10.
112. Murray, *op. cit.*, p. 50.
113. Heb. 9:25,26.

"And every priest indeed standeth day by day ministering and offering oftentimes the same sacrifices, the which can never take away sins: but he, when he had offered one sacrifice for sins forever, sat down on the right hand of God."[114] Again in verse 14, "For by one offering he hath perfected for ever them that are sanctified."

He only was able to perform the office of the high priest and offer himself as the sacrifice. Though we are called on to imitate him as our Example, nevertheless, even if we have to die for him, our death could not expiate guilt, propitiate wrath, reconcile the world to God or secure redemption. "All these categories belong exclusively to Christ."[115]

(b) The Efficacy of Christ's Atonement

The question here is whether he accomplished his purpose in laying down his life. The Bible represents that work as accomplishing each of the purposes for which it was designed. His obedience was not just a token obedience but he fulfilled all righteousness.[116] His obedience constituted us righteous.[117] His sacrifice purged our guilt.[118] He propitiated the wrath of God for our sins.[119] He actually bore our sins and the wrath of God for them.[120] He wrought reconciliation, so that the alienation of God was removed.[121] He purchased the Church with his own blood and obtained eternal redemption.[122] "The sum is that Christ by his own atoning work *secured* and *insured* the consummation that will be registered in the resurrection of life (cf. John 6:39)."[123]

(5) The Extent of the Atonement

(a) What the Question Is Not Addressing

The question to be answered in this section is, "For whom did Christ die?" Before seeking to find the Biblical answer to the question, it is well to indicate negatively what is not before us. It is not the question of the sufficiency of Christ's death. It is clear from the fact that the Gospel is to be offered to the whole world it must be sufficient to save any and all who come. An analysis of the nature of sin and of the requirement for salvation indicates that the same penalty would have been exacted of Christ had he been dying for just one person, or for all the world. The intrinsic efficacy of his Person gives to his sacrifice infinite worth. Thus it is not a question of sufficiency at all.

Second, it is not a question of the suitability of his work to save all. It is represented in Scripture as suitable for any and all sinners.

---

114. Heb. 10:11-12.
115. Murray, *Atonement*, p. 27.
116. Mt. 3:15; Heb. 5:9.
117. Rom. 5:19.
118. Heb. 1:3.
119. I John 2:2.
120. Is. 53:6, 11; I Pet. 2:24.
121. Rom. 5:9, 10; 8;32.
122. Acts 20:28; Heb. 9:12.
123. Murray, *Atonement*, p. 27.

Third, it is not the question of objective availability of and the offer of redemption. Even the casual reading of the passages of Scripture offering the Gospel to the world clearly show that it is sincerely offered, and is thus available for all to receive. The very fact that the atonement is of infinite sufficiency implies that it is objectively available to all.

Fourth, it is not the question of whether there are benefits for all from the death of Christ.

> The unbelieving and reprobate in this world enjoy numerous benefits that flow from the fact that Christ died and rose again. The mediatorial dominion of Christ is universal. Christ is head over all things and is given authority in heaven and in earth. It is within this mediatorial dominion that all the blessings which men enjoy are dispensed. ...Since all benefits and blessings are within the realm of Christ's dominion and since this dominion rests upon his finished work of atonement, the benefits innumerable which are enjoyed by all men indiscriminately are related to the death of Christ and may be said to accrue from it in one way or another. If they thus flow from the death of Christ they were intended thus to flow. It is proper, therefore, to say that the enjoyment of certain benefits, even by the non-elect and reprobate, falls within the design of the death of Christ. The denial of universal atonement does not carry with it the denial of any such relation that the benefits enjoyed by all men may sustain to Christ's death and finished work.[124]

Fifth, it is not even the question of who has redemption applied to them. All agree that it is applied only to those who are saved.

(b) The Question that Is Being Addressed

Positively the question is: For whom did Christ die? For whom did he propitiate the wrath of God? For whom did he bring reconciliation in his death? Whom did he redeem by his death? Whom did he contemplate as the objects of his atoning and redeeming work when he died on Calvary? Professor Murray puts the question thus:

> Did Christ come to make the salvation of all men possible, to remove obstacles that stood in the way of salvation, and merely to make provision for salvation? Or did he come to save his people? Did he come to put all men in a savable state? Or did he come to secure the salvation of all those who are ordained to eternal life? Did he come to make men redeemable? Or did he come effectually and infallibly to redeem? The doctrine of the atonement must be radically revised if, as atonement, it applies to those who finally perish as well as to those who are the heirs of eternal life. In that event we should have to dilute the grand categories in terms of which the Scripture defines the atonement and deprive them of their precious import and glory.[125]

We may answer these questions simply with just a quick reference to the words of Jesus, "I have come down from heaven, not to do my own will but the

---
124. Murray, *Redemption*, p. 72.
125. *Redemption*, pp. 73-74.

will of him who sent me. And this is the will of him who sent me, that of everything which he hath given to me I should lose nothing, but should raise it up in the last day."[126]

There are a number of Biblical passages that teach the limited or particular idea of the atonement. First the concept is explicitly taught by every one of the Old Testament sacrifices. They were all particular or limited in their design. With the weight of the Old Testament testimony that sacrifices are always definite, we can understand why there is no special case made for this idea in the New Testament. Rather, it is the assumed idea of the atonement.

(c) Biblical Evidence

(1) Old Testament Particularism

The great passage on the atonement in the Old Testament, namely, Isaiah 52:13-53:12 supports the doctrine of the limited design and extent of the atonement. At first 53:6 might seem to support the universal atonement, where it says, "The Lord hath laid on him the iniquity of us all." The parallel passage of verse 11, however, suggests the limitation of the "all" to the "many". Further, there is in verse 6 itself the limitation of Isaiah in which he says "*us* all." In other words, Isaiah is not saying that the Servant suffered for all the world, but for us all. Verses 4 and 5 have this limiting concept also: "He hath borne OUR griefs, carried OUR sorrows... But he was wounded for OUR iniquities; the chastisement of OUR peace was upon him, and with his stripes WE are healed." In these verses we have "a sustained series of possessive pronouns, and the same speakers are in view in verse 6. There is no universalism in verse 6 unless the CONFESSIONAL AFFIRMATIONS in the preceding verses are universalized, and that is not the case. We cannot extend the "all of us" in verse 6 beyond the confessional affirmations in the preceding verses."[127] As we go on in this chapter, we find in verse 8 the specific reference to "my people" which tells us who is in view in the rest of the chapter in verses 6, 11, and 12. Again verse 10 speaks of his seed. Here the idea of a substitution for the seed is clearly stated, "When his soul shall make an offering for sin, he shall see his seed, he shall prolong his days." There is in 52:15 an ethnic universalism, "So shall he sprinkle many nations," but there is no idea of a distributive, each and every one, universalism in this passage. On the contrary, there are clear limitations in the passage.

(2) New Testament Particularism

For example, when the angel announced to Joseph the name of Jesus, he said, "And she shall bring forth a son and thou shalt call his name Jesus: for he shall save *his people* from their sins."[128] Two things should be observed in this verse. First, Jesus is actually to save, not just make salvation possible. Second, his saving work is designed specifically for his people. Jesus described the pur-

---

126. John 6:38-39.
127. Murray, Class Notes, p. 41.
128. Mt. 1:21.

pose of his own work in Matt. 20:28, "Even as the Son of man came not to be ministered unto, but to minister, and to give his life a ransom *for many*." Here again there is the suggestion in the "for many" of a particular redemption, and not a universal one. Again in John 10 Jesus describes himself as the good shepherd, "the good shepherd layeth down his life for the sheep" (John 10:11,15). Here we see the specific design of the death of Christ as being for the sheep. This is particularly interesting for in the context Jesus speaks to the Jews, who, not being his sheep, do not accept him, "But ye believe not, because ye are not of my sheep" (John 10:26). A similar passage is found in John 15:13, "Greater love hath no man than this, that a man lay down his life for his friends." In Acts 20:28 the Apostle says of the death of Christ, "Take heed unto ... the flock, in which the Holy Spirit hath made you bishops, to feed the *church of God* which he purchased with his own blood." Here the design of the purchase is explicitly designated as the church of the Lord. Again in Ephesians 5:25 the Apostle names the Church as the object for which Christ died, "Husbands love your wives, even as Christ also loved the church, and gave himself up for it."

The great high priestly prayer of John 17 is explicitly stated as being in behalf of the elect, of those whom the Father gave the Son.[129] This is of particular significance because this prayer is recognized as an integral part of the priestly work of Christ. He was in this prayer sanctifying or setting himself apart to the death on the Cross (vs. 19). If he limits this aspect of his priestly work to the elect, then it may be assumed that the atonement itself, which was also a part of his priestly work was also limited in its design.

As in the case of Isaiah 53, the word "all" is limited by the context, so also similar limitations to the word "all" are found in Romans 8:32. "He that spared not his own son, but delivered him up for us all, how shall he not also with him freely give us all things?" On the surface again, it might appear that this is a universalist passage asserting that Christ was delivered for all. The context of the passage, however, indicates a limitation to this expression. Romans 8:30 has referred to the elect specifically. So also does verse 33. Also in verse 32 the all is modified by "us." The particularisms of the whole passage from verse 28 through 39 restrict our understanding of the "us all" of verse 32 to God's own. Verse 33 clearly uses the term "God's elect" in referring to those for whom Christ died. Moving on to verse 34 there is a reference to the efficacious intercession of Christ "for us." Thus "us" of this passage is limited again by the "us" of verse 31. Both the death and intercession of Christ for us are restricted to those of verse 30. Finally, the love of God which is celebrated in verse 35-39, which is the guarantee of the security of the believer, is the love which is in Christ Jesus.

> Now the inevitable inference is that this love from which it is impossible to be separated and which guarantees the bliss of those who are embraced in it is the same love that must be alluded to earlier in the passage when Paul says, 'He that spared not his own Son but delivered him up for us all, how shall he not with him also freely give us all things?' (vs. 32). It is surely the same love, called in verse 39 'the love of God which is in Christ Jesus,' that constrained the Father to deliver

---

129. John 17:2, 6, 9, 11, 12, 24.

up his own Son. This means that the love implied in verse 32, the love of giving the Son cannot be given a wider reference than the love which, according to verse 35-39, insures the eternal security of those who are its objects. If not all men enjoy this security, how can that which is the source of this security and the guarantee of its possession embrace those who enjoy no such security? We see, therefore, that the security of which Paul here speaks is a security restricted to those who are the objects of the love which was exhibited on Calvary's accursed tree, and therefore the love exhibited on Calvary is itself a distinguishing love and not a love that is indiscriminately universal.[130]

(3) Universalistic Passages Examined

i. General Considerations

Having seen that there are clearly some passages that teach the particularism of Christ's love and of his atonement, we must now examine some of the passages that appear to teach a universalism. It should be said at the outset that there cannot be any ultimate contradiction within the Word of God. Thus, it is incumbent upon the believer to let Scripture interpret Scripture, especially where apparent contradiction occurs. Before examining separate passages let us make some preliminary observations.

First, there are universal terms used in the Scripture which are obviously restricted in intent. For example, Gen. 6:12-13 says, "All flesh had corrupted their way; the end of all flesh is come before me." This is not distributively universal, for Noah and his family were excepted. Again in Mark 5:33 the woman who had touched the garment of Jesus and was healed is described as telling Jesus "all the truth." Clearly this is a limited use of all. No doubt it was the truth concerning her act, but not all truth in the universal sense. Mark used the term in connection with the ministry of John the Baptist, "And there went out unto him all the country of Judaea, and all they of Jerusalem; and they were baptized of him in the river Jordan..." (1:5). It is obvious that he means that a great many people of Judaea and Jerusalem went out, but he hardly means each and every one distributively went out. Other such passages include Acts 2:43; I Cor. 10:23; I Pet. 4:7.

Second, there is a distinction to be found in the Bible between *ethnic universalism*, and *distributive universalism*. We have already noted this in connection with our treatment of Isaiah 52-3. The fact that Christ's death was for all nations, for people of all tribes and kindreds, was a concept that had to be stressed with the Jewish disciples of the New Testament. The context of John 12:32 suggests this to be the meaning of the drawing of all men unto him. All sorts of men would be drawn to him, not each and every man of the world.

Third, there is an *indiscriminate universalism* to be found in the New Testament also. It is found in the fact that the Gospel is suitable for the salvation

---

130. Murray, *Redemption*, pp. 78-79.

of all, and the invitation is to be given to all. Paul's usage of all in some cases may have been to stress the undiscriminating nature of the Gospel as opposed to the classism of Gnosticism, e.g. I Tim. 2:7.

Fourth, the term "world" as used in the New Testament, and especially by John may best be understood in the distinctly ethical quality, rather than as a reference to the world as distributively understood.

Fifth, we must use care in exegeting passages not to press the universalism beyond the intent of the writer. For example, in Hebrews 2:9 the phrase "he should taste of death for every man (*huper pantos* [131])" is clearly restricted in the next verse by the phrase, "in bringing many sons into glory."

Having made these observations, let us now look at a few of the so-called universalistic passages.

ii. John 3:16

A careful analysis of this passage indicates that it is not intended to teach a universalism. The object of the love of God is described as the "world." We have already suggested that this term in John is frequently used in an ethical, rather than a quantitative sense. I John 2:16 reads, "Love not the world, neither the things that are in the world, the lust of the flesh and the lust of the eyes and the vainglory of life, is not of the Father, but is of the world." [132] The object of God's love in John 3:16 then is that which is utterly detestable to God, because it is contradictory to all that is holy and good. It is this kind of world that God so loved as to give his Son. Thus the love that this verse is celebrating is the quality of the love, the intensity of love that would send the only-begotten Son of God to bear the contradiction and curse of the despicable and hateful world. It is not so much a quantity, but a quality that is stressed. Further, it should be observed that the result of this act of love was the securing of salvation for those who believe in him. It was thus the giving of Christ to secure and insure something very definite, namely, eternal life.

> It would not be exegetically proper to say that he gave his Son that the elect might not perish. This in itself is true enough, but that is not what the text says. It would be a travesty to impose that interpretation on the latter part of the text. The text is intended to lay emphasis on the security attaching to faith in Christ; the security that has been obtained to that end by the giving of the Son; the security of those who believe in Christ, whosoever they may be. [133]

It should also be observed that the verse itself includes the restriction of the application of this salvation only to those who believe. If we universalize the term "world" in John 3:16, then we must do so in 3:17: "For God sent not his son into the world to condemn the world, but that the world through him might be saved." If we take the world as universally referring to each and every one, then we must posit on the basis of 3:17 that each and every one was saved. Yet in 3:16 there is a clear limitation of those who are saved to only those who believe.

---

131. ὑπὲρ παντός
132. Cf. John 14:17, 27; 15:18, 19; 16:11; I John 2:15; 3:1, 13; 4:5; 5:4, 19.
133. Murray, Class notes, p. 46.

If on the other hand, we understand the "world" as referring to the vileness of the object of God's love, that he was nevertheless willing to send his Son into, and from which there would be those who would believe and thus be saved, we have done full justice to the text, without any contradiction to the definite or limited atonement passages.

iii. II Cor. 5:14-15

"For the love of Christ constraineth us; because we judge, that one died for all, therefore all died; and he died for all, that they that live should no longer live unto themselves, but unto him who for their sakes died and rose again." Twice in this passage we see the statement that Christ "died for all." An examination of the passage indicates that those for whom he died also died with him. Romans 6:8 states that all who die with him shall also live with him. "But if we died with Christ, we believe that we shall also live with him." The passage before us implies the same in that it says, "He died for all, that they that live should no longer live unto themselves, but unto him who for their sakes died and rose again." If we understand those who live to be restricted in number, we may assume that this limits the "all" for whom he died. Romans 6:2-8 clearly limits those who died with Christ as those who walk in newness of life. Thus, from Paul's own teaching we conclude that the expression "died for all" in this passage is not intended to teach a universal atonement in a distributive sense.

iv. I John 2:2

"And he is the propitiation for our sins, and not for ours only but also for the whole world." This passage seems to teach the extension of the propitiatory work of Christ to the whole world in a universalistic sense. It should be said that this language would be perfectly in accord with a universal atonement, if this were the teaching of the rest of Scripture. The question, however, is whether this passage demands universal atonement. To put it in another way, can this passage be interpreted in accord with the doctrine of the limited atonement without doing violence to the principles of interpretation? Since we have found the limited atonement asserted so clearly in other parts of the Scripture, we may properly ask whether there is any way in which to interpret this passage in accord with this doctrine. Are there good reasons for John's use of the expression "for the whole world" that do not require a doctrine of universal atonement? There are several reasons that may be given for the expression, "and not for ours only, but also for the whole world." First, it may be a reference to the fact that the propitiation was for more than just the disciples who had seen, heard and handled the Lord,[134] or for the immediate circle of those who had believed through the Apostles' witness.[135] Second, it was necessary for the Apostles to stress the fact that the propitiation of Christ was for more than just the Jewish people. It had its ethnic universal application, for every nation, kindred and people were embraced by the work of Christ. Further, the context suggests the fact that the propitiation

---

134. I John 1:1-3.
135. I John 1:3-4.

of Christ was of lasting effect for all time and every age. "It is highly probable that this form of statement points to 'Jesus Christ the righteous' as not only the one who made propitiation once for all by his sacrifice on the cross but as the one who is the abiding embodiment of the propitiatory virtue accruing from his once-for-all accomplishment and also as the one who offers to those who trust in him an ever availing propitiation."[136] The limitation of the propitiation may be suggested by the advocacy of verse 1. "If we give to the propitiation an extent far beyond that of his advocacy we inject something which is hardly compatible with this complementation (of the two.)."[137]

As we conclude this section on the extent of the atonement, it might be well to remember that the Bible represents the death of Christ as accomplishing and securing the blessings of salvation, namely, expiation, propitiation, reconciliation and redemption. In none of these cases is the representation that of making these blessings just possible, but rather they all are actually accomplished by Christ. A universalism that would dilute these terms to just possible expiation, possible propitiation, possible reconciliation and possible redemption would be a compromise of the Biblical doctrine of the atonement. It is only when the atonement is viewed as actually accomplishing these blessings, that the fulness of Christ's work is seen. It is only a definite or limited atonement that preserves the fulness of the Biblical representation. As Professor Murray says, "the glory of the cross of Christ is bound up with the effectiveness of its accomplishment. Christ redeemed us to God by his blood, he gave himself a ransom that he might deliver us from all iniquity. The atonement is efficacious substitution."[138]

III. Christ as King

A. Introduction

As we consider the royal office of Christ, it should be observed immediately that the Kingship of Christ which is in view here is not that which he has in virtue of his deity. Rather, it is the kingly office that he has as the Mediator of the Covenant of Grace. It is the office which he received at the completion of his work of the cross, after he had risen from the dead. It is, therefore, the office of King that he executes as the God-man. All his royal acts are infinitely wise, righteous and powerful because he is God, and yet they possess the truly human qualities, for he has a feeling for all our infirmities.

B. The Origin of His Reign

1. Christ has been the Mediator of the Covenant of Grace since the beginning of time, for he was the Lamb slain from the foundation of the world.[139] He was the Prophet before Abraham and Moses, the Priest before Melchizedek and Aaron, and the King before David. He is the ground of their

---
136. Murray, *Redemption*, p. 84.
137. *Ibid.*, p. 85.
138. *Idem.*
139. Rev. 13:8.

offices. He established them as types of himself, and they take their meaning from him as Prophet, Priest and King. As King, Jesus was the Jehovah of the Old Testament. It is of interest to note that Paul's favorite title for him was Lord, the word used in the Septuagint to translate Jehovah. He was the Angel of the Lord. He reigned over all human affairs in history. He was the giver of the Law at Sinai. He brought Israel out of Egypt "with a mighty hand, and with an outstretched arm, and with great terribleness, and with signs and with wonder." [140]

2. Strictly speaking, however, the actual and formal assumption of the Kingly office came after the Resurrection, and with the Ascension to Heaven. He did not possess the God-man character until the time of the incarnation. Here his priestly work preceded his royal work. "This man, after he had offered one sacrifice for sins for ever, sat down on the right hand of God; from henceforth expecting till his enemies be made his footstool." [141]

C. The Nature of the Royal Office

This royal office is essentially the royal dispersion of grace by Christ as Saviour. This is seen in his royal command to the Church, "All power is given to me in heaven and in earth. Go ye therefore and disciple all nations." [142] The outpouring of the Holy Spirit at Pentecost, and thus the empowering of the Church to carry the Gospel to the world was the work of Christ, "This Jesus hath God raised up, whereof we all are witnesses. Being therefore by the right hand of God exalted, and having received of the Father the promise of the Holy Spirit, he hath poured forth this, which ye see and hear." [143] The nature of this kingship then is gracious in character.

D. The Object of his Kingship

The object of this kingship is to bring order into this sin-ruined universe, and in particular to bring salvation to his own. [144] He works all things for good for his people. [145] He establishes his kingdom for them. [146] He will eventually reduce all to subjection to himself, [147] and all shall worship him and acknowledge him as Lord. [148]

---

140. Deut. 26:8.
141. Heb. 10:12-13. See also Matt. 28:18; and Acts 2:32-36.
142. Matt. 28:18-19.
143. Acts 2:32-33.
144. Eph. 1:10,23; Col. 1:20.
145. Rom. 8:28.
146. Lk. 22:29; Jn. 14:2.
147. I Cor. 15:25; Heb. 10:13.
148. Phil. 2:7-11; Heb. 1:6; Rev. 5:2-13.

E. Aspects of His Kingship

1. His is a Kingdom of Power.

It embraces all of the universe. "All authority has been given unto him."[149]

2. His is a Kingdom of Grace.

He exercises a spiritual reign over his people. This is carried out individually, by his subduing us to himself, and by effectually calling us into his kingdom of grace. Further, he restrains and conquers all of his and our enemies. He is our present help in times of need. Further, he exercises his reign over us collectively. He is the sole ruler in Zion, the Church visible. He has established its laws, the conditions of its membership, its officers, and its discipline.

3 His is a Kingdom of Glory.

He is the one, who by his personal return, will usher in the glorious consummation of his kingdom.[150] He is the One who will sit upon the great white throne, and he will be the one to rule for all eternity.

---

149. Mt. 28:18.
150. Rev. 19:11-16; 22:3-4.

Chapter XXVIII The States of Christ

Introduction

The work of Christ was performed in his two different states, namely, his humiliation and exaltation. Berkhof defines a state as "one's position or status in life, and particularly the forensic relationship in which one stands to the law, while a condition is the mode of one's existence, especially as determined by the circumstances of life."[1]

The state of humiliation includes the incarnation, sufferings, death and burial of the Lord. The state of exaltation includes the resurrection, ascension, session at the right hand of God and return of our Lord. We have already considered some aspects of his humiliation under both the person and the Work of Christ. We shall examine areas that have not been previously covered under each of these states of Christ. Since the return of the Lord is to be considered under eschatology, we shall not deal with it here.

I. The Humiliation of Christ

A. The Incarnation

One of the most amazing facts of the Gospel is the fact of the incarnation. That is, God himself has assumed human nature. Hodge describes it thus:

> The incarnation of the Son of God, his stooping to take into personal and perpetual union with himself a nature infinitely lower than his own, was an act of unspeakable condescension, and therefore is properly included in the particulars in which he humbled himself.[2]

Lutheran theologians do not want to include the incarnation itself as part of the humiliation, since it continues in his present heavenly state. Philippians 2:7, however, speaks of the fact that he made himself of no reputation in his becoming man. It is true that his humanity was exalted in heaven, but the very act of the Creator assuming the nature of the creature is necessarily an act of condescension or humiliation.

The Old Testament, as we have already seen, predicted a Messiah who would be both divine and human. It indicated that this would take place through a virgin birth (Isaiah 7:14).

The very idea of the incarnation of one of the Persons of the Godhead raises several difficult questions. Accepting the orthodox doctrine of the Trinity, with the idea that Christ was essentially divine, how did the assumption of human nature affect this divine person? Or, to put it another way, in what do the incarnation and humiliation of Christ consist? Does the assumption of the human nature affect his Godhood? How could there be a conjunction of the Godhood and of the manhood without some modification of the Godhood? Does the incarnation interfere with the possession of divine attributes? Is there any sus-

---

1. Berkhof, *op. cit.*, p. 331.
2. C. Hodge, *op. cit.*, Vol. II, p. 611.

pension of the prerogatives and functions that belong to him as God? These questions were before the Church from the beginning. These were the questions with which she has struggled throughout the centuries. Attempts at a solution have sometimes resulted in heretical deviations.

It is a remarkable fact that during the fifteen centuries following Chalcedon the kenotic theory was not formulated in the Church. It is true that some theologians have used terminology which might lead to the kenotic idea, but no one during that period formulated the *kenosis* idea to explain the incarnation. The reason for this is clear. Catholic orthodoxy took as its starting point the immutability of the *Logos* in his divine nature and intra-divine relations, attributes, prerogatives and functions. It consistently maintained that there was no subtraction, suspension or surrender of the form of God, when he took on the form of a servant. He was made man, a change that involved the adding of manhood to Godhood, not a reduction of the integrity of his Godhood in any way. Continuing what he was, he took what he was not. This was the position of orthodoxy until the second half of the 19th century.

1. 19th Century *Kenosis* Theories

With the 19th Century we enter a new phase in the treatment of the incarnation. The kenotic principle is essentially that the Son of God, in becoming man, divested himself of his divine attributes, prerogatives and functions, or suspended his intra-divine relations, or some aspects of his intra-divine relations. That is, there was, to some extent, a denudation of the divine attributes, and consequently, a suspension of the divine prerogatives and functions. He ceased to be, for a time, what he previously was, ceased to possess what he previously possessed, and ceased to exercise what he previously exercised. Thus, the key idea of *kenosis* regarding the Deity in the incarnation was that of abandonment, self-divestiture, self-restriction.

a. Earliest Forms

(1) Thomasius of Erlangen wrote a book, *The Person and Work of Christ* (1852-1861), in which he set forth his view that Christ possessed relative or metaphysical attributes, such as, omnipresence, omnipotence and omniscience which were laid aside in the incarnation. His absolute attributes of love, truth, holiness, etc., were inalienable, and thus could not be set aside.

(2) A. M. Fairbairn in *Christ and Modern Theology* held substantially the same viewpoint as Thomasius.

b. W. F. Gess and Godet

These men went further than the earlier ones did. They maintained that the *kenosis* applied to the absolute as well as the relative attributes. Christ obliterated his eternal self-consciousness so that there was a suspension of the influx of eternal life from the Father to the Son, a suspension of eternal generation.

c. Ebrard of Erlangen, and Martenson of Denmark, and William Newton Clarke, liberal Baptist at Colgate Seminary, in America

These men went further yet. They conceived of the *kenosis* not so much as a laying aside of divine attributes, but an adaptation of the divine attributes to finitude. The metaphysical attributes were retained in an adapted form. Thus, there was really a metamorphosis, a transmutation, so that the divine attributes appear under the form of human attributes. We see in Christ not the naked God, but the fullness of God framed in the ring of humanity. The divine attributes were embodied in attributes of human nature. Instead of omnipresence we see his blessed presence. The divine attributes were thus no longer divine attributes.

d. Charles Gore of England

Gore maintained that Christ deliberately negated his divine attributes, emptying himself of Deity to assume permanent characteristics of the human servile life. Though he remained the Son of God, he had abandoned certain divine prerogatives in order to assume the human.

2. The Biblical Teaching

The *locus classicus* on the kenotic theory is Philippians 2:6-8. A careful study of this passage must be made to determine the Biblical teaching on the subject.

a. Form of God (*morphe theou*)[3]

The term "form" (*morphe*) is the Greek philosophical term that denotes the abiding essential form of something. That is, it refers to the specific character of a thing, without which a thing ceased to be. It is the sum of those characteristic qualities that make a thing the precise thing that it is. It does not in any way refer to the outward appearance. It has nothing to do with this, but rather with the specific nature of a thing. Thus, when Christ is said to be in the form of God, he is said to possess the sum of the characterizing qualities which make God specifically God. It is of interest to note that Paul refers to Christ possessing this with a present participle. This implies that he not only existed in this form-essence originally, but also that he continues to be in it. There is no suggestion that the state or condition of existing in the form of God (*en morphe theou huparchon*[4]) terminated with the action denoted by the principal verb. The present participle suggests "who being in and continuing in the form of God." This alone creates a strong presumption against the kenotic interpretation of the passage as a whole.

---

3. μορφῇ θεοῦ
4. ἐν μορφῇ θεοῦ ὑπάρχων

b. Being on an equality with God (*to einai isa theo*[5])

The question is just what relation this clause has to the earlier expression "form of God" (*morphe theou*) and to the principal verb of the passage. Some of the ablest opponents to the kenotic theory have maintained that this state of being on an equality with God is different from his being in the form-essence of God, and that it was this equality in majesty and glory that he set aside. E. H. Gifford argued that this clause designates circumstances and conditions of glory and honor peculiar and appropriate to his divine majesty, and that during the incarnation he laid aside such conditions and circumstances of glory and honor. J. B. Lightfoot held that the being on equality with God was the insignia of majesty, the prerogative of Deity, which for a time the Son gave up.[6] Both of these interpreters held that the being on an equality with God was not considered a prize that had to be tenaciously held, but one that he was willing to resign for the period of his humiliation.

In answer to this position, it must be asserted that the being on equality with God is much more integrally and indissolubly related to the form of God than these men thought. It is a designation of the station or status that belongs inevitably to him in virtue of his being in the form of God. The thought then is that Christ, who was and continues to be in the form of God, and therefore, did not consider the being on an equality with God robbery or a prize needing grasping, made himself of no reputation. That is, being on an equality with God is something conceived of as securely and unalterably his in virtue of his being in the form of God. Or again, his being on an equality with God was his by nature, by inalienable right and immutable possession, and thus he did not consider it something of precarious tenure. It was not, therefore, his sole object of preoccupation and interest. Instead he made no account of himself, since this was unalterably secure as a status. By reason of his being in the form of God, he did not need to be anxiously fretful about it. He did not need to consider it robbery or a prize that needed to be clutched as though it were of a precarious nature.

c. Emptied himself "Made himself of no reputation" (KJV) (*heauton ekenosen*[7])

The literal rendering of the verb *kenoo*[8] is "emptied". Once we allow this literal rendering, then we are faced with the question of what he emptied himself of. The preponderance of New Testament usage of the verb *kenoo* shows that the literal interpretation is not the preferred one. New Testament usage points to a figurative usage of the word, such as that found in the King James Version, "made himself of no reputation." Warfield in *The Person and Work of Christ* has most effectively marshalled the arguments against the literal interpretation.

---

5. τὸ εἶναι ἴσα θεῷ
6. J. B. Lightfoot, *Saint Paul's Epistle to the Philippians* (Grand Rapids: Zondervan Publishing House, 1953, reprinted from London: Macmillian and Company, 1913), p. 112.
7. ἑαυτὸν ἐκένωσεν
8. κενόω

(1) The verb *kenoo* when used elsewhere in the New Testament bears exclusively the figurative meaning: Romans 4:14, "For if they that are of the law are heirs, faith is made void (*kekenotai*⁹) and the promise is made of none effect"; I Corinthians 1:17, "For Christ sent me not to baptize, but to preach the gospel: not in wisdom of words, lest the cross of Christ should be made void" (*kenothe*¹⁰); I Corinthians 9:15, " ... than that any man should make my glorying void" (*kenosei*¹¹); II Corinthians 9:3, "But I have sent the brethren, that our glorying on your behalf may not be made void (*kenothe*) in this respect ..."

The adjective form *kenos*¹² occurs eighteen times, some twelve or thirteen of which are used in the figurative sense. The adverb *kenos*¹³ is used once in James 4:5 in the figurative sense, "Or think ye that the scripture speaketh in vain? ..." Thus out of the twenty-three instances of the usage of this word and its cognates the overwhelming usage is that of the figurative sense. Only in the adjectival sense is it used a few times in the literal sense of "empty". On the basis of the preponderant use in the New Testament the adoption of the non-literal translation of the word in Philippians 2 is favored. This is enforced when it is found to lead to a rendering without the theological difficulties that the literal translation raises. The figurative rendering makes perfectly easy reading. There is no question raised as to what he emptied himself of.

(2) The modal clauses which immediately follow, both with aorists participles, define how he made himself of no reputation "taking the form of a servant, being made in the likeness of men" (*morphev doulou labon, en homoiomati anthropon genomenos*¹⁴). The close conjunction of these two clauses to the main verb warns against any idea of divestiture or emptying, because these two clauses do not speak of divestiture, or self-emptying, but rather speak in terms of adding. It is the assumption of, or adding of the existence form of a servant to the existence form of God, the adding of being made in the likeness of men to the being on an equality with God that makes him of no reputation. This indicates that it was by addition, and not by subtraction that he *heauton ekenosin*.

(3) The position of *heauton* in the phrase is that of the emphatic. It draws the attention to "himself". This emphatic placing of himself interposed between the preceding clause and the verb rendered "emptied" builds a barrier over which we cannot climb backwards in search of that of which our Lord emptied himself. We might speak of him as emptying himself of something, but not of emptying himself of himself. If we want to understand the verb in the figurative sense while using the literal language, then we can say he emptied himself of himself. That is, he made no account of himself. This is con-

---

9. κεκένωται
10. κενωθῇ
11. κενώσει
12. κένος
13. κενῶς
14. μορφὴν δούλου λαβών, ἐν ὁμοιώματι ἀνθρώπων γενόμενος

sonant with the entire passage, which calls upon us not to look on our own things, not to make ourselves the exclusive object of preoccupation, but to follow the example of Christ, who made no account of himself. He did not make self or his own things the absorbing object of his interest. He came not to be ministered unto, but to minister. He did not look with greedy eyes on his being on an equality with God as a thing requiring all interest and concern. He did not make his own station the exclusive subject of thought, but considered the needs of others instead of self. We cannot speak of emptying himself in a literal sense, which would mean depersonalizing of himself, but the figurative sense gives the meaning, that he made no account of himself.

(4) The figurative rendering is consonant with the thought of the context. Paul is urging the Philippians to unselfishness (verse 4), and to enforce this he calls on the supreme example of Christ. It is unwarranted to think in terms of abandonment or divestiture. The thought of the *heauton ekenosen* can be illustrated as follows: Jesus was not concentrated on or anxious about his being on an equality with God. He was not so jealously absorbed in himself that he was unwilling to do the humblest service as a servant. For example, consider two men, both with a high and dignified position and unreproachable character, one of whom is so preoccupied with his position that he considers it inconsistent with his status and character to stoop to some form of humble and menial service for others; the other is merciful and compassionate in character, and has thought for others, so that he is prepared to stoop to perform the most distasteful and menial task. The latter does not set such an overrated store in his dignified position, but that he can and will perform the humblest service. He does not think of his station, but of the needs of others. As he does this task for others, does this man abandon his dignified position? He humbles himself, but does not abandon his station. The more secure he is in his position and the more irreproachable his moral character, the more freely may he perform the humblest of services. Thus it was with Christ. He did not consider his condition of being on an equality with God with such absorbing jealousy that he refrained from humiliation, which made no account of himself. Thus the literal rendering of the word as "empty" does not convey the meaning of the passage as well as the figurative "made himself of no reputation."

d. The Force of the Participles in Verse 7: Taking (*labon*[15]), and Being Made (*genomenos*[16]).

These participles come immediately after *ekenosen*. What is their exact force? There are three kinds of aorists: antecedent act, identical or coincident act, and subsequent act. The question is whether the aorist participles denote antecedent, coincident, or subsequent action to the principal verb. We shall examine each possible interpretation.

---

15. λαβών
16. γενόμενος

(1) Subsequent Action

Could these participles refer to subsequent actions, which took place after the action of the main verb? This is ruled out on the consideration inherent in the concepts expressed. The main verb certainly refers to an act of marvelous condescension. The participles describe such acts of condescension, and thus are not subsequent to the principal verb.

(2) Antecedent Action

It would make good sense to consider the acts of the participles as antecedent to the principal verb. "Having taken the form of a servant, and having been made in the likeness of men he made no account of himself." That is, having become incarnate, having adopted existence of the form of a servant, he carried out the implications of such humiliation. He made himself of no reputation. In that event, the principal verb has reference to what he did in the incarnate state, and presupposes the incarnation. If this interpretation were adopted, it would provide the strongest evidence against the kenotic theory, because the main verb reflects on consequences of the incarnation, and not on what was involved in the act of incarnation itself. *Kenosis* would then apply only to acts subsequent to the act of incarnation.

(3) Coincident Action or Identical Action

The argument for this understanding of the action is found in the parallelism that is found in the next verse, "He humbled himself becoming obedient even unto death" (*etapeinosen heauton genomenos upekoos mechri thanatou*[17]). Becoming obedient unto death cannot be regarded as antecedent to the principal verb, but rather must be seen as the supreme exemplification of self-humiliation. The self-humiliation consisted in his becoming obedient unto death. Thus, the self-humiliation is defined, at least climactically, in terms of becoming obedient unto death. This is not simply a coincident action, but the identical act. The one consists in the other and is definitive of the other. He humbled himself by obedience, which reached its climax in his death. In view of this parallelism of verse 8, we may expect to interpret verse 7 in the same way. That is, he made no account of himself by taking the form of servant and being made in the likeness of man. In other words, the main verb is defined in terms of "taking the form of a servant" and "being made in the likeness of men". They are modal clauses, which define the *kenosis*. This is not only supported by the analogy of verse 7 and 8, but is in thorough accord with the whole syntax and thought of the passage.

The kenosis spoken of in this passage is not to be understood in terms of abandonment, or divestiture of anything. He did not give up metaphysical or ethical attributes or function, nor did he adapt his divine function to the human, nor did he even relinquish the condition or circumstance of his divine mode of

---

17. ἐταπείνωσεν ἑαυτὸν γενόμενος ὑπήκοος μέχρι θανάτου

existence. Rather, the *kenosis* is to be understood in terms of the assumption of a new form essence, the addition of human nature and the form existence of a servant to the Godhood and to his being on an equality with God. The *kenosis* of this passage is to be interpreted as the entrance of the Son of God on a new mode of existence and a new existence form not antecedently his. Previous to the incarnation he had only one existence form, only one mode of existence, namely, the divine. Subsequent to the incarnation he has two forms and two modes of existence. This condition arose from the fact of addition of the human and servant forms. The human form and servant nature did not possess or exercise divine attributes. To assume that this was the case would be to deny the reality of the human nature. The human nature was and continued to be finite. Thus, he underwent change in the human nature, and was subject to human limitations in this nature. Because he really assumed the form of a servant, he became really a servant, and he subjected himself and was subjected by the Father to the condition of humiliation, poverty, misery and shame, which were not essential to the incarnation as such, but were essential to the special task that he came to perform. These peculiar conditions of humiliation, arising from the special task he came to perform, could not appear in the condition of glory and majesty peculiar to his divine dignity and majesty. There was real humiliation for him. Thus, his divine glory was veiled. He could, on all occasions, have given an overwhelming demonstration of glory and honor, such as he will give in his second coming in the human nature, but the conditions necessary for the performance of his task forbade this display of the divine prerogatives. He humbled himself and became obedient to death, even the death of the Cross.

We must not forget the other side of the matter also. Though it is true that as regards his human nature he subjected himself to the condition of shame and poverty, suffering and dishonor, it does not at all follow that in his other existence form, that was unalterably his, he did not enjoy and possess its prerogatives and functions, circumstances and conditions appropriate to the divine majesty. The endurance of poverty and human suffering in the one mode of existence does not exclude from the divine form and mode of existence the unabbreviated riches of glory belonging to that nature. II Corinthians 8:9 does not suggest that he ceased to be rich when he became poor. He was both rich and poor. The same principle which governs the incarnation applies here. He did not cease to be what he was, but became what he was not. There were two whole and complete natures in the one indivisible person.[18]

B. Christ as Servant - Made Under the Law

We have already examined under the work of Christ something of how his saving work was a work of obedience. We took note of the prophecies of Isaiah regarding the Messiah as Servant (Isaiah 42:1, 19; 49:6; 50:10; 52:13-53:12). Jesus submitted to the baptism of John as an act of obedience "to fulfill all righteousness."[19] Jesus also spoke of his ministry in terms of doing the will

---

18. Note: Material for this section was derived largely from class notes of a course on the Person and Work of Christ taught by Professor John Murray.
19. Matt. 3:15.

of the Father, "My meat is to do the will of him who sent me."[20] Of course, this is the essence of the idea of being a servant. In particular he saw his death as done in obedience to the Father, "Therefore doth the Father love me, because I lay down my life that I may take it again. No one taketh it away from me, but I lay it down of myself. I have power to lay it down, and I have power to take it again. This commandment received I from my Father."[21] Having treated these concepts under the work of Christ, it is not necessary to repeat them here, other than to note that this was a part of the state of humiliation of Christ.

C. The Suffering and Death of Christ

The Westminster *Larger Catechism* describes the humiliation of Christ in his death thus: "Christ humbled himself in his death, in that having been betrayed by Judas, forsaken by his disciples, scorned and rejected by the world, condemned by Pilate, and tormented by his persecutors, having also conflicted with the terrors of death, and the powers of darkness, felt and bore the weight of God's wrath, he laid down his life an offering for sin, enduring the painful, shameful, and cursed death of the cross."

1. Voluntary Suffering

As we consider his suffering and death, we should not think that it came upon him unexpectedly, or that he entered into it unwillingly. He said, "I have a baptism to be baptized with, and how am I straitened till it be accomplished."[22] His last journey to Jerusalem, he made openly. He made a public entrance into Jerusalem, riding in triumph, which one might expect would arouse the animosity of his enemies. That he voluntarily suffered is seen in his conduct in Gethsemane. "Jesus therefore, knowing all the things that were coming upon him, went forth, and saith unto them, 'Whom seek ye?' . . . When therefore he said unto them, 'I am he,' they went backward and fell to the ground."[23] It is evident that he was in control, and the soldiers could not do anything against him, unless he voluntarily gave himself to them. This he did.

2. Betrayal by Judas

The fact that he was betrayed by one of his own for the price of a slave added to his sufferings. It was a wound inflicted by one who pretended to be a friend.

3. Forsaken by the Disciples

Not only did Judas betray him, but once he was taken, all of the disciples forsook him and fled.[24] This certainly added to his suffering in that he had to

---

20. John 4:34.
21. John 10:17-18.
22. Luke 12:50.
23. John 18:4-6.
24. Matt. 26:56.

bear it all alone. There was no one there to assist or encourage him. A part of this abandonment by the disciples was the denial of Peter, who brought reproach upon his Lord with his curses and denials.

4. The World Rejected Him

He was the object of the scorn of the world, as though he was inferior to it. Psalm 22:6-7 says, "I am a worm and no man; a reproach of men, and despised of the people. All they that see me, laugh me to scorn; they shoot out the lip, they shake the head." He met with this reproach and rejection throughout his ministry. It comes to a climax in his trial and death, as his captors mocked him, placing a scarlet robe on him. The final note of rejection was the call for Barabbas to be released in the place of Jesus. Peter said, "Ye denied the Holy One, and the Just, and desired a murderer to be granted unto you."[25]

5. Condemned by Pontius Pilate

The condemnation of Pontius Pilate marked a particular stage of his suffering. Pilate acted against his own convictions. He knew that the chief priests had delivered him for envy. He sought to wash his hands of the guilt, and declared that he was innocent of the blood of this Just person.[26] He acted out of pure selfishness as he heeded the call of the Jews that he would not be a friend of Caesar if he did not condemn him. All of this added to the reproach and suffering of our Lord, who was thus unjustly condemned to death by a godless representative of the world.

6. Tormented by His Persecutors

Our Savior was tormented by his persecutors, scourged, buffeted, smitten with the palms of their hands, crowned with thorns, which may have pierced his head. He was compelled to carry his own cross until totally exhausted. We see in this something of the result of the persecution that he had undergone in the hours just preceding his crucifixion. "These things he endured, immediately before his crucifixion, from wicked men, divested of all humanity, as well as religion."[27]

7. Bore the Weight of God's Wrath

His death was in some things more formidable than the death of any of the sinners. All sinners deserve death as the just wage for their sin. Jesus was holy, righteous and undefiled, and yet our sins were laid upon him, and he had to suffer that which he did not deserve. The Catechism speaks of the powers of darkness being involved in his suffering.

---

25. Acts 3:14.
26. Matt. 27:24.
27. Thomas Ridgley, *op. cit.*, LC Q. 49, p. 305.

It is more than probable that the powers of darkness had a great hand in setting before his view the terrors of the wrath of God due to sin, which none are better able to do, than they who are the subjects thereof; and therefore it is observed in this answer, that he conflicted with the terrors of death and the powers of darkness. The devil is sometimes said to have *the power of death,* Heb. 2:14, that is, if the Spirit of God do not come in with his comforting presence, but Satan be suffered to do what he can to fill the soul with horror, he had certainly power to make death, beyond measure, terrible. His design herein, with respect to our Saviour, was either to drive him to despair, induce him to repent of his undertaking what he came into the world about . . .[28]

8. Painful, Shameful Death of the Cross

Crucifixion, which was the barbaric, Roman means of execution was one of the most painful deaths devised by man. Paul speaks of his enduring "even the death of the cross."[29] Sometimes the Romans used ropes to hold the person on the cross. In Jesus' case they nailed him to the cross. We know this to be the case as he later showed the print of the nails to Thomas (John 20:27). Our Savior bore the whole of this, without even the help of the wine mixed with myrrh, which could have deadened his pain.

Crucifixion was called "shameful." This may be due in part to the fact that the crucified was stripped and hung upon the cross. Of more import for our Savior is the fact that crucifixion was reserved only for those who were considered guilty of the vilest of crimes and for slaves.

The death of the cross is designated a cursed death. Paul speaks of the fact that Christ was made a curse for us, as it is written, "Cursed is every one that hangeth on a tree."[30] The idea involved in hanging one upon a tree is that of abandonment by both God and man. It was the sign of God's judgment against the individual so hung. Our Lord did not in any way deserve such treatment of either God or man, but as the Bible says, "Him who knew no sin he made to be sin on our behalf; that we might become the righteousness of God in him."[31] That is, our sins were imputed to him, and then he fell under the full wrath and curse due our sins.

After he had borne our griefs and offered his soul a sacrifice for our sins, then he came forth from the darkness to declare that he had finished the work. That is, he had finished the spiritual punishment for sin. He had yet to actually lay down his life. Again it is striking to observe that he was in control, and that he laid it down. He simply declared, "Into thy hands I commend my spirit." He gave up the ghost. Thus he literally met the wage of sin, namely, paying the price of death itself.

---

28. *Idem.*
29. Phil. 2:8.
30. Gal. 3:13. See Deut. 21:22-23.
31. II Cor. 5:21.

9. An offering for sin

To properly understand what he was doing on the cross, we must turn to Scripture. There have been those who see in him the great example of one committed to a cause, and who deny that it was a sacrifice for sin. We have already treated the work of Christ as a sacrifice under the Work of Christ, and will not repeat this at this point. (See page 404 and following.)

D. The Burial

The burial of Jesus was a part of his humiliation. It was not until he was raised from the dead that the humiliation ended. We know that his soul or spirit went to be with the Lord at the moment of his death, but his body was buried in a tomb. Thus, he suffered the humiliation of the intermediate state, of the separation of body and soul. As long as he was under the power of death this state continued.

The burial served to demonstrate that he had truly died. So much rested upon his having died that the Bible leaves no doubt about it. He was said to have bowed his head and given up the ghost.[32] His enemies were convinced of his death, so that they did not break his legs to cause death. The piercing of his side would have killed him, had he not already been dead. Pilate checked on his death. He "marvelled if he were already dead; and calling unto him the centurion, he asked whether he had been dead any while?"[33]

E. The Descent into Hell

Where did Christ go after his death and burial? The Apostles' Creed uses the phrase "he descended into hell" to describe this stage of his humiliation. This statement is one that has caused much controversy. Some churches today leave it out when reciting the creed. It is important to have a proper understanding of this phrase so that we can determine its place in the Creed.

The Apostles' Creed finds its origin in the Old Roman baptismal formula, to which later additions have been made. The disputed article is found first in a commentary on the Creed by Rufinus c. 390. He states that the article was not found in either the Roman or Greek editions of the creed. He indicates the addition of the phrase is not to add a new doctrine, but to explain an old one.[34] The Aquileian Creed thus omits the phrase "was buried" and substitutes the phrase, "he descended into hell." Thus in this earliest usage, it was equated with the burial.

The phrase appears again in the so-called Athanasian Creed of 430, and then again in the Creed of Venantius Fortunatus c. 570. This latter creed appears to be dependent upon the commentary of Rufinus. It became settled in the Creed around 700, which, according to Briggs was officially revised in Rome.[35]

---

32. John 19:30.
33. Mark 15:44.
34. Cited by W. G. T. Shedd, *Dogmatic Theology* (New York: Scribners, 1889), Vol. II, p. 604.
35. Charles A. Briggs, *Theological Symbolics* (New York: Charles Scribner's Sons, 1902), pp. 192-193.

As to the meaning of the phrase, there are a variety of opinions that have been given. "The interpretation having the greatest antiquity is surely the notion that Christ did in fact descend into the underworld of Hades between his death and resurrection, as references to the early churchmen clearly attest."[36] Otto points out that the interpretation of this phrase falls into two categories. The first rests on I Pet. 3:18-20, understanding that the descent involved a last preaching of the gospel, either to all the believers of the old dispensation or to the wicked dead. "Let it suffice here to assert that any preaching to the OT saints would be superfluous, since they had already believed the gospel and were thus justified (Rom.4:3; Gal. 3:6-9). Moreover, preaching to the impenitent dead would be against the entire tenor of Scripture, which pronounces judgment after death (Heb. 9:27) and condemnation to the wicked dead without review as, for instance, the parable of the rich man and Lazarus indicates (Luke 16:19-31)."[37]

The other line of interpretation of the phrase, which is held by many in the Western Church is that the descent was part of the defeat of Satan. This is the view of the Lutherans. The Formula of Concord says, "For it ought to be enough for us to know that Christ descended into hell, that he destroyed hell for all believers, and that we through him have been snatched from the power of death and Satan, from eternal damnation, and even from the jaws of hell."[38] Here we see the note of triumph over hell as taught by the Lutheran church.

Calvin, on the other hand, held it to be a description of the suffering of Christ. He argues for the inclusion of the article in the creed thus:

> But it is not right to omit his 'descent into hell,' which is of no small importance towards the accomplishment of redemption. . . . If Christ had merely died a corporeal death, no end would have been accomplished by it; it was requisite, also, that he should feel the severity of the divine vengeance, in order to appease the wrath of God, and satisfy his justice. Hence it was necessary for him to contend with the powers of hell and the horror of eternal death. We have already stated from the prophet, that 'the chastisement of our peace was upon him,' that 'he was wounded for our transgressions, and bruised for our iniquities;' the meaning of which is, that he was made a substitute and surety for transgressors, and even treated as a criminal himself, to sustain all the punishments which would have been inflicted on them; only with this exception, that 'it was not possible that he should be holden of the pains of death.' Therefore it is no wonder, if he be said to have descended into hell, since he suffered that death which the wrath of God inflicts on transgressors. . . . For the relation of those sufferings of Christ, which were visible to men, is very properly followed by that invisible and incomprehensible vengeance which he suffered from the hand of God; in order to assure us that not only the body of Christ was given as the price of our redemption, but that there was another greater and more ex-

---

36. Ronald E. Otto, "Descendit in Inferna: A Reformed Review of a Creedal Conundrum," *WTJ*, 52 (1990), p. 145. This article is a very helpful survey of this subject, which has been followed in the above discussion.
37. *Ibid.*, p. 146.
38. *Formula of Concord*, Article IX, as found in Philip Schaff's *Creeds of Christendom* (Grand Rapids: Baker Book House, 1966), Vol. III, p. 160.

cellent ransom, since he suffered in his soul the dreadful torments of a person condemned and irretrievably lost.[39]

The *Heidelberg Catechism* is in agreement with Calvin. Question 44 asks, "Why is there added: he descended into hell?" Answer. "That in my greatest temptations I may be assured, and wholly comfort myself with this that my Lord Jesus Christ, by his inexpressible anguish, pains, terrors and hellish agony in which he was plunged during his sufferings, but especially on the cross, has delivered me from the anguish and torment of hell."[40]

The Westminster *Larger Catechism* views "hell" as "hades" or the place of the dead. Question 50 reads, "Wherein consisted Christ's humiliation after his death?" Answer: "Christ's humiliation after his death, consisted in his being buried, and continuing in the state of the dead, and under the power of death, till the third day, which hath been otherwise expressed in these words, he descended into hell."[41]

Thus, in the history of interpretation of this phrase by the Reformed Church, we have two different views. The *Larger Catechism* fits better with the order of the articles in the Apostles' Creed, and also appears to be in accord with the earliest understanding of the phrase. This is not at all to deny what Calvin says of the suffering of Christ, that he must have suffered the anguish of hell itself, but it is to say that this is not the teaching of this phrase in the Creed.

II. The Exaltation of Christ

A. The Resurrection of Christ

Charles Hodge says of the resurrection, "The resurrection of Christ is not only asserted in the Scriptures, but it is also declared to be the fundamental truth of the gospel. 'If Christ be not risen,' says the Apostle, 'then is our preaching vain, and your faith is also vain' (I Cor. 15:14). 'If Christ be not raised, your faith is in vain; ye are yet in your sins' (verse 17)."[42] He goes on to indicate the importance of the resurrection. It arises first from the fact that "all his claims, and the success of his work, rest on the fact that he rose again from the dead. If he rose, the Gospel is true. If he did not rise, it is false."[43] Secondly, the mission of the Spirit depended on the resurrection of Christ. Thirdly, "as Christ died as the head and representative of his people, his resurrection secures and illustrates theirs. As he lives, they shall live also."[44]

1. The Biblical Presentation

a. The Old Testament predicted that the Messiah would be one who would conquer sin and its effects.[45] Since death itself is one of the ef-

---

39. John Calvin, *Institutes of the Christian Religion*, Book II, Chapt. XVI, Article X.
40. *Doctrinal Standards of the Christian Reformed Church*, (Grand Rapids: Publication Committee of the Christian Reformed Church, 1962), p. 29. Also in Schaff, *op. cit.*, p. 321.
41. Question 50.
40. *Op. cit.*, Vol. II, p. 626.
43. *Ibid.*, p. 627.
44. *Idem.*
45. Gen. 3:15; 22:17.

fects of sin, then it was to be expected that the Messiah would conquer death as well. Thus, the resurrection was implied in the general prophecies of the coming Messiah.

      b. The resurrection of the Messiah is specifically predicted in Psalm 16:10. "For thou wilt not leave my soul to Sheol (Hell); neither wilt thou suffer thy holy one to see corruption." Peter, under the inspiration of the Holy Spirit at Pentecost says that this was a prophecy of the resurrection, "Being therefore a prophet, and knowing that God had sworn with an oath to him, that of the fruit of his loins he would set one upon his throne; he foreseeing this spake of the resurrection of the Christ, that neither was he left unto Hades, nor did his flesh see corruption" (Acts 2:30-31). Christ cited the Old Testament from Moses on to prove that he would suffer and "enter into his glory."[46]

      c. Christ predicted his own resurrection.

> And as Jesus was going up to Jerusalem, he took the twelve disciples apart, and on the way he said unto them, Behold, we go up to Jerusalem; and the Son of man shall be delivered unto the chief priests and scribes; and they shall condemn him to death, and shall deliver him unto the Gentiles to mock, and to scourge, and to crucify: and the third day he shall be raised up.[47]

Earlier in his ministry he had given a veiled prediction of his resurrection, "Destroy this temple, and in three days I will raise it up" (John 2:19). Again in this same Gospel he is recorded as saying:

> Therefore doth the Father love me, because I lay down my life, that I may take it again. No one taketh it away from me, but I lay it down of myself. I have power to lay it down, and I have power to take it again. This commandment received I from my Father.[48]

      d. All four of the Gospels present the fact of the empty tomb on the third day after the crucifixion. All explain the empty tomb by the resurrection of Christ. An examination of the false theories regarding the tomb proves their ineffectualness to explain it.

(1) The Falsehood Theory

    This theory suggests that the disciples stole the body of Jesus and declared that he had risen. This is the story that the guards were paid to circulate.[49] The explanation given by the guards is clearly a falsehood itself, for it purports to be the account of what happened while they were asleep. This explanation of the empty tomb does not account for the change that took place in the disciples, who had fled or at best only followed afar off to the trial of Christ. Further, these disciples were willing to die for their message, a fact that would not be rea-

---

46. Luke 24:26-27.
47. Mt. 20:17-19.
48. John 10:17-18.
49. Mt. 28:11-15.

sonable if it was all a hoax. "Only the facts of the resurrection can explain the indomitable courage and power which they reveal in witnessing to the resurrection of Christ."[50]

(2) The Swoon Theory

This theory suggests that Jesus did not really die, but had only fainted. The cool tomb was said to have revived him. The Bible is quite explicit about his death. The soldier did not break his legs to kill him, for he found him already dead.[51] If there were any doubt about the matter, the spear thrust would certainly have finished him. Further, he was handled by friends who might have wished that he was yet alive, but who were convinced of his death. If he had simply revived from a swoon, and then permitted his disciples to believe that he had actually risen from the dead, he would have been guilty of a hoax. Further, he appeared in perfect health, and not as a sick man who had been half-dead for three days. He walked to Emmaus. This theory has so many difficulties that it cannot be taken seriously.

(3) The Vision Theory

There are two variations of this rather popular theory. The first is that the disciples had subjective visions of Christ since they thought about him so much, and became convinced that he was raised. Against the view is the fact that the disciples did not expect a resurrection. Further, the way in which Jesus appeared would not be that which one would expect if this were a valid theory. Either he would have appeared just as he had before his death, or in some sort of halo of glory. Neither is the case of the actual appearances. Finally, how could subjective visions occur to several persons at the same time? The second form of the theory is that God presented some objective vision for them to see. This seems to answer some of the difficulties of the first form, but it is still fraught with difficulties. First, why just visions, if the supernatural was needed? More difficult is the idea that God would send such objective visions to fool the disciples into thinking that Jesus was resurrected. They then went out and preached such a lie, and the book of Acts represents them as blessed of God in so doing. This would be inconsistent with the character of God.

(4) The Mythical Theory

This view suggests that the idea of a resurrection was part of the ancient culture, as found in various myths. The Church simply imported these mythological ideas into their thinking. This view does not take into account the factual account of the resurrection given in the New Testament. The representation there is that of complete surprise by the strange turn of events with the finding of the empty tomb. It fails to account for the actual beginnings of the Church as based on the preaching of the resurrection of Christ. This theory has the same

---

50. Berkhof, *Systematic Theology, op. cit.*, p. 348.
51. John 19:33-34.

weakness that we noted of the falsehood theory, for it suggests that the Apostles taught a doctrine that they knew to be only a myth.

e. Paul gives in I Corinthians 15 a list of appearances of Christ, and then arguments for the resurrection. He concludes that if Christ is not risen there is no Gospel, but now he is risen.

f. The Biblical eschatology presents Christ as not only risen, but also as returning in the same body in which he had ascended.[52] This implies the bodily resurrection.

From all of these representations of Scripture, we may conclude that the resurrection of Christ is a central part of its teaching.

2. The Nature of the Resurrection

The identity of the body in which he arose with that in which he died is clearly the representation of Scripture. He had the nail prints in his hands and feet, and the spear mark in his side.[53] On the other hand, he was not easily recognized. Mary Magdalene failed to recognize him until he spoke.[54] The men on the way to Emmaus did not know him until he broke bread before them.[55] As he stood on the sea shore, it was not until the evidence of the miraculous draft of fishes was seen that the disciples knew him.[56] The difference of this resurrected body was seen in its ability simply to enter a closed chamber, the doors being shut.[57] Paul described something of the change that we may expect in the resurrection,[58] and it may be assumed that Christ also experienced similar changes in his body, so that on the one hand, it was the same body, but, on the other hand, it was a changed body.

3. The Author of the Resurrection

The resurrection is ascribed variously to God in general,[59] or, more particularly to the Father.[60] Christ claimed that he himself would take again his life,[61] and that he was the resurrection and the life,[62] and that he would rebuild his body.[63] As the High Priest it was appropriate that he should rise from the sacrificial act, and present the shed blood in the Holy of Holies. The Holy Spirit was also involved in the resurrection.[64] Thus we see that the Triune God was active in all three Persons in this crowning event of the work of Christ.

---

52. Acts 1:11.
53. John 20:27.
54. John 20:15.
55. Luke 24:31.
56. John 21:7.
57. Lk. 24:36; Jn. 20:19.
58. I Cor. 15:42-44.
59. Acts 2:24, 32; 3:26; 5:30; I Cor. 6:14; Eph. 1:20.
60. Rom. 6:4; Gal. 1:1; I Pet. 1:3.
61. John 10:18.
62. John 11:25.
63. John 2:19-21.
64. Rom. 8:11.

4. The Significance of the Resurrection

a. For Christ the resurrection marked the transition from his state of humiliation to exaltation. It marked, therefore, the conclusion of his suffering and actual work of atonement. It was the vindication of his own claims that he would rise from the dead. Had he not risen, then his teaching would have been false, and he would have been finally a victim of death, and under its power. By rising he conquered sin and death, thus crowning his work on the cross.

b. By vindicating his claims to us, the resurrection also vindicated his claims of deity to us, and became a declaration of his deity.[65]

c. The fact of Christ's resurrection also attests to us the completion of the atonement, and the acceptance of the same by the Father. It thus became the crowning basis of our justification,[66] regeneration,[67] and final resurrection.[68] his and our enemies were defeated, even the last, namely, death.

B. The Ascension of Christ

The ascension of Christ back to heaven was the necessary completion of the resurrection. It is not attested in the Scripture as fully and frequently as the resurrection, but the record is clear enough.[69]

The ascension involved the visible ascent of the person of Christ in his human nature. As such the idea of the passage from one place to another is taught. It was necessary as a part of the priestly work of Christ to enter into the Holy of Holies with his own blood.[70] In this connection he was going to prepare a place for us, and a way for us to come to that place.[71] By taking our human nature to the throne of God, he gives us great assurance that we too may be made fit through his sacrifice to enter into the very presence of God. Further, the blessings that we now receive in the gift of the Holy Spirit were dependent upon his going away.[72] Thus, not only was it necessary that he accomplish redemption on the Cross, but it was also necessary that he apply that redemption to us through the Holy Spirit, which he sent forth from the throne of God, after he had ascended up to Heaven.

---

65. Rom. 1:1-4.
66. Rom. 4:25.
67. Eph. 1:19-20.
68. Rom. 5:10; Phil. 3:10; I Pet. 1:3.
69. Luke 24:50-53; Acts 1:6-11; John 6:62; 14:2, 12; 16:5, 10, 17, 28; 17:5; 20:17; Eph. 1:20; 4:8-10; Heb. 1:3; 4:14; 9:24.
70. Heb. 9:23-24.
71. John 14:2-3, 6.
72. John 16:7.

C. The Session of Christ at the Right Hand of God

The Scripture speaks of the session of Christ at the right hand of God. Christ predicted it of himself.[73] Peter spoke of it in his sermons, Acts 2:33-36; 5:31. Other passages mentioning this aspect of his work are, Eph. 1:20-22; Heb. 1:3; 10:12; I Pet. 3:22; Rev. 3:21; 22:1. Other passages speak of Christ's reigning as King, Rom. 14:9; I Cor. 15:24-28; Heb. 2:7-8.

The significance of the session is that of glorification, and of inauguration to the royal office as the God-man. It had been prophesied in Ps. 110:1, "Sit thou at my right hand, until I make thine enemies thy footstool." As we have already indicated, he was Lord by virtue of his deity, but the Kingship as Mediator is something that came as reward for his completed work on the Cross. The mention of sitting at the right hand of God should not be taken to mean that he is no longer active as our Mediator. The Scripture represents him in various forms of activity, sitting and being at the right hand of God,[74] and walking in the midst of the candlesticks.[75]

The work which he performs there includes the three offices that we have already observed him doing as our Mediator, namely, prophetic, priestly, and royal. As the Prophet he sends the Holy Spirit to guide his Church into all truth.[76] He gave the Scripture through the Holy Spirit. As the Priest he presents the blood of his own sacrifice, and makes continual intercession for us.[77] As King he rules over all the universe to set it in order, and to bring all things into subjection to himself.[78]

D. The Return of Christ

Though we shall cover the return of Christ more fully under the head of Eschatology, we should note the fact that this is a part of his exaltation. Hodge summarizes the clear teaching of the Scripture on this subject:
    1. Christ is to come again.
    2. It will be a personal, visible and glorious coming.
    3. He will come as judge of the world.
    4. The judgment will include all men, and will be based on the deeds done in this life, the standard being the Word of God. The sentence of the judgment is to be final, fixing the eternal destiny of all concerned.[79]

---

73. Mt. 26:64.
74. Rom. 8:34; I Pet. 3:22). On the occasion of Stephen's death he was seen standing as though to assist his first martyr (Acts 7:56).
75. Rev. 1:12-20.
76. John 14:26; 16:7-15.
77 Zech. 6:13; Heb. 4:14; 7:24-25; 8:1-6; 9:11, 24-26; 10:19-22; I John 2:2.
78. I Pet. 3:22; Ps. 2; 45; 72; 110; Is. 9:67; Dan. 8:14; Heb. 1:13.
79. C. Hodge, *Systematic Theology, op. cit.*, Vol. II, p. 638.

CPSIA information can be obtained
at www.ICGtesting.com
Printed in the USA
LVHW081944020323
740773LV00004B/184

9 781532 698453